5TH EDITION

BECOMING A TEACHER
KNOWLEDGE, SKILLS AND ISSUES

COLIN MARSH

To Glen – my ever-loving wife and soulmate.

Copyright © Pearson Australia (a division of Pearson Australia Group Pty Ltd) 2010

Pearson Australia
Unit 4, Level 3
14 Aquatic Drive
Frenchs Forest NSW 2086

www.pearson.com.au

The *Copyright Act 1968* of Australia allows a maximum of one chapter or 10% of this book, whichever is the greater, to be copied by any educational institution for its educational purposes provided that that educational institution (or the body that administers it) has given a remuneration notice to Copyright Agency Limited (CAL) under the Act. For details of the CAL licence for educational institutions contact:
Copyright Agency Limited, telephone: (02) 9394 7600, email: info@copyright.com.au

All rights reserved. Except under the conditions described in the *Copyright Act 1968* of Australia and subsequent amendments, no part of this publication may be reproduced, stored in a retrieval system or transmitted in any form or by any means, electronic, mechanical, photocopying, recording or otherwise, without the prior permission of the copyright owner.

Acquisitions Editor: Julie Tylman
Project Editor: Kathryn Munro
Development Editor: Jessica Sykes
Editorial Coordinator: Jennifer Trewin
Production Administrator: Rochelle Deighton
Copy Editor: Janice Keynton
Proofreader: Marie-Louise Taylor
Copyright and Pictures Editor: Liz de Rome
Indexer: Jo Rudd
Cover and internal design by Natalie Bowra
Cover images: Smiling teacher © Chris Schmidt/iStockphoto.com; Schoolchildren studying in front of computers © Catherine Yeulet/iStockphoto.com; adult male teacher © James Pauls/iStockphoto.com; Boys in school © SteveStone/iStockphoto.com; video player © Michael Brown/Dreamstime.com.
Clock icon image © Fazakas Mihaly / shutterstock.com
Typeset by Midland Typesetters, Australia

Printed in China (SWTC/01)

1 2 3 4 5 14 13 12 11 10

National Library of Australia
Cataloguing-in-Publication Data

Author:	Marsh, Colin J.
Title:	Becoming a Teacher: Knowledge, Skills and Issues.
Edition:	5th ed.
ISBN:	9781442523289 (pbk.)
Notes:	Includes index, bibliography.
Previous ed:	2008.
Subjects:	Teaching—Australia—Handbooks, manuals, etc.
	First year teachers—Australia—Handbooks, manuals, etc.
Dewey Number:	371.10994

Every effort has been made to trace and acknowledge copyright. However, should any infringement have occurred, the publishers tender their apologies and invite copyright owners to contact them.

PEARSON AUSTRALIA
is a division of

CONTENTS

Preface	ix
About the author	x
Acknowledgements	x
New features	xi
Supplements for students and educators	xii

Part 1 Introduction — 1
1 What is teaching all about? — 2
1.1 Introduction — 2
1.2 First impressions — 2
1.3 What is a 'good' teacher? — 3
1.4 The complexity of being a teacher — 6
1.5 Learning how to teach — 7
Concluding comments — 8
Key issues raised in this chapter — 8
Reflections and issues — 8
Special references — 9
Web sources — 9

2 The Education Revolution: national curriculum and equity — 10
2.1 Introduction — 10
2.2 A national curriculum for Australia? — 10
   2.2.1 Core curriculum — 11
   2.2.2 National collaborative curriculum development project — 14
   2.2.3 The Discovering Democracy Project — 16
   2.2.4 Statements of learning — 17
   2.2.5 History summit — 18
2.3 National Curriculum Board and the education revolution — 18
2.4 Reflecting on current progress of the NCB (ACARA) — 25
2.5 Equity in education — 26
   2.5.1 Some important terms — 26
   2.5.2 Indigenous Australians and equity issues — 28
   2.5.3 International rankings on equity — 29
   2.5.4 Problem areas — 30
2.6 Specific issues — 31
   2.6.1 Student disengagement and early leaving — 31
   2.6.2 Teacher quality and disadvantaged students — 32
2.7 Some solutions — 32
   2.7.1 Early childhood education — 32
   2.7.2 Primary education — 33
   2.7.3 Secondary education — 33
Concluding comments — 34
Key issues raised in this chapter — 35
Reflections and issues — 35
Special references — 36
Web sources — 36

Part 2 Student learning — 37
3 How students develop and learn — 38
3.1 Introduction — 38
3.2 Theories of cognitive development — 39
   3.2.1 Piaget — 39
Case study: How I use Piaget in my teaching — 41
   3.2.2 Implications of Piaget's theory for teaching — 42
   3.2.3 Criticisms of Piaget's theory — 43
   3.2.4 Bruner — 44
   3.2.5 Vygotsky — 45
Case study: How I use Vygotsky's theory in my teaching — 47
   3.2.6 Implications of Vygotsky's theory for teaching — 47
3.3 Theories of social, emotional and moral development — 48
   3.3.1 A theory of psychosocial development – Erikson — 48
   3.3.2 Critique of Erikson's theory — 51
   3.3.3 A theory of moral development – Kohlberg — 51
   3.3.4 Critique of Kohlberg's theory — 53
Case study: How I use Kohlberg's theory in my teaching — 54
Concluding comments — 54
Key issues raised in this chapter — 55
Reflections and issues — 55
Special references — 56
Web sources — 56

4 Learner motivation and developing self-esteem — 57
4.1 Introduction — 57
4.2 Intrinsic and extrinsic motivation — 57
   4.2.1 Intrinsic motivation — 57

	4.2.2 Extrinsic motivation	58	
4.3	Self-esteem	59	
4.4	Achievement motivation	60	
Case study: Achievement motivation		62	
4.5	Attribution theory of motivation	62	
4.6	Social motivation	63	
4.7	Motivation – influencing factors	66	
4.8	Pastoral care	68	
Concluding comments		69	
Key issues raised in this chapter		69	
Reflections and issues		70	
Special references		70	
Web sources		70	

5 Learning environments — 71

5.1 Introduction — 71
5.2 Classroom settings — 72
    5.2.1 Some considerations — 72
    5.2.2 Room arrangement principles — 72
    5.2.3 Floor space — 73
    5.2.4 Location of the teacher's desk — 74
    5.2.5 Arrangement of students' desks — 74
    5.2.6 Arrangement of furniture and equipment — 74
    5.2.7 Learning stations and work centres — 75
    5.2.8 Pin-up boards and bulletin boards — 77
    5.2.9 Smart Boards (interactive whiteboards) — 77
    5.2.10 Special items — 77
    5.2.11 Floating teachers — 77
5.3 Other physical and psychological factors in the classroom — 78
    5.3.1 Colour — 79
    5.3.2 Noise — 79
    5.3.3 Temperature — 81
    5.3.4 Seating — 81
    5.3.5 Class size — 82
    5.3.6 Psychosocial environment — 83
    5.3.7 Ability groupings — 83
    5.3.8 Single-sex schools and single-sex classes in coeducational schools — 83
    5.3.9 Private and public schools — 84
    5.3.10 Home schooling — 84
    5.3.11 Tutoring services provided by commercial interests — 84
5.4 Other learning settings — 85
    5.4.1 Community schools — 85
    5.4.2 Service learning — 85
Concluding comments — 86
Key issues raised in this chapter — 86
Reflections and issues — 86
Special references — 87
Web sources — 87

Part 3 How teachers organise and teach — 89

6 What is a curriculum? — 90

6.1 Introduction — 90
6.2 Meaning of the term 'curriculum' — 90
6.3 Examples of curriculum documents — 94
    6.3.1 Early grades – English – 'Our homes' — 95
    6.3.2 Primary school – Studies of Society and Environment — 95
    6.3.3 Primary school – Personal Development, Health and Physical Education — 96
    6.3.4 Senior secondary school – Economics — 98
Concluding comments — 98
Key issues raised in this chapter — 99
Reflections and issues — 99
Special references — 100
Web sources — 100

7 Planning and preparing for teaching — 101

7.1 Introduction — 101
7.2 Planning principles — 101
7.3 Digging a little deeper — 102
7.4 Practicum, teaching practice or internship — 103
7.5 Programs, units and lesson plans — 104
7.6 Developing a program — 104
    7.6.1 Planning the priorities — 104
    7.6.2 Primary school example — 105
    7.6.3 Secondary school example — 107
    7.6.4 Combining the priorities to provide a coherent approach — 108
7.7 Planning a unit — 110
    7.7.1 A new approach — 117
7.8 Lesson plans — 118
    7.8.1 A more detailed approach — 120
    7.8.2 Interactionist approach — 120
    7.8.3 Lesson study — 126
Concluding comments — 127
Key issues raised in this chapter — 127
Reflections and issues — 128
Special references — 128
Web sources — 128

8 Organising classroom structures and routines — 129

8.1 Introduction — 129
8.2 Typical school structures — 129
    8.2.1 Kindergartens and preschools — 129
    8.2.2 Primary schools — 130
    8.2.3 Secondary schools — 131
    8.2.4 Middle schools — 132
8.3 Pressures and demands on schools — 133

8.4	Organising tasks and elements	133		10.3.1	School Development Plans	167
8.5	Self-contained classrooms	135		10.3.2	Strategic Planning Frameworks	168
8.6	Open versus self-contained classrooms	135		10.3.3	Futures perspective	168
8.7	Individualised learning	136		10.3.4	Strategic intents	168
8.8	Heterogeneous versus streamed classes	137		10.3.5	Strategic plans	170
8.9	Whole-class instruction	137		10.3.6	Operational target setting	173
8.10	Using small groups	138	10.4	School plans and the school culture		175
8.11	Cooperative learning	141	10.5	Difficulties in doing school planning		176

8.11.1 Theoretical origins 141
8.11.2 Planning and conducting cooperative learning lessons 142
8.11.3 Student-teams learning approach 142
8.11.4 Jigsaw method 142
8.11.5 Research evidence 144

Concluding comments 144
Key issues raised in this chapter 145
Reflections and issues 145
Special references 146
Web sources 146

9 Planning to achieve goals, aims, objectives, outcomes and standards 147

9.1 Introduction 147
9.2 The importance of goals and aims 147
9.3 The importance of objectives 148
9.4 The importance of outcomes 151
9.5 The importance of standards 154
9.6 Reflecting on the relative merits of objectives and outcomes 157
9.7 A closer look at some advantages of using objectives 158
9.8 Types of objectives 158
  9.8.1 Behavioural objectives 158
  9.8.2 Instructional objectives 160
9.9 Classifying objectives 160
  9.9.1 Cognitive domain 161
  9.9.2 Affective domain 161
  9.9.3 Psychomotor domain 161
9.10 Critique of taxonomies 162

Concluding comments 162
Key issues raised in this chapter 162
Reflections and issues 163
Special references 163
Web sources 164

10 School development plans and Strategic Planning Frameworks 165

10.1 Introduction 165
10.2 Commonly used terms relating to school development and improvement 165
10.3 School Development Plans and Strategic Planning Frameworks 167

  10.5.1 Aims 176
  10.5.2 Partners 176
  10.5.3 Curriculum 176
  10.5.4 Organisation of teaching and learning 176
  10.5.5 Management 177
  10.5.6 Change 177
  10.5.7 Support 177
  10.5.8 Ethos 178
Case study: Collaborative planning at my school 178
Concluding comments 179
Key issues raised in this chapter 179
Reflections and issues 179
Special references 180
Web sources 180

Part 4 Teaching effectively 181

11 Communicating effectively 182

11.1 Introduction 182
11.2 The nature of communication 182
11.3 Models of communication 185
Case study: The need for communicating with warmth 186
11.4 Communicating effectively in the classroom 186
11.5 Explaining 187
11.6 Questioning 188
  11.6.1 Classifications 188
  11.6.2 Planning questions 189
  11.6.3 Asking questions 190
  11.6.4 Responding to answers 191
  11.6.5 Students asking questions 191
11.7 Listening 192

Concluding comments 193
Key issues raised in this chapter 193
Reflections and issues 193
Special references 194
Web sources 194

12 Pedagogy, teaching and learning 195

12.1 Introduction 195
12.2 Pedagogy 195
12.3 Matching teaching styles with students' learning styles 196

12.4	Impact of standards on teaching and learning	199	
12.5	Making use of technology	200	
12.6	Teaching and learning phases of instruction	202	
12.7	Teaching and learning modes	203	
	12.7.1 Lectures, teacher talks, expository talks and teacher presentations	204	
	12.7.2 Practice drills	206	
	12.7.3 Directed questioning	207	
	12.7.4 Direct instruction	209	
	12.7.5 Demonstrations	210	
	12.7.6 Online teaching	210	
	12.7.7 Constructivism	211	
	12.7.8 Discussion	212	
	12.7.9 Cooperative learning	213	
	12.7.10 Problem solving, inquiry and discovery	213	
	12.7.11 Role-playing and simulation games	215	
	12.7.12 Project-based learning and problem-based learning	216	
	12.7.13 Independent self-directed study	217	

Concluding comments 217
Key issues raised in this chapter 218
Reflections and issues 218
Special references 219
Web sources 219

13 Classroom management 220

13.1 Introduction 220
13.2 Beginning teacher concerns about classroom management 220
13.3 On-task/off-task behaviours 222
13.4 Establishing a positive classroom climate 223
13.5 Establishing routines 224
Case study: Managing a difficult child 226
13.6 Establishing effective communication channels 226
13.7 Gender and racial issues 227
13.8 Bullying 228
13.9 Attention Deficit Hyperactivity Disorder (ADHD) 229
13.10 Working with parents 230
13.11 Preventive discipline 230
13.12 Supportive discipline 230
13.13 Corrective discipline 231
13.14 A balanced system of classroom management 232
13.15 Classroom management models 232
13.16 Assertive Discipline Model 233
13.17 Decisive Leadership Model 234
Concluding comments 234
Key issues raised in this chapter 234
Reflections and issues 234

Special references 235
Web sources 235

14 Using resources creatively 236

14.1 Introduction 236
14.2 Resources available for use in schools 237
14.3 Print materials 237
    14.3.1 Textbooks 237
    14.3.2 Reference books 239
    14.3.3 Trade books 239
    14.3.4 Project kits 240
    14.3.5 Website sources and inexpensive materials 240
    14.3.6 Colour prints and posters 241
    14.3.7 Simulation games 241
    14.3.8 Maps, globes and models 241
14.4 Checklists for evaluating and selecting print materials 242
14.5 Multimedia 244
    14.5.1 Computers 244
    14.5.2 CD-ROMs 245
    14.5.3 The Internet 246
    14.5.4 Blogs 247
    14.5.5 Television, DVDs and videotapes 247
    14.5.6 Older-style resources 247
    14.5.7 PowerPoint projectors (LCD) 248
    14.5.8 Smart Boards and interactive whiteboards (IWBs) 248
14.6 Resources available beyond the school setting 249
    14.6.1 Cultural resources 249
    14.6.2 People in specific occupations and retired people 249
    14.6.3 Groups, associations and organisations 250
    14.6.4 Newspapers, documents and artefacts 250
Concluding comments 250
Key issues raised in this chapter 250
Reflections and issues 250
Special references 251
Web sources 251

15 Meeting the diverse needs of students 252

15.1 Introduction 252
15.2 Individuals and the school environment 252
    15.2.1 Individual differences and student achievement 253
15.3 The potential of differentiated classrooms 254
    15.3.1 Contracts 256
    15.3.2 Learning centres 258
    15.3.3 Computer-based instruction 258

	15.3.4	Lesson study	259	17.5	A parent participation continuum	299

15.3.4 Lesson study 259
15.3.5 Mastery learning 259
15.3.6 Multiple intelligences 260
15.3.7 Outcomes-based education 261
15.3.8 Standards-based education 263
15.4 Individual differences and curriculum materials 263
15.5 Individual differences and gender 264
15.6 Individual differences and exceptional students 266
15.7 Culturally different students 269
15.8 Abused and neglected students 270
Concluding comments 271
Key issues raised in this chapter 271
Reflections and issues 271
Special references 272
Web sources 272

16 Teaching, values and moral education 273

16.1 Introduction 273
16.2 Values and teachers 273
16.3 Values and students 275
  16.3.1 Some claims and counterclaims 277
16.4 A critical analysis of some alternative curriculum designs 278
  16.4.1 Values and moral education as a separate subject in the school curriculum 278
  16.4.2 Values taught as a set of valuing processes across the curriculum 278
  16.4.3 Values clarification approach 279
  16.4.4 Moral development approach 281
  16.4.5 Values analysis approach 283
16.5 Values and the national statements and profiles 284
16.6 National Values Education Project 285
16.7 Values and the National Curriculum Board (ACARA) 287
16.8 Civics and citizenship education 288
Concluding comments 290
Key issues raised in this chapter 290
Reflections and issues 291
Special references 292
Web sources 292

17 Working effectively with parents 293

17.1 Introduction 293
17.2 Parent involvement or participation? 293
17.3 Historical basis for parent and community participation in education 294
17.4 Some claims and counterclaims about parent participation 296

17.5 A parent participation continuum 299
17.6 Intended practices and actual outcomes 301
17.7 Training needs for parents 303
17.8 Training needs for teachers 305
17.9 School councils 306
Concluding comments 308
Key issues raised in this chapter 308
Reflections and issues 308
Special references 309
Web sources 309

18 Assessment and reporting 310

18.1 Introduction 310
18.2 Assessment 311
18.3 Reasons for assessment 311
18.4 Assessing for whom? 312
18.5 Important emphases in assessment 312
  18.5.1 ICT developments in assessment 312
  18.5.2 Assessment for learning 313
18.6 Important concepts in assessment 315
  18.6.1 Diagnostic/formative–summative 315
  18.6.2 Informal–formal 315
  18.6.3 Norm-referenced–criterion-referenced 317
  18.6.4 Process–product 317
  18.6.5 Learner judged–teacher judged 318
  18.6.6 Internal–external 318
  18.6.7 Inclusive–exclusive 320
  18.6.8 Technicist–liberal/postmodernist 320
18.7 Commonly used assessment techniques 320
  18.7.1 Direct observation 321
  18.7.2 Semantic differentials 322
18.8 Current trends in assessment 323
  18.8.1 Authentic assessment 323
  18.8.2 Outcomes-based assessment 324
  18.8.3 Performance assessment 327
  18.8.4 Examples of performance assessments 328
18.9 Record-keeping and reporting 333
  18.9.1 Trends in reporting 334
18.10 New developments in assessment and reporting 336
Concluding comments 337
Key issues raised in this chapter 337
Reflections and issues 337
Special references 338
Web sources 338

Part 5 The teaching profession 339

19 Professional and cultural dimensions of teaching 340

19.1 Introduction 340

19.2	Profession – meanings and interpretations	340	
19.3	Professionalisation and professional development	342	
19.4	Professions – lessons from history	343	
19.5	The Australian teaching profession	344	
19.6	Career structures	349	
19.7	Continuing issues for the teaching profession	352	
	19.7.1 Ageing of teachers	352	
	19.7.2 Women in teaching and the feminisation of teaching	354	
	19.7.3 Class relations	355	
	19.7.4 Empowerment	355	
	19.7.5 Teacher morale	356	
19.8	School culture and teaching	357	
19.9	Culture	357	
19.10	School culture	357	
	19.10.1 School culture and leadership	360	
	19.10.2 School culture and beginning teachers	360	
19.11	School culture and schooling over the decades	360	
	19.11.1 The 1960s	361	
	19.11.2 The twenty-first century (2010 and beyond)	362	
	19.11.3 Commonwealth–state relationships	362	
	19.11.4 Equity issues and international rankings	363	
	19.11.5 Assessment developments	363	
	19.11.6 Conditions for teachers	364	
Concluding comments		365	
Key issues raised in this chapter		366	
Reflections and issues		366	
Special references		367	
Web sources		367	

20 Ethical and legal issues in teaching 368

20.1	Introduction	368
20.2	The ethics of teaching	368
20.3	Teaching as a moral craft	370
20.4	Ethical relationships between the teacher and the education system	371
20.5	Ethical relationships between the teacher and the principal	371
20.6	Ethical relationships between teacher and students	372
20.7	Ethical relationships between a school and private industry	372
20.8	Legal issues in teaching	376
20.9	Rights of teachers	376
	20.9.1 Academic freedom	377
	20.9.2 Employment discrimination	377
	20.9.3 Freedom of speech	377
	20.9.4 Copying of published materials	377
	20.9.5 Defamation	378
	20.9.6 Negligence	378
	20.9.7 Discipline	379
20.10	Rights of students	380
	20.10.1 Discipline and punishment, exclusion from school	380
	20.10.2 Privacy: searches, confiscations and drug testing	380
	20.10.3 Property	381
	20.10.4 Use of camera/video phones in schools	381
	20.10.5 Wearing the hijab or jilbab	381
	20.10.6 Student rights regarding graduation	382
	20.10.7 Bullying	382
	20.10.8 Protection from paedophiles	382
20.11	Enforcement of rights	383
	20.11.1 Court cases and the provision of legal advice	383
	20.11.2 Discipline and punishment	384
	20.11.3 Searches and confiscations	385
	20.11.4 Exclusion from school	387
Concluding comments		389
Key issues raised in this chapter		390
Reflections and issues		390
Special references		391
Web sources		391

21 Teacher competencies and standards 392

21.1	Introduction	392
21.2	Quality of teaching – national inquiries and programs	393
21.3	Competency-based teaching	396
21.4	Advantages and disadvantages of competency-based teaching	398
21.5	Standards for teaching	402
21.6	Standards for teaching Mathematics	405
21.7	Standards for teaching of English	406
21.8	Standards for teaching of Science	406
21.9	'Teaching Australia' and the National Institute for Teaching and School Leadership	407
Concluding comments		409
Key issues raised in this chapter		409
Reflections and issues		409
Special references		410
Web sources		410
Bibliography		411
Index		450

PREFACE

Congratulations on deciding to become a teacher. The world of teaching and learning is not only fascinating and inspiring, but also challenging.

Being a teacher is all about having the passion, energy and commitment to enhance students' learning. Every student is valuable and important and our task is to give them all optimal learning opportunities. It is a two-way learning process in that we can also learn so much from our students.

Becoming a Teacher is intended to assist you in the process of becoming a capable, caring teacher. It includes a comprehensive range of chapters, and within each chapter there are questions ('Pause for thought' and 'Your turn'), and at the end of the chapter there are special references and reflections. In particular, the reader is invited to do follow-up reading using the special references listed at the end of each chapter. There is also an extensive and up-to-date bibliography in the last section of the book.

Remember it is most important to take the time to do your reading of additional references and to ponder those questions and issues – a reflective teacher is a successful teacher.

This is the fifth edition of *Becoming a Teacher*. Although it retains most of the chapters of the previous edition all have been revised and updated. The approach in this edition is more reflective, and gives readers an opportunity to interact much more with issues raised in the text. Additional case studies and examples are included. Various links to Internet sites can be found in all chapters. Many additional topics, new to this edition of *Becoming a Teacher*, are listed in the new features summary.

In this edition of *Becoming a Teacher* there is a brand new chapter, which examines the very important topics of national curriculum and equity issues (Chapter 2). These are likely to be two major areas of interest to beginning and practising teachers over the next few years. There is also a major emphasis on ICT (Information and Communication Technologies) in this edition of the book. Many of the chapters now include specific examples of how ICT can be used in teaching.

This book will have a most valuable supplement of online MyEducationLab videos termed 'Taking it to the Classroom', which will provide additional background and ideas about teaching.

My thanks are due to Everlyn Tan for her expert secretarial assistance in the preparation of the manuscript; to Julie Tylman, Senior Acquisitions Editor, and to Kathryn Munro, my Project Editor, who attended to many organisational issues very patiently, over many weeks.

I trust that you enjoy this fifth edition. I have found it very interesting and fulfilling. I welcome feedback about any aspects of the text. Please e-mail me: c.marsh@curtin.edu.au

ABOUT THE AUTHOR

COLIN MARSH

Colin Marsh is an Adjunct Professor at Curtin University, Perth. He has had extensive teaching experience as a primary school teacher, secondary school teacher and university lecturer in a number of countries.

He is a prolific writer and has published over 35 books. *Becoming a Teacher* and *Teaching Studies of Society and Environment* are two major texts published by Pearson Education Australia. His main interests are playing and listening to jazz music and playing tennis.

ACKNOWLEDGEMENTS

We gratefully acknowledge the following practising teachers who generously shared their ideas and experiences in the classroom on video in order to help prepare the next generation of teachers. We hope pre-service teachers (and the teacher educators who prepare them) will benefit from their insights.

Cameron Bacholer	*The Peninsula School*
Sally Brown	*Brighton Primary School*
Fiona Lane	*Wynnum West Primary*
Roshan Lee	*Melbourne Girls Grammar*
Andrew Moffat	*McClelland College*
Rachael Peterson	*Melbourne Girls Grammar*
Jason Smith	*Mount Alvernia College*

The publisher would also like to thank the following academics for their invaluable feedback and advice:

Angelina Ambrosetti	*Central Queensland University*
Richard Berlach	*Notre Dame University*
Denise Beutel	*Queensland University of Technology*
Tess Boyle	*Southern Cross University*
Gordon Brown	*University of Wollongong*
Matthew Campbell	*Australian Catholic University*
Tony Dowden	*University of Tasmania*
John Harris	*Flinders University*
Bruce Johnson	*University of South Australia*
Nina Maadad	*University of Adelaide*
Paul Nicholson	*Deakin University*
Karin Oerlemans	*University of Tasmania*
Judy Peters	*University of South Australia*
Noelene Weatherby	*University of Wollongong*

NEW FEATURES

- An expanded first chapter titled 'What is teaching all about?' including first impressions of a good teacher, ambiguities of teaching, risk-taking and creativity, and developing personal and professional attributes.
- A new chapter (Chapter 2) entitled 'The Education Revolution: national curriculum and equity', which analyses two major developments in Australia – the new national curriculum and what it will mean for teachers, and equity issues relating to disadvantaged students, student disengagement and international rankings on equity.
- Problems in applying Western developmental theories to Aboriginal children (Chapter 3).
- Adolescent students' decline in motivation, and how to re-engage students (Chapter 4).
- Extension of analysis of class size and effects on student achievement; home schooling, and service learning (Chapter 5).
- Planning and preparing for teaching – use of interactionist approaches and models such as Wiggins & McTighe (2005) (Chapter 7).
- The influence of computers on classroom organisation (Chapter 8).
- A new section on goals, the National Goals for Schooling in Australia over three decades up to 2009, the National Curriculum Board and ACARA (Chapter 9).
- A new section on Strategic Planning Frameworks (Chapter 10).
- Examination of media literacy skills (Chapter 11).
- A new section on pedagogy and pedagogical knowledge; examples of ICT applications included with each mode of instruction (ranging from lectures to independent study) (Chapter 12).
- A new section on cyber-bullying (Chapter 13).
- A new section on MP3 players and Smart Boards (Chapter 14).
- An extended section on differentiated classrooms (Chapter 15).
- The value of parents' home-based involvement and their children's achievement (Chapter 17).
- ICT developments in assessment; international student assessment tests, PISA and TIMSS; national assessment program in Literacy and Numeracy (Chapter 18).
- Latest figures (2007) on the Australian teaching profession in terms of gender, working hours per week, job satisfaction; schooling in 2010 (Chapter 19).
- A new section on commercial sponsorship in schools; school violence; drug testing; child sex abuse (Chapter 20).
- A new section on standards in Mathematics, Science and English; expanding role of the 'National Institute for Teaching and School Leadership' (Chapter 21).

Note: Each chapter in this edition contains 'Pause for thought' questions (identified by); 'Your turn' reflections; 'Key issues raised in this chapter'; 'Reflections and issues'; and 'Special references'. There is a comprehensive and up-to-date bibliography at the end of the book.

SUPPLEMENTS FOR STUDENTS AND EDUCATORS

New to this edition!

www.pearson.com.au/myeducationlab

We're taking it to the Classroom!

Through exciting new Australian video clips, posted within MyEducationLab, students can hear first-hand, from practising, local teachers. By connecting teacher education theory with actual teacher practise, students gain a better insight into the complexity of the classroom and into different teaching styles and approaches.

Created under the editorial guidance of teacher educators Dr. Leanne Crosswell and Jennie Duke from Queensland University of Technology, these original videos were carefully designed to specifically support the topics covered in *Becoming a Teacher, 5th edition*.

In addition to Australian videos, MyEducationLab includes:
- Chapter study quizzes, great for revision, created by Dr. Noelene Weatherby-Fell of University of Wollongong
- Reflection questions with each video relating back to the book content, created by Dr. Tony Dowden, University of Tasmania
- Additional web resources for each chapter
- An eBook

Becoming A Teacher, 5th edition MyEducationLab videos:

Part 1:
- Meet the Teachers: Fiona, Jason and Rachael
- Meet the Teachers: Andrew, Roshan, Cameron and Sally

Part 2:
- Student Learning
- Learning and social needs of students
- Equitable access and engagement

Part 3:
- Planning curriculum programs
- Planning issues
- Planning and student need
- Setting up the classroom environment
- Issues effecting classroom layout

Part 4:
- Effective pedagogical approaches
- Use of ICT
- Differentiating instruction
- Behaviour management approach
- Proactive approaches
- Student need and behaviour management
- Use of assessment
- Assessment for improving learning

Part 5:
- Managing the demands
- Professional learning needs

If this textbook did not come bundled with a MyEducationLab access code, access may be purchased at www.pearson.com.au/myeducationlab.

PART 1

INTRODUCTION

Taking it to the Classroom

www.pearson.com.au/myeducationlab

Number of years teaching: 3 years
Year level teaching now: Year 2

First day of teaching memories:

On the first day, there are a lot of new faces coming into your room and so many parents who want to meet you. To help the children settle quickly whilst waiting for the rest of the class to arrive, I make a word search which includes the names of each child in the class. I put a word search at each child's desk and as they come in, I can introduce myself, meet the parents and show the child where to sit. The children settle quickly to do the activity and it leaves me free to meet the next family who have entered the classroom.

Sally Brown
Brighton Primary School

chapter 1   What is teaching all about?
chapter 2   The Education Revolution: national curriculum and equity

1
WHAT IS TEACHING ALL ABOUT?

1.1 | INTRODUCTION

Welcome to the world of teaching. You have made a wonderful choice. At whatever level you finish up teaching, whether it is early childhood, primary, secondary or tertiary, you will never cease to be amazed by students' hunger for learning – an insatiable need which drives them forward and upward.

1.2 | FIRST IMPRESSIONS

Some impressions of the first students you teach will stay with you forever, such as the adoring eyes of a little five-year-old girl who is completely fascinated by what you say and do. Or perhaps it is the energetic eleven-year-old boy who doesn't often remain seated for very long but is burning with ideas that he wants to share with you.

Then again at the secondary school level there are the cool young males and females who observe you at a distance at first but can often be very forthcoming and articulate once they have decided that you can be trusted.

These first impressions of students you get as a teacher are all the more memorable, because for the first time you are the centre of attention rather than part of a group of 20 or more listening to someone else. You may think that you know all there is to be known about teaching, because after all you have experienced classrooms and teachers for many years – at least 11 or 12 years, or more than 12 000 hours. During that time you have observed all kinds of teachers. But now it is all different – you have the stage and are the focus of attention while the students are the observers.

Have you thought about what kind of teacher you want to be? In many cases you have in mind some picture of the 'good teacher' based upon your memories of teachers you have had in the past. You may be only vaguely aware of some of these past influences. As noted by Lortie (2002), 'The result is an accretion of views, sentiments and implicit actions that may be only partially perceived by the beginning teacher' (p. xi).

1.3 | WHAT IS A 'GOOD' TEACHER?

Hughes (2004) uses examples from his life as an educator to try to define the 'good teacher'. He emphasises the need for a teacher to have humanity and warmth – to know at all times what students in a class are doing and also to care about what they are doing.

Try to recall some of the special things that your 'good' teacher did.
- Was it his/her manners?
- How he/she gave instructions to the class?
- The way he/she listened to your problems?
- How he/she told interesting stories?

Make a list of things learnt from this good teacher that you might want to copy.

The cartoon in Figure 1.1, although in humorous vein, pinpoints just some of the many abilities found in a good teacher!

Yet it can also be argued that your views of past teachers may be incomplete and that perhaps they are not useful as role models. After all, as a thinking teacher, you surely cannot accept the concept that you want to become merely a clone of teacher X, some hero or heroine in your past.

Lortie (2002) goes further and argues that beginning teachers need to be freed of implicit dispositions developed in the past so that they can become 'more aware of what they do while teaching and to more readily consider practices to which they have not been previously exposed' (p. xi).

Latham *et al.* (2006) take a similar stance when they argue that new teachers should challenge habitual practices that are ingrained and are largely unreflective practice. Teaching is a very privileged profession.

The teaching profession has few clear-cut answers. There are so many ambiguities and uncertainties in teaching. According to Helsing (2002) teachers can only search for appropriate courses of action and perhaps even several less-than-good alternatives rather than clear-cut resolutions.

Yet this is not all bad. Teaching is about risk-taking, about openness and creativity, about striking out in new territory. As an example, Tomlinson and Germundson (2007) consider that successful teaching is like creating jazz. Jazz blends musical sounds – it uses blue notes and syncopation and swing – and it invites improvisation and unexpected outcomes. According to Tomlinson and Germundson teaching too makes music using different elements and blending different cultural styles with educational techniques and theories.

The author of this book identifies readily with the concept of teaching as jazz because it reflects his past professional life as a jazz piano player. In his teaching over the years he has used different rhythms and improvisations to challenge and excite his students.

> **YOUR TURN**
>
> Reflect upon a lesson you are planning in any subject but use jazz concepts as planners. For example, consider what you might do as an opening highlight. Do the planned activities that follow blend in harmoniously? Are the students encouraged to work actively and strongly, akin to a syncopated rhythm? Do you introduce some new elements (chords) during the activity to stir student interests?

FIGURE 1.1 Recipe for the 'perfect' teacher

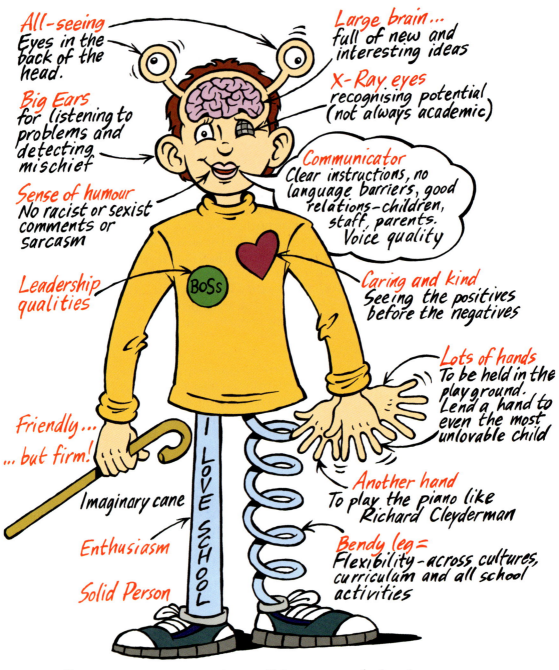

Source: Recipe for the 'Perfect' Teacher. Redrawn with kind permission from Moyles, J (2007) Beginning Teaching, Beginning Learning, 3rd ed, Open University Press, London, p. 314.

School is an important part of young children's lives. They may not always be able to express their ideas openly but they do have understandings about school life that affect their attitude to learning. According to Hayes (2008) young children enjoy many things about early childhood centres and primary schools – being with friends, learning interesting things, having fun, playing games and doing puzzles, painting and creating things, getting praise from adults and friends, feeling secure and knowing what is acceptable and unacceptable.

It is also important to remember that there are some things that young children dislike, such as being criticised in front of other children, the teacher displaying favouritism to some students, and not being given enough time to complete a task (Hayes 2008).

Lortie's (1975) research into adult memories of their time at school discovered that many of his subjects recalled incidents that probably seemed trivial to the teacher at the time but burned deeply into the child's consciousness. Teachers can be responsible for children's humiliation and guilt feelings as well as their positive times of feeling happy and delighted.

Wescombe-Down (2009) takes a similar stance when he states that teachers must pay sufficient attention to the fragility of students during the process of teachers' core business.

What activities might you do with one or two students in your class to encourage them to participate and to be engaged? For example, consider the benefits of using the two-by-ten strategy (Smith & Lambert 2008) where the teacher has a personal conversation with a difficult student for two minutes each day, ten days in a row.

At early childhood and primary school levels 'you are working with children whose cognitive development is advancing at the greatest speed in human life' (Brighouse 1995, p. x). The vocabulary they develop, their ideas, their understandings – it can be a really breathtaking discovery to observe just what young children can do. You will be learning too, on a very steep learning curve, but not as fast as your young charges.

At these stages of schooling it is important that children are allowed to behave as children – to enjoy time with their friends, to be involved in all kinds of make-believe games, to be able to interact in a safe, caring environment. Of course children bring to school various experiences from home which can be positive or negative. Children who have emotionally and physically distressed conditions at home will find it difficult to cope well at school without support and understanding from the teacher. As a professional, a teacher needs to be a keen observer of children and to be watchful of behaviours which might be linked to more serious matters.

There is an ongoing debate about whether cognitive development through the acquisition of a range of knowledge and skills should be emphasised in early childhood centres or whether play activities and informal socialisation should be the focus (Grieshaber 2009). What is likely to be preferred in the new national curriculum? Consider some of the issues from both perspectives.

Secondary school students are often vocal about what is wrong with schools. With good reason, they often complain about the deadening effects of covering content and the use of frequent testing. As a result, a number of secondary school students reject schooling and have little interest in becoming engaged in learning.

Secondary school students like to be with their friends, they tend to be concerned about their physical appearance and they want to give the impression of being cool and sophisticated.

Yet they can also display a depth of understanding on complex issues that may appear to be well beyond their years. This can happen if schools provide the opportunities for students to make meaning rather than simply teaching content. Wiggins and McTighe (2008) contend that secondary school students need to acquire important information and skills, but it is the making of meaning of this content and its effective transfer to new situations that is most important.

The secondary school teacher has to understand the personal joys, concerns and goals of developing adolescents. Somehow, through patient observing and support, a teacher and his/her students can develop respect and dignity (Smith & Lambert 2008).

Secondary schools are geared towards servicing the academic curriculum and examination regimes, rather than providing learning experiences that are relevant to young people (Wilson & Sproats 2009). Discuss.

Brighouse (1995) notes that a beginning teacher has to be both an optimist and a realist:
- you must have intellectual curiosity and a keen eye for change in students
- you will be energetic and a 'magpie' for ideas
- you will have the confidence to admit your weaknesses and you will be a risk-taker
- you will never stop learning yourself and you will take care to show this to the students you teach.

Chai (2005) makes the claim that a teacher has the opportunity to 'teach less, learn more'. She argues that teaching is not just 'delivering knowledge': teaching is about communicating – finding out what students like, their opinion about things, their hopes and fears. Teachers in turn need to share their ideas and feelings with their students.

Wolk (2008) advocates joyful learning as a necessary condition in schools to counteract dreariness and boredom. He refers to John Dewey's (1938) comment that learning vast amounts of information is useless if it destroys children's spirit to learn and their sense of wonder. Wolk (2008) suggests that teachers need to emphasise such joys as:
- finding the pleasure in learning
- giving students choices
- letting students create things
- making school spaces inviting
- having some fun together.

It may be very evident to you already that teaching can be rewarding – not necessarily in monetary terms but in emotional feelings of satisfaction about progress you have been able to make with certain students. Lortie (2002) uses the term 'psychic rewards' to refer to a teacher's work gratification: to have reached certain students, and to accomplish daily work tasks at a high level of success.

Kennedy and Hui (2003) contend that beginning teachers have to believe in their capacities to be able to influence students. They use the term 'self-efficacy' to explain why teachers are motivated to want to change students' behaviour. If a teacher does not have this self-belief then there will be little incentive to act.

1.4 | THE COMPLEXITY OF BEING A TEACHER

Teaching is enjoyable and brings many psychic rewards, but it is also complex (O'Brien & Goddard 2006). Jackson (1968) reports on the complexity of teaching and notes that a teacher can make over 200 classroom decisions daily!

Fortunately, you are able to draw on personal and professional knowledge and skills to assist you with this decision making.

Moyles (2007) refers to needed *personal attributes* such as:
- empathy with students
- respect for individuals
- positive outlook and attitude
- approachability
- sense of humour.

Moyles (2007) notes that *professional attributes* that are needed include:
- good organisation skills
- professional relationships with staff, parents and students
- appreciating others' skills.

Cruickshank, Jenkins and Metcalf (2009) take a similar stance when they discuss factors that influence how we teach. They include:
- personal characteristics, such as gender, age, experience, personality. For example, they quote Dunkin (1987): 'On balance, female teachers' classrooms more often are warmer and more nurturing, while male teachers' classrooms are better organised.' (You may dispute Dunkin's statement and want to disprove it. I hope you can do so!)
- experience and preparation in education – how the way we prefer to learn affects our teaching, and how our knowledge of subject matter affects our teaching
- context – the context in which you teach, including the number of students in the class and the availability of instructional materials and equipment.

So what does this all mean in terms of *why* you want to be a teacher? Some writers have emphasised the following. Which of these have special meaning for you?
- I want to teach because I want others to succeed.
- I want to teach because I consider I am receptive and perceptive about learning.
- I want to teach because I enjoy working with students.
- I want to teach because I know I can develop strong partnerships with students.
- I want to teach because I thrive on challenges.
- I want to teach because I know I can help students learn.
- I want to teach because I know this will enable me to continuously grow with new knowledge and skills.
- I want to teach so that I can reflect on my personal meaning and life goals.
- I want to teach so that I can grow and develop on the job.

Some of these statements might be more appealing to you than others. Select two or three and reflect upon why they seem especially relevant for you. Can you explain why this is the case?

Are there other statements in this list that you consider might be more relevant to you in the future? Perhaps you consider that you would need considerable teaching experience before you could support some of these statements.

Both 'why you want to teach' and 'how to teach' are perplexing.

1.5 | LEARNING HOW TO TEACH

Learning *how* to teach is also a complex matter. As noted by Ryan, Cooper and Tauer (2008), learning how to teach is as important as what you teach. How you teach will depend upon the purpose of a lesson, students' understanding of key concepts, and different degrees of direct or indirect teacher involvement.

In the following chapters of this book a major effort has been made to acquaint you with how to teach.

Two important and current issues, the national curriculum and equity, are introduced in Chapter 2 because these are crucial matters of concern to all teachers.

The early chapters focus especially on students' cognitive, emotional and moral development and levels of motivation (Chapters 3 and 4). Trying to establish a warm, caring environment for teaching and learning is the focus in Chapter 5. There are many chapters which explain how a teacher can plan, prepare and implement successful lessons (Chapters 6, 7, 8, 9, 10, 11, 12 and 14). Some of the complexities of teaching are also included, such as the very important topic of classroom discipline (Chapter 13), providing for individual differences (Chapter 15) and teaching values and moral education (Chapter 16). Assessment and reporting (Chapter 18) is a major focus in teaching, as are ethical and legal issues (Chapter 20). Professional elements of teaching are discussed in Chapter 19, working effectively with parents is covered in Chapter 17, and Chapter 21 deals with the impact of teacher competences and standards.

CONCLUDING COMMENTS

So there you have it. It is an ambitious task to take all the elements of an enterprise as dynamic as teaching and somehow collapse them into one book.

In this first chapter you have seen glimpses of what teaching is about and why it is a most rewarding and fulfilling professional career. Have you been encouraged to go further? If this is a realistic picture of what teaching is all about, do you see that this is for you?

Technological advances in ICT mean that traditional forms of teaching are being rapidly overtaken by new teaching approaches. You have to have the appetite and the desire to be part of this new wave of teaching and learning. Over to you.

KEY ISSUES RAISED IN THIS CHAPTER

1. Memories of good teachers we have had are likely to leave a lasting impression upon us.
2. There is a need to be reflective and strike out with new approaches.
3. Young children in early childhood centres and in primary schools have rapid cognitive development and need to be encouraged.
4. Students in secondary school need to be encouraged to gain understandings as well as factual knowledge, within an atmosphere of respect and trust.
5. There are many ways that a teacher can bring about positive learning situations.
6. You need to reflect on why you want to be a teacher as well as to find satisfactory answers about how to teach.

REFLECTIONS AND ISSUES

1. A teaching self-portrait
   In one paragraph describe what you think you will be like as a teacher.
   As a teacher I think I will be:
   _____
   _____
   _____

2. McKenzie *et al.* (2008) state that the top five factors in the decision to become a primary teacher are:
   - personal fulfilment
   - desire to work with young people
   - teaching makes a worthwhile social contribution
   - enjoyment of subject areas
   - passion for education.

   By contrast the top five factors cited by secondary teachers are:
   - enjoyment of subject areas
   - personal fulfilment
   - teaching makes a worthwhile social contribution
   - desire to work with young people
   - desire to pass on knowledge.

   Reflect upon these factors and the differences between primary teacher and secondary teacher decisions. Give a brief explanation.

3. Have you recollections about a teacher you experienced and who you considered at the time was the 'best' teacher you ever had? What qualities did this teacher demonstrate that made

them the 'best' in your eyes? Would you want to develop any of the same qualities? Might they still be relevant for teaching in the twenty-first century?
4 At this point, have you considered any ideas of specific approaches you might want to try out with a class? Explain how you might use these. Why did you choose these and not others?
5 Is it possible to be a creative teacher? What things might you do which could be described as being 'creative'?
6 Consider how rapid developments with ICT might cause teachers in the near future to make major changes in their teaching. Describe two or three examples.
7 Do you have personal teaching philosophies that are likely to affect how you might teach? For example do you consider that:
  - separate subject disciplines are more important than integrated subjects?
  - not all subject matter is created equal?
  - the curriculum should stress societal needs over individual needs?
  - curriculum should reflect current real-life situations?
  - the curriculum should provide the tools for individual survival in an unstable and changing world?
8 Explain the 'teaching platform' that describes your current thinking about teaching and learning.

Special references

Grieshaber, S (2009) 'Equity and quality in the early years of schooling', *Curriculum Perspectives*, 29(1):91–7.
Ryan, K Cooper, JM & Tauer, S (2008) *Teaching for Student Learning: Becoming a Master Teacher*, Houghton Mifflen, Boston.
Wise, B (2008) 'High schools at the tipping point', *Educational Leadership*, 65(8):8–13.
Wolk, S (2008) 'Joy in School', *Educational Leadership*, 66(1):8–15.

Web sources

For additional resources and tips on becoming a teacher, please go to: www.pearson.com.au/myeducationlab.

2

THE EDUCATION REVOLUTION: NATIONAL CURRICULUM AND EQUITY

2.1 | INTRODUCTION

Two major developments in teaching are covered in this chapter, namely the national curriculum and equity. They are two integral elements of the Education Revolution announced by the Rudd government in 2007.

A new national curriculum could have a major impact upon what teachers will teach and what students will learn for each year of schooling. The Rudd government is also emphasising equity as a major goal of its education revolution.

The development of a national curriculum is a major priority. National curriculum proposals have been attempted in the past but after a few years they have 'spluttered' and died. This time there does appear to be more commitment by the states and territories. The newly created legislation enacted by the Commonwealth Government, with related funding support, will act as a major incentive.

Equity issues have confronted educators in Australia over many decades, especially with regard to Indigenous Australians. Equity for all disadvantaged students has been highlighted over recent years as a result of the publicity given to large-scale international tests such as PISA and TIMSS. The Rudd government has committed itself to such priorities as lifting rates of retention to Year 12 or equivalent to 90 per cent by 2020; sharply increasing rates of participation in higher education for students from 'disadvantaged' backgrounds; and raising literacy and numeracy outcomes, especially for Indigenous students, where it has a target of halving the attainment gap in Year 12 by 2020 (Gillard 2008a).

2.2 | A NATIONAL CURRICULUM FOR AUSTRALIA?

There is a lot of 'déjà vu' about the current major push for a national curriculum in Australia. In each of the decades since the 1980s there have been similar initiatives and all failed. Whether the Rudd government's current major impetus through the National Curriculum Board (NCB) will fare any better is a fascinating question (Reid 2009). Certainly, this time around a number of safeguards for success have been included, such as financial inducements for non-government schools (*Schools Assistance Bill*), the creation of an *Education Act* to establish the Australian Curriculum, Assessment and Reporting Authority (ACARA), and wide-ranging consultations. Yet it is all happening at break-neck speed, as noted by Kennedy (2009) – 'Kevin Rudd's government is rushing headlong towards a national curriculum with framing papers in key subjects already developed and consultations in full swing' (p. 3). This new national curriculum is intended to be operating in all states and territories at the beginning of the 2011 school year. That surely is a very tall order!

As noted in Table 2.1, there have been several attempts at developing a national curriculum in Australia since the 1980s. Of course, there have been much earlier attempts to create 'broad fields' (Bellack 1964), 'core curriculum' (Alberty 1953) and 'common curriculum' (Lawton 1975).

The reasons for wanting a national curriculum in Australia have appeared and reappeared over the decade. For example some common reasons include:
- to promote a national cohesion in the curriculum through effective collaboration
- to enable economies and efficiencies in curriculum – state curriculum agencies could be wound down
- a national curriculum reduces mobility problems for children of the armed forces and related occupations
- to produce an excellent, high standard curriculum.

> **YOUR TURN**
>
> Is it ever possible to have a national curriculum if the Australian Constitution gives the states and territories responsibility for curriculum?

2.2.1 Core curriculum

The core curriculum, a slim 24-page document developed by the then national body, the Curriculum Development Centre (CDC), was largely the brain child of the Director, Malcolm Skilbeck. It attempted to reconceptualise the existing school subjects within a social-reconstructionist framework (see Table 2.1).

It was suggested that students would study nine broad areas throughout their schooling, in an attempt to break down the concentration by schools on traditional subjects. These areas were:
- Communication
- Mathematics
- Scientific and technological ways of knowing and their social applications
- Moral reasoning and action
- Social, cultural and civic studies
- Environmental studies
- Arts and crafts
- Health education
- Work, leisure and lifestyle.

The authors were also concerned about two other dimensions, namely learning processes and learning environments. They were clearly not putting forward merely a subject-oriented core. The learning process and experiences included:
- learning and thinking techniques
- ways of organising knowledge
- disposition and values
- skills or abilities
- forms of expression
- practical performances
- interpersonal and group relationships.

TABLE 2.1 Attempts to develop a national curriculum in Australia since the 1980s

Year	Title	Developed by	Major elements	Impact
1980	Core Curriculum for Australian Schools	Curriculum Development Centre (CDC)	Areas of knowledge and experience: • Communication • Environmental studies • Mathematics • Works, leisure and lifestyle • Health education • Arts and crafts • Moral reasoning and action • Social, cultural and civic studies • Scientific and technological ways of knowing and their social applications	1 Major daily papers were very positive 2 Workshops and seminars held in all states 3 Parts of program were implemented in NSW, WA, NT 4 Only short-lived. Funding for CDC greatly reduced in 1981 – core curriculum discontinued

1989–1993	National Collaborative Curriculum Development	Australian Education Council (AEC) and Curriculum and Assessment Committee	• Mapping of content across the states in traditional subjects
			• 8 learning areas created and national statements and profiles created:
			  – English
			  – Science
			  – Mathematics
			  – Languages other than English
			  – Technology
			  – Studies of Society and Environment
			  – The Arts
			  – Health
				1 Initial major support from all states
				2 Post-1993–95 comprehensive implementation in many states
				3 Post-1995 new variations developed

1994–1996; 1997–1999	Discovering Democracy	Office of the Prime Minister; Curriculum Corporation	A box of source material and readers for primary schools and a similar box for secondary school students Topics 1 Who rules? 2 Laws and rights 3 Australian nation 4 Citizens and public life	1 Copies were distributed to all schools in Australia 2 Teachers were likely to 'dip into' and use materials selectively 3 Materials were well supported by websites supported by the Curriculum Corporation 4 Unlikely that materials would continue to be widely used after the first few years

2003–2008	Statements of Learning in 5 subjects for all schools	• Ministerial Council on Education, Employment, Training and Youth Affairs (MCEETYA) • Australian Education Systems Officials' Committee (AESOC) • Curriculum Corporation	Essential knowledge and skills to be achieved by all students at end of Years 3, 5, 7 and 9 for English, Mathematics, Science, Civics and Citizenship, Information and Communication Technology	1 States and territories appear to have simply revised existing syllabuses 2 Could be budget implications if allocations to states are dependent on results
2006	History Summit	1 Prime Minister Howard 2 Minister for Education, Science and Training, Julie Bishop	1 Proposed that Australian history should be taught as a compulsory subject in Years 9 and 10 2 To develop a model curriculum in History	1 No action because of change of government 2 History is however one of the subjects to be developed by the National Curriculum Board
2008–2010	National Curriculum	National Curriculum Board (NCB interim) Australian Curriculum, Assessment and Reporting Authority (ACARA)	To develop world-class curriculum for students K–12 starting with English, Mathematics, Sciences, History	Work in progress

In total they represented an impressive array of desired skills.

Their orientation toward 'opening up' learning was also applied to learning environments. It was suggested that they should include a variety of environments in addition to the classroom, namely:
- field work visits
- workshop experiences
- outdoors
- community institutions.

It was considered that a diverse range of learning environments was needed to give all students an opportunity to perform well and not just the academic minority who excel in the classroom environment.

Although developed nationally, the core curriculum appeared to be favourably received by the states and territories. Major newspapers at the time such as *The Australian* (25 June 1980) and *The Age* (27 June 1980) were very positive and supportive (Marsh & Stafford 1988). Workshops and seminars were arranged in all states by the CDC. Several states and territories such as NSW, Victoria, Tasmania and the Northern Territory made commitments to implement the core curriculum.

Writing in 1980, Skilbeck (1980, p. 25) was optimistic about the impact the CDC document would have in generating discussion, debate and policy decisions.

> It is one step in this whole process of clarifying, enlarging and developing the idea of core curriculum. It promises to be with us for a long time.

But predictions have a habit of not being fulfilled. Dr Skilbeck left the CDC in 1981. The Committee Report on the Review of Commonwealth Functions recommended that the budget for the CDC be halved. In these circumstances 'the core curriculum debate faded away' (Marsh & Stafford 1988, p. 249).

2.2.2 National Collaborative Curriculum Development project

A more vigorous approach, yet again a top-down approach, was initiated by the Commonwealth Minister of Education, John Dawkins, in 1989. He raised various concerns expressed in crisis rhetoric about Australian schools and the need to strengthen them (Marsh 1994a). Aware of the constitutional powers of the states, Dawkins was able to orchestrate and fund the National Collaborative Curriculum Development project by using the Australian Education Council (AEC) (comprising all state Ministers of Education) and a sub-committee, the 'Curriculum and Assessment Committee' (CURASS) to drive the operation. Teams worked intensively on the development of national statements and profiles and were able to produce completed documents within a five-year period.

The CURASS committee was wedded to an outcomes-based approach and this became a dominant element across the total framework. Although the eight learning areas included traditional subject areas (English, Mathematics, Science, Languages other than English) there were also attempts to cut across subject boundaries, reminiscent of the 1980 core curriculum document. These learning areas included Studies of Society and Environment, Technology, The Arts and Health (Physical Education and Personal Development).

Teams of writers were selected to produce draft statements and profiles for each of the eight learning areas within a very tight time frame (a process that is currently being repeated by the ACARA). The teams of writers were distributed over a number of states and were mainly officers seconded from assessment and accreditation agencies and research departments.

For the national statements, the teams were instructed to develop curriculum principles and a rationale. Especially, they were to provide details on each strand (concept) selected and level of difficulty for each of the bands (lower primary, upper primary, lower secondary). The four learning areas which cut across traditional subject boundaries had additional issues to consider: namely deciding how subjects would be grouped and which strands would be included to represent all the subjects.

This was especially difficult to achieve in the Studies of Society and Environment (SSE) learning area. For example a discipline-based approach to SSE was accepted by a special meeting of CURASS members in June 1992 (Marsh 1994a). This decision came back to haunt state education systems several years later and it is worth noting that ACARA has only concentrated to date on separate school subjects or disciplines.

For the national profiles, teams of writers were again selected to produce, for each learning area, a set of outcomes for each strand (concept), exemplifying the student outcomes by producing pointers and work samples.

The stakes were now much higher when it came to developing national profiles rather than merely producing national statements. As noted by Marsh (1994b), 'educators and politicians realised the clout of assessment and evaluation and how these tools could drive the whole education enterprise' (p. 110).

At this stage in the National Collaborative Curriculum Development project, CURASS became very 'top-down', imposing its will on all the profile writing teams. In the interests of quality control, CURASS insisted on the same number of levels for each learning area and a similar number of strands and outcome statements, even though there might have been sound pedagogical reasons to allow for greater variability.

By 1991, CURASS was very aware of its self-imposed deadline (30 June 1993) to complete all the national statements and profiles, to be presented to the AEC meeting in July 1993. These two years were ones of intensive effort by writing groups and involved very heavy workloads.

In addition to completing the profiles, CURASS also required an empirical validation of each, using teacher observations of student learning to verify the pointers and the outcome statements. This task was undertaken very speedily by ACER within the time frame, but the depth of analysis of these validations might well have been very limited.

The non-negotiable deadline of June 1993 was fast approaching. In 1992 Directors-General from all state and territory education systems had confirmed their strong commitment to implementing the national statements and profiles. Yet, in early 1993 there was intensive lobbying by subject interest groups representing areas such as Mathematics, Science and Physical and Sport Education. The subsequent media outrage was predictable and included such headlines as 'A failed curriculum' (*The Age* 31 May 1993, p. 2) and 'Science gone mad' (*Herald Sun* 10 June 1993, p. 13) as reported in Marsh (1994a).

> **YOUR TURN**
>
> It has been stated that the 1989–93 national statements and profiles were merely politically correct, 'dumbed down', and a mediocre set of standards. Do you agree? Discuss this with reference to a particular key learning area.

Federal Ministers requested last minute revisions to profiles to try to dampen down the criticisms. In a last minute plea to state Ministers for Education, a joint letter of support for the national statements and profiles from the ACTU and the Australian Chamber of Commerce and Industry was distributed the day before the fateful AEC meeting in Perth on 2 July 1993 (Marsh 1994a, p. 158).

At the 2 July 1993 AEC meeting the non-Labor Ministers formed an alliance against Labor Ministers and the motion to defer accepting the national statements and profiles was accepted 5/4. This deferment meant, in reality, the death of the national curriculum yet again.

By July 1993, Victoria indicated it wanted major changes especially to the Mathematics, Science and Studies of Society and Environment statements and profiles. NSW initially made preparations to implement them but, after a change of government and a subsequent education report by Professor

Ken Eltis (1995), backed away completely from outcomes and national profiles, opting instead for a reversion to traditional syllabuses.

Some states and territories continued with the national profiles and implemented them in their respective systems, although in some states (for example, in WA) they merely rebadged them. In other states (such as South Australia and Tasmania) the national statements and profiles were implemented very comprehensively in the first few years. Victoria accepted only three of the learning areas with minor changes (English, Technology and Health and Physical Education).

Although members of CURASS were hopeful that the national statements and profiles would continue to have a major impact, it was not to be. Dr Ken Boston's final address, as Chairman of CURASS, was both poignant and prophetic:

> I thank you for your contribution to the largest single collaborative activity ever attempted in the history of education in this country, and one which I believe will, in due course, have a profound impact on Australian schooling. We have achieved a great deal. As the individual states and school sectors begin to mine our material, they will find some very rich lodes in which the silver far outweighs the dross. (Boston 1993, p. 2)

However by the mid-1990s states and territories appeared to want to throw off the 'shackles' of a national approach in favour of different, state-oriented, conceptualisations. The New Basics Project (Education Queensland 2000) promised to be a very innovative approach in Queensland. South Australia developed a new Curriculum Standards and Accountability Framework in 2005. Victoria developed Essential Learning Standards in 2005. Tasmania developed a new curriculum, Essential Learnings, also in 2005.

 Although the attempt to produce a national curriculum in 1989–1993 failed, did education systems mine the rich lodes described by Boston? What did teachers gain, if anything, from the experience?

2.2.3 The Discovering Democracy project

The Discovering Democracy project was an interesting Commonwealth Government initiative which commenced in 1994, soon after the demise of the National Collaborative Curriculum Development project. The then Prime Minister, Paul Keating, announced the establishment of a Civics Expert Group to provide a plan for a program of public education and information on the Australian system of government. Whether the government saw this as a 'safer' inroad into a national curriculum for schools or whether it was concerned about a deficit in civic knowledge (Kennedy 2001) is a matter of conjecture. A sizeable budget was provided to develop a new program of civics and citizenship education. Even though there was a change of government in 1996, the incoming Howard government supported the program and continued the funding to complete the project over three years.

The project materials for primary and secondary schools were completed by the Curriculum Corporation and distributed to all schools in 1998. An implementation phase was scheduled for 1999.

Various writers have subsequently provided critiques of the project. Carter, Ditchburn and Bennett (1999) argue that the project represented a traditional approach and reflected an establishment point of view. Hogan and Fearnley-Sander (1999) contend that the project was overly ambitious and if taken up by teachers would occupy a quarter to a half of the time allocated to social studies. Finch (1999) was even more cynical when she considers it was an educational product – a tangible educational product – that politicians could display as a lead-up to celebrating the centenary of federation. Gill and Reid (1999) contend that the project 'valorises a white, male, Eurocentric concept of citizen and marginalises other significant sections of people in Australia at this time' (p. 39).

Although 'civics and citizenship education continues to be of major concern to all Australians in an increasingly uncertain and unstable world' (Kennedy 2008, p. 407), it does not appear that this attempt to provide a national subject in civics and citizenship education was successful.

As concluded by Finch (1999), although some elements of Discovering Democracy might become 'naturalised' into the programs of some schools, most will languish in school storerooms.

> **YOUR TURN**
>
> Do you agree that the Discovering Democracy project was too ambitious and finished up being an unsatisfactory political and intellectual compromise?

2.2.4 Statements of Learning

This collaborative venture between the states and territories and the Commonwealth Government is a classic example of 'hard policy'. Brady and Kennedy (2010) differentiate between 'soft policy' (for example, inducements, persuasion and staff development) and 'hard policy' (for example, legislation and delivery requirements linked to funding). They used these terms to describe earlier attempts to develop a national curriculum in Australia.

Ministers of Education agreed at a Ministerial Council on Education, Employment, Training and Youth Affairs (MCEETYA) meeting in July 2003 that Statements of Learning would be developed in English, Mathematics, Science, and Civics and Citizenship. It was stipulated that essential knowledge, skills, understandings and capacities would be detailed and that young Australians should have the opportunity to learn these by the end of Years 3, 5, 7 and 9. At a May meeting of MCEETYA in 2005, Information and Communications Technologies was added to the list. These year levels were chosen because common testing standards could be linked to them, although this is still under consideration.

More significantly, the Statements of Learning were finally approved by MCEETYA in 2006 and then, under the *Schools Assistance Act 2004* all education systems and jurisdictions were to implement them and to develop common testing standards in the five domains by 1 January 2008.

> **YOUR TURN**
>
> Do you consider the 'hard policy' strategy of requiring by Act of Parliament all states and territories to use Statements of Learning, a success? What criteria would you use to judge this?

On the surface, at least, this was a classic example of hard policy. To legislate for their use in all jurisdictions made it an obligatory requirement, however the aim was for state and territory curriculum developers to use these statements when they implemented their own curriculum documents. The Statements of Learning are not for the general use of teachers and the community.

Several interesting questions arise from these MCEETYA decisions:
- Is this a clever way by the Commonwealth to extend national testing in literacy and numeracy?
- Why were these five subjects chosen and others excluded?
- How seriously did states and territories go about the process of listing statements for these four year levels?
- How will the Commonwealth be able to monitor whether curriculum developers incorporate these statements into their respective curricula? What are the penalties if they don't?

As noted above, this is a different level of policy implementation by the Commonwealth Government. Perhaps this hard policy will bring all the states and territories into line and we will soon experience a tightly controlled set of national testing standards across five subjects. An alternative scenario is that nothing much will change, especially if national testing in these subjects at primary and secondary levels is slow in getting started. A cynical response might be that curriculum developers in state and territory jurisdictions could undertake superficial moves to indicate acquiescence to the 2004 Act without any serious commitment. After all, state and territory jurisdictions have had plenty of experience fronting up to Commonwealth demands and looking for and finding ways of upstaging them!

2.2.5 History Summit

This was another example of hard policy by the Commonwealth that appeared to gain some momentum in 2006, but the change of federal government in December 2007 caused the initiative to collapse.

It started in January 2006 with the then Prime Minister, John Howard, calling for a 'root and branch renewal' of the teaching of Australian history in the nation's schools. The newly appointed Commonwealth Minster for Education, Science and Training, Julie Bishop, took up the call and announced that a summit for invited academics, curriculum experts and teachers would be held in Canberra on 17 August 2006.

A group of 23 invited 'summiteers' (including only three teachers) attended the summit and, not surprisingly, recommended that Australian history should be taught in Years 9 and 10 as a core and separate subject. They also recommended that a model curriculum be developed.

Following on from the Summit, Ms Bishop commissioned a well-known History academic, Tony Taylor, to develop an outline model national curriculum framework in Australian history for Years 3–10. An Australian History Curriculum Reference Group was established in June 2007 to continue the work.

All of these activities came to an abrupt end in the latter months of 2007 when the government was defeated and Kevin Rudd's government was elected.

Again a number of interesting questions can be raised:
- Did Prime Minister Howard raise an important issue about Australian history which struck a chord with many educators? After all the NSW education system had implemented a compulsory course in Australian history for Years 9 and 10 almost a decade earlier.
- If the previous government had continued in office, would they have succeeded in making Australian History a compulsory subject for all state and territory jurisdictions?
- By concentrating on just one subject, was this a smarter manoeuvre by the Commonwealth to force their way into state and territory jurisdictions? Could they have then moved to other subjects and picked them off one by one?
- Even though the initiative failed, it is interesting to note that History was selected as one of four key subjects by the newly appointed National Curriculum Board. In other words, the publicity given to History by the Summit in 2006 may have raised its status with the National Curriculum Board in 2008.

2.3 NATIONAL CURRICULUM BOARD AND THE EDUCATION REVOLUTION

Prior to the 2007 federal election, Kevin Rudd launched his Education Revolution. This was followed by a policy, 'Establishing a National Curriculum to improve our children's educational outcomes'. He proposed a national curriculum board be set up to establish national standards for English, History, Mathematics and Science by 2010.

Very soon after the election when Rudd was able to form government he and the Deputy Prime Minister, Julia Gillard, announced the creation of a National Curriculum Board with Professor Barry McGaw as its chairman. The rhetoric in the media release (20 January 2008) was very stirring:

> The Board will be established by 1 January 2009 and will oversee the development of a world-class curriculum for all Australian students …
>
> there has been a longstanding need for a single, high quality national curriculum …
>
> We need to ensure children get the basics right, but we also need to focus on the achievement of excellence …
>
> We want to develop a rigorous national curriculum that helps Australian students and Australian schools compete internationally …

These were high-sounding goals indeed – all to be achieved within three years. It is interesting to note that the reasons for needing a national curriculum in 2008 were very similar to those expounded in 1989 for the National Statements and Profiles, namely:
- the disparity of educational attainments between states and territories
- the need for mobility for children of families who move across state and territory borders
- to remove unnecessary differences in curriculum between systems
- to enable economies of scale and efficiencies.

YOUR TURN

Should the rich diversity that we have in education systems across states and territories be given up in favour of a national, one-size-fits-all curriculum?

Yet, as noted by Kennedy (2009), arguments based upon correcting deficits are not ideal for developing a new curriculum – the vision should be about 'creating a future for young people that can draw on the best that a nation has to offer'. However, to be fair to the new NCB, the initial planning documents produced to date do expand upon their conception (see Figure 2.1).

FIGURE 2.1 National curriculum development program

Table of contents
1. The role of national curriculum in building Australia's future
2. Principles for developing national curriculum
3. Approaches to developing national curriculum: questions for discussion
4. Content
5. National curriculum content: questions for discussion
6. Achievement standards
7. National curriculum standards: questions for discussion
8. Cross-curricular learnings
9. National curriculum and cross-curricular learnings: questions for discussion
10. Development process
11. Communication, consultation and engagement
12. National curriculum development and consultation: questions for discussion

Source: NCB (2008a), pp 1-35.

FIGURE 2.2 The shape of the national curriculum: a proposal for discussion

Principles and specifications for development
1. Curriculum documents should be explicit about knowledge, understanding and skills
2. The curriculum should be based on the assumption that all students can learn and that every child matters
3. The curriculum should build on the early years learning framework
4. The curriculum should build firm foundational skills
5. The curriculum should provide students with an understanding of the past
6. The curriculum should be feasible taking account of the time and resources available
7. The primary audience for national curriculum documents should be classroom teachers
8. Time demands on students must leave room for learning areas that will not be part of the national curriculum
9. The curriculum should allow jurisdictions, systems and schools to implement it in a way that values teachers' professional knowledge and reflects local contexts
10. The curriculum should be established on a strong evidence based on learning, pedagogy and what works

Source: NCB (2008b), <www.acara.edu.au/verve/_resources/The_Shape_of_the_National_Curriculum_paper.pdf>, p 4.

The membership of the National Curriculum Board was appointed expeditiously. The thirteen members are highly experienced educators representing all states and territories, although inevitably the major representations are from NSW and Victoria.

As a first step the NCB issued a National Curriculum Development Paper in June 2008 in which it set down a set of questions that needed to be answered (see Figure 2.1).

As part of its commitment to wide consultation and an open development process, a number of forums were held. A national forum was held in June 2008 attended by 200 people and follow-up forums were held in states and territories.

In October 2008 there followed a more detailed paper entitled 'The Shape of the National Curriculum: A Proposal for Discussion'. In this document ten principles were listed which appear quite laudable even though some might be difficult to achieve (see numbers 2, 4 and 6, Figure 2.2).

Also included in this document was reference to:
- educational goals for young Australians (MCEETYA 2008)
- knowledge, understanding and skills, especially deep knowledge
- general capabilities (generic competencies)
- achievement standards
- curriculum development
- implementation.

The details included in this document do provide a comprehensive overview of what the NCB intends to do. Subsequent NCB documents indicate the procedures to be followed (see Table 2.2). The impression is one of efficiency, carefully sequenced timelines, and the expectation of successful curriculum outcomes (see Table 2.3).

Less obvious are some of the implicit philosophical and pedagogical priorities. For example, it is evident that no groupings of subjects into interdisciplinary subjects will be countenanced. The emphasis is firmly upon the development of deep knowledge from the disciplines and a close monitoring of standards. The 'world-class' curriculum envisaged by the Deputy Prime Minister, Julia Gillard, has no place for integrated studies (for counter-arguments see Johnston 2009). Even the choice of the first four subjects to be developed (English, Mathematics, Science and History) emphasises that these basic subjects are really important and that social/cultural/aesthetic subjects will have to wait (see Figures 2.3 and 2.4 on pages 22 and 23). These figures indicate the attention to be given to these four subjects, although it is mentioned in a subsequent NCB media release that phase 2 will include Geography, Languages and the Arts.

TABLE 2.2 NCB procedures to be followed

June 2008	National Curriculum Development Paper (discussion paper)
October 2008	The Shape of the National Curriculum: A Proposal for Discussion
October 2008	Learning area forums
20 November 2008	Framing papers released for English, Maths, the Sciences, History
February 2009	National forums on equity and diversity and stages of schooling
March 2009	Achievement standards workshop
February – March 2009	Expressions of interest for curriculum writers and advisory panel members

Source: NCB (2008b), pp 2-10.

TABLE 2.3 Curriculum development timelines

Draft timelines for writing the national curriculum are set out below.

Stage	Activity	Timelines K–10	Timelines senior years (11/12)
Curriculum framing	Confirmation of directions for writing curriculum for the learning areas of English, Mathematics, the Sciences and History	April 2009	April 2009
Curriculum development	2-step process for development of curriculum documents • Step 1 – broad outline; scope and sequence • Step 2 – completion of 'detail' of curriculum	April – December 2009	June 2009 – January 2010
Consultation	National consultation on curriculum documents and trialing	January – April 2010	March – June 2010
Publication	Publication of national curriculum documents in print and digital format	June – July 2010	July – September 2010

Source: ACARA, <www.acara.edu.au/curriculum_development_timelines.html>, accessed 15th December 2009. Reproduced with permission.

YOUR TURN

Will a centralised national curriculum enable academic performance of students to rise and therefore enable us to achieve higher rankings on international tests such as PISA?

Unlike what happened with the 1989–93 development of national statements and profiles, this time there does appear to be a much wider consultation with key stakeholders, albeit a very controlled, top-down consultation process (see Table 2.4 on page 24). Initial forums were held in June 2008 to discuss the first document, the National Curriculum Development Paper. According to the NCB over 200 people attended the national forum and many attended the subsequent state and territory forums.

FIGURE 2.3 Tables of content from the initial advice papers, October 2008

National English (23 pages)
- Reasons for studying English
- Debates in English education
- The place of literature
- The teaching of grammar in English
- Elements
  - knowledge about the English language
  - informed appreciation of literature
  - growing repertoires of English usage
- A 21st century English curriculum
- Curriculum materials consulted

National History (17 pages)
- Why history?
- History for the 21st century
- The objective
- Historical thinking
- What the curriculum should look like
- Guidelines for skills, knowledge and understanding
- Cross-curriculum learnings
- Pedagogy and assessment

National Mathematics (15 pages)
- Goals and challenges facing schools
- Embedding a futures-orientation in the curriculum
- Describing the strands
- Incorporating the numeracy perspective
- Purposes and emphasis across the stages
- Streamlining the curriculum
- Setting high but realistic expectations for student achievement
- Categorising and describing the content
  - domains
  - strands

National Science (15 pages)
- Purposes of school science education
- Selection of science content
- Relevance of science learning
- General capabilities and science education
- Assessment
- Structure of the curriculum (across 4 stages)
- A proposed structure for the science curriculum

Source: NCB (2008c), pp 1–5.

Small numbers of experts formed advisory groups to assist each of the four writers recruited to write the brief initial advice paper and then the framing papers. It is interesting to note that the four chief writers selected were all highly experienced and well-respected professors. Perhaps this was another tactical move to try to impress educators and the general community. Further forums in each of the four subject areas were held in October 2008 to discuss the initial advice papers (Figure 2.3). The chief writers clearly had to move very fast after these forums to complete their respective subject area framing papers, which were made available on the NCB website on 20 November 2008.

FIGURE 2.4 National framing papers

National English Curriculum (30 pages)
- Aims
- A futures orientation
- Terms used
- Considerations
  - beginnings and basics
  - the teaching of grammar
  - the texts
  - understanding, analysing, appreciating, constructing
  - the place of literature and Australian literature
  - pedagogy and disciplinarity
  - general capabilities across the curriculum
- Structure of the curriculum
  - The elements
    - element 1   language
    - element 2   literature
    - element 3   literacy
  - stages of schooling
- Pedagogy and assessment
- Advancing the teaching and learning of English
- Curriculum materials consulted

National History Curriculum (28 pages)
- Aims
- Terms used
- Considerations
- Structure of the curriculum
  - stages of schooling
    - stage 1
    - stage 2
    - stage 3
      - unit 1   History – earliest human communities to end of ancient time
      - unit 2   History from end of ancient period to beginning of modern period
      - unit 3   Modern world and Australia (1750–1901)
    - stage 4   (typically from 15–18 years of age)

- Conclusions
- Research basis

National Mathematics Curriculum (19 pages)
- Aims
- Terms used – content strands, proficiency strands, numeracy
- Considerations
  - equity and opportunity
  - the need to engage more students
  - ensuring inclusion
  - challenge of creating opportunity
  - connections to other learning areas
  - clarity and succinctness
  - thinning out the crowded curriculum
  - the role of digital technologies
- Structure of the curriculum
  - Stages of schooling, stages 1–4
- Pedagogy and assessment
- Conclusion
- References

National Science Curriculum (17 pages)
- Aims
- Terms used
- Considerations
  - selection of science content
  - relevance of science learning
  - flexibility and equity
  - general capabilities
- Structure of the curriculum
  - Stages of schooling, stages 1–4
- Pedagogy and assessment
- Conclusion
- References

Source: NCB (2008d), pp 2-25.

As might be expected, initial reactions to these framing papers were mixed, as revealed by media headlines at the time:

'Spelling, grammar back at the heart of new English' (Hiatt 17 October 2008, p. 9)

'Maths curriculum guru queries use of calculators' (Hiatt 15 October 2008, p. 14)

'National plan to teach history from kindy' (Hiatt 13 October 2008, p. 11)

Individuals and groups, especially professional associations, were encouraged to provide in-depth feedback to the NCB over the period 20 November 2008 to 28 February 2009, using a pro-forma survey

TABLE 2.4 National Curriculum Board stakeholders

The Board's stakeholders
The table below provides a summary of identified stakeholders with whom the Board consults.

Stakeholder group	Group breakdown
School-based	Teachers Students Principals, school administrators, school leaders, support personnel
Education authorities	School authorities (state and territory, Catholic and Independent) Australasian Curriculum, Assessment and Certification Authorities (ACACA) agencies Department of Education, Employment and Work Place Relations (DEEWR)
Professional bodies	National/state professional associations, including subject associations and principal organisations Unions Business/employers
Community	Parents and Parents and Friends Associations
Tertiary sector	Universities Academics Industry training sector
Government	Deputy Prime Minister's office Council of Australian Governments (COAG) Premiers, state/territory ministers Ministerial Council on Education, Employment, Training and Youth Affairs (MCEETYA) Federal opposition State/territory opposition

Source: NCB (2008a), pp 1-8.

with a comprehensive set of headings. A number of these detailed submissions are listed on the NCB website. For example, the Australian Science Teachers Association (ASTA) listed the following points:
- a wider definition of scientific literacy is needed
- mandated times for science are needed
- the use of 'stages' is confusing
- there must be balance between the three core concepts of understanding, inquiry skills and human endeavour
- the framework must be flexible for teachers
- teachers will need appropriate professional development
- it is a complex matter to accommodate senior Secondary Science courses – a framework is needed
- the persons selected to write the units must be credible, highly experienced Science education practitioners.

Interestingly, a joint communiqué from the four professional associations representing English (AATE), Mathematics (AAMT), Science (ASTA) and History (HTAA) stressed the need for direct engagement of teachers at all stages of the national curriculum's development and implementation (see Figure 2.5). They were clearly raising issues about the apparent top-down approach by experts appointed by the NCB. In passing, it should be noted that this was also a major criticism levelled at CURASS and experts involved in developing the national statements and profiles in 1989–93.

The K–10 draft national curriculum documents for English, Mathematics, Science, and History were released on 1st March 2010 for discussion. It is likely that they will generate considerable debate and discussion but early signs are quite positive.

FIGURE 2.5 Joint Communiqué from AATE, AAMT, ASTA and HTAA

Principles
A national curriculum should:
- be forward-looking whilst also valuing existing successful practices
- be written for teachers, in consultation with teachers
- support professional decision making at the classroom level
- allow flexibility to enable teachers to address the needs of their students
- promote teaching practices that engage and challenge students
- balance the following elements of authentic learning: the acquisition of knowledge, skills development, application, innovation and creativity.

Recommendations
The National Curriculum Board should ensure that:
- the relevant subject associations have access to the Board in order to provide input throughout all stages of the process
- writing groups are expertise-based, with representation that includes teachers and academics
- subject associations have representatives on expert writing groups
- involvement of teachers in consultation must be adequately funded
- teacher educators are kept aware of and involved in all aspects of the Board's work
- ongoing evaluation and renewal of the national curriculum is built into the medium and long term.

Source: From a joint statement by AATE, AAMT, ASTA & HTAA *Educating Teachers... Educating Young Australians for the 21st Century*, 17 June 2008.[1]

2.4 | REFLECTING ON CURRENT PROGRESS OF THE NCB (ACARA)

Kennedy (2009) argues that elements of the NCB represent the government's use of hard policy. The interim NCB became a statutory body under a Federal Act of Parliament, later in 2009. Further, the brief of the NCB was extended to include not only 'curriculum' but also 'assessment' and 'reporting'. The new Board was renamed the 'Australian Curriculum Assessment and Reporting Authority' (ACARA). This might raise alarm bells for many educators if in fact the Commonwealth Government intends to operate and control curriculum, assessment and reporting via ACARA.

Further evidence of hard policy is the *Schools Assistance Bill 2008*, which requires non-systemic schools (non-government schools) to implement the new national curriculum if they are to receive funding from the Commonwealth. This kind of 'big stick' can be wielded by the Commonwealth upon non-government schools but not government schools, which by the Constitution are the responsibility of the states and territories. This could lead to public and private schools being treated very differently in terms of the national curriculum.

Clearly it is very early days yet in the development of a national curriculum by NCB and ACARA. The efficiency of the exercise and the production of papers within announced deadlines is impressive. Well-renowned educators are driving the enterprise, from the NCB Chairman and Deputy Chairman to key writers. Yet there are issues surfacing already about the lack of input from teachers and subject associations and the need for extensive professional development (Tym 2010).

Kennedy (2009) in his overview paper of national curriculum in Australia refers especially to:
- the vision
- the history of national curriculum conversations
- implementing a national curriculum.

These are useful headings in summarising the current situation with the national curriculum.

Vision

Over the decades various visions have been promoted, such as progressivist, neo-liberal, social justice vision, equity-based and cultural. Julia Gillard (2008b) in her espousing of a world-class curriculum is emphasising excellence and equity, productivity and participation. Which of these become dominant in the next few years is a very interesting question.

> **YOUR TURN**
>
> How would you describe the vision that the NCB has for a national curriculum? Is it wide-ranging, comprehensive and flexible? Discuss.

History of national curriculum conversations

National curriculum ideas have been around for at least 30 years! More recently the term 'national consistency' has been advocated by many writers including Kerr (2000) and Reid (2005). 'Collaborative federalism' (Dawkins 1988) is another term used for the idea of state, territory and Commonwealth governments working together on core areas and sharing the costs and benefits of reforms.

There have been many failures in attempting to produce a national curriculum in the past. Short of major constitutional changes in the education powers of states and territories, it is unclear whether the current exercise will be any more successful.

Implementing a national curriculum

Reference has already been made to the establishing of ACARA as a statutory authority and the *Schools Assistance Bill*. This hard policy approach is reminiscent of the hard policies adopted in the UK (*Education Act 1988*) and the 'No Child Left Behind' legislation (US Department of Education 2002) in the USA. Yet official announcements to date by ACARA indicate that the implementation policies (and costs) will be the responsibility of the states and territories. Clearly there will be massive costs to provide professional development for teachers involved in teaching the national curriculum subjects. For example, Harris-Hart (2009) argues that few primary teachers have a sufficient background in History and that they will require concentrated training to develop academic and pedagogical knowledge in History. The hard policy approach could be seriously jeopardised if there is no quality control on how implementation is carried out. Based upon rampant criticisms of implementation policies in the UK and USA, implementation of the national curriculum in Australia may be a very stormy affair.

There is also the issue of whether 'general capabilities' will be included in a detailed way or whether they will be given only superficial treatment. Informal comments from ACARA officers indicate that they intend to scope and sequence general capabilities, but as noted by Reid (2009), if writers are not briefed on this before they start their work, it will not happen. Reid concludes that there are serious design issues with the national curriculum – 'the approach to issues, problems and challenges of the contemporary world requires us to cross established disciplinary boundaries, not remain trapped within them' (p. 14).

2.5 | EQUITY IN EDUCATION

2.5.1 Some important terms

'Equity' is a term frequently used in education when discussing education provisions that are fair to persons of all backgrounds. The NSW Department of Education and Training (2008b) has the following equity principles included in all its education programs:

1. Everyone is entitled to high-quality education and training programs that provide recognised credentials and clear pathways to employment and lifelong learning. The outcomes of education and training should not depend on factors beyond the learner's control or influence.
2. In the allocation of public resources, priority is given to narrowing those gaps in education and training outcomes that reflect need and prevailing social inequalities.
3. All young people are entitled, as a minimum, to be able to complete their school education to Year 12 or a vocational education equivalent.
4. The diversity of the population is recognised and valued by inclusive approaches to the development, conduct and evaluation of programs.
5. A demonstrated commitment to these equity principles and practices is a core responsibility for all those involved in education and training.

McGaw (2006) argues that improved equity in education is important for social cohesion – if existing social arrangements are simply reproduced then conferring privilege will remain unchecked.

'Social justice education' or 'equality of opportunity' are also terms that are widely used (North 2008). She suggests that 'recognition' and 'redistribution' are key elements of social justice. Various cultural groups frequently want some recognition of difference (for example, calls for gay pride). There are also many calls for redistribution for a wide range of social goods such as material goods (for example, housing) and social services (for example, health care) and access to high-quality educational institutions and the opportunities offered within them (for example, small classes). These twin elements do of course lead to conflicts. For example, it might be argued that 'neo-liberal economic and neo-conservative social principles have seeped into our psyche and thus masked the need for redistribution policies' (Anyon 2005).

> **YOUR TURN**
>
> Reflect on the terms 'recognition' and 'redistribution' with regard to disadvantaged students and families. What can teachers and schools do to assist with recognition? Is it possible for schools to do anything tangible to promote redistribution?

'Disadvantaged' is another term frequently used in the literature. Griffiths (2009) analyses the social and economic characteristics of disadvantaged student populations. He concedes that in Australia efforts have been made to provide support for disadvantaged groups. He cites the Disadvantaged Schools Program and the literacy programs (National Assessment Program, Literacy and Numeracy, NAPLAN). Yet despite these efforts there are ongoing high rates of inequity within Australian systems, particularly for Indigenous and low-SES students. He is pessimistic about whether social justice can achieve its goals and bring about a more equitable redistribution of resources. He quotes Starr (1991): 'Some kinds of social justice are just not achievable because they are at odds with the political and economic forces which shape our society' (p. 24).

'Social inclusion' is a term widely used in the literature. The Deputy Prime Minister, Julia Gillard (2008b), speaking at the Australian Council of Social Service (ACOSS) National Conference in April 2008, explained that:

> social inclusion means coordinating policies across national, state and local governments and with the community sector to ensure no Australian is excluded from meaningful participation in the mainstream economic and social life of the country (p. 3).

The Deputy Prime Minister cited the policy initiatives being taken by the Council of Australian Governments (COAG) such as
- providing universal access to early learning for all four year olds
- lifting Year 12 or equivalent attainment to 90 per cent by 2020

- providing an additional 450 000 training places
- halving the Indigenous gap in reading, writing and numeracy achievements within a decade
- halving the gap in Year 12 or equivalent attainment between Indigenous and non-Indigenous students.

These are indeed bold goals. However, progress to date with Indigenous education has been very limited.

2.5.2 Indigenous Australians and equity issues

Although official reports (MCEETYA 2006b) state that educational outcomes of Indigenous Australians have improved over recent decades, there is still no parity with non-Indigenous Australians. Some of the ongoing education equity issues include:
- many Indigenous students 'drop out' before Year 10
- few remain at school to complete Years 11 and 12
- few gain entry into university or its vocational equivalent
- the limited first-school options and life choices of Indigenous students perpetuate intergenerational cycles of social and economic disadvantage.

There is an urgent need to challenge the prevailing view that disparity in the educational outcomes of Indigenous and non-Indigenous students is 'normal' and that incremental gains are acceptable (MCEETYA 2006b, p. 4).

There have been many attempts in the past to break down this disparity. A number of specific intervention programs, including their pilot projects and trials, have been successful but only a small proportion of the total population of Indigenous students have had access to them. Also, they were seen as peripheral rather than integral to core business. Schools and systems have in the past devalued the educational potential of Indigenous students – 'there has been a socio-historical construction of whiteness embedded in Australian (Western) society as an invisible, unmarked norm' (Hambel 2006, p. 3).

As part of the Rudd government's Education Revolution, a wide-ranging approach is to be taken to improving equity issues for Indigenous students. These programs include:
- early childhood education
- school and community educational partnerships
- school leadership
- quality teaching
- pathways to training, employment and higher education.

Universal access to high-quality early childhood education (ECE) services for Indigenous children aged 0–5 is an essential recommendation. Currently only about 50 per cent of eligible four-year-old Indigenous children are enrolled in preschool. It should be noted that the recommendation is to provide access to two years of high-quality early childhood education and to develop educational programs that respect and value Indigenous cultures, languages and contexts.

The Australian Education Union (2009) has welcomed this recommendation but cautioned that a solid funding commitment will be needed and that the role of Indigenous languages in ECE and the role of Indigenous teachers and teaching assistants will need to be considered.

The second recommendation is to phase in by 2010 agreements between schools with significant Indigenous student cohorts and local Indigenous communities which will enable community engagement in the selection of staff; establish agreement on school goals and policies; and provide flexibility in the operation of the school and use of resources.

The school leadership recommendation will encourage school principals to include learning outcomes for Indigenous students as a key part of their accountability framework and will include a public reporting of these outcomes.

The fourth recommendation, quality teaching, focuses on teachers explicitly teaching literacy to

Indigenous students and having cultural understandings to significantly improve outcomes for Indigenous students.

The 'pathways to training, employment and higher education' recommendation focuses on providing culturally inclusive and intensive support to Indigenous students and on improving the vocational learning opportunities for Indigenous students.

These recommended programs are comprehensive and ambitious. They seek to accelerate the pace of change by engaging Indigenous children and young people in learning.

In September 2009, the newly formed Ministerial Council for Education, Early Childhood Development and Youth Affairs (MCEECDYA) agreed upon an Indigenous Education Action Plan to drive improvement through key areas of readiness for school; attendance; school leadership and quality teaching; literacy and numeracy; parental and community engagement; and pathways to real employment opportunities.

> ### YOUR TURN
>
> To what extent do you think Indigenous education can be 'built in' to mainstream teaching rather than being something just 'bolted on'? How can schools do more to adequately engage Indigenous students?

Another important ongoing issue is how the new Australian Curriculum, Assessment and Reporting Authority (ACARA) will address the issue of equity. ACARA (NCB) has a major focus upon excellence and producing a world-class curriculum. There is also an emphasis upon social objectives and social justice, but whether this will be developed as a major initiative is uncertain. If the major thrust of the NCB is on high performance of students and ways to overcome student under-performance then this may not be a good solution in dealing with equity issues.

As noted by Connell (2009), there is an assumption here that the education system as we have it is fine – 'all that is needed is to bring the laggards up to scratch' (p. 7).

Reid (2009) is particularly critical of the lack of an equity priority in the national curriculum. 'It [national curriculum] assumes that knowledge is neutral and that concepts such as cultural and social capital do not exist; and it fails to acknowledge the ways in which the very structures of the curriculum can discriminate against certain groups of students' (Reid 2009, p. 14).

2.5.3 International rankings on equity

Issues of high quality or high equity have been publicised over recent years as a result of large-scale comparative tests in science, mathematics and literacy, such as those recorded as part of the Organisation for Economic Cooperation and Development (OECD) regimes of PISA (Program for International Student Assessment) (OECD 2005) and the International Association for the Evaluation of Educational Achievement (IEA) regimes of TIMSS (Trends in International Mathematics and Science Study) (TIMSS 2008).

Global rankings on PISA and TIMSS are readily quoted these days in education circles. In particular, data on the 30 OECD countries in PISA portrays not only rankings in the listed subjects but also performance differences between schools and the social clustering of school performance. This is possible because in PISA, 15-year-olds complete a questionnaire which asks about gender, parents' education and occupation, cultural artefacts in the home and activities at home and school (McGaw 2007). It is thus possible to develop an index of social background.

What is disturbing is that for Australian students the relationship between social background and achievement is stronger than in other 'like' countries such as Finland and Canada. That is, although there is a single comprehensive system of education in Australia there are distinct program types (public and private schools, independent schools, selective entry schools) and so it is much harder to achieve equity (OECD 2006).

By contrast, in Finland and Canada the relationship between social background and educational achievement is not so marked and so it is possible for students in these countries to maximise their potential more effectively.

As noted by Hayes (2009), 'if you are disadvantaged in Australia the education system does not serve you as well as systems in other comparable countries' (p. 2). Other structures and activities further exacerbate equity problems in Australia. For example, experienced teachers will gravitate toward schools that are well resourced and where students are highly motivated (Haycock & Crawford 2008).

> **YOUR TURN**
>
> The PISA data shows that even though Australia has high-quality education, equity is low because of the extent of the association between social advantage and higher educational performance. Why is this association so marked? What innovative schooling policies might help to reduce the association and thereby increase equity?

By contrast, concentrations of low socio-economic status students in specific areas and schools means that these schools will have the weakest students and the greatest need for responsive curriculum programs to support them. According to Black (2006), a significant number of government schools and a number of Catholic schools in Australia are not regarded as being able to provide stable learning environments.

The pressures by governments to establish league tables and performance-based pay for teachers is yet another move that does not affect the strong social networks of middle-income families but further disadvantages lower-income families.

These pressures are now upon us as revealed by the following two points.

The recent launching of the My School website has had a major impact and there have been positive and negative reactions to it. Teachers' unions have argued strongly against the use of the website. Parents tend to be very positive about it. It is already having an impact in some states, such as Victoria, with teachers being directed to practise examples of the tests with their students.

A recent MCEETYA (2009) paper, Reporting and Comparing School Performance, announced that from 2009 the new Australian Curriculum, Assessment and Reporting Authority (ACARA) will be responsible for publishing relevant, nationally comparable information on all schools. This will include publication of the 2008 National Assessment Program, Literacy and Numeracy (NAPLAN) data.

The assertions made in this paper are both profound and ominous and could have dire consequences for low-SES schools.

> The information available will enable comparison of each school with other schools serving similar student populations around the nation and with the best-performing school in each cohort of 'like schools'.
>
> Through better monitoring of performance at the student, school and system level, educational outcomes can be lifted across all schools. MCEETYA (2009, p. 2)

2.5.4 Problem areas

Inevitably there is now a concentration of high-SES students in the independent school sector and high concentrations of low-SES students in government and Catholic secondary schools. This tends to create a pattern of circular disadvantage. Disengagement with school and high rates of early leaving maintain the cycle of disadvantage.

Various writers have documented some of the negative impacts of poverty on student achievement. Australian students from low-SES backgrounds are:
- twice as likely as students from high-SES backgrounds to under-perform in literacy and numeracy
- more likely to have negative attitudes to school, truant, be suspended or expelled and leave school early
- more likely to struggle with the transition from school to work
- less likely to enter university or to succeed in vocational education courses
- more likely to live in public housing, which is associated with lower educational attainment due to overcrowding, poor resources and a lack of social networks
- less likely to have educationally supportive social and physical infrastructure at home
- unlikely to escape poverty while they are young: more than three-quarters of children born into low-SES families are still in low-SES families when they turn 12 (Keating & Lamb 2004; Teese & Polesel 2003; Watson & Considine 2003).

Writing in the US (Barton 2004) contends that poverty affects children 'before and beyond school' and 'in school'. He lists these factors as:

Before and beyond school
- birth weight
- lead poisoning
- hunger and nutrition
- lack of reading to young children
- excessive television watching
- lack of parent availability
- increased student mobility
- minimal parent participation.

In school
- lack of rigour of curriculum
- inexperienced teachers
- insufficient teacher preparation
- large class sizes
- limited ICT instruction
- issues of school safety.

2.6 | SPECIFIC ISSUES

2.6.1 Student disengagement and early leaving

Data from the US indicate that students who are disadvantaged come from low-income or single-parent families, get low grades in school, are absent frequently and often change schools. They make up the majority of the school drop-outs.

Black (2006) analysed data from the state of Victoria. She noted that over one-third of early leavers cited factors such as not doing well at school, not liking school or not liking what was on offer at school. She concluded that 'early leavers who do not take up further study or employment face a gradual path of exclusion from education, training and employment institutions and society at large' (Black 2006, p. 4).

For these early leavers there can be major personal costs (Black 2006; Dusseldorp Skills Forum 2005; Vinson 2004):
- lower wages and financial insecurity
- poorer mental and physical health

- a higher likelihood of child abuse and neglect when early leavers become parents
- higher instances of homelessness and drug and alcohol abuse
- mortality rates up to nine times higher than their counterparts.

2.6.2 Teacher quality and disadvantaged students

There seems to be an inclination by some writers and certainly by the media to blame teachers and schools for the lack of student engagement, poor performance and early leaving. For example, Leigh and Ryan (2008) in their studies conclude that Australian government schools and their teachers' productivity, as measured by output per dollar, declined by some 73 per cent with regards to literacy between 1964 and 2003. They assert that this may have been due to falling teacher quality. Zyngier (2009) in a detailed response questions the methodology they used and their findings. He strongly refutes the claim there is falling teacher quality.

Wescombe-Down (2009) contends that teachers in Australia do not pay sufficient attention 'to the fragility of students during the process of teachers' core business: discharging what we know as education' (p. 4). He asserts that children should be protected from the 'low-level, long-term and therefore far-reaching effects resulting from malpractices of inappropriate pedagogy and teacher behaviour in classrooms' (p. 4). These are stirring comments, even though the author provides little concrete evidence to support the claims.

The media too is quick to pounce upon reports of 'what makes for good teaching' and seems to enjoy 'teacher bashing'. On the one hand, educators try to provide school programs that are emancipatory and concerned with social justice and transformation (Gale & Cross 2007), but the media and conservative commentators 'attempt to lay the blame for many of society's problems at the feet of schools, teachers and the university faculties of education' (Zyngier 2009, p. 11).

> **YOUR TURN**
>
> How we value, nurture and educate young children is central to who we are as a community and a nation. This is especially the case for the most fragile and vulnerable children and families. What recommendations would you make to achieve progress?

2.7 | SOME SOLUTIONS

2.7.1 Early childhood education

Early childhood is acknowledged as a period of critical physical, emotional, intellectual and social growth. Recent evidence from the neurological sciences suggests that 75 per cent of brain development occurs during the first five years of life, much during the first three years.

> **YOUR TURN**
>
> Governments around the world are recognising the value of investing in early childhood education and the benefits that accrue for the child, the family and the community. Is this a critical area in which to concentrate on equity issues? Give details.

Grieshaber (2009) comments on the importance of equity of access in the early years – which means that all children have opportunities to access quality early childhood programs and are not restricted by family income, parental employment, special education requirements, or cultural, ethnic or language background (OECD 2006). She notes that 'at-risk' children and families need greater efforts to provide access for them.

As noted above, the Rudd government has provided for free, quality early childhood programs with qualified early childhood teachers for 15 hours per week for 40 weeks per year (Rudd 2008). The improvement of services to Indigenous children is included in this plan although it may be difficult to implement this in isolated and remote communities. The number of Indigenous children attending preschools has risen in recent years but is still only around 50 per cent. This means that many are less 'school ready' and have difficulty in the transition to primary schools.

ACARA has recently finalised the Early Years Learning Framework, which is part of COAG's reform agenda for early childhood education.

2.7.2 Primary education

Historically, the funding for primary schools compared with secondary schools has always been much lower (Angus *et al.* 1999). Data provided by the National Board of Employment, Education and Training in 1994 indicated that there were some improvements in resources allocated to primary schools.

However announcements by MCEETYA and MCEECDYA, and in particular the release of the 'National Goals for Schooling in the Twenty-first Century', will put considerable pressure on Australian primary schools. A study by Angus *et al.* (2004) found that a majority of the primary principals interviewed felt that they would be unable to meet the expectations placed on them by the new national goals. Angus and Olney (2009) are currently undertaking research with 30 low-SES schools to investigate how they can most effectively target their resources so that they can reduce the number of students failing to meet the national literacy and numeracy minimum standards.

The other major equity issue for primary schools (and lower secondary) is the standardised literacy and numeracy testing in Years 3, 5 and 7. It is argued by education specialists that the benchmark tests which make up the National Assessment Program, Literacy and Numeracy (NAPLAN) are seriously flawed. For example, Woods (2007) argues that these benchmark standards have major problems such as:

- the standard of the benchmarks keeps changing for political reasons; the standard was originally set high in 1996 but then it was lowered because too many children were unable to reach it – it is a subjective standard
- no consideration is given to contexts of learning in schools – the tests just measure a narrow set of universal skills regardless of the context
- the sub-categories of reporting are too simplistic and they just perpetuate stereotypes
- there is little evidence that minimum national standards will lead to improved outcomes for student achievement.

There are also wider pedagogical issues: high-stakes testing narrows instruction; it forces teachers to teach to the tests; it reduces teachers' professionalism; and it reduces students' engagement (Wyatt Smith 2008; Kerin & Comber 2008).

2.7.3 Secondary education

Equity is a major issue in many secondary schools. As stated by Black, Stokes and Turnbull (2010):

> At the beginning of the 21st century, the Australian education landscape reflects the deepening economic and social divides at work across the country. At one end of the spectrum, our school students are reportedly performing well in relation to the OECD average. At the other end, there is strong evidence to indicate that educational outcomes are worsening for many young people and that significant numbers are either underachieving or in danger of opting out of the schooling process. As the panorama of work, family and community undergoes sweeping change, Australia is becoming a high performing but low equity country (p. 1).

Australian students from low socio-economic backgrounds are increasingly clustered in schools with poor educational outcomes (Keating & Lamb 2004; Hay 2010). There is a worrying trend for schools to continue to reproduce and reinforce existing patterns of privilege and disadvantage. Indicators of this are problem areas of educational disengagement and early school leaving.

Various reports on secondary schools assert that what is needed is to transform the personal and social fortunes of people who are disadvantaged (Feeney & Feeney 2002). McGaw (2007) suggests that the differences between disadvantaged and advantaged schools might be bridged by co-location of schools, which would necessitate sharing of resources and considering the needs of the whole community. Hayes (2009) suggests service-based innovation that gets to the root of the teaching relationship by developing generic skills for students that will keep them engaged in their transition from school to full-time work. Black, Stokes and Turnbull (2010) refer to the City Learning Centre as a classroom without walls in the heart of Melbourne's Central Business District. Year 9 and 10 students from disadvantaged communities come to the City Learning Centre for one week after having spent 'pre-production' time at their respective schools working on a topic such as 'Melbourne has a bad graffiti problem'. After the one week at the City Learning Centre, the students have a 'post-production' period back at their schools where they reflect on outcomes.

Kerin and Comber (2009) take a positive stance on the recently introduced standardised literacy testing for Year 9 students (NAPLAN) by noting that the data could contribute to understandings and knowledge of individual student literacy. It could be a springboard for ongoing classroom interventions with 'at-risk' students.

By contrast other writers such as Zyngier (2009) and Millard (2003) contend that these attempts do not get at the heart of the problem. Zyngier argues that it is unfair for teachers to be blamed for the failures in our secondary schools. In an earlier paper, Zyngier (2003) argues that if our secondary schools do not promote relationships that foster self-expression and self-realisation, then schools will continue to contribute to injustice and oppression for 'at-risk' students. Millard (2003) concurs and states that 'making schools more inclusive may involve teaching and supporting staff to challenge their own discriminatory practices and attitudes' (p. 7). As an example, Penney and Walker (2007) refer to an endeavour to initiate a transformative curriculum for senior secondary students in Western Australia which had the potential to open up opportunities for less academic students. Unfortunately, interest groups of teachers were against these new, outcomes-based frameworks. They mounted a strong campaign, together with vocal support from the daily newspaper, to bring about its demise.

CONCLUDING COMMENTS

National curriculum and equity are two extremely important topics for teachers. If ACARA rolls out a binding curriculum, assessment and reporting model, to be implemented by all government and non-government schools, then this will indeed be all-encompassing and will greatly prescribe what teachers will do. Alternatively, if states and territories can find ways to reduce the national pressures, then perhaps the much-heralded national curriculum might become little more than a background discussion paper.

Equity issues have always been a major problem for schools, especially trying to find solutions for disadvantaged groups such as Indigenous Australians and minority groups. The recent interest in international ranking tests such as PISA is based upon governments' concerns about the data publicly available on student achievement and equity. Every country is trying to aspire to high-quality standards and high equity, but at present Australia's equity results are far from satisfactory.

KEY ISSUES RAISED IN THIS CHAPTER

1. National curriculum has been discussed and approaches put forward on several occasions over the last 30 years with little success.
2. The constitutional rights of states and territories to be responsible for schooling have always been a predicament for federal governments.
3. The current attempt by ACARA to develop and implement a national curriculum represents a 'hard policy' approach because of the accompanying legislation and funding compliance requirements.
4. NCB (ACARA) has made an impressive start in developing a national curriculum, but the three-year timeline is extremely tight and may lead to some conflicts between key players in the next few years.
5. Equity and related terms, such as 'social justice' and 'social inclusion', have been widely used in discussing equity problems in Australian schools.
6. Two terms, 'recognition' and 'redistribution', are fundamental elements but they have been difficult to achieve. Neo-liberal economic and neo-conservative social principles have limited opportunities for redistribution policies.
7. Equity access for Indigenous Australians has always been a major problem, but recent initiatives under the Rudd government's Education Revolution, such as two years of high-quality early childhood education and agreements between schools and local communities, may lead to some progress.
8. International rankings on equity such as PISA, which indicates that Australia is high on quality but low on equity, may force governments to look more closely at funding needs.
9. Student disengagement and early leaving are still major problems for secondary schools.

REFLECTIONS AND ISSUES

1. The drift of enrolments to non-government schools in all states and territories is increasing social segregation and causing equity problems. Do you agree? What major education policies might be initiated to reduce this drift?
2. Is there a major difference of opinion over the type of national curriculum that teachers and academics want and what politicians, media and members of the public want? In the current development of a national curriculum how are these opposing stances being addressed?
3. Over the last two decades successive federal governments have had an increasingly interventionist agenda. Make a list of some of these interventions and their impact on teaching.
4. 'The current content of school subjects is out of step with the kind of learning that is needed for all students to start to understand and make sense of the world and feel capable of contributing to how the future will evolve' (Cole 2007, p. 14). Reflect on this statement. To what extent is the current work on a national curriculum following this stance?
5. The National Curriculum Board states that it is committed to an open development process with substantial consultation with the profession and the public. To what extent is this happening so far? What further refinements to this open development process might be needed?
6. 'Principles of fairness and social justice demand that children from different social backgrounds have an equal start in adult life.' Consider this statement in terms of moral, social and economic arguments.
7. 'Reducing social inequity in education would provide a massive boost to skill levels in the workforce. The large disparity in school outcomes indicates a waste of talents, skills and resources' (Save Our Schools 2008, p. 4). Explain the argument being presented here. Give reasons for supporting or rejecting it.

8 A national Early Years Learning Framework (0–5 years) has recently being developed. How will issues of equity be addressed, especially reducing the gap in achievement between those from socially advantaged and disadvantaged backgrounds?
9 Secondary education dominates the agenda of governments and departmental officials and this has been reflected in greater resources and improved conditions of work compared with primary education. Angus *et al.* (1999) state that 'for every $100 spent on educating a student in a secondary school at least $23 less is spent on educating a student in primary school' (p. 5). Is this a reasonable stance for the twenty-first century? What might be done to alleviate the situation for primary schools?
10 'There is considerable evidence that secondary students from low socio-economic backgrounds are less likely to achieve academic success at school compared with students from high ones, and that working class students continue to exit formal education with fewer and less valuable qualifications' (Hay 2010, p. 2). What policy initiatives are occurring in your state or territory to try to alleviate these issues?
11 Rotherham and Willingham (2009) make a strong case for a twenty-first century curriculum for all students. The following quotation sums up some of the difficulties of changing a teacher's mind set – 'We don't yet know how to teach self-direction, collaboration, creativity and innovation the way we know how to teach long division' (p. 19).

Discuss the problems involved in moving to a twenty-first century curriculum.

Endnote

1 Reproduced with the permission of The Australian Association for the Teaching of English, The Association of Mathematics Teachers, Inc., The Australian Science Teachers' Association and The History Teachers' Association of Australia. Sourced from: www.asta.edu.au/freestyler/files/statement%2017%20June.doc. Accessed 22 December 2009.

Special references

Black, R (2006) *Equity and Excellence: Where Do We Stand?* An Education Foundation Fact Sheet, Education Foundation, Melbourne.
Kennedy, K (2009) 'The idea of a national curriculum in Australia: What do Susan Ryan, John Dawkins and Julia Gillard have in common?' *Curriculum Perspectives*, 29(1):1–9.
Kerr, D (2000) *Achieving a World Class Curriculum in Australia*, IARTV seminar series, No. 96, IARTV, Melbourne.
Marsh, CJ (1994a) *Producing a National Curriculum: Plans and Paranoia*, Allen & Unwin, Sydney.
McGaw, B (2007), 'Achieving economic and social objectives', *Professional Magazine*, 22, November pp. 11–17.
Reid, A (2005) 'The politics of National Curriculum Collaboration: How can Australia move beyond the railway gauge metaphor?'. In C Harris & CJ Marsh (eds), *Curriculum Developments in Australia*, Openbook, Adelaide.
Woods, A (2007) 'Searching for equitable outcomes for all students', *Curriculum Perspectives*, 29(1).

Web sources

For additional resources on achieving quality and equity in education, please go to: www.pearson.com.au/myeducationlab.

PART 2

STUDENT LEARNING

Taking it to the Classroom
www.pearson.com.au/myeducationlab

Number of years teaching: 2 years
Year level teaching now: Year 5

First day of teaching memories:

My classroom was very organised, displays up, desks arranged, little notes and treat (an eraser each) welcoming them into Year 5P. I was extremely excited to meet the students and have them all in 'my classroom'. I wanted to be knowledgeable about who they all were; I achieved this by looking at past class photos and discussing their background history when meeting with their past year teachers.

Rachael Peterson
Melbourne Girls Grammar

chapter 3	How students develop and learn
chapter 4	Learner motivation and developing self-esteem
chapter 5	Learning environments

3

HOW STUDENTS DEVELOP AND LEARN

3.1 | INTRODUCTION

Educators, and especially educational psychologists (such as Woolfolk 2008 and Santrock 2008), remind us that all students have basic human needs, although the intensity of any particular need varies from student to student. The needs are variously described but generally include physical, social, emotional and intellectual needs.

The term 'human development' is often used to refer to changes that occur in humans between conception and death. The emphasis is on changes that appear to occur in orderly ways in terms of physical development, personal development, social development, cognitive development and moral development.

Changes that occur in individuals are judged to be for the better in terms of being more adaptive and flexible and hence the term 'development' is used.

Teachers have the opportunity to observe at first hand how individual students develop and the nature of their present developmental tasks. Observation of students' work habits, manual skills and small group behaviour can be very revealing for the teacher and it is most important that checklists are used to systematically monitor students' coping behaviours. (For example, see the checklist in Figure 3.1.)

FIGURE 3.1 Checklist for observing individual students

How well do I know students in my class?
1. Have I started an individual record of behaviour for each student?
2. Do I know each student's general school achievement?
3. What are their specific achievement needs in terms of skills?
4. What have been some significant aspects of social behaviour for each student?
5. Which students have physical handicaps?
6. Which students have emotional difficulties?
7. Which students need particular help in social adjustment?

Source: Based on Byers and Irish 1961.

However, it is also important to note that there is a lot of disagreement about the way 'development' occurs. Although most developmental theorists agree that humans develop at different rates, that development is relatively orderly and that development takes place gradually, on other matters there is considerable disagreement. For example:
- Are the major forces influencing development due to the environment or are they determined at birth?
- Are there similar patterns of development for all children or are there many unique paths?
- Is development sequential and cumulative or is it best characterised by stages and developmental leaps?

Although several major developmental theories will be analysed in this chapter, it is important to remember that each theory is nothing more than a set of reasonable but tentative suggestions. They are useful in that they organise and give meaning to facts and make predictions about changes in children's behaviour over time, but they typically account for only some of the behaviour. These themes are plausible and need to be known by practising teachers, but they lack any substantial empirical testing.

As noted by Barrow (1984), developmental theories and generalisations have not been empirically validated and it is erroneous to adopt an exclusive, monolithic theory of development as the basis for planning curricula and organising teaching. Glassman and Wang (2004) remind us that developmental theories are dynamic and dependent on use. The way in which we might use a particular theory depends upon how we interpret it and use it as a tool.

Different cultural groups may not follow the developmental stages advocated in these theories. As a case in point, the circumstances and medical conditions of Aboriginal children can be major impediments to their development. For example, Zubrick *et al*.'s (2008) study noted that suboptimal foetal growth among Aboriginal children was high (20% compared with 13% for the total population); and that 24% of Aboriginal children were at high risk for significant emotional or behavioural difficulties. There is therefore not the same likelihood that these children will develop along the stages proposed by the developmental theories described below.

3.2 | THEORIES OF COGNITIVE DEVELOPMENT

3.2.1 Piaget

Jean Piaget and other psychologists, such as Bruner (1966) and Vygotsky (1978), developed cognitive theories that depict how individuals develop by a series of stages of cognitive development.

Jean Piaget (1896–1980) was the major pioneer of cognitive theory (Berger 2006; Heaven 2001). He was hired as a psychologist to field-test questions for a standard intelligence test for children. In checking the 'right' answers and 'wrong' answers children gave to specific questions he became interested in why children of the same age shared similar mistaken concepts. This led him to consider a developmental sequence that could explain intellectual growth.

Piaget believed there is a biological inevitability to how children develop. He undertook an intensive observation of individual children (especially his own children) and by this *clinical* method established his theoretical principles.

He used the term 'schema' to demonstrate how children actively construct their world. A schema is a concept or framework that exists in an individual's mind to organise and interpret information (Santrock 2001).

Piaget contended that there are two processes responsible for how children use and adapt their schemata: 'assimilation' and 'accommodation'. Assimilation occurs when a child incorporates new knowledge into existing knowledge. Accommodation occurs when a child adjusts to new information (Santrock 2008). That is, assimilation involves adjusting the environment into a schema, whereas accommodation is adjusting a schema to the environment.

Piaget also used the term 'cognitive equilibrium' to explain why children use the processes of assimilation and accommodation. Cognitive equilibrium is a state of mental balance. When a child has a new experience that does not fit into his/her existing understanding, then a state of 'cognitive disequilibrium' occurs. Initially this produces confusion, but it eventually leads to cognitive growth (Berger 2006).

Piaget considered that even young infants develop schemata. This is a lifelong process whereby all humans construct and modify their schemata and this development unfolds through stages.

Piaget's theory has had a major impact on educators and schooling because of the insights he has provided, namely that:

- children think differently (in qualitative terms) at various stages of their development. Their movement through these stages depends on the quality of their experiences
- learning requires active involvement, physically and mentally, between the child and the environment
- children build their own cognitive structures. They do not passively receive knowledge but organise and transform it according to their cognitive structures
- children think differently to adults and their thinking levels vary at different stages.

Piaget's theory is geared towards children and not adults. The focus is on children's actions. What does this mean in terms of the teacher's role?

Piaget saw cognitive or intellectual development as having four stages:

1 Sensori-motor (0–2 years)
2 Pre-operational (2–7 years)
3 Concrete operational (7–11 years)
4 Formal operational (11 years and above).

He considered that every individual passed through these four stages in the same order, although there would be variations in the ages associated with each stage. It should be noted that an individual does not end one stage suddenly and commence another. Rather, there is a gradual merging from one to another. In fact, it is possible that in certain situations an individual could display the characteristics of a certain stage and for other situations demonstrate characteristics of a higher or lower stage.

1 Sensori-motor stage (0–2 years)

Infants experience the environment as a result of their senses and from their body movements. At the end of this stage they can solve simple problems in their heads.

Children learn:
(a) that objects are permanent and still exist when they can no longer see them. They use images to stand for objects (mediation)
(b) to initiate goal-directed actions. They use physical and mental trial and error methods to manipulate objects.

2 Pre-operational stage (2–7 years)

Piaget considered that this stage represents a quantum leap because children start to use symbols. They make something to stand for something else. Language becomes increasingly important for them in developing their symbols. Experience is vital for students to develop their thought patterns. See Figure 3.2.

Children at this stage:
(a) classify objects based on a single characteristic
(b) form and use symbols such as words, gestures and signs
(c) mime or pretend actions such as combing their hair
(d) formulate primitive concepts
(e) are egocentric – that is, have difficulty in taking another person's point of view

(f) have difficulty in considering more than one aspect of a situation at a time (decentring)
(g) have difficulty understanding conservation (that the amount or quality of matter stays the same even though its shape or position can change).

3 Concrete operational stage (7–11 years)

At this stage individuals can apply logical thought processes but only with concrete objects or problems. They can think through particular actions without having to go through the process of trying each one by trial and error.

Individuals operating at this stage are typically tied to personal experience. If they can partake in activities with concrete objects they can produce all kinds of thinking. A major element is reversability – the ability to reverse one's thinking processes: to realise that a ball of clay can make a dog, but that it can be returned again to a ball of clay. See Figure 3.3.

Children at this stage:
(a) can use different classification systems. They can sequence numbers and classify objects by colour, shape or size
(b) can recognise the stability of the physical world
(c) can recognise that elements can be changed without losing their basic characteristics (conservation)
(d) can rank different objects in order, for example based on size (serialising)
(e) develop a more socio-metric and less egocentric approach when communicating with others.

case study: How I use Piaget in my teaching

With my Year 7 class I find Piaget's developmental theory an important guide to how I teach Mathematics. I know that some of my students are at a concrete operational stage while others are at a formal operational stage. Therefore I have to use a range of concrete examples (coloured circles, geometric shapes, plastic cards) to give my students hands-on experiences and to encourage them to discover the rules of addition, subtraction, multiplication and division.

FIGURE 3.2 Strategies for teaching the pre-operational student

1. Use concrete materials, e.g. blocks, rods
2. Use visual aids, e.g. pictures, overhead transparencies
3. Keep instructions brief, using gestures to highlight intent, e.g. explain by acting out a part
4. Provide hands-on practice, e.g. cut-out letters to build words
5. Provide a wide range of experiences to build up concept learning, e.g. visits to gardens, theatres

Source: Based on Woolfolk 2008 and Santrock 2008.

FIGURE 3.3 Strategies for teaching the concrete operational student

1. Keep using concrete materials, e.g. artefacts, objects
2. Keep using visual aids, e.g. timelines, overhead transparencies
3. Use familiar examples to go from the simple to the complex, e.g. compare the local environment with far-away places
4. Ensure presentations are brief and well organised, e.g. use a small number of key points
5. Give practice in analysing problems and activities, e.g. use riddles and brainstorming

Source: Based on Woolfolk 2008 and Santrock 2008.

4 Formal operational stage (11 years and above)

Individuals can now operate at a new level – that is, at a formal level. They can use hypothetico-deductive reasoning and focus on 'what if' and 'what might be' questions. Students operating at this stage are able to consider abstract possibilities; they can hypothesise and consider a range of alternatives. However, they may not be able to describe to others the system of reasoning they are using.

Students are able to imagine ideal scenarios for themselves and others. They often become very involved in egocentric activities such as analysing their own beliefs and attitudes. See Figure 3.4.

Students at this stage can:
(a) do formal thinking using abstract possibilities but may not be able to explain the thinking processes they use
(b) imagine ideal world scenarios
(c) become engrossed in adolescent egocentrism
(d) reason from general principles to specific actions
(e) systematically explore logical alternatives
(f) isolate individual factors and possible combinations of factors that can contribute to a solution.

It is problematic that formal operations thinking is so little widespread among adolescents and adults. Woolfolk (2008) suggests that many high school students are not able to cope with formal thinking, as in subjects such as Mathematics or Science. It is likely that many adults can use formal operational thought in only a few areas.

 How do you consider you could get all students in your class to reach the formal operational stage? Are they able to stay at this level?

FIGURE 3.4 Strategies for teaching the formal operational student

1. Keep using concrete operational materials, e.g. computer-based simulations
2. Provide opportunities for students to hypothesise, e.g. writing points of view on controversial topics
3. Provide opportunities for students to inquire, e.g. individual and group projects
4. Use broad concepts rather than facts, e.g. environment and pollution
5. Use activities that are highly relevant to students' interests, e.g. use modern songs to discuss a social problem

Source: Based on Woolfolk 2008 and Santrock 2008.

3.2.2 Implications of Piaget's theory for teaching

As teachers, it is important for us to observe and listen carefully to what our students say and do and try to analyse how they think. Some of the concepts and principles included in Piaget's theory have important implications for developing students' thinking.

Concrete materials

Especially at kindergarten and in the early primary years, students need to work with concrete objects – to manipulate, act, touch, see and feel things. As noted by Gage and Berliner (1998, p. 124) 'children who have not played with beads, rods and lumps of clay may have difficulty understanding addition, subtraction, multiplication and division'.

Open learning

Open classrooms, appropriately established, can enable students to work on various individual projects in keeping with their respective stages of development. They have opportunities to collect, structure and reorganise materials and produce various conclusions to puzzles or issues. Students can make decisions about their work and can develop responsibility for setting and meeting their educational goals.

Discovery learning

Thinking involves discovering answers to problems. Inductive approaches by children to particular problems can lead to important personal discoveries. This is very important for students in their staged development of acquiring an understanding of more complex concepts and principles (De Vries & Zan 1994) and social development (Becker & Varelas 2001).

Matching strategies to abilities

Piagetian stages provide some insights to assist teachers in providing learning experiences that match up with the respective abilities of students. The learning activities must create sufficient puzzlement (disequilibrium) to encourage students to think about solutions.

Pace of learning

Students need opportunities to work through activities at their own pace rather than being subsumed within a total group pattern. Because of different developmental patterns, students will vary considerably in how successful they are with certain tasks. Most important of all, students need time and opportunities to sort out for themselves their construction of knowledge.

3.2.3 Criticisms of Piaget's theory

Piaget's theory has had a major impact on educators concerned with cognitive development. Various educational programs have been designed around this developmental orientation, especially for primary school students.

However, recent research has uncovered data that disputes a number of Piaget's principles. According to McInerney and McInerney (2005) recent research has addressed the following problems:
- Are the stages Piaget described really universal?
- Do they cut across domains of knowledge?
- Do the various cognitive abilities associated with the stages emerge at the ages Piaget predicted?
- Are the developmental stages he described invariant across individuals and cultures?

Structurally distinct stages

There does not appear to be the consistency of thinking at each stage that Piaget asserted was the case. For example, students might use conservation of number effectively but not conservation of weight. Piaget maintains that conservation occurs at the same level of operations in all situations. Further, recent research studies have demonstrated that training programs can enable students to learn particular concepts before they have reached certain stages. The stages are nowhere near as distinct as Piaget considered them to be.

Understanding the intellectual abilities of young children

Piaget's clinical method of collecting data may have caused him to use problems with young children that were too difficult. Recent research indicates that preschoolers are much more competent than indicated by Piaget in his clinical studies. More advanced scientific equipment is now being used in experiments and the results indicate that Piaget underestimated children's ability to do specific tasks in different stages by between 6 and 12 months. He may have overemphasised the formal thinking skills of adolescents. Also, it appears that young children can be very social in their speech and not markedly involved in egocentric speech as asserted by Piaget.

Overlooking the effects of the student's cultural and social group

The stages developed by Piaget appear to be significant to Western cultures in that scientific thinking and formal operations are prized as worthy levels to be reached. Other cultures might have different priorities, including a much higher regard for basic concrete operations.

Minimising the primacy of social and cultural processes

Some recent writers (for example, Phillips 1995; Forman 1992) argue that Piaget's child is a solitary scientist who constructs knowledge outside of the social context and that this assumption limits his theory. Children do grow up in very different social environments that affect their experiences and their opportunities for cognitive development. Others, such as De Vries (1997), contend that Piaget did consider social factors in his developmental theory such as in his 'social cooperations'.

Berger (2006) notes that there have been three main developments by theorists in reaction to some of the limitations of Piaget's theory, as uncovered by recent research. A number of theorists have preserved those features of Piaget's theory that have been found to stand up to current debate and research. These theorists are termed *neo-Piagetian* adherents (see Case 1985; Halford 1993). A second development has been theorists who have re-emphasised the *constructivist* elements of Piaget's theory. These include such elements as: children are active and motivated learners; and children organise what they learn from their experiences. A third development has been the re-emphasis on the social elements of Piaget's theory in which cooperative social interactions function to promote cognitive, affective and moral developments (De Vries 1997).

Without doubt, Piaget is a giant in the field of developmental psychology. We owe to him the present state of the field of children's cognitive development. We owe to him a long list of masterful concepts of enduring power and fascination. We also owe to him the current vision of children as active, constructive thinkers (Santrock 2008, p. 57).

3.2.4 Bruner

Jerome Bruner (1966), a cognitive psychologist, also examined cognitive growth as a result of working with children. Some principles that he considered were of major significance in the developmental process included the following:
- Intellectual growth is directly related to a child's ability to become independent of responses from stimuli. At first, children react directly to stimuli. As they develop language they learn to modify responses to stimuli.
- A child's intellectual growth depends on an internal information-processing and storage system to represent the world. They need this symbol system, such as language, to predict, extrapolate and to hypothesise.
- Intellectual development involves a child's ability to be able to describe past and future actions.
- Children need systematic interactions with a tutor/adult to achieve cognitive development.
- Children need language to communicate with others, to question, to link the new with the familiar.

 Do you agree with Bruner that learning is an active process in which learners construct new ideas or concepts based upon their current/past knowledge? Have you observed this type of learning happening in classrooms?

Bruner emphasised that children gradually organise their environment into meaningful units or 'categories' (for example, categories for food, clothing and danger). Categories are built up through a process of coding – children encode their experiences working from the specific to the general (McInerney & McInerney 2005).

Based on his studies, Bruner identified three stages of growth. Although they have developmental characteristics similar to those posited by Piaget, it should be noted that Bruner did not stress their hierarchical nature.

1. The *enactive* stage is the first stage commonly experienced by children and is predominantly learning by doing. Children do things with objects – such as holding, moving, rubbing, touching – and this provides them with a necessary understanding of their environment. As noted by Slee (2002), the stage of enactive representation is equivalent to Piaget's sensori-motor period. Bruner argues that the infant gains knowledge of the world by actions and not from mental images. Bruner maintains that infants at this stage of growth perform actions but do not know they perform them.

2. The *iconic* stage involves the use of imagery but not language. Children decide on actions based on sensory impressions. As noted by Barrow (1984), this stage refers to the type of learning involved in the ability to recognise instances of something without being able to give an account of the concept, or to picture things that one could not describe. The word 'iconic' comes from the word 'icon', which is derived from the Greek word for likeness or image. It should be noted that a mental image is a genuine cognitive representation. There are a number of identifiable characteristics of iconic knowledge, according to Bruner (1966), such as it is inflexible; it focuses upon small details and it is self-centred. Slee (2002) notes that Bruner and Piaget disagreed about the role of iconic representation. Bruner thought the role of iconic knowledge was crucial to the explanation of conservation.

3. The *symbolic* stage is the final stage where children obtain understanding through the use of symbol systems. Various symbol systems are available to children, including language, logic and mathematics. These systems enable children to arrange ideas and store them so that they can be retrieved when needed.

Although Bruner contended that children tend to develop through these stages, he also stressed that an individual might employ the iconic, enactive or symbolic modes of learning at any time, and possibly concomitantly. Consequently, teachers will get a better result with learners if they combine concrete, pictorial and symbolic presentations of material (McInerney & McInerney 2005). Gage and Berliner (1992) suggest that the symbolic system usually becomes dominant but that some adults will have highly developed enactive coding systems (for example, great athletes) and iconic systems (for example, great artists).

In subsequent books, Bruner outlined the importance of *discovery learning* in terms of understanding the structure of a subject being studied, the need for active learning to make personal discoveries and the value of inductive reasoning (see Figure 3.5). Bruner's theory reflects many of the tenets of personal constructivism (Woolfolk 2008).

3.2.5 Vygotsky

Lev Vygotsky lived in the first half of the twentieth century in the USSR. As a psychologist, he focused on social interaction as the major determinant of human development.

His theory is basically a social constructivist approach (Santrock 2008). Translations of his work in English did not appear until the 1960s and 70s. He has had a major influence in recent decades.

Rather than the child developing as a miniature scientist, Vygotsky asserted that it is people, especially adults in the child's world, who influence cognitive development. Children are in constant contact with parents, teachers, peers, friends and relatives. Parents and teachers are important in that they read to them, explain points and hold conversations. Friends and peers are also significant because they encourage conversations and discussions. The media are relevant, especially television, for the development of intellectual skills. It is interesting to note that Vygotsky, living in the early

FIGURE 3.5 Discovery learning

Students must identify key principles for themselves. Teachers present examples and students work with the examples until they discover the interrelationships and hence the subject's structure.

Classroom strategies:

1 Present both examples and non-examples of the concepts you are teaching.
   Example: In teaching about mammals include people, kangaroos, cats and non-examples such as fish and frogs.
2 Help students see connections among concepts.
   Example: Get students to think about alternative names for concepts (Orange, Fruit).
   Use diagrams to point out connections.
3 Pose questions and encourage students to find anwers.
   Example: Why do some fruit have thick skins and others have thin skins?
4 Try to get students to make intuitive guesses.
   Example: Give out incomplete diagrams or sketches and ask students to complete them.

Source: Anita Woolfolk, Educational Psychology, 11th edn, 2008. Published by Allyn & Bacon, Boston, MA. Copyright © 2008 by Pearson Education. Reprinted by permission of the publisher.

twentieth century, only considered such intellectual skills as systems for counting, works of art, writing and maps. If Vygotsky had lived in the twenty-first century he would have no doubt included the computer as a major intellectual tool (Krause, Bochner & Duchesne 2003).

It is argued by some writers that although Vygotsky's theory applies to language learning in children it can be applied to learning in a digital era. Consider how the computer can be used to develop intellectual skills along with parents and teachers.

Vygotsky (1978) focused particularly on the social world of the child and noted that one's culture tends to determine the stimuli that occur. Children internalise certain aspects and not others, in keeping with the dictates of a specific culture. It is these social processes that lead children to behave in certain ways (Roth & Lee 2007). Vygotsky argued that children's talking/mutterings to themselves (private speech) plays an important role in cognitive development. Children use private speech to communicate with themselves and to guide their behaviour and thinking. Private speech (or inner speech, see Renshaw 1992) is typically abbreviated and fragmentary because it is an internal dialogue that only has to make sense to the individual. By contrast, outer speech has to be readily understood by others.

Vygotsky maintains that private speech has an important role in the development of thinking. He posits four stages in the development of thought:

1 non-verbal thought and conceptual speech
2 beginning of a merging between thinking and speech
3 egocentric speech (overt)
4 egocentric speech becomes covert.

At the first stage (the first two years of life) there is no relationship between thought and speech. By the second stage, at about the age of two years, children start to connect their thinking with their speech. They label common objects by their names and start to talk to other people. At the third stage, a child's speech starts to direct thinking and behaviour. Children at this stage often announce what they are going to do before they do it – 'I am going to ride my bike'. Children at this stage often talk to each other about what they are doing. During the fourth stage, the overt egocentric speech is gradually overtaken by private speech. Children start to use covert, abbreviated speech to talk about their actions.

For Vygotsky learning commences in the social world. Children learn language and ways of thinking from others. It is only when their speech becomes established from talking to others that they can begin to have covert speech – monologues with themselves. Children transform their knowledge of what others have said in dialogue into their own personal schemata (along the lines described by Piaget).

According to Vygotsky, if children encounter ideas that do not fit into their existing schema, then there is an imbalance and they need assistance from adults or others to return to a state of balance. He used the term 'zone of proximal development' to indicate that there is a boundary area where on one side children can cope independently with particular knowledge and skills but beyond that boundary they need adult assistance.

There are important implications here for teachers. Students may be able to do tasks at higher levels if they are given assistance to get them past the zone of proximal development. Teachers should provide instruction at a level just above a student's independent level of functioning but not so high that it becomes frustrating for the student.

McInerney and McInerney (2005) refer to this assistance by the teacher as 'scaffolded instruction'. Just as a scaffold supports a building until it is completed, scaffolded instruction provides initial support from the teacher for children's early efforts. 'As the children become more adept at performing tasks, the scaffolding is gradually phased out and the children eventually perform these tasks on their own' (McDevitt & Ormrod 2002, p. 135).

Gradually, through this process of teacher social interaction, the student increases in cognitive development. That is, instruction should be at a sufficiently high level to constantly push students and to operate beyond their actual level of cognitive development. Students will need support from a teacher and able peers as they grapple with more complex ideas, but this is a vital process. The knowledge students acquire through interacting socially with the teacher and peers becomes their individual knowledge. Students should be encouraged to use language to organise their thinking and to talk about what they are doing.

How I use Vygotsky's theory in my teaching

Use of scaffolding

In a high school geography lesson I ask my students to take notes during my short lecture. Before I start I give them a detailed outline so they can use this to organise their notes. During the lecture I remind them about important elements to include.

Giving young children the opportunity to play adult roles

In my primary school classroom I have a learning centre corner where I have set up a range of old equipment including a telephone set, an old typewriter, an old mantelpiece clock and an old portable radio. I encourage children to discover how things work.

3.2.6 Implications of Vygotsky's theory for teaching

McDevitt and Ormrod (2002) suggest that some of the implications of Vygotsky's ideas for teachers include:
1. present challenging tasks for students within cooperative learning frameworks
2. help students acquire the basic conceptual tools of various academic disciplines
3. scaffold students' efforts
4. assess students' abilities under a variety of work conditions
5. provide opportunities for students to engage in authentic activities

6 promote self-regulation in students by teaching them to talk themselves through difficult situations
7 give students the chance to play.

Vygotsky's theory emphasises that cognitive development is essentially a social process. This is of great importance to teachers who have to plan how to teach students with diverse social and cultural backgrounds.

Critics of Vygotsky assert that his concepts such as 'zone of proximal development' are too vague. Also, it should be noted that Vygotsky does not acknowledge the role of developmental influences such as physical maturation (Krause, Bochner & Duchesne 2003).

A summary of Piaget's, Bruner's and Vygotsky's cognitive development theories and their application to the classroom is provided in Figure 3.6.

FIGURE 3.6 Cognitive developmental theories and the classroom

To provide a focus for specific learning problems you encounter with individual students in your class, consider using the following questions, based upon the three theories described above.

Piaget
- What developmental level is the student working at?
- Do you consider that the student has the necessary schemata to learn the task?
- Are the material and techniques appropriate for the student's developmental level?
- Is the student just entering a new development stage and not yet ready to perform a particular task?
- Has the student had sufficient opportunity to explore new material, physically and cognitively?
- Is the material too unfamiliar or irrelevant to the student's past experiences?

Bruner
- Has the student had sufficient opportunity to have had sensory contact with the new material?
- Has the teacher presented examples and non-examples to the student?
- Has the student had the opportunity to ask questions about the concept?

Vygotsky
- Has the level of instruction been focused within the student's zone of proximal development or has it been too low or too high?
- Has the student's learning been too confined to solitary learning?
- Have the student's social needs been met?
- Have forms of teaching been used which were culturally unfamiliar to the student?

3.3 THEORIES OF SOCIAL, EMOTIONAL AND MORAL DEVELOPMENT

Schooling involves more than just cognitive development. Students gradually develop a sense of self and identity. They gain perspectives about personal social behaviours that often involve moral judgments. This typically occurs as a result of interactions with parents and peers.

Two theories have been selected for closer study – Erikson's Stages of Psychosocial Development and Kohlberg's Stages of Moral Development.

3.3.1 A theory of psychosocial development – Erikson

Erik Erikson spent his childhood in Germany and in adolescence was tutored by Freud in Austria (Berger 2000). He published important books in the 1950s and '60s in which he established his theory about a person's drive for identity. He argued that it is identity which is the basis for personality development and that our search for identity continues from infancy through to old age. Because children spend many important years at school it is a major social setting for all (Santrock 2008).

The eight stages in his theory are interdependent and any solutions to developmental identity crises made earlier in life will affect later decisions. If each of the crises is solved successfully, a person's personality becomes strong and vigorous and they are able to cope successfully with subsequent identity crises.

The alternative for some children is to resolve crises in a negative way. This can lead to difficulties and problems at later stages. Erikson saw the tension between negative and positive polarities as necessary for healthy psychosocial development (Krause, Bochner & Duchesne 2003; Price 2005). See also Table 3.1.

Childhood stages

1. *Basic trust v mistrust*
   At stage 1, babies soon find out who they can depend on and who they can trust. Babies have needs for food and care and perceive the world either as a predictable, trusting place or as a chaotic place where they develop mistrust.
2. *Autonomy v shame and doubt*
   At stage 2, toddlers are capable of doing much more on their own, such as feeding, dressing and walking. Becoming toilet trained is of particular importance. If young children achieve these levels of independence they have mastered this identity crisis positively. Conversely, if they do not achieve these skills, they can develop feelings of guilt and shame.
3. *Initiative v guilt*
   At stage 3, children of typically 4–5 years of age like to be active and want to engage in all kinds of activities. They want to initiate various activities, but this can cause conflicts if some activities are forbidden by adults. Children at this stage want to explore and develop their imagination through language and through physical activities. If adults control these initiatives too rigidly, children may develop feelings of guilt.
4. *Industry v inferiority*
   At stage 4, which corresponds to the years 6–12, children are faced with a myriad of demands, especially at school. If they are successful with academic tasks, and get on well with their peers, they are rewarded for their industry or competence. This applies especially to using basic skills such as literacy and numeracy in formal learning situations and wider social skills with their peers. Children who do not succeed feel rejected and develop feelings of inferiority.
5. *Identity v role confusion*
   Stage 5 is a critical identity crisis stage for adolescents. Adolescents at this stage have to make major decisions about who they are and who they want to become. It involves establishing a variety of identities, including a clear sexual identity, an occupational identity and a family identity.

Marcia (1966) argues that for each of Erikson's stages an individual could cope with a new crisis in four different ways, namely:
(i) Moratorium – they are actively exploring what a crisis stage means to them and working towards a solution.
(ii) Identity achieved – they have experienced a particular crisis and made commitments about what they will do.
(iii) Diffusion – they have not bothered to explore the particular crisis and are trying to avoid confronting the problem.
(iv) Foreclosure – they have come to particular commitments without really experiencing the crisis. They have followed a plan devised by parents or other adults without directly experiencing it themselves.

Mallory (1989) asserts that a healthy progression through a crisis is 'moratorium' followed by 'identity achieved'. By contrast, 'diffusion' and 'foreclosure' may lead to less positive outcomes. At the

TABLE 3.1 Eight stages of development

	Approximate age (years)	Psychosocial stage	Tasks associated with the stage
1	0–1	Trust v mistrust	Child's need for forming a trusting relationship with an adult.
2	2–3	Autonomy v shame and doubt	Children begin to do things on their own (e.g. feeding, dressing) which involves self-control (e.g. toilet training). If children don't do these things they have self-doubts and become ashamed of their inabilities.
3	4–5	Initiative v guilt	Children try out and play-act many new roles. If they are punished for acting without thinking they can develop feelings of guilt.
4	6–12	Industry v inferiority	Children begin to master all basic cultural skills and norms, including fundamental skills of literacy and numeracy. Failure can lead to feelings of inferiority.
5	13–18	Identity v role confusion	Adolescents and young adults have to adapt to puberty change, occupational choice.
6	19–25	Intimacy v isolation	Individuals develop deep and open commitment to others or run the risk of becoming psychologically isolated.
7	26–40	Generativity v stagnation	Adults bear and rear children and are involved in training future generations, or there is a risk of stagnating.
8	40 plus	Integrity v despair	Consolidation of identity and acceptance of self, or at risk because they despair of their existence.

adolescent stage, these four coping ways for dealing with an identity crisis are very evident, but they are also evident at Erikson's other stages.

Adult stages

6 *Intimacy v isolation*
Adults have to cope with intimacy identity crisis at stage 6 whereby they are prepared to develop deep, intimate relationships with others. Those individuals who cannot cope with this level of giving and sharing will retreat into isolationism.

7 *Generativity v stagnation*
Adults have to deal with the stage 7 identity conflict of caring for and guiding the next generation. That is, it involves a commitment to bear and rear children, to be a support to their development and to others in the community. It can extend to wider concerns about a nation or about the environment. Adults who do not make these generative commitments tend to stagnate.

8 *Integrity v despair*
Stage 8 refers to persons over 40 years of age and their ability to cope with subsequent life crises. A positive response involves making decisions that are consistent with their lifestyle and which uphold their credibility with others. Alternatively, there will be some adults who are not able to cope with these crises and they submit to ever-deepening levels of despair and they fear death.

Key to Erikson's theory is the understanding that at each stage of development individuals have positive and negative experiences and the total personality at any time reflects the balance struck between them. According to McInerney and McInerney (2005, p. 419) 'if children experience basically negative or confusing experiences, they may be unable to establish a sense of self-identity.'

3.3.2 Critique of Erikson's theory

Because Erikson's principles and stages are general and descriptive, it is difficult to use normal scientific procedures to test them. There is little direct research evidence to support or refute the theory. However, studies have examined the quantum crisis style for adolescents (Boyes & Chandler 1992); the effects of divorce on young children and their greater risk for depression and emotional disturbance (Doherty & Needle 1991); and the importance of trust between toddlers and their mothers (Sroufe 1988).

 Do you consider that young adults today are better able to deal with life crises than young adults who were brought up in the 1960s and 1970s? Consider in particular levels of youth suicide and depression symptoms.

3.3.3 A theory of moral development – Kohlberg

Lawrence Kohlberg was a student at the University of Chicago in the 1950s. He was strongly influenced by Piaget's work, especially his theorising about the development of morality. Kohlberg also used Piaget's methodology of clinical interviews to collect his research data (McInerney & McInerney 2005).

Piaget proposed that all children progress through two stages of morality, a stage of 'heteronomous morality' (where children's sense of morality is based on consequences of breaking rules) and a second stage of 'autonomous morality' (where children recognise that rules are invested by others and can be changed).

Kohlberg was influenced by these two stages and the stages of cognitive development that Piaget had developed, especially sensori-motor, pre-operational and concrete operational. Piaget used a series of simple experiments to obtain details of children's thinking at different stages. Kohlberg used moral dilemmas in the form of stories and told these to children of various ages as well as to young adolescents and adults in several countries. He used the reasons the interviewees gave for their solutions to a dilemma as the basis for constructing a sequence of stages of moral reasoning.

Kohlberg (1975) theorised that there were three main levels of increasingly complex and moral reasoning and that there were two sub-stages at each level. Further, he concluded that the stages were an invariant sequence. Kindergarten, preschool and young primary school children were mainly at stages 1 and 2. Second level moral reasoning occurred mainly at adolescent levels. Third level reasoning was usually found in adults.

Children will progress through these stages as they actively react to their environment. Some will move at faster rates than others and only a very few (perhaps 20 per cent) will ever attain the sixth level. The purported strength of this approach is its emphasis on a 'natural' sequence and therefore the role of the teacher is simply to enhance the child's development along a path that will inexorably occur over a period of time. See Table 3.2.

At a *pre-conventional level*, children behave because there are physical punishments if they do not! They do not necessarily conform because they consider it is desirable to do so.

At stage 1, children behave basically in terms of a punishment; that is, obedience orientation. There may be physical consequences if they are caught doing something that is not approved of by adults. They are aware of rules and they are especially aware of the punishments if they break these rules.

At stage 2, children are concerned about their own pleasures. They are motivated by self-interest or doing exchanges with others so that both parties gain. The relationships are chiefly reciprocal (one good turn deserves one in return) and not based on justice.

TABLE 3.2 Kohlberg's stages of moral development

Typical age levels	
(0–9 yrs)	**Pre-conventional level** (focus on self-interest)
Stage 1	Avoidance of punishment and unquestioning obedience to superiors are valued.
Stage 2	Right action consists of that which instrumentally satisfies one's own needs and occasionally the needs of others (instrumental relativist orientation).
(9–19 yrs)	**Conventional level** (focus on maintaining social order)
Stage 3	Good behaviour is that which pleases or helps others and is approved by them (interpersonal concordance orientation).
Stage 4	Authority, fixed rules and the maintenance of the social order are values.
(20 yrs and over)	**Post-conventional level** (focus on shared principles)
Stage 5	Values agreed upon by the society, including individual rights, determine what is right.
Stage 6	Right is defined by one's conscience in accordance with self-chosen ethical principles (universal ethical principle orientation).

At a *conventional level*, children and young adults behave because there is a desire to maintain the social order. Moral judgments are based on performing good and bad roles.

At stage 3, persons make judgments that will earn them approval for being 'good'. They are concerned about pleasing or impressing others. They are aware that they need to consider the feelings of others.

At stage 4, persons make moral judgments based on law and order. They feel that they have a duty to maintain the existing social order, even if some of these laws might disadvantage them. They must uphold the traditional values of the family, community and nation. These customs and laws are very important and absolute.

At a *post-conventional level*, which is reached by only a small proportion of individuals, the emphasis is on developing self-chosen principles and being true to them. It can involve the development of shared principles and standards that may not be in accord with traditional laws and customs.

At stage 5, individuals make judgments about right actions based on individual rights and standards. There is an emphasis on procedural rules for reaching agreement. Social contracts between individuals can be negotiated.

At stage 6, individuals focus on self-chosen ethical principles in terms of their conscience. They make a specific decision for a particular situation. Their conscience guides them as they interact with others and produce decisions that earn mutual respect.

To illustrate how individuals at different stages of moral development might react to a moral dilemma, consider the following account, which is a summary of a moral dilemma used by Kohlberg (1966, p. 64):

> In a European country a woman was suffering from a special type of cancer and was near death. Her doctor thought that there was a drug, a form of radium, that might save her. The local chemist had obtained this and was charging customers $4000 for a small dose. The husband of the sick woman went to his friends to try to borrow the $4000 he needed but all he could collect was $2000. He told the chemist his wife was dying and asked him to sell it cheaper or give it to him on time payment. The chemist refused to help. The husband became desperate and considered breaking into the chemist shop and stealing the radium.

Kohlberg (1966, pp. 64–5) posed a number of questions to this dilemma, which are summarised below:
- Should the husband steal the radium?
- Is it right or wrong to steal it? Why is it right or wrong?
- Does he have a duty to steal the drug? Why or why not?
- Is it important for a person to do anything to save another person's life? Why or why not?
- It is against the law to steal, but is it morally wrong in this case? Why or why not?
- What is the most responsible thing for the husband to do? Why?

Referring back to the six stages, some possible answers to the dilemma might be as follows:
- Stage 1 individuals might decide that the husband should not steal the radium from the chemist shop because the police would punish him.
- Stage 2 individuals might decide that the husband should steal the radium because he is worried about his wife and he would feel better if she recovered.
- Stage 3 individuals might decide that the husband should steal the radium because good husbands must take care of their wives and society expects this.
- Stage 4 individuals might decide that the husband should not steal the radium because stealing is against the law and laws must be obeyed.
- Stage 5 individuals might consider a range of options including stealing, encouraging and assisting the wife to commit euthanasia, stealing from others to pay for the radium.
- Stage 6 individuals might consider an even wider range of options including those listed in stage 5.

3.3.4 Critique of Kohlberg's theory

Although Kohlberg's stages were extensively researched to check the validity of the levels, there have been many critics. One major criticism raised is that the purported 'natural' progression that a person experiences through the six stages really only applies to the first four. Gibbs (1977, p. 44) argues that the last two stages represent ideological and cultural points of view and cannot be substantiated as universal to all cultures. For example, Tzuriel (1992) argues that some cultures emphasise the collective good rather than individual rights. If this is the case, then Kohlberg is simply perpetuating another form of value inculcation. Peters (1976) takes up a similar point when he criticises Kohlberg for advocating that a morality based on the concept of justice is the *only* type of morality that is defensible. Peters also argues that it may not be morally better for individuals to progress to stages 5 or 6. It may in fact be more important for citizens to be well bedded down in the other four stages. He makes the point convincingly:

> The policeman cannot always be present, and if I am lying in the gutter after being robbed, it is somewhat otiose to speculate at what stage the mugger is. My regret must surely be that he has not at least got a conventional morality well instilled in him. (Peters 1976, p. 678)

Gilligan and Attanucci (1988) are critical of Kohlberg's theory because he only used male subjects in his research and the moral dilemmas he used were very abstract. They contend that males view morality from a position of rights or justice rather than from a position of caring and consequently the stages give higher rating to males. Yet other researchers, such as Galotti, Kozberg and Farmer (1991), provide evidence that there is little difference in the thinking of males and females about moral issues.

Others, such as Bear and Richards (1981) and McDevitt and Ormrod (2002), criticise Kohlberg's theory because it focuses on moral thinking rather than moral behaviour. There is only a moderate correlation between the two, possibly because other non-moral factors affect how persons behave.

Over the last decade, a number of theorists have developed from Kohlberg's theory a new approach, which has been termed *neo-Kohlbergian*. This approach uses moral schemata as more concrete conceptions of the stages of moral development.

Numerous classroom applications have been developed using moral dilemmas and defining issues. For example, Rest *et al.* (1999b), who are considered to be neo-Kohlbergians, propose a four component framework, namely:

1. Moral sensitivity – students are given situations to assess and to judge whether it is a moral problem or not.
2. Moral judgment – students are encouraged to examine a number of possible responses to a problem and to decide which is the most moral solution.
3. Moral motivation – students consider all the concerns and decide whether a moral action can be justified over other personal solutions.
4. Moral character – students construct and implement actions and have the courage to continue a course of action.

Researchers and teachers have used moral dilemma stories especially in science lessons. For example Settelmaier (2002) undertook research involving the use of moral dilemma stories in science to transform the culture of science teaching.

The Science Teachers Association of Western Australia (2008) (STAWA) has produced a 'Socially Responsible Science' website, <www.dilemmas.net.au>, which includes dilemmas about wetlands, whale rescue, climate change and transplant of human organs.

Go to the website. Select one of the dilemmas and reflect upon how useful it might be in a class. How useful are the teaching resources provided with each dilemma?.

---

case study

How I use Kohlberg's theory in my teaching

In studying bioethics in Science I often use role-plays to examine moral issues. In this series of lessons with a Year 10 class I established a hospital ethics committee whose job was to select four patients who would receive a heart transplant. Students are given a list of 20 potential patients and the committee has to debate which four will get the life-saving heart transplant. Potential patients include those from minority groups, recent immigrants from overseas and physically disabled persons. Some of the reasons students give for selecting/rejecting particular applicants raise important moral issues that provide fruitful class discussions.

CONCLUDING COMMENTS

As noted at the beginning of this chapter, developmental theories can provide some reasonable principles that can guide our teaching. However, no single theory can provide all the answers and we should be mindful of enthusiastic scholars who distort a theory and ascribe positions to it which were never intended by the author (Gredler 2007).

Developmental theories emphasise how children think compared with how adults think. We need to be reminded of these differences and to appreciate how children react to problems and learn by working with concrete objects, materials and phenomena.

Children can develop at very different paces and levels. They need new experiences to stimulate, enhance and reinforce their development. To a certain extent they need opportunities to do their own learning, but the social side of learning is also very important. As noted earlier in the chapter, Western developmental theories applied to Aboriginal children have less relevance because of other pressing problems. For example Scott (2008) argues that there are pressing

issues for parents and their children in terms of inner and outer worlds. She states the issues as three propositions, based on Winnicott (1964):
- the inner worlds affect outer worlds – for example a depressed mother may withdraw from her child-rearing role, reducing verbal interaction with her child and causing safety risks for a young child.
- outer worlds affect the inner world – neighbourhoods with poor housing, poverty and violence can create high anxiety for developing children.
- past worlds affect the present world – parents carry with them experiences from the past, including trauma and disruptions which can affect their capacity to nurture their child.

Teachers of young Aboriginal children, along with community level services, have to nurture these children and to endeavour to 'enhance the resilience and well being of vulnerable children' (Scott 2008, p. 121).

KEY ISSUES RAISED IN THIS CHAPTER

1. Some major developmental theories are analysed in this chapter. It is important to remember that each theory is a set of reasonable but tentative suggestions.
2. Piaget's theory has had a major impact on educators and schooling because of his stage theory of cognitive development.
3. Bruner's theory highlights three stages of growth, namely enactive, iconic and symbolic.
4. Vygotsky's theory has had a major impact on educators and schooling. He emphasised that cognitive development is essentially a social process.
5. Erikson argues that it is identity which is the basis for personality development and that this occurs over eight stages.
6. Kohlberg theorised about the development of morality. He developed stages of moral reasoning and he argued that this was a natural sequence for all children and adults.

REFLECTIONS AND ISSUES

1. Reflect on your childhood and adolescent years. What were key events that happened to you that you can recall? Are you able to link them to any of the theories described in this chapter?
2. To what extent does Piaget's theory emphasise that children should act as amateur scientists rather than as social beings? Explain.
3. Crain (2005, p. 146) asserts that 'Piaget portrayed pre-operational children too negatively, focusing on their logical deficiencies. We need to consider the possibility that young children's thinking has its own qualities and distinctive virtues.' Discuss.
4. According to McDevitt and Ormrod (2002, p. 148) 'challenge, readiness and social interaction are central to the theories of both Piaget and Vygotsky.' Do you agree? How do the two theories differ?
5. Bruner contends that teachers should encourage 'discovery' and provide inductive learning opportunities. For a particular grade level, describe some resources or learning opportunities that you would provide to encourage children's personal discovery.
6. Do you agree with Crain (2005, p. 169) that 'Kohlberg's stages provide us with an inspiring vision of where moral development might lead'? Provide a critique of Kohlberg's theory.
7. How might cooperative learning situations provide good opportunities for peer interaction that could lead to moral growth?
8. How useful is it to use real moral dilemma problems to teach moral values to students?

Special references

Berger, KS (2006) *The Developing Person through Childhood and Adolescence*, 2nd edn, Worth Publishers, New York.
Crain, W (2005) *Theories of Development*, 5th edn, Prentice Hall, Upper Saddle River, New Jersey.
Daniels, H (2007) *Vygotsky and Research*, Routledge, London.
Jardine, DW (2006) 'Welcoming the old man home: Meditations on Jean Piaget, interpretation and the "nostalgia for the original"'. In DW Jardine, S Friesen & P Clifford, *Curriculum in Abundance*, Lawrence Erlbaum, Mahwah, New Jersey, pp. 73–86.
Lee, V (1990) (ed.) *Children Learning in School*, Hodder & Stoughton, London.
Murphy, P & Moon, B (1989) (eds) *Developments in Learning and Assessment*, Hodder & Stoughton, London.
Woolfolk, A (2008) *Educational Psychology*, 11th edn, Allyn & Bacon, Boston.

Web sources

For additional resources on how students develop and learn, please go to:
www.pearson.com.au/myeducationlab.

4

LEARNER MOTIVATION AND DEVELOPING SELF-ESTEEM

4.1 | INTRODUCTION

A common question that is asked by student teachers is: 'How can you get school students motivated about …?' It would be good if there was a simple answer, but there is not.

We probably have impressions about the processes of motivation, about what energises us and what does not. But what causes this flow and direction of energy? Is it due to instincts, needs, incentives, fears or social pressures?

4.2 | INTRINSIC AND EXTRINSIC MOTIVATION

Various definitions of motivation abound, such as 'motivation is an internal state that arouses, directs and maintains behaviour' (Woolfolk 2008, p. 336). Yet this does not tell us very much. What causes a person to initiate a particular action is a fascinating question. A useful dichotomy to discuss this is *intrinsic* and *extrinsic* motivation.

4.2.1 Intrinsic motivation

Intrinsic motivation refers to motivation without any apparent external reward – for example, the motivation for learning comes entirely from performing a particular task. Students will be motivated to undertake a certain task because of some personal factors – these may include needs, interests, curiosity and enjoyment. The activity in itself is the reward in these circumstances.

Intrinsic motivation can be capitalised on by using innovative teaching. For example, if a teacher can create puzzling questions, dilemmas and novel situations, and if this in turn puzzles the students in a class, they are likely to be intrinsically motivated to find solutions (see Figure 4.1).

 How important is it for students to be emotionally 'safe' in a classroom? How might this influence their levels of motivation in wanting to work on a task?

Montalvo, Mansfield and Miller (2007) contend that teachers who are liked by students are able to respond better to their needs and so this can also assist levels of intrinsic motivation. McCombs, Daniels and Perry's (2008) research on early schooling grades (K–3) came up with similar results.

Not all students will be intrinsically motivated about particular puzzles or dilemmas. Those

FIGURE 4.1 Strategies to encourage intrinsic motivation

- Present a novel situation to the class.
- Use an anecdote to engage students in a personal response.
- Use challenging questions.
- Provide contradictory information about a topic.
- Produce unfamiliar examples.
- Use case study accounts.

students who are strongly motivated to work on challenging tasks, often on their own, are likely to be students who are confident about their own self-worth and who have developed a strong interest in a particular subject or schooling in general. Different students will find different tasks/activities that will elicit particular forms of intrinsic motivation.

Research evidence about classrooms indicates that intrinsic motivation is only successful in certain situations for particular students (Borich & Tombari 1997). Extrinsic motivation also needs to be used to stimulate students.

4.2.2 Extrinsic motivation

Extrinsic motivation is experienced by students when they receive a reward, or avoid punishment, or in some other way unconnected with the task earn approval for particular behaviour. In technical terms we can refer to *reinforcement*, which is the external stimulus that follows as a result of a certain response. If it is a *positive reinforcer* then the stimulus or event results in improved learning. Examples of *primary reinforcers* include those items/events that satisfy our basic physiological needs, such as food and drink. *Secondary reinforcers* are behaviours or events associated with primary reinforcers, such as the supportive/friendly manner of persons giving out the items of food. It is evident that a lot of teacher behaviours are related to secondary reinforcement such as teachers' gestures and non-verbal behaviour. Primary reinforcers are also used by teachers, especially in earlier grades, and include items such as lollies, drinks and play-toys.

A problem for teachers is that we can never be certain which reinforcers will motivate particular students. Further, students' preferences for certain reinforcers can change over time. Above all, a teacher needs to have reflected carefully on his/her attitudes towards the use of acceptable and unacceptable types of external reinforcers. For example, do you consider that giving a student free reading time is a better reinforcer than releasing a student early to go to lunch? Do you place a high or a low value on consumable rewards?

It is evident that both intrinsic and extrinsic motivation are used in classroom learning. The perceptive teacher will always demonstrate why he/she is using external motivation and this can encourage students to become more confident and independent and hence more likely in the long term to become intrinsically motivated.

Research evidence provides conflicting advice on the use of intrinsic and extrinsic motivation. Deci, Koestner and Ryan (2001) in a major meta-analysis study conclude that tangible extrinsic rewards (for example, gold stars, best-student awards, honour rolls) 'do significantly and substantially undermine intrinsic motivation' (p. 2). They contend that these forms of motivation attempt to control behaviour and lead to a perception by students of reduced opportunities for self-determination.

By contrast, Cameron (2001), also using a major meta-analysis study, concludes that the negative effects of extrinsic rewards are minimal and can easily be prevented in applied school settings. She argues for the use of rewards to 'shape successful performance and to recognise student accomplishment' (p. 40).

Hide and Harackiewicz (2000) take a similar stance to Cameron (2001) when they argue that 'situational interest' (external rewards) can have long-term benefits. They conclude that those who argue against external rewards have been over-reacting to behaviourism, and as a consequence 'have ended up denying the importance of external influences that may be necessary for all students to get a decent, if not equal chance to achieve' (p. 169).

Vansteenhiste, Lens and Deci (2006) distinguish between extrinsic motivation which is 'autonomous' and that which is 'controlled'. Autonomous motivation involves the experience of volition and choice. In these situations the teacher allows opportunities for self-initiation and choice. Controlled motivation involves the experience of being pressured or coerced. In these situations, the teacher pressures students to think, act or feel in certain ways. According to Vansteenhiste, Lens and Deci, the more autonomy-supportive the classroom context, the more it maintains or enhances intrinsic motivation.

> **YOUR TURN**
>
> - When you are observing classrooms, do you see teachers using mainly intrinsic or extrinsic motivation? Which ones are most effective? How can you tell?
> - Which types of motivation do you intend to use? Why?

4.3 | SELF-ESTEEM

A number of educators assert that self-esteem is one of the most basic of human needs and that it is a powerful factor in classroom behaviour.

Maslow (1954) considered that motivation can be grouped into a hierarchy of needs, and self-esteem is included in this listing (see Figure 4.2). Our low-level needs are our physical needs (food and safety). These needs are fundamental in determining our behaviour, but once they have been met we are stimulated to fulfil higher level needs, namely social needs. Our social needs revolve around self-esteem (being special and different) and belongingness (knowing that others are aware of us and want to be a part of our group).

FIGURE 4.2 Maslow's hierarchy of needs

Self-actualisation needs
(fully functioning individual)

Aesthetic needs
(appreciation)

Need to know and understand
(access to information; wanting to know)

Esteem needs
(being recognised as unique)

Belongingness and love needs
(being accepted)

Security and safety needs
(regular, predictable)

Survival needs
(physiological)

Source: Abraham Maslow, Motivation and Personality, 3rd ed, 1987, Addison-Wesley. © Reprinted by permission of Pearson Education Inc., Upper Saddle River, NJ.

Once our social needs are more or less satisfied we will develop our intellectual needs in terms of needing to know and to understand. Beyond this in the hierarchy are aesthetic appreciation needs and, finally, self-actualisation. The highest need, self-actualisation, involves striving for the highest level of personal potential.

Maslow maintains that the four lower level needs (survival, safety, belonging and self-esteem) are needs that individuals will strive to satisfy. Striving for the three higher needs (intellectual achievement, aesthetic needs and self-actualisation) will only occur if a reasonable level of satisfaction has been attained with the four lower levels.

There are important implications here for teachers. Clearly, students who are on a deficient diet at home and come to school hungry will not be motivated by needs beyond the physiological ones. Students who feel lonely and insecure may be highly motivated to satisfy belongingness needs, rather than be very interested in intellectual pursuits. The teacher can assist students to satisfy their needs by a sensitive use of praise, recognition and approval.

An understanding of Maslow's hierarchy is also helpful in realising how conflicts can occur within a class. For example, a teacher may be aiming at satisfying students' intellectual, aesthetic or self-actualisation needs, when the students may be more concerned about lower level needs such as belonging or self-esteem.

Of course, it is important to remember that the hierarchy is an idealised model – not all students will behave according to the hierarchy. Perhaps most of us move quite readily between the hierarchical levels, depending on the situation and the persons with whom we interact. But, as noted by Woolfolk (2008), Maslow's hierarchy enables us to consider the whole person and how their physical, emotional and intellectual needs are interrelated.

McGrath (2003) notes that the self-esteem movement of the 1970s and 1980s emphasised feelings and everyone's right to happiness. Lerner (1996) concludes that this approach did not change anti-social behaviour nor improve relationships.

A newer self-esteem theory, according to McGrath (2003), 'stresses that competency achievement of personal goals and "pro-social" behaviour comes first and self-esteem follows' (p. 16). McGrath contends that having healthy self-esteem is linked to being resilient – being able to bounce back after adversity and disappointment. There are a number of classroom resilience programs that provide strategies to develop resilience (see Figure 4.3): packages available include MindMatters (2000).

FIGURE 4.3 Strategies to develop resilience

1 Emphasise pro-social values – these include honesty, fairness, support and concern for others.
2 Coping skills – how to normalise events in one's life rather than personalise them.
3 Courage – to persevere even when there are many difficulties.
4 Optimistic thinking – focusing on the positive aspects of a negative situation.
5 Managing feelings – how to manage 'bad' feelings.
6 Social skills – develop social skills and positive relationships.
7 Goal achievement – applying self-discipline in setting goals and achieving them.
8 Evidence-based self-knowledge – awareness of strengths and limitations based upon evidence.

Source: After McGrath 2003.

4.4 | ACHIEVEMENT MOTIVATION

Achievement motivation is a matter of considerable importance to many students and teachers. Writers have noted that family and cultural group motives appear to influence students who have developed high or low levels of achievement motivation (McMillan & Hearn 2008).

Classroom tasks offer students various opportunities for experiencing success or failure (Givvin et al. 2001). Those students who have a high achievement motivation will show greater persistence and effort and they typically perceive themselves as having a high ability and self-esteem. By contrast, students with low achievement motivation have feelings of inadequacy and are not willing to stick at a task until it is completed satisfactorily (see the case study on page 62).

 Select two or three students to interview the next time you visit a school. Invite them to talk about their aspirations and goals. Where appropriate and with necessary tact, explore their answers in greater depth.

The explanations that students give for their successes and failures usually focus on ability, effort, task difficulty and luck. For example, students' likelihood of high achievement may be attributed to such factors as ability or effort. These are controls internal to the student and which they can do something about.

External controls are those that students cannot influence, such as test difficulty (set by external experts) or mere luck or chance in terms of the items included in a test. Turney et al. (1992) state that students with low achievement tend to explain failure in terms of external attributions, such as luck and ability (a stable internal attribute), but which in turn tends to perpetuate failure.

Then there are other external factors such as state systems. Marks and Cresswell (2005) undertook a study of achievement levels in Reading, Mathematics and Science in different Australian states and territories. Their results provide alarming news for some states, especially Queensland, Victoria and Tasmania, where students scored much lower in proficiency levels in Reading compared with students in other states. By contrast, New South Wales students scored highest among all states in Reading, Mathematics and Sciences. Marks and Cresswell suggest that the states with the highest scores may provide better services to low achieving students.

As indicated in Figure 4.4, there are important considerations for the teacher desiring to increase students' achievement motivation levels. Establishing a classroom climate where students know that they can make mistakes without being ridiculed is an important consideration for a teacher. Some research studies have also revealed that it is possible to train teachers to encourage their students to take more personal responsibility for their achievements (internal control) rather than blaming external factors (Hattie & Fletcher 2005).

FIGURE 4.4 A checklist for teachers about achievement motivation

1. Do you set tasks that are attainable and that build upon students' current levels of skill?
2. Do you create a psychologically safe class environment where wrong answers and mistakes are accepted?
3. Do you encourage students to assume more personal responsibility for goal setting?
4. Do you use activities/exercises to improve students' self-esteem?
5. Do you have a high level of achievement motivation about excellence in teaching?
6. Have you considered any steps you might take to reduce the competitive nature of your classroom?
7. How might individual learning and cooperative learning approaches assist students with their motivation levels?

Then again, it may be possible to reduce the level of competition within a class by using forms of instruction that emphasise individual mastery or cooperative learning. Cooperative learning in particular enables low-ability students to be members of cooperative groups that achieve success (see Chapter 8).

Of particular concern within education systems in Australia are the levels of achievement of Aboriginal students and their associated motivational factors. McInerney's (1991) study noted that significant motivational variables were:

> **Achievement motivation**
>
> Helen very seldom completes her maths exercises. She is often distracted during maths lessons. She complains that maths is boring.
>
> The class teacher tries to make her maths lessons more interesting by developing everyday problems for students to solve that involve maths calculations. Although this strategy seems to work with many of the other students, little noticeable improvement is displayed by Helen.
>
> The teacher decides to have an exploratory interview with Helen to try to find out what is the problem. In this discussion Helen reveals that she feels bored with maths because she is unsure of what to do; she lacks confidence in her ability to complete the maths exercises.
>
> What might be done to assist Helen? Explain why you would use these strategies.

- their lack of confidence and self-reliance in the school setting
- their low level of goal-directed behaviour
- the level of parental support and encouragement for schooling.

He concluded that 'the cluster of influential variables determining the Aboriginal child's motivation at school, and ultimately his or her decision to continue with school beyond the minimum school leaving age, revolves around a sense of self: self-reliance, confidence and goal direction. These in their turn are influenced by facilitating conditions: first, parental support and help; secondly, school support through teachers and peers; and thirdly, general affect [like or dislike] towards schooling' (McInerney 1991, p. 167).

> **YOUR TURN**
>
> - What activities can a teacher use to encourage students to achieve at their highest levels?
> - From your classroom observations, why do some students want or not want to achieve at their highest levels? What would you do about it as a classroom teacher?

4.5 | ATTRIBUTION THEORY OF MOTIVATION

Achievement motivation is critical to effective teaching. In an endeavour to find out how and why it operates, various theories have been developed. The attribution theory (Weiner 1986) states that people inevitably seek to explain why they have succeeded or failed. These explanations are called *attributes*. Explanations might include:

- lack of effort
- lack of ability
- the teacher did not help me
- difficulty of the task
- other chance factors.

According to Weiner (1986), these explanations or attributes include emotional reactions regarding future performance and expectations for success or failure. Specifically, students make attributions or explanations based on:

1. *Situational cues*
   (a) A student's past experience with a similar task (for example, consistent success or failure in the past).

(b) A student's performance compared with peers.
(c) Time-on-task (for example, whether they spent a weekend preparing for a test or did no preparation at all).
(d) How much help they received during the task (for example, did another person help them do a project or did they cheat?).
2 *Prior beliefs*
Students have enduring beliefs about success and failure (enduring beliefs can be developed from reading or listening to parents).
3 *Self-perceptions*
Students with high self-esteem will consider that reasons for their success are due to effort or ability and not due to luck.

Taken together, these factors inform us about the level of motivation of students and what drives them. These various factors also demonstrate how complex motivational dispositions can be. There is no simple uni-dimensional basis for what motivates students. Each student's motivation to do a task can be very different – some may be eager and successful; some may demonstrate anger, guilt or shame.

Borich and Tombari (1997) suggest that teachers supporting an attribution theory approach should be doing everything in their power to ensure that students attribute their classroom accomplishments and failures in ways that bring out effort rather than discouragement. For example, they list the following as worthwhile strategies for teachers to adopt:

- Be very aware of how and what you communicate to each student – use encouragement rather than praise. For example: 'Your answers show thought' not 'You are a good thinker'.
- Try to get students to think about the learning processes they use as well as the product they are trying to achieve.
- Use small groups that are heterogeneous in terms of ability. Do not allocate students to groups based on ability, as this suggests that a teacher values ability over effort (Gallagher, Millar & Ellis 1996).
- Use cooperative learning arrangements where possible with students, rather than activities that are perceived to be competitive. (For examples of cooperative learning see Chapter 8.)
- Develop goals for each student that are realistic. If students keep on failing because they are aiming too high, they are likely to doubt their abilities (Page 1998).

Proponents of attribution theory argue that a learner's motivation for achievement is based on their attributions or reasons for success or failure. The task for teachers is therefore to convince students that factors of success are under their control. The attribution theory has been modified and refined by others such as Dweck and Elliott (1983) and Cobington (1984). Although there are many other theories of motivation, the attribution theory is widely supported in the literature.

4.6 | SOCIAL MOTIVATION

As noted earlier with regard to Maslow's hierarchy of needs, social needs are a major consideration for all students. Many students actively seek out support and attention from the teacher and from other students.

Support from the teacher is clearly a major management strategy – it can be used to reinforce desired behaviour by the teacher as well as build self-esteem and generally more positive relationships between the teacher and students in a class. Some research studies highlight how certain students are able to solicit far more support from a teacher than other students because of such factors as their high ability, confidence and social behaviour. By reacting positively to their teacher, these students are rewarding the teacher! The interaction patterns between teacher and students can indeed be very complex and sophisticated.

In the classroom situation, the use of support is very important for students and for the teacher. 'Both teachers and students need to be accepted and both seek out as well as react to praise'

(Sinclair & Hatton 1992, p. 100). The development of a positive climate within the classroom is dependent on this accepting behaviour, which may be achieved relatively painlessly or may be a very protracted process. Notwithstanding, it is up to classroom teachers to reflect on how and when they use support (and criticism), and to develop strategies to use it systematically and selectively, dependent on the needs of individual students.

 How important is it for teachers to be good role models if student motivation is to be fostered?

Harmin (1994) suggests that it is the role of the teacher to inspire new growth in dignity, energy, self-management, community and awareness (DESCA). Harmin provides some sound practical ideas for inspiring DESCA (Table 4.1) and strategies for motivating students beyond praise and rewards (Figure 4.5).

TABLE 4.1 Teacher messages to inspire new growth in dignity, energy, self-management, community and awareness (DESCA)

'I Appreciate' messages that inspire DESCA	'I'm With You' messages that inspire DESCA
Dignity	*Dignity*
I really like the way you just spoke up for yourself.	I can imagine how you felt after speaking up that way.
I like the way you defended your friend.	I think I know how you felt when you insisted on your rights.
I appreciate the way you look straight into people's eyes.	There was a time when I, too, could not get all the courage I wanted.
Energy	*Energy*
I like it when you pace yourself.	I need rest too.
I like it when you speak with energy.	I'm like you when it comes to taking initiative.
I like it when you go one more step when you are ready to give up.	It's not easy to eat well all the time, is it?
Self-management	*Self-management*
I like it when you make a time plan.	I, too, have trouble knowing when to speak up and when to say nothing.
I like it when you think it out for yourself.	I understand how you knew when you had had enough.
Community	Sometimes we need to look twice to see what must be done, don't we?
I like it when you respect the differences in others.	I, too, must sometimes remind myself not to be negative.
I like it when you find something to appreciate in people so different from you.	*Community*
I like it when you listen so well to others.	I understand how you felt about cleaning up a mess you didn't make.
Awareness	It's fun to cheer people on, isn't it?
Thank you very much for being so alert.	You feel good when you reach out to newcomers, don't you?
Thank you very much for reading with an open mind.	It feels good to me, too, when I can stand up for our class.
	Awareness
	I, too, sometimes do not manage myself as well as I want to.
	I, too, sometimes go too fast without noticing it.
	I, too, sometimes wonder about my feelings.

Source: Based on Harmin 1994, pp. 74–5.

FIGURE 4.5 Strategies for encouraging beyond praise and rewards

Strategy 1: 'I Appreciate' message

Description: A statement that communicates something honestly appreciated about students.

Purpose: To remind students that at least one adult appreciates them.

Examples:

I like the way you said that.

Thanks for giving that a try.

Strategy 2: 'I'm With You' message

Description: A message that communicates an empathetic acceptance or understanding of a student.

Purpose: To help students understand that they are not alone.

Examples:

Lots of us feel that way.

I can see how you would do that.

I think I understand how you feel.

I'd be proud to be in your shoes.

Strategy 3: Attention without praise

Description: Giving full attention to a student, as by listening carefully, without offering praise.

Purpose: To support and encourage students without making them overdependent on approval from others.

Examples:

Physical touch.

Eye contact.

Greetings after an absence.

Strategy 4: Plain corrects

Description: Straightforwardly informing a student that an answer is correct and then moving on.

Purpose: To confirm correctness without eliciting a distracting emotion.

Examples:

Yes, that's right.

Okay.

Yes, that's just what I wanted.

Just right.

Correct.

Yes, thank you.

Strategy 5: Plain incorrects

Description: Straightforwardly informing a student that an answer is not correct and then moving on.

Purpose: To inform students that an answer is incorrect without eliciting any distracting emotion.

continued

FIGURE 4.5 *(continued)*

Examples:

No, the correct answer is _____ .

You had the first name right. The correct answer is _____ .

Strategy 6: Silent response

Description: Making a mental note of a student error or problem, but leaving until later a consideration of what, if anything, is to be done about it.

Purpose: To avoid responding in unproductive ways to students' mistakes.

Strategy 7: Praise and rewards for all

Description: Praise or rewards offered to the group as a whole.

Purpose: To encourage a group without slighting any student and to build group unity.

Examples:

This group is making great progress. It's a pleasure for me to work with you.

Let's give ourselves a hand for the way we handled today's lesson.

You are all working so well together! I told the principal today how special you are.

Strategy 8: Honest delight

Description: A statement expressing spontaneous delight with a student.

Purpose: To allow oneself to be spontaneously expressive. Also, to demonstrate the reality that people have the ability to delight others.

Examples:

That was a really great paper you wrote yesterday, Lois.

What a good initiative you took, Jim.

I was delighted to see how you stuck with your friend, Billy.

You were truthful, and that was not easy, Sam. I was very happy to see that.

Great answer, Gloria. Very creative.

Source: Based on Harmin 1994, pp. 63–73.

Of course, teacher support and criticism is also an important means for students to receive feedback on their performance. According to Bloom and Bourdon (1980), few teachers (8 per cent in their research study) noticed consistent student errors and informed the students. Effective feedback for students should include specific details about errors, together with positive comments about ways to improve.

4.7 | MOTIVATION – INFLUENCING FACTORS

Student motivation is variable and complex and interrelated with many other factors such as anxiety, need for achievement, the need to be accepted, curiosity, and other needs outlined by Maslow.

At a school level, it is interesting to note some of the research on how student motivation is affected by the gender of teachers, the level of schooling (especially the problems in middle years) and the levels of school structure.

From classes you have observed do cooperative classrooms enable more student learning than competitive ones? Give points for or against this assertion.

Martin and Marsh (2005) studied middle and high school students in five Australian schools and concluded that 'boys and girls are no less or more motivated or engaged in classes taught by males than they are in classes taught by females' (p. 330). They demonstrated that the bulk of variance in motivation occurs at the student level and not because of the gender of the teacher.

Yeung and McInerney (2005) noted in their research that there is a decline in motivation of students during adolescence. In particular, there is a decline in effort motivation from Grade 7 to 9 in the Australian schools they studied. However, there is a rise again in Grade 11, when career aspirations appear to be a major motivating factor.

Black, Swann and Wiliam's (2006) study of UK students found that their opinions of learning in school declined between Years 6 to 9.

Anderson, Hattie and Hamilton (2005) concluded from their study that the structure of a school affects students' levels of motivation and achievement. Their results demonstrated that the ideal structure of a school is one that is sufficiently structured to be predictable but not so structured as to limit action alternatives for students.

To pinpoint factors that assist with motivating students is rather hazardous because of different motivational states of students, but some general factors are worth noting:

- *Warmth and enthusiasm*: Teachers who are enthusiastic about a subject and who can present the material in a sensitive, caring way are likely to strongly motivate their students.
- *Meaningful goals*: Teachers who set goals that are meaningful, realistic and achievable by students are likely to get their support. In these cases, students will become highly motivated because they can see how these instructional goals are relevant to their personal goals. This is especially the case if students perceive that they can achieve the goal or task and that they will not fail.
- *Fostering climate*: Teachers need to use a number of strategies to develop and maintain a positive social and psychological climate in the classroom. For example, they may need to develop cooperative team projects; they will want to initiate challenges that can be aired in a 'safe' environment; they will want to provide opportunities for students to enhance their self-actualisation. Fostering a positive climate is not only desirable for the students but also for the teacher, who also needs to receive support, recognition and acceptance.
- *Maintaining equity*: As noted above, students have well-developed skills in attracting particular kinds of teacher responses. To be fair and accepting to all students of varying levels of ability, commitment, personality and friendliness is a difficult task for any teacher and one that has to be monitored constantly. It is very easy to be selective in our praise and support and, perhaps unknowingly, ostracise certain students. Students are very aware of equity and will be quick to point out teacher behaviours or actions that do not appear to be even-handed and fair.

Some more specific principles for teachers to concentrate on are included in Figure 4.6. Several have been referred to earlier in the chapter, but it is useful to consider them as a complete list. A good time to review your strategies is at the beginning or end of each school term. Some of the strategies (for example, simulations and games) may need to be incorporated into your program for the following term. Other strategies may be used from time to time to add variety to your lessons (for example, the use of novel stimuli).

Finally, Figure 4.7 highlights some undesirable practices that a teacher should endeavour to avoid in order to keep students in the class highly motivated. Some situations are obvious (for example physical discomfort) but others (such as equity issues about students being tested on material not covered in class) can easily occur unknowingly. The list in total provides some timely reminders about situations that should be avoided whenever possible (see also Chapter 5).

FIGURE 4.6 General principles for motivating students

1. Use spoken and written support. Spoken support is particularly effective but so too are written comments.
2. Provide challenging and varied learning activities – there needs to be sufficient variety to maintain interest.
3. Attempt to match the instructional needs and interests of each student in your class.
4. Use short-term goals that are achievable – there is a higher sense of mastery of short-term goals.
5. Select reinforcers that are likely to be effective – this requires a teacher to monitor those reinforcers that are successful with particular students or groups.
6. Have clear outcomes – students will be more energised if they have been informed about the specific student outcomes required.
7. Use novel stimuli as springboards – students will be highly motivated by novel, complex or ambiguous stimuli; use this curiosity as a springboard into the lesson.
8. Use simulations and games – the research literature indicates that these are very motivating for students and promote student/teacher interaction (Marsh 2005).
9. Use familiar materials as stepping stones – any teaching situations should build upon persons, objects or events that are familiar to students.

FIGURE 4.7 Situations likely to bring about low levels of motivation

- Physical discomfort.
- Excessive demands from a teacher.
- A teacher conveys (knowingly or unknowingly) low expectations about individuals or groups.
- Students are assessed on material that has not been covered in class.
- A student's request for assistance from a teacher goes unanswered.
- Students have to work at a pace that is too fast for them.
- Students have to listen to an uninteresting presentation by the teacher.
- Failure (which may be publicly announced/referred to by the teacher).
- Loss of self-esteem due to failing to understand a topic or process.
- The teacher appears uninterested in the subject matter.
- The teacher uses criticism and sarcasm to motivate students.

YOUR TURN

- What techniques have you used with students who have low levels of motivation?
- Explain why you chose these techniques. Were they successful? Did you have a chance to follow up the issue of low motivation with the students concerned?

4.8 PASTORAL CARE

Pastoral care is closely related to the above sections on motivation. The term refers to all aspects of work with students in a school other than pure teaching (Cohen, Manion & Morrison 2004).

Teachers and administrators tend to portray pastoral care in terms of altruistic commitment and include such elements as:

- concern for the total welfare of the student
- schools providing a learning environment that is sensitive, warm and humane

- creating feelings of belonging for students
- enhancing the formation of positive relationships between the teacher and a student.

However, there are a number of research studies which reveal that a school's pastoral care structures are dysfunctional (Cruickshank, Jenkins & Metcalf 2009). House, year and sub-school systems and tutoring groups are just some of the structures used, especially in secondary schools, yet surveys of secondary school students reveal that many students do not perceive their schools to be caring institutions (Dynan 1980). In many cases, schools use these pastoral care structures for administrative expediency rather than for attending to the pastoral care needs of students (Lang & Hyde 1987). There is increasing concern over the quality of school life and the negative effects on students of organisational and administrative practices.

Lang and Hyde (1987) contend that pastoral care matters that need to be considered for students (and especially for secondary students) include:
- provision of specific actions to support the welfare of students
- giving support and guidance in coping with study, career choices, and personal and social problems
- helping students to acquire skills, understandings and aptitudes that will enable them to relate effectively to others.

CONCLUDING COMMENTS

Motivation is a very important force that affects and directs our behaviour. As a consequence, it is a vital factor for teachers to understand and to apply in their teaching.

By understanding different motivational needs of students and different forms of motivation, such as intrinsic and extrinsic motivation, we are better placed to provide classroom environments that are amenable to student learning. There are motivational techniques that we can use in the classroom. To a certain extent this involves us in trial and error and monitoring those strategies that are highly motivational with a particular class and those that are not. As noted by Gage and Berliner (1992, p. 381):

> Make your teaching experience cumulative. Don't be afraid to experiment but be sure to learn from the experience. Keep records. If something works, use it again; if it doesn't motivate your students, drop it. Teaching is a process that demands constant and careful revision.

Pastoral care needs of students are important but structures in many schools do little to service this need — many are based simply on administrative expediency.

KEY ISSUES RAISED IN THIS CHAPTER

1. Motivation energises, directs and sustains behaviour.
2. It is possible to intrinsically motivate students some of the time through innovative methods.
3. In classroom learning both intrinsic and extrinsic motivation is used.
4. Achievement motivation is especially important to many students and their families.
5. Many students actually seek out support and attention from the teacher and from other students.

REFLECTIONS AND ISSUES

1. What procedures can teachers use to develop intrinsic motivation? To what extent can extrinsic rewards support or undermine intrinsic motivation?
2. Students can control the effort they expend but have no control over innate ability, the difficulty of the task or luck and chance factors. Explain how an understanding of these factors in attribution theory can help teachers maximise the motivation of their students.
3. 'It is not which rewards or punishments that are most effective but how it is done and by whom.' (Caffyn 1989, p. 129). Discuss this statement.
4. How would you develop a positive classroom climate? Give examples of strategies you would use, including things to avoid.
5. Give examples of novel stimuli you might use as springboards for motivating students. If you have used any of these already in the classroom, comment on their effectiveness.
6. Which key principles are important to you in achieving high levels of motivation in the classroom? Which would be difficult to implement and why?
7. There are students in almost every class who are academically unmotivated. What strategies would you use to help them with their learning?
8. What kinds of information about individual students in your class would be helpful to you? How could this help you in motivating your students?
9. Examine some of the pastoral care structures in place at a nearby secondary school. Obtain feedback from teachers and students about their effectiveness.
10. What is a caring school? What can a teacher do to promote sound pastoral care?

Special references

Bottini, M & Grossman, S (2005) 'Centre-based teaching and children's learning', *Childhood Education*, 81(5), pp. 274–7.

McCaslin, M (2006) 'Student motivational dynamics in the era of school reform', *The Elementary School Journal*, 106(3), pp. 482–9.

Summers, J & Davis, H (2006) 'Introduction: The interpersonal contexts of teaching, learning and motivation', *The Elementary School Journal*, 106(3), pp. 189–91.

Web sources

For additional resources on learner motivation and developing self-esteem, please go to: www.pearson.com.au/myeducationlab.

5

LEARNING ENVIRONMENTS

5.1 | INTRODUCTION

Classroom environments are an integral part of the learning process and no teacher or student can be unaffected by their presence. It is the learning environment for both you and your students (Emmer, Evertson & Worsham 2006). For students, classroom environments represent sources of security and identity for individuals (Judson 2006). Teachers need to be able to adapt classroom environments for creative and innovative initiatives (Loi & Dillon 2006). Yet many classroom buildings are 'old and in poor condition, and may contain environmental conditions that inhibit learning and pose increased risks to the health of students and staff' (US Environmental Protection Agency 2006, p. 3).

In any school, the class teachers and students have to adjust to the building architecture – that is, the overall space, the position and number of doors and windows, the height of the ceiling and the insulation qualities of the walls. But as Bennett (1981, p. 24) reminds us:

> this does not indicate architectural determinism. Architecture can certainly modify the teaching environment, but teachers determine the curriculum and organisation.

Teachers and students have the opportunity to 'express their "personalities" through the arrangement and decor of the environment and the arrangement of space' (Ross 1982, pp. 1–2). However, creative arrangements need to be undertaken in the knowledge that specific physical conditions and space allocations can have important consequences on the attitudes, behaviours and even the achievements of students.

There is growing interest in very different classroom environments. Fully electronic learning environments are being planned and prototypes already exist. 'The Classroom of the Future', located at the National Institute of Education, Singapore, showcases how technology will influence pedagogical methods and improve the learning environment (Back Pack Net Centre 2005).

There is also interest in the planning of learning environments that move from a knowledge-transmission model to a knowledge-construction model (de Kock, Sleegers & Voeten 2004). Barab and Roth (2006) emphasise that knowing as participation in rich contexts (knowledge construction) does motivate students. Educators such as Edwards (2006) argue for 'green schools' which use passive solar heating and natural cross-ventilation. Allen (2007) uses the terms 'high performance schools' or 'sustainable schools' to describe efforts to make these schools more energy efficient, less costly to operate, environmentally safe and healthier for students and staff.

5.2 | CLASSROOM SETTINGS

5.2.1 Some considerations

How an area of space is used in a teaching–learning situation is clearly important, but often taken for granted. The particular pattern of juxtaposing furniture and spaces within the confines of a classroom (or open teaching area) is done for a variety of purposes. In some instances, the teacher arranges a particular pattern because they are convinced that this configuration aids learning. As examples, single rows of desks might be considered to be most useful for students listening to an expository, teacher-directed Science lesson; a grouping of desks in clusters of four might be far better for sharing materials in an Art lesson; and a circle of chairs with the desks pushed to the sides might be the most appropriate arrangement for a Literature lesson.

However, the teacher may have other reasons in mind that explain a particular pattern. Perhaps the teacher is concerned about a general atmosphere of restlessness in the class and wants convenient aisles and spaces so that 'seat work' can be continuously surveyed. In this case, the classroom spaces take on a greater significance than the furniture, because the opportunities for supervising are uppermost in the teacher's mind. It is impossible to separate these 'emotional climate' needs from the physical setting (Konza, Grainger & Bradshaw 2001).

Schools are contradictory places. As noted by Cullingford (2006) 'the emphasis of school, the organisation of classes, the physical conditions and the ambience of schooling are based on an industrial model of inputs and outcomes' (p. 211). Students, in the main, are very critical of this system even though they give the impression of politeness and submission.

5.2.2 Room arrangement principles

The following guidelines may be helpful in making decisions about the classroom – your special learning environment along with 30 or more students!

Use a room arrangement that facilitates your teaching and learning style and doesn't impede it

The classroom teacher needs to be aware of whether the physical environment they have provided facilitates the student behaviours desired. That is, unless the two are interrelated or congruent (the technical term is *synomorphic*), then undesirable effects are likely to result. Obvious examples would include a teacher planning for small group discussions between students but maintaining students in linear rows, thus impeding a lot of face-to-face contact.

Each teacher needs to design and plan the kinds of instruction needed in specific activity segments so that congruency does occur. Care must also be taken with the in-between activities, the *transitional periods* between lessons. Some activity segments lead naturally into others with a minimum of disruption and relocation of furniture and equipment, while others may not. For primary school teachers there are considerable opportunities for rescheduling activities. Secondary school teachers have less opportunity to do so except when they are operating on double periods.

Somehow, each teacher has to be aware of these instructional planning options, to produce rational decisions yet be prepared to launch out into creative ventures that enable the students to be extended and fulfilled. The particular mix of rational planning and creative endeavours comes down finally to the particular purposes a teacher wishes to achieve.

In broad terms, a teacher may desire to organise the class on the basis of *territory* or by *function*; the former focuses on a teacher-dominated purpose while the latter emphasises a resource specialisation, student-initiated focus.

In classrooms organised by territory, the major decision is how to allocate and arrange student desks and chairs. It is assumed that each student has their own domain or work space and that this is the basis for considering how certain learning activities will occur. The teacher may produce some rather different configurations of desks in their efforts to encourage particular kinds of interactions between students, but the focus of each activity segment and the location of the desks will be such that the teacher remains the central figure. The students are viewed predominantly as receivers (Tessmer & Richey 1997).

Classrooms organised on the basis of function enable students to engage in generative learning (Harris & Bell 1990). They are commonly found in early childhood centres and in junior grades in primary schools. They are also found in specialist subject areas (for example, Media or Science) and in subjects using computer-based projects (Anderson-Inman & Horney 1993). In this case, the allocation of space is based on what specialist materials or activities can be accommodated in a given area, and the matter of the location of desks is only of minor consideration. If several different functional areas are to be included in the one room, additional considerations need to be made about how each area should be arranged in relation to the others.

Ensure that high traffic areas are open and not congested

There are always high traffic areas such as around doorways, the pencil-sharpener, computers, certain bookshelves and the teacher's desk. According to Emmer, Evertson & Worsham (2008), high traffic areas should be kept away from each other, have plenty of space and be easily accessible.

Ensure clear lines of sight between students and the teacher

Every teacher is faced with a management issue of ensuring that all students are undertaking the tasks required. This is related, of course, to students being able to see teacher presentations without moving their chairs. Don't have seating that encourages students not to pay attention!

Have frequently used teaching materials and supplies readily available and accessible

Easy access for students will enable them to start and conclude the teaching and learning activities promptly and will minimise disruptions and delays.

YOUR TURN

From your observations in classrooms, how do teachers use classroom space?
- What areas are left vacant and why?
- What are the peak activity areas? Why?
- Would you arrange your classroom differently?
- Explain why you would do this.

5.2.3 Floor space

There are numerous classroom shapes and sizes, but it is possible to highlight the common elements of classrooms. The typical classroom is 12 metres long and 8 metres wide and is designed to accommodate approximately 30 students. One wall is typically taken up with blackboards or whiteboards and another wall often contains several pin-up boards. The teacher's table is usually at the front of the room and students' desks are arranged in four rows of seven to eight.

In this relatively formal classroom situation it is likely that the 'action zone' (Brophy 1981) for interaction between the teacher and students will be in the front and centre. That is, students seated near the front and centre desks facing the teacher are more likely to be the focus of the teacher's attention, rather than the students seated on the margins or at the rear of the room.

Many teachers are able to devise very different, creative patterns of use within the confines of the standard classroom (Cohen, Manion & Morrison 2004; Loi & Dillon 2006). Small group activities are facilitated by clusters of desks. A common area formed by the combination of five to six desks may be ideal for spreading out documents and charts as well as for providing close physical contact between a small group of students. The desks can still be oriented towards the blackboard and the teacher, or they can be located at points in the room that maximise space between groups.

In some classrooms, students have some input into decisions about the location of furniture and the use of space. Students might have concerns about being seated adjacent to other students with compatible interests and work habits. It is often in a classroom teacher's best interests to take note of these students' interests so that a congenial classroom atmosphere can be attained. Students might also have suggestions about the use and location of specialist furniture for displays. Student interests in developing such areas in the room can also lead to their willingness to supervise the use of these resources.

5.2.4 Location of the teacher's desk

Clearly, the location of your desk must be where it is most functional. If you use it as a storage place for instructional materials used during presentations, the desk needs to be at the front. If you prefer to watch the activities of students from the rear of the room then this is the ideal location for your desk (see Figure 5.1).

5.2.5 Arrangement of students' desks

Depending on space available many different arrangements are possible, as depicted in Figure 5.1 (and in relation to furniture, in Figures 5.2 and 5.3).

In devising the location of student desks it is important to remember students' needs, including:
- Their need to be seated at points in the classroom where they can comfortably undertake the learning activities. This might include being close to the teacher to see and hear him/her clearly without straining; to be able to read the whiteboard or overhead or PowerPoint projection in comfort; to be close enough to the teacher and centrally located to ensure that they will be fully engaged in the interactions (questioning, discussions) with the teacher.
- A need for them to be located at desks or tables adjacent to peers with whom they have a close and mutually positive relationship (Woods 1990a).
- A need for them to have access to the resources in the room. Student needs with regard to the learning activities reflect the desirability of congruence between physical and behavioural components. Some students will make a conscious effort to be seated close to the teacher so they are able to interact verbally and non-verbally with him/her. Other students may, of course, have no such intention and will do their utmost to ensure that they distance themselves from the teacher. The teacher has to ensure that as many students as possible are located at appropriate positions in the room so that they gain maximum participation in the ongoing activities.

5.2.6 Arrangement of furniture and equipment

Large items of furniture such as cupboards can be used as dividers within a room. Pieces of pegboard can be used to cover the sides of a cupboard and thereby provide additional display space. It is also helpful to have one or two large tables in a classroom, even though they take up a lot of space. These tables can be used for a multitude of purposes including storing audiovisual materials, storing unfinished work or for displays of completed projects. Figure 5.2 illustrates how cupboards and tables can be used as dividers in a single room.

FIGURE 5.1 A room arrangement for whole-class instruction

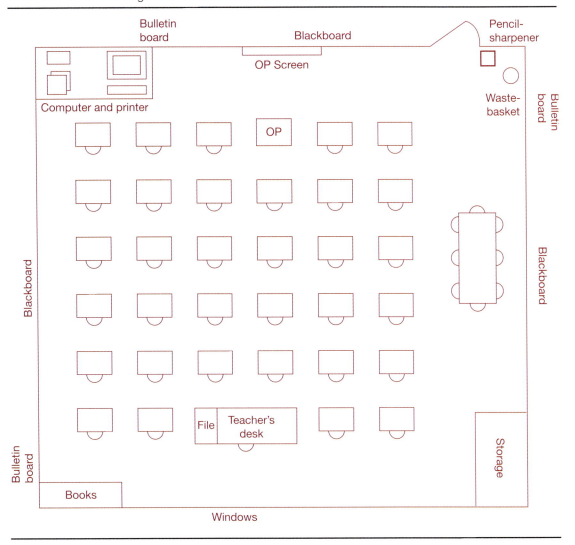

The placement of computers in the room is an additional complication. A single computer might be located in any convenient corner, but a pod of five or more computers can cause difficulties in an already crowded room. A possible layout is depicted in Figure 5.3. Some primary schools have all their computers located in a separate computer laboratory.

5.2.7 Learning stations and work centres

These are areas where a small number of students come to work on a special activity. These areas need to be located so that they do not distract from major learning activities.

Learning stations are examples of functional areas that are often established in early childhood centres and primary schools. A learning station is simply an area in a room where a group of students can work together at well-defined tasks. Usually, all resource materials are provided at the one location and tasks are included on colour-coded cards so that individuals or groups can involve themselves with minimal supervision by the teacher. Materials can be at different difficulty levels to provide for differentiated instruction (Tomlinson 2008a). Many educators applaud the use of learning

FIGURE 5.2 A classroom using cupboards as dividers

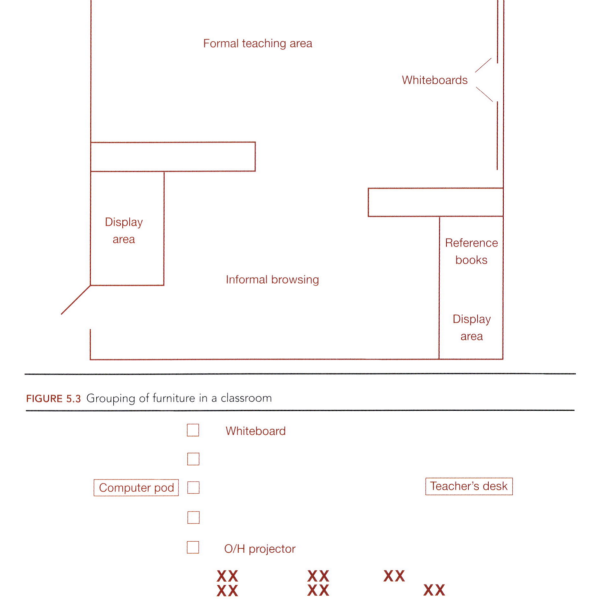

FIGURE 5.3 Grouping of furniture in a classroom

centres – 'they provide children with opportunities for making choices, working with others, being involved in hands-on activities and becoming fully engaged in learning' (Bottini & Grossman 2005, p. 274).

Tablet PCs, laptops and other computer products are ideal for using at learning stations. Students can work individually, in pairs, or in small groups on projects (Bitter & Pierson 2005).

A classroom might contain three or four learning stations, located so that there is sufficient space between each to minimise noise interruptions and provide convenient access to other support areas, such as a 'conference' section where the teacher can discuss completed work units with students.

In addition to the traditional specialist rooms in secondary schools such as Design and Technology centres, Home Economics Rooms and Science laboratories, it is interesting to note how this has been extended over the last decade to include sophisticated language laboratories, media centres and computer laboratories (Cohen, Manion & Morrison 2004; de Castell 2000).

5.2.8 Pin-up boards and bulletin boards

Pin-up boards are a major element in any classroom because they can be used to display various items of interest, such as student work, charts, posters, class rules and routines. Primary school students might have class banners, class photographs, birthday charts or monitor charts (Konza, Grainger & Bradshaw 2001). Secondary school students might prefer posters on media topics, environment and sporting figures.

5.2.9 Smart Boards (interactive whiteboards)

The interactive whiteboard is being used now in a number of schools (Cross 2006). It is essentially a large computer screen that is sensitive to touch. The content of the computer screen is displayed on the board using a data projector. Interactive whiteboards can be used to replace blackboards and overhead projectors. Students can display their work, add notes, and even include video, music and picture files. They are a boon to student-initiated activities and small group work.

5.2.10 Special items

Plants can add a very positive effect to a classroom and of course students learn to be responsible for their watering. At primary school level, various animals may be kept such as fish, birds, tadpoles and mice. They add novelty and colour and are further opportunities for students to develop responsibilities for the safety and welfare of pets.

The task for each teacher is to work out how to make the best use of available furniture and facilities. It is often amazing how the rearrangement of particular desks or cupboards leads to unforeseen increases in space and access. Mezzanine floors suspended above the tables and chairs and withdrawal areas complete with lounge chairs and occasional tables are just some of the more adventurous schemes that have been implemented by some teachers. The checklist included in Figure 5.4 provides useful reminders about space utilisation.

5.2.11 Floating teachers

At the secondary school level, but also for specialists in a primary school, it is highly likely that teachers will not have their own room. They may be required to share or co-teach with another teacher at the primary school level, or at the secondary school level go to three or four rooms each day.

This requires different organisational arrangements. For each of the rooms you will be using it is necessary to try to arrange the following:
- an overhead projector in place for daily use, or access to a projector and laptop computer to present PowerPoint slides
- a regular space on the blackboard
- a pin-up board available for your class announcements, assignments, and so on
- a shelf or cabinet for placing teaching materials (Emmer, Evertson & Worsham 2008).

Another useful device is either a wheeled airport-type bag or a more robust trolley with sufficient space to carry reference books and audiovisual aids.

FIGURE 5.4 Checklist to evaluate the use of classroom space

1. Is there too much furniture?
2. Is the best use made of the whole space of the school?
3. How does the use of space reflect the range and nature of different activities?
4. How effectively is shared space used?
5. How attractive and stimulating is the space?
6. How does the grouping of tables and work areas reflect the needs of the students and the tasks, especially computer-based tasks?
7. How well do students understand the classroom organisation?
8. How appropriately and effectively are the resources deployed?
9. How accessible are resources and spaces?
10. How easy is pupil and teacher movement?
11. How effectively does the organisation of space promote pupil interaction?

Source: Based on Morrison and Ridley 1988.

YOUR TURN

- Do you consider that the use of space in classrooms really caters for the needs of students?
- What aspects are not considered?
- Have you observed effective alternative arrangements?

5.3 | OTHER PHYSICAL AND PSYCHOLOGICAL FACTORS IN THE CLASSROOM

Winston Churchill once remarked: 'We shape our buildings, and afterwards our buildings shape us'. This statement underlines the importance of the physical buildings in which we work and play and especially the environments in which school children spend at least 12 years of their lives. However, Churchill also appears to be attributing a considerable degree of determinism to the physical buildings, and it is far from clear whether this stance can be supported.

Proshansky, Ittelson and Rivlin noted in 1976 that physical settings were being reconsidered by scientists after a number of decades in which it had been (naively) assumed that the effects of the physical environment were predictable and controllable. They stated that the view hitherto had been that:

> an appropriately designed physical setting could be expected to evoke, or at least to serve as the locus of, a range of behaviours … Thus, for the child to learn, he needs to feel at ease, comfortable, and secure. It follows, therefore, that schools must be light, airy, colourful and roomy. (p. 171)

Research evidence indicates that relationships between the physical environment and students are far from clear (Allen & Fraser 2007). There are some patterns emerging related to crowding, privacy and territoriality (Sebba 1986), but few conclusive studies relating to specific physical environment factors. In fact, it is very difficult to disentangle the physical from the psychological factors. The research studies that have provided conclusive results are those that have demonstrated particular interrelationships between the two, such as the relationship between the density of students in a classroom with student attitudes of dissatisfaction. The examples that follow indicate the interrelationships between physical environment factors and affective states of students rather than direct influences on achievement measures.

5.3.1 Colour

> The communications media are very aware of the use of colour and it is little wonder that colour television, colour inserts in daily newspapers, glossy colour magazines and full colour computer games and graphics are so popular. (Cohen, Manion & Morrison 2004)

So it is in classrooms. The list of items that can add colour to a classroom is endless and is not just limited to those listed above. Newspaper clippings, pamphlets and photographs are an integral part of many classrooms and they can add to the visual impact. So, too, can three-dimensional models (for example, of landscapes, buildings and animals) and dioramas. Personal computer nooks and cubicles found in many classrooms add to the diversity of colours. However, a variegated assortment of colours, vying for students' attention in a classroom, needs to be considered in terms of educational purposes (Emmer, Evertson & Worsham 2008). Colours may be used by the teacher to gain students' attention and motivation, but they are also included to provide satisfaction and a sense of belonging to the student members of each classroom (Konza, Grainger & Bradshaw 2001). As Field (1980, p. 197) notes, 'classrooms belong to the children, and teachers need to help them identify with it more readily'. If students are involved in the planning of materials to be displayed and in the regular changing of them, then it is likely that they will identify far more readily with their teacher and the classroom endeavours he/she is trying to pursue.

Despite the many assertions from education writers about the value of colour in classroom environments, there is little research evidence to support or refute its use.

Horowitz and Otto (1973) compared the scholastic achievement of tertiary students in a traditional classroom with a room that was specially designed to include a great deal of colour (and also a complex lighting system, flexible, comfortable seats and moveable wall panels). Although no differences in achievement were noted between the two groups, there was a definite difference in classroom behaviour. The group of students who used the experimental room participated more fully in class sessions, attendance rates were higher and there was more group cohesion.

At the primary school level, Santrock (1976) studied first and second grade children in a specially designed room that was decorated alternately with happy, sad and neutral coloured pictures. The results indicated that the type of pictures in the room had a strong influence on the children and that they worked longer at a task when they were in the setting with the happy pictures.

Related to colour is the amount of natural light available to students in a classroom. Rosenfeld's (1999) research demonstrated that primary school students in Seattle, USA, who studied in light-filled schools scored higher in maths and reading tests than those students working in classrooms with least light.

5.3.2 Noise

Sounds are all around us, but when certain sounds are unwanted they are generally termed 'noise'. Bell, Fisher and Loomis (1976) make this point when they emphasise that noise involves a physical component (by the ear and higher brain structures), but also a psychological component when it is evaluated as unwanted.

As far as the classroom is concerned, it is important that the physical environment provides acoustics that enable participants to hold discussions in a normal conversational voice. The level of desirable noise will vary in different settings such as from a manual arts workshop with noisy lathes and electric drills to an extremely quiet library. Each instructional setting has its own noise level requirements to the extent that each person needs to be able to hear clearly what is needed to be heard and is not distracted by other noises (Erikson & Wintermute 1983).

Every classroom environment has a background noise level due to the operation of various ventilation and audiovisual appliances (such as oscillating fans, recorders, computer keyboards, printers). Background noise level (BNL) is typically measured in decibels. According to the Department of Education and Science (1975) in the United Kingdom, a teacher can communicate clearly in a quiet voice when the BNL rises to 35 dB. A normal voice will carry quite well over a BNL of 40 dB, but once a BNL of 45 dB or 50 dB is reached, a teacher (or student) has to speak in a very loud voice. Inevitably the exchange of conversation in a loud voice can lead to irritation, stress and fatigue. Anderson (2001) notes that teachers talk for 6.3 hours, on average, per school day and often experience vocal fatigue. Of course, the irritation is generated by disagreements over what is being said as well as by the level of noise that is being created by the sender. A particular noise may or may not be wanted. More often, it is the unpredictability or lack of control over the source of the noise that is the major cause of the frustration.

Research studies on the effects of noise in classrooms have been considerable over the last six decades, but the results are inconclusive and often contradictory. Some of these studies have examined short-term exposure of students to noise within the school, while other studies have monitored long-term exposure to severe noise from external sources.

As an example of the former, Slater (1968) examined seventh grade primary school children's performance on a standardised reading test under three conditions. The first classroom of students was isolated from surrounding background noise, the second had normal background neighbouring noise of 55–70 dB, and in the third room additional noise sources were used (lawn mower, tape recordings) to maintain a BNL of 75–90 dB. The results indicated that the students' performance on the reading test was not affected either positively or negatively by the different levels of noise. In another study of primary school students, Weinstein and Weinstein (1979) compared the reading performance of fourth grade students under quiet (47 dB) and normal (60 dB) background noise and also found that there were no significant differences in performance.

More conclusive results have been obtained in long-term studies using extreme external noises. For example, Bronzaft and McCarthy (1975) compared the reading scores of students attending a school that was located adjacent to an overhead train line. The scores of the students located in classrooms on the noisy side of the building nearest the train line were significantly lower than the scores of students located on the other side of the building. It is difficult to interpret the reasons for this difference. The major cause of the difference might have been that the students were unable to hear the teacher and thereby missed important periods of instruction; or perhaps the teacher paused whenever a train went by (every four minutes) and thereby lost valuable instruction time; or perhaps the students became accustomed to screening out noises and filtered out relevant as well as irrelevant sounds.

In their study, Cohen *et al.* (1979) did not replicate this finding but raised other issues. They studied primary school students located at four schools in the air corridor of Los Angeles International Airport. Children from these noisy schools and a set of control group quiet schools were not significantly different on tests of mathematics and reading achievement, or on auditory discrimination. However, children at the noisy schools did not perform as well on problem-solving tests and their social behaviour indicated a greater tendency to be distracted easily.

Crandell (1995) undertook research on the attention spans of young children and concluded that skills of figure-ground discrimination (listeners paying attention to a specific sound such as a teacher's voice) do not mature until approximately age thirteen. Younger children require speech to be much louder before they can recognise words accurately.

Noise affects all teachers and students, but the problem is compounded for students with hearing problems (Anderson 2001). Ray (1992) noted in his study that 20 to 43 per cent of primary school students had minimal degrees of permanent or fluctuating hearing impairment that could adversely affect listening and learning. The problem is especially acute with special education students, many of whom have significant histories of hearing loss (Reichman & Healey 1993). Dockrell and Shield

(2006) note that poor classroom acoustics can create a negative learning environment for many students, especially those with learning impairments.

One solution for problems associated with noisy classrooms is to have a sound amplification system. Teachers in many Asian classrooms use microphones because of the size of the classes.

According to Anderson (2001), an obvious benefit of a sound amplification system is that teachers do not have to raise their voices above a conversational level to be heard clearly throughout the classroom. Just as an overhead projector helps students focus on the teacher's written presentations, an amplification system helps all students focus on verbal instruction (p. 78).

Excessive noise can also affect the wellbeing of teachers. Grebennikov and Wiggins (2006) studied 25 teachers working in 14 preschool settings in Western Sydney. They concluded that 40 per cent of the monitored teaching staff were exposed to daily or peak noise rates in excess of the Australian standard. There were statistically significant positive relationships between doses of noise received and levels of teacher interpersonal stress.

YOUR TURN

- How detrimental is classroom noise to an effective learning environment? What are 'acceptable' and 'unacceptable' noise levels?
- How do students react in classrooms that are excessively noisy?

5.3.3 Temperature

Common sense would indicate that there is a fairly limited temperature range in which school students might be expected to work at their best. High temperatures will tend to make some students irritable and uncomfortable. In extreme cases students can become lethargic and even nauseous. Then again, cold temperatures seem to bring out aggression and negative behaviour in some students.

Judgments about temperature control in schools are typically made at head office, in that decisions about the architectural design of schools and the use of specific building materials are made at this level. The use of particular designs, the siting of buildings and the use of insulating material will clearly affect maximum and minimum temperatures.

Within each school, a principal may be able to seek additional equipment to maintain the temperature at moderate levels. For example, oscillating ceiling fans are commonly used in many schools and the traditional hearth and wood fire have given way to oil and gas-fired heaters. Extremes of temperature are only experienced in a few areas of Australia to the extent that central heating of schools is required in winter (for example in the ACT) or airconditioning is required in summer (for example schools in the Pilbara in Western Australia and some Northern Territory schools).

The majority of research studies on the effects of temperature have been laboratory ones and many relate to the military. As was mentioned earlier with regard to noise, the perception of temperature involves physical and psychological components. The thoughtful teacher needs to be aware of the possibilities of temperature stress if abnormally high or low temperatures prevail, and adjust his/her instructional activities accordingly. Some students are easily prone to discomfort from temperature excesses while others are not unduly affected.

5.3.4 Seating

Having comfortable seating in classrooms is of major importance. If students are confined to uncomfortable seats for extended periods of time they become distracted from the learning task (Gay 1986). Uncomfortable seating may also lead to negative attitudes about the teacher (Emmer, Evertson &

Worsham 2008). Mann (1997) reports on a study where students were given modular, modern furniture and noted major changes in attitude. Lieble (1980, p. 22) states the problem succinctly: 'the mind can only absorb what the seat can endure'.

5.3.5 Class size

Of course interactions between the teacher and students can be increased when class numbers are small (Blatchford 2003). This results in less desk space and therefore more free space is available for informal activities or for specialist equipment.

 Reflect upon the size of classes you have experienced as a student in primary and secondary schools. Have you any suggestions about what is an optimal class size? Why?

Research evidence is contradictory on whether class size impacts on student achievement. For example, Murphy and Rosenberg (1998) and Davies, Hallam and Ireson (2003) contend that there is compelling evidence that reducing class size, especially for younger children, will have a positive effect on student achievement.

Finn, Pannozzo and Achilles (2003) studied 15 primary school classes in the United States. They concluded that when class sizes are reduced, major changes occur in students' engagement in the classroom. In the smaller classes students are more visible to the teacher. There is also a greater sense of belonging and group cohesiveness.

Konstantopoulos (2008) studied students in 79 primary schools in Tennessee, USA, as part of Project STAR. He concluded that higher achieving students benefited more from being in small classes in early grades than other students. However he also concluded that reductions in class size did not reduce the achievement gap between low and high achievers.

In a major synthesis of research studies on class size, Biddle and Berliner (2002, p. 20) make several conclusions:

- Small classes in the early grades generate substantial gains for the students and those extra gains are greater the longer students are exposed to those classes.
- Extra gains from small classes in the early grades are larger when the class has fewer than 20 students.
- Students who have traditionally been disadvantaged in education carry gains forward into the upper grades.
- The extra gains appear to apply equally to boys and girls.
- Evidence for the possible advantages of small classes in the upper grades and high school is inconclusive.

State governments in Australia have recently taken steps to reduce classes. For example, New South Wales aimed at class sizes of 20, 22 and 24 in the first three years of schooling for all state schools by 2007. Results in 2009 indicated positive achievements with class sizes for the first three years reduced to 19.3, 21.3 and 22.6 (NSW Department of Education and Training 2009). Victoria has reduced classes in the first three years of school to an average of 21 students (Pollard 2002).

Yet there is also evidence which does not support the stance that smaller classes lead to better outcomes. Rees and Johnson (2000) conclude that there is no evidence that smaller class sizes alone lead to higher student achievement. A study of over 1500 Victorian primary and secondary schools showed that academic achievement was unrelated to the number of students in the class (Jensen 2004).

Hattie's (2006) meta-analysis research concludes that effects are small unless there are concerted efforts by teachers to refrain from using the same teaching methods regardless of class size. Yeh (2007) contends that it is many times more cost-effective to use rapid formative assessment (computer-based immediate feedback to a student, for example 2–5 times per week) to improve student outcomes rather than reducing class size. In an international study, Wofmann and West (2004) concluded that there were minimal class size effects in school systems around the world.

5.3.6 Psychosocial environment

A number of studies have been done on students' perceptions to get information on a better person–environment fit in classrooms (Fraser & Walberg 1991; Fisher & Khine 2006; Allodi 2007).

At the primary and secondary school levels, students can be surveyed to get data on their present levels of personal satisfaction and adjustment and their respective teachers can then use this information to make changes where appropriate (Griffith 1997).

A number of student inventories have been developed that provide this information. The *Classroom Environment Scale* (Moos & Trickett 1974) has been widely used in the US. This instrument measures nine different dimensions of the classroom environment, including students' interpersonal relationships, personal growth and teacher control.

My Class Inventory is an instrument developed by Australian researchers Fisher and Fraser (1981) and Fraser and Goh (2003), which is used to gain information about primary school students' perceptions of classroom goals and value orientations. The items require students to make ratings on actual classroom environments as well as preferred environments. This information can be of great interest to class teachers who are concerned about providing instructional environments that are more in accord with those preferred by students.

A further questionnaire instrument was developed by Fraser, McRobbie and Fisher (1996) to measure students' perceptions of their classroom environment. Items are included that provide data on the seven dimensions: student cohesiveness, extent of teacher support, extent of student involvement, investigative activities, task orientation, cooperation and equity.

Numerous studies have been undertaken within specific subject disciplines and cross-nationally (for example, Dorman, Adams & Ferguson 2002; Henderson, Fisher & Fraser 1998; Fraser & Ferguson 1999; Wolf & Fraser 2008) and in classrooms using new information technologies (Zandvliet & Fraser 2005). It is very evident that a student's perception of classroom environment has an important role in learning.

5.3.7 Ability groupings

Ability groupings and cross-setting arrangements have been the subject of considerable controversy over the years. Although some educators argue that homogenous ability groups have many benefits for teachers and students, others argue that it leads to unfair stigmatising of some students and inappropriate allocations to groups, with little hope for these students to be moved to higher ability groups.

Davies, Hallam and Ireson (2003) note that there has been an increase in the use of ability grouping in primary schools in the UK because of the increased pressure on schools to raise the performance of their students. They conclude that many factors need to be considered when embarking upon the setting up of ability groups, such as the physical layout of the school, staff levels and the availability of resources.

5.3.8 Single-sex schools and single-sex classes in coeducational schools

In many Western countries over the last decade there have been growing concerns about boys' apparent underachievement relative to that of girls. Within the UK, governments have highlighted the underachievement of boys in national assessments at 7, 11, 14 and 16 years of age (Younger & Warrington 2006). In Australia the boys' lobbies have been very successful in demonstrating that boys are the new disadvantaged group (Ailwood 2003).

Independent single-sex schools have been popular in many countries and achievements of boys and girls in their respective schools have been noteworthy. The emergence of single-sex classes within coeducational schools in the UK and Australia has been marked. Those arguing in favour of single-sex classes for boys assert that these classes enable boys to share their feelings and emotions without embarrassment; and they are less distracted by girls (Sukhnandan *et al.* 2000; Swan 1998; Cox 2006).

There is evidence also that single-sex classes can benefit girls as much as or more than boys (Herr & Arms 2004). According to Younger and Warrington (2006), such an approach enables teachers to challenge some girls' stereotypical responses to subjects such as Mathematics and Science and enables girls to develop confidence in their own abilities. Yet there are concerns that many of the initiatives for the single-sex classes for boys are 'rooted in the agenda of male disadvantage and repair and situated strongly within recuperative masculinity politics' (Younger & Warrington 2006; Karlsson 2007).

It is evident that the use of single-sex classes in coeducational schools is a complex matter and for it to be successful there must be wide-ranging staff development programs and appropriate teaching and learning strategies that engage and motivate students (Martino & Pallotta-Chierolli 2005). In the short term, recuperative masculinity agendas are unhelpful and do not address the real needs of girls currently being failed by the school system (Younger & Warrington 2006).

5.3.9 Private and public schools

Debates continue to rage over whether private schools provide a better education than do government schools (Loader 1999; Townsend 1999; Blackmore 1999). Some education experts clearly think so as revealed by Caldwell's (2006) reported comment by CC Leung in *The Age* (5 July 2006, p. 3), 'ageing public school buildings across Victoria must be "bulldozed" and replaced by cutting-edge facilities to help stem the flow of students to private schools'. A study by Buckingham (2000) noted that the learning environment was a major factor why parents were opting for private schools. Parents cited such reasons as the following:
- better discipline in private schools
- smaller classes
- more individual attention given to students.

5.3.10 Home schooling

An option that is becoming increasingly popular among parents is to home school their children.

According to Gaither (2008) home schooling in the USA is now a political movement, being fuelled by the Countercultural Left (wanting an alternative society for their children) and the Countercultural Right (conservatives and evangelicals wanting religious-based teaching).

In Australia, the motivations for home schooling are less pronounced but are possibly a combination of Countercultural Left and the problem of distance from well-resourced schools for families in rural areas. All state and territory education systems in Australia have made provision for home schooling. Parents are required to develop a curriculum based upon the relevant syllabus documents. Typically, education officers will inspect the parents to check the progress of children. There can be a number of reasons why parents might take this option, including moral and religious grounds, and a strong motivation to develop the perceived or actual special talents of a child.

Various organisations are available to provide resources for home schooling. With current major developments in computers it is now possible for home schoolers to undertake electronic learning.

5.3.11 Tutoring services provided by commercial interests

Although tutoring of primary and secondary school students is not a major industry in Australia, it is expanding rapidly. In Asian countries it is widely practised and in the US it has increased dramatically as a result of the *No Child Left Behind Act* (NCLB). For example, schools in the US that miss the NCLB goals are provided with free tutoring by the state. Such is the pressure on states to meet the NCLB targets (ASCD 2005, 27 October; 2006, 18 March).

5.4 | OTHER LEARNING SETTINGS

The school is not the only learning environment for young and older children. There are other non-formal agencies such as church and youth groups that provide organised, systematic and educational activities.

5.4.1 Community schools

Dryfoos (2004) has evaluated a number of community schools in the US. These are schools that are jointly operated through a partnership between the school system and community agencies. These schools typically emphasise community services and community learning. He concludes that community schools are having a positive impact and reducing social barriers to learning.

Participation in these community activities enables students to realise the value of life skills – they develop self-confidence and understand more about personal dependability (McLaughlin 2001).

Full-service youth and community centres provide additional learning environments apart from classrooms. They have family resource centres, health care facilities, preschool, before- and after-school child care, auditoriums and other facilities. These sites are open day and night and capture the spirit of a community school (Dryfoos 2000).

Bowker and Tearle (2007) refer to a Gardens for Life project practised in 67 schools in England, Kenya and India. They contend that gardening, as a form of experimental learning, showed a positive impact on learning in these countries.

5.4.2 Service learning

Service learning has become an important priority in recent years, whereby students visit other environments (such as senior citizen homes, or disabled hostels) and provide caring services to others in need. Doing these community services gives students an opportunity to reflect on their own development (Dinkelman 2001). Seitsinger (2005) researched the use of service learning in middle schools in the US and concluded that these experiences enabled students to develop their higher order thinking skills.

In Canada, Ellis (2003) reports how a Storefront School has been working out of a shopping centre in Ottawa. This is a creative partnership between the school board and the shopping mall owners. It provides a valuable opportunity for 19–21 year old students with disabilities to have a work experience and life skills program.

Yet there are issues with service learning. Butin (2003) argues that there are at least three major problems:
- there is limited research evidence on community impact resulting from service learning even though it might provide knowledge and insight to some students and teachers
- research on students involved in service learning shows only small increases in academic, social and personal outcomes
- it is difficult to undertake rigorous and authentic assessment of service learning.

Butin (2003) contends that service learning must be 'understood through multiple conceptual frames – technical, cultural, political and post-structural' (p. 1690).

There are indications that service learning will become a significant focus in national curriculum developments in Australia. For example, Cole (2008) asserts that 'we need to ensure that community and service learning experiences are able to be pursued and recognised within the senior secondary curriculum' (p. 4). The National Curriculum Board's (2008a) 'Initial Policy Proposal' emphasises flexible and critical thinking in a range of contexts, including local communities.

CONCLUDING COMMENTS

Descriptions of classroom environments run the full gamut from invective criticism:

> Judging from what is said and from what is available as a measuring stick, schools are architecturally and environmentally sterile ... Their structure is insipid, cavernous and regimented. They are only now and then really creature-comfortable. Their designs maximise economy, surveillance, safety and – maybe – efficiency. (George & McKinley 1974, p. 141)

to unbridled praise:

> [Open planned classroom environments] are a liberatory measure capable of emancipating children from the authority of teachers. (Cooper 1982, p. 168)

In this chapter an attempt was made to place judgments about classroom environments on a more substantial footing and not to subscribe to either extreme view. Classroom instruction is affected by different uses of space and physical conditions. It is not possible to have knowledge of all the interrelationships, but it would be less than professional to ignore the evidence that is available. Creative arranging of the classroom is one thing, but it must be tempered by careful consideration of the effects of the classroom environment in all its complexities.

KEY ISSUES RAISED IN THIS CHAPTER

1. Classroom environments are an integral part of the learning process. Every teacher and student is affected by it.
2. Computer equipment such as laptops, tablet PCs and smart boards are now replacing some of the fittings traditionally found in classrooms.
3. Physical and psychosocial factors can affect student interest and achievements.
4. There are ongoing debates about the value of single sex schools and classes.

REFLECTIONS AND ISSUES

1. 'Effective teachers carefully and consciously craft the environment in their classrooms' (Ryan, Cooper & Tauer 2008, p. 93). What aspects would you concentrate on in the first few weeks of starting with a new class?
2. If learning activities are the main focus of your teaching then this should be a major consideration in how you arrange furniture and resources in your classroom. Discuss.
3. 'In my space there must be a wide range of ways to succeed, multiple interests to pursue, a variety of possible contributions to make. This means the room is decentralised and characterised by lively work stations or interest areas, rather than by straight rows.' (Ayers 1993, p. 60). How achievable is this? Describe how you have developed classrooms in terms of multiple interests.
4. To what extent is it possible to cater for students' individual learning styles in terms of environmental elements such as noise, temperature and colour? Give examples from your classroom experiences or classes you have visited.
5. A certain level of adequacy must be attained in seating, acoustics, temperature and lighting for high level learning to occur (Tessmer & Richey 1997). Explain, giving examples from your classroom experiences.
6. 'Machines change relations within the traditional classroom. Film, video, computer software and websites act as teachers and partially displace the human teacher' (De Vaney 1998, p. 3). Discuss.

7 'School is diffusing spatially, merging into the physical backdrop of society. Schools are losing their architectural individuality, becoming increasingly difficult to recognise as places of learning' (Hopmann & Kunzli 1997, p. 261). What are other places of learning? Are schools losing their individuality? If so, what will the impact be in the short and medium term?
8 'Children's attitude and behaviour is determined, to a considerable extent, by the design of school grounds' (Titman 1997, p. 2). What messages do the quality of school grounds convey to school children? What are positive and negative elements of school grounds for children? How might this affect their behaviour in and out of the classroom?
9 'Teachers have little training in how to arrange a room. Perhaps every new teacher should receive an empty classroom and then plan what they want to do in it and how they want it to operate.' If you were given an empty room, explain how you would arrange it.

Special references

Allen, R (2007) 'Green schools: Thinking outside the schoolroom box', *Education Update*, 49(11):1–8.
Hattie, J (2006) 'The paradox of reducing class size and improving learning outcomes', *International Journal of Educational Research*, 43(6):387–425.
Tessmer, M & Richey, RC (1997) 'The role of context in learning and instructional design', *Educational Technology, Research and Development*, 45(2), pp. 85–116.
Titman, W (1997) 'Special places, special people: The hidden curriculum of school grounds', *Set 1*, 1–4, Winchester, UK.
Tuijnman, A & Bostrom, A (2002) 'Changing notions of lifelong education and lifelong learning', *International Review of Education*, (48)1/2:93–110.

Web sources

For additional resources on learning environments, please go to:
www.pearson.com.au/myeducationlab.

PART

HOW TEACHERS ORGANISE AND TEACH

3

Taking it to the Classroom

www.pearson.com.au/myeducationlab

Number of years teaching: 7 years
Year level teaching now: Year 12

First day of teaching memories:

I can remember turning up to my classroom for my form group about a half hour or 45 minutes early and being greeted by my first Year 7 student who'd beaten me there by about 15 minutes. Just seeing how nervous he was did a lot to settle my nerves for the day because I could sort of see that as difficult as this is for me, at least I'm in control. Whereas here, you've got a boy, the age of 12, who doesn't really know quite what is in store for him. Then, at the end of the day, to see him leave with a smile on his face, happy – exhausted, but happy – made me feel like it was a good day done.

Cameron Bacholer
The Peninsula School

chapter 6	What is a curriculum?
chapter 7	Planning and preparing for teaching
chapter 8	Organising classroom structures and routines
chapter 9	Planning to achieve goals, aims, objectives, outcomes and standards
chapter 10	School Development Plans and Strategic Planning Frameworks

6

WHAT IS A CURRICULUM?

6.1 | INTRODUCTION

Teaching is an art. Numerous skills are needed in terms of planning WHAT, HOW and WHEN to teach – and the overall aim is to produce coherent, purposeful teaching and learning activities. This requires a lot of thought and creativity.

 Are you up to this task? What skills do you think you already have? Who can you turn to if you need help in producing good lessons?

Fortunately we do not have to do all these tasks by ourselves. There are many other educators who can assist us.

This chapter examines the product of creative planning by others – the written curriculum. Curriculum documents come in all shapes and sizes and they all represent carefully planned and presented approaches to guide the teacher. It is important that we are fully conversant with curriculum documents before we get down to the task of lesson planning and creating our own lessons. It is also important to look for the overt and covert values incorporated in these documents.

6.2 | MEANING OF THE TERM 'CURRICULUM'

The term 'curriculum' (and its synonyms) is used in myriad situations and most would consider that they know its meaning. For example, the 'curriculum' for training sessions for netball or basketball might consist of such things as specific physical exercises, endurance trials and 'pep-talks'. Even parents follow a 'curriculum' of sorts in terms of the required activities and responsibilities they undertake for their children, including looking after their daily hygiene, food needs, love and support, and discipline.

The term is also used very loosely to mean expectations about roles or tasks undertaken by persons to achieve certain goals or standards.

One useful starting point when studying what curriculum is, is to consider three levels, namely the 'planned curriculum', the 'enacted curriculum' and the 'experienced curriculum' (Marsh and Willis 2007).

The planned curriculum is all about what knowledge is of most worth – the important goals and objectives. Campbell (2006) refers to this as 'curricular authority' – the legitimacy of standardised curricular guidelines.

The enacted curriculum deals with professional judgments about the type of curriculum to be implemented and evaluated. Teachers have to judge the appropriate pedagogical knowledge to use. As noted by Campbell (2006) teachers' professional authority in enacting the curriculum may cause conflicts with the planned curriculum. Harris (2005) describes some of the contestation that can occur between a curriculum plan (for example, a history syllabus) and how it was implemented (enacted).

The experienced curriculum refers to what actually happens in the classroom. As noted by Smith and Lovat (2003), lived experience defies complete description either before or after it happens – it is individual, ongoing and unpredictable (Marsh & Willis 2007). Kennedy (2005) notes that curriculum experiences are no longer confined to the classroom. There is 'an increasing gap now between "official" school knowledge and real-world knowledge to which students have access through information technology' (p. 37). He suggests that a major issue for school curriculum in the twenty-first century is how to 'create a sense of community and common values in a context where knowledge cannot be restricted in any way and where individual control is much more powerful' (p. 37).

McNeil (2003) concentrates on the enacted curriculum but takes it further by highlighting the live curriculum rather than the inert, dead curriculum. He contends that the live curriculum is when teachers and students engage in classroom activities that are meaningful.

Much earlier, Whitehead (1929) used the metaphor of romance to characterise the rhythm of curriculum. As reported in Walker and Soltis (2004), he argued that 'we should begin an engagement with any subject in a romantic way, feeling excitement in its presence, being aroused by its attractiveness, and enjoying its company' (p. 44).

Tomlinson and Germundson (2007) elaborate on the rhythm of curriculum by comparing teaching to creating jazz. The enacted curriculum for these authors is characterised by a teacher blending musical sounds: 'blue notes for expressive purposes and syncopation and swing to surprise … to create curriculum with the soul of jazz – curriculum that gets under the skin of young learners' (p. 27).

When we focus on 'curriculum' in schools we are still likely to encounter a variety of different interpretations. Here is a very small selection of definitions of 'curriculum':

- Curriculum is that which is taught in school.
- Curriculum is a set of subjects.
- Curriculum is content.
- Curriculum is a set of materials.
- Curriculum is a set of performance objectives for student learning at a variety of learning sites.
- Curriculum is that which an individual learner experiences as a result of schooling.
- Curriculum is everything that is planned by school personnel.
- Curriculum is that which the student constructs from working with the computer and its various networks such as the Internet.
- Curriculum is questioning areas of authority and searching for more complex views of human situations.

To define 'curriculum' as 'that which is taught in schools' is, of course, very vague. People often talk about the 'school curriculum' in this general way and they tend to mean by this the range of subjects taught and the amount of instruction time given to each in terms of hours or minutes.

In an increasing number of countries this definition has been strengthened to include specific knowledge and skills to be acquired by a certain grade level. For example, benchmarks have been established in literacy and numeracy at Years 3, 5 and 7 across all eight state and territory systems in Australia (Woods 2007). In the US, the *No Child Left Behind Act* (NCLB) of 2001 requires standards to be achieved by all students in reading and mathematics at specific grade levels (Kim & Sunderman 2005).

Curriculum defined as 'content' is an interesting emphasis and brings into question another term, namely the 'syllabus'. A 'syllabus' is usually a summary statement about the content to be taught in a course or unit, often linked to an external examination. This emphasis on WHAT content is to be taught is a critical element of a 'syllabus', but a 'curriculum' includes more than this. For example, HOW you teach content can drastically affect what is learned. Also, the extent to which students are sufficiently prepared and motivated to study particular content will very greatly affect what is learnt.

Curriculum is quite often defined as a product – a document that includes details about goals, objectives, content, teaching techniques, evaluation and assessment, and resources. Sometimes these are official documents, issued by the government or one of its agencies, that prescribe HOW and WHAT is to be taught. Of course it is important to realise that a curriculum document represents the ideal rather than the actual curriculum. A teacher may not accept all aspects of a written curriculum and/or not be able to implement a curriculum exactly as prescribed due to lack of training and understanding. There can be gaps between the intended, ideal curriculum and the actual curriculum. It may be that the level and interests of the students or local community preferences may prevent a teacher from implementing a curriculum as prescribed.

Defining a curriculum as a 'set of performance objectives for student learning at a variety of learning sites' is a very practical orientation to curriculum. This approach focuses on specific skills or knowledge to be attained by students. Proponents of this approach argue that, if a teacher knows the targets that students should achieve, it is so much easier to organise other elements to achieve this end, such as the appropriate content and teaching methods (Willis & Kissane 1995). Few would deny that another strength of this approach is the emphasis on students. After all, they are the ultimate consumers and it is important to focus on what it is anticipated they will achieve and to organise all teaching activities to that end. It is also important to note the emphasis on a variety of learning sites. Given the learning opportunities available outside of school (the Internet and industry work experience programs, for example), this adds a wider dimension.

However, it must also be remembered that this approach can lead to an overemphasis on behavioural outcomes and vocational objectives that can be easily measured (Perkinson 1993). Some skills and values are far more difficult to state in terms of performance objectives. Also, a curriculum document that is simply a listing of performance objectives would have to be very large and tend to be unwieldy.

To define 'curriculum' in terms of 'that which an individual learner experiences as a result of schooling' is an attempt to widen the focus (Clandinin & Connelly 1991). The emphasis here is on the student as a self-motivated learner. Each student should be encouraged to select those learning experiences that will enable them to develop into a fully functioning person (Short & Burke 1991).

Barab and Wolff-Michael Roth (2006) contend that students learn by action – participating in life-world experiences. Gitlin and Ornstein (2007) take a similar stance when they argue that the curriculum should enable us to explore our human potential.

In the United Kingdom, the Education Secretary recently announced that students aged 11 to 14 would soon solve mathematics problems with real-world applicability to fields such as sports and fashion. The plan is designed to keep students' interest in maths during the early years of secondary school (*The Independent*, 30 June 2006).

However, it should be noted that each student acquires knowledge, skills and values not only from the *official* or *formal* curriculum but also from the *unofficial* or *hidden* curriculum. As noted by McCutcheon (1997), the hidden curriculum is implicit within regular school procedures, in curriculum materials, and in communication approaches and mannerisms used by staff. It is important to remember that students do learn a lot from the hidden curriculum, even though this is not intended by teachers (Kelly 2009).

The definition that refers to curriculum as 'everything that is planned by school personnel' is yet another orientation that emphasises the planning aspect of curriculum. Few would deny that classroom learning experiences for students need to be planned, although some unplanned activities will always occur (and these can have positive or negative effects). This definition also brings to bear the distinction that some writers make between *curriculum* and *instruction*. Some writers argue that curriculum is the WHAT and instruction is the HOW or – expressed in another way – 'curriculum activity is the production of plans for further action and instruction is the putting of plans into action' (MacDonald & Leeper 1965).

Although it can be important to separate out the two functions of WHAT and HOW, it tends to obscure the interdependence of curriculum and instruction. Classroom teachers do not separate the two functions because they are constantly planning, implementing and monitoring in their classrooms. That is, it is not practical to separate intentions from actions – there is really a fluid movement of interactions between plans, actions, changes of plans and different actions.

The definition of 'curriculum' as 'that which the student constructs from working with the computer' is now a reality for many students. Tapscott (2007) contends that the curriculum is now dominated by the Internet. The Internet affects everything we do. As far as students are concerned this can be very positive – the new technologies enable learners to enjoy enhanced interactivity and connections with others. The Internet is the ultimate interactive learning environment.

Computers are everywhere – in the home, school and office – as is digital technology in the form of cameras, video games and CD-ROMs. According to Tapscott (2007), the new Net Generation of students considers that computers and the related technology is their natural landscape. The new computer technologies have helped create a culture for learning (Papert 1996) in which students experience enhanced interactivity. However, Budin (1999) reminds us that technology is not a neutral tool.

To define 'curriculum' in terms of 'questioning areas of authority and searching for more complex views of human situations' highlights a postmodernist orientation (Waks 2006). Proponents of this approach contend that fixed notions of knowledge and reality should be rejected. Schooling is far more complex and ambiguous than traditional curriculum writers describe it. Teachers need to enter into dialogue about the uncertainties, the concerns, the doubts and the questions that pervade teaching, including those that surround selecting and enacting curricula (Pinar 2004; Rizvi, Lingard & Lavia 2006).

To conclude this section, it is important for me as the author of this book to state my preferred definition of curriculum, which I have used elsewhere: 'an interrelated set of plans and experiences which a student completes under the guidance of the school' (Marsh & Willis 2007).

This definition needs amplification and illustration (see Figure 6.1). The phrase 'interrelated set of plans and experiences' refers to the point that curricula that are implemented in schools are typically planned in advance but, inevitably, unplanned activities also occur. Therefore, the actual curricula that are implemented in classrooms consist of an amalgam of plans and experiences (unplanned happenings). The curriculum as experienced in the classroom is not a one-way transmission of ideas and information from the teacher to a group of passive recipients, but a series of communications and reactions and exchanges between both groups.

The phrase 'which a student completes under the guidance of the school' is included to emphasise the time element of every curriculum. That is, curricula are produced on the assumption that students

FIGURE 6.1 An illustrative definition of curriculum showing main components

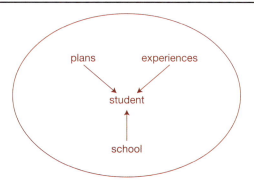

will complete certain tasks and activities over a period of time. 'Under the guidance of the school' refers to all persons associated with the school who may have had some input into planning a curriculum. It might normally include teachers, school councils and external specialists such as advisory inspectors.

Above all, the definition presupposes that conscious planning is possible, and indeed desirable, and that there are some important elements that are common to any planning activity, regardless of the particular value orientation (Hlebowitsh 1998). It also assumes that the learning activities experienced by students in classroom settings are managed and mediated by teachers so that intended outcomes can be reconciled with practical day-to-day restrictions.

Furthermore, the definition emphasises the importance of including school level personnel in the curriculum decision-making process. That is, teachers in particular can improve their teaching by taking increased responsibility for curriculum decisions – to expand their thinking and to interact more with others about school level curriculum decision making (Caldwell & Spinks 1998). Johnston (1994) argues that curriculum decision making at the school level leads teachers into critically examining current practices and addressing issues, and in the process they become empowered and are more willing to experiment.

 Do you have some definite ideas of what you would include in a definition of curriculum? Try to write your chosen definition in 3–4 lines. Can you justify why you have chosen it?

6.3 | EXAMPLES OF CURRICULUM DOCUMENTS

The definitions of 'curriculum' given above illustrate the diversity of interpretations of curriculum and how it applies to classroom interactions between teachers and students.

Notwithstanding this, teachers working for a particular education system, whether it is a government or non-government school system, will be required to follow to a greater or lesser extent curriculum documents that have been produced, and often mandated, for each school subject.

For example, at kindergarten and preschool levels curriculum documents are broadly based and provide suggestions for a range of activities.

At primary school levels, curriculum documents tend to be comprehensive but not mandatory. There are no external examinations that require certain content or skills to be taught, and primary school teachers have considerable freedom in planning their teaching. In some education systems, school-based planning is encouraged at the primary level whereby minimal guidelines are provided across the system (*generic*) but the curriculum material that is produced is only relevant for a particular school (*site specific*).

It requires considerable planning effort by individual school staff to produce coherent curriculum materials.

Some criteria they must keep in mind when formulating their curricula include:
(a) **Integration**
 – To what extent will facts, ideas and skills be integrated across subjects?
 – Many primary school teachers have the flexibility with their classes to use an integrated teaching approach, but it needs to be carefully planned.
(b) **Sequence**
 – How will the content be broken down into manageable parts?
 – Are there any criteria to be used in determining the order of content?
 – When should students acquire certain content?

This is a very complex problem to resolve and there are few guidelines or criteria available, apart from such principles as:
- going from the simple to the complex
- treating ideas chronologically
- whole-to-part learning – that is, understanding the whole before understanding specific components

- going from the concrete to the abstract – that is, starting from a student's experiences and proceeding to more remote learning
- spiral sequencing – that is, revisiting a concept repeatedly at a more difficult level each time (Oliva 2008; Brady & Kennedy 2010).

(c) **Variety and relevance**
  – Does the curriculum allow for a variety of methods to be used?
  – Is it appropriate to students' interests and levels of development?

6.3.1 Early grades – English – 'Our homes'

The Board of Studies NSW provides a number of topics, one of which is 'Talking about our houses and homes'.

Prior to a lesson on 'Our homes', children are asked to bring in any photographs of where they live. The teacher will need to have additional photographs of homes available.

Using a large poster or a doll's house, the teacher will label parts of a house (such as the roof, door, windows, fence).

Children will be invited to compare homes in the photographs. The teacher might use such questions as:
- What shape are the windows?
- What colour is the roof?
- Where is the front door?

The children will be encouraged to compare shapes and sizes of different houses. The teacher will organise a short neighbourhood walk to locations where there are a range of different types of houses (Board of Studies, NSW 2006).

What values are being emphasised in this curriculum? Is it just informational about homes or is it more experiential – wanting students to express ideas about what a 'home' means to them?

6.3.2 Primary school – Studies of Society and Environment

Rationale

The Studies of Society and Environment (SOSE) in Victoria (in Curriculum Standards Framework II – CSFII) is a study of human progress, how people have organised themselves into societies over time, examining how humans organise themselves into communities and states, form institutions and systems, and how they have interacted with their physical environments.

The study of societies at a local, national and international level is critical for young people to develop an understanding of their world and its historical development.

Goals

SOSE focuses on the complex range of knowledge comprising a mix of traditional disciplines and vocational and integrated studies, including the disciplines History, Geography, Economics, Legal Studies and Political Studies (see Figure 6.2).

The knowledge that is the basis of the SOSE key learning area is accompanied by the development of skills that enable students to:
- identify, collect and process data from a range of sources, including electronic media
- use the inquiry process to plan an investigation, analyse data and form conclusions supported by evidence
- reason and solve problems to assist them in making meaning of their society and environment
- clarify values and attitudes about issues affecting society and the environment, in particular tolerance of people from many cultures and commitment to the democratic process
- participate in activities that enhance community life, particularly in making decisions about civic projects and in ways of achieving ecologically sustainable development

- use information technology to support learning about society and environment and in investigating and communicating ideas.

Studies in the SOSE key learning area assist students to develop knowledge, skills and values that enable them to participate as active and informed citizens in a democratic society and the global community. While emphasising an understanding of Australian culture, SOSE gives schools the flexibility to select topics that encourage students to develop an international perspective and a commitment to lifelong learning.

FIGURE 6.2 Six important conceptual areas of knowledge (Victoria, CSFII)

---

1. *Australia and all of its people* – knowledge of the economic, historic, geographical, environmental, social and cultural development of the Australian continent.
2. *Civics and citizenship education* – the role of responsible citizens and an understanding of the values that underpin Australian society, including tolerance and mutual respect, and a knowledge of the development and functioning of Australia's political, legal, electoral and judicial systems.
3. *Environmental awareness* – knowledge of ecological systems and their relationship with human populations, and resource distribution and management.
4. *Global understanding* – knowledge of major issues facing the world community and especially Australia's near neighbours in Asia.
5. *The economy* – knowledge of the major aspects of economics, structure of the economy, and the impact of economic decision making on society.
6. *Enterprise skills* – enterprise skills applicable in a wide range of situations in personal and professional life include collaborative decision making, problem solving, exploring issues and the creating of work and business opportunities.

Approaches to teaching and learning in SOSE

SOSE provides a framework for integrating knowledge, skills and values into a coherent and effective program on which to base both course planning and student learning. The knowledge content provides a balance between acquiring knowledge and developing the intellectual skills of inquiry and critical thinking, and using that knowledge to further develop and communicate understandings.

Learning in SOSE is based on two interrelated sets of activities:
- *Investigation:* This develops students' skills in researching, processing and interpreting data. It is the foundation for analysing events and issues, constructing hypotheses and making informed judgments.
- *Communication:* This develops students' skills in using various forms of communication – spoken, written, graphical, statistical and electronic. Students learn to collect, process, analyse and present information using a range of formats and a variety of media (Curriculum and Standards Framework 2002, pp. 1–3).

This is a very detailed curriculum document which sets out major goals, rationales for these and teaching approaches you might use. What might a teaching topic look like based upon these parameters? Provide a brief summary of a lesson you might develop.

6.3.3 Primary school – Personal Development, Health and Physical Education

Rationale

Personal Development, Health and Physical Education (PDHPE) is one of the six key learning areas in the New South Wales primary curriculum (2006).

The PDHPE syllabus provides a broad contribution to developing the student as a whole person and encompasses various health-related topics including social, mental, physical and spiritual health. There is also a major focus on students developing appropriate skills to enable them to lead healthy lives. Teaching and learning in this syllabus also examines health priorities for young people including drug education, fitness and physical activity, child protection and nutrition.

Objectives

The objectives are wide ranging and cover values and attitudes, skills, and knowledge.

Values and attitudes – to develop students' appreciation of, and commitment to, healthy and socially just ways of living.

Skills – to develop students' skills in:
- making, communicating and acting upon health decisions
- moving with competence and confidence
- forming and maintaining positive relationships.

Knowledge – to develop students' knowledge and understanding about:
- ways to enhance personal and community health and wellbeing
- the composition, performance and appraisal of movement.

Subject matter

The subject matter is organised into eight interrelated strands. In each stage of primary education, students are taught aspects from the eight strands. The strands include:
- active lifestyle – encouraging students to adopt activity patterns that promote their wellbeing
- dance – getting students to communicate and express themselves through movement
- games and sports – developing student competence and confidence in a broad range of games and sports
- growth and development – students' understanding their own physical, social, cognitive and emotional development
- gymnastics – experiencing a variety of movement experiences and challenges
- interpersonal relationships – developing an understanding of the nature of relationships
- personal health choices – examining the process of making lifestyle decisions
- safe living – promoting safe environments and the protection of individuals.

It can be seen that these eight strands provide valuable opportunities for teachers to integrate widely across subjects using a diversity of materials. The skills are also sufficiently broad to enable teachers to incorporate them into integrated topics. The essential skills include:
- communicating – being able to use a variety of communication skills
- decision making – making sound decisions about healthy personal and lifestyle choices
- interacting – being able to relate positively to others
- moving – being able to move effectively in response to a variety of stimuli
- problem solving – being able to use a range of problem-solving strategies.

It is argued that PDHPE is an important key learning area for primary school students as it:
- encourages an understanding and valuing of self and others – students can identify and express a range of feelings
- promotes physical activity – this is a critical element given current attention to the need for students to have at least 30 minutes of moderate physical activity each day for health benefits
- emphasises informed decision making – students are given opportunities to consider responsible action regarding their own lifestyle.

A very detailed range of foundation statements (essential learnings), outcomes and indicators are set out for the four stages of primary school. Early stage 1 (Kindergarten); Stage 1 (Years 1 and 2); Stage 2 (Years 3 and 4); Stage 3 (Years 5 and 6).

These foundation statements are all linked to the eight subject matter strands, five skills and six values. The total number of outcomes and indicators is very large (over 500) and could be overwhelming for the newly appointed teacher. Details of content to be taught at each primary school level across all the strands is also included.

On the one hand it might be argued that PDHPE is an exciting syllabus and conducive to very rewarding integrated learning opportunities. Yet it is also very demanding in its detailed requirements of essential foundation statements and outcomes.

6.3.4 Senior secondary school – Economics

At the senior secondary school level, the impact of matriculation entry to universities and technical and vocational education institutions causes major restrictions on the scope of curriculum development, even though there have been various attempts to break down the barriers (Marginson 1993; Reid 1998). In most states and territories there is a dichotomy of subjects – those that are accepted by higher education institutions for tertiary entrance and secondary graduation and those that are accepted for secondary graduation only. The former group tends to rely on highly academic syllabus statements that provide specific details for students about course aims, content, forms of assessment and examinations.

For example, the Year 11 Economics Syllabus (Western Australia) contains detailed requirements of Economics knowledge, understandings and process skills to be acquired by students in a typical 120 hours of structured instruction over one school year. The syllabus consists of compulsory content areas (40 per cent) and three alternative sections (each between 15–25 per cent).

A new outcomes-based Economics syllabus was due to be implemented in 2007, but strong appeals by teachers and the media have caused it to be delayed. It has recently been discontinued.

 How do you react to these four curriculum examples? Perhaps you are impressed by the level of detail that planners have included? Perhaps you are a little over-awed by it all. Don't be! Go over each of the four examples again and try to develop lessons that would be meaningful for you.

YOUR TURN

- Do you find curriculum documents issued by education systems helpful in your planning of lessons? How do you use them?
- To what extent do you follow the curriculum guidelines very closely?
- To what extent are the documents restrictive and not helpful?

CONCLUDING COMMENTS

For a number of educators the term 'curriculum' is non-controversial. It is WHAT is taught in schools. However, curriculum documents can vary considerably because of different value orientations and perspectives. Curriculum is in fact very problematic. We need to be aware of earlier and present concepts of curriculum and how they are being played out in Australian primary and secondary schools.

The development of eight key learning areas, initially outcomes-based but now based on standards and essential learnings, is causing changes for teachers in planning the WHAT, HOW and WHEN of teaching. These learning areas have the potential to provide greater coherence and continuity of learning experiences, and greater flexibility for teachers and students

(Piper 1997). Yet others argue that they have caused greater confusion for teachers and have been counterproductive (Wilson 2002; Donnelly 2007).

KEY ISSUES RAISED IN THIS CHAPTER

1. Curriculum is central to a school. Schools could not exist without a curriculum.
2. Each curriculum is very value-laden. Educators have very different priorities for what is a desirable curriculum, as revealed by diverse definitions of curriculum.
3. Curriculum planners can devote many hours to developing a curriculum, but how it is experienced by teachers and students is the crucial phase.

REFLECTIONS AND ISSUES

1. Why is it important that you develop a critical perspective in your approach to curriculum?
2. Reflect upon the challenges of providing an appropriate curriculum for all students.
3. Comment on the role that teachers can play in defining the curriculum. Ideally? In practice in Australian schools?
4. Is the selection of content an adequate basis for designing a curriculum? On what bases should content be selected?
5. There are very divergent views about the nature of curriculum. What definition of curriculum do you support? Justify your choice.
6. Search out and read an existing school curriculum document. How is it organised? Describe the elements and its coherence and sequencing. What are some apparent desirable and undesirable features?
7. Explain the advantages and disadvantages of adopting an outcomes-based approach to curriculum planning.
8. Examine a curriculum document for one of the eight learning areas. Select a specific outcome and describe how you might develop some innovative approaches for teaching it.
9. 'If the curriculum is to be the instrument of change in education, its meanings and operational terms must be clearer than they are currently' (Toombs & Tierney 1993, p. 175). Discuss.
10. Trying to clarify central concepts by proposing definitions for them has been popular in many fields (Portelli 1987). Have these concepts and definitions proven useful in the field of curriculum?
11. 'The struggle over the definition of curriculum is a matter of social and political priorities as well as intellectual discourse' (Goodson 1988, p. 23). Discuss.
12. To what extent do you consider that the eight learning areas included in the Australian curriculum frameworks are distinctive and viable? What are some of the problems of combining subjects into the one learning area?
13. Glatthorn and Jailall (2000) contend that the curriculum for the twenty-first century must:
    - have greater depth and less superficial coverage
    - focus on problem solving
    - emphasise both skills and knowledge
    - provide for students' individual differences
    - offer a common core to all students.

    What views of curriculum are being advocated by these authors? Provide arguments for or against their stance.

Special references

Harris, C & Marsh, CJ (2005) (eds) *Curriculum Developments in Australia: Promising Initiatives, Impasses and Dead-ends*, Openbook, Adelaide.
Hayes, D (2006) *Primary Education: The Key Concepts*, Routledge, London.
Kelly, AV (2009) *The Curriculum: Theory and Practice*, 6th edn, Sage, Los Angeles.
Louden, W (2006) *In Teachers' Hands: Effective Literacy Teaching Practices in the Early Years of Schooling*, Department of Education, Science and Training, Canberra.
McLeod, JH & Reynolds, R (2003) *Planning for Learning*, Social Science Press, Sydney.

Web sources

For additional resources on curriculum, please go to:
www.pearson.com.au/myeducationlab.

7

PLANNING AND PREPARING FOR TEACHING

7.1 | INTRODUCTION

For a student teacher, being able to prepare and execute effective lessons to a class of students is a major goal. Experienced teachers may have forgotten about the stresses they experienced in first planning their lessons – the successes and the flops that happen to us all.

Good lessons don't just happen. It is crucial to do the planning of topics and lessons to ensure that what is taught in lessons is meaningful and appropriate. There is no single, perfect solution to planning because there are so many different factors to consider. A range of practical ideas are presented in this chapter, but only you can decide what is best for you.

7.2 | PLANNING PRINCIPLES

Student teachers and beginning teachers always worry about their planning. For example:
- How much detail do I need to write up? If I provide too much detail will this stifle creative moments?
- How do I ensure that awkward silences do not occur in my teaching?
- Do I have enough knowledge about the topic to cover all questions that students might ask me?
- What happens if I run out of time and do not complete all that I intended to do?

There are no fixed, immutable rules for planning teaching (McLeod & Reynolds 2003). All kinds of documents might be used such as diaries, weekly planners, daily notebooks and folders. As noted by Groundwater-Smith, Cusworth and Dobbins (1998), these are mere artefacts. It is the mental processes that count – that is, the values, priorities and leaps of imagination.

The following set of guidelines conveys something of the spirit needed to prepare adequately for teaching:
1 *Planning is largely a mental and verbal activity*: Teachers need to think through their priorities and to make the major links between what they present, how and why (Henniger 2004). It may involve working backwards from desired outcomes. McCutcheon (1980) refers to the mental rehearsing and imagining that is undertaken. Hansen (1998, p. 171) notes that planning 'is not only, or even mainly, drawing up a formal document to be followed'.

2. *Planning requires reconciling different priorities and goals*: Teachers have to search for and persuade themselves and others that what they are planning to teach is relevant and challenging (Ness 2001). There is no clear-cut answer to 'What must I teach?' Each teacher has to deliberate about this (Reid 1994) and somehow reconcile different priorities. There is no clear formula for success. The amount of searching and creativity undertaken by a teacher will depend no doubt on the extent to which they feel they are constrained by official documents and syllabuses, school policies and community expectations – their decision-making space may be relatively open or relatively constrained (Lovat & Smith 1995). Moyles (2007) argues that every teacher has to somehow reconcile three aspects, namely: students' individual and collective learning interests; system level guidelines and policies; and a teacher's own interests and motivations. These three elements can both constrain and support.

3. *Planning requires critical reflection*: Teachers need to think carefully about the planning decisions they make both prior to and after they have given their lessons. Brookfield (1995) notes that critical self-reflection is a crucial habit for teachers to develop. It helps teachers undertake informed action and provides a rationale for practice – teachers need to be able to express what they stand for and why they believe certain values are important (Burn *et al.* 2000). Critical reflection also enables teachers to avoid self-laceration (Brookfield 1995). Serious teachers may unwittingly blame themselves if students are not learning, when in reality there may be wider societal factors responsible.

> **YOUR TURN**
>
> - What are your major priorities in planning?
> - Can you justify why you hold these priorities?
> - What do you expect to be the results of having these priorities?
>
> Jot down your responses – we will return to these questions later.

4. *Planning requires risk-taking*: Teachers must consider flexible approaches to learning and this can involve using resources with which they have limited expertise. They sometimes have to choose between well-cushioned, comfort-zone planning and planning that is innovative but risky (Chubbuck et al. 2001). For example, many teachers lack confidence and competence in doing computer-based instruction (Brummelhuis & Plomp 1994). All kinds of organisational problems can occur but, if mastered, computer-based instruction can provide wide benefits for students (Albion 1996). A number of teachers worldwide now focus on student-centred learning using computers and various CD-ROM packages and the Internet (for example, Peha 1995; Newhouse 1998). Yet unless teachers have sufficient training and technical support, early innovative efforts may not be successful; therein lies the challenge for new teachers.

7.3 | DIGGING A LITTLE DEEPER

Luke, Weir and Woods (2008) point out that there are 'informed prescription' ways of teacher planning and 'informed professionalism'. By that they mean that informed prescription lists essential knowledge and skills within a strong accountability framework. By contrast, informed professionalism involves teacher autonomy in interpreting and adapting what is to be taught.

John (2006) takes a similar stance when he criticises teacher planning that uses a linear model that begins with specification of objectives and ends with a lesson evaluation. He argues that these information processing models are not to be encouraged because student teachers have to conform to a rigid template for their lesson planning. John also argues that the planning of a lesson is not an unalterable event but that it is associated with unpredictability, flexibility and creativity. He asserts that an interactionist approach to planning, which he titles a 'dialogical' model, is far more useful in developing pedagogical intelligence.

These matters will be considered again later in this chapter. However, the point being made here is that a rigid, linear approach to lesson planning might seem to be desirable because of its simplicity but in fact is quite limited. Various examples of lesson plans will be described, but it is up to the reader to ascertain what will help him/her in the creative, problem-solving aspects of their planning and teaching.

7.4 | PRACTICUM, TEACHING PRACTICE OR INTERNSHIP

Student teachers enrolled in a teacher education program typically look forward to the opportunities of practical experience with real live students in schools. The term 'teaching practice' is used in some programs, although the majority use the term 'practicum' or 'internship'.

There is some justification for using the latter term. When student teachers simply apply specific theoretical principles and techniques to classroom situations it is reasonable to use the term 'teaching practice', especially if it is based upon concurrent one-day visits to schools.

The term 'practicum' indicates that the classroom environment is the venue where all kinds of teaching and learning take place. The experiences are different for each student teacher as they assimilate and develop their personally owned professional knowledge (Meere 1993; Weiss & Weiss 2001). Furthermore, the learning that takes place in a practicum is very different from learning on an academic campus – it requires much more personal involvement and reflection by each student teacher.

The length of time for a practicum is usually between three and four weeks, each year of the pre-service program. There are indications that the federal government, which provides funding for practicums, is intent on reducing the total number of weeks, presumably as a cost-saving measure.

The interactions and support for a student teacher can also vary considerably. Usually two student teachers are assigned to a class teacher and this has benefits in providing moral support for the two student teachers. A supervisor from the university teacher education program visits each student and observes a number of lessons. The classroom teacher may also observe a number of lessons and give feedback to the student teacher.

This is clearly a period of intense activity for each student teacher and can often be exhausting. Sometimes the advice from the class teacher and the visiting supervisor can be conflicting. Inevitably, each student teacher will perform well with some lessons but not in others. A student teacher's self-esteem may take a 'battering' during a practicum. They have to be willing to listen to advice and to reflect deeply upon their lessons.

 How did you feel during your first practicum? Were you accepting of different kinds of advice or did a lot of the advice seem pointless to you? What lasting impressions have you of this first practical experience?

There are very many different forms of practicum across the country with variations occurring in the number of weeks, block versus concurrent days and the range of personnel involved.

The block period of four to six weeks is most common, but there are also a number of teacher education institutions that provide a full term or semester of practicum.

The term 'internship' usually applies to a longer period of time in a school of eight to ten weeks, where the student teacher is more actively involved as an assistant teacher. There is less intensive observation of lessons and the student teacher has the opportunity to experiment with different teaching approaches. For the confident and able student teacher, an internship (previously named the Assistant Teacher Program) can be an extremely rewarding experience. However, for many it is a desperate time because teaching can be overshadowed by convoluted planning requirements and little guidance in the documentation regarding mandatory content (Power & Berlach 2005).

 During your internship have you been able to understand more fully the context of your school? What are some of its unique features in terms of student interests, community values, and special strengths of staffs? Have you been able to work on any collaborative projects with other staff at the school?

A key element of the practicum is the humanness of the learning process. Unlike other experiences at a tertiary level, experiencing a classroom of students is a very stirring, never-to-be-forgotten event. There are the thrills of having 30 pairs of eyes and ears hanging on every word you utter. There are also the disappointments when a lesson isn't successful or when you are unable to persuade a student to try harder on a piece of work.

To be successful in the classroom you need to develop skills in planning lessons that will be well received and relevant to students. The sections that follow provide guidelines for developing programs, units and individual lessons.

7.5 | PROGRAMS, UNITS AND LESSON PLANS

Although education systems vary in terms of new requirements and preferences, most educators acknowledge the need for teachers to develop programs of teaching units (over a term, semester or year) and daily or weekly lesson plans.

A program is a teacher's creative representation or interpretation of a curriculum. It should follow the broad principles of the curriculum, but the emphases and combinations of activities will represent each teacher's judgments about what they consider to be important for their particular class.

A unit is for a smaller planning period, typically 2–6 weeks. There is a tighter focus and theme than for a program.

Lesson plans are even more personal in that the teacher creates learning activities for specific periods of time, usually half an hour up to two hours, which optimise student learning of particular objectives or enable students to demonstrate particular outcomes. They are important because they enable each teacher to:
- develop a clear idea of the main purpose of a lesson
- present coherent and interesting ideas
- select and structure relevant content
- use a variety of activities.

7.6 | DEVELOPING A PROGRAM

Programs will vary in style and emphasis for different teaching subjects and, as described above, will be dependent upon the personal style of each teacher. Although each school may establish some constraints about how a program is to be set out, there is ample opportunity for a teacher to plan creatively. To this end, it is useful to make a distinction between two elements:
1. Planning the priorities.
2. Combining the priorities to provide a coherent approach.

7.6.1 Planning the priorities

It is important that major organisers or headings are included in a program, but it is up to each teacher how they structure the process. That is, there is no reason whatsoever for teachers to follow slavishly, in lock-step fashion, a series of programming headings.

Let us consider some headings that are typically included in programs. The examples included in Table 7.1 cover a wide range and they have been sorted into comparable groupings.

TABLE 7.1 Examples of program headings by two major authors

Topic	Topic
Time	Time
Goals and objectives	General objectives and pre-assessment of student prior knowledge
Content	Content
Learning activities	Activities
Resources and materials	Instructional materials and resources
Evaluation accommodations (for students with learning difficulties)	
Reflection	
Source: Moore 2009b, p. 100	*Source: Cruickshank et al. 2009, p. 178*

The headings described below have been selected because they cover major areas of importance to the author. Other headings may be more relevant to the reader.

Topic: This refers to a brief description of a unit, such as 'Local Community Study'.

Time: This can be expressed in number of months, number of weeks or total number of lessons.

Rationale: This provides an explanation about why this topic is being included – perhaps mandated in the curriculum or of special significance to the school or the class.

Objectives or outcomes: Objectives provide the focus for what it is intended students will learn or will be will be able to demonstrate.

Content: The content may be expressed in terms of themes or issues, or in terms of specific knowledge, concepts, skills and values.

Learning experiences: These can be quite diverse and might include specific strategies (such as role playing); ways of grouping the students (whole group, small groups); and the physical arrangement of the classroom (circles, open space).

Evaluation: This will consist of methods used to assess student achievements (using formal and informal methods) and also making evaluative judgments about the teaching (for example, self-reports) and about the curriculum materials used.

Some educational experts seem to have a habit of showing us neat logical ways to plan our activities. For programming they would no doubt insist that it is a linear exercise in which we start with objectives, then work through to content, learning experiences and evaluation. But creative planning can take many forms. Creativity can come from sudden flashes of intuition while taking a shower or working out at the local gymnasium. Therefore, there seems to be no harm at all in commencing programming at any point in the sequence and then working either forwards or backwards, as depicted in Figure 7.1.

7.6.2 Primary school example

Let us try creating some examples. The Health Education Curriculum in most states and territories includes concepts or themes about community and environmental health, with special reference to road safety. For example, the West Australian Health Education Curriculum in Year 4 primary refers to 'bicycle safety'.

FIGURE 7.1 Alternative routes in programming

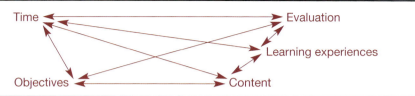

> **YOUR TURN**
>
> - If you were to develop a program about community and environmental health, with special reference to road safety and bicycle safety, what specific objectives would you include?
> - How will you assess if students have achieved your objectives?

Perhaps a teacher has been reading the 'Constable Care' rhymes in the daily paper or is reminded of the potential dangers for young cyclists coping on busy roads with huge tankers and fast cars and of the need for cyclists to be ever-vigilant when crossing roads – 'at a stop sign, put your foot on the road'; 'look back before turning right'; 'ride straight, one metre out' (NSW Road Traffic Authority 2009).

The teacher feels that the important message in all of this is the attitudes of children to road safety; if the right kinds of learning activities are provided, students will acquire more positive attitudes. This leads the teacher to concentrate on the theme of 'sharing the road with others' and to consider which activities to include.

Some possibilities include:
- using a videotape to illustrate all the different road users – for example, *It's Smart to be Safe* (NSW Traffic Authority 2005)
- using a CD-ROM encyclopaedia such as Grolier, Compton or *Encyclopaedia Britannica* or Internet information such as <www.rta.nsw.gov.au>, <www.vicroads.vic.gov.au> or a Handbook for Bicycle Riders <www.rta.nsw.gov.au>
- role-playing the different road users
- an excursion to a local, congested traffic area to undertake a survey
- an awareness of your bicycle and how to look after it
- competency tests on your bicycle including practice braking tests
- competency tests on road behaviour including scanning, warning and checking.

By the time the teacher has brainstormed about these possible learning activities (which could involve lessons given over a term or longer) it is then possible to firm up on the objectives for the program – What outcomes do I want students to achieve by the completion of the unit? This will depend of course on the backgrounds of the students, their needs and their abilities. Informal discussions with the class would be essential to find out:
- Who owns a bicycle and rides it frequently?
- Who knows the road rules?
- What causes road accidents?
- How can cyclists help to make roads safer?

By ascertaining what the students already know about road rules and using bicycles, the teacher should then be able to produce some appropriate program objectives or outcomes. These might include the following:

'By the completion of the teaching unit students will:
- demonstrate their understanding of road rules and how they apply, especially to riding bicycles
- give detailed accounts of road users and how sharing rules must operate
- demonstrate competence in bicycle riding, braking and turning
- give detailed accounts of defensive strategies that bicycle riders can use.'

The listing of these objectives might lead the teacher automatically to consider how these objectives or outcomes will be assessed. Will simulated activities be appropriate, or is it necessary to have on-the-road tests? What are the time constraints or personnel and safety constraints for each alternative? Would paper and pencil, multiple choice tests be appropriate? How can you really tell whether the students have developed more positive attitudes to road safety?

It may be that the teacher uses a combination of these forms of assessment in their program, namely:
- a multiple choice test to assess basic knowledge of road rules
- a small group project on 'sharing the road'
- an on-the-road test as a culminating activity, supported by parent volunteers.

By this stage the teacher is well on the way to completing the remaining elements of their program. The content has already been foreshadowed by the decisions made above. It will consist of viewing a videotape or a CD-ROM; images from the Victorian Road Traffic Authority (VicRoads) will be downloaded; Bike-Ed instructional booklets will be purchased; and role-playing simulations will be obtained.

The allocation of time for the unit will need to be carefully planned. The teacher may decide to program the unit so that in the first eight weeks single periods of 30 minutes per week are used, whereas in the final six weeks double periods of 60 minutes scheduled next to lunch hour are used to enable the practical testing to be carried out.

So the teacher has finally completed all the elements of the program and, although further refinements may be necessary, it has the potential to be a very successful teaching unit.

7.6.3 Secondary school example

Let us now consider another example aimed at *secondary school students*. At the secondary school level most Health Education Curriculum documents include concepts about alcohol and road use – for example, in Year 10 one curriculum theme listed is 'students' social pressures and drink-driving'.

Perhaps a teacher seizes upon this theme and begins to ponder about how it might be assessed. It is an important social issue that involves developing positive attitudes about not drinking when you are driving and a realisation of the problems associated with the excessive use of alcohol. But how to assess it? Ideally a simulation game where participants role play particular parts and then reflect on value stances in debriefing periods would be very appropriate, but how could you assess each student's participation? If this would not be a fair method of assessment, what would be some other alternatives?

Another option might be to get groups of three to four students to select a project on a particular aspect of drink-driving and be assessed on the impact of their presentation to the rest of the class. Each member of the small group would receive the same assessment mark (that is, a group mark).

In their presentations, groups might use the following strategies to maximise their impact on the class audience:
- Presentation of statistical details. For example: over 60 per cent each year of car drivers aged between 18 and 20 killed in a road crash had a blood alcohol concentration over 0.52; females between 15 and 24 years of age comprise over 12 per cent each year of car passenger deaths.
- Newspaper photographs, police or traffic department photographs of horrific vehicle crashes.

- Case study accounts by victims who have survived devastating motor vehicle crashes.
- Perspectives on road crashes from external 'carers' such as casualty ward doctors or traffic police officers.

Having settled upon an appropriate form of assessment, it would then be necessary to ensure that proper content was provided. In terms of the theme of the program unit, it would be necessary to provide content about groups and group behaviour and drink-driving behaviour. Examples of content might include:
- small group behaviour – group standards, group identification
- media influences on group behaviour
- individual and group attitudes about cars
- vehicle stopping time
- reaction time of drivers (without alcohol and those affected by alcohol).

The *learning experiences* required to teach this content would need to concentrate on valuing and value clarification activities. Some excellent videotapes such as *The Physics of Car Crashes* (1999), *Dead Cells do tell Tales* (2005) or *You are never-ever the same person* (2006) could be used to introduce the topic, followed by small group discussions. Presentation of statistics on road fatalities and drink-driving could be undertaken by the teacher or prepared as a set of graphs by students. It would be useful to combine these activities with working models to obtain approximate figures on vehicle stopping time (brakemeters). This data could be graphed and compared with official statistics.

Role-playing could be a very useful learning experience. An existing commercial simulation game could be used or the teacher could prepare a simple role-playing model involving a son/daughter, parents, police officer, doctor and hospital staff.

To illustrate graphically the loss of life caused by road accidents, a simple dice board game could be played by students based on a scoring system such as:

'Six' means that the person dies.
'Five' means they suffer severe injuries – for example, becomes a quadriplegic.
'Four' means they are injured to the point of needing to be hospitalised.
'Three' indicates some injury, but not serious enough to require hospitalisation.
'Two' or 'one' means that the person escapes unharmed. (Edwards 1985, p. 43)

The dice is thrown once for the driver and once for each of the passengers. If the person is wearing a seatbelt, a point is taken off the score. Students working in small groups could record results of a number of dice throws and then reflect on the outcomes.

Values clarification exercises could be undertaken on topics dealing with recognition by peers, popularity, alcohol and individual differences and group pressures. The Leisure Grid (see Figure 7.2), where students give details of particular leisure activities they have experienced and also reasons for doing these activities, can be a good basis for discussing group pressures and could lead to some important explorations of values by students.

By this stage, it is a relatively easy task for the teacher to firm up on objectives for this program unit. For example, they might include the following:
By the conclusion of the unit students will be able to:
- provide factual content to dispel common myths and misconceptions about alcohol
- describe commonsense strategies for minimising or avoiding potentially unsafe situations
- make a considered choice about behaviour and attitudes towards drink-driving.

7.6.4 Combining the priorities to provide a coherent approach

There is an art involved in orchestrating the various components of a program. As commented on above, creative brainstorming is very necessary to elicit the ideas and the relationships, but considerable fine tuning is needed to put all the ideas together.

FIGURE 7.2 The Leisure Grid

	Fun	Thrills	Peer group approval	Parent approval	Earning money	Making new friends	Trying to be more interesting
Parties							
Going to pop concerts	X		X			X	
Discos							
Bike riding							
Trail bikes							
Driving around							
'Wheelies'							
Drinking		X	X				X
Smoking							
Hitch-hiking							
Camping							
Surfing	X	X				X	
Babysitting							
Saturday jobs							

Source: based on The Leisure Grid, in Edwards, E. Teenagers, Alcohol and Road Safety, *RTA, Melbourne, 1985, p. 61.*

There are very few guidelines available to assist the teacher in doing this fine tuning, but a few caveats can be raised:

Time: Be realistic in the time you set for teaching a topic. Few teachers ever complete a topic within the time allocated. Don't be too ambitious about what will be covered.

Rationale: Have you considered any potential problems in undertaking the unit in terms of:
- resources?
- parental concerns?
- school ethos?

Objectives/outcomes: Are the objectives you use consistent with each other? Are they attainable by students?
Are they sufficiently specific and not ambiguous?

Content: Is the content used essential or basic?
Is the content authentic (valid)?
Does the content have social relevance?
Does the content have utility for individual students?
Does it have interest for students?

Learning experiences: Are a variety of strategies used?
Are they optimal ones for the objectives to be achieved?
Do the strategies involve active learning by students?
Is there continuity in the learning experiences?
Do the learning experiences provide a unified and integrated experience for the student?

Evaluation/assessment: Are a variety of strategies used?
Is regular feedback provided to students?
Are the strategies directly related to the objectives/outcomes?

Returning to the two brainstorming examples sketched out above, final versions are included in Tables 7.2 and 7.3 to provide examples of the fine tuning needed to produce a coherent approach to programming.

7.7 | PLANNING A UNIT

Teaching in units is widely recommended because it provides students with a focus, rather than letting them just experience isolated lessons.

The use of units can also be very rewarding and stimulating to teachers. It enables teachers to select materials from a variety of sources and to be able to produce dynamic, creative lessons.

In some circumstances a teacher may have complete freedom in choosing a unit, but in most cases choices are limited by:
- education system curriculum framework
- availability of textbooks
- needs, interests and abilities of students being taught
- availability of resources.

Units in the early childhood and primary school are planned typically to be completed in two to three weeks, whereas those at secondary school level can last six weeks or longer. The length of time is partly dependent on the extent to which the unit is integrated. If a number of different subject areas are included, then the length of time needed will be much greater. Many schools have a curriculum policy about the selection and sequence of units.

Experienced teachers will modify teaching units as they become involved in teaching them. They will make decisions on some occasions to extend particular activities and on other occasions to terminate them sooner than planned. On subsequent occasions they will make further refinements to these units. In specific classes they may need to make a number of modifications to allow for the needs of students with impairments or for gifted and talented students.

The planning of units is a personal activity and there are many different approaches, but the general phases can be characterised as:
1. Unit title.
2. Description of the grade level and student population.
3. Rationale for the unit.
4. Goals, objectives, outcomes.
5. Content.
6. Selecting and sequencing learning activities.
7. Evaluation.
8. Resources.

No set format exists for writing units. Some teachers prefer to use columns so they can be more aware of the interrelationships between the major headings, while others prefer to put each heading on a separate page.

Furthermore, there is no special starting point for developing a unit. Although it might be logical to start from the beginning, there may also be benefits in starting off with areas that have greatest appeal, such as forms of assessment (point 7) or a consideration of specific learning activities (point 6), as described earlier in section 7.6 Developing a program.

YOUR TURN

Reflect on a unit title that is exciting to you and which you think would be very rewarding to students. Jot down some key points about your nominated unit.

TABLE 7.2 Program in health: road safety class of Year 4

Topic/time	Rationale	Objectives	Content	Learning activities	Resources	Evaluation/assessment
Sharing the road with others One term 30 mins/week for weeks 1–6 60 mins/week for weeks 7–10	• Health syllabus, Year 4, p. 26 • Parent Council concerned about recent accidents involving bicycles	Students will: • Demonstrate their understanding of road rules for riding bicycles • Demonstrate competence in bicycle riding • Give detailed accounts of defensive strategies for bicycle riders	• Road rules • Traffic regulations • Bicycle components and characteristics • Defensive strategies for cyclists	• View/discuss videotape • Discussions on road users • Role-playing activity • Local excursion • Demonstration of bicycles/components/limitations • Competency tests • On-road tests under supervision	• Videotape *It's Smart to be Safe* (NSW Traffic Authority) • Bike Ed kits (RTA, Vic) including posters, student booklet, activities	• Small group project to be completed • Multiple choice test • On-road bicycle test

TABLE 7.3 Program in health: road safety class of Year 10

Topic/time	Rationale	Objectives	Content	Learning activities	Resources	Evaluation/ assessment
• Dangers of drink-driving • 40 min. period/week for 12 weeks	• Health syllabus Year 4 • Parent concern about recent road accidents involving teenagers	Students will: • Provide factual content to dispel misconceptions about alcohol use • Describe commonsense strategies for avoiding unsafe situations • Demonstrate well-reasoned choices about drinking and driving	• Small group behaviour, students' norms • Vehicle stopping time • Reaction times of drivers • Common causes of road accidents • Media influences on group behaviour • Values analysis	• View videotapes – small group discussions • Analysis of statistics – discussion • Operate working models on vehicle stopping time • Role-plays and board games • Values clarification exercises • Small group major project	• Videotapes/films: *The Physics of Car Crashes* (15 mins), a documentary on basic facts about alcohol and its effects; *Dead Cells do tell Tales*, raises the issue of drinking and driving; *You are never-ever the same person*, points to the long-term effects on health and well-being • Working models of vehicle stopping time	• Multiple choice test • Small group project and presentation

1 Unit title

The titles should be succinct and, where possible, challenging and interesting. Examples in the primary school might include 'Our Class Newsletter', or 'Treasure Hunt'. Examples in the secondary school might include 'What is Prejudice?', or 'Living in Cities'.

2 Description of the grade level and student population

Brief details need to be included about the intended age or grade details, to ensure that diverse student needs are accommodated (Fuller & Stone 1998). Many of the outcomes-based planning documents refer to academic levels rather than grade levels.

3 Rationale for the unit

This is an important element and a number of issues should be considered by a teacher intending to use a new unit. These might include:
- What contribution does the unit make to the learning area?
- Does it relate to system-level curriculum guidelines?
- Is it likely to be interesting and challenging to students?
- Is it feasible in terms of time, available materials and students' abilities?
- Does it have more potential than the unit it replaces?
- Are there any possible negative effects of including the unit, in terms of other classes and teachers and parents?

Reflecting on why a particular unit is being developed is of course an important matter. There must be a close relationship between assumptions and beliefs about content and learning activities and the actual format of the unit.

4 Goals, objectives, outcomes

Goals are general statements that provide teachers and students with a vision – the big picture. They tend to be medium- to long-term and are usually directed towards student achievement.

Objectives are typically a statement of intent about anticipated changes in learners. An objective identifies how students should change their behaviour as a result of certain learning experiences.

Instructional objectives are objectives that are relatively specific and describe desired learning outcomes in terms of student activities or behaviours, but do not reduce all classroom activities to behaviourist outcomes.

Instructional objectives are very useful in planning a unit because they provide a specific focus and a basis for evaluating the effectiveness of students' learning. If strong action verbs are used in the objectives (see Table 7.4), this helps provide a very specific guide to the activities required.

Outcome statements tend to be quite broad, but they do incorporate concepts that have been categorised into progressive levels of difficulty. Concrete examples ('pointers') and work samples provide more detailed advice for planning.

YOUR TURN

- Write down two or three objectives that you consider would be appropriate for your nominated unit.
- Reflect on how this unit will benefit your students.

TABLE 7.4 Some strong action verbs for instructional objectives

Knowledge objectives	Skills objectives	Attitude objectives
to describe	to draw	to choose
to identify	to illustrate	to relate positively to
to list	to conduct	to respond to
to compare	to measure	to approve of
to contrast	to locate	to disapprove of
to solve	to translate	to believe in
to match		to acclaim
to label		to question
to recognise examples		to dispute
to interpret		

5 Content

To develop quality units, a lot of thought must go into the selection of content. Some criteria to use when selecting content include:
- Does the content assist students to identify and reflect on important issues?
- Can the content be developed in such a way that each student will have opportunities for success?
- Is the content suited to the developmental levels and abilities of students?
- Can this content be developed in the classroom with the use of a variety of teaching strategies?

As noted above, concepts are an extremely important tool for teaching and typically provide the basis for selecting content (Banks & Banks 2008). Concepts vary in their scope and difficulty. Those that are related to a student's concrete, observable experiences are easier to understand than abstractions. The building of concepts from easy to complex is a difficult task and must be carefully planned.

Generalisations are statements relating two or more concepts. For generalisations to be understood, the concepts need to be grounded in concrete factual cases. Thus facts do have a role in providing concrete examples for concepts and generalisations. Consider these examples:

Concepts

scarcity – needs – wants – goods – services – markets – competition

Generalisation

In a competitive market, an increase in supply of a particular good or service will result in a lower market price.

Facts

Australian spending on specific consumer items such as video recorders in 1992 and 2002 was $XX and $YY respectively.

The content of a unit therefore is likely to include factual information across time, cultures or periods, which has been carefully sampled to illustrate particular concepts and generalisations. The factual content selected will also be dependent on system-level guidelines and syllabuses.

A wide range of materials is available from which appropriate content can be selected. A variety of print and multimedia materials is available, including those that can be accessed from the Internet and computer-managed instruction (CMI) packages.

6 Selecting and sequencing learning activities

A teaching unit needs to include a variety of learning activities. One way to ensure a wide range is to plan for particular teaching techniques and to link these with the teaching of specific concepts. For example, the following teaching techniques have considerable potential:

- lectures and presentations
- practical demonstrations
- inquiry and problem solving
- simulations and role-plays
- questions and discussions
- model building
- multimedia presentations
- library research
- community-based research
- individual and group projects
- self-instructional activities.

Unless mindful of it, teachers will tend to use a small number of techniques with which they have had direct experience. Although it is more stressful to experiment with new approaches, these need to be incorporated into teaching units because students have very different learning styles (Tomlinson & Kalbfleisch 1998). By providing a variety of learning activities, teachers keep not only their students stimulated but also themselves.

Teacher-directed stimulation is of course not the only approach. There are a number of student-directed approaches that can develop students' independence and motivation. Individual projects and library research projects are useful approaches to develop student skills and to provide a variation from the regular teacher-directed forms (Saye 1998).

Banks and Banks (2008) assert that it is activities that are the heart of units. Each teacher needs to develop a range of interesting and useful activities that link the unit together. They can be generated from a variety of sources including newspapers, television and the Internet. The trick is to find particular topics and then use a little creativity to develop them as integrated units, spanning a number of teaching areas.

YOUR TURN

- What do you consider will be some key activities for your unit?
- How will you present these key activities so that they integrate across learning areas?
- Do you think the students will react positively to these activities?

A simple way to develop each activity is to put the basic details on a separate palm card (see Figure 7.3 and Figure 7.4). All that is needed is a brief, one-sentence description, an allotted time and the necessary materials. Not all activities will turn out to be useful and a number may need to be eliminated eventually.

As noted earlier, it may be desirable for teachers to commence planning their unit by concentrating first on activities; that is, to devise activities that students might enjoy doing and then work backwards to formulate appropriate objectives.

7 Evaluation

Evaluations are undertaken to determine the relative effectiveness of teaching units, in terms of the teacher activities and the learning accomplished by students.

FIGURE 7.3 An activity example (primary)

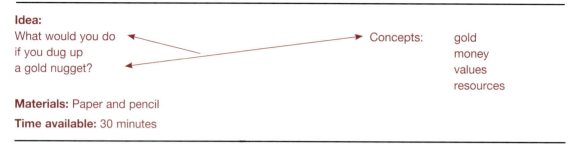

Materials: Paper and pencil

Time available: 30 minutes

FIGURE 7.4 An activity example (lower secondary)

Idea – choosing between options

Students are to establish reasons for choosing why five of the following projects will each receive $50 million in government funding:

1. Project on 'wave power' to see if action of the sea can generate 'power'
2. Project on 'test tube babies'
3. Project on car safety
4. Project on space flight equipment
5. Project on weather control
6. Project on new weapon system
7. Project on retarding old age
8. Project on turning sea water into good drinking water
9. Project on producing abundant quantities of enriched food
10. Project on rat control

In terms of student performance there are a range of assessment strategies that should be included in a unit. They need to be varied and, above all, they should provide feedback about students' development as reflective, competent and concerned citizens (Wiggins and McTighe 2005). A number of useful assessment strategies are listed in Table 7.5.

During the running of a unit and after its completion it is most important for teachers to evaluate its effectiveness. This can take the form of self-evaluation questions as listed in Figure 7.5 or more formal approaches as depicted in Table 7.6.

TABLE 7.5 Some commonly used assessment strategies to obtain data about student achievement

• autobiographies	• cooperative learning outcomes	• rating scales
• activity records	• interviews	• role-play enactments
• attitudinal measures	• observation records	• teacher interviews
• checklists	• questionnaires	• teacher-made tests
• class projects		

TABLE 7.6 Some commonly used evaluation strategies to obtain data about the effectiveness of a unit

• external ratings	• portfolio samples
• group discussions	• student questionnaires
• peer ratings	• student ratings

FIGURE 7.5 Self-evaluation questions about a unit

1. Is the theme and content appropriate for the age group?
2. Is there a variety of activities for the students?
3. Is there integration with other subject areas of the curriculum?
4. Is there a progression of experiences and activities that lead to a satisfactory culmination in the unit?
5. What are the overall strengths and weaknesses of the unit?
6. What skills might a teacher need to enable that unit to be taught effectively?

> **YOUR TURN**
> - What do you consider will be appropriate forms of assessment to include in your unit?
> - Do these forms of assessment cater for different student backgrounds and interests?

8 Resources

A teaching unit typically includes a comprehensive listing of resources. This should include not only textbooks and reference books but also the ever-increasing range of non-print materials such as videotapes, CD-ROMs, DVDs, computer software packages and the Internet. Access, for example, the website <www.ambitweb.com/computer/compinfo.html>.

In addition, there are many other potentially useful resources available in children's literature, music and art. These sources enable students to travel vicariously to other times and places. They add important dimensions to student learning and, in the process, provide further opportunities for students to develop listening, speaking, writing and reading skills.

Every teacher is able to build up his or her range of resource materials using appropriate storage boxes and folders and via USB modems, CDs, CD-ROMs and DVDs. Students can be encouraged also to collect relevant resources and to assist with 'learning centre' tables in their classrooms.

7.7.1 A new approach

An approach to planning units which has been widely used in a number of countries is Wiggins and McTighe's (2005) *Understanding by Design*. It is termed a backward design model because it is argued by the authors that teachers should identify the desired results and then work backwards to identify acceptable evidence and then to plan the learning experiences desired. Wiggins and McTighe contend that if the design is done backwards it is more powerful. It is like task analysis. You settle on the task to be accomplished and then you work out how to get there.

The model has proved to be very popular because of its clarity and its connection with current educational issues such as standards and authentic assessment.

Stage 1: identify desired results

In this first stage goals and established content standards are analysed. The authors suggest that four filters or criteria should be used in helping decide what ideas and processes should be included. The filters include:
- Filter 1: to what extent does the idea, topic or process represent a 'big idea' having enduring value beyond the classroom?
- Filter 2: to what extent does the idea, topic or process reside at the heart of the discipline?

- Filter 3: to what extent does the idea, topic or process require uncoverage (a word the authors use to refer to stripping away the values unconsciously brought to planning)?
- Filter 4: to what extent does the idea, topic or process offer potential for engaging students?

These are certainly very useful criteria. The emphasis on the idea of enduring value is important to select out concepts of major significance. The authors are also mindful that the disciplines have a major role to play as it is important to select insights from these sources. The authors also talk about misconceptions or 'uncoverage' and this is a useful concept to remind teachers about the values they might bring to planning without necessarily being aware of them. The need for ideas to engage students is a major element and one that is very significant for all teachers.

Stage 2: determine acceptable evidence

This stage is all about planning what kinds of evidence will be needed to indicate that students have reached a particular proficiency in understanding. The authors are mindful of using a range of assessment methods and they consider that a variety should be used. The authors consider both formal and informal assessments. They are also concerned about the need to use performance tasks to enable students to demonstrate their levels of understanding.

Stage 3: plan learning experiences and instruction

The authors argue that teachers, having experienced the first two stages, would then be in a good position to make decisions about what will be included in their curriculum design.

They contend that there are several key questions that must be considered at this stage, namely:
- What enabling knowledge (facts, concepts and principles) and skills (procedures) will students need to perform effectively and achieve desired results?
- What activities will equip students with the needed knowledge and skills?
- What will need to be taught and coached and how should it best be taught, in light of performance goals?
- What materials and sources are best suited to accomplish these goals?
- Is the overall design coherent and effective?

The Understanding by Design (UBD) approach has been heavily marketed by the US curriculum professional association, Association for Supervision and Curriculum Development (ASCD). A range of workshops and training manuals on UBD are available for teachers (see <www.ascd.org/>).

7.8 | LESSON PLANS

As indicated above, the mental planning of lessons is of critical importance. The lesson plan, according to Cohen, Manion and Morrison (2004), is the clearest example of short-term planning. There is no single format; it depends on a number of factors, such as:
- the school's pro forma for lesson planning
- the students
- the curriculum area
- the type of lesson
- the level of detail required
- the level of detail that is useful.

Lesson plans are very personal in that the teacher creates learning activities for specific periods of time, usually half an hour up to two hours, which optimise student learning of particular objectives or enable students to demonstrate particular outcomes. They are important because they enable each teacher to:
- develop a clear idea of the main purpose of a lesson
- present coherent and interesting ideas

- select and structure relevant content
- use a variety of activities.

Lesson plans may be needed for a variety of reasons. Lessons can:
- be introductory
- continue work from a previous lesson
- build on and develop the work from a previous lesson
- practise skills learnt in previous lessons
- be designed to enrich and extend points made in earlier lessons
- be concluding lessons
- be diagnostic.

The amount of detail included in a lesson plan varies with the individual teacher and their experience. Student teachers are advised to provide very clear details, not for the sake of it but to enable them to have a very clear understanding of every aspect, and the sequence, of the lesson. With experience, teachers will use plans that are greatly reduced in length and perhaps limited to one or two lines in a daily planning schedule.

There needs to be a careful match between lesson plans and the teaching unit. That is, the overall goals of the unit should be kept in mind when constructing daily lesson plans.

Producing lesson plans is an art form. Teachers need to be able to produce lesson plans that will enable meaningful learning to occur. To do this they also need to capture students' interest and involvement.

Beginnings of lessons are most important. They are a major factor in shaping the motivation of students. There needs to be a smooth transition from what students know and what they have already studied. The lesson plans need to be sufficiently detailed so that the procedures are clearly recognisable. During the running of lessons it may be necessary for a teacher to make changes to these procedures because of unforeseen developments. It might also be necessary to change the proposed closure of a lesson.

So daily lesson plans are important because they:
- help teachers to build up confidence in their teaching
- enable teachers to be better prepared for instruction
- enable teachers to consider different options and to be more flexible
- assist with evaluating instruction.

Typical headings used in a variety of lessons include:
- objectives and outcomes
- time available
- materials needed
- learning activities – introductory, developmental and concluding
- evaluation.

Each lesson should have a small number of objectives or outcomes. These are derived from the teaching unit and the relevant system level syllabus or curriculum guide.

The time available for lessons is never sufficient! Where units are integrated in nature, it is possible to spill over into other subject times, especially at the primary school level. Double periods are needed for some activities.

It is necessary to list all the materials needed and to ensure that they are available at the appropriate time. This is especially the case with multimedia materials.

Learning activities are the centrepiece of each lesson. The introductory activities are used to motivate students and to present new ideas or topics. This often involves showing items (such as charts or pictures), or posing questions, or raising an issue based on a current event in a newspaper.

Developmental activities grow out of the introductory, opening activities. They may involve using a range of resources involving class discussions, individual reading, group viewing and many other approaches, as described above.

The concluding activities involve some closure for the lesson or for a series of lessons. They may involve some reporting back by small groups or individuals or a concluding summary by the teacher.

Evaluation activities, in terms of specific data collection, do not necessarily occur with every lesson. If it is a culmination of a number of lessons, then a student assessment may be included (such as a multiple choice test). Informal evaluative data may be collected by the teacher based on conversations with students or general observations of the class in action.

7.8.1 A more detailed approach

A more elaborate list was developed recently by Marsh (2009) for use with teachers in Singaporean schools, namely:
- Purposes
- Anticipated outcomes
- Student orientation
- Task engagement
- Task sequencing and timing
- Assessment activities
- Closure
- Resources and organisation
- Extension activities
- Encouraging reflection and evaluation
- Following up.

Details of each are as follows:
- Purposes – What do I really hope to achieve in this lesson? What activities and experiences will best enable these purposes to be achieved?
- Anticipated outcomes – What do I expect the students to be able to do as a result of this learning experience? How will they demonstrate this?
- Student orientation – What have the students completed in this area or topic prior to this lesson? How can I build on their prior knowledge in developing further understandings?
- Task engagement – How best can I engage and involve students in the learning experience? What questions or activities are important initially? What questions might the students ask?
- Task sequencing and timing – Is there an optimal way of sequencing the learning tasks and experiences? How much time is available for each aspect of the lesson? Are there any potential difficulties in this organisation?
- Assessment – What formative and summative techniques might I use?
- Closure – How can I draw this lesson to a close effectively so the students are clear or challenged or surprised?
- Resources and organisation – What resources and materials are needed? How can I make best use of available space? What equipment will each student need?
- Extension activities – How will I provide meaningful activities for those students who finish the tasks quickly? Or who will need extra time?
- Encouraging reflection and evaluation – What strategies will help me and my students reflect on the successes or difficulties with this lesson?
- Following up – How can I best build on these learning experiences?

7.8.2 Interactionist approach

Another approach to planning lessons, as indicated earlier, is the interactional method. Rather than following a linear series of steps, the emphasis is upon processes – in many cases it is a simultaneous consideration of a number of elements, especially content and activities, rather than starting with objectives. John's (2006) dialogical approach to lesson planning involves problem-level processes –

you have an overall goal but then interact with a number of sub-processes such as age and ability, learning styles, ICT, tasks and activities, and classroom control, to name just a few. John contends that this model is very helpful for inexperienced student teachers because it makes the crucial connection between classroom management, subject content and the curriculum.

The production of lesson plans involves personal choices about the amount of detail and the format. Some teachers use a column format for each teaching week so they can ensure they are using a variety of approaches and resources (see Table 7.7). Others tend to use a full-page format. Lesson plan examples at primary and secondary levels are included in Tables 7.8 and 7.9. The primary school example is based on the road safety program described earlier in this chapter.

TABLE 7.7 A summary of lesson plans for the week

Monday	Tuesday	Wednesday	Thursday	Friday
DVD on Japan	Mapping activity	Small group activity using literature audiotapes	Reading and written assignment	Guest speaker to visit

TABLE 7.8 A sample lesson on 'Sharing the Road with Others' (road safety) for primary schools

Subject:	Sharing the Road with Others, Year 4, March Lesson: Let's Get Visible
Objectives:	On completing the lesson each student will be able to: • demonstrate the benefits of wearing light, bright clothing when cycling • list, label and discuss bicycle safety aids.
Student background:	Students have light coloured bicycle helmets. Many have yellow raincoats.
Preparation:	Large pictures showing a camouflaged animal, young children riding in yellow raincoats. Videotape *It's Smart to be Safe* Hand-out sheet on road users

Procedure introduction:
(5 mins)
 	
(10 mins)
(10 mins)
 	
(15 mins)
	1 Show picture of camouflaged animal. Ask questions about camouflage. Discuss examples.
	2 Make a list on blackboard of clothing they typically wear when riding their bicycles.
	    List the colours of these items.
	3 Discuss safety clothes available, colours, reflective material.
	4 View videotape *It's Smart to be Safe* (7 mins).
	    Discussion on main characters
	What lessons are there for us?

Work: (20 mins)	1 Give out sheet, which is a sketch of young cyclists and other road users. 2 Students colour in the drawing. 3 Display completed drawings. 4 Obtain comments from students.
Evaluation:	Questioning undertaken during the viewing of the large pictures, the videotape and after the drawing activity.
Self-evaluation:	(To be completed by the teacher)

> **YOUR TURN**
>
> Select a lesson to be taught from the unit you have developed.
> - Reflect on the major focus for the lesson.
> - What headings will you use to set out your lesson plan?

TABLE 7.9 A sample lesson plan on Japan (secondary/middle schools)

Objectives/outcomes:	1 Students are able to describe the location of Japan and map natural resources. 2 Students are able to describe how people's use of natural features has changed over time.
Time available:	1 hour
Year level:	Years 6–8
Materials needed:	• wall map of Japan, hand-out outline maps • DVD on Japan • news stories, clippings, photographs of Japan's natural environment • section in students' textbook on Japan.
Learning activities **Introductory activities:**	• Show large photographs of scenes in Japan. • Compare with Australia. • What are the main features of Japan's natural environment? • List students' responses on whiteboard.
Developmental activities:	1 Show 10-minute DVD on the natural resources of Japan. 2 Ask students to read textbook and consult atlas and then locate major features on the hand-out outline map of Japan. 3 Read out excerpts from literature/books about Japanese culture and the natural environment. 4 Ask students to write a paragraph about how the Japanese have adapted to their natural environment.
Concluding activities:	Select three students to read their paragraphs out to the class.
Evaluation:	1 Observe students doing the mapping activity. Collect completed maps to be marked and returned during the next lesson. 2 Observe students writing the paragraphs. Provide individual feedbacks as required.

Some other formats are included in Tables 7.10 and 7.11. Formats for grouped classes require, of course, additional columns.

In this section a variety of guidelines and examples has been presented about lesson planning. What is important for student teachers is to obtain feedback about the progress they are making with their teaching.

One form of feedback for student teachers is to use a checklist to evaluate the progress they are making in developing successful lesson plans. The comprehensive checklist on planning and preparation (Figure 7.6) could be used as a self-report checklist or completed by several teachers or student teachers.

TABLE 7.10 A standard lesson planner guide

Subject/topic	Time		Date	
Objectives/outcomes				
Resources/equipment				
Teacher's activities	Students' activities		Assessment data	
Introductory activity				
Main activity			Formative data	
Concluding activity			Summative data	
Teacher reflection on lesson				

Source: Based on Cohen, Manion & Morrison, A Guide to Teaching Practice, 5th edn, 1998, Taylor and Francis Books Ltd, p. 113.

TABLE 7.11 A more flexible lesson planner

Date: Time: Groups:

Teaching area:

- Intended learning outcomes:

- Resources/equipment:

- Major teaching points:

- Activities/content:

- Assessment:

- Follow-up activities:

- Lesson review:

Source: Based on Cohen, Manion & Morrison, A Guide to Teaching Practice, *5th edn, 1998, Taylor and Francis Books Ltd, p. 114.*

FIGURE 7.6 Checklist for student teachers

		Agree	Agree to a limited extent	Disagree
1	The teacher has planned adequate means for motivating the students.	☐	☐	☐
2	The teacher has prepared instructional objectives that are clear and appropriate.	☐	☐	☐
3	The teacher has included content that is appropriate for the objectives and the skills to be learnt.	☐	☐	☐
4	The teacher has included content that is interesting for the students.	☐	☐	☐
5	The teacher has included content that helps develop positive attitudes.	☐	☐	☐
6	The teacher has planned activities where the voice can be used effectively and is clearly understood.	☐	☐	☐
7	The teacher has planned activities that will promote order and good behaviour in the class.	☐	☐	☐
8	The teacher will use a variety of instructional techniques.	☐	☐	☐
9	The teacher has planned adequate communication links with students by questioning, responding and explaining.	☐	☐	☐
10	The teacher has planned different stages of the lesson and for there to be a smooth transition between each stage.	☐	☐	☐
11	The teacher has planned to pace the different activities in the lesson.	☐	☐	☐
12	The teacher has planned to develop a good rapport with the students.	☐	☐	☐
13	The teacher has developed key teaching points in the lesson plan.	☐	☐	☐
14	The teacher has planned to use space effectively for different activities.	☐	☐	☐
15	The teacher has prepared overviews and hand-outs on key ideas.	☐	☐	☐
16	The teacher has alternatives prepared if the lesson plans do not go as intended.	☐	☐	☐
17	The teacher has included effective means of collecting assessment data about students.	☐	☐	☐
18	The teacher has included techniques for collecting formative assessment information.	☐	☐	☐
19	The teacher has selected teaching resources that are relevant to the purpose of the lesson.	☐	☐	☐
20	The teacher has collected together resources that will be stimulating and attractive for the students.	☐	☐	☐
21	The teacher has developed comprehensive ways of monitoring the progress of students.	☐	☐	☐

> **YOUR TURN**
>
> All teachers need to reflect on the effectiveness of specific lessons.
> - For the teaching topic(s) you have worked on in this chapter, were your original priorities justified?
> - Use the checklist in Figure 7.6 as a basis for deciding your progress to date with lesson planning.

It is important for teachers, but especially student teachers, to do a *post-lesson* analysis. Cohen, Manion and Morrison (2004) emphasise that if student teachers are to become reflective practitioners, they need to be able to isolate significant issues.

This can be done by some simple self-reflection on such matters as:
- How did students react to the lesson?
- Which activities were well done, and which poorly done?
- Why did these problems arise?
- Were the outcomes realistic?
- Which students seemed to gain most and who did not? Why?

Alternatively, a more detailed checklist for self-evaluation can be used, as depicted in Figure 7.7.

It is very helpful for a teacher to jot down any thoughts on the margin of the lesson plan for future reference. Lesson planning is an incremental process. Refinements need to be added at the time specific lessons are taught. Planning skills have to be continually checked and honed if marked improvements in teaching skills are to occur.

FIGURE 7.7 Checklist for evaluating lessons

1. Did the lesson motivate my students in the introductory stages?
2. Was my questioning clear? Did my students respond actively to the questions?
3. Were all stages of my lesson successful?
4. Were the timing and pacing of different activities appropriate?
5. Were the resources used appropriate?
6. Did I get across the key teaching points?
7. Were the activities undertaken by the students successful?
8. Did the lesson provide positive relationships between me and the students?
9. Did the lesson promote good student behaviour?
10. Did I obtain important assessment data about the students during the lesson?

7.8.3 Lesson study

A very recent development that may be of benefit to beginning teachers is 'lesson study'.

'Lesson study' is an action research (teacher-focused) based approach to lesson planning that is now being actively practised in a number of countries. The idea of lesson study was derived from Chinese and Japanese teachers who conducted systematic and in-depth investigations into their own lessons (Matoba, Crawford & Arani 2001).

The use of lesson study has subsequently spread to many other countries including the USA (Lewis, Perry & Murata 2006), Hong Kong (Lo, Pong & Pakey 2005) and Singapore (Lee & Yamping 2006).

Lesson study is premised on the idea that students will have a diverse range of ideas about a topic. The processes involved in doing lesson study highlight ways of uncovering these differences and then producing lessons that are more viable. For example, the typical sequence is as follows:
1. A group of teachers decide to work as a team to analyse and produce better lessons for a subject or topic.
2. Students in a class are given a pre-test to find out critical elements of learning that are typically misunderstood or perceived differently.
3. The group of teachers collectively plan a lesson that they consider is more pedagogically sound and likely to be more effective with a greater number of students.
4. One teacher is selected to teach the lesson while other teachers observe.
5. The lesson is videotaped and/or other teachers make observational records.
6. The students in the class are given a post-test to ascertain their levels of understandings of the topic.
7. The total group of teachers review the lesson and make plans for revising it.
8. Another cycle begins. Several cycles may be completed before the teachers are satisfied with the lesson plans they have produced.

In a number of countries, lesson study teams have embarked enthusiastically on refining lesson plans for specific topics or subjects. Research studies have demonstrated that students show improvements in a number of outcomes as a result of experiencing the 'refined' lessons. It is also a valuable source of professional development for teachers and especially for beginning teachers (Pang & Marton 2003; Stigler & Hiebert 1999; Lo, Pong & Pakey 2005).

CONCLUDING COMMENTS

Programming units and lesson planning are critical activities for teachers at all levels. Teachers who spend insufficient time on planning inevitably present lessons that lack coherence, are of minimal interest to students and will lead to a lack of credibility for the individuals concerned.

Although there are basic headings and strategies that can be used, planning is a very creative activity. There is no single approach. It is up to each teacher to develop strategies that best suit their talents, energy and interest.

KEY ISSUES RAISED IN THIS CHAPTER

1. Being able to prepare and execute successful lessons is a major goal for every teacher.
2. Although linear steps provide a simple template, it is important that pre-service teachers take time to reflect on a range of issues and develop their own approaches.
3. Practical experiences are extremely valuable for pre-service teachers if they approach them openly and self-critically.
4. Developing a teaching program is essential but the style and emphasis will depend upon the level, subject and the personal style of each teacher.
5. Planning a teaching unit provides a clear focus for students and the teacher.
6. A new approach to planning, Understanding by Design (UBD), may have considerable merit.
7. Lesson planning involves developing personal, short-term plans.
8. The interactionist method of lesson planning allows for the simultaneous consideration of a number of planning elements.
9. Lesson study is a new approach to developing more effective lessons based upon systematic research procedures.

REFLECTIONS AND ISSUES

1. 'The better the teacher plans, the better the teacher.' Do you agree? Explain the planning (mental and written) you do prior to giving a lesson. How could it be improved?
2. What special strengths do you have as a teacher? Do you incorporate these in your lesson plans? What do your students say about the strengths and weaknesses of your lessons? Explain how you intend to build on your strengths and to work around your limitations.
3. Why is pacing so important in developing a program?
4. Do differences between the programs of teachers mainly depend on differences in how prescriptive are curricula? Are there other reasons?
5. How useful are teachers' guides in planning a program? Do they promote good teaching or simply inhibit a teacher? Give examples.
6. 'The rise of information technology introduces the possibility of new individualised planning for students' (Cohen, Manion & Morrison 2004). Do you agree? Give examples.
7. Reflect on a teaching unit you have used or observed recently in classrooms. What was the major focus of the unit? To what extent did the learning experiences support this focus? What were its strengths and weaknesses as a teaching unit?
8. Observe the learning space in a colleague's classroom. Note in particular the location of furniture and resources and what opportunities are available for student group activities. Establish some general principles about effective use of classroom space.
9. How useful is the backward planning approach of the Understanding by Design (UBD) model? Take a particular teaching topic and follow through with the three steps of UBD.
10. Take a particularly difficult concept to teach in Mathematics and then discuss with two or three colleagues different ways of teaching it. Use a lesson study approach to practising different ways of teaching the concept.

Special references

Moore, A (2004) *The Good Teacher*, Routledge Falmer, London.
Moore, KD (2009b) *Effective Instructional Strategies*, Sage, Thousand Oaks.
Moyles, J (2007) (ed.) *Beginning Teaching: Beginning Learning*, 3rd edn, CA, Open University Press, Buckingham.
Orlich et al, (2007) *Teaching Strategies*, 9th edn, Wadsworth, Cengage learning, Boston.

Web sources

For additional resources on planning and preparing for teaching, please go to:
www.pearson.com.au/myeducationlab.

ORGANISING CLASSROOM STRUCTURES AND ROUTINES

8.1 | INTRODUCTION

The use of the term 'the grammar of schooling' (Tyack & Cuban 1995) is a perceptive way of describing the taken-for-granted structural features of how we try to use schools (Farrell 2001).

Classrooms around the world are remarkably similar. Watkins (2005) refers to such observable similarities as classroom walls, rows of students, status, gender and power. Cuban (1993) and Sarason (1993) point to three reasons for classrooms remaining relatively stable over the decades (some would say centuries!):
- the characteristics of the classroom situation
- the power relations between teachers and students
- the dominant view of learning and learners.

In this chapter we are examining the classroom situation and various ways it can be organised.

A major problem for teachers is the chaotic nature of interactions in all classrooms and the difficulties of learning to live in a crowd (Jackson 1968). To offset these problems various structures and routines are developed and maintained by classroom teachers. In the frantic and complex activities associated with teaching, it is essential for the teacher and students that some order be visible and effective. There is of course no best structure or routine. The issues are multidimensional (Hewitt 2006). It is important to analyse some of the options available and to consider their relative merit in particular contexts.

8.2 | TYPICAL SCHOOL STRUCTURES

There is not a single Australian education system. Each state or territory has an Education Department and political responsibility is with a Minister of Education. The organisation of schools will vary somewhat between government and non-government schools (that is, schools run by religious organisations and alternative schools).

8.2.1 Kindergartens and preschools

Kindergartens typically provide learning experiences and social activities for four-year-old children, and pre-primary education is available for five-year-olds. There are currently variations between states and territories despite recent Commonwealth Government initiatives to standardise them.

A Commonwealth Government initiative, the Early Years Learning Framework draft was released in February 2009. It attempts to provide a standardised curriculum for all toddlers and preschoolers but early reactions have been far from positive: 'It will see young children being taught politically correct messages in play time' (Tillett, 15 April 2009, p. 13).

Attendance in kindergartens and preschools is not compulsory, but increasingly parents are taking advantage of these opportunities for their children (over 90 per cent in Western Australia).

Both kindergartens and preschools enable young children to learn social and academic skills through play and active involvement with other children and adults. Numbers per group are small (10–20) and children can typically do a range of activities including working on their own, in groups and as part of a whole group (Department of Education and Training 2006a). Learning centres, both indoor and outdoor, are especially useful as they allow children to interact freely and to do tasks that are developmentally appropriate (Kostelnik, Soderman & Whiren 2007; Dodge, Colker & Heroman 2002).

Some of the activities that children may participate in include:
- designing and creating cubbies
- dressing up
- climbing
- dancing
- doing puzzles
- making collages
- listening to and playing music
- painting
- drawing
- reading books and storytelling
- playing with clay, dough and blocks. (Department of Education and Training 2006b)

Reflect upon activities that typically occur in kindergartens. Is there evidence that staff involve children in creative activities, develop their physical skills and develop their positive self-confidence and self-awareness?

8.2.2 Primary schools

Primary schools have similar structures in each state or territory, but there are differences in terms of 'age of eligibility to enrol at school and whether pre-primary years are built into the formal schooling system' (Lokan 1996, p. 1).

Primary schools typically have an enrolment of 100 to 600 students ranging from kindergarten (pre-primary) through to Years 6, 7 or 8, depending on the organisational patterns of secondary schools. Typically, the school principal allocates the human and material resources to optimise student learning. This usually means that one teacher is allocated per year level or grade although, dependent on total school numbers and specific educational policies, other variations do occur, such as team teaching, grouped classes and streamed classes. There may be several specialist teachers on staff such as an Art teacher, Music teacher or Physical Education teacher. One or more secretaries will be available to assist with clerical tasks and there will be one or more deputy principals to assist with management of the school.

YOUR TURN

Do you agree or disagree with the statement that whole-class teaching provides the order, control, purpose and concentration that is needed in today's primary school classrooms? Give reasons.

Each school will typically have a school council and, depending on its powers, it may be very dominant and hire staff and determine the curriculum or play a relatively subservient, advisory role. A typical organisational pattern is illustrated in Figure 8.1.

At the primary school level in particular, the organisational patterns can exert a powerful influence on both teaching and learning (Cohen, Manion & Morrison 2004). Angus and Ainley (2007) argue that the culture of primary schools sustains extraordinarily high levels of commitment, efficacy and goodwill. A recent report in Australia concluded that 92 per cent of teachers surveyed claimed to enjoy their primary school teaching and felt they were making a difference (Angus & Ainley 2007).

There is often government pressure on primary schools to set ambitious goals for literacy and numeracy. Have you seen evidence of this in any visits you have made to primary schools? The Deputy Prime Minister has added pressures by stating recently (*Weekend Australian*, 28 March 2009) that the 'Government is committed to transparent reporting of school performance' (p. 3).

FIGURE 8.1 Primary school organisation

		Region/District Superintendent		
		Principal – School Council		
		Deputy Principal		
Classroom teachers	Art teacher	Music teacher	Physical Education teacher	Secretary

8.2.3 Secondary schools

Secondary schools usually have higher enrolments, ranging from 500 to 1200 or more students. The principal has an administrative team of several deputies and a bursar to manage the school policies, budget and deployment of teachers and resources. Secondary schools are usually organised into subject departments and senior teachers in charge schedule teaching loads and use of specialist equipment. There are a number of specialists including a guidance officer, youth education officer and chaplain, as well as visiting specialists in languages.

Secondary schools are now also linked with vocational courses, both on and off campus. Secondary students will typically take some academic courses on campus and also do work placements with local industry and community groups.

Some secondary schools specialise in a particular curriculum area such as Mathematics, Dance or Music and tend to have a wider catchment area than the usual secondary school. As noted above for primary schools, secondary schools will typically have a school council but the powers bestowed on it vary considerably from state to state. A typical organisational pattern is illustrated in Figure 8.2.

FIGURE 8.2 Secondary school organisation

		Region/District Superintendent		
		Principal – School Council		
	Deputy Principal		Deputy Principal	
		Senior Teachers/Heads of Departments		
Specialists	Teachers		Secretaries	Principal's Secretary

> **YOUR TURN**
>
> Secondary teachers have to have:
> - academic subject knowledge
> - pedagogical knowledge
> - effective interpersonal skills
> - organisational skills
> - enthusiasm and motivating skills
> - pastoral care skills
> - assessment skills.
>
> Do you consider that secondary teachers are caught up in a web of different and conflicting demands?

Compared with primary schools which are generally lauded as being successful and relevant, secondary schools are frequently criticised. Wise (2008) argues that education reforms in the USA have largely ignored secondary schools – too many secondary school students drop out of school and too many graduates are unprepared for tertiary study or employment. McGaw (2007) notes that Australia ranks poorly in terms of the total population finishing secondary education.

Is the problem that secondary school teachers are still often trained to be isolated content lecturers and that students are pushed into one-size-fits-all courses?

Hayes and Vivian (2008) argue that primary schools are sites of private space that represents a supportive, family environment. By contrast, secondary schools introduce students to a public space – a social space where the relatively anonymous spaces are occupied by strangers. Hayes and Vivian (2008) present a telling picture of public space in secondary schools – 'it is a hybrid social arena where students affiliate with others but often in groups whose boundaries are tightly defined and aggressively policed' (2008, p. 24).

Based upon your experiences in secondary school did you feel isolated and under pressure to succeed academically? How supportive was it compared with your primary school experiences? Is it possible to make secondary schools more inclusive and valuing of interpersonal development?

8.2.4 Middle schools

Middle schooling tries to address the specific developmental needs of young adolescents. It has been developed since the 1990s in Australia. Hill and Russell (1999) argue that the challenge for middle years education is to provide a more student-focused approach to teaching. Carrington (2004) contends that middle schooling has to address student orientation and disengagement.

The number of middle schools in each Australian state has grown rapidly over the last several decades. The schools can range in size from 300 to 800 students. They cater for 10- to 15-year-olds and have a major emphasis on an integrated, learner-centred curriculum.

In some cases, existing buildings have been converted into middle schools (often having 'houses' or 'school within school' models). Custom-built premises for middle schools have the advantage of providing areas for interdisciplinary teams, media and computing resources.

Middle schools typically use interdisciplinary teams of teachers who share the same students, the same schedule and the same part of the building (George, Lawrence & Bushnell 1998). Larger blocks of time enable teachers and students to explore topics in detail.

Since the early 1990s there have been a large number of key reports on the middle years. Of these the most significant and influential have been those by Eyers, Cormack and Barratt (1992), the Australian Curriculum Studies Association (1996) and Barratt (1998). All of these reports argued for 'more supportive learning environments where teachers and students are able to experiment with new pedagogies and approaches to curriculum' (Carrington 2004, p. 33).

YOUR TURN

What skills are needed to be an effective middle school teacher? Consider the following, and make a list of those items that you consider are the most important:
- Personal qualities – being secure and flexible, and having respect for the dignity and worth of the individual.
- Understanding the nature of the young adolescent learner.
- Instructional skills, including facilitating problem solving and group work.

Recent research studies on middle schooling include those completed by Hayes and Chodkiewicz (2006); Wallace *et al.* (2007) and Black, Stokes and Turnbull (2010).

The typical organisational pattern of middle schools is illustrated in Figure 8.3.

 What are some of the root causes of student alienation? Is it the rapidly changing socio-cultural, economic and technological landscapes that students experience in schools now? Can middle schooling alleviate student alienation?

FIGURE 8.3 Middle school organisation

Region/District Superintendent
Principal – School Council

Interdisciplinary teams of teachers   Support staff
(specialists and generalists)

8.3 | PRESSURES AND DEMANDS ON SCHOOLS

Schools at each of the levels of kindergarten, preschool, primary, middle and secondary have to cope with ever-increasing pressures. There is a need to provide organisational patterns of learning that can cope flexibly with different ethnic and racial groups and students of differing abilities. In addition, there are the constant clamourings from the media and the public for higher student achievement levels (McGaw 2007).

Economic rationalist policies in many states have caused low-enrolment schools, especially rural schools, to close because they were deemed to be inefficient (McCollow 2007). There has been a tendency to create larger primary and secondary schools, although there is little evidence to indicate that larger schools provide more effective education (Perrone 2000).

There are indications already that technology will affect the organisation of schools. The 'Classroom of the Future' developed at the National Institute of Singapore is student-centred and relies entirely on students using tablet PCs to interact with different programs. The role of the teacher is minimal (Back Pack Net Centre 2005). It is highly likely that schools will have to offer more flexible hours and more individualised instruction. Much of the instruction for students will occur on the home computer. The resources available at schools will need to be greatly extended. The role of the teacher will change from instructor to co-learner and facilitator.

8.4 | ORGANISING TASKS AND ELEMENTS

Notwithstanding these possible future scenarios, the tasks for organising schools at present can be summarised according to Danielson (2002) in terms of:

- high-level learning for all students – through the school's organisational pattern, the staff convey to students and their parents that learning is important
- a safe and positive environment – a physically safe environment, given recent tragedies in schools, is of paramount importance at all levels
- a culture of hard work and opportunities – a good school organisation offers challenges to students, stretching them but also ensuring that they can succeed.

The staffs of schools at all levels typically inherit organisational patterns from previous years, but it is important to highlight elements that are common and often taken for granted (Danielson 2002).

The *master timetable* structures the pace of the activities. Even in primary schools where other specialists operate alongside the one teacher/one class pattern, the master timetable is still dominant. In many schools, a minimum period of time for core subjects is built into the timetable, and this reminds teachers and students about what is important and what isn't!

The *deployment of staff* is another major factor. In primary schools it is normally one teacher per year level (as described above) but the management team can decide on a variety of alternatives including split grades, withdrawal groups and team-taught groups (especially in middle schools) (Burns & Mason 2002). In secondary schools, the staff is being increasingly involved in teaching and/or supervising students at industry locations as well as on school campuses.

The *grouping strategies* used in a school can be based on traditional patterns or innovative practices. This might include ability grouping of students for core subjects (short-term remedial or long-term) or groupings based on student interests and abilities. It can be related to management decisions about the maximum size of classes (Blatchford *et al.* 2002).

The *time available in schools* is never sufficient! Arends (2009) notes that the effective use of time is just as important as the amount of time spent on a topic. Moore (2009b) and Marks (2000) are mindful of the various types of time in schools: there is the mandated (required) time allocated to particular subjects; there is the engaged time or 'time-on-task', which is the actual amount of time that individual students spend on assigned work (and this may be far less than the designated instructional time); and there is 'academic learning time' where students are actually concentrating, thinking, reflecting and not merely pretending to be using their materials or to be listening to the teacher.

YOUR TURN

- What are the advantages of block scheduling of 90-minute classes over the normal 40-minute class?
- Does it engage students more deeply?
- Does it force teachers to employ different approaches?

Educators have recently given more attention to the concept of 'engaged learning'. For example Theroux (2004) notes that engaged learners are:
- responsible for their own learning
- energised by learning
- strategic
- collaborative.

Students are 'engaged' when:
- conducting authentic and multidisciplinary tasks
- participating in interactive learning
- working collaboratively
- learning through exploration.

What does engaged learning mean to you? How would you characterise what you do when you are 'engaged'? How does that compare with when you are 'disengaged'?

It is important to analyse some of the major organisational patterns found in schools so that we can judge their appropriateness for specific school contexts and teaching situations.

8.5 SELF-CONTAINED CLASSROOMS

A self-contained classroom is one in which one teacher is responsible for all the instruction in all subject areas. This provides optimal flexibility for the teacher because he/she can decide what, when and how material will be taught. However, the quality of the teaching depends to a large extent on the individual teacher.

Moore (2009b) contends that most teachers lack the content knowledge in all the core curriculum areas to make the self-contained classroom pattern a viable option. Cohen, Manion and Morrison (2004) suggest that many teachers in self-contained classrooms follow a formal approach to their teaching.

8.6 OPEN VERSUS SELF-CONTAINED CLASSROOMS

The physical environment does not prevent teachers from rearranging furniture to create an open teaching environment in their room. If, on the other hand, a teacher is working in an open classroom building with large areas in which students can move around freely and where teachers can team up for tasks, an informal approach is likely to predominate.

Informal teaching or open education can be considered as an *organisational* emphasis or as an *ideology*. Over the decades, but especially in the 1960s and 1970s, open education was extolled as the very best way to bring about student learning (Oliva 2008). The following Chinese proverb was often cited to encapsulate the spirit of open education:

> I hear, I forget, I see, I remember, I do, I understand.

As portrayed by its exponents in *ideological* terms, open education tends to emphasise such principles as those listed below:
- We should provide child-centred activities using a variety of materials in informal settings and the teacher should act as a facilitator.
- Children should have opportunities to individually discover things.
- We should encourage the development of the whole personality of children, to satisfy their curiosity and develop their confidence, perseverance and alertness (Central Advisory Council for Education 1967, pp. 493–507).

Notwithstanding, *organisational* aspects of open learning can be included in classrooms by teachers to suit particular groups of students. For example, it is possible to organise some elements of open learning to have:
- learning stations where students can work individually or in groups (including, for example, a quiet station, music station, viewing station, computer pod, or investigation station)
- formal teaching in the mornings and informal teaching in the afternoons
- morning tasks completed in a set time but no fixed time for afternoon activities.

It is important to realise that organising activities in an open classroom is quite complex and, if anything, is more difficult than in formal classrooms where rules are well established. Some points to consider when organising an open classroom include:
- Do students understand the tasks they will be doing (either individually or in small groups)?
- Where will students be moving to and from?
- Will resources be available for all their needs?
- How will you resolve any disagreements or conflicts between students?

Critics of open education, such as Pratt (1980); Hunt and Yarusso (1979) and Cuban (2004) contend that proponents greatly underestimate the audible and visual distractions of open classrooms. Oliva (2008) notes that there is little evidence to support open education on the grounds of academic achievement. Kranz (2002) notes that the fad of open classrooms has fallen out of favour. Problems of students being easily distracted by nearby noises and activities, such as other students watching movies; lack of security and inability to lock down classrooms; difficulties in wiring classrooms for a wide range of technologies and not being able to have conduits in walls to stop students tripping over wires all helped to bring about its demise. Open education classrooms have not produced the results that were hoped for.

 Are you a supporter of open education? Are there advantages in having child-centred activities in a variety of informal settings where children can discover things? What are some of the disadvantages?

8.7 | INDIVIDUALISED LEARNING

Ideally, if teachers could work with students on a one-to-one basis it would be possible to optimise all the unique qualities of each student. Even though this is not possible in the normal teaching situation, it is desirable to plan and organise some opportunities for students to work individually.

Individual projects can be organised in which each student has the task of researching a particular topic, searching out information from a library and interviewing community personnel. Or individual projects may be based on journal writing, where each student reflects on particular happenings and writes down their reactions (Quek 2006).

Personal computers in schools offer increased opportunities for individualised learning. For example, in many secondary school classes all students have laptop computers or tablet PCs and they can work away on their individual projects (McDonald & Ingvarson 1997; Newhouse 1998). Most schools have pods of computers in classrooms, which allow students to work on projects independently.

By using CD-ROMs and the Internet, students can individually research a variety of topics, they can solve problems – for example, using a computer simulation such as Bush Rescue (Matson & Smith 1987) – and they can create stories and images – (for example, creating a visual narrative on the bombing of Darwin during World War II).

The Internet enables individual students to explore a wealth of data. According to Hackbarth (1997) it has emerged rapidly to become the prime electronic medium. It provides access to a vast array of data and people, and it enables global sharing and communication.

Some caveats need to be mentioned. On the one hand it can be argued that it is highly desirable for students to master the complex skills of accessing information, because this is needed by everyone in the twenty-first century (Dede 1998). However, on the other hand, access to the Internet can also enable students to access objectionable materials (Futoran, Schofield & Eurich-Fulmer 1995; Norton & Wiburg 2003).

Without doubt, the explosion of material on the Internet has created additional problems for teachers – both beginning and experienced – who have only rudimentary knowledge of the computer and are finding it difficult to upgrade their skills (McFarlane & Jared 1994; Norton & Wiburg 2003).

Notwithstanding all this, computers offer enormous opportunities for individualised learning. There has been increasing attention over recent years to differentiated classrooms and how they can cater more adequately for individual differences. Tomlinson (1999) argues that differentiated classrooms allow teachers and students to work together in a variety of ways. She outlines how it is possible to differentiate by:
- teaching difference levels of content according to a student's readiness
- using activities and pace of learning according to student needs
- having different requirements for products or targets for students to achieve
- varying the types and difficulty levels of assessment.

In classrooms you have visited recently to what extent are students using computers? Do they seem to have sound information retrieval skills? What are some examples of projects or activities they are engaged in on the computers?

8.8 | HETEROGENEOUS VERSUS STREAMED CLASSES

The issue of streamed versus heterogeneous or non-streamed classes is an ongoing one. In Australia, primary classes are typically non-streamed, whereas some streaming does occur for core subjects such as Mathematics, English and Science in a number of schools. By contrast, there are many countries where streaming is widespread in both primary and secondary schools (for example, Singapore, Hong Kong, US, UK, Netherlands).

The arguments for streaming include:
- It is easier for teachers.
- Students of similar ability gain from being together in the one class.

The arguments against streaming include:
- It is inherently unfair and creates inequalities within our society (Slavin 1995).
- Students in the lowest streams are demoralised and demotivated (Yonezawa & Jones 2006).

> **YOUR TURN**
>
> Reflect upon classes that you have taught which have been streamed, based upon ability. What have been the goals and aspirations of students in the lower ability streams? Can streaming be justified on grounds of equity and opportunity?

Proponents of heterogeneous (non-streamed) classes argue that there are a number of best practices that can be undertaken to promote learning and motivation for all students. They include:
- using multiple points of entry for students
- building a classroom community that includes all learners (Watanabe 2006)
- providing targeted and effective support for all students
- building students' skills of analysis and self-assessment (Rubin 2006).

These are major issues of equity that all schools have to address. It can be argued that classrooms are made up of individuals with varying interests, attitudes and talents. To attempt to create homogeneous groups through ability streaming means that students do not receive the same quality of education.

 If streaming is so unfair and creates inequalities among students, why is it still widely practiced? Can it be justified by countries that want to achieve high scores in international rankings such as PISA and TIMMS?

8.9 | WHOLE-CLASS INSTRUCTION

There will be occasions when whole-group instruction is needed and is the most effective method (see Chapter 12). Some teachers argue that whole groups are easier to manage – certainly the planning of these lessons is more focused because the initiatives are all taken by the teacher. It can, however, lead to lack of student involvement and boredom. To counteract this occurring, some ways to maintain whole-class attention include:
- keeping the teacher talk presentations brief – intersperse them where possible with a student activity

- enhancing the talks with visual aids or music
- trying to include concrete and personal student examples in the talk
- asking questions during the presentation and pausing sufficiently ('wait-time') to give the expectation that student responses are really wanted
- seating potentially disruptive students at locations that are easily accessible by the teacher.

Whole-class sessions can add greatly to the atmosphere or 'climate' of a class because students feel a sense of belonging and of cohesion. However, a steady diet of whole-class lessons, although this is the typical pattern in many schools, should be reserved for those activities that are best suited to this approach. For example, useful activities and topics for whole-class sessions include:
- an introduction to a new teaching unit
- an activity of general interest such as a videotape, film or slide presentation
- a demonstration of a technical process
- a briefing talk for an excursion or field trip
- the teaching of a complex concept or skill.

8.10 | USING SMALL GROUPS

Within each school students can be grouped homogeneously (based on ability), heterogeneously (based on mixed ability) or for special programs (for example, intellectually talented, English as a second language). It is also possible to plan for groups within a class (intra-class groupings). Groups are important to all of us. As noted by Johnson *et al.* (1994), we learn, work, worship and play in groups. Orlich *et al.* (2009) assert that students who work in small groups learn to work harmoniously and create an atmosphere in which information sharing can take place. A major reason why teachers opt for using small groups within their classes is that it creates opportunities for students to develop personally and socially. In ideal situations, group work should enable all students to be challenged (Benjamin, Bessant & Watts 1997). This may involve having high-ability students working together in a small group and lower-ability students working in separate groups, or it might be advantageous to have individuals of different abilities located within each small group.

Decisions about using groups should be made carefully and not for simplistic reasons. For example, you might want to weigh up the following matters before making a decision about using groups:
- What are my intended objectives and to what extent will they be achieved by using small groups?
- Is the lesson content conducive to being learnt through group activities?
- Is the time allocated sufficient for group activities to be undertaken satisfactorily?
- Is the teaching setting appropriate for undertaking group activities?
- Are specific materials and resources available for each group to undertake specific group tasks? (Cooke & Nicholson 1992)

These are important questions and it may be that for many lessons and subjects, group work is not appropriate. Where group work is undertaken, the following categories or types are most common:
- groups of students with a similar achievement level (for example, reading groups, spelling groups)
- groups with the same skill level (for example, in physical education)
- friendship groups that allow friends to work together
- interest groups.

Reading groups are found in most primary schools and consist of students who are comparable in reading ability. There may be three or four reading groups within the one class. Reading groups usually follow set routines for oral reading or comprehension activities, but they still require careful supervision by the teacher.

Not all students in a reading group are highly motivated – some may be wrongly graded while others may be lacking in motivation. The effective teacher needs to be able to spend time with each group and yet to be aware of what is happening in the rest of the room. Strategic positioning by the teacher – for example, sitting in corners of the room so he/she can talk to a small group and still be able to observe the activities of the rest of the class – is one way of achieving this.

Friendship groups can be effective in some situations. Certainly, students are very keen to work with their friends – friendships and shared interests are significant in the lives of students (Cooke & Nicholson 1992, p. 47). Yet if students self-select their group members, then the teacher is not able to control the composition of each group and some groups may be very happy but most groups may be non-productive or even disruptive. For example, the difficult students in a class might all endeavour to be placed within the one group because of strong friendships and this could lead to a very explosive situation for the teacher. There is also the probability that friendship groups will further alienate individuals in a class who are ignored by the others, are unpopular and, as a result, have a low self-concept.

It is up to each teacher to find out about friendship patterns within a class before groups are selected (Dillon 1994). This can often be achieved through observation and informal conversations; the teacher can then make some judicious choices to ensure that 'loners' are catered for and that 'troublemakers' are not all concentrated in the one group.

However, it is also true that friendship patterns within a class are sometimes well hidden. One way to find out the social structure of a group is to gather socio-metric data and produce a sociogram (Salvia & Ysseldyke 1998). This technique is based on students' choices of companions from among the class in specified situations. Specific situations may be presented to the children in either a written or verbal form, provided the following criteria are observed:

1. The choices should be real choices that are natural parts of the ongoing activities in the classroom.
2. The basis for choice and the restrictions on choosing should be made clear.
3. All students should be equally free to participate in the activity or situation.
4. The choices each student makes should be kept strictly confidential.
5. The choices should be actually used to organise or rearrange groups (Gronlund 1981, p. 460).

Once the children have indicated their preferences, the teacher should record the results in a useful fashion. Sociograms indicate which students have been chosen by their classmates as working partners (see Figure 8.4). A strength of this particular form of recording is that it reveals to the teacher not only those who are most consistently chosen, but also possible compatible groupings. A disadvantage is that the teacher can only assume that the children will respond honestly and even then their choices may change.

Interest groups are another type of classroom organisation that can be very effective. For example, students might be asked to list three topics that are of most interest to them and this information can then be used to divide up the interest groups. The teacher then encourages students of differing achievement levels and ethnic origins to work together and students contribute according to their particular knowledge, skills or talents.

Above all, we should be reminded that every student has different predispositions about group work; some students thrive on group work, some positively hate it. Further, group activities can be confusing for some students. It does not follow that all students are enthusiastic about working in small groups. To have small groups operate effectively it is important to note that:
- group goals must be clearly understood
- all members of a group must have an opportunity to participate and to take leadership roles
- members must be encouraged to communicate their ideas and feelings accurately and clearly to each other
- any conflicts that arise should be talked through and not avoided
- group cohesion is a major task that has to be worked on by the teacher and students.

FIGURE 8.4 Sociogram showing working partners in a Social Science unit

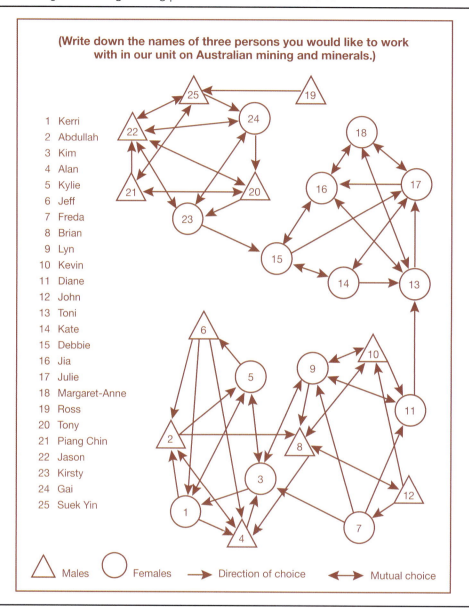

The role of the teacher in supervising group work requires careful planning and sensitive supervising. It is useful to get students to express their feelings about working in small groups – to impress upon them that it is the process of group learning that is just as important as completing specific tasks (Galton & Williamson 1992).

 Have you observed classrooms where small groups were used? How well did the students work on their allotted tasks? Did you notice any special techniques the teacher used to ensure the small groups worked satisfactorily?

8.11 | COOPERATIVE LEARNING

Cooperative learning is a form of small group instruction that has become especially popular with teachers and students. It is advocated as a complement to direct instruction and to teaching – these approaches often create a highly competitive environment. Research evidence indicates that students gain considerably from cooperative learning across all grade levels of schooling (Ellis & Fouts 1997).

A number of different approaches to cooperative learning have been developed, but most share the characteristics listed in Figure 8.5. Cooperative learning is a technique whereby a group is given a task to do that requires efforts from all students. Students need to interact with and support each other in completing the overall task and the sub-tasks.

FIGURE 8.5 Characteristics of cooperative learning classrooms

- Most classroom activities involve using small groups of 3–5 students.
- Each group is as heterogeneous as possible in terms of gender, ethnicity, and knowledge and ability.
- The teacher and students set clear, specific, individual and group goals.
- Each student has to achieve certain individual goals as well as being accountable for group success.
- The teacher provides worthwhile group rewards on the basis of group members' individual achievements.
- Each group divides up group work into individual tasks.
- Each group member soon learns that interdependence is needed for the group to function effectively – this involves a considerable amount of face-to-face interaction.
- Each group member learns effective listening and communicating skills as well as group-processing skills.
- Each group evaluates its levels of success.

8.11.1 Theoretical origins

Cooperative learning has an interesting pedigree in terms of contributions from educational theorists.

John Dewey's pedagogy required teachers to use democratic procedures in their classrooms. The students were encouraged to inquire about issues that involved social and interpersonal problems. Arends (2009, p. 316) concludes that 'The specific procedures described by Dewey (and his latter-day followers) emphasised small, problem-solving groups of students searching for their own answers and learning democratic principles through day-to-day interaction with one another.'

So it might be argued that Dewey in his writing (such as *Democracy and Education* 1916) was an early advocate of a form of cooperative learning. Herbert Thelen was another early advocate who theorised about group dynamics. He worked closely with Ralph Tyler on the Eight Year Study (Aiken 1942).

Thelen conceived of the classroom as a social laboratory. In his book *Education and the Human Quest* (1960) he advocated four models that teachers might use. They were:
- personal inquiry – a quest for selfhood or integration
- group investigation – students building up rules and agreements with others
- reflection action – transacting businesses with the environment
- skill development – facilitates all other kinds of inquiry.

Thus Thelen, writing in the 1960s, provided more structures on the pedagogy of group investigation. These developments also facilitated the growth of cooperative learning several decades later.

Arends (2009) contends that another important event in the US was the Supreme Court ruling in 1954 that public schools must become racially integrated. Arends claims that much of the recent interest in cooperative learning grew out of attempts by educators to structure classrooms so that students gained more positive regard for other students, especially minority groups. He cites Slavin's (1978) work in inner city schools on the eastern seaboard as a valuable contribution to a better understanding of integration in schools.

> **YOUR TURN**
> - Search out more information on the intellectual roots of cooperative learning. For example, read some of Dewey's accounts in Marsh and Willis (2007).
> - Some educators argue that cooperative learning should be part of every beginning teacher's repertoire. Why would educators take this stance? Do you agree?

Johnson and Johnson (2009) claim that cooperative learning has been so successful because it is closely linked to social interdependence theory. They claim that positive interdependence enables individuals to achieve higher than when they work individually.

Johnson and Johnson (2009) contend that cooperative learning has progressed to become one of the dominant instructional practices throughout the world.

8.11.2 Planning and conducting cooperative learning lessons

According to Cruickshank, Jenkins and Metcalf (2009) cooperative learning occurs when learners work together in small groups and are rewarded for their collective accomplishments (see Figure 8.6).

Groups or teams of 4 to 6 work on particular tasks. The members of the group are selected so that they are heterogeneous in terms of gender, academic ability, race and other traits. The rules of behaviour for participants involve responsibility and accountability to oneself and the team, and a willingness to encourage peer help and cooperate with other team members. The rewards or marks are based on the team's achievement.

A number of different cooperative learning models have been developed and used in school settings, including *Student-Teams Learning* (Slavin 1978) and *Jigsaw* (Aronson *et al.* 1978).

FIGURE 8.6 Benefits of cooperative learning

- Improves learning of academic content.
- Improves student strategies for acquiring information.
- Develops social skills.
- Boosts students' self-esteem.
- Allows student decision making.

8.11.3 Student-teams learning approach

The *Student-teams learning* approach involves the following:
- The teacher divides the class into 4 or 5 member teams.
- Each team is heterogeneous in ability levels; new content is introduced by traditional large-group instruction.
- Each team is then given worksheets describing tasks to be done and problems to be solved.
- Team members tutor each other and interact to ensure that all have completed their tasks.
- When all tasks have been completed, the team members take individual tests.

The scores of the individual team members are combined to yield a team score.

8.11.4 Jigsaw method

The *Jigsaw* method involves the following:
- The teacher divides the class into teams of 5 or 6 students, ensuring that there is a mix of abilities in each team.

- The assigned team activity has sub-tasks so that there is one task (labelled A, B, etc.) for each team member.
- The persons assigned to do task A in each team come together and form a new team. New teams are also formed for B, etc.
- The newly formed teams (A team, B team, etc.) work on completing their tasks by discussing issues and then working individually or collectively.
- When the tasks have been completed, the students reassemble in their original teams. Each team member shares their information and this is compiled into the overall assignment which is then submitted to the teacher.

Once a teacher has selected a particular approach it is then necessary to undertake the following planning steps:
1. Develop materials – this may involve a mini-lecture to be given by the teacher for the preparation of text, worksheets and study guides for each group to use directly.
2. Plan the tasks and roles for students in each group – students need to have a clear understanding of their roles; it may take several sessions before students are familiar with what to do.
3. Plan for the use of time and space – don't underestimate the time needed for cooperative learning lessons.

Once the planning sequence has been completed the actual lessons include the following steps:
- Teacher goes over goals for the lesson.
- Teacher presents information to students either verbally or with text.
- Teacher explains to students how to form their learning teams.
- Teacher assists learning teams as they do their work.
- Teacher tests knowledge of learning materials or groups present results of their work.
- Teacher finds ways to recognise both individual and group effort and achievement (Arends 2009).

YOUR TURN

- To what extent is the selection of appropriate study materials crucial to the success of cooperative learning lessons?
- Teachers should not assume that all their students possess the social skills needed to work effectively in small groups. What can the teacher do to assist students with limited social skills?

Not all lessons are conducive to cooperative learning. Ideally, topics are used that require the searching out of answers and exploring of alternative solutions. The teacher also has to make organisational decisions that may only be possible in certain circumstances – for example, rearranging the room furniture and organising materials. There can also be difficulties in assigning students to groups; the intent is to form truly heterogeneous groups, but personality conflicts still occur (Chan 2004). Students may need considerable help in developing problem-solving skills (Barry et al. 1998) (see Table 8.1).

To overcome some of these difficulties, especially with lower grades, it may be necessary for the teacher to assign roles. Chapin and Messick (1999) suggest the following:
- One student as chairperson to organise the group's work.
- One student as recorder or secretary to write down the group's answers.
- One student as the check person to check that everyone can explain and agree with completed answers.
- One student as encourager to keep participants interested and excited.

TABLE 8.1 Some problems encountered using cooperative learning techniques with small groups

Problems	Possible solutions
(a) No-one says anything	• Wait the silence out. • Ask what the silence means. • Go around the table asking for comments. • Break the group up into smaller ones.
(b) Uneven participation	• Reiterate procedures whereby all have opportunities to speak. • Assign new roles for low-status students.
(c) Victimisation of a student	• Reiterate procedures of group work. • Teacher intervenes in a non-threatening way.
(d) Discussion becomes biased	• Teacher provides additional resource information. • Teacher intervenes with additional perspective.

8.11.5 Research evidence

The research evidence on cooperative learning is extremely positive and includes literally hundreds of published studies (see, for example, Ellis & Fouts 1997; Menges & Weimer 1996; Emmer & Gerwells 1998; Orlich et al. 2009). Some of the major findings include:
- Achievement effects of cooperative learning are consistently positive – that is, experimental groups have significant positive results compared to control groups.
- Positive achievement effects occur across all grade levels from 2 to 12, in all major subjects, and the effects are equally positive for high, average and low achievers.

 Cooperative learning is rated very highly in the literature as a successful way of grouping and teaching students? What are your reactions to it? Will you try it in the near future? What are some safeguards that you will try to use?

CONCLUDING COMMENTS

It is unlikely that a class of students will be receptive to a steady diet of individualised instruction or small group work or whole-class instruction. The key to success is knowing when to use a particular organisational pattern and why. A typical day in a primary classroom might consist of whole-class activities followed by small group work with some opportunities for individualised instruction. At the secondary school level there are likely to be more whole-class activities with occasional group activities.

Traditional classroom structures may become less dominant in the future. It is quite possible that students will spend an increasing proportion of their time working on individual computer projects and interacting with their peers and teachers by electronic means, such as email, rather than face-to-face. Furthermore, their computer-based learning activities may occur at home or in other community settings, rather than in formal school settings.

KEY ISSUES RAISED IN THIS CHAPTER

1 Different levels of schooling have varying successes, and in some cases, failures. It is generally recognised that primary schools are successful but that there are serious problems with many secondary schools. Middle schooling appears to be a promising development in some cases.
2 The use of technology is requiring new organisational structures and different forms of pedagogy.
3 Open education techniques are based on a sound educational philosophy but there can be practical problems in practicing them.
4 Whole-class teaching techniques are still widely practiced and they do have value. However more student-centred approaches are being tried out by teachers.
5 Cooperative learning has been widely reviewed in many countries. The evidence indicates that this is a highly successful small group technique.

REFLECTIONS AND ISSUES

1 With reference to a school you have visited recently, briefly describe the following:
   (a) Who is responsible for what?
   (b) How are decisions made and who is involved?
   (c) How do the staff communicate with each other?
2 In schools that you have visited, what are the overt and covert expectations about how classes will be organised?
3 In what circumstances should teachers attempt to use friendships among students as a basis for organising groups?
4 Good teacher teamwork brings together people with different skills and experience, enhancing communication and learning for its members and for the school. Reflect on examples you have seen of good teacher teamwork. What were the critical elements?
5 What guidelines or support do you need to give small groups so they can work largely unsupervised? Provide a list of these guidelines.
6 What are some time problems in using group activities and how can they be overcome?
7 Do you think the skills for cooperative group work can be taught to all students? Give examples.
8 What different strategies would you use in large group teaching compared with small group teaching? Discuss some of the advantages and disadvantages of each.
9 To what extent should learners be grouped according to their similarities and differences? For example, what might be the advantages and disadvantages of grouping learners according to their cultural background, gender, learning style or learning ability?
10 'If we want students to be able to function in a cooperative society – indeed a cooperative world – when they reach adulthood, we need to teach them the skills they will need to do so' (George, Lawrence & Bushnell 1998, p. 73). Do you agree? Explain what these skills are and how they can be developed.
11 Do you consider that middle schools have the potential to intellectually engage and inspire young adolescents (Beane & Lipka 2006)?
12 Some educators such as Banks (2004) argue that middle schools should provide young adolescents with opportunities to participate in service learning and to learn values, citizenship and social skills. Do you agree? Consider how this might be organised.
13 Which of the present ways of organising classroom structures and practices do you consider will be short-lived and which will be enduring? Give reasons for your answer.

Special references

Cruickshank, D, Jenkins, D & Metcalf, K (2009) *The Act of Teaching*, 5th edn, McGraw Hill, Boston.
Danielson, C (2002) *Enhancing Student Achievement*, ASCD, Alexandria, Virginia.
Department of Education and Training (2006b) *Small Steps, Giant Leaps Forward*, Department of Education and Training, Perth.
Johnson, DW, Johnson, RT & Holubec, EJ (1994) *The New Circles of Learning: Co-operation in the Classroom and School*, ASCD, Alexandria, Virginia.
Marsh, CJ & Willis, G (2007) *Curriculum: Alternative Approaches, Ongoing Issues,* 4th edn, Prentice Hall, Columbus, Ohio.
Oliva, PF (2008) *Developing the Curriculum*, 6th edn, Longman, New York.
Tomlinson, CA (1999) *The Differentiated Classroom*, ASCD, Alexandria, Virginia.

Web sources

For additional resources on organising classroom structures and routines, please go to: www.pearson.com.au/myeducationlab.

9

PLANNING TO ACHIEVE GOALS, AIMS, OBJECTIVES, OUTCOMES AND STANDARDS

9.1 | INTRODUCTION

Learning within a school environment is typically goal-directed. Students are at school because they want to learn certain things, attain specific standards, and perhaps satisfy the requirements for a particular diploma or award. The majority of students are not there, as described mischievously by Postman and Weingartner (1987), to serve out a sentence! Teachers, too, are not serving 'time' in schools but are wanting their students to achieve particular goals or ends.

9.2 | THE IMPORTANCE OF GOALS AND AIMS

Goals and aims are extremely broad statements that are used to describe the purposes of schooling or the purpose of a particular program. Most writers in education agree that the terms 'goals' and 'aims' can be used interchangeably (Moore 2009; Cruickshank, Jenkins & Metcalf 2009). However, others such as Ornstein and Hunkins, (2003) contend that 'aims' are starting points that suggest an ideal vision whereas 'goals' are statements of purpose.

 Do you consider that educational aims are expecting schools to do too much? Are schools the ideal agencies to solve the nation's problems?

Goals refer to the desired outcomes for students as a result of experiencing a particular curriculum, but they don't address how teachers would instruct students to attain these goals. Examples might include:
- The student will become a knowledgeable citizen.
- Each student will understand and practice democratic ideas and ideals.

According to Ornstein and Hunkins (2003) goals should have a degree of timeliness about them. That is they should address particular times but the wording should also be appropriate for future times.

Common and Agreed National Goals for Schooling were approved by the Australian Education Council in 1989. At the time this was considered a remarkable achievement because up until then state and territory education systems had developed their own educational goals. These goals were significant because they formed the basis for the National Statements and Profiles produced during the period 1989–93, even though this attempt at a national curriculum failed.

How useful are these goals for guiding teaching in Australian schools? Some would argue they are too conservative and academic. What do you think?

The 1989 goals were revisited ten years later and the Adelaide Declaration in 1999 produced some revised National Goals of Schooling (MCEETYA 1999).

Ten years later in 2008 the Melbourne Declaration produced yet another set of National Goals of Schooling. Ministers were mindful that there had been some major changes in the intervening period that had implications for education, especially:

- global integration and international mobility had increased rapidly
- there was a need to become 'Asia literate' by building strong relationships with Asia
- globalisation and technological change were placing great demands on education and skill development
- complex environmental, social and economic pressures such as climate change posed unprecedented challenges
- rapid and continuous advances in information and communication technologies (ICT) were changing the ways people share, use, develop and process information and technology (MCEETYA 2008).

It was opportune for the National Curriculum Board, created in 2008 (now widened to become the Australian Curriculum Assessment and Reporting Authority) to be able to base their program on the national goals agreed upon in Melbourne in 2008 (see Figure 9.1).

 How relevant are the national goals produced in 2008? Do they cover important areas of teaching for you? What is missing?

In 2008 the National Curriculum Board produced various policy documents. One of these, *The Shape of the National Curriculum* (NCB 2008b), stated the major outcomes for the Board (see Figure 9.2), which were derived in turn from the National Goals (MCEETYA 2008).

It is interesting to note that the term 'aims' is used by the NCB for each of its papers produced to guide the writing of the national curriculum in English, Mathematics, Science and History. For example, *The Shape of the Australian Curriculum: Mathematics* (NCB 2009) contains the following three aims:

- 'to educate students to be active, thinking citizens, interpreting the world mathematically and using mathematics to help form their predictions and decisions about personal and financial priorities'
- to be able to critically examine substantial social and scientific issues 'by using and interpreting mathematical perspectives'
- to enable students to 'appreciate the elegance and power of mathematical thinking' (NCB 2009a, p. 5).

These are interesting aims (goals) and hint at the ideal visions and the take-off point for the intended national curriculum in Mathematics.

9.3 | THE IMPORTANCE OF OBJECTIVES

Objectives provide an answer to what it is that students want to learn and what it is that teachers are trying to teach them. Objectives greatly assist the planning process for teachers. In Chapter 7, reference was made to planning associated with developing programs and lesson plans. The foundation for these planners is unquestionably clearly stated objectives.

Some teachers resist using objectives because they consider they are too limiting or inappropriate for certain content that cannot be specifically defined or evaluated. Yet measurement experts, such as Mager (1984, p. 5), point out that:

FIGURE 9.1 National Declaration on Educational Goals for Young Australians

Successful learners . . .
- develop their capacity to learn and play an active role in their own learning
- have the essential skills in literacy and numeracy and are creative and productive users of technology, especially ICT, as a foundation for success in all learning areas
- are able to think deeply and logically, and obtain and evaluate evidence in a disciplined way as the result of studying fundamental disciplines
- are creative, innovative and resourceful, and are able to solve problems in ways that draw upon a range of learning areas and disciplines
- are able to plan activities independently, collaborate, work in teams and communicate ideas
- are able to make sense of their world and think about how things have become the way they are
- are on a pathway towards continued success in further education, training or employment, and acquire the skills to make informed learning and employment decisions throughout their lives
- are motivated to reach their full potential.

Confident individuals . . .
- have a sense of self-worth, self-awareness and personal identity that enables them to manage their emotional, mental, spiritual and physical wellbeing
- have a sense of optimism about their lives and the future – are enterprising, show initiative and use their creative abilities
- develop personal values and attributes such as honesty, resilience, empathy and respect for others
- have the knowledge, skills, understanding and values to establish and maintain healthy, satisfying lives
- have the confidence and capability to pursue university or post-secondary vocational qualifications leading to rewarding and productive employment
- relate well to others and form and maintain healthy relationships
- are well prepared for their potential life roles as family, community and workforce members
- embrace opportunities, make rational and informed decisions about their own lives and accept responsibility for their own actions.

Active and informed citizens . . .
- act with moral and ethical integrity
- appreciate Australia's social, cultural, linguistic and religious diversity, and have an understanding of Australia's system of government, history and culture
- understand and acknowledge the value of Indigenous cultures and possess the knowledge, skills and understanding to contribute to, and benefit from, reconciliation between Indigenous and non-Indigenous Australians
- are committed to national values of democracy, equity and justice, and participate in Australia's civic life
- are able to relate to and communicate across cultures, especially the cultures and countries of Asia
- work for the common good, in particular sustaining and improving natural and social environments
- are responsible global and local citizens.

Source: Ministerial Council for Education, Employment, Training and Youth Affairs, *Melbourne Declaration on Educational Goals for Young Australians, December 2008, pp. 8–9. Full declaration available at www.mceecdya.edu.au.*

FIGURE 9.2 Intended educational outcomes from the Formal Curriculum for Young Australians

A solid foundation in knowledge, understanding, skills and values on which further learning and adult life can be built:

The curriculum will include a strong focus on literacy and numeracy skills. It will also enable students to build social and emotional intelligence, and nurture student wellbeing through health and physical education in particular. The curriculum will support students to relate well to others and foster an understanding of Australian society, citizenship and national values, including through the study of civics and citizenship. As a foundation for further learning and adult life the curriculum will include practical knowledge and skills development in areas such as ICT and design and technology, which are central to Australia's skilled economy and provide crucial pathways to post-school success.

Deep knowledge, understanding, skills and values that will enable advanced learning and an ability to create new ideas and translate them into practical applications:

The curriculum will enable students to develop knowledge in the disciplines of English, Mathematics, Science, Languages, Humanities and the Arts; to understand the spiritual, moral and aesthetic dimensions of life; and open up new ways of thinking. It will also support the development of deep knowledge within a discipline, which provides the foundation for interdisciplinary approaches to innovation and complex problem-solving.

General capabilities that underpin flexible and analytical thinking, a capacity to work with others and an ability to move across subject disciplines to develop new expertise:

The curriculum will support young people to develop a range of generic and employability skills that have particular application to the world of work and further education and training, such as planning and organising, the ability to think flexibly, to communicate well and to work in teams. Young people also need to develop the capacity to think creatively, innovate, solve problems and engage with new disciplines.

Source: Ministerial Council for Education, Employment, Training and Youth Affairs, Melbourne Declaration on Educational Goals for Young Australians, December 2008, p. 13. Full declaration available at www.mceecdya.edu.au.

> If you are teaching things that cannot be evaluated, you are in the awkward position of being unable to demonstrate that you are teaching anything at all. Intangibles are often intangible because we have been too lazy to think about what it is we want students to be able to do.

In terms of the teaching role, objectives provide the opportunity for teachers to formulate, and hopefully act on, clear statements about what students are intended to learn through instruction.

We are probably all aware of anecdotes that refer to the guessing games that can occur between a teacher and students. For example, 'What does our teacher want us to learn? Is it to memorise or regurgitate certain content, or is it to apply and explain it?' Objectives, if conveyed to students, can eradicate a lot of these misunderstandings and can lead to a higher level of communication between the teacher and students.

Objectives are also likely to lead to higher levels of achievement by students, but only under certain conditions. For example, objectives can lead to better learning in lessons that are loosely structured, such as research projects or a film. However, for lessons that involve very structured materials, such as a tightly sequenced laboratory experiment or a computer program, objectives seem to be less important (Tobias & Duchastel 1974).

Objectives assist teachers and students to focus on what will be evaluated. There should be a close relationship between the assignments, tests and checklists used by the teacher and the objectives for the particular teaching unit or lessons. The feedback received by students from particular assessments lets them know whether they are achieving the standards required.

9.4 | THE IMPORTANCE OF OUTCOMES

Since the late 1980s a number of state and territory school systems undertook trials with outcome statements with varying degrees of success. Subsequently most states and territories have changed their nomenclature from 'outcomes' to 'standards' and 'essential learnings' (see section 9.5 The importance of standards).

Willis and Kissane (1997) define outcome statements as 'broad descriptions of student competencies which reflect long term learning of significance beyond school, and which are superordinate to the details of any particular curriculum content, sequence or pedagogy' (p. 21).

Outcome statements concentrate on the outputs rather than the inputs of teaching. Exponents of this approach argue that objectives only concentrate on the inputs of teaching.

To a certain extent, the approach represents a recycling of earlier movements, especially in the United States, such as mastery learning and competency-based education. Yet it does not incorporate specific behavioural statements. Rather, the emphasis is on broad outcome statements to be achieved, 8 to 12 statements per learning area (which typically comprises several teaching subjects).

A very successful and leading exponent of outcomes-based education in the US has been William Spady. According to Spady (1993), outcomes-based education (OBE) means focusing and organising a school's entire program and instructional efforts around the clearly defined outcomes we want all students to demonstrate when they leave school (p. ii). That is, the intended learning results are the start-up points in defining the system (Hansen 1989). A set of conditions are described that characterise real life and these are used to derive a set of culminatory role performances. Students are required to provide a culminating demonstration – the focus is on competence as well as content, but not on the time needed to reach this standard (students can cover a common set of requirements in varying periods of time, McGhan 2005).

Specifically, an outcome is an actual demonstration in an authentic context.

Moore (2009) notes that in the US there have been many versions of outcomes-based education (OBE), but all of them promote system-level change – 'observable, measurable outcomes; and the belief that all students can learn' (p. 98). This may have been their major attraction and the cause for their demise. They promised far-reaching reform but could not deliver.

Some states within the US were enthusiastic about OBE at first, such as the Pennsylvania Department of Education, which recommended it be used throughout the state (Glatthorn & Jailall 2000). However, by the mid-1990s OBE was being widely criticised in terms of:
- its overemphasis on outcomes rather than processes
- schools inculcating values that conflicted with parental values
- no hard evidence that OBE worked
- fears that OBE would 'dumb down' the curriculum and lead to lower standards
- concerns that content becomes subservient under an OBE approach
- student outcome statements being difficult and expensive to assess.

 Do you consider that outcomes-based education (OBE) creates too heavy a workload for teachers in terms of having to continually monitor each student's work to determine what skills and tasks each student has mastered?

As a result, OBE in the US rapidly declined in the 1990s, to be overtaken by standards-based (content standards) and constructivist approaches (Glatthorn & Jailall 2000; Berlach & McNaught 2007).

The genesis of outcomes statements and OBE in Australia is intriguing. The Quality of Education Review Committee Report (1985) gave a national impetus to accountability and outcomes. This

committee recommended a shift from educational inputs to educational outcomes (Woods 2007). In some states, such as South Australia and Victoria, the initiative appears to have been motivated by at least two major factors:
1 a concern for greater accountability and control over teaching
2 a desire for a viable alternative to initiatives by some pressure groups to introduce state or nation-wide achievement testing.

The outcomes-based approach became a nationwide philosophy under the direction of the Australian Education Council and its Curriculum and Assessment Committee (CURASS) during the period 1991–93. All states and territories worked collaboratively on the development of national statements and profiles for eight learning areas that encompassed all school subjects. Outcome statements were developed for each learning area and relegated to one of eight levels spanning the school-age continuum K–12. Each national statement included a listing of the outcome statements and sub-categories, termed strands, based on 'conceptual' or 'process' emphases to be achieved at levels 1–8 and bands A–D (junior primary, upper primary, lower secondary and post compulsory).

> **YOUR TURN**
>
> Select an outcome statement and think about how you would develop it for use in one or more lessons.
> - Discuss your ideas with a colleague to see how they interpret the outcome statement.
> - If their ideas are very different, how does this affect what you will teach?

Although the documents were completed in 1993, states and territories decided against using this national curriculum and instead generated their own variations. Despite variations in titles such as 'frameworks' in the Australian Capital Territory and 'levels of student performance' in Queensland, there was a common outcomes-based approach operating in most states and territories.

The profiles provide specific guidance to teachers about how they might assess students. This was done by producing a total package for each learning area that consists of:
- a number of strands or concepts based on knowledge/process skills, which are categorised into progressive levels of difficulty across eight levels
- the inclusion of one or more outcome statements for each strand at each of the eight levels
- the use of pointers and more specific, concrete examples of a strand, to help the teacher appreciate the meaning of an outcome statement and to make judgments about the achievement of an outcome
- the inclusion of students' work samples to provide further illustrative examples of the standard for each level.

To illustrate the use of outcome statements as developed by CURASS, consider the example in Figure 9.3 selected from the learning area Studies of Society and Environment, Curriculum and Standards Framework, Victoria (Board of Studies, Victoria 1995).

FIGURE 9.3 An example of an outcome statement

Outcome statement: Time, continuity and change

'Portray an event or occasion from a particular perspective.'

TABLE 9.1 Recommended steps in planning to teach an outcome statement

Key questions	Steps
1 Understanding the outcome	Clarify what the outcome means to you
2 Consider how this outcome is linked to other outcomes or key learning areas (KLAs)	What other outcomes or KLAs are linked to this outcome? In what ways? Are there opportunities for integrated learning?
3 Break down the outcome	Consider some major concepts, skills or values What big ideas underpin it?
4 What ideas in the outcome are likely to be new for students?	What did the students cover last term, last semester?
5 Consider the extent to which students are already achieving this outcome	Check on students' current understandings, skills
6 Investigate why students are not achieving this outcome or aspects of it	What diagnostic information on the students is available?
7 Consider whether a different sequence of learning is needed for this outcome	Will different student activities be needed? Why?
8 Investigate any changes needed to assessment strategies	How will the new student activities necessitate changes to the form and/or frequency of assessments?
9 Modify or change any planned learning experiences	Are there any other changes that will be needed? Why?
10 Evaluate students' achievement using the outcome	How successful were the students in coping with this outcome statement? What evidence did you compile about student activities?
11 Continue the cycle of reflection	What were successful and unsuccessful features of teaching this outcome statement? What changes will you make next time?

Curriculum officers in various states have provided resources to help teachers get started with outcomes. As noted by Hargreaves and Moore (1999), teachers feel 'overwhelmed by the prospect of mastering the number and complexity of outcomes' (p. 4) and largely this is due to the statements in the policy documents being relatively cumbersome and opaque.

Teachers do need considerable help in unravelling outcome statements and deciding how they might plan their teaching. As an example, the 'getting started' series produced for teachers by the Curriculum Council in Western Australia provides some specific guidance (see Table 9.1). It is evident from these steps that teachers need to do a lot of reflecting before they start organising their lessons.

Given the considerable lack of support for OBE in the US since the mid-1990s it is interesting to reflect on the apparent continuance of outcomes in Australia. Furthermore, there has been little public consultation or research into its potential use in schools in Australia. Perhaps Blyth (2002) is accurate when he states that curriculum planning in Australia has been mainly 'outcome-setting' – what has occurred in practice beyond outcome-setting is varied and unclear.

There have certainly been concerns from various quarters about implementation of outcomes (Berlach & McNaught 2007; Andrich 2006). The then CEO of the Curriculum Corporation, Bruce Wilson (2002), declared 'let's get beyond outcomes fetishism. The present form of outcomes has probably outlived its usefulness. Indeed it is difficult to find a jurisdiction outside Australasia which has persevered with the peculiar approach to outcomes which we have adopted' (p. 8).

Griffin (1998) concluded from his evaluation of Australian schools' implementation of OBE that 'perhaps OBE cannot be fully implemented system wide. The changes needed are too radical and disruptive for whole systems of education to accommodate' (p. 19).

Pointers

There are a number of pointers which are supplied to assist the teacher in selecting content and learning experiences for this outcome statement. Evident when, for example, the student:

- empathises with people in the past through role play (class drama, letters from the Gallipoli Peninsula)
- discusses different ways of presenting stories of the past, including oral history (interview or tape), visual history (magazines, films), and written history
- writes a television news item describing the events at the opening of Federal Parliament in 1901.

Work samples

Work samples are supplied to assist teachers in pinpointing the standard required. For example, a work sample could be provided about how students researched information about life in Sydney Town in the first few years of settlement and then used this data to compose an imaginary letter written by a female convict, Mary Ann Allen.

It is argued that the philosophy of OBE has not been comprehensively thought through (Towers 1992) and that the assessment protocols are excessively time-consuming and insufficiently competitive, resulting in a dumbing-down of standards (Berlach 2004). Explain these statements. Do you agree?

O'Neil (1994) referring to OBE in the US noted that it could not be used for high stakes examinations until outcomes were more clearly defined or until performance-based assessments improved their technical qualities. It was this aspect that has created considerable public scrutiny and debate in some states, especially in Western Australia and Tasmania. In Western Australia a major media campaign was waged against the proposed introduction of OBE in Years 11 and 12. This led in turn to a parliamentary review and some considerable modifications by the Premier. In Tasmania there were also heated media reports about Essential Learnings.

Donnelly (2002, 2007) is very critical of outcomes-based developments in Australia and concludes that many Australian senior officials are now admitting that 'outcomes-based education has failed and that it is time to adopt a standards approach for student learning' (p. 10).

Table 9.2, based on Donnelly (2002), depicts purported differences between syllabuses, outcomes and standards approaches.

9.5 | THE IMPORTANCE OF STANDARDS

The raising of educational standards is a constant cry in educational reform. In the US there was a major impetus in the 1990s to create 'unified national standards that would ensure consistent delivery and outcomes across diverse state systems and districts via the *Educate America Act* 1994' (Blyth 2002, p. 7).

Do you agree that standards developed by external experts are limited because they don't consider the needs of teachers at the school level?

Knowledge experts in the various subject fields have produced standards for their respective subjects (see Table 9.3). These standards have been taken up by individual states in the US and incorporated into state curriculum frameworks and mastery tests. According to Arends (2009) 'state frameworks have an important influence on what is taught in schools because mastery tests are usually built around the performance standards identified in the frameworks' (p. 54).

TABLE 9.2 Differences in curriculum approaches between syllabus, outcomes and standards statements

Syllabus	Outcomes	Standards
Focus on what students should be taught/expected to learn	Focus on what students should achieve or be able to do	Identify what students should know and be able to do
Based on established disciplines/categories of knowledge	Mixture of established disciplines and a multidisciplinary approach	Based on established disciplines/categories of knowledge
Relate to specific grades/year levels	Address levels that incorporate a number of grades/year levels	Focus generally on specific grades/year levels
Expectation that essential knowledge, understanding and skills are mastered at key stages (high stakes tests and streaming)	Developmental, constructivist approach to learning	Expectation that essential knowledge, understanding and skills are mastered at key stages (some states expect students to repeat a year if standards not met)
Greater emphasis on teacher-directed, whole-class teaching	An individualistic, child-centred approach to teaching and learning	Greater emphasis on teacher-directed, whole-class teaching
Common curriculum, or within distinct and separate curricular pathways, based on a core plus electives where a pathways approach is employed	Common curriculum	Core/elective curriculum
Discrete areas of study and topics	Particular topics (such as literature or geometry) often dispersed across strands	Discrete topics
Mandated number of hours	Number of hours not stipulated	Number of hours not stipulated

Source: Dr Kevin Donnelly, Director Education Strategies Institute. A Review of New Zealand's School Curriculum, 2002, p. 7, Education Strategies, Melbourne, <www.edstandards.com.au>

TABLE 9.3 Examples of subject matter Curriculum Standards (USA)

English	Standards for the Assessment of Reading and Writing
Foreign Languages	Standards for Foreign Language Learning
History	US History Standards
Mathematics	Curriculum and Evaluation Standards for Social Mathematics
Science	National Science Education Standards

See also <project2061.aaas.org>; <putwest.boces.org/standards.html>.

A distinction needs to be made between content and performance standards. Content standards declare knowledge to be acquired, whether it is process or content knowledge. Performance standards are tasks to be completed by a student where the knowledge is embedded in the task and where a student has to use the knowledge and skills in a certain way.

Marzano, Marzano and Pickering (2003) contend that both content and performance standards need to be used. Further, they suggest that the content standards are articulated at a general level but with specific sub-components at developmental levels or 'benchmarks'. As noted by Blyth (2002) 'benchmarks are essential in describing the developmental components of the general domain identified by a standard' (p. 35).

In the US, apart from the use of detailed content standards in specific subjects, the *No Child Left Behind Act* (NCLB) of 2001 is a set of academic standards in reading and mathematics to be achieved by all students regardless of race or minority status by the 2013–14 academic year. Schools have the responsibility of reaching annual targets, as determined by each state. There are sanctions if schools do not attain these targets (Kim & Sunderman 2005). Although many educators support the concept of reducing achievement disparities in reading and mathematics, it does raise many issues, such as:

- Are the standardised tests a reliable and valid means of measuring achievement in reading and mathematics?
- Which indicators should be used?
- Should standards be written generally or specifically?
- Does NCLB force teachers to concentrate on these tests and ignore other subjects?
- Are free tutoring opportunities a desirable method for schools falling behind in their targets? (Hamilton & Stecher 2004; Platt 2005; ASCD 2004, 7 September; ASCD 2006, 14 February; Placier, Walker & Foster 2002)

Yet, standards seem to be welcomed by many teachers and citizens. Various writers extol the virtues of the new standards – they are a better way to develop conceptual understanding and reasoning (Goldsmith & Mark 1999). Rosenholtz (1991) asserts that standards provide a common focus, clarify understanding, accelerate communication and promote persistence and collective purpose.

However, other educators are more cautious. Schmoker and Marzano (1999) raise the question, will the standards movement endure? They contend that educators have to be very disciplined about writing clear standards and that the standards should be limited in number. Moore (2009) notes that the standards must be carefully linked to assessment. Glatthorn and Jailall (2000) assert that many of the standards are too vague about content.

Top-down school reform by the use of state or national standards is arrogant and unwarranted. The failure to bring teachers into the reform effort decreases the likelihood that standards reform will be effective (Nelson *et al.* 2004). What do you think about this statement?

In Australia, all states and territories have established standards or 'essential learnings' from Year 1 to Year 10. These standards define what students should know and be able to do at different stages of learning. Although the terms vary, it is evident that similar structures have now been developed in all states and territories (see Table 9.4).

With the creation of the Australian Curriculum Assessment and Reporting Authority (ACARA) in May 2009 it is clear that standards will be a major focus in the development of assessments in Mathematics, English, Science and History. However it is too early yet to be certain about which form these will take.

A possible indication is that in the *The Shape of the Australian Curriculum* documents for each of the four subjects, the term 'strand' is used to describe major content concepts and proficiency concepts. Strands were the major concept used in the national profiles developed for the eight learning areas in 1991–93. So it is possible that strands will be the focus point again and content and proficiency standards will be developed for each.

For example, in Mathematics the listed strands are as follows:

Content strands	*Proficiency strands*
Number and algebra	Understanding
Measurement and geometry	Fluency
Statistics and probability	Problem-solving
	Reasoning

TABLE 9.4 Structures for standards in Australian states and territories

South Australia	
South Australian Curriculum, Standards and Accountability	Essential learnings for each area. Standards defined for Years 2, 4, 6, 8 and 10.
Victoria	
Victorian Essential Learning Standards	Standards by Domain, includes Physical, Personal and Social Learning; Discipline-based learning; Interdisciplinary learning
Tasmania	
Essential Learnings Framework	Five essential learnings with outcomes and standards for each but not tied to age or grade.
New South Wales	
Syllabuses developed by the Board of Studies for its NSW Curriculum Framework	Board of Studies has developed statements for each syllabus
Northern Territory	
Northern Territory Curriculum Framework	Four domains and identified learning outcomes
ACT	
ACT Curriculum Framework	Essential learning statements with four bands of development
Queensland	
Queensland Curriculum Assessment and Reporting Framework	Essential learning outcomes linked to syllabuses
Western Australia	
Outcomes and Standards	Learning areas have sets of outcomes; grades are allocated by teachers based on levels set out in Outcomes and Standards Framework

How confident are you that if strands are used as national standards for assessment by ACARA, that they will be accepted fully and implemented effectively by teachers? Will it create similar problems to what occurred with the use of national profiles in the 1990s?

9.6 | REFLECTING ON THE RELATIVE MERITS OF OBJECTIVES AND OUTCOMES

In the 1970s, various educators criticised what they perceived to be undue attention being devoted to objectives in teaching, and especially behavioural objectives. For example, Eisner (1979) developed the term *expressive objective* and later *expressive outcome* to demonstrate that not all teaching requires the same degree of certainty.

Eisner (1979) noted that expressive outcomes are the consequences of curriculum activities that are intentionally planned to provide a fertile field for personal purposing and experience.

It is evident that outcome statements have some advantages for teachers in planning their teaching but also a number of disadvantages, as indicated by the fact that all states and territories have moved towards a standards paradigm.

Some possible advantages of outcomes include:
- They allow teachers more flexibility in planning their teaching.

- There is less emphasis on content to be covered and more emphasis on skills or competencies to be achieved.
- They can address higher order thinking skills.
- They acknowledge differing learning styles and forms of intelligence.

Educators in state and territory education systems had some major problems with outcomes such as:

- enormous workloads for teachers (especially for primary school teachers) to assess students on outcome statements even when using special computer software (Berlach & McNaught 2007)
- providing sufficient professional development training for teachers on the outcomes-based approach. Teachers needed substantial training to arrive at a shared commitment to the achievement of a common set of outcome statements (Griffin 1998)
- developing indicators that were meaningful and assessable. It cannot be assumed that all teachers will interpret them in the same way (Willis & Kissane 1997)
- developing an economical system to monitor whether the outcomes had been achieved or not (Brady 1996)
- obtaining evidence that an outcomes approach would lead to improved learning (Darling-Hammond 1994).

9.7 | A CLOSER LOOK AT SOME ADVANTAGES OF USING OBJECTIVES

It can be argued that objectives share many of the advantages listed for outcomes without incurring the disadvantages. For example, objectives enable teachers and students to focus on major concepts; they can be communicated easily to parents and students; and they enable assessment procedures to be directly related to the objectives. Furthermore, objectives do not have some of the inherent weaknesses of outcome statements in that there are no assumptions about developmental or growth levels or semi-arbitrary areas of knowledge to be divided into strands.

 Reconceptualist curriculum theorists such as Pinar (1999) and Giroux (1988) do not argue for the use of objectives at all. Instead they focus on a political and social critique of schooling. Read further about these theorists and other postmodernists and take a stance for or against their views.

9.8 | TYPES OF OBJECTIVES

Objectives can range from the general to the highly specific. It can be argued that the two extremes have relatively little impact on teachers. General abstract statements about such affairs as intellectual development or citizenship provide few insights for the teacher. On the other hand, objectives that are so tightly focused that they concentrate on low-level, insignificant facts or processes are also of very limited use to teachers.

9.8.1 Behavioural objectives

Behavioural objectives are perceived by some educators to be at a middle position between these two extremes. These objectives focus on observable and measurable changes in students. Typically, adherents of behavioural objectives require three criteria to be met, namely: evidence of achievement, conditions of performance and acceptable levels of performance.

Evidence of achievement

The performance by learners must be stated as an observable student behaviour. Hence it is suggested that teachers should use terms that are observable, such as:

- list
- define
- add
- calculate
- demonstrate.

Example: Students will *list* the states and territories of Australia.

Although this could lead to simplistic objectives being set by the teacher, this criterion does make the task of evaluation so much easier.

Conditions of performance

This criterion requires that the important conditions under which the behaviour is expected to occur must also be specified. The conditions might vary with the subject matter but could include such conditions as with or without class notes, in oral or written form, at home or in class, with or without certain tools.

Examples: Using a compass and a ruler, construct two tangents to a circle of 6 cm diameter from an external point 12 cm from the circle centre.

Given a box of eight crayons, students will select the three primary colours.

Acceptable levels of performance

It is also necessary to state the minimum acceptable level of performance or, in other words, the criterion for success. It defines the desired performance and may be expressed in terms of speed (amount of time taken), accuracy, or quality.

Examples: Students must spell accurately 90 per cent of the 15 words presented.

They must select the three primary colours at the first attempt.

Combinations

By combining these three criteria, we get detailed behavioural objectives that can be readily observed and measured.

Examples: Students will match up accurately 90 per cent of the rivers listed with their locations in states of Australia without using their workbooks.

Without notes, the student should be able to write down the five main causes of World War I and write an explanatory account of each, all within a period of 30 minutes.

On a level surface, the student should be able to do 15 bunny-hops in three minutes.

This particular form of behavioural objectives is typically attributed to Mager (1984), but there are other variations that have considerable value. For example, Gronlund's (1981) approach is to state objectives first in general terms and then clarify this by listing a few sample behaviours that would provide evidence that the student had attained the objective. It is interesting to note that the general objective with the attendant sample behaviours is very similar to outcome statements (general) which are produced with attendant specific examples of pointers.

Example: General objective:
For Year 12 Geography, students can efficiently solve real-life problems involving stream erosion, transport and deposition.

Specific examples:
1 Distinguish between erosion, transport and deposition on a stream table.
2 Identify examples of stream erosion.
3 Identify material transported by the stream.

4   Identify examples of stream deposition.
5   When observing a real-life stream, state measures used to reduce problems caused by erosion, transport or deposition.

 Supporters of behavioural objectives argue that learning needs to be reinforced in a sequenced and step-by-step procedure. Is this a major reason why behavioural objectives should be used?

9.8.2 Instructional objectives

A case can be made for instructional objectives (behavioural or non-behavioural) to be used by teachers to assist with the instructional process. They provide a clearer direction and overcome vague ideas that may not have been fully developed. Further, they assist the teacher in selecting appropriate content, teaching strategies, resources and assessment. Having instructional objectives can also assist the teacher in demonstrating accountability to the principal, to parents, and to the head office education system personnel (Cohen, Manion & Morrison 2004).

For each major unit of instruction it is reasonable and useful for a teacher to develop a number of instructional objectives – for example, two to six. Of course, the teacher will have help in formulating objectives – help from national and state, governmental and professional, local district and school resources. And these objectives should be statements of the major purposes to guide the teacher and the student through the curriculum. As noted earlier, objectives can act like a road map. A road map need not specify every town and creek to be useful. So objectives for a unit of instruction need not specify every change in student behaviour.

Without following the strict criteria described above for behavioural objectives, there are some criteria that enable teachers and curriculum developers to produce effective instructional objectives. These include:

- **Scope**: the objectives must be sufficiently broad to include all desirable outcomes, presumably relating to knowledge, skills and values.
- **Consistency**: the objectives should be consistent with each other and reflect a similar value orientation.
- **Suitability**: the objectives should be relevant and suitable for students at particular grade levels.
- **Validity**: the objectives should reflect and state what we want them to mean.
- **Feasibility**: the objectives must be attainable by all students.
- **Specificity**: the objectives should avoid ambiguity and be phrased precisely.

To follow each of these criteria closely would be an exacting task. Nevertheless, it is important to keep them in mind when devising appropriate instructional objectives.

YOUR TURN

- How important is it to write well-stated instructional objectives? Are these needed for every lesson you teach?
- Do you inform the students of your objectives? How do you do this? Why?
- How do objectives make your teaching more effective?

9.9 CLASSIFYING OBJECTIVES

During the 1970s experts in educational evaluation, led in particular by Benjamin Bloom, began exploring the possibility of classifying objectives in terms of cognitive, affective and psychomotor behaviours. Cognitive objectives deal with intellectual processes such as knowing, perceiving, recognising and reasoning. Affective objectives deal with feeling, emotion, appreciation and valuing. Psychomotor objectives deal with skilled ways of moving, such as throwing a ball, dancing and handwriting. Of course, it is important to remember that in real life, behaviours from these three domains occur simultaneously. Notwithstanding, by focusing on one domain at a time we can gain important insights about planning lessons.

9.9.1 Cognitive domain

Bloom *et al.* (1956) produced six basic objectives for the cognitive domain. They consist of:

1. **Knowledge**: Remembering, recalling or recognising.
   Example: Students should be able to provide the date when Australia became a Federation.
2. **Comprehension**: Receiving what is being communicated without relating it to other materials.
   Example: Students should be able to explain the causes of sunburn.
3. **Application**: Using general concepts to solve specific problems.
   Example: Students should be able to use a weather vane to predict weather changes.
4. **Analysis**: Ability to break down some communication into its parts.
   Example: Students should be able to infer the moral of a short story.
5. **Synthesis**: Producing something new by combining pieces or elements.
   Example: Students should be able to produce a proposal for a new recreation hall at their school.
6. **Evaluation**: Judging the value of materials or methods.
   Example: Students should be able to critique a short story or play.

Although there have been debates over the years about whether or not the six levels constitute a hierarchy with each skill building on those below it, it is a useful device to help teachers plan their range of objectives (Borich & Tombari 1997). It also is of considerable value to teachers in guiding the types of questions they ask in class. Various studies (for example, Trachtenberg 1974) have shown that teachers typically use knowledge or comprehension questions and very few of the higher levels of the taxonomy. Teachers need to remember the value of including questions at the higher levels of the taxonomy if they want to extend their students.

9.9.2 Affective domain

Krathwohl, Bloom and Masia (1956) produced five basic objectives ranging from least committed to most committed for the affective domain. They consist of:

1. **Receiving**: Being aware of or attending to something.
2. **Responding**: Revealing a new behaviour as a result of experience.
3. **Valuing**: Showing some commitment.
4. **Organisation**: Integrating a new value into one's set of values.
5. **Characterisation by value**: Acting consistently with the new value.

The cognitive domain objectives are relatively easy to adapt for classroom use; however, the same is not true for affective domain objectives. These objectives could be used by teachers to ascertain values students hold as a basis for planning further lessons, but they should not be used to assess students.

9.9.3 Psychomotor domain

Several taxonomies have been produced (for example, Harrow 1972) that go from basic perceptions to creative movements. These objectives would be of special interest to teachers of the Arts, Technology, Physical Education and Special Education.

9.10 | CRITIQUE OF TAXONOMIES

To celebrate the fortieth anniversary of the publication of *Taxonomy of Educational Objectives, Handbook 1, Cognitive Domain* (Bloom *et al.* 1956), notable educators in the US produced critiques that were included in the volume edited by Anderson and Sosniak (1994). Some of the conclusions made by these authors are worth noting.

- Teacher educators at universities have used the *Taxonomy* to help teachers plan their lessons, prepare their tests and ask questions.
- Teachers have made little of the *Taxonomy* because it is too time-consuming, it is not practical to spend time on the higher order objectives (takes away time from content), and it is too rational and complex.
- The *Taxonomy* concentrates on categorising and does not provide any guidance about how to translate these objectives into teaching programs. As a result it has had limited impact.
- The major enduring influence of the *Taxonomy* has been to convey the notion of higher and lower level cognitive behaviours.
- The *Taxonomy* has been used extensively by experts preparing tests.
- Although the *Taxonomy* purports to be descriptive and neutral, it concentrates on overt student behaviours only.
- The *Taxonomy* has been a major focus for discussion in most countries of the world; it has forced educators to raise questions as to whether they have varied the cognitive level of tasks, exercises and examinations they propose, and whether they sufficiently stimulate their students to think.

Wiggins and McTighe (2005) have produced a similar classification, which they list as 'explaining', 'interpreting', 'applying', 'taking a perspective', 'empathising' and being 'aware of self-knowledge'. This list includes both cognitive and affective elements. Acquaint yourself with the details in Wiggins and McTighe's book. Is this a more relevant classification?

CONCLUDING COMMENTS

Teachers undertake purposeful activities in schools. To give direction to what the teacher and students are doing involves the communication to all parties of particular intents. Over the decades, 'objectives' in their various forms have been used to communicate intent. 'Outcomes' and 'standards' have now been highlighted as a more user-friendly approach to communicate intent. It is uncertain whether their popularity will continue into the next decade.

KEY ISSUES RAISED IN THIS CHAPTER

1. Goals and aims are broad statements used to describe the purposes of schooling.
2. The National Goals of Schooling was an important milestone to get agreement from the states and territories. The original statement was published in 1989 and revised versions have been published in 1999 and 2009.
3. The National Curriculum Board (NCB), recently expanded to become the Australian Curriculum, Assessment and Reporting Authority (ACARA), will have a major role in developing national goals, aims, objectives and outcomes.
4. The use of outcomes predominated in the 1990s because it appeared to have major benefits for teachers and students.

5   In recent years the use of outcomes has declined and there is now a major emphasis upon content and performance standards.
6   Standards and essential learnings appear to have been welcomed by administrators and the public, but there can be difficulties for teachers in using them.
7   It is uncertain what ACARA will use when curricula have been produced in 2010, but it is likely to be a combination of content and performance standards.
8   Behavioural and instructional objectives both have their uses.

REFLECTIONS AND ISSUES

1   Reflect upon the objectives you might write for the following teaching methods:
    (a) a lecture
    (b) a group discussion
    (c) inquiry.
    How would they differ? Why?
2   Collect samples of instructional objectives used by teachers. Analyse them in terms of the criteria listed in section 9.8.
3   In outcomes-based education (OBE) you start your planning by examining the output intended. How difficult is this to do? Take an outcome statement and explain how you would plan learning activities to achieve it.
4   'The hardest part of introducing essential learning outcomes is to work out how to assess them.' Discuss.
5   Does an outcomes-based approach enable more creative and efficient forms of assessment to be used? Give examples to support your argument.
6   'System administrators are enthusiastic about the outcome approach but there is a lukewarm response from schools and teachers.' Is this an accurate account? Explain the reasons for these different perspectives.
7   Compare and contrast the benefits of 'behavioural' objectives and 'instructional' objectives.
8   Compare the advantages and disadvantages of using an outcomes-based and a standards-based approach to curriculum planning.
9   What are some of the problems in breaking knowledge and content down into outcomes? What is the basis for creating levels of outcomes? Does an outcomes-based approach trivialise knowledge and discriminate against capable students?
10 How are standards established by central policy makers more desirable than standards currently set by texts and high-status tests?
11 Do you consider that outcomes and levels are too crude for ranking students for tertiary entrance? Discuss.
12 Does the nomenclature of OBE help or hinder communication of student results to parents? Discuss.
13 By international standards, countries that perform highly on TIMSS typically use syllabuses and not outcomes. Is there a stronger relationship between the use of syllabuses and student achievement? Discuss.

Special references

Glatthorn, AA & Fontana, J (2002) *Standards and Accountability: How Teachers See Them*, National Education Association, Washington DC.
McLeod, JH, Reynolds, R & Weckert, C (2001) *Enriching Learning*, Social Science Press, Sydney.

O'Shea, MR (2005) *From Standards to Success*, ASCD, Alexandria, Virginia.
Singer, AJ (2003) *Teaching to Learn, Learning to Teach*, Lawrence Erlbaum, Mahwah, New Jersey.
Whitton, D, Sinclair, C, Barker, K, Nanlohy, P & Nosworthy, M (2004) *Learning for Teaching: Teaching for Learning*, Thomson, Melbourne.
Willis, S & Kissane, B (1997) *Achieving Outcome-Based Education*, ACSA, Canberra.
Woods, A (2007) 'What's wrong with benchmarks? Answering the wrong questions with the wrong answers', *Curriculum Perspectives*, 27(3):1–10.

Web sources

For additional resources on planning to achieve goals, aims, objectives, outcomes and standards, please go to:
www.pearson.com.au/myeducationlab.

10

SCHOOL DEVELOPMENT PLANS AND STRATEGIC PLANNING FRAMEWORKS

10.1 | INTRODUCTION

In the 1990s school development planning was undertaken by many schools, largely in terms of a list of activities or priorities – some might even characterise them as a wish list! Since then the tasks have become more complicated and degrees of accountability have increased. There are now many more factors to consider such as Information and Communication Technology (ICT) development plans, strategic target plans, curriculum improvement plans and staffing plans.

It is argued that Strategic Planning Frameworks (SPFs) are of greater value than School Development Plans (SDPs) because there is more emphasis on futures and intents rather than a simple list of actions to be achieved.

However with both SDPs and SPFs there are many issues to be addressed in the process of doing the planning. Not least is the matter of whose interests are being served. For example, should the main emphasis with SDPs and SPFs be on market strategies for attracting particular kinds of parents and their children; or should it be higher achievement results for all students, especially in literacy and numeracy; or the provision of an inclusive holistic education program for students; or a learning community where teachers and administrators work collaboratively to achieve common goals?

It is difficult to separate the rhetoric from actual practices. There are many tensions and contradictions between the stakeholders and embarking on school planning can be a hazardous journey. Some of the major issues are examined in this chapter.

10.2 | COMMONLY USED TERMS RELATING TO SCHOOL DEVELOPMENT AND IMPROVEMENT

During the 1980s and 1990s in many countries of the world, new initiatives were taken to bring about improved student learning. In the United States the *effective schools* movement was an initiative to improve student learning, especially in inner-city schools (Reynolds *et al.* 1994). Researchers identified a range of different variables that correlated highly with student achievement. Schools that exhibited these variables were seen to be 'effective schools'. Some of these variables and characteristics included:
- a pervasive academic focus
- an orderly, safe climate conducive to teaching and learning

- school site management
- school-wide staff development
- maximised learning time
- measures of student achievement as the basis for program evaluation
- curriculum based on clear goals and objectives.

School improvement initiatives were also a feature of the 1980s. Miles and Ekholm (1985, p. 48) define school improvement as 'a systematic, sustained effort aimed at change in learning conditions and other related internal conditions in one or more schools, with the ultimate aim of accomplishing educational goals more effectively'. The emphasis here is on processes and collaborative decision making among teachers.

In the United Kingdom during the 1980s the term *School Based Review* (SBR) was used to emphasise British school improvement endeavours. As noted by Hopkins (1989, p. 154), 'SBR places greater emphasis on effective staff collaboration which means that in most schools, skills in communication, problem solving, and team building have to be consciously developed' (see also Chapter 19).

A major international project sponsored by the OECD, the International School Improvement Project (ISIP) commenced in 1982 and continued until 1986. The aim of the project was to share and develop understandings cross-nationally about what it takes to make school improvement work (Van Velzen *et al.* 1985).

These developments worldwide were all aimed at improving schools, and variations have continued into the 1990s and in the first decade of the twenty-first century. The restructuring of education that has been occurring in Australia is part of this same process. It is complicated because there are various tensions between democracy and bureaucracy (Dimmock & O'Donoghue 1997). There are pressures for democratic participation at the school-site level but equally strong pressures to maintain centralised controls in the interest of educational standards, equity and accountability (Boyd 1990).

Various solutions have been attempted in the different states and territories to provide for a coexistence of central direction and maximum school-level autonomy (Angus 1998). Examples include: 'Schools of the Future', 'Schools of the Third Millennium', 'Self-Governing Schools' (in Victoria), 'Leading Schools' (in Queensland) and 'Directions in Education' (in Tasmania). An ongoing example in Victoria is the creation of 'Schools of the Third Millennium'. These are government schools that are given greater autonomy and can choose to specialise in particular subjects. Professional bodies such as 'Principals Australia' continue to provide workshops and forums for principals for the third millennium.

A number of educators argue for autonomy at the school level; that school-based management by teachers, students and parents is important because many key decisions have to be made at the local, school level; that school-based management is consistent with trends in modern business management; and that it activates all the stakeholders (Ladbrooke 1997; Davies 2007; Day 2000).

Angus (1990, pp. 5–6) asserts that state education authorities across Australia have adopted similar machinery in order to put their devolution proposals into effect. For example:
- a mandatory development plan in each school (in effect, the school's corporate plan)
- single line budgets or block grants for schools containing funds previously allocated centrally for specific purposes
- formally constituted school decision-making groups, containing staff and community representatives, which endorse plans and authorise budgets
- an external auditing capacity that has an educational as well as a financial remit
- central offices more focused than in the past on defining policy parameters and standards
- decentralised support services for schools to be based either in schools or in local offices.

Caldwell (1997) argues that self-management of schools has now become an international phenomenon and that major transformations are imminent. Further, he asserts that technology will enrich and support the work of teachers and, in many situations, liberate them from present demands. He maintains that evidence from the 'Schools of the Future' reform in Victoria indicates 'that teachers' knowledge about learning and teaching has been enhanced through school self-management' (Caldwell 1997, p. 73).

Davies (2007) notes that self-management of schools is a major focus in many countries because schools have to seek multiple revenue sources. There is now a mixed economy of various providers.

 Reflect upon the planning considerations that senior school staffs have to make. To what extent is marketing and advertising preventing a school from concentrating on a quality program?

The literature provided by government and non-government schools clearly reveals the new emphasis on attracting parents and students. For example, Stromlo High School in the ACT provides a very informative and attractive folder containing a message from the school principal and information about their mission statement, student services, philosophy and management, student involvement, key learning areas, curriculum and timetable (Stromlo High School 2001).

However, Davies and Ellison (2000) caution about the application of the term 'market economy' to schooling. They contend that the features of a full market economy for schools would include:
- a price mechanism
- open and effective choice on the part of consumers (students, parents)
- relatively easy entry for new educational providers
- freely available, comprehensive information about different providers and their products
- minimal regulation by government authorities (p. 8).

In practice, such a market system in terms of schools does not exist. For example, a price differential does not operate between government schools. Neither is there open choice, easy entry for 'new player' providers nor freely available information about their products.

YOUR TURN

What can you do individually and as a member of a school team to solve the following?
- Demands for schools to cater better for students with individual differences.
- Demands from market forces for schools to be more efficient and to raise standards.
- Demands that schools keep up with technological developments.

10.3 SCHOOL DEVELOPMENT PLANS AND STRATEGIC PLANNING FRAMEWORKS

10.3.1 School Development Plans

All Australian state education systems now require schools to produce and implement a school-based plan. Non-government schools such as independent and Catholic schools also require school-based plans although their scope and resources may be very different (see, for example, Figure 10.1).

The chief purpose of a school plan is to involve the school community in practical planning activities, to participate in important decisions about a school's operation, to clarify the division of responsibilities between schools and their communities and to raise their credibility in the local community.

A very significant benefit of producing a school plan is for participants to experience the process. The completed plan is of course important but so too are the meetings, discussions, arguments and resolutions that will inevitably occur in making decisions (Sparks & Hirsh 1997).

FIGURE 10.1 School development plan – Catholic school, Queensland

- College mission statement
- Learning framework
- Community values statement
- Strategic priorities 2007–2010

Another important feature of school plans is that the planners (especially teachers and parents) have considerable control over what aspects they want to change – it can relieve the stress caused by hectic change initiatives. The planners are able to arrive at the priorities they consider are important for their school.

As an example, a West Australian government primary school, Parkerville, has published its School Development Plan on the Internet (see Figure 10.2). The authors have provided full details about their school, particular values (for example, a commitment to the pursuit of knowledge and achievement of potential), detailed priority strategies for the achievement of literacy and numeracy, and targets for each of eight learning areas.

Many schools still use the term 'School Development Plan' for describing the planning they undertake. The use of the term 'Strategic Planning Framework' might sound rather grandiose and idealistic. Perhaps it is. However it acknowledges that school-based planning has become very complicated and it is now far more involved than just adding a few activities to be undertaken.

10.3.2 Strategic Planning Frameworks

A Strategic Planning Framework (SPF) is an overall plan of initiatives, policies and priorities for a school. It can take many forms – predominantly a working document produced by a school's staff and community to guide decision making and not for wider circulation, or it can be a public document which is provided to system officials and is distributed widely.

Most education systems do not provide detailed principles or guidelines for doing an SPF. There is good reason for this. Every school is unique with its particular combination of staff and students, resources and community involvement. One size does not fit all. The level of any guidelines is usually pitched at general considerations (see Figure 10.2).

SPFs can range in detail from a brief list of targets or activities to well-integrated, detailed, planning frameworks. An example of a brief listing might be as depicted in Figure 10.3.

Authors such as Davies (2009) argue that School Development Plans (SDPs) are too linear, and too limited in their time scale and focus.

Strategic Planning Frameworks (SPFs) are more comprehensive and futures oriented, but no doubt they would be very time consuming to accomplish.

The components of the SPF which are considered to be essential include those in Figure 10.4.

10.3.3 Futures perspective

It can be argued that a *futures* perspective is most important for an SPF. Development plans that only take into consideration plans for a 1–2 year period can only apply a very short-term focus. Developing ideas and trends need to be considered to ensure that students currently at a school, and future enrollees, will be given every possible opportunity for development.

10.3.4 Strategic intents

Strategic intent is a crucial element and involves looking at ways of enhancing the capability of a school. It is suggested by Davies (2009) that a school should limit itself to a small number of intents (perhaps four or five) and then try to specify what these might be. An example of such

FIGURE 10.2 School development plan (Western Australia)

Concept

An SDP is a school's public statement of its current situation and its plans for the foreseeable future. The SDP will be:
- a mechanism for assisting schools to meet the educational requirements of all students
- the management device through which the school's development intentions and progress towards achieving them are articulated
- the means through which the Ministry and community priorities are expressed in school policies
- a means through which formal staff and community participation in the development of school priorities and policies is sustained
- the means of evaluating school performance by measuring achievement against the stated objectives
- a formal link in the supervisory relationship between the District Superintendent and the school.

Principles

1. The SDP should be an outcome of participative decision making in the school.
2. The plan should be regarded as a 'working document', updated as the cycle of planning, implementing and reviewing continues.
3. The plan should be functional; it becomes the key reference point for decision making, shaping actual developments in the school.
4. The plan should provide an overview. It should be limited to simple, clear statements which can be easily prepared. Policies, programs, submissions for additional funding and evaluations might exist as supporting documentation to the plan itself.
5. The form and scope of school plans should be variable according to the school's current circumstances and planning intentions – there is no prescribed format.

Source: School Development Plans and School-Based Decision-making Groups, *Ministry of Education, Western Australia, 1988.*

FIGURE 10.3 Strategic planning framework (school)

- Our school vision
- Aims of the school
- Targets
- Review of previous school development plan
- Operational plans for 2009–2010 and success criteria

a capability might be related to ICT infrastructure in the school and ICT skills levels of all teachers. Such an intent could not be achieved quickly but it illustrates the need for a fundamental rethinking about what is needed in a school. Davies (2009) describes the process of strategic intent as 'leveraging up performance to a significantly higher level by building capacity in the organisation' (p. 3).

The three sub-categories of strategic intent are all important. The *ICT development plan* would include intents about:
- using ICT as a teaching and learning aid
- having an infrastructure that enables staff to access valuable content
- developing the infrastructure of hardware and software.

 In your visits to schools have you observed any evidence of an ICT plan? What did you notice about the number and range of ICT equipment, levels of teacher competence with ICT and how it is used?

FIGURE 10.4 Essential components of a Strategic Planning Framework

The *curriculum improvement* intents could include:
- finding out about curriculum planning understandings and skills of staff and seeking ways of upgrading them (Marsh 2009)
- getting staff to be able to analyse statistical data readily available on a student and school performance (Schmoker 2003; Rudner & Boston 2003)
- providing learning environments for teachers that are more conducive to student-initiated, small group learning.

The *staffing* intents could focus upon:
- how to maximise staff teaching expertise and interests
- how to vary full-time and part-time participation to maximise student learning.

It is contended that strategic intents are meant to be imaginative and creative in seeking new ways to develop capability. It is the thinking about and problem solving over the intents that is so important. If it is evident that a particular intent can be established then the school staff move on to the next phase of doing the strategic planning to achieve it. If, alternatively, it becomes clear after considerable discussion that a particular intent cannot be achieved then it becomes necessary to reframe the intent so that a more achievable result can be produced.

10.3.5 Strategic plans

The *strategic plan* is where the more predictable and concrete details are outlined. However, it should not be a simple 'shopping list' but a carefully categorised grouping of priorities, costed out and with rubrics of success criteria.

An ICT strategic plan is an essential element for today's schools. ICT equipment is expensive and it needs to be carefully managed and coordinated across a school. Any ICT plan has to demonstrate how its use will help a school to be better managed and enable students to learn more effectively. It has to be credible (an integral part of the school plan); manageable (involving senior staff); and sustainable (having the support of all stakeholders).

It is important that an ICT strategic plan has a clear vision for the future with measurable targets and clear operational actions. Table 10.1 illustrates some of the key elements that could be included

TABLE 10.1 Example summary of an ICT strategic plan

Key action	Main action points Year 1	Main action points Year 2	Main action points Year 3	Responsibility and monitoring	Success criteria	Impact on student learning	Costings
1 Resources and infrastructure	Create ICT suite New Internet cabling	Furnish ICT suite	Install interactive Smart Boards	Senior teachers and ICT officer	School has well equipped and functional ICT suite	More focused teaching	$155 000
2 Hardware updates	Purchase new printers	Lease hardware to update classroom computers	Purchase two scanners	Monitor lesson plans	ICT lessons will be taught	Enable students with different learning styles to learn more effectively	$75 000
3 Raising student ICT skills	Develop a cross-curricula subject	Ensure all students receive ICT	Ensure adequate assessment of ICT	ICT officer collects student data Heads of dept. analyse data	Evidence of success in progression of using ICT	Children work at own pace	N/A
4 Curriculum development	Implement a new integrated subject	Use new software for integrated subject	Evaluate impact on subject	Do an audit of all software on computers	Ensure continuity across rooms	Children find ICT work interesting	N/A
5 Inclusion	Purchase new PCs for remedial classes	Purchase software	Further training for remedial teachers	Senior teacher (remedial) and ICT officer jointly plan	Evidence of student uptake	Students enjoy working with ICT	$55 000
6 Staff development	Train staff to download resources	Train staff to use new software	Train staff to use Smart Board	Curriculum senior teacher and ICT officer organise workshops	Evidence of improved teacher confidence	Students' enjoyment in working with ICT	N/A
7 Community links	To install Internet Create school website	Invite parents to view and use ICT suite	Update school website	ICT officer and Principal arrange parent seminars	Evidence of parent support	Parent support for ICT activities students complete at home	N/A

Source: After Thomas Buxton Infant School 2009; Department for Education and Skills, 2009

TABLE 10.2 Example summary of a curriculum improvement strategic plan

Key objectives	Main activities Year 1	Main activities Year 2	Main activities Year 3	Responsibility and monitoring	Success criteria	Impact on student learning	Costings
1 Improved school focus – staff and student inputs	Needs analysis of future directions, surveys of staff and students	Sharing of draft plans	Implementation	Principal and heads of departments	Level of interaction between staff	Extent to which staff and students share new vision	N/A
2 Development of staff strengths	Appoint external facilitator to explore staff strengths	Individual staff provide workshops	Further sharing of ideas	Principal and external faculties	Extent to which new staff strengths are identified	Examples of innovative approaches and students' reactions	$50 000
3 Improved results in literacy and numeracy	Initiate new programs including staff training	Consolidate	Consolidate	Curriculum supervisor and heads of departments	Teacher support for new programs; student achievements	Improved literacy and numeracy results	N/A
4 Development of networks for planning and interacting	Establish and develop new working groups	Increase the range of activities of each working group	Further consolidation	Heads of departments	Improved working atmosphere in school	Improved student engagement	$400 000
5 Planning of functional learning areas for innovative teaching	Engage planners to assist with plans for new academic resource areas	Undertake first stage of building	Complete building activities	Principal and heads of departments	Satisfaction with new purpose built resources	Improved student engagement when working in new environments	$150 000
6 Involve staff with experts on curriculum planning	Invite staff to enrol in professional development courses	Increase number of staff enrolled	Further secondments	Principal and curriculum supervisor	Enthusiasm of staff when return from course	New innovative ideas used with students	$15 000
7 Celebrate successes via Special Days, Events	Undertake planning of special events and awards	Review activities from previous year – expand on range of celebrations	Further consolidation	Principal and curriculum supervisor	The extent of support from teachers, students and parents	The extent of positive reactions to celebrations	$90 000

in an ICT strategic plan. As noted by the Department for Children, Schools and Families (2009), an ICT strategic plan should demonstrate how a school will:
- raise standards of students' achievement in ICT
- maintain and develop the infrastructure of hardware and connectivity
- ensure that the infrastructure enables staff to access valuable content
- develop and sustain practice, including ongoing staff training.

A curriculum improvement strategic plan is also an essential element in a period of curriculum reform and increased attention to standards and accountability measures (see Table 10.2).

Each school has its own unique distribution of staff interests and strengths, student capabilities and interests and parent-community strengths. Any strategic plan must give full consideration to the major players (such as teachers, administrators, students, parents, external consultants) to maximise curriculum improvement. There is no one single solution that fits all schools.

For one school the emphasis might be on developing and extending a school improvement plan involving a number of key teachers. For another school the emphasis might be upon creating new learning areas which facilitate student-oriented, small group activities and this could involve the erection of new buildings and rooms. In another school the emphasis might be upon teacher, student or parent involvement in community-based projects and ensuring that their achievements are recognised through special events.

The staff is of course a major element in any school environment and a strategic plan for staffing and resources is critical. Changing demands for subjects by students requires flexibility in staffing and may require short-term and long-term discussions. To maximise flexibility, a careful blend of full-time specialist staff, full-time generalists and part-time staff may be needed. Staff use of ICT in daily teaching has become increasingly important and this must be linked to the ICT strategic plan. Health and safety measures affecting staff and students are important considerations.

Table 10.3 illustrates some of the key elements that could be included in a staff and resources strategic plan.

10.3.6 Operational target setting

The final element in a strategic planning framework is the listing of specific targets – the operational target setting for a school for 1–2 years. It is desirable to have a small number of targets, well-costed and covering whole-school and individual department needs that can become a major focus for all school personnel. An example is listed in Figure 10.5.

 When you next visit a school inquire about the school develop plan and the specific targets they have for the next two years.

FIGURE 10.5 Example operational target-setting plan

Teaching and learning
1. Provide professional development for all staff on teaching and learning needs of gifted students.
2. Build a new ICT lab for 30 PCs.
3. Increase library facilities to include 30 networked computers.

Students
4. Initiate a Year 7 Peer Monitoring Program.
5. Extend the pastoral care program.
6. Trial of electronic student attendance monitoring.

School leadership and management
7. Complete planning and documentation for refurbishing Science laboratories.
8. Open forum time at staff meetings for staff to share best practice.

Source: After Lyncham High School Development Plan 2006; Department for Children, Schools and Families 2009.

TABLE 10.3 Example staffing and resources strategic plan

Key objectives	Main action points Year 1	Main action points Year 2	Main action points Year 3	Responsibility and monitoring	Success criteria	Impact on student learning	Costings
Review of staffing needs for core functions	Examine current ratios and plan for increased staff	Appoint additional staff	Review	Principal and vice principal	Feedback from senior staff	N/A	$150 000 in 2nd and 3rd years
Specialist staff needed for academic areas	Examine requirements in terms of curriculum improvement plan	Make appointments	Review	Principal and vice principal	Support from senior staff	N/A	$120 000 in 2nd and 3rd years
Room availability and use	Review of room usage, timetabling requirements, part-time staff needs	Implement new room use plan	Consolidate	Vice principal	Support from senior staff	N/A	N/A
Use of ICT resources	Examine requirements in terms of ICT plan						
Uses and availability of part-time staff	Examine current use and future needs	Recruit additional staff if needed	Consolidate	Vice principal	Feedback from staff	Obtain feedback from full-time staff	N/A
Health and safety provisions	Examine staff work loads and safety standards in teaching areas	Implement new health and safety provisions	Consolidate	Vice principal	Feedback from staff	N/A	N/A

10.4 | SCHOOL PLANS AND THE SCHOOL CULTURE

The human element cannot be taken for granted. There are tasks to be done, data to be collected and decisions to be made. Yet the personnel involved – the principal, teachers, parents (and in some cases, students) – may not be highly motivated and may even distrust, or even despise, the whole process and the leaders involved (Loader 1998). For example, studies of the culture of teaching stress the autonomy of the teacher in the classroom. It can be extremely difficult for teachers to work on tasks where they must share with and depend upon others. Creating a positive school culture is critical if the stakeholders are going to work together successfully in developing school plans (see Chapter 19).

'School culture' is a term difficult to define. Deal (1985, p. 605) describes it as 'the way we do things around here'. It is, of course, a combination of values and beliefs (intangibles) and tangibles such as words used, behaviours demonstrated and buildings used by the major stakeholders (Slee, Weiner & Tomlinson 1998).

For stakeholders to be actively involved in school planning SDPs, relationships within the school culture have to be worked on. Cavanagh and MacNeil (2002) contend that stakeholders must be passionate about their school's vision – to use their 'creative energy to include scenarios that would not have emerged through rational planning processes' (p. 15). Caldwell and Spinks (1993) maintain that empowerment, trust, synergy, responsibility and subsidiarity are important notions. (The term *subsidiarity*, as used by Caldwell and Spinks, refers to the value of doing planning at the school level, as these activities are more appropriate at the heart of learning than at higher levels in an education bureaucracy.)

Leaders of school planning endeavours have to ensure that all persons in a school community have an opportunity to be involved in decision making and generally make contributions that will advance their full development or *empowerment* as individuals.

Trust is a major factor in school planning. For example, teachers need to be aware of the expertise of others and to be satisfied that they can provide high-quality inputs.

Synergy refers to the total impact of a group working together compared with the output of individuals working separately. Effective collaboration brings out many desirable qualities in individuals and enables the resulting group endeavour to be of a very high standard.

In school level planning there are various responsibilities for participants and they complement each other. It is not possible to avoid difficult decisions or to ascribe them to head office officials.

YOUR TURN

- What qualities do you consider are necessary to be an effective member of a school development team?
- How important are the following qualities:
    - being a good listener
    - tolerance for uncertainty and ambiguity
    - sensitivity to others
    - commitment to collaborative planning
    - being willing to take risks
    - having a secure sense of self?
- Give yourself a ranking between 1 and 10 for each of the above. Reflect on your rankings.

10.5 | DIFFICULTIES IN DOING SCHOOL PLANNING

Although it is relatively easy for procedures and sequences to be established for doing school planning, it is quite possible that a number of schools may not be able to respond positively and effectively to the advice. The difficulty may be largely a school culture problem as described above, or it might be multi-faceted and involve problems associated with aims, partners, curriculum, organisation of teaching and learning, management, change, support and ethos. Each of these factors warrants further analysis.

10.5.1 Aims

A very difficult aspect of any SDP is to get agreement on the overriding aims or purpose. The education system may espouse a general mission (such as to develop the cognitive and social skills of students), but it is difficult to translate this into operational goals that reflect the needs of the local school community (Hargreaves & Evans 1997).

10.5.2 Partners

Partnerships have to be established if the principal, teachers and parents are all to be involved in developing school plans. The principal may not be the central actor any longer but rather a member of the executive team (Caldwell & Spinks 1998). The principal will need to develop additional inter-personal skills and in particular must acquire a high level of understanding of adult development and learning as well as of the range of strategies and techniques that can be used when working with adults (Murphy 1991).

A number of teachers may take on leadership roles in the development of school plans. This might be expected if teachers at a school have specialised knowledge, skills or simply powers of persuasion.

Parents may be actively involved in school planning (Roesner 1995) but this will depend greatly on their levels of professional training and expertise, as detailed in Chapter 17.

Again, it will be necessary for team-building sessions to be initiated to build up trust and support between these partners. It is extremely likely that misunderstandings and conflicts will occur. The only positive way forward is for these differences of opinion to be talked out in informal, face-to-face sessions (Gold & Evans 1998).

As noted by Hargreaves *et al.* (2001), if the principal and teachers perceive the addition of parents as interference and a lack of trust in their professionalism, conflicts will occur. On the other hand, if the school becomes so committed to the priorities of the different partners that it loses its sense of identity and unity, other problems will also occur. A middle position requires recognition of the contribution of all the partners, while trying to achieve a balance worked out in a spirit of collaboration.

10.5.3 Curriculum

In most state education systems in Australia over recent years there have been enormous pressures to change the curriculum. Major changes have been initiated at lower secondary and post-secondary levels in particular. The introduction of outcomes-based and standards approaches for the eight learning areas represent a major change.

The dilemma for school-based teams is how to incorporate these new curriculum changes into their respective school plans without losing the continuity of existing practices. As noted by Fullan (1993) about change in general, it is prudent if school planners include small, incremental curriculum changes rather than have major changes as their targets.

10.5.4 Organisation of teaching and learning

Many teachers tend to be very protective about the forms of teaching and learning they use. However, a school plan with a new target or focus might be dependent on different forms of teaching for it to be successful. For example, a school plan with a major focus on creating good self-esteem in students might require very informal and non-traditional forms of teaching.

There are further difficulties for a school-based partnership when it comes to discussions about methods of teaching. Although parents may have wide experience in terms of educational policy, they tend not to have professional expertise in methods of teaching. Teachers might perceive it to be very threatening and inappropriate for parent members of a planning team to offer advice or recommendations to be included in the school plan.

10.5.5 Management

The operation of planning groups involving approximately equal representation of the stakeholders presupposes equality and partnership codes of behaviour. Yet every task requires some form of leadership or management. It appears that many of the site-based school planners have been confused about who is responsible for what.

During the 1980s and 1990s in Victoria considerable hostility occurred due to a perceived lack of opportunity for principals to have a major role in management. The 'Schools of the Future' program also had an imbalance between parent and teacher representatives on school councils. Knight (1995, p. 270) observes that the regulation for the composition of school councils states that there must be 6–12 members, no more than one-third of whom can be teachers. He suggests that:

> on some school councils there may even be no classroom teachers, as the one-third applies to all Department of School Education employees. The coalition between parents and teachers nurtured during the previous decade will be broken.

Grundy and Bonser (1997b) contend that restructuring in Victoria has been characterised by fragmentation and individualisation. Project teams work on separate projects and are subject to individual performance contracts. This has created 'work practices among teachers which placed them in competition with one another, rather than in cooperative, collegial relationships' (Grundy & Bonser 1997b, p. 163).

10.5.6 Change

For many participants the process of developing a school plan at the school level is a major change in itself and they will want to minimise any other changes. If the school plan consists of new goals it could lead to many additional changes. In Western Australia, the introduction of school-based decision-making groups is 'the fulcrum of the education department's attempts to provide both quality and accountability' (Dimmock 1990, p. 202). This is a major change for teachers and parents and it has been a traumatic one (Forlin & Forlin 1996).

The inclusion of innovatory elements into a school plan may largely be due to the enthusiasm of one or two people. These elements are likely to be aborted if the originators depart. Alternatively, change may be so strongly resisted that the existing structures and programs are maintained. Ideally, innovations should be carefully considered and only selected ones included in a school plan after there has been extensive deliberation and support.

There are also many ongoing changes at central system levels, such as trends to move towards an entrepreneurial, consumer-oriented approach for schooling. According to Caldwell and Spinks (1998, p. 161):

> self-managing schools are emerging in times of dramatic restructuring in education around the world. While changes to roles and responsibilities at the school level are challenging enough in themselves, there are concomitant changes at the central and other levels of the system which are even more far-reaching in terms of their impact on people.

10.5.7 Support

In most education systems, the support required to undertake change is vastly underestimated. It is indeed a vicious cycle. Quite often, major restructuring is initiated because of budget downturns. The resulting new structures require financial support to get them started, but of course there are minimal provisions in the budget for them.

It is interesting to note that in many US school districts, largely due to funding from the 'Goals 2000 initiative', seed money was made available to many districts to run workshops to help teachers develop skills for school planning. In Idaho, school districts that encourage collaborative planning on curriculum alignment received a monetary bonus (Allen 2002a).

In Western Australia, Angus (1998) and Dimmock and Hattie (1994) all refer to the lack of support and the enormously increased workloads and stress for teachers and principals. Another concern about lack of support in Western Australia arose because of the removal of subject superintendents (senior subject teachers assigned to head office who visited schools regularly) at the time of the restructuring in 1987. Various teachers and especially the teachers' union expressed dismay about the sense of isolation after the loss of subject superintendents (Chadbourne & Quin 1989). In this case, moral support was being sought by teachers in terms of the traditional central model into which they had been socialised. In time, it might be argued that teachers would need to accept responsibility for their own professional development. This example simply highlights some of the human elements of educational change and the pressures that can be experienced by teachers.

10.5.8 Ethos

The ethos is the shared values and commitments of a school. It is a slow, painful process to build a positive ethos among the stakeholders of a school community. For some, the most powerful aspects of a school ethos involve a willingness to be innovative and to develop a school plan that fully reflects what the school community would like to be. For others, ethos might be portrayed as stability and maintenance of the things we like doing and are good at doing.

These are just some of the difficulties experienced in developing a school plan. They are not insurmountable but they clearly require time, a considerable amount of discussion, sensitivity to different points of view and a willingness to take action.

A case study account of an innovative school, as depicted below, perhaps epitomises what is required.

---

case study

Collaborative planning at my school

At my primary school of 200 students things have been different over the last three years. A lot of this has been due to the new head, Nancy. She gets in and works alongside us. She doesn't try to dominate us yet she gently prods, encourages, supports us.

We no longer have the conventional boundaries between school head and teachers. We work together on achieving shared goals, especially with regard to developing student outcomes.

Yes, of course we strike our dead-ends. We are not happy with each other all the time. Yet we do share responsibilities and there is a cooperative commitment and ownership to the school's ethos.

There is a focus on learning between teachers (and parents) which is educationally holistic (Cockburn District Education Office 1994, p. 8).

CONCLUDING COMMENTS

School development plans (SDPs) and Strategic Planning Frameworks (SPFs) are important links in shaping more relevant school programs based on students' and community needs. Participation in the process is extremely valuable for teachers' professional development. It is also of considerable benefit to parents and community members who are able to gain a greater understanding of school-level decision making.

Throughout Australia various types of SDPs are required by different education systems. Some schools are experimenting with a form of SPF. There is no best structure or set of procedures. The processes of decision making, in some ways, are more important than the product. Students will clearly benefit if school plans can be produced that reflect community priorities, have connections with system-wide reforms and are supported and promoted by all the stakeholders (Watson, Fullan & Kilcher 2000).

KEY ISSUES RAISED IN THIS CHAPTER

1. School Development Plans (SDPs) are required in most education systems but there are now additional planning considerations to include.
2. Strategic Planning Frameworks (SPFs) are more comprehensive and include a futures orientation and intents rather than just a shopping list of actions.
3. Additional plans that are necessary for schools now include Information and Communication Technology (ICT) development plans and curriculum improvement plans.
4. Strategic intent plans examine ways of enhancing the capability of a school – they need to be imaginative and creative.
5. ICT development plans are especially important and must include ICT as a teaching and learning tool, staff access to valuable ICT content, and developing and maintaining an infrastructure of hardware and connectivity.
6. A significant benefit of producing a school plan is for participants to experience the process.
7. Creating a positive school culture is critical if stakeholders are going to work together successfully in developing school plans.

REFLECTIONS AND ISSUES

1. School plans can be considered as part of an annual cycle of planning and review. What do you consider to be the main purposes of a school plan? Is it feasible to produce a school plan annually?
2. What role should a newly appointed teacher play in developing a school plan? What university training experiences might be of benefit to the planning team? Do you envisage some possible impediments to active participation by newly appointed teachers?
3. The challenge for staff involved in developing a school plan 'is not to be subverted by existing [school] conditions or expectations. The power of visioning lies in its capacity to transcend reality and explore what could be' (Cavanagh & MacNeil 2002, p. 15). Do you agree?
4. 'A school plan captures the long-term vision for the school within which manageable short-term goals are set. The priorities contained in the plan represent the school's translation of policy into its agenda for action' (Hargreaves & Hopkins 1991, p. 6). Discuss the extent to which school plans can achieve this.
5. In New Zealand, school-site management and initiation of school plans has caused much

higher workloads for teachers, especially in terms of administrative and accountability demands (Wylie 1995). Is this likely within the Australian contexts? What are some measures that might be introduced to reduce this problem?

6 'Market forces in education have often been discussed, but seldom, if ever, have they existed' (Davies & Ellison 2000, p. 9). Use some local examples of schools to support or refute this statement.

Special references

Davies, B & Ellison, L (2000) Site-based management – myths and realities, paper presented at the Annual Conference of the American Educational Research Association, New Orleans.

Davies, B (2007) *Developing Sustainable Leadership*, Sage, London.

Day, C (2000) *The Life and Work of Teachers*, Routledge, London.

Fullan, M (2001) *Leading in a Culture of Change*, Jossey-Bass, San Francisco.

Hargreaves, A, Earl, L, Moore, S & Manning, S (2001) *Learning to Change*, Jossey-Bass, San Francisco.

Hargreaves, DH & Hopkins, D (1994) *Development Planning for School Improvement*, Routledge, London.

Ladbrooke, A (1997) School *Development Manual: A Practical Guide for School Improvement*, Pearson, Sydney.

Townsend, T, Clarke, P & Ainscow, M (1999) *Third Millennium Schools: A World of Difference in Effectiveness and Improvement*, Swets & Zeitlinger, London.

Web sources

For additional resources on school development plans and strategic planning frameworks, please go to:

www.pearson.com.au/myeducationlab

PART 4
TEACHING EFFECTIVELY

Taking it to the Classroom
www.pearson.com.au/myeducationlab

Number of years teaching: 1 year
Year level teaching now: Years 7–12

First day of teaching memories:

My first day as a teacher was my first day on rounds where my supervising teacher actually didn't show up for my first class. I was left to take a Year 12 music class, which was quite a shock to begin with, but I think being thrown in the deep end early on was a really good experience and I think that's probably shaped me as a teacher more than anything else at university.

Andrew Moffat
McClelland College

chapter 11   Communicating effectively
chapter 12   Pedagogy, teaching and learning
chapter 13   Classroom management
chapter 14   Using resources creatively
chapter 15   Meeting the diverse needs of students
chapter 16   Teaching, values and moral education
chapter 17   Working effectively with parents
chapter 18   Assessment and reporting

11

COMMUNICATING EFFECTIVELY

11.1 | INTRODUCTION

Communicating is a complicated and vital aspect of teaching and learning. Interactions occur between various players – students, teachers, the principal, parents and community members. Messages can be sent and received in the form of verbal, non-verbal or written communication, and the different types can occur simultaneously.

11.2 | THE NATURE OF COMMUNICATION

Communication is the basis for all human interaction. Communication is a process – an activity that serves to connect senders and receivers of messages through space and time (Dillman 2006). Although we are mainly concerned with human communication, the process is present in all living animals – it is fundamental and universal.

Communication is not merely passive connection. It is the *process* of connecting (Dillman 2006). It happens between or among at least two persons and it involves an exchange of 'messages'.

As noted by Latham *et al.* (2006), communication is not always easy, neither is it typically simple and effortless.

In the classroom it is a constant exchange of information involving a number of persons receiving and sending messages. The classroom teacher often has to communicate regularly with a wide range of people, each with a different background and interests (see Figure 11.1).

YOUR TURN

Do a classroom observation of another teacher at work. Make notes on the following:
- Could the teacher be seen by all the students?
- Could all the students hear what the teacher was saying?
- Did the teacher vary the tempo, pace and pitch of his/her voice?
- Did the teacher communicate in an interesting manner?

FIGURE 11.1 Communication links within a school

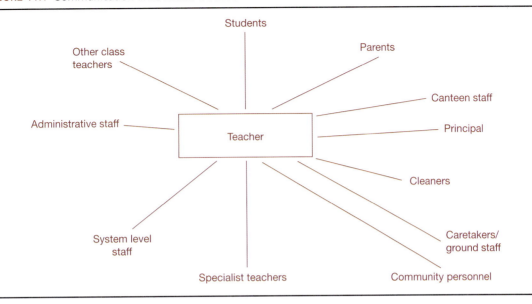

One way of trying to analyse communication is to categorise it in terms of three sets of skills: language skills, social skills and cognitive skills. That is, communication requires people to use language skills, to be able to interact socially with receivers and to know something about the subject under consideration (Pollard & Tann 1997).

Of course, we need to distinguish between the types of language used, as it may be verbal and/or non-verbal. Any verbal communication will involve the displaying of certain non-verbal expressions, whether these be limb movements, head nodding or eye movements. Meaning is conveyed by *how* we say something as well as *what* we say.

Verbal communication is what most teachers do most of the time. Various research studies have demonstrated that teachers do most of the talking in classrooms (Flanders 1970; Bennett *et al.* 1984; Cruickshank, Jenkins & Metcalf 2009). Further, a lot of the talking done by teachers is about management and supervision of tasks. Very little time is directed at posing questions about content and generally challenging students to become involved in problem solving and higher order thinking.

 In classrooms you have observed, are the questions raised by a teacher mainly about management and supervision of tasks? When, if at all, do they try to challenge students about their thinking? What happens when a teacher challenges students?

The teacher often uses verbal communication (knowingly or unknowingly) to maintain a superordinate position (McCormick & Pressley 1997). The language demands of each subject can be very challenging and many students have difficulty mastering the technical phrases of certain subjects such as Science. The vocabulary expectations of specialised subjects can be a very heavy load on students and can be devastating to their confidence levels and self-esteem.

Learning does not always result from verbal communication by the teacher. According to Moore (2009a), non-verbal variables often determine whether or not something is learned.

Non-verbal communication is used by teachers to support their verbal communication, but on occasions conflicting messages are conveyed. Amidon (1971) refers to four non-verbal dimensions of teacher behaviour in classrooms:

1. Classroom setting – the physical arrangement of desks, tables and chalkboards provides clues about what type of teaching will occur.

2 Curriculum materials – the presence or absence of textbooks, paper, crayons and audiovisual aids provide further clues about the type of teaching.
3 Non-verbal behaviours – the use of particular gestures, facial expressions and physical movements.
4 Combinations of the above symbols as a replacement for verbal behaviour.

The examples of non-verbal communication given in Figure 11.2 provide a useful checklist for teachers to reflect upon. We all need to ask what non-verbal clues we are giving with our particular style of teaching. More importantly, how carefully do we check to ensure that our non-verbal behaviour (such as body language) supports our verbal behaviour?

 What kinds of non-verbal communication do you typically use? With a close friend, sit down somewhere in a relatively formal situation and try to teach your friend about a particular topic that you know a lot about in three minutes. Ask your friend to comment on the verbal and non-verbal cues you used. If your friend is willing to do the same, ask them to present a brief talk of three minutes to you. Give feedback on your friend's communication styles.

FIGURE 11.2 Non-verbal items that provide clues to students

Room arrangement

Teacher's desk	– Location
	– Contents on the desk
Students' desks	– Location
	– Contents placed on each desk
Chalkboards	– Location
	– Content
Display tables	– Location
	– Content

Materials
Printed items

Textbooks	– availability or absence
Dictionaries	– availability or absence
Library and resource books	– availability or absence
Magazines	– availability or absence

Multimedia aids

Laptop/tablet PC	– availability or absence
Videotapes	– availability or absence
DVDs	– availability or absence
Digital viewers/audio tapes	– availability or absence

Special supplies

Objects	– availability or absence
Creative instruments	– availability or absence
Tools	– availability or absence
Manipulative instruments	– availability or absence

Non-verbal behaviours

Gestures	– presence or absence, frequency
Facial expressions	– presence or absence, frequency
Vocal expressiveness	– presence or absence, frequency
Position in the room	– presence or absence, frequency
Physical movement	– presence or absence, frequency
Posture	– presence or absence, frequency

Source: Based on Amidon 1971.

According to Miller (1981) the face is second only to words in communicating internal feelings. The use of the eyes is probably the most meaningful channel of non-verbal communication available to us (Moore 2009a). That is why the use of eye contact is so important for teachers.

Gestures with the head, arms, hands and other body parts are important non-verbal communicators. A tense body communicates insecurity to students. A relaxed torso denotes openness and friendliness (Kougl 1997).

There are other ways of classifying communication. For example, Conran (1989) refers to:
- proactive communication – that is, a direct form used mainly by the teacher to order, instruct, or structure a task
- interactive communication – this permits students and teachers to explore matters in an open form but requires trust and respect.

YOUR TURN

Observe another student teacher or teacher in a classroom and focus on their non-verbal communication.
- How did they use facial expressions and especially their eyes?
- How did their posture change during the lesson?
- To what extent did they use gestures?
- How did the classroom environment reinforce their non-verbal actions?

11.3 | MODELS OF COMMUNICATION

Various writers have provided simple and complex descriptions of the process of communication. A very simple one developed by Lasswell (1948) is based on the 'Five Ws':

Who says What to Whom in Which channel with What effect.

Cole and Chan (1994) produced a model consisting of the sender (who is responsible for formulating, encoding and transmitting messages), and the receiver (who decodes and interprets messages and gives feedback to the sender).

Johnson, Johnson & Holubec (1994) use the following processes to describe interpersonal communication:

Person 1
Sender:
(a) encodes – translates ideas, feelings and intentions
(b) transmits the message

Channel 1–2 (noise)

Person 2
Receiver:
(a) decodes – interprets the meaning of the message
(b) makes an internal response to the message

Person 2
Sender:
(a) encodes – translates ideas, feelings and intentions
(b) transmits the message

Channel 2–1 (noise)

Person 1
Receiver:
(a) decodes – interprets the meaning of the message
(b) makes an internal response

It should be noted that the message could be any verbal or non-verbal symbol. The channel is a means of communication and it could be the human voice or printed material. Noise is any element that interferes with accurate messages, such as attitudes or language used.

> **case study**
>
> **The need for communicating with warmth**
>
> Mary is very task-oriented. She has been teaching grade 3 classes for just two years. She comes across to students in her class as being very strict, perhaps distant and lacking warmth. Yet, Mary's natural communication style is to be explicit and precise in what she says to her students. She hasn't considered any socio-emotional aspects of her relationships with her class. A recent observation visit by her school principal has caused her to rethink her communication skills. He has recommended to her that she should show more empathy and warmth in how she communicates with her students.
>
> What steps should Mary take to redirect or modify her communication approaches? Should she try to work on her approaches with small groups as a starting point? Should she ask colleagues if she can observe some of their lessons? Should she ask an experienced teacher to develop a mentoring role with her?

11.4 COMMUNICATING EFFECTIVELY IN THE CLASSROOM

Given the constraints of classroom activities and the typical number of students per room (15–35), the types of classroom communication tend to be limited to:
- expository teaching – that is, communication by the teacher
- question-and-answer sessions – that is, communications directed by the teacher with some student responses
- discussion sessions – that is, relatively open exploration and communication of ideas by all participants.

Each situation requires different roles for the 'senders' and 'receivers' and the rules vary for each. Some of these classroom communication types are described in more detail in Chapter 12.

There are now a variety of computed-based classroom communication systems (CCSs) available (Scardamalia & Bereiter 2001; Berge & Collins 1995). These technology products support communication and interactivity in classes. For example, the University of Massachusetts has developed a CCS which:
- allows a teacher to present a problem or question
- allows students to enter their answers via a tablet PC
- instantly aggregates and summarises student answers for a teacher
- allows students to answer in small groups (Beatty 2004).

Students learn about communication through a variety of 'literacies' (Luke 1995). McLeod, Reynolds and Weckert (2001) emphasise the use of 'critical literacy' and 'media literacy'. Critical literacy involves a meta-textual level of understanding – it requires readers to reflect upon what a particular text is trying to do and to analyse its effects. Media literacy is being able to gain understanding from a variety of print, visual and graphic media (Abate 1994).

More and more students need to be able to use multiple literacies in dealing with topics and projects.

How confident and competent are you in terms of critical literacy and media literacy? Give an example to demonstrate your media literacy about a specific event or happening reported in the media.

11.5 | EXPLAINING

Operating effective communication systems in a classroom requires an open and trusting environment with ample opportunities for communication by all students and the teacher (Ryan, Cooper & Tauer 2008). The communication flows are likely to be mainly *downward*, but encouragement should be given to *upward* and *horizontal* flows. In most classrooms the teacher initiates downward communication by face-to-face contacts or by written directives. Yet it is possible for students to initiate upward communication to the teacher on matters of concern. Further, it can be most desirable for students to have horizontal communication with other students or for teachers and parents to have flows of information.

Explaining is an important aspect of sending information, particularly for teachers but also for students. Newly appointed teachers and student teachers often have difficulty in presenting clear explanations to their respective classes (Kougl 2006). A number of strategies to improve teachers' explanations are given in Figure 11.3.

A major point is to ensure that the content is well known and that the sequence to be used to introduce information is clear, logical and not too technical. It is often very advisable for the teacher to mentally rehearse the major points to be used in the explanation.

Explanations need to be given at a pace that students can follow and in a sequence they can understand. It is often useful for the teacher to have an outline on the whiteboard or overhead transparency that provides an overview of what information will be covered. Very complex explanations usually need to be given orally so that students have the opportunity to ask questions. Routine items of information are typically communicated by a written statement, letter or newsletter.

Oral explanations have to be presented in a lively manner, confidently and enthusiastically by the teacher, if the information is to be communicated effectively to all students (see Figure 11.3). Non-verbal communications (for example, gestures and eye contact) may be very significant in putting across a forceful explanation. The effective teacher will vary the tone of his/her voice and vary the speed (including judicious amounts of 'wait-time') to ensure that students' attention is maintained throughout the presentation. In every classroom students should also have the opportunity to give explanations to others, either in small groups or to the whole class (see Figure 11.4). In any explanations or reporting back sessions by students, it is important that they are aware of basic points of presentation such as getting the attention of the class and ensuring they know their subject matter and the three or four key things they want to present.

FIGURE 11.3 Effective explaining techniques for teachers

1. Use clear, logical steps to explain a topic/issue – mentally rehearse the order and sequence you will use.
2. Use direct language and avoid jargon.
3. Present information at a pace appropriate to the students.
4. Use examples to illustrate points.
5. Repeat points that are difficult to understand.
6. Use multiple communication channels simultaneously (e.g. overhead projector transparencies and oral comment).
7. Use an interesting lively tone of voice.
8. Use eye contact to hold attention.
9. Allow opportunities for students to ask questions throughout the explanation.

FIGURE 11.4 Effective explaining techniques for students

1 Ensure that they obtain the attention of the whole class.
2 Ensure that they understand the content to be explained.
3 Encourage them to provide an introduction that motivates the listeners.
4 Suggest that they use visual aids to assist their explanation.
5 Suggest that they vary their pace.

11.6 | QUESTIONING

Questioning is a central tool for both teachers and students. Teachers can ask questions of students as a means of testing understanding about a topic. Students can ask questions of the teacher to clarify meaning about the topic. Questions from both the teacher and the students prompt thinking. They should account for a high proportion of teacher talk and a high proportion of student talk, but various school constraints tend to minimise these opportunities.

Teachers ask questions of students for a variety of purposes, not all of which are directly related to the topic being taught. Some examples of purposes include to:
- get a particular student to pay attention and to participate
- test a student's knowledge of the topic
- review understanding of a topic
- diagnose a student's weakness
- motivate students
- stimulate particular kinds of thinking
- build up a student's security when the teacher is confident that the student will respond correctly
- control the behaviour of particular students or the whole class.

11.6.1 Classifications

One useful way of thinking about questions is to classify them into two main categories: *psycho-social* questions, which reflect relationships between students and the teacher or between students; and *pedagogical* questions, which focus on the teaching and learning of specific knowledge, skills and values.

Example:
Psycho-social: Does anyone have a puppy or kitten?
What is its name?
Pedagogical: What is the capital city of New South Wales?

Another way of classifying questions is to put them into analytic, empirical and valuative groups. Analytic questions probe students' understanding of the meaning of terms, symbols or concepts. Empirical questions require verification by evidence from our senses. Valuative questions elicit responses from students that praise, blame, criticise or somehow represent a value orientation.

Example:
Analytic: What is the square root of 49?
Empirical: If you put an ice-tray from the refrigerator onto the bench, will it sweat or remain dry?
Valuative: Who is your favourite Australian explorer and why?

A classification developed by Bloom *et al.* (1956) that has been used widely for 40 years is the *cognitive domain taxonomy* (see also Chapter 9). The six major areas included in this taxonomy have been used extensively by curriculum planners and teachers in planning a comprehensive array of classroom questions. The six major areas are as follows:

Level 1 – Knowledge requires the student to recognise or recall information.
Example: What year did Captain Cook land in Australia?

Level 2 – Comprehension requires the student to receive what is being communicated and to organise and arrange it mentally and describe it in their own words.
Example: What is the main idea that is presented in this graph?

Level 3 – Application requires students to apply a rule or process to particular, concrete situations.
Example: If $x = 2$ and $y = 4$ then $2x + 3y = ?$

Level 4 – Analysis requires students to think critically and in depth; to break down the communication into its constituent elements.
Example: Now that we have concluded our simulation game, what experiences did you have which support the principle that cooperation between nations is viable?

Level 5 – Synthesis requires students to work with elements or parts and combine them to form new patterns or structures.
Example: If we were to establish a student government for our class, what would it look like?

Level 6 – Evaluation requires students to make judgments about the merit of an idea, a solution or a problem, according to certain criteria.
Example: What are the significant arguments about whether Australia should or should not become a republic?

The six areas of the taxonomy have helped educators enormously with their curriculum planning and especially with the construction of tests and test items (Cruickshank, Jenkins & Metcalf 2009). Various research studies (for example, Ellis & Fouts 1997) have noted that teachers tend to use only the lowest levels of questions with their students (knowledge and comprehension) and rarely use the higher levels. Although there have been criticisms of the hierarchy of six levels (see Kreitzer & Madaus 1994), the levels have been an invaluable source for teachers and curriculum planners in planning a comprehensive range of questions that extend student thinking.

A simpler classification, which some educators contend is equally effective, is WHAT, WHEN, HOW, WHO and WHY. Taken collectively, these words enable a teacher to pursue a range of ideas and issues with students.

What questions elicit knowledge, recall of ideas
What is the population of Australia?
When questions elicit information about a temporal sequence
When did ethnic groups from Asia represent more than 10 per cent of the total population of Australia?
How questions elicit information about procedures
How did 'The White Australia Policy' operate?
Who questions elicit information about persons or groups involved in certain events
Who is the current minister responsible for migration policy?
Why questions elicit reasons for particular actions or events
Why do we trade more with Asia than with the European Common Market?

11.6.2 Planning questions

Planning of questions you intend to use in a lesson is vital, especially for beginning teachers. It is so important to ensure good phrasing and appropriate types of questions. It can be very useful to write many of the critical questions into your lesson plan because:
- this is likely to ensure that you give an interactive lesson
- it will remind you to develop more advanced levels of thinking (Cruickshank, Jenkins & Metcalf 2009).

The list in Figure 11.5 provides some helpful hints for the preparation of clearly understood and key questions. Of course other questions will emerge during the actual lesson and these will be incorporated in your planned list.

11.6.3 Asking questions

As noted earlier, it is important that questions are asked confidently and briskly and that the non-verbal activities – such as posture and facial expressions – support the questions you are posing to the class (see Figure 11.6). Although the speed at which you ask questions will depend on the nature of the material, it is useful for you to ask a question and then wait before requesting an answer. The sequence listed in Figure 11.7 is a useful guide.

Wait-time 'is the pause between a teacher's question and the student's response and between the response and the teacher's subsequent reaction or follow-up question' (Arends 2009, p. 383). Many teachers pause only briefly, often less than a second before calling on a student to respond. Tobin (1987) discovered in his research that effective teachers paused from three to four seconds.

For beginning teachers it is difficult to wait – they are concerned about management issues and the pace of their delivery. Cruickshank, Jenkins and Metcalf (2009) suggest the following for beginning teachers:

- After asking a question, count to five in your head while scanning the room.
- Do not repeat or rephrase or add to the question you have asked until at least several seconds have passed.

FIGURE 11.5 Reminders about planning questions

1. Prepare a number of key questions in advance which are directly related to the purpose of your lesson.
2. Include questions that involve higher and lower levels.
3. Ensure that the sequence of the key questions is logical to the students.
4. Make sure that the wording of the questions is clear and suited to the level of the students.

FIGURE 11.6 Reminders about asking questions

1. Write the key questions on a palmcard or sheet of paper and refer to it during the lesson.
2. Ask one question at a time and if necessary rephrase it.
3. Provide adequate time (including wait-time) for students to respond to each question.
4. Avoid rhetorical questions.
5. Avoid asking questions of a selective sub-group – distribute questions widely to class members.

FIGURE 11.7 A possible sequence for teacher questioning

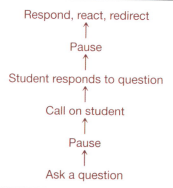

Source: Based on Cruickshank, Jenkins and Metcalf 2005.

A necessary skill in asking questions is to be able to **probe** – to ask additional questions to help raise the level of understanding. Probing is especially helpful in prompting students to use higher order thinking.

Redirecting is when a teacher asks another student to answer the same question. It is particularly effective with high-ability students but less so with insecure and weaker students (Coladarci & Gage 1984).

A teacher may sometimes **rephrase** a question in different terms. It may be necessary to rephrase on some occasions if the teacher initially phrased the question poorly. However, if the teacher has planned the questions in advance there is little need for rephrasing. This technique should be used sparingly. It is far more effective to probe rather than to rephrase.

Each teacher establishes class procedures for the way students are to respond to questions, but common expectations are that students will not call out but will signal their desire to answer by putting up their hand. It is important that the teacher acknowledges each student's answer and, where possible, provides positive support and praise.

11.6.4 Responding to answers

In theory, it is possible for a teacher to respond in a number of ways to a student's answer – it can be rejected, modified, ignored, corrected or accepted. The sensitive teacher is unlikely to reject or ignore an answer unless there are other behavioural factors that have elicited the response, such as a student acting as the class clown and deliberately making a provocative answer.

In practice, a teacher should accept student answers and this can be done in various supportive ways. For example, a teacher may hold it over with other responses for general consideration; or the teacher may ask for further clarification or extension; or the teacher may give partial praise but suggest that other aspects need to be considered.

Above all, the teacher should respond in ways that are seen to be friendly, supportive and non-threatening. Some students will need special help if they are shy and retiring and have great difficulty in offering responses to questions. Students should be encouraged to strive for more adequate answers by being supplied with hints and cues by the teacher.

> **YOUR TURN**
>
> In lessons you observe, what is the quality of the questions asked and the frequency? Develop a sample chart to record the following about a lesson you observe:
> - What levels of questions are used and how frequently?
> - Are the questions clear?
> - Is reinforcement used effectively?
> - Is wait-time used between questions?

11.6.5 Students asking questions

Research evidence (Galton, Simon & Croll 1980; Galton & MacBeath 2002; Cotton 2000; Jackson 1992) indicates that teachers continue to dominate the questions asked in classrooms, yet with the use of small group activities and whole-class discussions there should be opportunities for more student-initiated questions. It is a complex problem. For a start, teachers need to be aware of the extensive amount of talking they do in a classroom. This can be confirmed by a simple check using a tape recorder! Finding ways to restrain, contain or limit the amount of talking we do is very difficult and requires considerable self-discipline.

There are also the traditions and expectations about classroom behaviour. Parents may expect their children to be predominantly passive listeners and for teachers to do most of the talking. School procedures and policies require teachers to initiate and manage most classroom activities.

Notwithstanding this, the teacher can encourage students to ask more questions by giving them opportunities during class sessions, being available out of class time to respond to student questions and, in general, supporting a classroom climate that encourages students to question one another.

With Internet resources, students have the opportunities to pose questions to peers and to the teacher via email and chat lines (Jackson 2002; Norton & Wiburg 2003).

Simkins *et al.* (2002) highlight the role of multimedia as a communication tool. Students are able to choose pictures, text, video sounds and animation in their individual or group projects. These projects not only enable the student to provide information but they can, in addition, raise questions and issues that students have discovered.

11.7 | LISTENING

Listening is a very important element of communicating, yet it is the least researched and the least specifically taught (Johnson, Johnson & Holubec 1994). For two-way communication it is essential that the receiver of the message be an active listener.

Listening requires the receiver to listen to the message and to respond to the content and feelings being expressed. Some strategies for improving listening skills include:

- taking brief notes on what is being conveyed
- listening to the whole message – not prejudging its value
- concentrating on the main ideas
- not getting distracted by emotional words used by the sender
- maintaining eye contact with the sender
- providing support to the sender by verbal or non-verbal cues (Smith & Laws 1992, p. 45).

In many classrooms, as noted above, the bulk of the listening is done by students and the bulk of the talking is done by the teacher. However, there are different types of listening, which serve specific purposes. The effective teacher must be aware of these different purposes and demands. Pollard and Tann (1997) refer to four types, namely:

1. Interactive listening (for example, during a discussion).
2. Reactive listening (for example, following a set of instructions).
3. Discriminative listening (for example, listening to musical sounds).
4. Appreciative listening (for example, listening for aesthetic pleasure).

Each of these types of listening requires different skills for students (and for teachers). As teachers, we often do insufficient planning about the types of listening that are needed. Further, we tend to limit the opportunities for discriminative and appreciative listening.

Moore (2009a) uses the term 'reflective listening' rather than 'appreciative listening'. He refers to reflective listening as listening with feeling as well as with cognition – 'it calls for careful attention to both the verbal and non-verbal cues given by the speaker' (Moore 2009a, p. 172). He urges teachers to concentrate especially on reflective listening and to be sensitive to what students are communicating both verbally and non-verbally.

Interactive and reactive listening can require skills that are difficult to master by some students. For example, what strategies can a student use to indicate to another student (or the teacher) that he/she wants to speak – do they raise their hand, do they make certain body movements, do they start to talk? Students need to have developed particular social skills before they have the confidence to bid to speak.

Paraphrasing is a useful way of checking what a person is saying. It involves the listener in restating the message in their own words, and usually as a brief summary of what was said. It is a very helpful way of letting a person know that you understand them. It is also a valuable way of establishing rapport with the person.

Communication in school settings tends to be very evaluative, with the teacher using a variety of questions to probe what students are doing or thinking. As noted by Pollard and Tann (1997), it is unlikely and inappropriate in non-school settings for interactive communication to be as probing as is often the case in school settings.

 The next opportunity you have to observe a teacher with his/her class, select a five-minute period at the beginning, middle and end of the lesson and make a tally of the number and type of questions asked by the teacher and by students. What did the results indicate?

CONCLUDING COMMENTS

Communication is a key component of classroom life. Communicating effectively in the classroom requires giving particular attention to the elements of explaining, questioning and listening. It is important to remember that communication is a two-way process and that teachers and students need to acquire skills associated with sending and receiving messages.

KEY ISSUES RAISED IN THIS CHAPTER

1. Planning how to communicate information and instruction is as important as planning what to teach students.
2. Verbal and non-verbal forms of communication are both important.
3. ICT can assist the teacher by providing a range of interactive communication opportunities.
4. Questioning is a central tool for both teachers and learners. Students need additional opportunities to ask questions.
5. For two-way communication it is important that teachers and students are active listeners. Students need training in being interactive and reflective listeners.

REFLECTIONS AND ISSUES

1. One of your most important teaching tools is your speaking voice. By manipulating your voice efficiently and effectively, you can not only engage students and keep their attention but also safeguard your vocal cords. Do you agree? Using a short written piece, practice speaking it using different speeds and pitches.
2. Reflect on how confident you are when using:
   - Oral communication
   - Written communication
   - Visual communication
   - Non-verbal communication.
3. Tape-record part of a lesson. Calculate the total amount of teacher talk and the time spent by students talking to the teacher and to each other. Where was the talk directed? What was the talk about? How would you want to vary these time allocations in future lessons?
4. Select a current affairs topic and plan a series of questions that represent lower and higher levels of thinking. Present the topic to a class or to a small group. Reflect on the reactions you received to this presentation.
5. What listening activities are typically undertaken by students in a classroom? During a lesson, or a day, try to note how much time a teacher and students spend on interactive, reactive,

discriminative and appreciative forms of listening. How different is listening for the teacher and the students? What are the implications?
6   To what extent does non-verbal communication assist teachers to communicate with their students? Can non-verbal cues be misinterpreted by students from different cultures and backgrounds? What can a teacher do to reduce these misunderstandings?

Special references

Berge, ZL & Collins, MP (1995) *Computer Mediated Communication and the Online Classroom*, Collins, London.
Cooper, P & Simonds, CJ (2002) *Communication for the Classroom Teacher*, Allyn & Bacon, Boston.
Fowler, K & Manktelow, J (1995) *Improve your Communication Skills*, <www.mindtools.com> extracted 23 April 2009.
Kougl, K (1997) *Communicating in the Classroom*, Waveland Press, Austin, Texas.
Moore, KD (2009a) *Classroom Teaching Skills*, 2nd edn, McGraw Hill, Boston.
Ryan, K Cooper, JM & Tauer, S (2008) *Teaching for Student Learning*, Houghton Mifflin, Boston.

Web sources

For additional resources on communicating effectively, please go to: www.pearson.com.au/myeducationlab.

12

PEDAGOGY, TEACHING AND LEARNING

12.1 INTRODUCTION

'Pedagogy' is a term which has many meanings and perspectives, all related to particular practices of teaching and learning. Although pedagogy has referred in the past to traditional teaching and learning practices, it is evident that new communication technologies give teachers and students access to very different modes of working (Leach & Moon 2008).

Pedagogy is more than just teaching. According to Teaching Australia (2008) 'it is defined as the art and science of educating children, the strategies for using teacher professional knowledge, skills and abilities in order to foster good learning outcomes' (p. 3).

Teaching and learning modes used in schools reflect directly on the preferences of teachers and students. It is crucial for teachers to match their preferences with student preferences and to be willing to be creative in exploring new, exciting pedagogical opportunities.

12.2 PEDAGOGY

Shulman (1986) initiated considerable debate in the 1980s with his use of the phrase 'pedagogical content knowledge', and the importance of this knowledge for successful teaching. Shulman (1986) argued that pedagogical content knowledge consisted of a synthesis of three elements, namely:
- subject matter knowledge – 'deep' knowledge of the subject
- pedagogical knowledge – special knowledge of how to transfer knowledge in a comprehensible form to others
- knowledge of context – understanding of learner needs and local school environment.

Beginning teachers especially have to wrestle simultaneously with issues of pedagogical content (or knowledge) as well as general pedagogy (or generic teaching principles) (Ornstein & Lasley 2004).

Shulman (1992) developed a model of Pedagogical Reasoning which he argued was essential for teachers to master. It consists of:
- comprehension – teachers need to understand subject matter structures, 'big' ideas, deep meanings

- transformation – teachers must be able to transform this content knowledge into forms that are pedagogically powerful and adaptive to student abilities
- instruction – this includes various teaching and learning acts include whole class presentations and student-centred activities
- evaluation – this includes checking for students' understanding during and at the end of the lessons
- reflection – teachers must review, reconstruct, re-enact and critically analyse their own teaching
- new comprehension – through going about this cycle of activities the teacher achieves new comprehension about pedagogical content knowledge.

As noted by Jones and Moreland (2005), if teachers have sufficient content and pedagogical knowledge they can respond to students productively.

Acquiring appropriate pedagogical content knowledge is a challenge for all teachers – it involves using the Shulman processes (1992) listed above but also vigorous creative explorations. Leach and Moon (2008) focus especially on the following capabilities if teachers are going to take centre stage in transformative teaching and learning. They consider that teachers need to understand the complex factors that influence the process of learning and teaching, and in particular to understand and appreciate that:
- the mind is complex and multifaceted
- learning is a social process
- the development of knowledge is inseparable from the process of participating in a culture of practice
- pedagogy needs to imaginatively consider the wide range of tools and technologies
- pedagogy must build the self-esteem and identity of learners
- pedagogic settings should create the conditions for reflection and dialogue.

It is most significant that Teaching Australia (2008) is currently exploring the feasibility of establishing a National Centre for Pedagogy. The key features of a National Centre for Pedagogy will be to:
- initiate, conduct and broker research into pedagogy
- disseminate relevant findings to teachers and principals
- develop an evidence base to support teachers
- develop a relationship with teacher education institutions
- provide and inform professional learning activities
- foster partnerships and collaborative research.

 Reflect upon what the term pedagogy means to you. To what extent should imagination and creativity be used in developing appropriate pedagogy? Is the building of self-esteem and identity important? How can all these factors be included in classroom pedagogy?

12.3 | MATCHING TEACHING STYLES WITH STUDENTS' LEARNING STYLES

The teacher who works at developing a varied combination of teaching and learning modes is moving strongly to becoming a flexible teacher, and most likely to becoming a very effective one. We tend to prefer particular modes for a variety of reasons. It is less than professional to remain in a state of inertia with regard to a small number of teaching and learning modes when there are a number of exciting options available. Just a few of the possibilities are listed in Table 12.1 and in the Wheel of Instructional Choice (Figure 12.1). A number of them are described in detail in this chapter.

It might appear to be merely commonsense to match teaching styles with students' learning styles. However, we have all experienced at first hand teaching situations where the teacher's style

TABLE 12.1 Overview of alternative instructional modes

- constructivist learning
- cooperative learning
- debates
- demonstrations
- direct instruction
- discussion
- field work
- independent study
- inquiry
- lectures and presentations
- learning centres
- mastery learning
- online learning
- oral reports
- practice drills
- project learning
- questioning
- simulations and role-plays
- small group brainstorming

FIGURE 12.1 Wheel of Instructional Choice

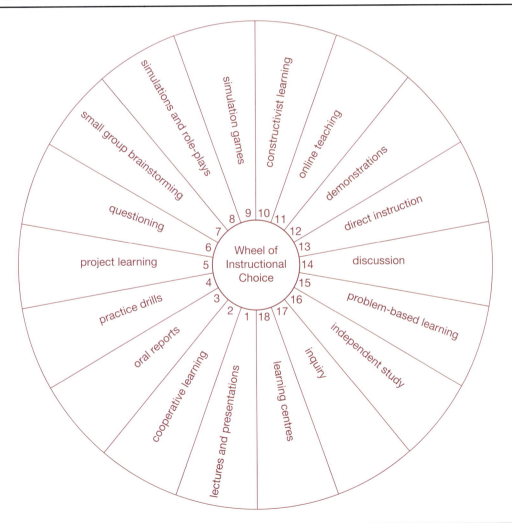

Source: Based on Cruickshank, Jenkins and Metcalf 2009.

and students' learning styles have been very different and even – according to some 'war' stories – diametrically opposed!

Various authors such as Dunn, Beaudry and Klavas (1989) and Hendry *et al.* (2005) contend that it is crucial for teachers to match up their styles with students' learning styles.

> Every person has a learning style – it's as individual as a signature.
>
> Knowing students' learning styles, we can organise classrooms to respond to their individual needs.

There is research evidence to support their stance (Lui & Read 1994; Witkin *et al.* 1977) but then again there is research evidence that does not support learning styles.

A study by Ford and Chen (2001) concluded that students who learned in matched conditions scored significantly higher in conceptual knowledge. However, their study also found that males outperformed females in matched conditions, so there are other complications to consider in this issue of matching and mismatching.

McIntyre, Pedder and Rudduck's (2005) study of pupil voice concluded that pupils who offered ideas, where teachers responded to these ideas, were able to develop highly consensual views about learning – that is, by a process of interaction they developed a closer matching. Zembylas (2007) takes a similar stance with his emphasis on teachers and students developing emotional understanding of each other or of the subject matter they explore.

 It can be very difficult to diagnose learning styles of students. What criteria do you use? For example, is performance in certain subjects more important than potential? How do you take account of students' needs and interests? Although it might be laudable to argue that you match learning tasks to the needs, interests, abilities and previous experiences of students, how do you do this in practice?

Slack and Norwich (2007) refer to the reliability and validity of Smith's (2001) student self-report inventory, which focuses on visual, auditory and kinaesthetic styles. Their study of 160 students in south-west England in Key Stage 2 mixed-age classes found that the visual and auditory scales were directly related to learning mode preferences. They concluded that the use of this inventory to match students' learning styles was a promising way of bringing about government policy on inclusive, differentiated and personalised learning.

YOUR TURN

From your observations of students in a classroom, can you notice several different learning styles?

- How would you label these learning styles?
- Do they seem to recur often with the same students or do they vary with the subject matter being taught?

Another question to consider is: do students care about learning? What invites students to learn? Tomlinson (2007) and McIntyre, Pedder and Rudduck (2005) contend that students seek an affirmation that they are significant in the classroom. As a consequence, matching factors should be couched in terms of:

- students' acceptance in the classroom
- how safe they feel – physically, emotionally and intellectually
- how they consider people care about them and listen to them.

Morrison and Ridley (1988) use a similar argument when they suggest that teachers need to consider the following questions when matching their students:

- How is each student's self-concept being developed?

- How is each student's motivation being developed?
- How do teachers meet students' individual differences of need, interest, ability and skill?
- How do teachers develop individual learning styles and rates of learning?
- How is autonomy being developed in each student?
- How does the organisation of the class and school facilities foster security in each student?

The other side of the equation is to consider the teaching styles of teachers, which are often the result of personal attitudes and values, personality, previous experience and availability of resources. Hargreaves (1972) distinguishes between three major teaching styles, which he labels 'lion tamers' (firm discipline, teacher as expert); 'entertainers' (multiple resources, active group work); and 'new normalities' (negotiated, individualised teaching).

Ryan and Cooper (2008) use the terms 'concrete sequential', 'abstract sequential', 'abstract random' and 'concrete random' to categorise four dominant teaching styles. 'Concrete sequential' teachers rely on hands-on materials, working models and displays to help students learn, and tend to use task-oriented lessons. 'Abstract sequential' teachers value depth of knowledge and help students think about topics and to generate ideas. 'Abstract random' teachers capitalise on student interest and enthusiasm rather than adhering strictly to a lesson plan. 'Concrete random' teachers rely on a variety of resources and organise their classes so that students operate independently or cooperatively.

These are just a few of the many groupings and stereotypes that have been produced to describe teaching styles. The major point to stress is that there are many differences and we need to be aware that teaching styles will be dependent on such factors as:
- type of activity in the classroom
- type of organisation of the classroom
- use of resources
- grouping and organisation of students
- students' roles in the classroom
- criteria used for assessing students
- nature and amount of student and teacher talk.

Yet it is also important to heed Joyce and Weil's (1986):433–4) caveats about learning styles, namely:
- It is not possible for teachers to assess the developmental levels of all their students and then create totally personalised curricula exactly matching their levels.
- Students can and will adapt to different teaching styles if we give them the chance.
- The simplest way to discover the environments in which students progress best is to provide them with a variety and observe their behaviour.

These authors are emphasising the adaptability that is displayed by teachers and by students. No teacher has a fixed style of teaching and no student has a fixed style of learning. In teaching–learning situations it is crucial that participants be flexible and adaptable.

Joyce and Weil (1986) provide additional insights to learning and teaching styles by their use of the term 'discomfort'. They argue that a discomfort factor is necessary for teachers and students. If an environment is perfectly matched to the developmental levels of learners, it can be too comfortable and there will be little advance beyond that level. That is, discomfort is a precursor to growth (see also Chapter 5). Teachers need to be constantly trying out new teaching styles even if they are unfamiliar and cause discomfort. For their part, teachers must assist students to acquire the necessary skills to adapt to new, unfamiliar learning styles.

12.4 | IMPACT OF STANDARDS ON TEACHING AND LEARNING

The impact of standards and standards testing has been most notable in the United States and the United Kingdom. In the US the *No Child Left Behind Act* (NCLB 2001) aims to improve the standards of accountability by the use of standardised assessments (Fuhrman & Elmore 2004). If a school does not meet the proficiency standards for all sub-groups of the student population (including African Americans, Latinos, low-income students and special education students), corrective action is taken such as acquiring additional tutoring for students or transferring poorly performing staff.

As might be anticipated, the NCLB has put teachers under considerable pressure to 'teach to the test' and to use teaching and learning modes involving direct instruction and practice drills (Marsh & Willis 2007).

In the UK, national initiatives such as the National Literacy and Numeracy Strategies have been implemented to improve learning and to raise standards. Teachers are encouraged to use up to 15 minutes of whole-class teaching in literacy and numeracy each day for primary school students. Myhill's (2006) study concludes that the whole-class discourses are typically teacher directed, to lead students to a predetermined destination. Burns and Myhill (2004) conclude that teaching in the UK is now 'a heavily accountable teaching culture, highly instructional, objectives-based pedagogy' (p. 47).

There are indications that the national testing of literacy and numeracy in Australia may also be leading to restrictive modes of teaching and learning (*The Age*, 9 February, 2010, p. 2).

12.5 | MAKING USE OF TECHNOLOGY

All teaching and learning modes of instruction make use of some form of technology, ranging from chalk to elaborate computer packages. Some forms of technology we take for granted – such as chalk, marker pens and whiteboards – especially if they do not interfere with a well-proven, traditional mode of instruction. Even overhead projectors and LCD projectors give minimal interference to teacher-directed forms of delivery.

It is when major behavioural changes are called for that teachers espouse concerns about using technology. There may be good reason for this technophobia if it involves different grouping patterns of students, if the authority of the teacher role is reduced, or if the teacher has to learn new skills. Fear of using computers in schools – 'cyberphobia' (Russell & Bradley 1996) – may be quite deep-seated and may occur in young teachers as well as older, highly experienced teachers.

There are currently many proponents who extol the virtues of incorporating computers into classroom activities; that is, technology infused instruction. 'It will become as integral a part of the classroom as the whiteboard' (Gardner P, 1997, p. 6). 'Multimedia [computers] create rich learning environments where kids really thrive' (Betts 1994, p. 20).

Within a few short years, computer technology for educational use has expanded rapidly. There is now available a range of software programs that can provide highly sophisticated functions relating to computer-managed instruction (CMI) and computer-assisted instruction (CAI).

CMI assists teachers with various organisational tasks ranging from recording student activities, conducting resource investigations and presentations and recording student assessments.

Instructional opportunities for students (CAI) are forever increasing (Williams 2000). Consider the following examples:
- Skills software for drilling and practising – skills software programs offer interactive experiences, generally with immediate feedback about performance.
- Computer graphics programs enable students to experience the world other than through verbal and print language. According to Norton and Wiburg (2003, p. 53), 'shape, size, proportion, relationship, scale, surface, texture and rhythm are all expressed more rapidly through image making than through using words'. As an example, Franklin (2004) uses the floating staircase in Harry Potter movies as a video clip to demonstrate how figures ascending and descending stairs can be drawn in art classes.
- Word processors, desktop publishers and web-based editors – word processors are computer programs that allow the student to write, edit, revise, format and print text. Documents can

include text and graphics at a standard similar to that of professional printers. Web-based editors enable students to create web pages for publication on the Internet.
- Databases – text-based databases include only text information; hypermedia databases provide information with access through links; multimedia databases include a variety of media forms including pictures, video clips, text and sound.
- Telecommunication opportunities include email messages; listservers distribute a single message to multiple receivers; bulletin boards post a public message to multiple receivers; chat rooms allow online conversations with multiple participants; synchronous communication allows two or more people to interact at the exact same time.
- Blogs (weblogs) are websites that provide commentaries or news on particular subjects. Many teachers are now encouraging students to develop blogs as personal online diaries (Richardson 2006; Ohler 2006).
- Internet access to information is available through the use of various search engines. Students develop information searching skills and also evaluative skills.
- Internet access to teaching and learning programs is readily available and these are fun to use. For example, Grey (2001) refers to 'The Human Race', an interactive Internet site that encourages students to enjoy regular physical activity away from their computers.
- Simulations – many educational software publishers produce simulations. 'Students are given the power to "play" with a model of the subject being studied and to experience the effects of changing different variables in the model' (Norton & Wiburg 2003, p. 57).
- Mathematical devices provide students with the opportunity to explore real-time data. For example, probeware allows students to measure temperature, humidity, distance and many related variables. Large amounts of data can be collected in a class period.
- Spreadsheets are computer programs that allow students to create charts and graphs that provide a visual representation of data.
- Assessment of student performance software is increasing rapidly. There are now programs available that create a variety of rubrics. (Criteria for judging performance are provided; electronic portfolios of work can be created; problem-solving processes of students can be observed and recorded; and a new set of interpretive tools is being created to monitor higher-level thinking and group collaboration.)
- Online courses are being developed at all levels of schooling. Ford (2001) describes a Virtual Enrichment Program for primary students living in outback areas of New South Wales. Secondary students living in small towns and outback areas of Queensland are being offered online (asynchronous) and real-time (synchronous) forms of instruction (Hansford 2000).

Cross (2006) notes how the Promethean Interactive White Boards (Smart boards) have a student response system whereby students can answer teachers' questions using hand-held keypads without their fellow students knowing. It encourages shy children to voice opinions and become more engaged.

In summary, computer technology greatly benefits classroom instruction because it:
- provides the flexibility to meet the individual needs and abilities of each student (Norton & Wiburg 2003; ASCD 2005, 21 October)
- provides students with immediate access to rich source materials beyond the school and beyond the nation – that is, it fosters cross-cultural perspectives (Khan 1997)
- presents information in new, relevant ways (Thornburg 2002)
- encourages students to try out new ideas and to problem solve (Grabe & Grabe 2000; Means 2000; Christophersen 2006)
- encourages students to design, plan and undertake project-based multimedia learning (Simkins et al. 2002)
- motivates and stimulates learning (Norton & Wiburg 2003)
- enables students to feel comfortable with the tools of the Information Age

- enables teachers to move from information-giver or instructor, to facilitator of learning (Carey 2006).

However, it is evident in many schools that modes of instruction have been little affected by computer technology:

> with all of the investment of time and money that has gone into putting the hardware and software in place in schools, students still spend most of their school days as if these tools and information resources had never been invented (Becker 1998, p. 24).

Various reasons have been given for the limited amount of take-up in schools, including the following:
- Teachers are unfamiliar with the equipment, and time and resources are not available to obtain comprehensive, ongoing training.
- There is an insufficient school budget for sufficient numbers of personal computers, software, network wiring and support technicians to be available (Cradler & Bridgforth 2004).
- There is limited pre-service preparation of teachers in the use of computer technology (Albion 1996) and the result is student teachers' anxiety about using computers (Russell & Bradley 1996).
- There is no overwhelming research evidence that teachers can be more effective using computer-based lessons rather than non-computer-based lessons (McQuillan 1994).
- It could heighten problems of equity for poorly funded schools.
- Computer-based technology threatens teachers – they are likely to lose more and more control over the work they do (Bigum 1997).
- Long use of computers by young children may rob them of important social and physical experiences (Monke 2006).
- Computer technology is not a neutral force in the classroom. It concentrates on speed and power and downplays student reflection and ethics (Schwartz 1996).
- There is increasing evidence that it may discourage social interaction and lead to solitary behaviour.
- There are reports of considerable health risks for teachers (eye strain, wrist and shoulder pain) and for students (effects of carrying heavy laptops to and from school) (Gibson 2002).
- A growing number of cases of student cheating (cyber cheating) and cyber bullying are occurring at all levels of teaching (Varnham 2001; Poole 2004; Franek 2006).

Perhaps Lundin's (2003) warning is timely: 'We should reflect on "Online and offline: Getting the mixture right", or expressed another way "E-world and R-world: Getting the mixture right"' (p. 13).

> **YOUR TURN**
>
> What examples of CAI have you observed in schools you have visited?
> - Does it appear to be used more and more by teachers or is it quite limited?
> - Talk to classroom teachers about their interest in and use of CAI.

12.6 TEACHING AND LEARNING PHASES OF INSTRUCTION

Before embarking on a detailed analysis of specific teaching and learning modes, it is important to note that within each mode there are relatively common phases that tend to occur. Referring back to the Herbartian steps (McMurry & McMurry 1926), these consist of:
- *Preparation*: the teacher readies the students for what they are about to learn.
- *Presentation*: the teacher transmits the new knowledge.

- *Comparison and abstraction*: students and the teacher examine the new particulars and make comparisons.
- *Application*: the general principles developed are put to use.

There are many other variations that have been developed since that period but all have some introductory phase, a main activity phase, and a concluding or application phase. The amount of emphasis given to each phase will depend upon the orientation and value stance of the mode of instruction. Some illustrative examples are included in Table 12.2.

The example provided by Broudy and Palmer (1965) in Table 12.2 is very teacher-dominated and Herbartian in outlook, in terms of the lock-step set of procedures. Joyce and Showers' (1986) set of phases is far more cyclical in nature. The pre-active activities involve planning but also guessing about interactive phase activities that may occur. The interactive phase activities can be partly planned but they also involve on-the-spot decision making and reacting to student responses. Teachers need to be able to 'read' students' responses to the mode of instruction, using skills that Joyce and Showers (1986, p. 14) refer to as the 'invisible skills of teaching' – that is, the ability of the teacher to read 'in-flight' information from the students and the construction of responses to student behaviour (and, most importantly, the ability to withhold or delay responses).

This issue will be discussed later with reference to individual modes, but suffice to say it emphasises the point that various influencing patterns are in operation in every classroom, in activities where the teacher influences students, and in activities where the students influence the teacher. As a result, tactics initially planned by a teacher may need to be aborted, revised or continued as a result of student reactions. Students, in turn, either overtly or covertly accept a teaching and learning mode, or attempt to modify it or, on rare occasions, reject it outright.

TABLE 12.2 Examples of phases of instruction

1	Preparation for instruction	1	Preactive phase
2	Motivation		
3	Presentation of the learning task		
4	Inducement of the trial response	2	Interactive phase
5	Correction of the trial response		
6	Fixation of response	3	Post-active phase
7	Test response and evaluation		

Source: Broudy and Palmer, 1965   Source: Jackson, 1968; Joyce and Showers, 1986

12.7 | TEACHING AND LEARNING MODES

Teachers are often urged to use a variety of modes to ensure that diverse student interests and abilities can be accommodated. Yet teachers can be limited in the modes they can use because of:
- restricted student abilities and interests
- the high number of students in a class
- the limitations of the teaching room
- insufficient background or knowledge about a specific instructional mode
- the type of technology available.

The last point is especially important in that technology has varied application for all modes. Simplistically, it might be argued that the computer is used as a tutor for teacher-directed lessons (knowledge instruction setting) and as a tool in student-centred lessons (knowledge construction setting) (Gibson 2002).

It is evident from Table 12.3 that a wide variety of modes is available and most teachers have the opportunity to expand their repertoire. Some major modes are described below.

TABLE 12.3 Teacher-directed/student-centred emphasis in lessons

Modes of instruction	Intro	Major activity	Conclusion	Teacher role	Student role	Organisation mode
Lecturing or teacher talks	T	T	T	present information	listen and respond	total class
Practice drills	T	T/S	T	repeat examples until skills mastered	respond and practise	total class or small groups
Directed questioning	T	T/S	T	present question	respond with answer, occasional questions	total class or small groups or individual
Discussion	T	T/S	T/S	question, listen, respond	listen, respond, question	total class or small groups or individual
Demonstration	T	S	T/S	present information materials	observe, listen, practise	total class or small groups
Direct instruction	T	T/S	T	direct activities, monitor	respond and practise	total class
Constructivism	T	S	T/S	introduce, question	participate, respond, question	small groups
Cooperative learning	T	S	T/S	introduce, monitor	interact, engage in activities	small groups
Problem solving or inquiry	T	S	T/S	direct activities	engage in activities	small groups or individual
Role-playing, simulation games	T	S	T/S	introduce, monitor	Participate or act out	small groups
Small group activity	T	S	T/S	introduce, supervise	participate, interact, report	small groups
Independent study	S	S	S	facilitate, monitor	initiate, engage in activities	individual

T = Teacher directed
S = Student centred

12.7.1 Lectures, teacher talks, expository talks and teacher presentations

A lecture is an oral presentation usually given by the teacher. Cruickshank, Jenkins and Metcalf (2009) prefer to describe it as a teaching method where the lecturer talks, acts, persuades and cajoles.

It can be a formal lecture, which tends to be long, uninterrupted and highly structured; or an informal lecture, which tends to be brief and includes some student participation. Both types tend to include various multimedia supports such as overhead projector transparencies, slides, posters or artefacts. At primary and secondary school levels, most would agree that informal lectures of up to 20 minutes are the preferred version of the two forms.

Lectures can be effective. Some of the advantages are listed below.
- They enable information to be transmitted quickly and directly.
- They are a useful way of introducing a new topic.
- They are successful if the main purpose is to disseminate information (rather than to develop skills or values).
- They can be very valuable if the material is not available elsewhere.
- They can be adapted at short notice.
- They can enthuse and motivate students.

Contrary to popular opinion, which tends to denigrate lectures as passive, boring and ineffective, research studies have demonstrated that lectures are at least as effective as other instructional modes (Gage & Berliner 1976; Rosenshine & Stevens 1986). For example, research by McKeachie and Kulick (1975) on 21 studies concluded that the lecture method was superior in 12, about equal to the discussion method in 4 and inferior to the discussion method in 5 – however, there were methodological problems in making these comparisons.

Although lectures have survived as an instructional mode over centuries, there are specific aspects that must be considered for them to be effective for primary and secondary school students.

The good lecture is one in which the students work with the teacher – it challenges the imagination of each student (Cruickshank, Jenkins & Metcalf 2009). It must be sufficiently open for students to ask questions and the teacher must build on these questions and responses.

It is important to remember that computer graphics, such as those included in lectures that involve PowerPoint presentations, can add considerable impact to the lecture and are being used increasingly by teachers. Norton and Wiburg (2003) provide a number of interesting examples that can be used at primary and secondary school levels.

Important characteristics of good lectures include:
- keeping your voice at an interesting pitch, using expression and making sure all students can hear you
- encouraging students to ask questions
- using a number of multimedia aids, models, hand-out sheets and whiteboard drawings (to focus the attention of the student, serve as a reference point and to make the subject understood) at the beginning, stating the key points to be made
- presenting the lecture in a lively, vibrant manner so as to engage students
- ensuring that the lecturer demonstrates their own intense interest in the topic
- limiting the lecture to 20 minutes and keeping the content appropriate to the interests and abilities of the students
- following key statements and questions with strategic pauses
- interposing students' names into the lecture and relating content to areas that interest the students
- using notes sparingly to ensure optimal dramatic effect.

There are of course many potential problems in using lectures. Some of the disadvantages of lectures include:
- not allowing for student creativity or problem solving
- at the worst, becoming an 'ego-trip' for the teacher
- leading to student boredom
- providing minimal opportunity for social development.

Lectures, or 'teacher-fronted instruction' as Patthey-Chavez (1998) terms them, continue to be widely used by teachers. In many cases, classroom discourse continues to be teacher-dominated and the lecture mode maintains this power relationship.

ICT applications

Lectures can certainly be made more appealing by incorporating computer-mediated presentations. In particular PowerPoint presentations can be very effective. Computer programs are available that help teachers to add all kinds of visual and auditory aids.

Susskind's (2008) study compared using PowerPoint presentations to overhead slides. He concluded that there were positive effects on student attitudes from using computer-mediated PowerPoints.

A study by Savoy, Proctor and Salvendy (2009) on the use of PowerPoint presentations compared with traditional lectures concluded the following:
- for retaining complex graphics and figures, PowerPoint presentations had an advantage
- for retaining information and concepts that are best conveyed through dialogue, traditional presentations are best.

Poo and Thye (2006) compared e-lectures with normal lectures with Junior College students. There was no significant difference but high-ability students had a slight preference for learning through e-lectures.

Das and Rahimah (2006) discuss the effectiveness of using animated PowerPoint lectures (using Vox proxy software). They concluded that Year 8 students were very positive about using these lectures and worked on them at their own pace.

Babb and Ross (2009) studied the value of giving students online lecture slides before the lecture. They concluded that students were happier having the online lecture slides in advance – it enabled them to have a better understanding of materials.

Stiler (2007) examined the potential for using MP3 players for recording lectures and talks. He noted the play-back potential if MP3 players are used.

Schmid (2008) researched the use of multimedia lectures using Smart Boards and concluded that multiple representations were only useful if students actively processed the information.

12.7.2 Practice drills

The term *practice drills* probably conjures up all kinds of negative memories about learning tables, but the fact of the matter is that practice through repetition is very necessary in certain areas, such as mathematics, spelling, grammar and skills development.

The purpose of practice drills is to achieve mastery and perfection to the extent that students can recall quickly and reliably. Computer software programs and language laboratories greatly extend the opportunities for students to undertake (and enjoy) drill sessions.

ICT applications

Computer programs are available mostly in Mathematics, Spelling, Foreign Languages and other subjects where the content is well structured. For many of these subjects, a direct instruction model is used (see later in this chapter): namely, a problem situation is presented, students are asked to find a solution, and they are given feedback on their level of success. Correct solutions enable students to move on to more difficult situations. Incorrect answers prompt remedial problems (Arends 2009).

Yeh and Lo (2008) used an online corrective feedback and error analysis system with students in an English as a Second Language class. With this system teachers can mark error corrections on online documents and students can receive corrective feedback instantly.

Tan and Pakiam (2006) used video presentations to communicate ideas to young writers in Primary 2 classes and found it to be very successful.

Boon and Yong (2006) used 'The Maths Story' software to help weak students to learn how to use trigonometric ratios in lower secondary classes.

Other computer programs enable skills of information literacy to be developed. For example, skills in retrieving data from CD-ROM encyclopaedias need to be practiced. Students at primary and secondary school levels enjoy learning the procedures because the multimedia presentations occur in the form of audio, video clips and still pictures. Similarly, students enjoy practising their retrieval skills with CD-ROM dictionaries, atlases and almanacs (Gardner P, 1997). Opportunities to practise the sending of email messages, together with graphics enclosures, are also widely enjoyed by students of all ages (Lifter & Adams 1997).

Practice drills can be effective with students if the following points are observed:
- Keep practice drills short – 10–15 minutes.
- Vary the amount and kind of drill according to the needs of the students.
- Encourage students to record their progress in practice drills.
- Use practice drills incidentally and interspersed with other activities.
- Use games for practising drills.
- Ensure that students understand why it is necessary to gain mastery of specific concepts or skills.

Too often practice drills can be:
- very boring
- too long and too frequent
- of negative interest to many students.

12.7.3 Directed questioning

The use of questions to students, both oral and written, is a very common mode of instruction. There are various reasons why teachers use questions and not all are related to student learning! Questions are used to:
- get immediate feedback during a demonstration
- focus a discussion
- pose a problem for solution
- help students sharpen their perceptions
- attract a student's attention
- get a particular student to participate
- diagnose a student's weaknesses
- allow a student to shine before his/her peers
- build up a student's security to an extent where the teacher is quite sure the student will respond correctly.

Questions can be used in rapid-fire succession or they can proceed more slowly with time for thoughtful responses. The types of questions you ask will determine the kind of thinking you want your students to do. Various writers have provided different classifications of questions. Some of these include:
- *high and low order questions*:
  - low order – mainly recall of facts and specifics
  - high order – mainly application, analysis
- *convergent and divergent or closed and open questions*:
  - convergent/closed – leads to expected answers
  - divergent/open – allows new directions in answers
- *what, when, how, who and why*:
  - a useful range to use, which proceeds in sequence from low order to high order.

Asking appropriate questions is a difficult task and requires considerable practice. A useful starting point is to choose an appropriate topic and then write down a range of questions that cover the sequences listed above. Ensure that the questions are concise and at an appropriate level of difficulty for students. Eliminate questions that appear to be ambiguous or vague. Table 12.4 provides some useful beginnings for questions based on the purposes you have in mind.

It is timely to remember that preparing good questions is only part of the exercise. Knowing how to present the questions to the class and responding to their reactions is of major importance. A basic rule is to ask the question, pause and then call on a specific student by name to respond (Orlich *et al.* 2009). Using eye contact; distributing questions around the room; giving your students plenty of time to answer (wait-time of three to five seconds); extending thinking by using further probes such as 'Are you sure?' or 'Give me an example' are just some of the techniques to ensure successful use of directed questioning.

Moore (2009b) has a more detailed list of guidelines to help teachers refine their skill at questioning, namely:

- Ask clear questions.
- Ask your question before designating a respondent.
- Ask questions that match your lesson objectives.
- Distribute questions about the class fairly.
- Ask questions suited to all ability levels in the class.
- Ask only one question at a time.
- Avoid asking questions too soon.
- Pause for at least three seconds following each question.
- Use questions to help students modify their responses.
- Avoid too many questions that give away answers, and avoid one-word-answer questions.
- Reinforce student answers sparingly.
- Listen carefully to student responses.

Often students are very anxious about teacher questions and, in particular, their answers, because they realise that they will be judged by their peers as well as the teacher. They may be cautious in answering because of a lack of self-confidence. If the climate of the classroom is positive and supportive, students may be more prepared to take personal risks. It is up to the teacher to support students who are not confident about answering questions by using rephrasing of questions, asking supplementary questions or providing additional information.

YOUR TURN

Have you analysed your questioning technique in the classroom?

- Are you confident that your range and level of questions are appropriate for the class?
- Do the students appear to be comfortable with the questions you ask or do they often display puzzlement or even embarrassment?
- Tape-record about 30 minutes of one of your lessons and then analyse the questions you ask.

ICT applications

Andrade *et al.* (2008) used Kipling's (2002) questions (What must one learn? Why must one learn? How must one learn? When must one learn? Where must one learn? Who must learn?) in an e-learning system with students. These proactive questions proved to be very effective.

TABLE 12.4 Some examples of question beginnings

To assess knowledge	Define, Describe, Tell, List, Who, When, Identify, Where
To check understanding	How do you know? Explain, Compare, Contrast
To help analyse problems	What causes, How, Why?
To explore values	How do you feel? Why do you prefer? Why do you feel?
To encourage creative thinking	What if, How else, Just suppose
To evaluate	Select, Judge, Evaluate
To apply knowledge	Demonstrate, Use the information to, Construct

Source: adapted from Roe et al. (1989), p. 169.

12.7.4 Direct instruction

Direct instruction is a teacher-centred mode of instruction. The focus is on promoting student learning of knowledge by having lessons that are well structured and can be taught in a step-by-step process (Arends 2009). Killen (2006) refers to it as the use of 'well scripted lessons' (p. 80).

The purpose of direct instruction is to help students learn basic academic content (such as reading or mathematics) in the most efficient way. According to Arends (2009) there are five steps involved, namely:

- establishing set
- explanation and/or demonstration
- guided practice
- feedback
- extended practice.

Cruickshank, Jenkins and Metcalf (2009) contend that direct instruction is characterised by three words – practice, practice, practice! Researchers working in the area of direct instruction have compiled some of the key elements, as listed in Figure 12.2.

The planning of direct instruction lessons requires specific behaviours and decisions. It could be argued, therefore, that direct instruction is based on behavioural principles.

The *planning* involves the following:

- The teacher prepares objectives that are student-based and specific, specifies the testing situation and identifies the level of performance.
- Task analysis is used to define precisely what a learner needs to do to perform a specific skill. It will involve dividing the overall skills into sub-skills and putting these into logical order.
- Managing of time by the teacher is most important; he/she needs to ensure that it is sufficient to match the abilities of the students.

FIGURE 12.2 Key elements of direct instruction

- Teacher centrality – teacher exerts strong instructional direction and control.
- Task orientation – major emphasis is on academic learning (not social learning or higher level thinking).
- Positive expectations – the teacher is concerned about the academic progress of each student and he/she expects each student to be successful.
- Student cooperation and accountability – students are held accountable for their academic work.
- Non-negative affect – the teacher ensures that the learners feel psychologically safe and secure and are not threatened.
- Established structure – the teacher establishes class rules and ensures that they are implemented.

Source: After Weil and Murphy 1982; Murphy, Weil and McGreal 1986.

The actual *conducting* of direct instruction lessons involves the following:
- The teacher explains the objectives of the lesson and how it follows from previous lessons.
- The teacher demonstrates the particular skill to be learnt.
- The teacher assigns short, meaningful amounts of practice. This may involve over-learning to establish complete mastery.
- The teacher checks understanding and provides feedback.

A number of studies (Peterson 1979; Rosenshine 1986) have demonstrated that direct instruction is very effective when the content to be learned is well structured, clear and unambiguous (Cruickshank, Jenkins & Metcalf 2009). Peterson (1979) concludes that direct instruction is superior when the goal is to improve achievement in basic skills as measured on tests. Peterson (1982) contends that direct instruction is very effective for teaching younger, less able students.

There are of course limitations with direct instruction. Slavin (1999) concludes that it de-emphasises students' autonomy. Peterson (1979) contends that the approach does not promote creativity and problem solving. Arends (2009) notes that, although direct instruction is widely used in American classrooms, it places far too much emphasis on teacher talk.

ICT applications

Luik and Mikk (2007) studied the use of electronic textbooks for high-achieving and low-achieving students in four schools, using a direct instruction teaching mode. They concluded that the design of the software should be different for learners with different achievement levels.

12.7.5 Demonstrations

Demonstrations by the teacher can be used with students of all ages and across all subjects. They can range from an elaborate scientific demonstration to the total class to demonstrations of a skill to a single student. Demonstrations can be especially appealing to students, and not simply because they represent a change from the usual classroom routines. However, it is important that the teacher is not only knowledgeable about the topic but also uses a variety of aids to ensure that students understand what is being demonstrated.

Some reminders to ensure successful demonstrations include the following:
- Make sure that it is kept simple, at an appropriate difficulty level and focused – do not try to teach too many concepts.
- Ensure that all students can see and hear the demonstration.
- Check frequently during the demonstration to ensure that students are following.
- Make sure that a wide range of objects and models are used to aid the demonstration.
- Where appropriate, students should be encouraged to also demonstrate the activity or process.
- Use a lively, enthusiastic style.
- Ensure that all safety considerations have been met.

ICT application

Sun, Lin and Yu (2007) used a web-based virtual science laboratory to demonstrate natural science to primary school students. Students were very positive about the web-based virtual laboratory.

12.7.6 Online teaching

Online teaching can range from the use of multimedia resources accessible from digital repositories to complete instructional courses (Freebody 2005). The online environment is unique because of the capacity to shift the time of delivery and the place of delivery compared with traditional teaching (Jury 2004).

Yet developing online teaching courses is expensive and there are a number of issues to consider:
- Does the need exist?

- The design of the course must consider the existing technology available, and how to maintain interactivity between instructors and students (Melton 2004).

Yet it is evident that electronic online communities are developing rapidly. Synchronous tools (such as chat rooms and instant messaging) and asynchronous communication tools (such as email, discussion boards and blogs) are now available to facilitate the implementation of online courses.

ICT applications

Ford (2001) describes a Virtual Enrichment Program for primary students living in outback areas of New South Wales. Secondary students living in small towns and outback areas of Queensland are being offered online (asynchronous) and real-time (synchronous) forms of instruction (Hansford 2000).

Vighnarajah, Wong and Bakar (2008) surveyed secondary school students' use of self-regulated online community discussions. There was general positive perception in using the forum, chat and dialogue tools.

King and Robinson (2008) used an electronic voting system to enliven the classroom and to enable large numbers of students to respond to questions in real time during class.

Ramos and Yudko (2006) concluded from their study that the number of hits rather than discussion posts were the better predictors of student success in online courses. They considered that students who engaged in online discussion had a tendency to engage in shallow discussion.

Yon, Ling and Aik (2006) used online questions to motivate lower secondary students learning science. They concluded that students became more motivated in terms of spontaneity in asking questions and taking initiatives.

12.7.7 Constructivism

Constructivism, or *problem-based learning*, focuses on maximising student understanding. According to Woolfolk (2008), it is a mode of instruction that emphasises the active role of the learner in building understanding and making sense of information. There is also a very strong emphasis on collaborative learning among students and the teacher whereby all are actively engaged in formulating questions, addressing complex issues and resolving problems (Holt-Reynolds 2000).

Constructivism can be traced back to the philosophical principles enunciated by Dewey, to psychologists such as Piaget and Vygotsky, and educational movements such as progressive education and inquiry-discovery learning (Cruickshank, Jenkins & Metcalf 2009).

Figure 12.3 provides details of major characteristics associated with constructivism. It is often stated that constructivism is one of the most challenging yet rewarding approaches to teaching. The

FIGURE 12.3 Characteristics of constructivism

- Learners construct their own meaning.
- Active learning rather than passive learning is emphasised.
- Learners engage with concrete (authentic) tasks rather than the abstract – they use raw data and primary sources along with manipulative interactive tasks and physical materials.
- Learners are encouraged to engage in dialogue with the teacher and other students – learning is more effective in 'communities of learners'.
- Learners are encouraged to relate new information to what they already understand through bridging.
- Teachers must provide learners with assistance or scaffolding to help them progress.
- Teachers provide time for students to construct relationships.

Source: After Marzano 2000; Cruickshank, Jenkins and Metcalf 2005.

characteristics listed in Figure 12.3 indicate the active learning processes and the need for collaborative dialogue and searching for creative solutions within a community of learners. According to Arends (2009), the school's curriculum becomes 'a set of learning events and activities through which students and teachers jointly negotiate meaning'.

There are many proponents of constructivism, but their calls for pedagogical reform have generally not been widely accepted. Constructivism can create a variety of problems with classroom management, provision of support, materials, time required for covering the curriculum and teachers' limited understanding of students' developmental knowledge (Brandt & Perkins 2000; Kirschner, Sweller & Clark 2006).

ICT applications

De Leng *et al.* (2008) used a constructivist e-learning model to foster critical thinking on basic science concepts and they concluded that this was successful.

Alonso, Manrique and Vines (2009) compared the use of constructivist e-learning in distance mode with face-to-face traditional teaching. They concluded that achievement grades were similar for both methods.

Yong, Gene & Abaullah (2006) used a social constructivist model of teaching with 4th grade primary students. They concluded that the ICT interface they used was a good platform for the integration of social constructivism across subjects.

Wee and Woo (2006) used a constructivist software package 'Fun with Construction', to encourage students to explore topics in geometry and to use the virtual geometric instrument to understand and solve simultaneous equations.

12.7.8 Discussion

Discussion in large or small groups is an effective mode of instruction, especially for controversial or low consensus topics (Killen 2006). Discussions can be largely teacher-dominated – as in the case of whole-class discussions – or students can be delegated the task of small group leaders.

A discussion can serve a variety of purposes. The major purposes include:
- To ensure mastery of a subject – to further discuss a topic that has been taught to ensure that the details are firmly grasped by students (Parker & Hess 2001).
- To have students examine questions that have no simple answers and require opinions, ideas and debates. An example of such a question could be 'What can be done about the growing world population?' (Moore 2009b).
- To have students solve a problem. Students can be given political, economic or social problems to discuss and resolve (Cruickshank, Jenkins & Metcalf 2009).
- To have students discuss issues that are strongly affective in nature. For example, discussions could focus on student attitudes towards drug use or civic duty.
- To help students improve their face-to-face or interpersonal communication skills. Small group discussions can help students develop skills in leadership, being active listeners, and handling disagreements and conflicts.

It should be noted that this instructional mode is of less value with young children, who generally do not have the levels of reasoning required (Creative Curriculum Net 2006).

To be effective, it is important that the physical layout of furniture is conducive to group discussions. Circles of chairs, horseshoes and other configurations are usually the most effective to ensure face-to-face communication.

When using this mode of instruction, it is essential that the teacher is willing to relinquish some authority and to tolerate various directions (and dead-ends!) that a discussion might take. Accepting low degrees of structure and organisation can be difficult for some teachers and may require considerable adjustment.

It is essential that student leaders are aware of different points of view about a topic prior to commencing small group discussions and that they ensure all members of the group have opportunities to express their opinions. It may be necessary to formulate some minimal rules of procedure – for example, the right to request a student to clarify a point that was made or to ask additional questions for clarification.

In small group situations the teacher's role is largely to monitor the activities and to be a resource person. Most of the time it may be appropriate just to remain silent; however, on occasions it may be necessary to interject a comment. It is useful for the teacher to take notes on processes and achievements of each small group and this can provide valuable data for feedback to the students at the completion of the activity.

ICT applications

Discussions now occur frequently *online* as a result of the Internet. Students can enter Internet 'chat rooms' and 'discussion forums' and express their views on a variety of topics. These may be teacher-initiated discussions or simply peer-initiated, informal discussions in out-of-school time. There are also popular discussion software programs such as ICQ and Instant Messenger.

Online discussions increase student participation. Some students may be motivated to continue talking about important topics after the class lesson has ended. One difficulty with online discussions at this point in time is that students can't see the participants and therefore can't appreciate the nuances of body language. This technological barrier is already being overcome for discussion between pairs. For example, Yamada (2008) studied four kinds of synchronous computer-mediated communication namely videoconferencing (image-voice); audioconferencing (voice but no image); text chat with image (image but no voice) and plain text chat (no image and no voice). He concluded that image and voice options best promoted consciousness of natural communication and relief.

12.7.9 Cooperative learning

This is discussed in detail in Chapter 8, section 8.11.

ICT applications

Suan (2006) used an ability-grouped buddy system within a cooperative learning model to teach English to a secondary (Year 10) class. Interviews undertaken after the research period revealed that students appreciated the system of support from the Buddy Team groupings.

Lau (2006) used a cooperative learning approach to teach a Geography unit to a secondary (Year 10) class. The results indicated that students were more engaged in the cooperative learning strategies than in traditional groupings.

Yeo, Thiagayson, Cheah and Khiang (2006) used a cooperative learning model to teach algebra to a secondary (Year 8) class. The researchers used a peer tutoring structure where within each cooperative learning group there was a peer tutor and two tutees. Although peer tutoring did not improve students' test marks, students were very positive about the approach.

12.7.10 Problem solving, inquiry and discovery

Problem solving, inquiry and discovery modes of instruction enable students to learn by doing. Students can use inquiry activities in a variety of subjects and at all ages, although more abstract versions are more suited to secondary school students (Hoek & Seegers 2005). Some advantages of this instructional mode include that it:
- is economical in its use of knowledge – only knowledge relevant to an issue is examined
- enables students to view content in a more realistic and positive way as they analyse and apply data to the resolution of problems
- is intrinsically very motivating for students
- enables the teacher to become a facilitator of learning
- provides superior transfer value compared with other forms of instruction.

ICT applications

CD-ROM packages and the Internet provide excellent opportunities for students to undertake inquiry projects (Killen 2006). For example, at primary school level, CD-ROMs such as *Dangerous Creatures* provide a range of opportunities. Internet sites such as 'Royal Park Melbourne Zoo', 'The Electronic Zoo' and 'Zoonet' provide valuable sources of data. Norton and Wiburg (2003) provide many examples, demonstrating that current multimedia and hypermedia programs and writing tools have 'promoted the integration of sound, video, print and animation into a giant web of information' (p. 105). Simkins *et al.* (2002) provide practical steps for teachers who want to get started using multimedia for inquiry projects.

Yang, Newby and Bill (2007) investigated the effectiveness of structured web-based bulletin board discussions in problem-solving units in science. Their findings were that critical thinking skills were greatly advanced using the bulletin board discussions.

Li and Lim (2007) examined the use of scaffolding for online History problem solving for lower secondary students. They concluded that where students interacted with the scaffolding, they achieved a higher performance.

Kao, Lin and Sun (2008) developed a computer-based integrated concept mapping system to assist students develop conceptual self-awareness.

Poi *et al.* (2008) developed a software package in science, 'Physhint' to help students by providing them with structured hints at appropriate intervals in their problem solving.

Wang, Chang and Li (2008) developed an automated grading scheme to assess science students' performance in undertaking creative problem solving tasks.

Hoban and Littlejohn (2009) describe how Year 9 students were required to select a problem area about the Sovereign Hill goldfields. They were to use computer-based hardware such as digital cameras, mobile phones and web sources to create a Photo Story about their chosen problem.

Stiler (2007), in a similar vein, explores the potential use of MP3 players for students to undertake problem solving in lower secondary schools.

However, it is also evident that the problem solving, inquiry or discovery mode is not a popular instructional mode with all teachers (Cruickshank, Jenkins & Metcalf 2009). Some of the purported disadvantages include:

- it takes an inordinate amount of class time and out-of-school time compared with other forms of instruction
- many students prefer passive learning approaches
- it can lead to embarrassing situations if controversial topics are examined within local communities
- it is difficult to assess compared with traditional modes.

Inquiry, problem solving and discovery can be largely non-structured, using various concrete materials with lower grades – such as Maple's (2005) example with an Early Childhood class – or it can extend to relatively rigorous testing out of specific hypotheses with older students. The typical processes of inquiry involve:

- examining an issue/problem/dilemma and involving questions such as
    - Why should we investigate this?
    - What do we already know?
    - What do we want to find out?
- deciding directions and forming hypotheses and involving questions such as
    - What would happen if … ?
    - How can we explain … ?
    - What questions do we need to ask?
- organising the study and the team and involving questions such as
    - How are we going to conduct our inquiry?
    - What type of information do we need and how do we find and collect it?

- finding out and involving questions such as
    - How are we going to find out about this?
    - Who, what, where has/is the information?
- sorting out, collecting and processing the data and involving questions such as
    - What similarities and differences can we see?
    - What connections can we see?
- drawing conclusions and communicating them to others and involving questions such as
    - What can we now say about … ?
    - What general conclusion can we make?
- considering social action and involving questions such as
    - How can we contribute to decisions made about … ?
    - What should be done about this?

Inquiry, problem solving and discovery can be very rewarding experiences for teachers and students. Computer software is enabling students, individually and in small groups, to proceed with exciting inquiry projects (Travers 1997; Arends 2009; Frid 2001; Lang 2006).

> **YOUR TURN**
>
> Have you tried a problem-solving/inquiry lesson with your class?
> - Was it difficult to get organised and to get the students started?
> - Did the students enjoy the lesson?
> - What would you do differently next time?

12.7.11 Role-playing and simulation games

Role-playing and the use of simulation games (simulations merged with game rules) can be very powerful ways of exploring values and interpersonal issues (White 2006). This instructional mode was popularised in the Humanities and Social Sciences, but has been used widely in recent years across a range of subjects.

Role-plays are usually teacher-directed and may involve a limited number of students playing or miming a specific role for a short period of time, usually 2–15 minutes. Simulation games include numerous, elaborate commercial productions (including an increasing number of computer-based simulation games) and teacher-developed versions. Simulation games are usually classified into board games (such as Monopoly) and role-playing games (including designated role-players, scenarios, procedures and win-criteria).

Although there is not substantial research evidence to demonstrate that simulation games are more effective than other instructional modes, there is considerable support for them as a teaching tool, from both teachers and students. Some of the common advantages advanced include that they:
- allow students to get fully involved in learning
- encourage self-development in students
- enable students to communicate more confidently
- allow students to see events occurring over accelerated time
- allow concepts to be more easily understood
- provide students with immediate reinforcement
- reduce classroom discipline problems
- enable students to become more aware of their own values.

However, others argue that simulation games are very time-consuming in terms of preparing and playing them, and that they can become very competitive.

Games (board and role-playing versions) do require careful preparation and supervision by the teacher. Some particular points for the teacher to note include the following:
- If there will be excessive noise or movement of furniture, it is prudent to advise other teachers in advance!
- Provide each student with a summary sheet describing the purpose of the simulation game, the role-players and the scenario.
- Develop a simple system for casting the players or participants.
- Provide the necessary recording materials in advance to the players, such as blank paper, marker pens, role cards and recording sheets.
- Once the simulation game has commenced, do not interrupt unless absolutely necessary.
- Once the simulation game has concluded, ensure that sufficient time is available for debriefing. Questions that students need to reflect on include:
  – What happened?
  – What decisions were made and why?
  – What were your greatest frustrations or successes?

ICT applications

With the growth of computer-based simulation games making good use of colour, graphics, sound and action, it is very evident that they are highly motivating for students. They have the added advantage that a student can interact with the computer at different time periods without interrupting others, which negates the argument that this instructional mode is very time-consuming.

There are many published accounts of computer-based simulation games, especially in Mathematics and Science. For example, Chang *et al.* (2008) compared the used of computer-based simulations with traditional laboratory learning in the teaching of Physics. Learning achievements were significantly better with the computer-based simulations.

Yaman, Nerdel and Bayrhuber (2008) studied the use of computer-based simulations in science and concluded that they were only successful if the teacher provided instructional support through worked-out examples.

Ke (2008) used computer-based simulation games in a summer Maths program for 4th and 5th graders. He concluded that these games provided significant cognitive Maths achievement and meta-cognitive awareness.

Kim, Park and Baek (2008) used a commercially available computer-based simulation game, 'Gersang', with lower secondary students in History to develop meta-cognitive strategies. They concluded that the problem-solving abilities of students were greatly improved by playing the simulation game.

Wall and Ahmed (2007) used a computer-based simulation game, MERIT, to develop lifelong learning skills.

A number of researchers have examined new possibilities for computer-based simulation games such as incorporating animation in Maths computer games (Taylor, Pountney & Baskett 2006) and the use of teacher-created video games to teach genetics (Annetta *et al.* 2009).

Kebritchi and Hirumi (2008) studied the pedagogical foundations of 22 computer-based simulation games. They concluded that where games were based on established learning theories, they were more successful with students.

12.7.12 Project-based learning and problem-based learning

According to Katz and Chard (2000) a project is an in-depth investigation of a topic worth learning more about, undertaken by a small group of students within a class, the whole class or individual students. The key feature of a project is to focus on finding out answers to questions posed by the teacher or by the students. It is typically undertaken by early childhood and primary school children.

According to Katz and Chard (2000), doing projects enables children to make genuine choices, including choices of when to carry out the tasks, where they want to work and who they work with on the project.

ICT applications

The Internet offers a wealth of opportunities for young children and older students. For project-based learning in particular, browsers such as Internet Explorer enable students to use search engines to locate and use a variety of information related to the topic they are using (Simkins *et al.* 2002).

As an example, Milentijevic, Ciric and Vojmovic (2007) describe computer-based generic models to assist teachers develop a range of project-based learning approaches.

12.7.13 Independent self-directed study

Independent study activities can take various forms, but the common element is that the focus of responsibility for learning changes from the teacher to the student. 'Independence' is the key term, although the amount of independence given to students will depend on their level of maturity, commitment and ability (Cruickshank, Jenkins & Metcalf 2009).

An independent study usually involves individual students fulfilling contracts or doing projects that last over several days or even weeks, and which are largely unsupervised. Examples include individualised learning kits (for example in reading or spelling) when students proceed in a set sequence through learning tasks at an individual pace and according to their level of proficiency.

In ideal situations, independent learning by students is strongly supported, especially if this entails students:
- doing activities that are worthwhile and meaningful to them
- disciplining themselves to do the work.

In actual practice it is likely that most students will need some assistance with their self-directed studies. Gage and Berliner (1992) suggest that students can be categorised at three levels: those at the level of guided study need considerable assistance; those at the cooperative planning level can direct their own activities but need assistance from time to time; those at an individual pursuit level can already define topics – they can make decisions, locate resources and keep to deadlines.

To assist students undertaking independent studies, the teacher can facilitate the process by:
- ensuring that resources are available for the projects to be undertaken
- including independent study activities along with non-independent modes of instruction for all students so that they gain in confidence in this approach
- providing explicit directions or a list of steps to be covered.

ICT applications

Churchill and Churchill (2007) examined the benefits of using PDAs for independent self-directed study. Stiler (2007) considered the potential use of MP3 players for individual projects.

CONCLUDING COMMENTS

Pedagogy is a vogue term currently because it highlights the range of traditional and new communication technologies which can be used to bring about student learning.

Teachers and students both benefit from initiating and experiencing a range of modes of instruction. How a particular mode of instruction is used in a classroom is dependent on a number of factors and there will be many variations and hybrids from an idealised mode. Further, it is a learning process for all participants and early experimentations with different instructional modes are likely to cause discomfort – for both the teacher and the students. Yet it is essential that a varied combination of modes is used to ensure that all students are exposed to at least some approaches that are closely amenable to their interests and preferred ways of learning.

Project work complements the more formal aspects of teaching. Unlike systematic instruction, which concentrates on children acquiring skills, project work concentrates on children applying skills, using intrinsic motivation.

Activities engaged in for project work for young children include drawing, writing, reading, recording observations and interviewing experts (Katz 1994).

The phases of project work include:
- Phase 1, planning and getting started – talking about the topic, engaging in dramatic play.
- Phase 2, projects in progress – the teacher's role here is to get the children to learn new information and knowledge.
- Phase 3, children share their understanding of the topic through play, wall displays, music, drama and dance, games, class books, folders of individual work (Katz & Chard 2000).

It is essential that a varied combination of modes is used to ensure that all students are exposed to at least some approaches that are closely amenable to their interests and preferred ways of learning.

KEY ISSUES RAISED IN THIS CHAPTER

1. The use of the term pedagogy is important because it gives a wider and more creative orientation to teaching and learning.
2. It is crucial for teachers, where possible, to match up their presentation styles with students' learning styles.
3. The current impact of standards and testing is likely to cause teachers to use a narrow range of teaching and learning approaches.
4. Computer technology is greatly benefiting classroom instruction.
5. A number of teaching and learning modes are detailed including expository talks and lectures, practice drills, directed questioning, direct instruction, demonstrations, online teaching, constructivism, discussion, cooperative learning, problem solving and inquiry, role-playing and simulations, project-based learning, and independent self-directed study.
6. For each mode examples are given about how ICT-based lessons have been given by teachers.

REFLECTIONS AND ISSUES

1. When deciding which modes of instruction to use, what is the relative importance of teacher versus learner needs?
2. Reflect on the modes of instruction you have used or typically use in the classroom. Why do you prefer these approaches? List some possible advantages and disadvantages for each.
3. 'Students are not failing because of the curriculum. Students can learn almost any subject matter when they are taught with methods and approaches responsive to their learning style strengths' (Dunn 1990, p. 15). Do you support the view that students have dominant learning styles? Should students be 'matched' with modes of instructions that suit their learning styles? Give details of how this might be achieved.
4. 'Teaching cannot simply consist of telling. It must enlist the pupil's own active participation since what gets processed gets learned' (Tomlinson & Quinton 1986). What modes of instruction can a teacher use to encourage more active pupil participation?

5 Plan a unit that could be taught using cooperative learning. How would the plan differ from other approaches? What might be some possible advantages and disadvantages?
6 Teachers must be familiar with the workings of a variety of computer hardware tools and must understand the uses of several types of software. Do you agree with this statement? To what extent have you achieved this standard or even surpassed it?
7 Discuss how modern technology can enrich modes of instruction. What are some of the problems for teachers and students in using computers in classrooms? What personal goals do you have for using computers in your various modes of instruction?
8 How do you react to the following statements?
'When I think of using computers in the classroom, I feel anxious.'
'I am unable to evaluate educational software.' (Russell & Bradley 1996, p. 237).
Describe your level of competence and confidence in using computer-based instruction. Are you actively trying to upgrade it? Give details.

Special references

Adams, ME (1997) *Integrating Technology into the Curriculum*, Hawker Brownlow, Melbourne.
Allen, RH (2010) *High-impact Teaching Strategies for the 'XYZ' Era of Education*, Allyn & Bacon, Boston.
Gardner, P (1997) *Managing Technology in the Middle School Classroom*, Hawker Brownlow, Melbourne.
Killen, R (2006) *Effective Teaching Strategies*, 4th edn, Thomson, Melbourne.
Leach, J & Moon, B (2008) *The Power of Pedagogy*, Sage, London.
Moore, KD (2009b) *Effective Instructional Strategies*, 2nd edn, Sage, Thousand Oaks, CA.
Orlich, DC, Harder, RJ, Callahan, RC & Gibson, HW (2009) *Teaching Strategies*, 9th edition, Wadsworth, Cengage learning, Boston.
Ornstein, A & Lasley, TJ (2004) *Strategies for Effective Teaching*, McGraw-Hill, Chicago.

Web sources

For additional resources on pedagogy, teaching and learning, please go to:
www.pearson.com.au/myeducationlab.

13
CLASSROOM MANAGEMENT

13.1 | INTRODUCTION

When you first observe a classroom teacher at work it may all seem so overwhelming. There seems to be so much going on! How does the regular class teacher cope with all the interactions that appear to be occurring simultaneously? How can a teacher remain so calm when chaos seems so likely?

Without doubt, the greatest worry of new teachers is being able to manage a class and prevent student misbehaviour. As noted by Cruickshank, Jenkins and Metcalf (2009), 'feelings of inadequacy are compounded by the realisation that teachers are *expected* to be good classroom managers. Administrators often equate control of students with good teaching.'

This chapter is about classroom management and focuses on strategies that can be used to ensure that students are actively involved in learning and that they feel successful in their endeavours. There is no simple or correct formula. A teacher has to choose and adapt from a variety of strategies and approaches the ones that best suit their personality and the members of class. The over-arching skill is to be able to recognise what is happening in a class and to be able to use coping strategies that are needed immediately, before major problems arise.

13.2 | BEGINNING TEACHER CONCERNS ABOUT CLASSROOM MANAGEMENT

Almost any survey of the concerns experienced by beginning teachers reveals a very high concern about classroom management – particularly student misbehaviour and discipline (Charles 2004; Arends 2009; Arthur, Gordon & Butterfield 2003). It is not surprising. School environments are very different and challenging. The teacher engages in many interpersonal exchanges each day – to a large extent he/she acts as a gatekeeper, deciding who shall and shall not speak (Ryan, Cooper & Tauer 2008; Marzano, Marzano & Pickering 2003).

Some of the typical misbehaviour problems that can occur in a class can cover the spectrum from serious to relatively insignificant:
- aggression – physical and verbal attacks, displays of violence
- immoral acts – cheating, lying and stealing
- defiance of authority – refusing to obey the teacher

- disruptive behaviour – talking loudly, calling out, tossing objects
- off-task behaviour – daydreaming, fooling around (Charles 2004; Remboldt 1998).

At the preschool level misbehaviour problems can occur in the form of:
- children being excessively noisy
- children playing roughly with others in confined areas
- children from different cultural backgrounds behaving differently and often creating challenges for the teachers (Grebennikov 2006; Walker-Dalhouse 2005).

Australian researchers have concluded that the most frequent and the most troublesome student behaviours at primary school level are:
- students being easily distracted
- students not listening to directions
- students talking out of turn
- students hindering other students (McDonald & Wilks 1994; Little 2005; Edwards & Watts 2004).

At the secondary school level, talking out of turn and hindering other students are the two most troublesome behaviour problems in the first four years of high school, but idleness becomes a concerning behaviour problem for teachers dealing with Year 11 and 12 students (Little 2005).

It is vital for teachers to reflect on their everyday teaching experiences and to make meaning out of the various problems that occur. Ideally, teachers need to work through classroom problems with their peers, with whom they can raise questions and respond to issues (Singh *et al.* 1997). Checkley (2006) refers to the importance of teacher teammates as mentors. In practice, this is often difficult to organise and a teacher may have to resort to self-analytical devices such as diary writing and self-reflection sessions.

A useful reference for reflecting and working through problems is depicted in Figure 13.1. Although the four attributes of family, student, peer and school are all interdependent, it can be

FIGURE 13.1 Factors affecting school behaviour

Family attributes
- care and concern
- parental attitudes to school
- family stresses

Student attributes
- temperament
- social skills
- peer acceptability

Student's behaviour at school

Peer attributes
- authority
- social prejudice

School attributes
- positive leadership by the principal
- school climate
- partnership with parents

Source: Adapted from Rigby 1996.

helpful to try to isolate major factors. For example, is a student's misbehaviour due mainly to family stresses? Or are they in a gang that actively disrupts school activities? What support is likely to be obtained from the principal in dealing with the problem?

Misbehaviour in schools, despite our best efforts, is increasing (Cowley 2001). For example, student bullying is now recognised as a major problem (Rigby 1996; Fox & Boulton 2005; Roberts 2006).

 Reflect upon various forms of student bullying you have observed. Have you heard about problems of cyber-bullying? What are some strategies you might use to reduce bullying?

Teacher drop-out rates in some education systems are increasing and, to a large extent, teachers seem to be leaving because of negative behaviour experiences they have had with specific students. Perhaps the increases in student misbehaviour reflect changes in society and problems associated with unemployment, self-centred versus group-centred approaches to life problems, increased violence and antisocial behaviour, and the scourge of drugs in society.

Positive action can and must be undertaken to overcome concerns about class management. Some educators (such as Barry & King 1998; Moore 2009a; and Hendrick 2001) argue that management problems can be prevented by:
- thorough lesson planning
- establishing good relationships with students
- conducting lessons effectively.

Cruickshank, Jenkins and Metcalf (2009) contend that a comprehensive management plan is needed that includes proactive (preventive) and reactive (disciplinary) management strategies. They suggest that 'effective teachers begin early in the school year to systematically implement a carefully developed plan' (p. 42).

Other educationalists assert that specific approaches or models are needed to achieve a classroom atmosphere where misbehaviour problems are minimised (Lovegrove & Lewis 1991; Charles 2004). Examples of two such approaches, the Assertive Discipline Model and the Decisive Leadership Model, are described later in this chapter.

13.3 | ON-TASK/OFF-TASK BEHAVIOURS

Classroom management is not about surviving another hour with a particular class, although on occasions we have all felt and suffered these situations. Rather, classroom management aims to provide effective learning opportunities for students on planned activities – that is, *on-task* activities. The more time a student can spend each day dealing with on-task activities, whether they are teacher-directed or student-initiated, the greater the learning (Ryan, Cooper & Tauer 2008). Conversely, the time spent by students during *off-task* activities is non-productive in terms of the school curriculum and reduces their opportunities for learning.

For example, Marzano, Marzano and Pickering (2003) have undertaken a major meta-analysis of 100 classroom management research studies and concluded that effective management techniques can enable classes of students to achieve at up to 20 percentile points higher than classes where effective management techniques are not employed. Infantino and Little (2005) note that up to 76 per cent of secondary school teachers' time in Australia is taken up with controlling the disruptive behaviour of students and therefore greatly reducing the on-task time available.

This is not to suggest that some off-task activities will not occur in each teaching day – for example, movement to other rooms, informal time and casual social interactions. It is when the time spent on off-task activities becomes a significant part of the school day that serious questions must be asked about a teacher's management skills.

It is possible to differentiate off-task behaviour further into *disruptive* and *non-disruptive*. Disruptive behaviour occurs when a student interferes with other students doing their assigned activities.

These students not only fail to cooperate with the teacher but also prevent or distract others. Also of concern are the non-disruptive, off-task students who do not appear to be motivated or to be concentrating – the stereotype who is turned off and oblivious, apparently, to almost everything that is going on around them but is not consciously distracting others.

There are of course many factors responsible for students' behaviours, only some of which can be influenced by the activities of the teacher. In any discussion of students who are on-task or off-task, it is important to remember that all class members, including the teacher, are influenced by the classroom environment and, in particular, the physical, social and educational components.

The *physical* surroundings of the classroom (see Chapter 5) may have a major impact on how students behave (Cruickshank, Jenkins & Metcalf 2009). The spaces between desks, the location of equipment, the colours in the room, the noise levels and the temperature can all influence students' behaviours. For example, research undertaken by Gunter *et al.* (1995) confirms that physical surroundings affect the behaviour of students.

 Reflecting upon your experiences as a student at all levels, are there some physical factors which spur you on or have a negative impact upon you?

Some of these physical factors can influence, in turn, such social factors as the arrangement of groups, formal and informal work areas and class rules. Further, the educational component affects the social and physical components in establishing what will be the major priorities, the time allocated for each, what knowledge and skills will be taught, to whom, and when. The educational priorities established for certain students may be of little interest to them and, as a result, they become quite hostile in their reactions to the teacher.

As illustrated in Table 13.1, these three components interact and influence each other. They provide a useful background in helping teachers understand why on-task and off-task behaviours occur among specific class members.

TABLE 13.1 Environmental factors influencing classroom behaviours

Physical factors	Social factors	Educational factors
Seating arrangement	Students work individually or in groups	Teacher's modes of instruction
Noise levels	Students' behaviour towards each other	Teacher's acceptance/rejection
Space provisions for working and movement	Group sizes and composition	Types of educational tasks required
Heating/cooling	Students' concentration/on-task behaviours	The pattern of activities required

Source: adapted from Bull and Solity, Classroom Management: Principles to Practice, 1987, Taylor and Francis Books Ltd.

13.4 | ESTABLISHING A POSITIVE CLASSROOM CLIMATE

A major factor in being a successful classroom manager lies in establishing a favourable classroom climate. What does this mean? There are many interpretations, but it relates to the 'feeling' that permeates a classroom. Arthur, Gordon and Butterfield (2003) refer to the need to establish a classroom ecology. Some observers may opt for terms such as 'businesslike' or 'task-oriented' to describe the feeling of a successful classroom, while others may prefer terms such as 'friendly' or 'warm'. Most educators can agree on classroom climates that are not successful – namely those that are cold, unfriendly, threatening or disruptive.

There are many preferred stances on how to develop a positive classroom climate (Slee 1992; Boynton & Boynton 2005; Smith & Lambert 2008). It depends largely on personal judgments. Cangelosi (1992), for example, argues for a businesslike approach: 'your students are in the "business of learning", you are in the "business of teaching"' (Cangelosi 1992, p. 130). He suggests the following:

- In your initial encounters with a new class, give directions that are simple and not likely to confuse; give them activities that almost all students will succeed in doing; have all students engage in the same activity; and structure the activity so you are free to monitor the conduct of students.
- Demonstrate that you are well organised by preparing materials (such as hand-outs and name cards) in advance.
- Administrative matters that are not central to teaching (collecting monies, checking the roll) should be done expeditiously.

Charles (2004) also stresses the need for a good classroom climate but emphasises a number of human relations skills.

1. *General human relations skills*
   - friendliness: even with students who displease us; achieve this by smiling and speaking gently
   - positive attitude: look for solutions rather than dwelling on problems
   - ability to listen: showing that we value other opinions
   - ability to compliment genuinely.
2. *Human relations skills with students*
   - giving regular attention: speak frequently but briefly to students
   - reinforcement: showing support and encouragement
   - continual willingness to help
   - modelling courtesy and good manners: demonstrating in your own behaviour what you want to see in students' behaviour.
3. *Human relations with parents*
   - communicate regularly: use notes, telephone calls and letters
   - communicate clearly: make the messages clear and simple
   - describe expectations clearly
   - emphasise the student's progress rather than dwelling too much on the student's shortcomings.

Charles (2004) is clearly emphasising a classroom climate characterised by positive communications, warmth and support and one that would be likely to enable productive, enjoyable activities to occur.

Positive climate can also be considered as a whole-school priority (Hue 2007). Luiselli *et al.* (2005) contend that whole-school positive behaviour support on discipline problems can be extremely successful and can benefit student academic performance. These researchers studied a primary school in the mid-west of the United States and examined the benefits of developing a behaviour support team that operated school-wide.

13.5 ESTABLISHING ROUTINES

Establishing routines is also closely linked to developing a positive classroom climate, but the number and range of routines will depend on the preferred style of interactions between the teacher and the students. The balance between having too many or not enough rules and routines is a difficult one to achieve. On the one hand, it is necessary to have a certain number of routines so that activities can be completed efficiently. It would be physically impossible for a teacher to give their undivided attention to each student all the time. Yet, if the number of routines appears to the students to be excessive and too formal and authoritative, they may not respond very positively to their teacher – that is, the classroom climate will become more unfriendly.

For the beginning teacher, however, it is important to err on the side of establishing a number of routines, because this can reduce the chance of major disciplinary problems occurring (Cohen, Manion & Morrison 2004). It can be very useful to plan in advance the kinds of routines you might need to implement.

For example, for an early childhood or preschool group you may need to think about the physical layout of play areas and resources in your room.
- How will the formal areas be arranged? Will the blackboards be visible for all students?
- How will the play areas be designated?
- What will be the preferred areas of student movement in your room? How will you ensure that this occurs?
- Where will you store materials so that access will not be inhibited?

It may then be useful to consider the routines you feel are needed for daily classroom activities. This might entail establishing routines for entering the classroom or cleaning up after a lesson. Some basic examples are included in Figure 13.2.

At the primary school level students can play an important role in setting routines and rules within a classroom (Lewis 2000). In so doing, they can further promote student ownership of the rules and more student responsibility for their own behaviour (Emmer & Gerwells 2006). They can be involved in discussing reasons for particular routines and clarifying their meaning. For senior grades, a teacher may permit some student choices with regard to particular routines.

With the widespread use of computers in schools, it is necessary to establish new routines to provide students with easy access, especially for secondary school students but also for lower grades (Cruickshank, Jenkins & Metcalf 2009). Points to consider include:
- positioning of work stations and research space for students
- storage arrangements if laptop computers are used by all or many students
- attention to noise-deadening materials around work stations.

 From your observations does students' use of computers in the classroom help produce a more cooperative environment? What routines do you consider are essential to enforce when students use computers?

Various educators remind us that, whatever collection of routines is decided on by a teacher (and in some cases by students), it will take some time for students to become acquainted and comfortable with them. For example, Dembo (1991) contends that at the beginning of the school year a teacher

FIGURE 13.2 Illustrative examples of routines

Routines for all students to follow when entering the room: e.g. take out their books and materials or read silently from library books.
Routines for cleaning up at the end of a lesson: e.g. procedures for packing away materials.
Routines for working in small groups: e.g. listening politely to comments from others.
Routines for working as a whole group: e.g. students raise their hand before asking a question.
Routines for handing in completed work: e.g. students place completed work in a special tray.
Routines for using class monitors/prefects: e.g. monitors distribute and collect materials.
Routines for working on individual and group projects: e.g. providing a summary of tasks to be covered.
Routines if the teacher is called away from the room: e.g. to read silently from library books.
Routines for going to the toilet: e.g. not going until the previous student has returned.
Routines for taking attendance: e.g. students read silently while this task is completed.

must set aside time during the first day of teaching and on subsequent occasions to discuss the specific class rules and routines. Some useful do's and don't's include:
- Do teach the routines and rules systematically and frequently.
- Do start with simple rules first.
- Don't assume that students will remember a routine after being informed once.
- Don't use activities other than whole-group activities for the first few days of teaching to avoid introducing too many rules.

The effective teacher will, of course, monitor the routines that are established to see whether they are still appropriate after a few weeks or months. Consider, for example, the problem posed in the case study below. Some routines may be too prescriptive and quite unnecessary. For some activities additional routines may need to be established. It is often very useful to discuss possible changes with your students and enlist their support in making modifications. By 'owning' the changes, they will be more prepared to follow the routines and rules.

An essential point for teachers to remember is that they must be consistent in following the rules themselves. There is nothing more demoralising for students than to discover that their teacher is capricious in enforcing rules, or is selective in how they interpret rules for 'special' students.

Routines, then, are an important element of classroom management. They do not have value in themselves, but they enable important educational activities to be carried out efficiently – they save time and energy for the teacher and the students.

Managing a difficult child

Sam is a physically mature boy in a Year 7 class. He is very boisterous and likes fun. Out in the playground he goes out of his way to tease smaller boys from his class. The more they object the worse he becomes.

Just recently, Sam has become more challenging within the classroom. He makes loud noises for no apparent reason. His attention to tasks is intermittent at best. In small group activities he tends to dominate.

He has started to challenge some of the instructions in class – mainly through his non-verbal shrugs and sighs. You wonder whether his behaviour is going to deteriorate even further.

When he comes to your table, he towers over you. Is he trying to establish some power relationship over you too?

What are some strategies you might use? Give details of actions you would take if you were in this situation.

13.6 | ESTABLISHING EFFECTIVE COMMUNICATION CHANNELS

Another important element of classroom management is being a good communicator – that is, what we communicate and how we do it.

 Do you consider you are a good communicator? Reflect upon the non-verbal cues and verbal cues you give to others. What do you consider are aspects that you need to improve?

Let us take the non-verbal communication element first, as it provides a powerful set of cues for the perceptive eyes of students (see Figure 13.3). Students will react positively to a teacher who faces them and makes direct eye contact. Such body language tells a student: 'I'm serious about what I'm saying and I want you to listen carefully.'

Body movement can also give cues to students. When teachers sprawl across their desk or sit informally it may tell the students that their teacher is being friendly and informal or it may indicate that this teacher is insecure and lacking in confidence, and should not be taken seriously. Again, it is up to each individual to develop body stances and movements that engender confidence and respect, without going to the extreme of being very formal and aloof (see Figure 13.3).

A teacher can also communicate very effectively by using a variety of signals that students quickly recognise. Arends (2009) and Konza, Grainger and Bradshaw (2001) suggest the following:
- bell signalling
- arm signals
- finger signals
- signalling with extended thumb (thumbs up, thumbs down)
- head signalling
- whisper signal
- 'secret' signals to specific students.

How verbal communication is used is also important. Research evidence indicates that teachers who inform or describe are held in higher esteem than those who are judgmental. For example, a teacher who points out good or bad points about a student's work in a neutral, informative way is likely to be received more positively than one who uses comments that are judgmental, negative and perceived to be a rebuke.

It is often very tempting to make short, sharp rebukes, especially in the heat of the moment, but this should be resisted. Without doubt, students will gain more diagnostic information and support from descriptive comments than judgmental ones. Some useful reminders about effective verbal communication include the following:
- Communicate clearly in a logical way using language that students can understand.
- Positive approach: use communication to support students' efforts.
- Demeanour: be professional in your posture, movement, conversations and discussions.
- Assertive approach: send consistent messages, being neither intimidating nor intimidated.
- Being responsible: remind students that they are in control of and responsible for their own conduct.

Aitken (1999) refers to the concept of the Emotional Bank Account. Teachers who are good communicators will ensure that they 'deposit' frequently into students' emotional accounts by finding out about students' interests, enjoying a laugh with students and being able to laugh at and apologise for the mistakes they make as a teacher.

FIGURE 13.3 Some do's and don't's about non-verbal communication

Do:
- make eye contact with students when you are speaking
- scan students frequently while you are talking
- face the class when you are talking
- use a number of positive expressions and gestures
- direct your body to the specific students you are addressing
- move systematically to students in different locations in the room.

Don't:
- look away when you are talking to students
- adopt 'sloppy' positions in the room; for example, sitting on tables or leaning against a door when talking
- make all your directions from a single location in the room.

13.7 | GENDER AND RACIAL ISSUES

Another important element is the relationship established between male and female students and the male or female teacher, and relationships between different races within a classroom.

As noted by Leach & Mitchell (2006), it has to be recognised that virtually all forms of violence against children are entrenched in gender roles and inequities that follow children throughout their short childhood and formative years into adulthood (p. ix).

Some studies have shown that female students have lower self-esteem and confidence than males (George 2006; Tullock 1995). Bartky (1996) argues that female students display feelings of inadequacy in school settings, as revealed by the tentative character of their speech and body language. Hall's (1995) research concludes that female students are less likely to be called upon directly by teachers than males; teachers talk to males wherever they are in the room, to females only when they are nearby; and teachers tend to remember the names of male students better than female students.

Gilbert and Gilbert (1998), Kenway (1997), and Keddie & Mills (2008) have monitored the behaviours of boys in schools and their struggles to achieve a satisfactory form of masculinity. They point to the efforts by boys to create 'macho' images of power or superiority, but these are not usually associated with academic school values.

Males are the chief culprits of disruptive behaviour in classrooms. The reasons for their misbehaviour can be varied, such as:
- they want to create a popular image of being funny
- they are bored by school work and do not like school
- they are asserting forms of aggression
- they are trying to seek attention and to show off in front of the females
- they want to assert their independence.

Masculinity issues are also related to matters of race and culture. Males from immigrant minority groups can have great difficulty establishing themselves in classes where the dominant culture has very different customs and mores (Leach & Mitchell 2006; Mills 2006).

At the preschool level, Walker-Dalhouse (2005) notes that 'many children of colour and children in poverty do not display the behaviours or experience the type of success of middle class students' (p. 24). Consequently they create challenges for the teacher. Dockett and Perry (2005) refer to the problems of starting school in Australia for families and children from culturally and linguistically diverse backgrounds. Malone, Bonitz and Rickett (1998) conclude that primary school students from low-income homes have the highest potential for behaviour problems. Walker-Dalhouse (2005) recommends that teachers need to recognise their own ethnocentrism and biases and increase their knowledge of their students' cultural backgrounds.

Aboriginal males and females can experience a range of forms of disadvantage in schools ranging from 'verbal to physical harassment and the myriad forms of put-downs, snubs and embarrassments' (Gilbert & Gilbert 1998, p. 150).

Simpson and Clancy (2005) note the inequities for young Australian Aboriginal learners when they experience early childhood literacy practices. They argue that teachers must avoid negative stereotyping and try to understand the cultural-historical contexts of these learners.

Having male/female and racial tensions within a classroom can cause major management difficulties for a teacher (Leach & Mitchell 2006). Solutions sometimes need to include recourse to school-wide policies on gender equity and conflict resolution (Luiselli *et al.* 2005).

13.8 | BULLYING

Bullying by students can occur within the classroom as well as in the school grounds and outside of school. Within the classroom bullying is likely to be mainly verbal harassment, but physically injurious actions can also occur (Bullock 2002). Various forms of physical bullying by males have become widespread in many schools (Rigby 1996). Females often appear to become involved in indirect bullying (Suckling & Temple 2001).

It is important that students of all backgrounds have the opportunity and the capacity to interact successfully with other students. It is a necessary developmental task for all students to achieve.

Fox and Boulton's (2005) study in the United Kingdom noted that, in a sample of six junior schools (330 students), victims of bullying displayed a behavioural vulnerability ('looks scared'; 'gives in to the bully too easily when picked on'; 'tends to be quite withdrawn and solitary in their behaviour' (p. 322)).

Lambert *et al*'s. (2008) survey of over 26 000 children aged 11–16 in South Wales concluded that reports of being a bully were higher amongst boys and that reports of being a bully and being bullied were higher in the lower school years.

According to Eckman (2001), bullying in the US has become a serious problem; Eckman cites evidence from the National Institute of Child Health and Human Development that 30 per cent of children in Grades 6 to 10 had been involved in bullying either as a victim or a perpetrator. Eckman contends that bullying cannot be solved by individual classroom teachers – it requires whole-school policies and commitment. For example, Arthur, Gordon and Butterfield (2003) refer to a Safe and Friendly Environment (SAFE) whole-school policy at a high school. This involves:
- introducing awareness-raising strategies for staff, students and parents
- designating a male and a female staff member as SAFE coordinators
- implementing procedures for dealing with incidents
- identifying strategies for supporting victims.

Delfabbro *et al.* (2006) studied peer and teacher bullying and victimisation at 25 government and private schools in South Australia. They concluded that students who reported peer victimisation typically showed high levels of social alienation and had poor self-esteem. Victims of teacher victimisation were typically less able academically and more likely to be involved in high-risk behaviours such as drug use and under-age drinking. Most of the bullying was found to occur at school and usually manifested as verbal aggression rather than physical harm. Boys were significantly more likely to be bullied than girls.

Cyber-bullying is an insidious and covert form of emerging social cruelty among adolescents (Shariff & Govin 2006). There is an ever-widening arsenal of weapons available for cyber-bullying including cell-phones, blogs and online chat rooms. Cyber-bullying can be persistent and relentless and it can involve hundreds of perpetrators who can remain anonymous behind the technology.

Fortunately various community groups in Australia provide support for students who are the victims of cyber-bullying. For example, over 200 Year 10 school students in Western Australia attended a Cyber Friendly Student Summit in October 2008. Police departments in all states have Cyber Predator teams who track down cyber-bullying perpetrators.

13.9 | ATTENTION DEFICIT HYPERACTIVITY DISORDER (ADHD)

A major problem for some parents (and their teachers and peers) is coping with children who have ADHD (around 3 to 5 per cent of children). There are three main types of ADHD:
- ADHD that displays mainly inattentive behaviour
- ADHD that displays hyperactive-impulsive behaviour
- ADHD that displays a combined type.

In a typical class there is usually at least one student who has ADHD, usually a boy. A major responsibility for all teachers is to help with diagnosing behaviour and to pass on this information to parents and specialists. If ADHD students are using medication (and it is carefully administered) then this reduces inattention and hyperactivity.

Some techniques that a teacher can use with ADHD students include:
- Use reinforcement for appropriate behaviour by the child (Cruikshank, Jenkins & Metcalf 2009).
- Have more breaks in academic learning time.
- Use visual aids to keep the child on task (Cowley 2001).
- Redirect the student rather than ordering them to stop what they are doing.

- Watch for initial signs that a student is becoming upset.
- Build relationships with these students (Little 2003; Boynton & Boynton 2005).

13.10 | WORKING WITH PARENTS

Effective teachers accept the important role that parents play in students' lives (Jones & Jones 1998). Parents can make a major contribution by reinforcing desirable school behaviour. When students misbehave, whether with minor occasions of inattention or with more serious forms of aggression and bullying, parents need to know.

Many teachers are not enthusiastic about working with parents. Parent contacts can often be very time-consuming and it is understandable that teachers do not want to burden themselves with additional hours.

However, according to Jones and Jones (1998), teachers can develop attitudes and skills that will make parent contacts much more enjoyable and productive. Some methods for involving parents include:
- making early contacts in the school year by using an introductory letter
- having an initial evening meeting, such as a 'back to school' night
- keeping parents informed by the use of regular newsletters about such things as future field trips and long-term projects
- having the students make personalised stationery at school, which is used by the teachers to send home positive notes about the students
- making personal telephone calls to a parent
- encouraging parents to serve as volunteers in the classroom
- organising formal parent conferences.

13.11 | PREVENTIVE DISCIPLINE

Most teachers will agree that it is far better for all concerned if misbehaviour can be prevented from occurring, but how do you do this? There are many possible solutions. One is for the teacher to be especially alert and perceptive – having 'with-it-ness' or, in other words, having eyes in the back of their head. This might be a tall order perhaps, but by scanning students constantly and not allowing unsupervised events to start, a teacher can prevent a lot of potential misbehaviour from occurring.

Another possible solution is to plan for diversity, variety and versatility in your lessons (Arthur-Kelly et al. 2006). This could entail the following:
- *Diversity*: make your lessons as worthwhile and enjoyable as possible for all students. Consider how you will cater for the faster and slower students. Prepare materials to cater for all ability levels.
- *Variety*: include a variety of activities within a lesson so that students do not become bored. Plan in advance to include such activities as listening, writing, discussing, reading, solving problems and illustrating.
- *Versatility*: consider some contingency plans in case the lesson does not go well. Do not persist with a topic if you are having major problems. Keep in command of the activity – if necessary, switch to another activity.

If you have developed a positive class climate, as described above, then students should be clear about the behaviour expected of them and they should be fully aware of the class routines and rules.

13.12 | SUPPORTIVE DISCIPLINE

From time to time students will err in terms of misbehaviour. Whether it is the windy weather or a bad night's sleep or a student argument carried over from lunchtime, misbehaviour can and will occur in every classroom.

Given sensitivity and common sense, minor indiscretions can be overcome without being allowed to develop into a major issue (Lovegrove & Lewis 1991). In fact, it is essential that they do not develop beyond a minor incident. The task for the teacher is to isolate the problem and communicate his/her awareness of it to the student concerned without making it a whole-class issue. Every teacher will develop their own set of techniques to use, but the list in Figure 13.4 is illustrative of techniques that might be used. It is useful to reflect on this list. How many have you used previously – a head-shake, a frown, a pause? Their effectiveness will of course depend on using them sparingly but also consistently.

FIGURE 13.4 Techniques for elementary minor misbehaviour

- Use eye contact to stare at the offending student.
- Pause in mid-sentence and stare at the offending student.
- Pause in mid-sentence and move to a different part of the room and then resume talking.
- Move quietly to the offending student and quietly and firmly demand that his/her behaviour changes.
- Use non-verbal signs to offending students such as a shake of the head, frowns, hand signals.
- Move up close to the offending student(s) and continue with the lesson.
- Remove objects that are being disruptive, if this can be done quickly and without drawing attention to them.
- Assign a whole-group activity to give you time to have individual talks with the offending students.
- Ask students to ignore the misbehaving student.
- Thank the class when they have behaved well.

13.13 | CORRECTIVE DISCIPLINE

Corrective discipline by the teacher may be necessary if repeated forms of minor misbehaviour are produced by a student or a group of students. If the misbehaviour is likely to disrupt your lesson or the tone you are trying to establish in your class, then sterner measures are needed.

The major need is of course to end the misbehaviour. It is usually necessary to name the student, identify the misbehaviour and indicate what behaviour is needed. The command should be quietly spoken, if possible at close quarters to the offending student, and spoken succinctly and clearly. It is important that the event is not carried over to the rest of the class ('ripple effect'), who may support the misbehaviour or reject it.

In certain cases it will be necessary to inform the student about the consequences of persistent misbehaviour and these should be followed through consistently. All students should be aware of the class 'punishments' that might be incurred, such as demerit points, working in isolation or staying after school to complete work.

However, some of these forms of punishment may impinge upon school policy and have an impact on after-school commitments such as school buses and related matters. It is essential, therefore, that teachers newly appointed to a school are conversant with routines associated with student discipline and punishment.

Again, every teacher will develop a set of techniques that work best for them. Some useful do's and don'ts include the following:

Do:
- be consistent in terms of the punishment you give to students
- get the offending student to state how he/she should behave
- stop the offending behaviour as inconspicuously as possible.

Don't:
- give additional school work as a punishment
- give punishment to a whole class when only one or two individuals are to blame

- use sarcasm and ridicule
- send the offending student to the principal or deputy principal – only do this as a last resort.

Little (2005) contends that at the primary school level in Australia, students tend to become involved in minor violations of rules and that advice to teachers on how to deal with specific classroom behaviour problems ('tip sheets') can be very effective. Little (2005) also notes that 'tip sheets' do not appear to have been used widely in Australian secondary schools but that they could be of great benefit to high school teachers.

13.14 | A BALANCED SYSTEM OF CLASSROOM MANAGEMENT

Ideally, every teacher should have well-formulated ideas about how they will manage a class. As noted above, a lot of planning can be done prior to meeting the class for the first time, including planning the physical layout of the room, student movement and placement of resources. Once you have met your class you are then in a position to develop specific routines and to work collaboratively on producing a positive classroom climate. This will involve establishing specific rules and consequences if these rules are not followed. It will be necessary also to ensure that the rules and routines you establish for your class are in accord with the whole-school policies and procedures. Most important, ensure that the school principal is conversant with your rules and routines and is supportive of them.

A classroom management system needs to be reviewed regularly by the teacher. Some questions that might need to be asked include:
- Is there a relaxed but purposeful working atmosphere?
- Do the students feel safe and secure?
- Do most students feel a sense of achievement?
- Are the students coping well with the class rules?
- Do the students have any suggestions about possible modifications?
- How effective are the rules in controlling misbehaviour?

Charles (2004) suggests that it is a salutary exercise for each teacher to write down and reflect upon 'my needs', 'my likes' and 'my dislikes'. 'My needs' might consist of an orderly classroom appearance or particular routines. 'My likes' might revolve around having enthusiastic students. 'My dislikes' might include excessive noise or rude conduct. By writing down preferences under these headings, teachers are enabled to reflect upon how appropriate some of these preferences might be for a particular class. For example, am I encouraging character development with my Early Childhood group? Am I being too authoritarian for my Year 4 class? Am I being sufficiently flexible for my Year 10s?

It is also useful to write down the punishment measures that you are prepared to use, if required. Do they represent a logical progression in terms of severity? Are they appropriate for a particular class of students? How do students react to the list and the sequence? Am I prepared to modify some of them after a fair trial?

13.15 | CLASSROOM MANAGEMENT MODELS

A consistent approach to classroom management is essential. Although the tips described above may help in formulating a personal position on how to prevent misbehaviour and how to redirect it, they do not constitute a complete model. There are some benefits in reflecting upon specific models or approaches to classroom discipline (Edwards & Watts 2004; Lee 2007).

Programs that have been used widely include the following:
- Traditional programs based on reinforcement theory. An example is the Assertive Discipline Model developed by Canter and Canter (1992).
- Programs that aim toward self-management and community. An example is Glasser's (1992) Classroom Meeting.

- Programs for a caring classroom based on constructivist, child-centred principles. Examples include Kohn (1996) and Noddings (1992).
- Programs with a strong emphasis on inquiry-based activities and student accountability and self-organisation responsibilities. An example is the Classroom Organisation and Management Program (COMP) developed by Evertson and Harris (1999).
- Programs that emphasise decisive teacher leadership: Rogers (1992) is an Australian example.

13.16 | ASSERTIVE DISCIPLINE MODEL

Canter and Canter's (1992) Assertive Discipline Model has been chosen here for further study because it enables a teacher to deal with students positively and to teach with little interruption (Charles 2004; Arends 2009; Edwards & Watts 2004).

This model highlights the rights of students and of teachers, namely:
- Students need and want to learn in a calm, safe environment and they want to know their limits with regard to proper conduct.
- Teachers have the responsibility to set and enforce these limits and they have the right to have support from school administrators and cooperation from parents.

The role of the assertive teacher is to:
- inform students of class expectations about behaviour
- establish good class rules of behaviour
- help students understand exactly what is acceptable and unacceptable and the consequences of unacceptable behaviour
- develop trust and respect in the classroom by modelling positive behaviour
- communicate positively with parents.

Good discipline is based on:
1. Developing a solid basis of trust and respect, for example:
   (a) listen carefully to students and speak respectfully to them
   (b) greet students by name with a smile.
2. Teaching students how they are expected to behave, for example:
   (a) give students specific instructions about how to behave in a certain situation
   (b) use positive recognition by praising students who follow directions closely.
3. Establish a discipline plan, for example:
   (a) use rules that state exactly how students are to behave
   (b) give positive recognition to students who behave appropriately
   (c) have a discipline hierarchy with each consequence more unpleasant than the previous one – for example, give a warning the first time a student disrupts and on the second or third time a student disrupts, impose a five-minute time out at the back table.

With misbehaving students, the model suggests that it may be very difficult to change their behaviour. However, attempts can be made to help them achieve by trying to:
- gain their trust
- anticipate what a misbehaving student will do and say and think through how you will respond
- stay calm but firm.

The Assertive Discipline Model should ideally be introduced at the beginning of a school year or school term (Orlich *et al.* 2007). Behaviours expected from students have to be discussed and agreed upon. Details about positive recognitions and a hierarchy of consequences need to be explained. It is a good idea to provide the school principal with a copy of the plan. A copy of the discipline plan should also be sent home to parents.

Charles (2004) notes that this model is used widely because it relieves teachers of the annoyance of verbal confrontations and it preserves their instructional time. Some educators (for example, Render, Padilla & Krank 1989) are critical of the extensive use of praise and other rewards because it reduces intrinsic motivation.

13.17 | DECISIVE LEADERSHIP MODEL

Rogers' (1992) model, as reported and developed by Aitken (1999), provides a set of principles to guide a teacher's responses to misbehaviour.

Principle One: *Respect* – this is the most fundamental right of a class member.
Principle Two: *Mutual rights and responsibilities* – Rights for students come with responsibilities. Rules develop from mutual rights and responsibilities.
Principle Three: *Collegial support* – Teachers need a wide support base of colleagues and parents.
Principle Four: *Begin as unobtrusively as possible* – Use private comments; avoid public denunciations of students.
Principle Five: *Use the language of expectation* – A calm, clear manner is needed with clear expectations about the end result.
Principle Six: *Maintain your focus on the primary misbehaviour* – Don't be put off by students trying to steer the conversation in different directions.
Principle Seven: *Emphasise choices and consequences* – Help students to see that their actions have consequences.
Principle Eight: *Go for certainty not severity* – Try to impose consequences that match the behaviour.
Principle Nine: *Re-establish a positive working relationship* – Once the student is back on task then it is time to move on with the lesson (Aitken 1999, p. 17).

CONCLUDING COMMENTS

Classroom management is of major concern to all teachers but especially to student teachers and newly appointed teachers. Strategies for developing a positive classroom climate, class routines and sound communication channels can be established cooperatively between the teacher and students. Misbehaviour can never be eliminated, but the trauma and unpleasantness associated with misbehaviour can be channelled appropriately if the teacher plans carefully and demonstrates a role model that is fair and consistent.

KEY ISSUES RAISED IN THIS CHAPTER

1. Classroom management is always a major concern for preservice teachers, but there are successful ways to manage students' behaviour.
2. How to achieve a high level of on-task student behaviours is a major priority.
3. Establishing a positive classroom climate is crucial.
4. Using simple, regular routines can be very effective.
5. Being a good communicator is essential.
6. Gender and racial issues need to be sensitively treated.

REFLECTIONS AND ISSUES

1. Classroom management is the biggest challenge that new teachers face. Do you think this is the case for you? What strategies do you consider you might use?

2. Reflect on your experiences in the classroom. Jot down, in note form, points that you would list for the following headings:
   (a) My needs
   (b) My likes
   (c) My dislikes.
3. How would you rate yourself in terms of managing a classroom? Be specific about your strengths and weaknesses. What might you do to strengthen your skills?
4. What can a teacher do to establish and maintain good teacher–pupil relationships?
5. Should the school principal be expected to support a teacher's classroom management practices?
6. Should teachers share with students details of their personal lives and interests?
7. Do students have rights in the classroom? Do teachers have rights in the classroom? Make two columns and provide a list for both.
8. Reflect on one or two students you have noted were very disruptive in class. Why were they so disruptive? In retrospect, what could you have done to change their disruptive behaviour?
9. What kinds of non-verbal cues do you typically use in managing a class? How effective do you think they are? What changes might you make? Why?
10. 'The concern is not only for ways of dealing with disruption but also for prevention – by establishing, throughout the school, practices and programs that exhort acceptable social relations' (Slee 1992, p. 7). Discuss.
11. How useful is the Assertive Discipline Model for you in your classroom? What aspects would you vary and why? Suggest alternative models.

Special references

Cowley, S (2001) *Getting the Buggers to Behave*, Continuum Press, London.
Edwards, CH & Watts, V (2004) *Classroom Discipline and Management: An Australasian Perspective*, John Wiley, Brisbane.
Jones, VF & Jones, LS (1998) *Comprehensive Classroom Management*, 5th edn, Allyn & Bacon, Boston.
Konza, D, Grainger, J & Bradshaw, K (2001) *Classroom Management: A Survival Guide*, Social Science Press, Sydney.
Leach, F & Mitchell, C (2006) *Combating Gender Violence in and around Schools*, Trentham Books, Stoke on Trent.
Little, E (2003) *Kids Behaving Badly*, Pearson Prentice Hall, Sydney.
Partington, G (ed.) (1998) *Perspectives on Aboriginal and Torres Strait Islander Education*, Social Science Press, Katoomba.
Roberts, WB (2006) *Bullying from Both Sides*, Corwin Press, Thousand Oaks, CA.

Web sources

For additional resources on classroom management, please go to:
www.pearson.com.au/myeducationlab.

14

USING RESOURCES CREATIVELY

14.1 | INTRODUCTION

Resources are a critical element in the interactions that occur between teachers and students in classrooms. In fact, it could be argued that the teacher, students and resources comprise the three major elements of classroom learning, even though wider contextual factors of school environment and community also influence the learning process.

The tremendous increase in resources, especially computer programs and the Internet, expands the range of resources available for use in the classroom. Although costs are certainly a major factor, many schools have the finances available to purchase an array of resources if teachers make the effort to systematically select suitable materials. Herein lies a major problem. Resources are only valuable to a school if they are carefully and continuously used, up until the point at which they are judged to be obsolete and no longer appropriate. Teachers tend not to use a wide range of resources and the limited number they do use are recycled year after year (Williamson 1995).

In this chapter, the following issues are raised:
- What are some reliable criteria to use when selecting resources?
- Who should be responsible for selecting resources in schools?
- How do the resources reflect the range and focus of the curriculum?
- How are the resources organised?
- How stimulating are the resources?
- How accessible are they?
- What are the respective merits of material resources (such as computer software programs) and human resources (such as guest speakers)?
- What are some of the problems in using community resources and visiting community venues?

Learners in the twenty-first century are surrounded by an information-rich environment. To access the resources available to them will require students and teachers to be information literate (Commonwealth Department of Education, Science and Training 2001). Students need to be competent in using the Internet and other ICT applications. In many cases their technical computer skills may be ahead of those of their teachers (Kuiper, Volman & Terwel 2005). Resources used in the classroom are often designed to promote teacher learning as well as student learning. For example,

Davis and Krajcik (2005) suggest that many curriculum materials can help teachers develop more general knowledge that they can apply flexibly in new situations.

Creative use of resources is applicable to both teachers and students. It is up to teachers to broaden their instructional base and to explore the use of different resources and methods. Students need to be given opportunities to use a variety of resources to broaden their learning base. Ideally, all students should have the appropriate literacy skills to access information and the ability to use it in particular learning situations (Hunt 1997). This applies especially to the assessing of electronic resources (de Castell 2000; Macdonald, Heap & Mason 2001).

14.2 | RESOURCES AVAILABLE FOR USE IN SCHOOLS

The range of resources available for use in the classroom is constantly growing, and each type has particular merits for certain teachers and students in specific learning situations.

As noted by Davis and Krajcik (2005), resources are especially valuable for teachers to use with their students but also are *educative* for teachers in terms of:
- helping them learn how to anticipate and interpret what learners may think about in response to instructional activities
- helping them learn the subject matter
- helping them to consider how the resources could be used with other units during the year.

Resources are extremely valuable for students, especially if they are involved in student-initiated activities such as project work and portfolios. This might involve them in accessing a variety of Internet tools and communicating with others via blogs.

Any attempt to classify resources is always fraught with problems.

In this chapter a category system is used that endeavours to give equal weight to print and multimedia resources and, in addition, gives considerable emphasis to community resources. This classification system is depicted in Figure 14.1.

14.3 | PRINT MATERIALS

14.3.1 Textbooks

Textbooks are a most important resource for many teachers (Ball & Cohen 1996). As noted by Altbach (1987, p. 159):

> in an age of computers and satellite communications, the most powerful and pervasive educational technology is the textbook. Even in classrooms where 'computer literacy' is the watchword, textbooks are used, and there is little evidence so far that their influence has declined.

Many beginning teachers are told what texts to use, but a number of teachers do have opportunities to make a choice. The purported advantages of a textbook include the following:
- They define the curriculum to be taught.
- They provide essential facts and techniques for learning.
- They provide up-to-date information.
- They provide an overview of particular topics.

Textbooks are usually very popular with teachers because they bring together a massive amount of important material in the one volume and thus save the busy teacher a considerable amount of time. For teachers lacking adequate background in certain topics, a comprehensive textbook can also be a boon. A textbook can be a very useful stepping-off point for teachers – a springboard from which they can get their students to follow up particular ideas, issues and problems (Fan & Kaeley 1998).

There is also considerable evidence available to indicate that textbooks are misused by teachers and that the content of the textbooks is often bland, poorly organised and inappropriate for many

FIGURE 14.1 Resources list for teachers

Resources available for use in the classroom/school

1. **Print materials**
   - Textbooks
   - Reference books
   - Project kits
   - Pamphlets and inexpensive materials
   - Study prints and posters
   - Simulation games
   - Maps, globes and models
2. **Multimedia**
   - Personal computers
   - Tablet PCs
   - PDAs
   - MP3 players
   - The Internet
   - CD-ROMs
   - DVDs
   - Blogs
   - Television and videotapes
   - Films
   - Radio
   - Slidetapes and film strips
   - Overhead projectors
   - PowerPoint projectors
   - Interactive whiteboards
   - Smart Boards

Resources available beyond the school

3. **Cultural resources**
   - Museums
   - Art galleries
   - Libraries
   - Archives
4. **Persons**
   - People in specific occupations
   - People now retired
   - Groups, associations and organisations
5. **Materials and artefacts**
   - Newspapers
   - Documents and reports
   - Photographs
   - Recordings
   - Miscellaneous personal items

students (Nelson 1992). Too often, teachers tend to rely on the textbook as the sole basis for organising a teaching unit, even to the extent of requiring their students to complete each exercise as listed in the textbook.

 Do textbooks still have a major role in student learning? Are Internet texts a viable alternative? What are some gains and possible problems in using Internet texts?

The selection of appropriate textbooks is clearly a very important task and one that must be undertaken very conscientiously by a teacher or groups of teachers at a school. It is also evident that textbooks must not be over-used in the classroom situation and that teachers and students should consider them as only one of the many types of resources available (Cruickshank, Jenkins & Metcalf 2009).

There is also the issue of whether textbooks are improving in terms of their pedagogical impact. Though publishers continue to strive for better quality products (through the use of colour, organisers, supplements, web pages) they are also striving for lower production costs. Research studies undertaken by Calfee and Chambliss (1988) and Chambliss, Calfee and Wong (1990) indicate that a number of texts are poorly conceptualised and provide few linkages between topics. Kesidou and Roseman's (2002) study noted that many textbooks in science were not accurate, complete or coherent in terms of content.

Online textbooks have been available for some years, but it is interesting to note that few publishers have expanded into this field. A variation on this which has been used extensively by several major book publishers is Internet-linked content. Holt, Rinehart and Winston (2006) are a leading publisher in this area, publishing a number of online texts in Language, Arts, Science and Health, Social Studies and Mathematics, but only for Years 6–12. There are also a number of online Mathematics textbooks at senior secondary level, for example Cain and Herod's (2002) *Multivariate Calculus*.

14.3.2 Reference books

A myriad of reference books is available in most libraries, ranging from world encyclopaedias and Australian encyclopaedias to specialist volumes dealing with topics such as industrial development, environment and Aborigines.

With the development of CD-ROMs there is now an enormous amount of general reference material – including encyclopaedias, dictionaries and atlases, and content-specific material – available electronically as e-learning. For example, there are now 57 companies who produce general reference encyclopaedias that have interactive CD-ROMs with full colour photographs, animation, sound and movie clips. Students can search for material by using title, subject, keywords and a number of different indexes.

There are a number of government publications that provide valuable information and statistical data. Examples include publications of the Australian Bureau of Statistics (Yearbooks, State and Australian), and social security, education and employment statistics. A lot of this material is also available on the Internet.

 Go to a library and look up the CD-ROM for a major encyclopaedia. How easy was it to search out a topic and follow through with various links?

14.3.3 Trade books

Trade books are those books that are intended for sale to the general public, including fiction and non-fiction, rather than for use in classrooms. Some publishers now have special divisions dealing with trade books (for example, Harcourt Trade Publishers 2006). There are literally thousands of trade books – children's books, travel books, hobby books. A number of these trade books can be of benefit to students.

As described by Gregory (1997) with regard to multicultural trade books, 'they bring children into a natural, non-threatening, experience of other people that cannot help but broaden and enrich their perspectives of the world' (p. 1).

Some of the benefits in using trade books include that they:
- can be used as supplementary readers for students
- provide background material for teachers
- can be used as reference material.

However, it is important to note that trade books will reflect the biases of the authors including, for example, 'the negative or absent representation of females, people of colour, non-Christian and non-Western religions, people from lower socio-economic backgrounds, and people with disabilities' (Boutte 2002, p. 150).

Davis and Palmer (1992) maintain that trade books are more lively and provide a vehicle for humanising and adding personal components to the teaching program (Goodwin 2008). However, it can be very difficult to choose appropriate trade books. Some useful criteria to use as a guide are listed below.
- Is valuable information presented?
- Is the material developmentally appropriate for a class?
- Is the material of literary value?

Library staff are usually willing to assist in the selection of trade books for particular teaching topics. A number of professional associations in the United States now have book review panels who recommend outstanding trade books for students K–12, such as the National Science Teachers Association (2006) and the National Council for the Social Studies (2006). The effort involved in using trade books is certainly worth it. As noted by the author elsewhere:

> Few teachers would miss using some of AB Paterson's poetry such as 'The Man from Snowy River' or Henry Lawson's stories such as 'The Loaded Dog' to convey impressions of life in outback Australia. At the secondary school level, there are numerous examples available, such as a German soldier's letter written during the invasion of Stalingrad in 1944 in *Last Letters from Stalingrad* by Schneider and Gullans (1962) or accounts of the atomic bomb being dropped in Japan in Hachiya's *The Agony of Hiroshima* (1955), or accounts of cultural clashes in Forster's *A Passage to India* (1924). (Marsh 2004, p. 113)

Again, a lot of trade books are now available on CD-ROM and this enables the text to be supplemented with media clips.

> **YOUR TURN**
> - Think about some favourite fiction stories you have read over the years. Could excerpts from any of these be used to enliven a lesson or series of lessons?
> - Are trade books a useful resource for teachers to use? What are some advantages and disadvantages to consider?

14.3.4 Project kits

Project kits continue to be produced by government and commercial firms. They are often packaged in attractive containers and typically include information sheets, booklets, charts, and audiovisual and computer disc software on specific themes.

The project kit 'Discovering Democracy' has been distributed to every school in Australia. The green and blue boxes have been supplemented by a set of readers providing original source material for the primary and secondary years. The 'Discovering Democracy' materials are well supported by a website maintained by the Curriculum Corporation <www.curriculum.edu.au/ddunits/index.htm>. This site provides access to online versions of the units, extensive teacher notes and links to other resources.

There are now many multimedia software packages available on a range of project topics (Simkins et al. 2002).

14.3.5 Website sources and inexpensive materials

A number of firms now provide websites where topics of interest to schools can be downloaded. For example, the Queensland Environmental Protection Agency's site <www.epa.qld.gov.au>, and Carbonfund.org's site on carbon emissions <www.carbonfund.org/?gclid=coswhat_7jkcfzgtpaodis40sg>.

These sources can be very useful for teachers as they are kept up-to-date, they are colourful, informative and often interactive. Nevertheless, it is important to realise that firms provide websites for particular reasons and that the content may be biased. There is always the possibility that students will not get all points of view about an issue. The alert teacher may need to balance any perceived biases.

Various checklists are available to assist busy teachers check out possible biases in websites. The following questions provide a useful starting-off point.
1. What organisation produced the materials?
2. Do the materials teach any unstated objectives?
3. Is the identification of the product or brand necessary to teach the objectives of the lesson?

4   Are the sources of the facts in the materials identified?
5   What important facts are omitted from the materials?
6   Do the materials use half-truths to support their viewpoints?
7   Do the materials use emotionally loaded words or pictures?

A valuable exercise for upper primary and secondary school students is for them to develop their own checklists for appraising websites. Such exercises are excellent concrete opportunities for students to apply their critical thinking skills.

14.3.6 Colour prints and posters

Study prints and posters can be very useful to stimulate discussion or for introducing a new topic. Although commercial firms still produce prints and posters free of charge or at a nominal cost, teachers can now use Smart Boards, Visual Imagers and LCD PowerPoint projectors to display digitally enhanced colour prints. These images can be used for all-class teaching or for small group activities.

14.3.7 Simulation games

Simulation games are games that resemble reality and include board games and role-play games. They are a most valuable resource for teachers whether they are simple, teacher-made examples, elaborate commercial versions, or computer-based versions (Wolfe 2000).

Some of the advantages of using simulation games include the following:
- they promote active learning
- students can see events occurring over accelerated time
- they encourage students to develop decision-making skills
- students can get immediate feedback on their decisions
- they are very useful in focusing on value issues.

Further details were provided in Chapter 12.

14.3.8 Maps, globes and models

Maps are pictures of reality and can portray a vast amount of information. It is important that students master the necessary skills to be able to read and understand maps. Various special purpose, political and travel maps are available that can be used very effectively in lessons. A variety of maps is now available on the Internet and can be easily accessed by students.

Globes are especially important because they provide the only accurate representation of the Earth's surface. For primary grades, a globe enables them to differentiate between areas of land, water, the two hemispheres, cardinal directions, and latitude and longitude. Secondary school students are able to use more elaborate physical and political globes.

Models can be created to represent various phenomena and can range from model relief maps made out of paper strips and paste, to elaborate dioramas (three-dimensional models) used to illustrate historical or contemporary events or actions.

All kinds of 'junk' materials can be used to add impact to models, and especially dioramas. For example, Christensen and Green (1982) suggest that the following have a variety of uses:
- cardboard boxes – kit storage, storing overhead projector transparencies
- fabric, drapes – cloth-backed maps, displays
- mailing tubes – map storage, cardboard furniture
- meat trays – mounting of pictures, collection displays
- scrap building materials – display boards
- shoe boxes – dioramas, puzzles
- broom handles – displays, mobiles
- coat hangers – mobiles, wire sculpture
- egg cartons – storage of collections.

14.4 | CHECKLISTS FOR EVALUATING AND SELECTING PRINT MATERIALS

All teachers involved in the process of purchasing new materials for their classrooms somehow have to discriminate between useful and unsuitable resources. Although intuition, recommendations from others and subjective reactions to physical appeal are some of the criteria that may be used, the importance of the selections warrants a process that is more rigorous and soundly based.

Harlen (1994) argues that it is very important that teachers use curriculum materials as intended. She urges groups of teachers (for example, in professional subject associations) to undertake a comprehensive series of steps in evaluating K–12 curriculum materials. The steps she considers are essential include:

- deciding on the criteria to be used
- gathering information by studying how the curriculum material is used in classrooms (for example, making notes during lessons; discussing the work with students; making sound and video recordings)
- analysing the information – use a grading scheme for each of the criteria
- reporting the judgments – profiles of the curriculum materials can be produced or full reports written.

Clearly, this would be a major undertaking. Analysis schemes devised in the US for Mathematics (Kulm & Grier 1998) and Science (National Science Resources Centre 1999) are also extremely comprehensive, time-consuming and expensive.

By contrast, there are less complex versions available that are still extremely useful, even though they are dated. A simple checklist, developed by Piper (1976), consists of 10 general headings with brief yes/no questions for each. It is included in Table 14.1.

The Piper scheme is easy to use and is applicable to a wide range of print materials, but it is predominantly teacher-directed and highly structured. Other schemes have been developed – for example, Gall (1981) – which provide for a wider variety of teacher styles.

Of course, with the advent of computer-based products it is necessary to evaluate these products too. School library media specialists can provide assistance to teachers in assessing the quality of computer-based packages (Cohen, Manion & Morrison 2004). Nationally, there are general appraisal and retrieval systems available to assist teachers, such as The Education Network Australia (EdNA). Packages are described in terms of such categories as format, language level, coverage and user level.

More detailed evaluations of packages are provided by overseas agencies such as the California Software Clearinghouse. This clearinghouse evaluates CD-ROM and DVD programs and instructional videos using the criteria of curricular match, instructional design, content, student interest and technical quality (Bakker & Piper 1994; Rethinam, Pyke & Lynch 2008).

YOUR TURN

- If you were asked to assist with selecting new student textbooks for your class or school, what criteria would you use? Price? Number of pages? Level of vocabulary? Multimedia inserts such as CD-ROMs?
- Construct your own checklist based upon Piper's list, included in Table 14.1.

TABLE 14.1 Checklist for evaluating print materials

Headings	Sample questions	
1 Goals		
(a) Aims and objectives	Are the aims and objectives adequate in scope and definition?	Yes/No
(b) Rationale	Is the rationale consistent with the aims and objectives of the unit?	Yes/No
2 Format		
(a) Practicality	Is the material practical in terms of:	
	(a) school facilities?	Yes/No
	(b) equipment skills/personnel required?	Yes/No
	(c) convenience of handling?	Yes/No
	(d) class size/age/ability range?	Yes/No
(b) Design	Does the material communicate effectively?	Yes/No
(c) Content	Is the content relevant to the needs of:	
	(a) the students?	Yes/No
	(b) the teacher?	Yes/No
	(c) the community?	Yes/No
3 Process		
(a) Student activities	Is there adequate provision for student activities in the unit?	Yes/No
(b) Teacher procedures	Are there special skills required of the teacher?	Yes/No
4 Outcomes		
(a) Student outcomes	Are there benefits for the student in terms of:	
	(a) knowledge/understanding?	Yes/No
	(b) skills?	Yes/No
	(c) attitudes/values?	Yes/No
	(d) perceptions?	Yes/No
	(e) interests?	Yes/No
(b) Teacher outcomes	Are there benefits for the teacher in terms of:	
	(a) satisfactions?	Yes/No
	(b) achievement of aims and objectives?	Yes/No
	(c) better relationships with pupils?	Yes/No
	(d) better teaching?	Yes/No
	(e) interest?	Yes/No
	(f) professional development?	Yes/No
(c) General outcomes	Does the unit achieve its aims and objectives?	Yes/No

Source: Piper 1976, pp. 84–8, Commonwealth of Australia copyright, reproduced with permission.

14.5 | MULTIMEDIA

Information technology (IT) equipment has developed so rapidly that it is now possible to have multi-sensory classroom environments. Students can experience highly sophisticated visual images, text, animation, sound – all sorts of sensory experiences. The commonly listed advantages include the fact that students:
- can learn and develop at different rates
- can become proficient at accessing, evaluating and communicating information
- can increase the quantity and quality of their thinking and writing
- can develop artistic expression
- become globally aware and access resources outside the school
- become more comfortable and familiar with computer tools of the Information Age.

There are now technologies that are revolutionising learning opportunities in schools still further, such as:
- computers that translate text-to-speech and speech-to-text
- pen-based computing
- virtual reality programs
- wireless connectivity
- videoconferencing using live audio and video on the Internet.

However, it is important to keep these assertions in perspective. Non-computer-based teaching can often be equally effective with students. The aim of learning situations is for students to develop a love of learning, not a love of multimedia per se (Atkins 1993). Also, the initial purchase and maintenance costs to schools of computing equipment are very high. There can be significant equity issues for many school communities where funding sources are very limited.

14.5.1 Computers

Table-top computers are present in almost all schools. In some cases there may be a single computer per classroom, or pods of four or five, or complete computer laboratories. There are different varieties of computers available such as laptops, tablet PCs and PDAs.

Laptop computers

In many schools, entire classes have their individual laptop computers (McDonald & Ingvarson 1997; Newhouse 1998).

An ACER study (Ainley 2000) examined Year 7 students' use of laptops at a Melbourne high school, continuing with the same groups over a two-year period. Students were asked to keep a diary about the way they used a laptop for schoolwork, homework and out-of-school activities. Some interesting findings included:
- both boys and girls stated that the computer was a useful means of getting work done
- they considered that understanding how to operate computers was part of their learning
- they considered laptops affected how classes were run – they were now more likely to make presentations and to work on individual research topics

but they didn't consider that the computer was useful as a means of assessing knowledge and information. This study highlights students' acceptance and use of laptops and how teaching methods are changing as a result. Yet it also demonstrates some resistance to using computers as an alternative source of knowledge.

Tablet PCs

These are fully functional laptop PCs, but they are equipped with a sensitive screen designed to interact with a complementary pen. The pen can be used directly on the screen and operates just like a mouse to select, drag and open files. A person can take notes at a meeting or in a class – the handwritten notes can be easily converted into text.

Tablet PCs may replace laptops in schools in the near future. This is happening already in a number of schools in Singapore. At the National Institute of Technology they have created 'The Classroom of the Future' which is a fully functioning classroom. Tablet PCs are a major feature of this classroom and are used by teachers and students in all activities (Ministry of Education, Singapore 2005).

Personal digital assistants (PDAs)

These are hand-held devices that combine computing, telephone and fax, Internet and networking features. They have a touch screen for data entry and many incorporate handwriting recognition features.

PDAs enable digital note-taking. They allow students to quickly spellcheck, modify and amend their class notes. Teachers can distribute course material to students with PDAs through the use of their Internet connectivity.

Yong *et al.* (2006) used PDAs with a Year 5 primary school class in Singapore involved in experiential learning in Science. They concluded that the students were more motivated and self-driven than in normal lessons.

MP3 players

MP3 players are widely used by teens and young adults as a medium for entertainment (Stiler 2007). However teachers and students are realising that MP3 players can be used very effectively for data storage, language learning and lecture recordings. Stiler's (2007) study of six teachers at a secondary school in California concluded that teachers became aware of the potential for MP3 players to better match the learning style of students. However the teachers also noted the need for a comprehensive and sustainable technology plan to support the infusion of MP3 players into classroom learning.

14.5.2 CD-ROMs

CD-ROMs (Compact Disc–Read Only Memory) are similar in size and appearance to music CDs but they have many additional features. They can include on the one disc vast amounts of information including text, graphics, voice recordings, music, maps, photographs and animation. The information can be retrieved easily, usually by a keyword search and then by clicking on highlighted words.

There is now a huge range of CD-ROMs available, including information products such as encyclopaedias, reference materials and interactive games.

As an example, *Convict Fleet to Dragon Boat* (Ripple Media 1998) is a CD-ROM that covers a 200-year period of Australian history. It provides video clips, interviews, profiles, music and games about the Aborigines, early Dutch explorers, convicts and recent immigrants from Europe and Asia. Video Education (2006) provides in-depth analyses of 'Australia and the Great Depression' and 'Australia and the Vietnam War'.

Wassermann (2001) describes how she and her secondary school students, together with assistance from a technician, created their own CD-ROM *Presumed Enemies*, which told the story of Japan from the mid-nineteenth century covering immigration trickles to North America, World War II, internment of Japanese during World War II and redress.

Fill and Ottewill (2006) describe how video streaming can be very powerful – learners can dip into a video resource, as they would a book, in search of relevant information. Teachers can enhance their impact by adding audio, visual and textual components to their PowerPoint presentations.

As well as commercially produced CD-ROMs, teachers are producing their own interactive CD-ROMs. As an example Soon and Leng (2006) developed and used a highly effective interactive CD-ROM for the teaching of Chinese vocabulary to a Year 5 class in Singapore.

14.5.3 The Internet

The Internet is a worldwide connection of computers that can communicate (Gardner P 1997). Small contributing networks are connected across the world and they all speak the same language, known as TCP/IP.

Galbreath (1997) contends that the Internet is moving at breakneck speed. As noted by Hahn and Stout (1994), the 'Internet is the first global forum and the first global library. Anyone can participate at any time: the Internet never closes' (p. 4).

As noted in Wikipedia (2006):

> the Web is the most far-reaching and extensive medium of personal exchange to appear on Earth. It has probably allowed many of its users to interact with many more groups of people, dispersed around the planet in time and space, than is possible when limited by physical contact or even when limited by every other existing medium of communication combined. (p. 1)

It is a major boon to teachers and students because users can access information and media from all over the world almost instantaneously for individual or cooperative projects (Jones 2002; Norton & Wiburg 2003). It allows teachers to practise open learning. Distances and platforms are no barriers to access (Anderson & Alagurnalai 1997).

Yet Kuiper, Volman and Terwel (2005) and Coiro (2005) warn that the Internet helps the learning processes of students only under certain conditions. For example:
- Students must have good searching skills and know what they are looking for.
- Students need to be able to assess the reliability of Internet texts.
- Students must learn to scan information quickly to ascertain what is useful.
- Students must be able to make purposeful use of the information they find.
- Students should avoid being distracted by sites such as eCheat.

The Internet can be used to communicate via electronic mail; transfer files such as documents and software; or to publish – for example, on a website.

Electronic mail can be sent to and received by others on the network. It can be used for exchanging private messages or for group-based communication. Garner and Gillingham (1996) suggest that email activities are very social for students. They are conversations written down and hence they can add considerably to students' communication skills. Email can also be a very valuable way to maintain interactions between the teacher and students in different learning settings.

When information is located on the Internet it can be downloaded onto the hard disk on the computer and then printed.

Yet there can be problems in accessing the Internet because of delays in transmission. Sometimes searches can be very long-winded and they are not always successful (Coiro 2005). There is the additional problem that some Internet sites contain material that may be offensive to students and their parents (Wolfe 2000).

 Do Internet technologies raise new issues about the authenticity of online information? For example read the following online hoax 'California's Velcro Crop under Challenge' <www.umbachconsulting.com.miscellany/velcro.html>.

The Internet now has a major role as a teaching tool. Internet videoconferencing (Fetterman 1996) is just one example of a development that could be an inexpensive boon for teachers and students. With the Internet students can log on at any time of the day or night. Internet-based instruction is likely to occur more and more in schools, whether we like it or not (Tapscott 1999). As noted by Brooks (1997), costs are lower with the Internet. Officials in education systems are likely to opt for greater use of Internet-based instruction.

14.5.4 Blogs

Blogs (or weblogs) are websites where entries are made in journal style. In the commercial world blogs provide commentaries or news on particular subjects.

Many teachers are now encouraging students to develop blogs as personal online diaries. A blog can contain text, images and links to other blogs. Blogs can be run using blog software such as WordPress or by subscribing to a dedicated blog history service such as Xanga.

14.5.5 Television, DVDs and videotapes

Television is a very powerful resource, as it is such a major element of students' culture. Television programs that pose problems, stimulate curiosity and raise value issues are especially useful for instructional purposes. Videotaping of desired programs (done within the bounds of copyright) is far easier for the classroom teacher than endeavouring to synchronise instruction with advertised times for educational television programs.

The introduction of cable television into Australia has enabled a wider range of educational programs to be made available, provided schools have the funds to access this resource. Special educational reports on global and international issues and specific elements of science and the arts are available together with various news reports.

14.5.6 Older-style resources

Films

Television has clearly overtaken films as a teaching resource, yet films still have a place in the classroom. An enormous range of topics is available for purchase or loan. The short 16-millimetre film (10–15 minutes) can provide an excellent stimulus or introduction to a topic.

As with all audiovisual resources, it is crucial that the teacher preview the resource to see whether it is suitable or not and to plan key points to emphasise.

Radio

For many students, listening to the radio is a very common pastime. It is an important resource for teachers because it has the potential to develop students' listening skills. Listening to a radio enables students to develop their own visual imagery. They are not limited by the visual/sound confines of the television screen. It can lead to very stimulating discussion sessions as students provide varied reactions to what they have heard.

Students can prepare their own class radio programs. This involves students in planning activities, scripting and the production of appropriate sound effects and can be extremely satisfying and a lot of fun.

Also, MP3 players with FM radio recording capabilities extend the uses of radio because live broadcasts can be downloaded and then analysed.

Students can also be engaged in making podcasts, which may be in a similar form to a radio program, but for Internet distribution.

Overhead projectors

Most classrooms have access to an overhead projector. Overhead projections enable teachers to write on transparent plastic or to point to items and diagrams while facing the class in a normally-lit classroom.

Although various, highly colourful commercial transparencies are available, teachers can produce their own on photocopying machines (subject to copyright regulations). Teachers wanting to build up

a transparency during a lesson can use soluble coloured marker pens. Davidson, Rowland and Sherry (1982) provide some useful reminders when preparing classroom transparencies:
- *Visibility*. Write, print and type large. Letters should be at least 0.5 centimetres high.
- *Clarity*. Everything on a visual chart should be instantly recognisable. If it is not, it should be labelled. Colour can be used to emphasise certain points.
- *Simplicity*. Keep it crisp and uncluttered. Use a maximum of six or seven lines per transparency.

14.5.7 PowerPoint projectors (LCD)

Although overhead projectors continue to be used in many classrooms, more sophisticated diagrams, charts and headings can be presented in dazzling colours by using LCD projectors linked to PowerPoint programs on a personal computer (Simkins *et al.* 2002; Norton & Wiburg 2003). Elaborate graphics and video clips can be projected in full daylight conditions and the teacher can direct the projections by remote control (Badge *et al.* 2008).

Russell (2006) notes that digital projectors were taking the place of older filmstrip, slide and movie projectors in classrooms. They typically produce brighter images from wider angles to the screen, are far more portable and have higher levels of resolution.

14.5.8 Smart Boards and interactive whiteboards (IWBs)

A Smart Board or interactive whiteboard is essentially a large computer screen that is sensitive to touch. To operate an IWB you need a computer and a PowerPoint projector. The board can be either fixed in the one location or portable. Any program that can be used on a computer can be projected onto the screen, which then becomes a touch screen for the whole class (Sweetnam 2005).

Smart Boards have many advantages, including:
- they provide a large display for students to see and interact with
- they provide a focus for students' attention
- the teacher remains in control of what happens
- they can be used as an overhead projector and as a whiteboard – unlimited pages are available to be used as a flip chart
- a variety of background colours are available
- students can demonstrate points on the board using a special mouse pen or their fingers
- any student work can be displayed on the IWB and saved or printed out
- material can be personalised so that a class has ownership of it (for example, constructing an audio book about themselves) (Gage 2005).

IWBs are widely used in the United Kingdom and Singapore and are now used widely in schools in Australia, especially in New South Wales and Victoria. Promethean and Smart Boards are the two major suppliers of IWBs and they both provide a range of files for most subjects, and especially literacy, across the curriculum.

As concluded by Sweetnam (2005), the 'possibilities of the IWB seem to be only limited by the imagination and creativity of the classroom teachers'. Students also seem to be very positive about the use of Smart Boards (Erikson 2007).

Yet a recent study on the use of IWBs in the UK is not so glowing (Smith, Hardman & Higgins 2006). These researchers observed teachers' use of IWBs and teacher–student interaction in English literacy lessons. They concluded that IWBs encouraged students to use more open-ended questions, but that there was no fundamental change in the teachers' underlying pedagogy. 'IWBs will not provide some technological fix – there needs to be a fundamental change in understandings about whole-class teaching' (Smith, Hardman & Higgins 2006, p. 456).

A BBC Report (2007) concluded that there was little impact on pupils' performance in the first year of using IWBs. In some cases IWBs slowed the pace of whole-class learning.

Do you agree that using Smart Boards has the potential to make lessons more interesting for students and enables them to be more directly involved in their learning? Give some points for and against this statement.

14.6 | RESOURCES AVAILABLE BEYOND THE SCHOOL SETTING

One resource that is available to all teachers is the local community. Nelson (1992) considers that there are a number of reasons why local communities should be studied.
- They provide a unique, rich resource of materials.
- They enhance cooperation between school and the community.
- They promote a sense of pride and fulfilment in students.
- Theories developed in the classroom and observed in the community make learning more relevant to students.
- Studies of community allow for a diversity of learning modes.

A variety of investigations can be undertaken by students ranging from formal to informal, in large or small groups, and in school time or non-school time.

14.6.1 Cultural resources

In the words of Harris (2005, p. 44), 'Cultural institutions such as museums, libraries, galleries and archives provide teachers with a rich variety of resources and pedagogical opportunities.'

Sydney Olympic Park is one of the many facilities in different states to offer educational experiences to students. Bagshaw (2005) coordinates school visits to the Sydney Olympic Park, where students are provided with information not only about the Olympic movement and Olympic legacy but also details about land and water management and sustainability for that area.

The IT revolution has greatly affected the operation of these cultural institutions, not only in terms of storage but also in the interactive digitised presentation formats that can be used. Many of these institutions now employ education officers to develop and implement a range of education programs. 'Increasingly, cultural institutions seem to have re-cast themselves (or been re-cast by others?) in the role of education providers' (Harris 2005, p. 3).

Yet it should be noted that these education officers have priorities to provide self-motivational informal learning, which may or may not support a program that a teacher is following. There is still the need, therefore, for teachers to plan innovative visits (Blain 2001) and not to abdicate responsibility for facilitating effective learning to the cultural institutions (Harris 2005).

14.6.2 People in specific occupations and retired people

Usually there is a wide range of resource personnel available but it is useful, as described elsewhere (Marsh 2004), to consider two main categories:
1. people who are of long standing in the community and have a wide general knowledge
2. people who have specialised knowledge, even though they may not have lived in the community for very long.

Once resource people have been identified, it is important to give them guidance before they speak to the students. Some personnel are outstanding communicators and relate very well with students, but many need some level of assistance. Some useful guidelines include the following:
- Give the resource person a time limit and be specific about the topic you would like presented.
- Provide background information to the resource person about the students in terms of abilities and interests.

The class also needs to be attuned to the resource person's presentation. They need to have sufficient background about the topic to be discussed. It is often useful to get students to prepare written questions they can put to the speaker at the end of the session.

14.6.3 Groups, associations and organisations

There are numerous local organisations whose members are available and willing to talk to school groups. The telephone directory provides an enormous number of possibilities, ranging from business groups (for example, the National Safety Council) to recreational groups (like the Scout Association), from social welfare groups (such as the Red Cross) to cultural and educational groups (such as the Oral History Association of Australia).

14.6.4 Newspapers, documents and artefacts

Daily and local newspapers are an important resource. Local papers often provide historical and current accounts of the local community and of major figures in the community. The study of these local, current events can be a valuable stimulus for students to create their own class newspaper.

In the local community there is a wealth of material available ranging from historical documents to old domestic appliances and tools. If asked, parents and local citizens are usually very willing to lend items to a school. Special events at a school such as a centenary are occasions when these items can be displayed. They can also be very valuable as in-class items for study by small groups or individual students.

CONCLUDING COMMENTS

There is now a bewildering diversity of resources available to the classroom teacher. Creative teachers will access a wide range of resources to accommodate the diverse range of interests and learning styles of their respective students.

A difficulty for all teachers is to make informed choices from the wide range available. An ability to be skilled in searching (information literacy) is crucial. Although computers and CD-ROMs are likely to have a major impact in the twenty-first century, there are many other important resources including print material and community resources.

KEY ISSUES RAISED IN THIS CHAPTER

1. We live in an information-rich environment and it is important that teachers use a variety of print and computer-based resources.
2. Textbooks still continue to be an important resource and they still have a number of advantages over other resources.
3. Websites can provide a vast array of stimulating sources for teachers.
4. Checklists are useful for evaluating and selecting appropriate resources.
5. Teachers need to be competent in the use of various computer-based resources such as blogs, Smart Boards (interactive whiteboards), LCD projectors, PDAs and MP3 players.

REFLECTIONS AND ISSUES

1. Visit a local school other than the one you teach in or with which you are closely associated. Note the following:
   (a) library resources typically used for two subject areas (e.g. English and Science) including encyclopaedias, references, literary selections, periodicals and other resources
   (b) multimedia equipment and software and how they are used.
   Give details of each type.

2   Teachers should keep in mind that students' preference for lessons involving media may be due to a variety of reasons, including their perception that it will reduce cognitive demands placed on them. Do you agree or disagree? If it is a potential problem, what strategies would you use to ensure that students use media-based lessons as serious learning experiences?
3   Examine one or more websites promoting an educational topic or process. Appraise the websites in terms of the seven criteria listed in section 14.3.5.
4   Using the checklist depicted in Table 14.1, evaluate a textbook that you intend to use or currently use for a particular teaching subject. Did this checklist cause you to consider other selection factors? Do you consider that additional items need to be added to the checklist?
5   Select a teaching topic relevant to a chosen class level and then make a list of the resources you might use that would illustrate a teacher-centred approach or a learner-centred approach. What factors would be important to you in choosing a preferred approach?
6   Some enthusiasts consider that in the second decade of the twenty-first century the major way of learning at all levels, and in all subject areas, will be through interactive use of computers. List some of the factors that could accelerate or inhibit this prospect. What is your personal stance on this assertion?
7   'Today's students are part of the Net Generation. This generation is using the new electronic techniques to help create a culture of learning, where the learner enjoys enhanced responsibility, interactivity, and connections with others' (Norton & Wiburg 2003, p. 15). To what extent is this occurring in Australian schools? Discuss.
8   'The potential of information noise and information overload from using computers is very real' (Gibbs & Krause 2000, p. 105). Elaborate on this statement.
9   Search on the Internet for details about Smart Boards and how they might be used to enhance student learning. If the school you are visiting has a Smart Board arrange with a teacher to develop a simple lesson to use with it.

Special references

Christensen, A & Green, L (1982) *Trash to Treasures*, Libraries Unlimited, Littleton, Colorado.
Cruickshank, DR Jenkins, D & Metcalf, K (2009) *The Act of Teaching*, 5th edn, McGraw Hill, Boston.
Gage, J (2005) *How to use an Interactive Whiteboard*, David Fulton, London.
Goodwin, P (2008) *Understanding Children's Books: A Guide for Education Professionals*, Sage, Thousand Oaks, CA.
Lifter, M & Adams, ME (1997) *Integrating Technology into the Curriculum*, Hawker Brownlow, Melbourne.
Ryan, K Cooper, JM & Tauer, S (2008) *Teaching for Student Learning*, Houghton Mifflin, Boston.

Web sources

For additional resources on using resources creatively, please go to:
www.pearson.com.au/myeducationlab.

15

MEETING THE DIVERSE NEEDS OF STUDENTS

15.1 | INTRODUCTION

It is very apparent that students have increasingly diverse needs and it is up to the teacher to recognise these to tailor programs that can optimise students' talents. In this process of personalising learning (Keamy & Nicholas 2007) teachers must recognise and value each students' unique interests, experiences and abilities, needs and backgrounds (NSW Dept of Education and Training 2008b).

Providing personalised instruction for exceptional students, gifted, physically and intellectually disabled, and culturally different students is an important commitment and challenge for teachers. Some strategies and guidelines for these students are also discussed.

15.2 | INDIVIDUALS AND THE SCHOOL ENVIRONMENT

Each individual student is different. Yet in some ways, each individual has some characteristics identical to others; some that are similar to others; and some that are different from every person born or ever to be born. For example, there are identical characteristics such as the need for oxygen and the need for food. Individuals are similar in that they share a common blood type or speak a common language. They are unique and different in terms of their experiences and genetic make-up.

The school environment can also be described in terms of being identical to other school environments in its use of school buildings, classrooms and playing fields; similar to others in terms of teachers' role and equipment used; and unique in that each serves a very different clientele including student population, parent and community groups.

Frymier (1977) suggests that for the individual and the environment it is useful to separate out the factors characteristic of each (see Figure 15.1). Although these are not 'either/or' distinctions, it is useful to consider a continuum in which at one end there are the constant factors that are very difficult if not impossible to change, and at the other end factors that are variable.

It is the variable aspects of the individual and the school environment that are the leverage points where interventions can lead to change.

It is important to remember that intelligence is multifaceted and that 'there are different ways of knowing and different ways of learning' (Lo & Pong 2002, p. 3).

FIGURE 15.1 Individual and environment factors

1. Individual
   (a) Constant factors – e.g. blood type, race
   (b) Constant variable factors – e.g. height, age
   (c) Variable factors – e.g. experience, motivation
2. School environment
   (a) Constant factors – e.g. time available for instruction each day
   (b) Constant variable factors – e.g. age of textbooks
   (c) Variable factors – e.g. sequence of subject matter

Thus, for any teaching and learning task, students will differ in how they acquire the capability.

Teachers therefore need to be mindful of what they want to teach (a carefully defined object) and must have a thorough understanding of the different ways by which students attain the learning (Lo & Pong 2002).

Having students with very different learning capabilities in a class can be an advantage to the teacher. A diverse range of thinking by students will create a learning atmosphere that is more creative and open-ended. Students gain from understanding and valuing other students' capabilities and interests.

Over the decades various approaches have been developed to cater for individual differences, ranging from ambitious endeavours to reconceptualise instruction; through the use of a curriculum-materials basis for accommodating individual differences; to specific programs to support gender differences; and specialised programs for exceptional student groups. Despite myriad attempts and enormous costs involved, the number of successes have been extremely limited. In fact, the rhetoric on innovatory approaches has not been matched by visible, practical outcomes.

Yet the challenge is there and is a must for all teachers and administrators. We cannot do other than accommodate the needs of each individual learner. We must consider the whole child – as teachers we must comprehend the totality of the whole learner (Noddings 2008). We must provide quality experience and interactions for every one of our students (Eisner 2005). Fullan, Hill and Crevola (2006) refer to the need to produce personalised programs and for teachers to be diagnostic practitioners.

15.2.1 Individual differences and student achievement

It is very evident that student achievement varies enormously between students of the same age. Although many studies have been done on specific factors such as race or gender, few have provided a comprehensive picture. One such meta-analysis was done by Barton (2004) based upon data he analysed in the United States. In developing his research framework he used the following categories:

- identifying life experiences and conditions that research showed were associated with school achievement
- noting how race, ethnicity and income affected these factors.

Barton concluded that there are a number of factors that correlate with student achievement:

Before and beyond school:
- Birthweight – infants with low birthweights are at risk of impaired development.
- Lead poisoning – lead paint found in old homes affects the development of children living in these houses.
- Hunger and nutrition – hungry, malnourished children are harmed in their cognitive development.

Home learning conditions:
- Reading to young children at home by parents provides major gains in language acquisition and general success at school.

- Television watching – watching a lot of television is associated with lower achievement and can lead to attention problems.
- Parent–child ratio – parents' availability as resources to their children is a significant factor.
- Student mobility – children who change school frequently score lower on school tests.

Home–school connection:
- Active parent participation between parents and the school is linked to fewer behaviour problems for these children.

School factors:
- Curricular rigour – there is a strong connection between advanced courses perceived by students to be of a high standard, and levels of achievement.
- Teacher experience – having experienced teachers with at least five years of experience is linked to student achievement.
- Teacher preparation – students in high poverty schools are often taught by relief teachers who are poorly prepared.
- Class size – there is no unequivocal evidence of optimal class size, but it is clearly an important factor.
- Technology-assisted instruction – the use of computers and Internet research is linked to student achievement.
- School safety – a positive disciplinary climate is directly linked to higher achievement (Barton 2004; Hart & Risely 1995; Landsman 2004; Taylor 2006; Hardre & Sullivan 2007).

This is a formidable list, but it underlines the importance of non-school and school factors. In particular, Barton (2004) concluded that children from minority races and those whose parents are on low incomes tend to be affected negatively by all these factors. 'The conclusion is clear: achievement gaps by race/ethnicity and income mirror inequalities in those aspects of schooling, early life and home circumstances that research has linked to school achievement' (Barton 2004, p. 9).

Reflect on your own development and consider the extent to which home learning conditions, home-school connections and school factors have played major roles in your development.

15.3 THE POTENTIAL OF DIFFERENTIATED CLASSROOMS

The predominant mode of instruction that occurs in classrooms involves the total class or small groups (see Chapter 12). Only occasionally are students given the opportunity to undertake independent learning and to be able to work by themselves (Tomlinson 2008a). There are of course many reasons for this. Teachers would have a very difficult time preparing separate activities for 30 or more students; there would be problems in finding sufficient resources and space to cater for all the individual activities; there would be major supervisory problems; and it would lead to misbehaviour and discipline problems – the list is endless!

Yet educators are becoming increasingly dissatisfied with conventional ways of instructing whole groups. The literature reinforces the need for all students to develop skills in learning how to learn – to be able to undertake independent, self-directed study. As noted in Chapter 8, technological innovations including the Internet now offer many more opportunities for students to undertake independent study.

Various terms have been proposed such as differentiated instruction (Hall 2002; Theroux 2001), differentiated learning (Wormeli 2007) and differentiated classrooms (Tomlinson 1999).

Tomlinson (1999) uses the term 'differentiated classroom' as a valuable concept to study ways of catering for individual differences. She defines a differentiated classroom as one where 'teachers provide specific ways for each individual to learn as deeply as possible and as quickly as possible, without assuming one student's road map for learning is identical to anyone else's' (p. 2). This can involve differentiating the content, the learning activities and the form of assessment used with different students (see Figure 15.2).

Using the term 'differentiated classroom' as defined, it is quite revealing to compare traditional and differentiated classrooms (Table 15.1). Even allowing for the fact that many of the items in the differentiated classroom are 'ideal', the table highlights the differences in emphasis and perhaps philosophical differences in approach.

A differentiated classroom is a different way of thinking about instruction. For a beginning teacher (or an experienced teacher), it is important to ponder some basic questions, as noted by Tomlinson (1999):

- Does it make sense for you to do most of the work in the classroom? Should students be the primary workers and thinkers?
- Does it seem more likely to you that everyone should always need the same book?
- Do students all seem to learn in the same way or at the same pace?
- Do students become independent learners in classrooms where they are always told what to do?
- Do learners care if they have choices about what and how to learn?
- In general, are you more effective and efficient at teaching with small groups of students and individuals, or are you more effective with the whole class?

These are very important considerations. Of course there can be a variety of constraints preventing you from working towards a differentiated classroom. However, it is worth making a start, even if you start small. Consider some of the following approaches and examples:

- As a preliminary before providing differentiated instruction, assign an 'anchor' (core) activity for all students and then allow some individuals to break off and do other tasks.

FIGURE 15.2 Dimensions of differentiation

- Content – vary the detail and difficulty level of concepts
- Learning activities – use a variety of instructional techniques to enhance and motivate students
- Assessment – provide different levels and assessment modes

TABLE 15.1 Comparing classrooms

AN IDEAL DIFFERENTIATED CLASSROOM HAS:

- instruction based on student readiness
- a range of modes of instruction
- individual achievement as a major goal
- has mainly diagnostic and formative assessment

A TRADITIONAL CLASSROOM HAS:

- whole–class instruction by the teacher
- mainly summative assessment
- the teacher controlling classroom activities
- a major emphasis on using a single textbook

- Try a differentiated task for only a small block of time.
- Take notes on your students. Note what works and what doesn't for individual students.
- Try creating one differentiated lesson per unit.
- Find multiple resources for some key lessons (Tomlinson 1999).

> **YOUR TURN**
>
> - How do you relate to the concept of a 'differentiated classroom'?
> - Would it be possible to establish the concept in classrooms you have visited?
> - What might be some early problems to overcome?

15.3.1 Contracts

Contracts encourage self-directed learning and they give students the choice when they will do certain activities (McLeod & Reynolds 2003). They permit individual pacing and they can be highly motivating for students (Saskatoon Public Schools 2008). They are relatively easy to construct (see Figure 15.3).

Students can gain considerably from being involved in individual contracts, but the level of complexity will need to be carefully judged for each student (see Figure 15.4). Some students will already have the level of maturity and information literacy skills to cope with contracts very easily, while others may have extreme difficulty. Some students may be very uncomfortable with contracts and positively dislike them!

Gage and Berliner (1992) suggest that it is possible to gauge the readiness of a student to do contracts by ascertaining the extent to which the student:

- can nominate a topic, clearly and concisely
- can state what activities would be needed to complete the contract
- is able to identify which resources would need to be used
- is able to establish a reasonable deadline for completing the contract.

At the primary school level the contracts will, by necessity, start with simple, daily checklist contracts, but they can be extended to include more complex weekly contracts (see Figure 15.5). At the secondary school level they can involve major projects (Hiemstra & Sisco 1990). For example, a Personal Interest Project is a required contract for all Year 11 and 12 students in New South Wales undertaking the Society and Culture course, as part of the Higher School Certificate examination. Each student is required to select a personal interest topic, preferably cross-cultural in emphasis, and gather appropriate primary and secondary source data to systematically analyse it. There are now a

FIGURE 15.3 Components typically included in contracts

Outcomes – they specify what is to be accomplished and the standard required

Resources – students will have access to print, media and human resources (for example – experts from the local community)

Learning alternatives – flexibility is necessary in choosing the activities. It could include reading, writing, viewing, creating, interviewing

Reporting alternatives – different ways of presenting outcomes including presentations, portfolios, products

FIGURE 15.4 Strategies for using contracts with individual students

Purpose of individual contracts

To encourage the use and development of the students' decision-making and self-management capabilities.

Strategies

- When you offer choices make sure that each one is acceptable to you.
- Give students time to explore the available choices – allow them to change their minds if their initial choice does not work out.
- Contracts work best if rewards are provided for completed tasks.
- There should not be punishments for contracts not completed.
- If a student finds it difficult to fulfill a contract it may be necessary to renegotiate the tasks or the deadline.
- Start with contracts offering limited choices and then move to more complex ones.
- Contracts can be developed for a specific subject for a class period, a day, or on a weekly basis or longer.
- The student can state what activities would be needed to complete the contract.
- The student is able to identify which resources would need to be used.
- The student is able to establish a reasonable deadline for completing the contract.

FIGURE 15.5 Examples of contracts

Primary school level

Daily contract

Date
Student
Reading Workbook
p. 49

Handwriting Unit 7

Weekly contract

Date
Student
Social Studies Contract

– 3 map skills cards
– read pages 27–39, half-page summary
– 3 community tasks cards
– free time for self-selected activities

Secondary school level

Personal interest project contract

Date
Student
Title of topic
Procedures to be undertaken
Resources to be used

number of computer software packages that can be used by students in planning and completing a contract (Wolfe 2000).

 Reflect upon a learning contract you experienced at secondary school. Was it enjoyable and fulfilling or really quite stressful? Explain your reaction.

15.3.2 Learning centres

Learning centres provide for self-directed learning for mixed ability groups (McLeod & Reynolds 2003).

Learning centres, as noted in Chapter 12, are places within a school or within a particular classroom that allow different students to work with different tasks.

According to Tomlinson (1999), 'learning centres can be informal or formal; they can be distinguished by signs, symbols or colours, or the teacher simply can ask groups of students to move to particular parts of the room' (p. 62).

A learning centre is usually separated from the main part of a classroom by pin-up boards, furniture, curtains or shelves. They typically contain materials and instructions for tasks relating to a particular subject (for example, Science or Maths), particular themes (such as the environment), particular skills (for example, handwriting), or certain kinds of instructional materials (such as newspapers or audiovisual materials).

With the increased use of computers, computer pods (mini labs with three to four computers) are now common in classrooms, or in the media centre of school libraries (Gardner P 1997; Norton & Wiburg 2003).

Learning centres can provide many opportunities for individual students to work undisturbed on contracts or self-directed study. They are usually stimulating and colourful environments and provide a welcome relief from the traditional, formal environment of lines of desks and chairs (Scott 1999).

However, successful learning centres require good classroom management and well-known rules and procedures. For example:
- decide how many centres you need and how many students are allowed in each centre
- establish rules of behaviour at each centre including cleaning up after they have finished their activity
- alternate lessons related to centres so students do not miss any classroom instruction
- start small with centres such as:
  - Maths centre – maths activities, pegboards
  - Computer centre – load learning software
  - reading centre – have a comfortable rug and a bookcase
  - Art centre – include paint, colours, paper
  - Music centre – set up a CD player with headphones.

15.3.3 Computer-based instruction

Computers offer the facility of CD-ROMs, Internet, hypertext and hypermedia which can be used by students to search out a wealth of data for specific teacher-directed inquiry projects or for self-directed study (see also Chapter 12). The Internet in particular provides almost limitless data options for individual students and gives them maximum flexibility (Hackbarth 1997; Wolfe 2000; Norton & Wiburg 2003; Connolly & Maicher 2005).

Silver-Pacuilla and Fleischman (2006) note that technology can help struggling students in a mixed group. They include a number of examples of ways to build literacy and language skills and independence for students such as:
- text to speech – to increase the amount of reading by the use of digital story books

- speech recognition – use speech recognition technology to help struggling writers and spellers
- graphic organisers – use these to tap into students' visual and spatial abilities.

> **YOUR TURN**
>
> Think about a learning centre you would like to establish in a classroom.
> - What would be the theme?
> - What materials would you locate at the centre?
> - What student activities would you prepare?
> - How useful might it be?

15.3.4 Lesson study

Lesson study is becoming a valuable tool in a number of countries, especially the UK, USA, China, Japan, Singapore and Hong Kong, to cater for individual differences (Davies & Dunnill 2008; Chokshi & Fernandez 2004; Lewis, Perry & Hurd 2004) (see also Chapter 7). This approach is based on the premise that there are critical differences between different students' ways of seeing things at school, especially their intuitive understanding and the understanding that is embodied in the notations and concepts of schools (Lo Mun Ling 2007).

Advocates of lesson study try to identify and address these student differences by carefully planning, teaching and then reteaching lessons (Stigler & Hiebert 1999; Marton & Booth 1997). Lo, Pong and Pakey (2005) advocate a pedagogy based on variation. That is, teachers in a team plan for lessons that help students to discern patterns of variation in objects based on contrast, generalisation, separation and fusion. Lessons are constructed based upon the following:

- choose the object of learning (purpose)
- ascertain students' prior understanding of the object of learning to find out what are the critical learning difficulties – use pre-lesson tests and student interviews with a sample of students
- plan and implement the research lesson
- evaluate the lesson using a post-lesson test with all students and post-lesson interviews with a sample of students
- report and discuss results
- move to a second cycle involving possible reteaching.

 Look up some lesson study examples on the web <www.tc.columbia.edu/lessonstudy/tools.html>. Are you surprised at some of the difficulties that students have in learning concepts? Consider how you might use lesson study.

15.3.5 Mastery learning

The examples given above indicate how instructional approaches can be modified to cater more widely for individual differences. There are other options that involve major changes to the way classes are organised and one example of this is mastery learning.

Mastery learning is extolled by many educators as a very worthy method of instruction because a greater percentage of students are able to achieve at high levels. It can assist individual students because under traditional methods many of them do not achieve high grades in their class work. Students will be interested in learning because they achieve levels of success (Bottoms 2007; Costa 2008).

The basic assumption behind mastery learning is that, given sufficient opportunity to learn and time spent actually learning, the vast majority of students can achieve some specified expected level of performance (Cruickshank, Jenkins & Metcalf 2009).

Features of the mastery learning approach include the following:
- Initial instruction of small units with related specific objectives.
- Teachers provide parallel short tests at frequent intervals. After a first failure and a new period of studying, each student is tested again. This cycle of studying and testing continues until a criterion for acceptable work has been reached, usually 80–90 per cent of correct responses.
- Remedial instruction is provided to students by the teacher, who generally provides encouragement as well.

Many forms of mastery learning are titled 'individualised instructional packages'. They are individualised to the extent that every individual has the opportunity to reach the required standard. Yet it can be argued that they are strongly teacher-centred. The teacher directs the flow of learning through the carefully sequenced activities, the reinforcement, the monitoring and the feedback (Arends 2009).

A current example of individualised instruction and mastery learning is the K–12 Accelerated Christian Education (ACE) curriculum in use in several Australian states. Students use a series of workbooks for each subject in the curriculum. For each unit there is a test that a student may take as many times as needed to reach the 80 per cent mastery criterion. Over the 13-year period of K–12 some students will complete all subjects in less time while others will require a longer period (see ACE 2008).

The research literature is generally very positive about mastery learning. Bloom (1968) argues especially for the effect it has on a student's self-concept – it can be a powerful source of reassurance and reinforcement. The findings are consistently positive across subject areas – for example, Guskey and Pigott (1988), Walberg (1985), Garner (2008) and Davis and Sorelli (1995).

Yet it does appear to benefit slower-learning students at the expense of faster-learning students (Slavin 1987). Gage and Berliner (1992) note that it is the classroom teacher who provides supplementary assistance to the slower learners and, while they are providing this help, the faster students may have to contend with 'busy' work.

15.3.6 Multiple intelligences

Studies on multiple intelligences over the last two decades (Gardner 1983; Armstrong 2000) have provided educators with different approaches to learning. Gardner (1983, 2006) described a set of intelligences (he selected seven initially; an eighth one, 'naturalist' intelligence, was added in 1993) based on studies in child development and cognitive science (see Table 15.2).

Teachers have seen the opportunities whereby they plan projects, lessons and interdisciplinary curricula and assessment tasks around the multiple intelligences. Teachers are able to help students discover and develop their individual talents across the eight intelligences (Campbell 1997; Gibson 2002; Smith, MK 2008; Nolen 2003).

To illustrate with some examples:
- A teacher teaches geometry kinesthetically by building models.
- Students close their eyes and see pictures of what they have just read – afterwards they draw or talk about their experiences.
- Students are invited to create songs or chants that summarise major principles from a subject area.

TABLE 15.2 Exploring our multiple intelligences

According to Gardner (1993) there are eight intelligences:
- Verbal linguistic intelligence – the capacity to use language, to express what is on your mind.
- Logical–mathematical intelligence – the capacity to manipulate numbers, quantities and operations and to understand principles.
- Spatial intelligence – the ability to represent the spatial world internally in your mind.
- Bodily–kinaesthetic intelligence – the capacity to use your whole body or parts of your body to solve a problem.
- Musical intelligence – the capacity to think in music, to hear patterns, to recognise them and to remember them.
- Interpersonal intelligence – the ability to understand other people.
- Naturalistic intelligence – the ability to recognise patterns among living things.
- Intrapersonal intelligence – the capacity to have an understanding of yourself, of knowing what you can do.

In some classrooms, teachers set up eight learning stations reflecting the eight multiple intelligences, and students rotate through them over a week. Some teachers ask students to select the type of intelligence they want to concentrate on for a particular topic. Others use the list as a basis for homework exercises such as doing their homework on one night musically. In some schools, teachers plan and teach in teams based on their intelligence strengths.

Forte and Schurr (1996) suggest that a useful planning device is to list some 'action verbs' that are appropriate for each of the eight intelligences and then use these as the trigger to develop student activities (see Table 15.3).

Multiple intelligence-based lessons can take many different forms and it is up to each teacher to produce meaningful learning experiences (Jensen 1998b). This is indeed the challenge for individualising learning. On the one hand, it can be argued that an awareness of multiple intelligences reminds the teacher that classrooms typically rely far too much on one or two intelligences (linguistic and logical–mathematical) and largely ignore the others. Yet it could also be very demanding for a teacher to try to regularly include activities that span the eight intelligences. Tomlinson and Kalbfleisch (1998) suggest that teachers need to deliberately plan for differentiated classrooms by:
- providing learning environments that are emotionally safe where participants accept and appreciate one another's similarities and differences
- providing varied learning options at different degrees of difficulty
- giving students choices about topics of study, ways of learning and modes of expression
- presenting information to students in varied ways including orally, visually and through demonstration
- allowing for varied assessment options.

15.3.7 Outcomes-based education

These approaches also involve major changes to the structuring of a school program in that desired outcomes or standards become the controlling factor in determining what is taught to students.

Outcomes-based education involves focusing and organising a school's entire program and instructional efforts around the clearly defined outcomes we want all students to demonstrate when they leave school. Outcomes-based education has been a rallying point around the Western world (Berlach 2004) – supposedly it places the learner and their needs at the 'hub' of curriculum planning (Smith, MK 2008). A set of conditions is described that characterises real life and this is used to derive

TABLE 15.3 Action verbs and students activities

Intelligence		Action verbs		Student activities
Verbal–linguistic	examples	debate explain recite memorise	examples	reports story telling speeches plays
Logical–mathematical	examples	calculate deduce measure test	examples	computer products graphs time sequence charts
Spatial	examples	design rearrange represent transform	examples	computer graphics pamphlets maps
Bodily–kinaesthetic	examples	demonstrate touch participate jump	examples	mimes role-plays sports
Musical	examples	hear recognise perform practise	examples	sound effects rhythm games songs
Interpersonal	examples	discuss empathise listen motivate	examples	role-plays group projects conflict resolution
Intrapersonal	examples	analyse reflect interpret judge	examples	autobiographies journals reflections

a set of culminatory role performances. Students are required to provide a culminating demonstration – the focus is on competence as well as content, but not on the time needed to reach this standard.

An outcomes-based education (OBE) approach is closely related to mastery learning, as revealed by the following characteristics. It:
- includes clearly defined and publicly derived exit outcomes that reflect changing societal conditions
- includes a variety of methods that assures success for students
- incorporates criterion-referenced procedures
- is future-oriented.

Most state and territory education systems in Australia actively promoted OBE in the 1990s but reduced their support in the early 2000s. The general nature of outcomes can be appropriate for primary and lower secondary classes because they promote teacher creativity and experimentation. However, at the upper secondary school levels it is extremely difficult to produce high-stakes assessments based upon broad outcomes. Most systems have moved to content standards and syllabuses at the senior secondary level. Exceptions include Queensland (Education Queensland 2008), where regions such as Toowoomba are heavily involved with OBE, and Western Australia, where the Ministers for Education have been embroiled in a long-running dispute over the use of OBE in Years 11 and 12 (Hiatt (2006) *West Australian*, 13 September, p. 5). In December 2007, the then Minister announced that new syllabuses would replace OBE (*Perth Now*, 12 December 2007). The new Minister for Education has established an independent review of OBE in Western Australia. She recently announced that the contentious 'levels' will be dropped (S O'Neill, Director-General 2009). The respective ministers were actively opposed by a vocal pressure group, PLATO (2008; *West Australian*, 22 October 2008).

15.3.8 Standards-based education

Standards-based education is a major priority, developed especially in the US where there is currently a major focus on performance standards (Ryan, Cooper & Tauer 2008; Moore 2009b) (see also Chapter 21). For example, Moore (2009b) contends that standards-based education is a process for planning, delivering, monitoring and improving academic programs. The clearly defined academic content standards provide the basis for content in instruction and assessment. There are strong advocates of standards (for example, Arends 2009; Cruickshank, Jenkins & Metcalf 2009). They contend that some of the advantages include that it:
- measures its success based on student learning
- aligns policies and initiatives with clearly defined academic standards
- uses assessment to inform instruction.

Notwithstanding, there are many other educators (for example, Plitt 2004; Cawelti 2003) who argue that standards-based education provides little incentive for teachers to engage their students in relevant, authentic and challenging learning experiences.

Standards and essential learnings are now very prominent in most education systems in Australia. These are linked specifically to syllabus documents in New South Wales. In Victoria, the Essential Learning Standards are divided into Physical, Personal and Social Learning, Discipline-based Learning and Interdisciplinary Learning. In Queensland, syllabuses and outcome levels are used together with standards for essential learnings in Years 4, 6 and 9.

> **YOUR TURN**
>
> What do you understand to be the differences between 'outcomes' and 'standards'? Which are the most helpful in trying to prepare learning experiences for students with diverse abilities?

15.4 | INDIVIDUAL DIFFERENCES AND CURRICULUM MATERIALS

Over the decades various curriculum packages have been proposed to individualise instruction. In many cases, the structure and range of materials has not enabled individualised instruction to occur. Because of the lack of appropriate curriculum materials or lack of incentive to do so, many teachers profess to support the principle of individualised instruction but do little in practice to further this goal.

Langrehr (1983) argues that many educators still think of curriculum materials as simply being passive 'sprayers of content'. He maintains that teachers typically select curriculum materials using the sole criterion of suitability of content matter, and that the materials are selected to support the content outline of a proposed syllabus. Little consideration is given to other qualities of curriculum materials that might be collectively termed the psychological characteristics, such as media format and the message design.

Learner characteristics or aptitudes such as their cognitive, affective and physiological learning style, together with their mental ability, can interact significantly with instructional materials (an example is listed in Table 15.4). Teachers must be aware that students with different learning styles will react very differently to a given set of curriculum materials (Silver, Strong & Perini 1997).

In the United States, methods for analysing curriculum materials have been developed for Mathematics and Science by the Advancing Science, Serving Society Project 2061 (Kulm & Grier 1998). This rating scheme for curriculum materials was put through extensive trials to ensure high levels of reliability, and it is used by teachers to analyse middle-grade Mathematics and Science textbooks. The rapid growth in the use of the Internet by teachers and students has also spread numerous new ideas about what can be included in checklists of curriculum materials and how they can be used (Means 2001). In particular, the Internet has become a huge new resource for teachers and students (Molnar 2000; Schofield & Davidson 2000).

With sophisticated computer-based retrieval systems now available, it is possible that an individualised curriculum materials program could be developed and maintained at a school level.

TABLE 15.4 Classification system

Curriculum materials Major dimensions	High, medium or low descriptors
1 Experience	H/M/L
2 Intelligence	H/M/L
3 Motivation	H/M/L
4 Emotion–personality	H/M/L
5 Creativity	H/M/L
6 Social	H/M/L
7 Verbal expression	H/M/L
8 Auditory perception	H/M/L
9 Visual perception	H/M/L
10 Motor perception	H/M/L

15.5 | INDIVIDUAL DIFFERENCES AND GENDER

Although research studies do not reveal any gender differences in general intelligence between boys and girls, there do appear to be differences for specific tasks. For example, girls tend to score higher on verbal abilities whereas boys do better on reasoning and spatial skills. Boys also tend to be more aggressive and have higher expectations of success (Gilbert & Gilbert 1998; Keddie 2005; Cruickshank, Jenkins & Metcalf 2009).

There is fascinating research evidence to support this, based upon position emission tomography and MRI technologies, which demonstrate that inside the brains of boys and girls there are structural and functional differences that greatly affect human learning. Furthermore, these gender differences in the brain do not differ significantly across cultures (Gurian & Stevens 2004). As examples, Gurian and Stevens cite the following:

- 'Girls have more cortical areas devoted to verbal functioning, listening and mental cross talk and so the complexities of reading and writing come easier to the female brain' (p. 22).
- 'Because boys' brains have more cortical areas dedicated to spatial–mechanical functioning, males use, on average, half the brain space that females use … The spatial–mechanical functioning makes many boys want to move objects through space …' (p. 23).

However, it is difficult to disentangle how societal expectations and sex stereotyping affects the achievement of boys and girls (Frawley 2005). The literature contains many examples that indicate that girls are disadvantaged.

Schools tend to add to sex stereotyping by using classroom routines that treat boys and girls differently (Knupfer 1998), such as:

- classroom seating arrangements based on sex
- using management techniques based on sex – for example, boys wait behind and the girls can now go out to recess
- creating needless competition between the sexes.

National programs, such as the National Action Plan for the Education of Girls (Australian Education Council 1993), have highlighted major discriminatory practices in schools.

The ultimate goal is for schools to treat all students equally and to provide instructional equity (Smith 2001). Every teacher has to work very hard to even make some progress toward this goal. Orlich *et al.* (2009) suggest that it is the daily activities that teachers have to be careful about, such as calling on girls as often as they call on boys; rotating classroom responsibilities and leadership roles between girls and boys; and placing equal numbers of girls and boys in small discussion and cooperative learning groups.

Often, a teacher is not aware that they favour boys or girls. Sanders and Nelson (2004) give several examples in Science where a male teacher spent 80 per cent of his time responding to boys and 20 per cent to girls, even though he had thought he was using the time allocation fairly to both sexes. According to Sanders and Nelson (2004) it is necessary for teachers to make changes to their teaching practice, which often means addressing a 'number of gender-based patterns that are below most teachers' level of conscious awareness' (p. 76). Jones and Dindie (2004) did a meta-analysis of 32 studies in the US and concluded that teachers had more overall interactions and more negative interactions with male students than with female students.

Yates, McLeod and Arrow (2007) undertook a longitudinal study of students at four schools in Victoria beginning at the age of 12 and continuing interviews with them until they turned 18 years of age. They made a number of conclusions about self and gender including:

- 'students now take the language of "equal opportunity" and "non-sexist education" for granted' (p. 4)
- 'both girls and boys think that it is "normal" for boys to "muck around" in schools and that body image is much more important for girls than it is for boys' (p. 4).

In terms of practical strategies that a teacher might use to reduce sex stereotyping, consider the examples given in Figure 15.6.

Of course, male and female teachers are perceived differently by students. Dunkin's (1987) research indicates that female teachers' classrooms are warmer and more nurturing while male teachers' classrooms are better organised and more task oriented (Cruickshank, Jenkins & Metcalf 2009).

Yates, McLeod and Arrow (2007) noted that students spoke about the benefit that they had gained from particular teachers and this affected their thinking about their future directions. Conversely, negative experience with teachers affected students emotionally.

FIGURE 15.6 Teacher strategies to reduce sex stereotyping

1. Ask students to describe their image of the typical male and the typical female. Get students to share their views with the rest of the class.
2. What adjectives would you use to describe men? What adjectives would you use to describe women? Put answers on the whiteboard/blackboard using two columns. Have a follow-up discussion on male and female stereotypes.
3. Show students sexist cartoons depicting masculinity and femininity. Get students to discuss the attitudes expressed in each cartoon. Encourage students to produce their own cartoons on 'Being a Boy' or 'Being a Girl'.
4. In small groups get students to do an analysis of social studies texts, focusing upon the following:
    (a) the number of men listed in the index
    (b) the number of women listed in the index
    (c) the number of illustrations depicting men
    (d) the number of illustrations depicting women
    (e) the number of illustrations depicting both.
5. Discuss with students whether they consider the following occupations are done mainly by men or by women:

librarian	doctor
electrician	farmer
chemist	nurse
pilot	bank manager
journalist	politician
jockey	lawyer
secretary	lecturer

    (a) What are the qualities a person needs to be successful in the jobs you have marked male?
    (b) What are the qualities a person needs to be successful in the jobs you have marked female?

15.6 | INDIVIDUAL DIFFERENCES AND EXCEPTIONAL STUDENTS

Every person is distinctive in terms of abilities, interests and limitations and to that extent we are all 'exceptional'. In this chapter we are using the term 'exceptional students' to refer to those students who have exceptional learning abilities or problems and require special services to reach their potential. They include gifted, physically and intellectually disabled and culturally different students.

There can be great variation in the degree and severity of the learning problem (or ability) and this provides considerable challenges for teachers. The labels we use for exceptional children should be perceived as diagnostic and tentative. Unfortunately, the labels are often used derogatively to the extent that they become self-fulfilling prophecies (Sireci 2005). *Gifted and talented students* are often poorly served in traditional classrooms. Renzulli (1982) notes that there are the academically gifted (who score highly on tests of intelligence) and the creatively gifted (who solve problems in new ways). This author defines giftedness as a combination of three characteristics:

1. above-average general ability
2. high motivation to achieve in certain areas
3. high level of creativity.

Gifted students are often not well catered for in standard school settings because they are not extended and as a result they become bored and frustrated (Freeman 2007). They can have very different interests from their peers.

Being able to pick out gifted children from a class is difficult because of differences of degree. It is not usually sufficient to base it on such characteristics as those students interested in books and reading, or those who have relatively large vocabularies or those who are curious to learn (Sternberg 2007). The checklist in Figure 15.7 is a useful guide. There are of course specialised achievement, intelligence and creativity tests available, usually undertaken by psychologists. Case study approaches to identifying gifted students are also commonly used.

Teaching gifted children calls for teachers to have imaginative and flexible strategies and, most important, not to be personally threatened by the enormous capabilities of these students. Various enrichment activities are often needed, although in some schools acceleration through the grades may be the school policy. Special programs often need to be implemented including student contracts within or external to the school, community programs, after-school or summer institute programs, honours classes and special-interest clubs. Multiple intelligence programs have a lot of potential for gifted students (Samples 1992).

Intellectually disabled students can vary considerably in terms of the degree of disability, ranging from mild to severe. There is now a variety of diagnostic assessments available to determine range

FIGURE 15.7 Questions to assist in selecting out gifted children for further testing

1. Who learns easily and rapidly?
2. Who uses a lot of common sense and practical knowledge?
3. Who retains easily what he or she has heard?
4. Who knows about many things that the other children do not?
5. Who uses a large number of words easily and accurately?
6. Who recognises relations and comprehends meanings?
7. Who is alert and keenly observant and responds quickly?

Source: Adapted from Walton 1961.

TABLE 15.5 Diagnostic assessments available to ascertain special needs of students

Category of disability	Type of assessment information required
Mentally retarded behaviour	Degree of intellectual ability, adaptive language functioning and medical history
Hard of hearing/deaf	Audiological, intellectual, language, speech, and social and emotional development
Speech impaired	Audiological, articulation, fluency, voice, language, and social and emotional development
Visually handicapped	Ophthalmological, intellectual, and social and emotional development
Seriously emotionally disturbed	Intellectual, medical, and social and emotional development
Orthopaedically impaired and other health impairments	Medical, motor, adaptive behaviour, and social and emotional development
Deaf-blind medical	Audiological, ophthalmological, language and adaptive behaviour
Multiple handicapped	Medical, intellectual, motor, adaptive behaviour, social and emotional development, language, speech and audiological and ophthamological when appropriate

and type of disability (Hehir 2007) (see Table 15.5). The criteria used in defining such deficiencies are typically:
- intellectual function significantly below average
- individuals do not meet the standards of personal independence and social responsibility expected at their age level
- the deficiencies must have appeared before the age of 18 years. (Woolfolk 2008)

Teaching intellectually disabled students requires additional and special skills in the classroom teacher (Villa & Thousand 1992; Tannock & Martinussen 2001). Even mildly affected students will require highly structured lessons. Sireci, Scarpati and Li (2005) point out that extended time in class for these students can lead to improved performance. Some of the strategies listed in Figure 15.8 focus on structured approaches that are effective. Learning goals for these students tend to be based on basic reading, writing and arithmetic, and on social, vocational and domestic skills (see Fowler 2008; Gargiulo 2008).

There are available a number of computer-assisted technologies to assist exceptional students (Arends 2009). For example, there are computer-assisted large-print Braille translations, speech synthesisers, modified keyboards for one-finger typists, and voice recognition programs.

Physically disabled students include those with visual or hearing impairments and other physical impairments, communication disorders and emotional or behavioural disorders (Levine 2003). The range of impairments is very wide and specialist assistance is available for most of them. Mainstreaming of these exceptional students in regular classrooms is a positive step forward for the emotional and social wellbeing of students and is now common in most countries. Nevertheless, it adds additional responsibilities for classroom teachers, many of whom may be concerned about their lack of training or lack of support from administrators in dealing with these students (Schirmer & McGough 2005; Norris 2008).

There are also many other complexities associated with mainstreaming (inclusive schooling) including the need for multiple teaching strategies, multiple learning sites, and a recognition of identity and difference issues (Slee 2000; O'Connor & Fernandez 2006; Thompson 2008).

Schuster, Hemmeter and Ault's (2001) research revealed that students with low-incidence disabilities in mainstream classes received fewer teaching opportunities than students without disabilities. Furthermore, there can be limits in a classroom teacher's ability to cope, given limited resources and their inability to simultaneously meet the unique needs of students (Podell & Tournaki 2001).

The strategies listed in Figure 15.9 provide some guide to the sensitivities needed with these students and with their parents.

It is important that the teacher treats each disabled student as an individual (Goy 2000). There will be tremendous diversity among disabled students. The critical task for the teacher is to look for particular strengths and to build up a learning profile of each student (Ryan & Cooper 2008; Arends 2009).

FIGURE 15.8 Strategies for teaching intellectually disabled students

1. Carefully develop readiness for each learning task.
2. Present material in small steps.
3. Develop ideas with concrete, manipulative and visually oriented materials.
4. Be prepared for large amounts of practice on the same idea or skill.
5. Relate learnings to familiar experiences and surroundings.
6. Focus on a small number of target behaviours so that students can experience success.
7. Motivate work carefully.
8. Ensure that the material used is appropriate for the physical age of the student and is not demeaning.
9. Every time students complete a task successfully they should be rewarded.

FIGURE 15.9 Strategies for teaching physically disabled students

1. Let disabled students know that you care – build a strong rapport with each one.
2. Tailor your instruction to meet the needs of each student – build on their strengths.
3. Give rewards for tasks successfully completed – provide positive, supportive feedback.
4. Be prepared to use new sets of materials or new methods of instruction.
5. Develop ideas with concrete, manipulative and visually oriented materials.
6. Be sensitive to the pressures and frustrations of parents of disabled children – use teacher–parent conferences frequently.

15.7 | CULTURALLY DIFFERENT STUDENTS

Teachers working in Australian schools require a broad understanding of our cultural diversity – diversity due to race, ethnicity, socio-economic status, geographic region, religion and gender. Many students enrolled at school do not have English as their first language. A number belong to minority ethnic groups.

The diversity of students in our classrooms is both a strength and our greatest challenge (Orlich *et al.* 2009). The challenge for each classroom teacher is to reduce prejudice and foster tolerance (Brennan 1998).

Aronson (2004) contends that stereotyping is all too familiar in schools. Those students who are stereotyped in unflattering allegations of inferiority become even more anxious when doing tests because they are fearful of confirming the stereotype. Cummins *et al.* (2005) advocate the welcoming of a student's home language, which facilitates the flow of knowledge, ideas and feelings between home and school and across languages.

The minority ethnic groups have a wealth of experience to contribute to classroom discussions and to assist the process of building a commitment to pluralism and democracy (Ryan & Cooper 2008).

School materials, especially textbooks, can exhibit cultural bias. Teachers need to help students identify bias and to seek information from a wide variety of sources so that many different viewpoints can be considered. The strategies included in Figure 15.10 provide some guidelines for working with students from different cultural backgrounds.

FIGURE 15.10 Strategies for teaching students from different cultural backgrounds

- Respect the ethnic and racial backgrounds of students – encourage and support them.
- Use role-plays to provide student empathy for different cultures.
- Ensure students from different cultures have opportunities to work with others in small group activities.
- When asking questions adjust wait-time for students from different cultures to make contributions.
- Use culturally responsive and respectful approaches in character education.
- Use curriculum resources that highlight multicultural perspectives.
- Provide opportunities for students to examine, in depth, particular values, beliefs and points of view relating to cultures.
- Use media examples to highlight undesirable bias and discrimination.
- Encourage students to be open and willing to evaluate their values.

Hambel (2006) writes forcefully about the plight of Indigenous peoples in Australia and especially the Aboriginal children attending school. She argues that 'a socio-historic construction of whiteness has become embedded in Australian (Western) society as an invisible, unmarked norm' (p. 3). White people see themselves as morally neutral, normative and average. Hambel contends that teachers must use critical dialogue to engage students in discussions that help deconstruct whiteness.

Reynolds (2005) argues that lack of proficiency in Standard English is a fundamental barrier to Aboriginal and Torres Strait Islander people's participation and education. He notes that 'two-way' schooling is needed in which Aboriginal education and culture are taught as legitimate ends in themselves.

Simpson and Clancy (2005) have examined learning models used in mainstream classes and argue that many of these are inappropriate for Indigenous students. They contend, for example, that most Indigenous learners prefer learning by observation and invitation rather than by verbal instruction.

At the Swan View Senior High School in Western Australia, a special access program, built around accommodating Indigenous cultural diversity and learning styles, has reversed the previous chronic pattern of student drop-out before graduation (Holt 2005). Holt (2005) notes that the three Rs for this Indigenous group are 'Respect, Responsibility and Resilience' (p. 3).

15.8 | ABUSED AND NEGLECTED STUDENTS

There are, unfortunately, many cases of child abuse in Australian society (Walsh & Farrell 2008). Abuse and neglect is typically defined as 'physical or mental injury, sexual abuse, negligent treatment or maltreatment of a child' (Cruickshank, Jenkins & Metcalf 2009, p. 28). In many cases child abuse occurs in families where the parents were themselves abused or where there are high levels of stress due to unemployment and poverty.

Alderman (1990) asserts that these students need special help to break the cycle of failure. Some practical guidelines include:

1. Hold high expectations for these students. Let them know you want and expect them to succeed.
2. Assist them to establish reachable goals.
3. Make sure they link their success to their effort.
4. Focus on the assets that students bring to the classroom – resilience, perseverance and hope.
5. Find ways to help them with their physical needs – warm clothing, a place to wash clothes – look to the community for resources.
6. Find respectful ways to survey students about their home situations.
7. Ask students to do jobs for you to help them feel important and in control of something in their lives.
8. Build a network of colleagues who are finding ways to assist neglected students (Alderman 1990; Landsman 2006; Rooney 2006).

More recently, there are growing numbers of students who have had to cope with violence, domestically within family groups and also beyond national borders as a result of terrorist attacks. Ravitch (2002) comments on the impact of the September 11 2001 terrorist attacks in the US and how this has forced educators to rethink their teaching about citizenship and global issues. Further terrorist attacks in Spain, Bali and London highlight the urgency of support structures for students. Dunn (2002) argues that students need a new set of inquiry skills and knowledge to make sense of international acts of terrorism.

Above all, pastoral care must be a high priority for all teachers in trying to re-establish caring, safe environments for their students by re-establishing schools as democratic, peaceful communities (Perlstein 2000; Winter 2000; Perkins-Gough et al. 2002).

CONCLUDING COMMENTS

Catering for individual differences in the classroom is a major commitment. Although a lot of rhetoric occurs about what might be done, the typical school structures and teaching behaviours do not do very much towards individualising learning.

There are approaches that can be successful in individualising instruction, including major structural changes (mastery learning, outcomes-based education) and teacher-organised initiatives such as individual student contracts. Computer-based software offers new, exciting possibilities for individualised instruction. Curriculum-based attempts to individualise learning have been developed, but they require considerable resources and commitment to implement and to maintain. The term 'exceptional student' covers many different abilities and impairments. These students provide a major challenge for the classroom teacher in individualising instruction.

KEY ISSUES RAISED IN THIS CHAPTER

1. Teachers must recognise and value each student's unique interests, experiences and abilities, needs and background.
2. A differentiated classroom is a different way of thinking about instruction – it is worth making a start even if you start small.
3. Contracts can be a valuable way of encouraging self-directed learning.
4. Computer-based instruction offers unlimited opportunities for students to learn as individuals.
5. There are useful teacher strategies to reduce sex-stereotyping.
6. Exceptional students (gifted and disabled) have special needs and require creative and flexible strategies by the teacher.

REFLECTIONS AND ISSUES

1. In any classroom there are students with a range of interests, abilities and commitments. What strategies have you used, or do you intend to use, to challenge, help and understand students so as to enable them to develop their individual talents to the full?
2. 'Training in social skills, cooperative learning and individualised instruction are important methods of educating exceptional students' (Dembo 1991, p. 212). Discuss.
3. To accommodate students from culturally diverse backgrounds, teachers should use activity centres and contracts, small mixed-ability groupings and opportunities for children to contribute individually through sharing and project work (Eckerman 1994). Have you used any of these approaches with a class recently? Describe the successes and problems you experienced.
4. Contracts provide a powerful motivating force for individual students. They shift responsibility for learning from the teacher to the student. Do you agree with this statement? What are some do's and don'ts in using contracts?
5. Choose one of the 'eight intelligences' that you do not usually use in your teaching. Select a teaching topic and give details about how you would incorporate activities to develop this intelligence.
6. 'Learning contracts are especially effective for online learners who are relatively isolated from other students' (Twigg 2003). Explain how they could be useful for online learners.
7. What are some of the unique abilities and interests of students in your class? Do you actively monitor the nature of these interests? What experiences do you provide to foster their development?

8   How do we teach our students to embrace multiple loyalties to our communities, nations and the planet so that terrorism can be greatly reduced?

Special references

Gardner, H (2006) *Changing Minds*, Harvard Business School Press, Boston.
Gargiulo RM (2008) *Special Education in Contemporary Society*, Sage, Los Angeles.
Saklofske, D & Eysenck, S (1997) *Individual Differences in Children and Adolescents*, Transaction Publishers, London.
Tomlinson, CA (1999) *The Differential Classroom*, ASCD, Alexandria, Virginia.
Wormeli, R (2007) *Differentiation*, Stenhouse, Portland.

Web sources

For additional resources on meeting the diverse needs of students, please go to: www.pearson.com.au/myeducationlab.

16

TEACHING, VALUES AND MORAL EDUCATION

16.1 | INTRODUCTION

There are many phrases used by educators to describe the importance of values and moral education:

> 'Shared values are part of Australia's common democratic way of life.' (Curriculum Corporation (2005) National Framework for Values Education in Australian Schools, p. 2)
>
> 'Morals are caught not taught. They take shape not through precept, but rather through the uncountable ordinary and informal contracts we have with other people.' (Hansen 1995, p. 59)
>
> 'Morals and morality pervade every aspect of our lives.' (Devine 2009, p. 1)
>
> 'Teachers and schools tend to mistake good behaviour for good character.' (Holt 1964, p. 2)

These quotations give some indication of the difficulties involved in addressing values and moral education within a teaching environment.

16.2 | VALUES AND TEACHERS

Values and attitudes relate to the feeling component of human behaviour. Values tend to be relatively stable in terms of our dispositions to behave in certain ways. Various factors influence the development of our values including parents, our religious involvement, peers, media and many others (Webster 2009).

In terms of teaching, it is impossible for teachers to avoid imparting values in one way or another (De Leo 2003). As noted by Cox (2004), the basic question with regard to values is not whether they should be taught but how best to carry out the teaching. According to Beyer (1997), teachers are moral agents who transmit values overtly or covertly. They make explicit pronouncements such as 'You must not cheat in tests' or 'You must not hit each other' and by their body language and non-verbal communication they express many other values on issues such as punctuality, academic achievement and behaviour.

Ryan and Cooper (2008) contend that people lose their freedom to do as they please when they become teachers. Thenceforth they have made commitments to ethical behaviour – for example, they might like to respond to a student by using sarcasm, or to shout with anger, but there are constraints

on teachers in relation to how they behave. Instead, teachers are expected to use their 'power' in a classroom by extolling and acting upon such values as:
- establishing rapport and developing special relationships with students
- expressing empathy for students and their problems
- protecting the rights of all parties when moral dilemmas arise in the classroom
- confronting major ethical issues with courage and conviction
- relying on effective communication skills to resolve problems.

> **YOUR TURN**
>
> Have you experienced the feeling of losing your freedom in front of a student? Do you consider that the constraints on a teacher's behaviour are reasonable and achievable?

Buzzelli and Johnston (2001) take a similar stance when they contend that:
- Teaching involves constraint, complex moral decision making and a sensitivity to contexts and individuals.
- The ways in which moral issues are realised in the classroom are complex and subtle.
- There will always be discrepancies between moral values played out in the classroom – discrepancies will be seen as conflicts, moral dilemmas and contradictions.

Fenstemacher (2001) uses the term 'manner' to explore how teachers foster virtue in students. He argues that there are a number of methods teachers can use:
- constructing classroom communities by setting rules and expectations and even by arranging the furniture and physical environment of the classroom
- didactic instruction of the students on what is morally or intellectually desirable
- getting students to engage in tasks that require them to think deeply and imaginatively
- giving verbal reminders and directions to students – calling out for conduct of a particular kind
- incorporating private conversations between the teacher and the student that can be corrective or affirmative and nurturing
- showcasing specific students as a way of signalling to other students what is praiseworthy conduct.

Hill (2003) prefers to use the term 'committed impartiality' to describe a teacher's desired manner. He suggests that a teacher should encourage values discussions, especially helping students to understand different world views and to learn skills of empathy and evaluation. He adds that assessment of students should not be directed to commitment but to whether they have developed the capacity to make informed choices.

A teacher cannot be value-neutral. This is a nonsensical, oxymoronic phrase (Yost 1997). Instead, teachers need constantly to reflect on key issues about their role and their very being, such as:
- What are my values?
- How do these values guide my actions?
- Who am I?
- How do I resolve the value conflicts within myself and with others as I perform the role of teacher?
- Which outcomes or consequences do I label as rewards?
- Which outcomes or consequences do I label as punishments? (Hamberger & Moore 1997)

 How can a teacher provide authentic, practical experiences through which students can live and enact values that the school fosters? Give some practical examples to highlight your answer.

Rolheiser, Hundey and Gordon (1998) focus on the values that teachers bring to the classroom, to the community of school staff and to the local community. They use the term 'educational citizenship' to describe the role of teachers in the wider context beyond the classroom. To be a good citizen in this professional world, teachers need to be able to cooperate with others on program teams and school management councils and take part in community development projects.

Pascoe (2002) focuses on global citizenship and the need to address issues and values associated with recent acts of global terrorism such as September 11 2001 in New York, the nightclub bombings in Bali in 2002, and the bombings on the London Underground in 2005.

Studies of pre-service teachers indicate some of the difficulties involved in including moral education in the curriculum. Reynolds' (2001) survey of Bachelor of Education students revealed that 'students come to universities with sets of personal and social values largely unexamined' (p. 38). It is therefore very difficult to get them to develop additional professional and societal values.

Reynolds (2001) highlights in particular the need for pre-service teachers to examine civics and citizenship, and their attitudes to Indigenous people and multiculturalism. Aveling (2002) and Hill (2003) both cite difficulties in getting pre-service teachers to reflect on diversity, race and racism. A number of students demonstrate a resistance to examining their cultural, social and political assumptions. Cummings *et al.* (2001) concluded from their study that pre-service teacher education students had significantly lower scores on moral reasoning tests (for example, the Defining Issues Test) than non-education students.

> **YOUR TURN**
>
> Terrorism is now a fact of life in many countries and this has serious implications for teachers. How would you introduce a discussion on this topic? What are some of the sensitivities to be mindful about in any such discussions? Is it really a matter of getting back to core values (ASCD 2006, May) or is it a global malaise due to the breakdown of the family and rampant greed (Ikemoto 2006)?

16.3 | VALUES AND STUDENTS

Various values are highlighted by interest groups as being the most desirable priorities for schools to teach their students (Aspin 2003). For example, there are some proponents who assert that it is the task of the school to assist students to understand the world of work so that they are better placed for their future adult roles. The various government and community groups who have been furthering this point of view are basing their perspective on such values as a work ethic, high productivity and role specialisation.

However, there are other interest groups that have been demanding a greater emphasis on the teaching of moral values in schools (Helwig, Turiel & Nucci 1997; Berkowitz 1998; Ozolins 2009). They cite the increasing crime and delinquency rates, a lack of moral standards in adolescents, pornography advances and drug abuses as just some of the reasons why moral education should have a major place in the school curriculum. But perhaps it is already a part of the school curriculum, although hidden. For example, Purpel and Ryan (1976, p. 9) recognise that:

> it is inconceivable for the school to take the child for six or seven hours a day, for 180 days a year, from the time he is six to the time he is eighteen, and not affect the way he thinks about moral issues and the way he behaves ... Moral education goes on all over the school building – in the classrooms, in the disciplinarian's office, in assemblies, in the gym ... For the educator, it comes with the territory.

Various terms have been used in educational circles to describe this emphasis, such as 'moral education', 'values education', 'values clarification' and 'moral development'.

'Values education' has received considerable support in the United States, but as a slogan for rallying curriculum support rather than for its importance as a concept. 'Values education' includes many dimensions of values, such as aesthetic values and values of technical efficiency, in addition to the term 'moral'.

Only a few of the American writers have preferred the term 'moral education' – for example, Purpel and Ryan (1976), Hansen (1993) and Leming (1993) – whereas this has been the predominant term used by British specialists such as Wilson (1990), Hirst (1974) and May (1981). Australian academics appear to support the use of the terms 'moral education' (Hill 1991; Crittenden 1981; Bullivant 1973) and also 'values education' (Lovat 2009a; Hill 2003).

Moral education has been derisively labelled as a 'name for nothing clear' (Wilson, Williams & Sugarman 1967, p. 11). Devine (2009) contends that if we want to show that certain kinds of education produce 'morally educated people' we must first identify a 'morally educated person'! Perhaps this is so. However, most would agree that moral education is partly about ethics (theories of moral behaviour) and partly about actual conduct. That is, moral education 'takes into account both the student's capacity to think about moral problems and the way in which a student actually behaves in situations involving right and wrong behaviour' (Purpel & Ryan 1976, p. 5).

 Are we experiencing a moral crisis in Australia with increased violent juvenile crime, teen pregnancy, widespread drug use and suicides? What roles can schools play in the moral development of students?

In some countries, such as the United Kingdom and the United States, there have been endeavours to teach moral education directly, as a distinct subject. For example, *character education* is a dominant model in many schools. Children learn to be good by being exposed to virtuous deeds and actions through models of famous people (via texts and multimedia) and being further reinforced by the teacher's moral and ethical judgments and behaviours.

For example Power (1997) refers to the revival of character education in primary schools where teachers can concentrate on the moral basics for which there is wide public consensus. Yet some of the activities can be rather dubious, such as Kohn's (1997) example that a different value is assigned for each day of the week – if it is Tuesday, this must be honesty!

According to Santrock (2001) it is a direct approach to moral education that involves teaching students basic moral literacy 'to prevent them from engaging in immoral behaviour and doing harm to themselves or others' (p. 108).

Proponents of this approach contend that every school should have an explicit moral code that is clearly communicated to students. If students do not conform to this code there are sanctions and penalties.

The task for the teacher is difficult because he/she must understand and model ethical behaviour. Young teachers tend to have received training in pre-service teacher education institutions where there were few if any courses on moral and character education.

There are further complications for the teacher in deciding whether to stress the ethic of justice or the ethic of care. The ethic of justice involves being impartial and neutral. The ethic of care involves demonstrating feelings of empathy and support. Campbell (2001) contends that justice aims at a society in which people are treated fairly, where they get what they are due and in which they are respected as equals. Caring aims at society and at personal relationships – 'caring is situational and context sensitive' (Campbell 2001, p. 8).

In addition, there are various indirect methods of teaching values, as is the case in Australian schools, via particular patterns of school organisation, the range and content of offerings of academic subjects, and the provision of extracurricular activities such as team games (Lovat 2009b).

> **YOUR TURN**
>
> Does it complicate your task as a teacher if you have to decide whether you stress the ethic of justice and fair play or the ethic of care and emotional support? Can you use both on all occasions or just some occasions?

16.3.1 Some claims and counterclaims

Interest in values and moral education has heightened considerably over recent decades. This has been partly due to pressure groups pushing their case for a return to traditional values such as 'respect for moral authority and decency, equity, civility, integrity and responsibility along with freedom, justice, the rule of law and due process' (Nyquist 1976, p. 272). Such groups have blamed declining moral standards on the influences of mass media, advertising, urbanisation, industrialisation and immigration, and many other processes (Nucci 2008).

But it may also be possible to attribute some of the blame for declining moral standards to incongruities subsumed within traditional social values. Individuals are now being encouraged to re-examine hitherto absolute values and, where appropriate, to substitute relativistic positions (Campbell 2001). For example, in the US, the California Senate recently endorsed a Bill that would require social science textbooks, beginning in 2012, to include the historical contributions of lesbian, gay, bisexual and trans-gender individuals (ASCD 2006, 13 May).

The Protestant work ethic has been challenged in the present era of considerable wealth yet chronic unemployment. Many young people are asking such questions as: Why work? Why save?

An economics-oriented ideology, which has hitherto dominated school subjects and the content to be learned, is now being questioned in periods of changing employment futures and leisure opportunities. The choices to be made by today's youth are also more complicated as a result of increased technology. Knowing about the merits and demerits of various options in consumer products and health programs, for example, goes beyond simple adherence to absolute values of integrity and justice.

 There is growing consensus on the need for moral education of the young but there is little agreement on proper aims, content and methods. Explain why this is the case. What are some possible solutions?

Education planners are therefore faced with a dilemma. There are pressures from all kinds of interest groups to re-establish cohesion and stability in our society after a period of considerable turbulence (Payne 2009; Webster 2009). Yet the traditional values no longer appear to be relevant in the new millennium. New directions have to be found and in some quarters this has led to renewed interest in core curriculum. But it also entails new directions in the methodology to be used for moral education. Somehow new content and methodology must be developed that reflect the pluralist morality and a more individualistic perspective on life that seems to be so much a part of Australian society.

Some attempts to achieve this have been undertaken by the Australian National Framework for Values Education (Curriculum Corporation 2005) and related teaching packages such as 'Building Values Across the Whole School' (Curriculum Corporation 2009).

16.4 | A CRITICAL ANALYSIS OF SOME ALTERNATIVE CURRICULUM DESIGNS

Numerous curriculum designs have been applied to values and moral education, especially with regard to two major patterns. Materials tend to be incorporated either into a separate subject curriculum package or as a set of processes that are incorporated across the curriculum into many different subjects. In terms of the latter, it is possible to distinguish between several designs that have been developed and used extensively over recent years, namely values clarification and moral development.

16.4.1 Values and moral education as a separate subject in the school curriculum

The direct teaching of moral education as a special subject has not been widely accepted within Australian education systems, apart from the schools that have close religious affiliations and where it is taught as part of Religion or Religious Studies. As a result, opportunities for teaching moral issues tend to occur across a wide spectrum of subjects, but especially in Studies of Society and Environment, Home Economics, Health Education, English and History.

Of course the subjects English and English Literature have enabled teachers to explore various moral issues and dilemmas as expressed by authors and poets. Home Economics, with its emphasis on consumer education and family roles and responsibilities, also lends itself to a discussion of a number of values issues. The Board of Studies in New South Wales (2006) has recently developed a new Studies of Religion Stage 6 syllabus, which examines values through a study of major religious traditions such as Buddhism. Studies of Society and Environment in Australian schools is an ideal subject to incorporate values issues because of the wide range of materials available and the integrated nature of the subject. However this might all be coming to an end in the near future. The Council of Australian Governments (COAG 2007) in a 2007 report were extremely critical of the SOSE framework and stated that the traditional disciplines of History, Geography and Economics should be reinstated in all states and territories. The National Curriculum Board (now the Australian Curriculum, Assessment and Reporting Authority) clearly had this in mind when deciding to select only traditional disciplines for the first four national subjects to be developed and only one of these (History) was a SOSE subject.

In other Western countries, and especially in the UK, there has been far greater support for teaching moral education as a separate subject, although the introduction of the National Curriculum in 1988 reduced the opportunities for schools to teach Personal and Social Education. Emphasis is now on traditional academic subjects to the exclusion of values teaching. The *Education Act* of 1992 requires all schools to provide for 'the spiritual, moral and cultural development of students' (Haydon 1998).

Yet it should be noted, in the wake of recent terrorism attacks, that the British government is currently reviewing the curriculum of 11- to 16-year-olds to see whether instruction in 'core British values' could help unify society (ASCD 2006, 17 May).

16.4.2 Values taught as a set of valuing processes across the curriculum

There have been some examples of curriculum projects in the US that have established a specific set of universal values to be taught – for example, the Harvard Project, which emphasises the values of self-respect, sympathy, love and justice (Oliver & Newman 1967; Shaver 1985). However, the majority of writings from this country over recent years have been on the *process of valuing and general methodologies* that might be used in classrooms. Educators have designed a variety of practical exercises and theoretical approaches to values clarification and moral development that can be used as brief 'warm-up' activities or prolonged discussion sessions, and which are viable in a number of different subject settings (Shelton 2000).

According to Harshman and Gray (1983) and Wynne (1986), these approaches all share a number of perspectives:
- The purpose is the development of decision-making skills.
- The content of decision making is problematic situations.
- The development of reason in value situations will influence action.
- The teacher has the responsibility for developing a classroom environment that is conducive to the non-judgmental exchange of ideas.
- Student value decisions are not to be part of any student assessment or grades.

These procedures are seen by their developers as complementing any direct inculcation of values. Of course, inculcation of values continues to occur in all classrooms, whether consciously undertaken by the teacher or not (Hansen 1993). The classroom teacher's behaviour, especially his or her language, provides positive or negative reinforcement to the students and greatly influences their behaviour. Students will also tend to identify with the role model provided by their respective teachers. The degree to which effective inculcation occurs in a given classroom depends partly on the relationship between the teacher and students, but also on the competing influences of other external forces such as the media (especially television), peer groups, family and church (Rogers & Renard 1999). Because it was realised that these external forces are so powerful, educators worked on the development of procedures that might be a competing force in their own right, but avoided the sermonising and didactic methods of value inculcation.

It is argued that 'education for values' is very important because students are engaged in issues and learn to apply values to select and promote solutions. How does this compare with approaches titled 'education about values' where students identify and recognise values? Which approach do you consider is the most meaningful?

16.4.3 Values clarification approach

The values clarification approach, as devised by Raths, Harmin and Simon (1966), is one method that has achieved support from teachers in the US and other Western countries (Leming 1993). It draws on the non-directive psychotherapeutic approaches of Carl Rogers (1969). Thus, students examine their personal behaviour patterns by a series of processes and by communicating their emotional feelings through a series of public affirmation exercises. Raths, Harmin and Simon (1966) advocate that the processes (although not a rigid step-by-step set of procedures) include the following:
1. *Choosing from alternatives* – helping students to discover, examine and choose.
2. *Choosing thoughtfully* – helping students to weigh alternatives carefully.
3. *Choosing freely* – encouraging students to make choices freely.
4. *Prizing one's choice* – encouraging students to support what it is they prize and cherish.
5. *Affirming one's choice* – providing opportunities for students to make public affirmation of their choices.
6. *Acting on one's choice* – encouraging students to act, behave and live in accordance with their choices.
7. *Acting repeatedly, over time* – helping students to establish repeated patterns of actions based on their choices (adapted from Raths, Harmin & Simon 1966, pp. 38–9).

These procedures are incorporated into a number of simple exercises and activities and it is these that have had tremendous appeal for teachers. Raths, Harmin and Simon (1966) concentrated on developing a number of new and different activities, including the use of rank orders and forced choices; hypothetical, contrived and real dilemmas; sensitivity and listening techniques; songs and artwork; games and simulations; and public interviews and values voting.

One example of the approach is included in Figure 16.1. Complete the statements in Figure 16.1. You may write one sentence or a whole paragraph. Write 'nothing' for any sentence for which you have no answer, or 'pass' if you would prefer not to say.

Although proponents of the value clarification approach stress that it is the valuing process that is the main emphasis, it does establish its own set of values to be imposed, and in this sense provides a 'content' as well as a 'process'. Purpel and Ryan (1976, p. 122) take up this point when they state that:

> values clarification definitely values thinking, feeling, choosing, communicating and acting. Moreover, it values certain types of thinking, feeling, choosing, communicating and acting non-critically. Considering consequences is regarded as better than choosing glibly or thoughtlessly. Choosing freely is considered better than simply yielding to authority or peer pressure.

Other criticisms have also been levelled at the values clarification approach because it emphasises conformity (coercion to the mean) of students, and it relies on questionable practices such as students having to affirm their stand publicly. Hall (1973) highlights the problem of privacy of students in that, too often, they are under pressure to participate in values clarification exercises. An additional problem is that personal data revealed in the classroom can sometimes float outside to informal peer situations when classroom norms for respecting privacy have not been developed by the group.

Szorenyi-Reischl (1981) criticises the approach because it does not take a broad perspective of the social causes behind certain moral issues and argues that the analysis of problems of individuals, although challenging and stimulating to students, is no real substitute for a wider orientation. Fraenkel (1977) also makes this criticism when he contends that values clarification exercises are directed primarily at helping students become more aware of their own personal commitments. Sheridan (1985), in a series of inflammatory articles in *The Australian* newspaper, tilted at teachers' moral values, their inept teaching, and the use of the values clarification approach, which he labelled as 'moral egoism (me and my feelings)'.

Other writers, such as Kazepides (1977), Paske (1986) and Santrock (2001), criticise the simple relativism of the approach. There are no hierarchies of values and one value is as good as the other. By holding this relativism stance, the values clarification approach seems to be ignoring the historical and cultural bases of our society, in which values are not all relative.

Ikemoto (1995) criticises values clarification approaches because they only deal with intellectual skills and pay little attention to moral action or how one ought to behave.

The values clarification approach to moral education, however, should not be dismissed entirely, because it is a powerful tool that appeals to students (Gore 1998). It seems to have a therapeutic influence on students because it enables them to sort out their own personal commitments without being influenced by teachers resorting to didactic methods of inculcation (Santrock 2001). The values clarification approach is used by some teachers in the US and Canada. Examples of the approach have appeared in curriculum materials produced for Australian schools, particularly in the learning areas of Studies of Society and Environment, Technology and Health and Physical Education.

YOUR TURN

- Try several very simple value statements with your students such as:
  I really like to do_____
  I don't see why I should do _____
  I will always do _____
  I don't like doing _____
- What were the reactions from the students?
- How did you feel about their reactions?

FIGURE 16.1 Values clarification exercise

1 I would be willing to die for _____
2 I would be willing to physically fight for _____
3 I would argue strongly in favour of _____
4 I would quietly take a position in favour of _____
5 I will share only with my friends my belief that _____
6 I prefer to keep to myself my belief that _____

16.4.4 Moral development approach

Another approach that has gained some support from researchers and teachers is 'moral development' or 'moral reasoning'. The emphasis is on reasoning and thinking because proponents of this approach consider values to be cognitive moral beliefs or concepts. A leader in this field has been Lawrence Kohlberg of Harvard University, who conceptualised six stages of moral development (see Chapter 3 for details).

Kohlberg (1975, pp. 670–1) maintains that each individual is an active initiator and reactor to his or her environment and that each will progress through these stages, although he is careful to point out that some will move at faster rates than others and that only a very few (perhaps 20 per cent) will ever attain the sixth level. The purported strength of this approach is its emphasis on a 'natural' sequence and therefore the role of the teacher is simply to enhance the child's development along a path that will inexorably occur over a period of time.

A child's structural bases are such that he or she first undergoes a stage of 'no morality', behaving according to the physical consequences involved (rewards and punishments). Kohlberg terms this a pre-conventional level; children behaving at this level are not conforming because they consider it is desirable to do so but because of the physical consequences to them if they do not! At the conventional level the individual has developed to the point where he or she wants actively to support and maintain the society's laws and expectations. If an individual reaches the last two stages, classified as the post-conventional level, he or she is developing a personally defined, autonomous morality. Kohlberg maintains that this last stage is the highest in the hierarchy and that it is morally better than lower-stage reasoning (Kohlberg 1975, p. 673). It is only at this highest stage that individuals are capable of organising information to make moral judgments according to an integrated and systematised framework.

Kohlberg's doctoral dissertation, completed in 1958, was the basis for his cognitive-developmental theory of moralisation (Henry 2001). There have been many critics of his theory over the years (see Chapter 3). A hotly debated criticism of Kohlberg's theory is that the stages are biased in favour of males and do not represent the way moral reasoning develops in women (Woolfolk 2008). Gilligan (1982) argues that Kohlberg's stages emphasise fairness and justice but omit other aspects of morality, especially compassion and caring for those in need, which are characteristic of the moral reasoning and behaviour of females (McDevitt & Ormrod 2002). Reed (2009) contends that Kohlberg's approach is a genetic epistemology which tends to ignore an individual's interactions with other individuals.

Cultural differences also can cause different standards about what constitutes right and wrong behaviours. Woolfolk (2008) contends that at stages 5 and 6 moral reasoning is biased in favour of Western, male values that emphasise individualism.

There have been neo-Kohlbergian approaches to moral development (Rest *et al.* 1999a) that use more concrete examples of behaviour, termed moral schemata, rather than using stages of moral development, but they also have their critics.

Notwithstanding the problems of applying Kohlberg's theory based on an individual level of analysis to the social sphere of schools (Henry 2001), a number of teaching units were developed but none has been produced recently. The teaching kits that have been produced include the *Holt Social*

Studies Curriculum (Holt Publishing 1975); *First Things: Social Reasoning* (1974); and *First Things: Values* (1972) for primary school students.

At the secondary school level it is suggested by various authors such as Ryan and Cooper (2008) and Arends (2009) that the teaching sequences should be:
1. Presenting the dilemma
   (a) Introduce the dilemma.
   (b) Define the terms used.
   (c) State the nature of the dilemma.
   (d) Divide the students into small groups where possible.
2. Stating a position
   (a) Help students to establish individual positions.
   (b) Help students to establish reasons for their individual positions.
   (c) Use probe questions and role taking where necessary.
3. Class discussion
   (a) Reconvene the class in a large group.
   (b) Encourage reports from small groups.
4. Closing the discussion
   (a) Summarise different positions.
   (b) Ask students to make a final choice.

Settelmaier (2002) provides some useful ideas for the teaching of moral dilemmas in science to secondary school students. From her research study she concluded that dilemma stories can be a useful pedagogical tool, but it is often difficult to determine which dilemmas will engage students. She contends that it can be more effective for the teacher to tell the story freely rather than for students to read about the dilemma from an overhead transparency or a photocopy.

A similar teaching sequence can be used with primary school students, except that they may need more support in commencing the discussion and some special assistance in working in small groups. The dilemma may need to be introduced via a series of warm-up questions, to get the children started. Primary school children are very receptive to visual stimuli and so multimedia presentations may facilitate the presentation of a particular dilemma. See the website <re-xs.ucsm.ac.uk/ethics> for a fascinating list of possible topics such as 'Animal Rights', which could be easily presented through multimedia presentations.

The division of the children into small groups should not occur until the alternatives to the dilemma have been fully discussed by the class as a whole. Even then, each small group will require specific instructions about what their tasks are to be.

Perarsky (1980) criticises the approach because it relies on the use of identifiable dilemmas. He maintains that in actual life situations, moral issues worth taking up are often camouflaged and that it takes considerable skill and sensitivity to even recognise that there is a moral problem that needs to be addressed. Haan *et al.* (1985) and Scott (1985) take a similar stance when they argue that practical morality should be the focus for students and this requires an interaction morality – that is, a morality of dialogue and negotiations between individuals.

Turiel, as quoted in Nucci and Weber (1991), argues that some of the many anomalies in Kohlberg's stage sequence are due to other domains of social knowledge such as social convention. That is, a child's developing concepts of morality are not just confined to a moral domain but can also be influenced by social conventions and cultural mores.

Reservations have also been raised about some pedagogical implications of the moral development approach. Rest (1975) and Fraenkel (1976) maintain that teaching sequences involving moral dilemmas do not take sufficient notice of optimal curriculum matching and sequencing. Surely some dilemmas are more effective at particular age levels? Perhaps some dilemmas could be used to build upon previous dilemmas. These writers suggest that dilemmas should be sequenced, becoming increasingly more complex, abstract and difficult.

Then, again, criticisms have been levelled about how teachers use moral dilemmas. Is it the dilemmas themselves that bring about stage movement? (Fraenkel 1976) Are moral dilemmas just too difficult for younger students, especially primary school children? Surely a teacher needs to have at his or her disposal a range of models and strategies for promoting moral development rather than relying on one approach?

However, empirical classroom studies using the moral development approach have been encouraging. Leming's (1981, p. 160) meta-evaluation of 59 empirical studies concluded that there was significant growth by the treatment groups ('mean class growth of between one-seventh and two-thirds of a stage in cases where the approach was used for 16 to 32 weeks'). Schlaefi, Rest and Thomas (1985) completed a meta-evaluation of 55 studies that had used Kohlberg's Defining Issues Test and concluded that the moral development approach did produce modest increases in stage growth, although the increases were more marked with adult groups.

McDevitt and Ormrod (2002) suggest that teachers can play a significant role in the moral development of their students, but they should not slavishly follow stage theories. They offer the following guidelines:

- Clarify which behaviours are acceptable and which are not and help students understand the reasons for various regulations and prohibitions.
- Expose students to numerous models of moral behaviour – teachers teach by what they do as well as by what they say.
- Engage students in discussions about social and moral issues – these will often arise at school.
- Challenge students' moral reasoning with slightly more advanced reasoning – teachers are more likely to create disequilibrium regarding moral issues and hence facilitate moral growth when they present moral arguments one stage above the stage at which students are currently reasoning.
- Expose students to diverse viewpoints about moral issues through class examples and literature.

Kohlberg's dilemmas are a valuable method for getting students to discuss specific values. Some experts argue that these lessons can be very effective if a teacher tells a story freely about a dilemma.

How do you react to the Kohlberg approach?

16.4.5 Values analysis approach

Various educators, such as Banks (1973), Fraenkel (1977), Tomlinson and Quinton (1986), Lemin, Potts and Welsford (1994) and Amundson (1991) have advocated a values analysis approach for discussing values issues in the classroom. The approach relies on the use of logical thinking and scientific investigation to decide value issues that are of importance. Students are encouraged to use rational, analytical processes in discussing, interrelating and conceptualising their values.

1. Students identify the issue or describe the problem.
2. Students identify alternative solutions to the problem or alternative positions on the issues.
3. Students hypothesise and/or collect data on the likely consequences of each alternative.
4. Students make a decision.
5. Students justify their decision. (Hahn & Avery 1985, p. 48)

Fraenkel's (1977) approach to values analysis, and especially his intake–organisational–demonstrative–expressive sequence, has been widely disseminated in curriculum documents to Australian teachers. Although he indicates a preference for a logical thinking emphasis in analysing values, he also extols the virtues of using a variety of learning experiences through simulation games, value surveys, songs, poetry and photography.

Lemin, Potts and Welsford (1994) developed a sequenced inquiry process involving six complementary, interdependent stages. According to the authors, this process provides students with a balanced exploration of values because as they experience the combined processes they encounter different viewpoints and have to weigh up alternatives and reflect on their value positions. The six-stage inquiry process is listed in Figure 16.2.

Critics, such as Hahn and Avery (1985), suggest that the values analysis approach is difficult for teachers to adopt unless they receive adequate training sessions. It has also been noted that not all students are motivated to use, or are capable of using, this approach. However, researchers such as Ehman (1977) have noted that the approach can bring about significant gains for students.

There are many examples in education journals such as *EQ Australia* and on the Internet that illustrate how individual schools are reflecting and analysing their values.

For example, Scalfino (2003) describes the process at a school in South Australia where the governing council, comprising council members, staff and senior students, arrived at agreed values and statements. They developed three values pathways:

- for learning – to ensure there is alignment of methodologies and learning values
- for individual responsibility – to ensure values include self-control, respect
- for working together – to ensure values include having a safe environment, communicating and working together.

Johnson and Jan (2003) describe a thinking–feeling approach they used at a school in Victoria. Using historical topics such as farming in the colonial years, they asked children to imagine the emotions and beliefs of the families of farmers, shopkeepers and miners. They used emotion and values issues that arose as a basis for detailed analysis.

FIGURE 16.2 A sequenced inquiry process for values teaching

1. Identifying and clarifying values – interpret and analyse issues from a range of sources
2. Comparing and contrasting values – use role-plays to compare and contrast values
3. Exploring and understanding feelings – explore and interpret based on real or fictional accounts
4. Exploring conflicting values – identify intrapersonal and interpersonal conflicts
5. Considering alternatives and implications – consider the range of possibilities in response to an issue
6. Making a plan of action – use various processes listed above and Venn diagrams, Future Wheels

Source: After Lemin, Potts and Welsford (1994); Henderson (2008).

16.5 | VALUES AND THE NATIONAL STATEMENTS AND PROFILES

The national statements and profiles developed collaboratively by states and territories over the period 1986–93 were intended to be frameworks for curriculum planning and not prescriptive. The emphasis in each of the eight learning areas was on the teaching of concepts and skills arranged sequentially over eight levels. Specific values were not included in the sequential development of concepts (strands) but, as indicated above, it was impossible for the teacher not to include them.

In 1989, the Hobart Declaration on National Goals for Schooling provided for the first time a set of national goals for schooling (MCEETYA 1989). These goals provided a framework for the subsequent development of eight learning areas and the teaching of concepts and skills arranged sequentially over eight levels. It is interesting to note that the values included in the national goals (see Figure 16.3) were not explicitly included in the development of concepts (strands) but were clearly embedded.

In a number of the key learning areas developed by 1993, explicit details were provided about values. For example, the *Studies of Society and Environment Statement* identified three clusters of shared values as 'democratic process', 'social justice' and 'ecological sustainability' and teachers were encouraged to use these values as criteria for selecting content in developing the specific strands in this learning area.

FIGURE 16.3 A range of values included in the national goals (1989)

- To enable all students to develop self-confidence, optimism, high self-esteem, respect for others and achievement of personal excellence (no. 1)
- To provide students with a respect for learning and positive attitudes for long-life education (no. 5)
- To develop in students a capacity to exercise judgment in matters of morality, ethics and social justice (no. 6)
- To develop knowledge, skills, attitudes and values which will enable students to participate as active and informed citizens (no. 7)
- To provide students with an understanding and respect for our cultural heritage including the particular cultural background of Aboriginal and ethnic groups (no. 8).

The *Mathematics Statement* referred to attitudes and values associated with 'a willingness and ability to work cooperatively with others and to value the contribution of others' and 'that rigorous justification of intuitive insights is important'.

The *Science Statement* urged teachers to 'uphold attitudes and values such as openness to new ideas, intellectual honesty, commitment to scientific reasoning and to striving for objectivity, respect for evidence and for the tenacious pursuit of evidence to conform or challenge current interpretations'.

In the mid-1990s Boards of Studies in respective states produced state-oriented documents about the statements and profiles. Most included specific sections dealing with values. For example, the West Australian Curriculum Council (1998) had a section on core shared values which included:

- a pursuit of knowledge and a commitment to achievement of potential
- self-acceptance and respect of self
- respect and concern for others and their rights
- social and civic responsibility
- environmental responsibility.

However, it should be noted that there was no intention for teachers to adopt an indoctrination approach to these values. Rather, the aim was to get students to critically interrogate the values that they and others had experienced to arrive at decisions about which values they would uphold (Reynolds 2001).

In New South Wales, specific publications on values education have been developed for teachers. *The Values We Teach* (Department of School Education 1991) provides examples of values relating to self and others and to civic responsibilities. Another resource is the *Values of NSW Public Schools* (Department of School Education 2001), which was distributed and placed on the Internet to stimulate discussion among teachers, students, parents, carers and school communities (Pascoe 2002).

By the close of the century most Boards of Studies had moved on to more state-focused learning areas. For example, the Curriculum and Standards Framework in Victoria now has a major focus on essential learning and combines studies of generic and specific discipline subjects. Yet there remains a strong emphasis on values. In Tasmania, an Essential Learning Framework was established, which includes a core set of values. This has subsequently been modified to become the Tasmanian Curriculum.

16.6 NATIONAL VALUES EDUCATION PROJECT

In 2002 a very comprehensive examination of values taught in Australian schools was initiated by Brendan Nelson, at the time the Minister for Education, Science and Training. It involved a literature review and a series of action research based case studies. The final report (2003) was well received by all political parties and a massive allocation of $29 million was allocated to a National Values Education Project, to be managed by the Curriculum Corporation. Nelson, in various press statements, made it clear that he wanted basic values prescriptively taught. Yet other experts argued that students must engage in moral action rather than just clarifying values (Aspin 2003). Gilbert (2004) argued that any values program must use the knowledge about abstract ideas of values and apply it to an engagement in moral action.

The National Framework for Values Education in Australian schools was released in 2005, drawing upon the 2003 final report (see Figure 16.4). The framework identified nine values (see Figure 16.5) which 'have emerged from Australian school communities and from the National Goals' (National Framework 2005, p. 4). The National Framework for Values Education has been strongly endorsed in many schools because it enables students, parents and teachers to work as partners on meaningful value issues in their local community.

 Are you aware of schools you have visited who are working successfully with the national framework? What might be some possible benefits and likely problems?

The Curriculum Corporation has a website, Curriculum Communities <www1.curriculum.edu.au/communitiesabout.htm>, which provides a comprehensive and exciting array of ideas for school communities to experience and develop.

There is an enormous range of websites linking values education themes. For example browse the following:

- BeCAL, The Belief, Learning and Culture Information Gateway
- Building Character through Cornerstone Values
- Bullying. No way!
- Earth Charter
- Living Values: An Education Program.

Furthermore, the production and distribution of a range of teaching and learning units in 2009, (Building Values Across the Whole School), has the potential to provide important professional development opportunities for teachers. The detailed teaching and learning units span early years through to later adolescence.

FIGURE 16.4 National Values Education Project: chronology of events

2002	The Commonwealth Minister for Education, Science and Training commissioned a detailed study of the values taught in Australian and overseas schools • Literature review • Action research case studies of 69 Australian schools
2003	The final report that there could be two approaches • Character education – development of specific 'virtues' • Reasoning, problem solving about values
2005	National Framework for Values Education in Australian Schools • Made links with the National Goals for Schooling • Nine values were identified • Copies of the framework, a poster and resources kit distributed to all schools • Established National Values Education website
2004–2008	• Clusters of schools involving teachers, parents and students were funded to be part of Good Practice Schools Project Stage 1 • Good Practice Schools Project Stage 2 implemented • Values in Action Schools Project

2009	• Professional Learning provided through 'Building Values Across the Whole School'
	• Teaching and learning units developed for
	  – Early years
	  – Middle childhood
	  – Early adolescence
	  – Later adolescence

FIGURE 16.5 Nine values for Australian schooling

1. Care and compassion
   Care for self and others
2. Doing your best
   Seek to accomplish something worthy and admirable, try hard, pursue excellence
3. Fair go
   Pursue and protect the common good where all people are treated fairly for a just society
4. Freedom
   Enjoy all the rights and privileges of Australian citizenship free from unnecessary interference or control, and stand up for the rights of others
5. Honesty and trustworthiness
   Be honest, sincere and seek the truth
6. Integrity
   Act in accordance with principles of moral and ethical conduct, ensure consistency between words and deeds
7. Respect
   Treat others with consideration and regard, respect another person's point of view
8. Responsibility
   Be accountable for one's own actions, resolve differences in constructive, non-violent and peaceful ways, contribute to society and to civic life, take care of the environment
9. Understanding, tolerance and inclusion
   Be aware of others and their cultures, accept diversity within a democratic society, being included and including others

The framework puts the onus on individual schools to have a whole-school approach in planning with students, teachers, parents, caregivers and families. Although the nine values are emphasised, it is evident that the range of good practice approaches provided as resources by the Curriculum Corporation encourage a wider exploration of values and a practising of skills.

Dialogue between experts, teachers and community groups has been maintained over the period 2004–09 through the use of school values education forums and drug education forums in most schools and annual conferences.

At the 2009 conference 'Shaping positive futures', it was evident that although most presenters were positive about the developments with the Values Education Project, some were critical. For example, Webster (2009) argued that the framework doesn't promote democratic participation through inquiry but has an overtly nationalistic agenda and this stifles the capacity of persons to pursue global understandings and world peace. Ozolins (2009) contends that there is not just one way (as favoured by a government in power) to become fully fledged members of civic society. He argues that the emphasis in schools should be on developing 'good persons' rather than the development of 'good citizens'.

By contrast, Lovat (2009a) argues that values education has the potential to re-focus teachers and their desire to provide quality teaching and to remind them that commitment and care for students is a sound basis for developing their personal character and effective citizenry.

16.7 | VALUES AND THE NATIONAL CURRICULUM BOARD (ACARA)

As described in detail in Chapter 2, an 'Education Revolution' was announced by Prime Minister Rudd in 2007 and within a short space of time a National Curriculum Board was established to develop and implement a national curriculum for all Australians. A very tight timeline was announced whereby K–12 curricula will be produced for English, Mathematics, Science and History and be ready for implementation by schools in 2010. The interim National Curriculum Board has now been replaced by the Australian Curriculum, Assessment and Reporting Authority (ACARA).

An analysis of the NCB documents produced so far reveal that the major emphasis for each of the four subjects is upon knowledge, skills and understandings with little emphasis upon values. Of course, value judgments are implicit in the choices and sequencing of concepts and skills, but it might be argued that values provide 'background' and not 'centre stage' in these planning documents.

At the 2009 National Values Education Conference in Canberra, the title for a presentation was 'The Australian Context: Where does Values Education fit within the "Melbourne Declaration on Educational Goals for Young Australians" and the National Curriculum.' In this interactive session the presenter argued that there were strong resonances between values education and:

- Educational Goals for Young Australians (MCEETYA 2008)
- Cross-curricular perspectives.

It is certainly the case that the Melbourne Declaration on Educational Goals for Young Australians (2008) has a much greater emphasis on values than the Hobart Declaration (MCEETYA 1989) and the Adelaide Declaration (Department of Education, Employment and Workplace Relations 2008). For example the Melbourne Declaration emphasises the need to develop personal values and attributes; to have the knowledge, skills, understandings and values to establish and maintain healthy, satisfying lives.

Various NCB documents (for example, *The Shape of the Australian Curriculum*, NCB May 2009) state that the National Curriculum closely follows the Melbourne Declaration (2008) goals. A close examination of the separate subject documents (*The Shape of the Australian Curriculum, Mathematics* (May 2009); *Science* (May 2009); *English* (May 2009); *History* (May 2009)) revealed little evidence of this.

Furthermore, any references to cross-curricular perspectives were also very limited. For example the cross-curricular perspectives in *The Shape of the Australian Curriculum, History* (May 2009) included a small section dealing with literacy, numeracy, ICT, Languages and Studies of Asia, the Arts, Civics and Citizenship Education. *The Shape of the Australian Curriculum, Mathematics* only referred to perspectives from the other three subjects of English, Science and History. *The Shape of the Australian Curriculum, English* had no specific section on cross-curricular perspectives. *The Shape of the Australian Curriculum, Science* had a small section on cross-curricular perspectives relating to Indigenous education, sustainability and Australia's links with Asia.

Based upon this evidence, it might appear that the new National Curriculum subjects will not give a major emphasis to values education, but this will become clearer when content details for each subject are made available later in the year.

Attempts in other countries to include values-oriented topics through cross-curricular offerings have had limited success. The creation of a national curriculum in the UK in 1988 envisaged the implementation of a wide range of cross-curriculum subjects, but this had limited success (Goodson & Marsh 1996). In Australia, the Hobart Declaration (MCEETYA 1989) recommended the introduction of six cross-curricular areas but the only two to become established were literacy and numeracy. Developers and writers of the eight learning areas were reminded to include cross-curricular areas but no guides were ever produced (Marsh 1994a).

16.8 | CIVICS AND CITIZENSHIP EDUCATION

At the present time in Australia, and in many other countries such as the US, the UK and Japan, civics education is on the policy agenda of government. The Australian government initiated civics as a major priority as a result of the report from the Civics Expert Group, *Whereas the People* (1994). The rationale for substantial Australian government funding was that civics and citizenship education is needed so that students can become active citizens throughout their lives. Education systems in all states and territories have made substantial efforts to include civics as part of their curriculum.

> **YOUR TURN**
> - What do you think it means to be an active citizen?
> - What values do you consider are most helpful for students in these turbulent times?
> - What activities and strategies would you use to teach citizenship?

Considerable funds have been expended on civics and citizenship education. The Curriculum Corporation had responsibility for a four-year program, 1997–2000, to develop teaching units for the 'Discovering Democracy' schools materials project (see Chapter 2). The specific values studied in the teaching units include:
- tolerance
- acceptance of cultural diversity
- respect for others
- freedom of speech, religion and association.

The learning units are built around four themes:
- Who rules?
- Laws and rights?
- The Australian nation
- Citizens and public life.

The learning materials have been designed to stimulate student interest and encourage active engagement. All government and non-government primary and secondary schools in Australia have been provided with copies of the Discovering Democracy kits, which include books of teaching and learning on the four units, videos, posters and cards and two CD-ROMs.

Additional resources on related topics have been produced and distributed to all schools. These include:
- Parliament at work CD-ROM
- One Destiny! The Federation Story Centenary Edition
- Assessment Resources
- Australia's Democracy: A short history.

A wealth of information is also available on the Civics and Citizenship Education website <www.civicsandcitizenship.eduau/cce/default.asp?id=9067>.

Yet it is not unexpected that many teachers would do little more than dip into 'Discovering Democracy' materials from time to time. As noted by Kennedy (2008), 'Civics and Citizenship is not a school subject like English, Mathematics and Science … This means the actual "curriculum" is less extensive, less explicit and less likely to be followed strictly' (p. 399).

Perhaps the MCEETYA ministers were hoping for a stronger commitment to the teaching of civics and citizenship by endorsing 'Statements of Learning for Civics and Citizenship' in 2006 (Curriculum Corporation 2006). These statements require all states and territories to produce specific learning outcomes by grades 3, 5, 7 and 9, but unless assessments are linked to demonstration of outcomes it might be expected that little would change.

More influential are likely to be the National Civics and Citizenship Assessments for Year 6 and Year 10 students, which commenced in 2004 and will be repeated every three years.

Key performance measures have been developed, namely:
- civics: knowledge and understanding of civic institutions and processes
- citizenship: dispositions and skills for participation understandings <www.mceetya.edu.au/taskfrce/civics.htm>.

An analysis of the 2004 and 2007 results reveals very disappointing outcomes (MCEETYA 2007). On average, only 50 per cent of Year 6 students and just 39 per cent of Year 10 had a satisfactory level of proficiency in civic and citizenship assessment tasks in 2004. There were no significant improvements in 2007.

Kennedy (2008) notes that a lot more attention must be given by teachers to teaching civics and citizenship education – 'civics and citizenship education is now of central concern to all Australians in an increasingly uncertain and unstable world' (p. 407).

There are many problems to be overcome. Some of the difficulties include a perceived lack of attention to ESL and Indigenous students; insufficient support being given to pre-service teachers; and an implementation timetable that is too rushed (Zbar 1998).

A final note on monitoring and assessing values: any teacher would tell you that this is a 'dynamite' topic, and must be treated sensitively. As noted by Hill (2003), assessing values is not assessing whether students are committed to certain values but whether they have developed the capacity to make informed value choices.

Forster and Anderson (2003) report on the trialling being undertaken by ACER to develop instruments to measure student's moral and ethical development. They developed an Attitudes and Values Questionnaire (AVQ) that includes 'five core dimensions of emotional growth, compassion, social growth, service to others and conscience, as well as two optional dimensions for Christian schools' (p. 13).

Popham (2005) agrees with the need to assess student affect and to include it in curriculum outcomes, but he is cautious about methods that might be used. He recommends that self-report inventories (respondents indicate agreement or disagreement on a series of statements) with absolute anonymity be provided to students and used over a period of time. This could provide valuable data for teachers on affective targets they might use.

CONCLUDING COMMENTS

Values and moral education are an integral part of teaching. A supportive classroom environment is an important basis for effective student discussion about moral conduct. Didactic methods and exhortations are likely to have minimal influences on values development. Some of the models described in this chapter can be effective approaches to moral education, but they need to be introduced with care and sensitivity.

The current emphasis and funding support for civics and civics education may enable Australian students and teachers to actively discuss and reflect on democratic values, and in the process become informed, active citizens in the civic community.

KEY ISSUES RAISED IN THIS CHAPTER

1. Teachers are moral agents who transmit values overly or covertly.
2. Teachers in classrooms have to make a commitment to ethical behaviour.
3. Character education is taught directly in some schools, especially primary schools.
4. Studies of Society and Environment has been an ideal opportunity to incorporate values issues, but there are pressures for this subject to be replaced by separate subjects such as History and Geography.
5. Values clarification is a popular approach for students to examine their personal behaviour patterns by using a set of procedures.
6. Kohlberg's moral development approach is used in some schools, especially for secondary school students.

7 A values analysis or inquiry developed by Lemin, Potts and Welsford (1994) is used in a number of Australian schools.
8 Values were included in the Australian national statements and profiles developed in the 1990s, especially for Society and Environment.
9 The new national curriculum with its emphasis upon separate subjects may leave little opportunity for the examination of values.
10 The National Values Education Project is an attempt to combine the teaching of specific Australian values and developing approaches to clarifying values. It is being strongly promoted by the Curriculum Corporation.
11 Civics and Citizenship Education units, such as those developed for 'Discovering Democracy', have been widely advocated at a national level.
12 The national assessments of Civics and Citizenship for Year 6 and Year 10 students to date demonstrate that student proficiency levels were quite low. The results in 2007 did not show any marked improvement.

REFLECTIONS AND ISSUES

1 Moral education is about the teacher and students sharing and reflecting on experiences together. The skilful teacher is one who can develop these sharing experiences without resorting to empty preaching and crude didacticism (Ryan 1993). Discuss how feasible this is for the classroom teacher.
2 Hansen (1993) argues that teachers have a 'moral influence' on students by their teaching style (gestures, body movements, facial expressions and tones of voice) and expectations over long periods of time (a term or semester or year in a classroom with the one person). How evident is this 'moral influence' in classrooms you have observed? Do teachers appear to plan for it or does it occur spontaneously? What are the implications for good teaching?
3 The teaching of values is about raising the questions, not giving the answers. Discuss with reference to teaching approaches you might use.
4 Do teachers have a major responsibility of transferring our basic values to our children? What are these basic values? Societal? Personal? Democratic? Discuss.
5 What is a values-rich environment? Is it the case the values determine what is taught?
6 How do we help young children in their valuing? What should be the aim of values education in a pluralistic society? Give details of how you would address these issues with a class.
7 What are some of the major pressures on students due to the youth culture? Are these issues addressed in traditional subjects? How might civics education address these issues?
8 It has been argued that a major lesson for pre-service teachers is to learn to reflect critically on student, school and community issues and make ethical decisions. Discuss.
9 What have been the three or four main values that have directed some of the key decisions in your life? What influences were significant in the development of those values? Have your values changed over time? How? If needed, refer to the values included in the National Framework for Values Education in Australian Schools.
10 Do young people think about democracy? Do they expect to vote and take part in other civic activities as adults? What can teachers do in their classrooms to build more civic-minded students?
11 'Is it a very un-Australian idea that government specifies what our values are for us and that we must display these values in our school to get Commonwealth funding?' <www.eurekastreet.com.au/article.aspx?aeid=3488>. Reflect on this question. What are some points for and against this stance?

12 Do you consider that the National Framework for Values Education has an overtly nationalistic agenda which stifles the capacity of persons to participate in a pursuit for global understandings and world peace? (Webster 2009) Discuss.
13 Values education forums in schools are providing a range of professional development opportunities for teachers and parents. Discuss.
14 Should there be professional ethics for teachers – codes of conduct as required in many other professions? Try to outline what would be included in such a code of conduct? Can you envisage merits or problems with such an initiative?
15 'A values dimension can serve as a corrective to those technicist approaches to teaching that serve to reduce teaching performance to mechanistic and instrumental criteria' (Lovat 2009a). Discuss.
16 'A country has a vested interest in ensuring that its citizens are equipped with the values and skills for them to be functionary members, but it does not follow that there is only one way in which they can become fully fledged and contributing members of civic society' (Ozolins 2009). Discuss with reference to the National Framework for Values Education.

Special references

Brown, M (2009) *Foundation Blocks: Personal, Social and Emotional Development*, Curriculum Corporation, Melbourne.
Curriculum Corporation (2004) *Values Education in Action: Case Studies from 12 Values Education Schools for the National Values Education Forum*, Curriculum Corporation, Melbourne.
Leicester, M Modgil, C & Modgil, S (2000) *Classroom Issues, Practice, Pedagogy and Curriculum*, Falmer, London.
Lovat, T & Toomey, R (2007) (eds) *Values Education and Quality Teaching: The Double Helix Effect*, David Barlow Publishing, Sydney.
Ryan, K & Cooper, JM (2008) *Those Who Can, Teach*, 9th edn, Houghton Mifflin, Boston.
Stevenson, J Ling, L Berman, E & Cooper, M (1997) *Values in Education*, ACER, Melbourne.
Tomlinson, P & Quinton, M (1986) *Values Across the curriculum*, Falmer, London.

Web sources

For additional resources on teaching, values and moral education, please go to:
www.pearson.com.au/myeducationlab.

17

WORKING EFFECTIVELY WITH PARENTS

17.1 | INTRODUCTION

There is widespread support among educators and the community for the view that parents have a major role to play in education and in schooling in particular (Cavarretta 1998). What is more difficult to get agreement on is how to nurture a collaborative relationship between parents and teachers to enhance students' learning.

Hayes and Chodkiewiez (2006) contend that the 'interface between schools and communities is a boundary that contains and excludes while affording limited views across it' (p. 3). Those positioned on opposite sides of this interface (teachers on one side and parents on the other) 'have limited opportunities for dialogue and for understanding each other' (p. 3).

Katyal and Evers (2007) provide a provocative comment when they state that '[t]he new reality of education is that schools are no longer the primary learning sites, at least for more senior students, and students view homes that are wired as the place where they learn in a meaningful manner' (p. 74). If this is the emerging pattern, then it will create different relationships between teachers and parents.

There are various interpretations about activities that are perceived to be effective or ineffective. In this chapter some of the historical and political contexts are examined, along with existing practices in various states and territories.

17.2 | PARENT INVOLVEMENT OR PARTICIPATION?

The ways in which parents work with schools can vary enormously. For many parents, their role is of limited involvement via attendance at:
- parent–teacher nights
- school sports days
- fetes
- tuck shops
- working bees
- Parents and Citizens or Parents and Friends meetings
- School Council meetings.

McGilp and Michael (1994) suggest parents can be involved 'as audience, spectators, fundraisers, aides, organisers, instructors, learners, policy makers, decision makers and advocates of school happenings' (p. 2).

As noted by Vick (1994), parents are usually on the sidelines when it comes to their children's education. 'Involvement' means very limited opportunities whereby parents undertake activities that have been designed and initiated by the school principal and staff. 'Participation' is to do with sharing or influencing decisions on policy matters and includes an active decision-making role in such areas as school policy, staffing and professional development of staff, budget, grounds and buildings, management of resources and the school curriculum. Participation can involve students, too, especially at middle and secondary schools.

> **YOUR TURN**
>
> When you attended a primary or a secondary school, what involvement did your parents or carers have with these schools?
> - What activities were they involved in?
> - Did they ever talk about how they assisted or would like to assist?
> - Did the principals of these schools encourage involvement by your parents?

There have been a number of initiatives developed federally and at state levels to increase the amount of parent participation in schools, but this needs to be viewed in terms of the unique Australian context – that is, the historical antecedents and contemporary issues.

17.3 | HISTORICAL BASIS FOR PARENT AND COMMUNITY PARTICIPATION IN EDUCATION

Historical accounts of schooling in Australia indicate that parent and community participation never became established as a dominant pattern in the nineteenth century and, for that matter, for the first 50 years of the twentieth century. Local church groups established the first colonial schools, but lack of funds and suitable teachers required successive governors to intervene and establish state schools.

The governments of the 1860s and 1870s, by a series of education acts, brought about a termination of funds to parish church schools and established secular schools controlled by an education department in each colony, responsible to a minister of the colony's government. The centralised state education system, controlled and directed by education officials and teachers, was the dominant pattern until well into the twentieth century. Where parents had any involvement in their children's school it was largely in the form of assisting with fundraising or making an annual visit to the school to view a parents' day program.

Excerpts from the annual reports for the Western Australian Education Department in 1907 and 1909 provide some indication of the degree of parent involvement.

> Parents' days – On these days parents are invited to attend and see the school in actual working order. Such occasions can be made most useful ... Many teachers frequently visit the homes of the settler until they have worked up sufficient interest to get a fair response to their invitation to the 'parents' day' at the school. This parents' day is quite a different thing to the school picnic day, with its sports and its feast, finishing up with a dance at night. I mention this advisedly, because these picnics are the only occasions in some places where parents and teacher meet. (Education Department, Western Australia 1909, p. 75)

Search out an historical account of schooling in your state or territory. To what extent are parents mentioned as key players? Describe some of the typical activities that parents undertook during that period.

The 1960s appear to have been a watershed for various individuals and groups in seeking a greater share for parents and community in educational decision making. It is too simplistic to refer to a single cause. O'Donoghue and O'Brien (1994) argue that increased parental involvement occurred in the 1960s because of a realisation that democratic principles and democracy in education were needed to replace the rigid thinking of centralised education.

Undoubtedly, a major impetus for national democratic reform was the Karmel Report (Karmel 1973) recommendations and the subsequent creation of the Commonwealth Schools Commission.

The Commonwealth Schools Commission, created in 1973, lost no time in providing substantial funds to support new programs that emphasised a devolution of educational decision making to schools and the greater involvement of community members. Examples of these programs included the Special Projects Program (Innovation Grants Program); the Disadvantaged Schools (Priority Schools) Program; Development Program; and the Choice and Diversity (School and Community) Program.

There were other influences too. The Report on Poverty and Education in Australia (Fitzgerald 1976) argued strongly for an increased role for the local community, including students and parents, to produce curricula that more adequately catered for underprivileged groups such as migrants, Aboriginal children and country children.

The creation of the Curriculum Development Centre in 1975 under the directorship of Dr Malcolm Skilbeck resulted in numerous curriculum projects being initiated, many of which had a school-based and community-involvement emphasis.

The concerted push in the late 1960s and early 1970s by Australian Capital Territory (ACT) parents was also a stimulus for democratic participation, according to Harman (1990). This newly created education authority established a precedent, moving away from the traditional, highly centralised bureaucratic model. Other states and territories followed suit: the Northern Territory created its own decentralised education system in 1976, and Victoria drastically changed its centralised system for a decentralised system in 1982.

Parents appointed to school councils in Victoria in the 1980s were given the legislative right of advising principals on school policy and, according to Chapman (1990), by the end of the 1980s parents had achieved the potential of becoming at least equal partners in the education process.

A significant program to be initiated by the Commonwealth Schools Commission in 1984 was the Participation and Equity Program (PEP), which emphasised the development of teacher–student levels of interaction. A number of the 'target' schools supported by PEP funds established interesting examples of community participation such as neighbourhood councils and training programs for parents on decision making and stress management (Marginson 1993).

Community organisations such as the Australian Council of State School Organisations and its state affiliations became very active in the 1980s in promoting an enlarged decision-making role for parents and citizens. In addition, other community organisations such as the Australian Association for Community Education were very active, especially in the state of Victoria. These perceived the school as being an integral part of the community, and that therefore it was only logical that the operation and management of each school must be open to the active participation of local community members.

But it was also apparent during the mid-1980s that economic, political and corporate management policies were emerging in all state and territory systems. A number of state education systems produced reviews such as the Keeves Report (Keeves 1982) in South Australia and the Scott Report (Scott 1989) in New South Wales. The Keeves Report recommended a de-emphasis of school-based, devolutionary structures in favour of more centralised control. The Scott Report focused on organisational reform to achieve greater efficiency, although it did provide greater scope for parental involvement.

School councils at state and territory national levels have continued to grow, despite the drastically reduced education budgets in the 1990s. For example, the Victorian Council of School Organisations provides advice and information to affiliated school councils. The Federation of Parents' and Citizens' Associations of New South Wales is very active and its *Parent and Citizen* journal is distributed widely.

 How active is the school council in your state or territory? What are its responsibilities at the school and community level? Are there other organisations that pursue parental issues and rights?

At the national level, the Australian Council of State School Organisations (representing government schools) and the Australian Parents Council (representing non-government schools) are currently actively involved on national committees dealing with literacy and numeracy, benchmarking and values education.

17.4 | SOME CLAIMS AND COUNTERCLAIMS ABOUT PARENT PARTICIPATION

A major reason for parent participation in schools is a powerful pedagogical one: 'The closer the parent is to the education of the child, the greater the impact on child development and education achievement' (Fullan 1991, p. 227). Of course this is a gross generalisation and, although many educators support it, can it be verified? There are likely to be all kinds of variations related to the age and gender of students and cultural, ethnic and class differences.

It can also be argued that parents are also teachers and can and should support the teaching that goes on in classrooms. Finn (1998) asserts that parents have their own curriculum and teaching styles, which are used in out-of-school learning situations. Hence the need for close collaboration between parents and teachers if children are to gain the full potential from their in-school and out-of-school learning experiences (Epstein & Salinas 2004).

Without doubt, parents possess a variety of skills, talents and interests that can enrich the curriculum in so many ways beyond the capabilities of any one classroom teacher, no matter how talented he or she happens to be (Stevenson 1998). With increasing specialisation of employment for adults and accompanying technological developments, it is likely that the skills they have to offer will increase substantially and, more importantly, they will have greater periods of leisure time to be able to share these talents with the local school. Having a number of parents as active participants in a school will create a multiplier effect because of the energies, enthusiasm and motivation generated by these additional adults (Lee & Bowen 2006).

 As a parent or a future parent, what role do you think you might play at the school where your children might attend? Do you consider that you have any special skills that would be keenly sought after by the school?

Another important consideration is that, if parents become involved in schools, they begin to understand the complexities of the teaching roles and structures. Too often parents are swayed by media coverage, which often presents derogatory accounts about schools, teachers and students (Dodd 1998). If parents can experience at first hand the complicated issues that can arise in the school environment, they are less likely to be influenced by superficial media accounts. By being well informed about school activities, it is likely that parents will be more willing to support the role of education and, specifically, the activities of their local school. Parents with experience working with schools can serve as dependable defenders of teachers (Comer 2005). The spin-offs are many, not the least being that parents will support education by their votes for the political party that is more likely than others to allocate a high priority to education.

Another claim is that parents have a democratic right and responsibility to further their children's education in whatever ways they can (Warwick 2007; Reay 1998). Some take this issue further, arguing that the decision making in schools should reflect the democratic decision making of the wider society – forging authentic family partnerships (Cavarretta 1998). Howard (2007) contends that educators of all racial and cultural groups need to develop new competencies and pedagogies to successfully engage our changing populations.

 Based upon a school you have visited recently, to what extent do you think the school policies and activities support and develop children from minority racial and cultural groups? Give details.

Most would support the contention that parents need access to decision making along with teachers and principals; if parents take time from their schedules to become involved in decision making, this is a signal to the rest of the community of how highly they value education. Other writers argue that democratic decision making rarely operates in other institutions and agencies, so why should it apply to schools? (Lareau 1986).

From time to time innovative attempts are made to provide for more democratic decision making. For example, in the United Kingdom in 2005 a radical white paper outlined a plan by the British government to allow every primary and secondary school to become an independent entity run by 'trusts' of parents, businesses, faith groups and charities (ASCD 2005, 27 October). According to Knight (2008) the trust model has captured the imagination of schools and organisations.

In the United States a National Network of School Learning Communities was established in 1996. The Network provides assistance to individual schools to customise and improve their programs of family and community involvement (Epstein & Salinas 2004).

The assertion is often made that parent participation on school councils and in the general governance of a school contributes to student learning at that school. Research evidence undertaken in the US (Bowles 1980) and the UK (Mortimer *et al.* 1988) did not find any empirical support for this contention. Fantini (1980) noted that the participating adults on councils benefited from their experiences, but there was no evidence to confirm or disprove any impact on student learning. Hatch (1998) argues that increases in student learning do occur when parents, teachers and students participate in intensive projects (see Figure 17.1).

There are also a number of *counterclaims* about why parents should not participate actively in school decision making (see Figure 17.2).

A commonly expressed argument is that schools are dominated by middle-class norms. In schools where there is active participation by parents, they tend to include articulate, well-educated parents. Parents who cannot speak English, who have difficulty communicating well in groups, or who are poorly educated, are usually not represented (Zady, Portes & Del Castillo 1998; Lee & Bowen 2006). That is, a significant number of parents are poorly equipped to be active participants in school decision making (Wadsworth & Remaley 2007). Some parents from non-dominant groups may encounter psychological barriers to involvement at school – they lack confidence in their interactions with the education system (Reay 1999).

FIGURE 17.1 Claims in favour of parent participation

- Parent participation will generally lead to improved student learning – intellectually, socially and emotionally.
- Parent participation increases the richness and variety of the school learning environment because of a wide range of skills that can be provided by parents.
- Parent participation increases the sense of identity for the local school community.
- Parent participation enables parents to understand education processes more fully and to support the goals of schooling.
- By increasing the number of interest groups involved in education, there is greater likelihood that the interests of all students will be taken into account.
- Parents and other citizens have the right in democratic countries to participate in school decision making.

> **FIGURE 17.2** Claims against parent participation
>
> - Many parents do not have the necessary problem solving and communication skills to be effective participants.
> - Many parents make conscious decisions not to participate, and as a result a small number of articulate parents can monopolise the decision making.
> - School staff are sometimes reluctant to consider, or opposed to, parent participation activities.
> - Governments have not devolved professional authority to parents and community – the rhetoric is stronger than the reality.
> - Parents are being encouraged to be individual consumer–citizens and to see schooling as another product in the marketplace.

McGowan (2005) provides an interesting argument that the neo-liberal strategy promoted by education authorities to have community-run schools might appear to be liberal, but it puts more pressure on parents to be responsible for a range of school level decisions.

Another point that is frequently raised is that any opening up of opportunities for parent participation places additional burdens on the time of teachers. There is more likelihood that parents will be contacting teachers during out-of-school hours – teachers could be constantly on call to various demands, both trivial and important, and teacher exhaustion and 'burnout' is a very real problem.

> **YOUR TURN**
>
> How do you react to the claim that teachers are too busy to get involved with parents; that teachers are typically exhausted without also having phone calls or emails from parents to deal with?

What is involved, of course, is a new set of relationships when parents become active participants in decision making. Katyal and Evers (2007) argue that the relationship should be that of a professional and client association, where both parents and teachers are aware of their responsibilities.

Small wonder that research studies indicate that only a minority of teachers in schools have goals and programs for parent participation. For example, Rosenholtz's (1989) study showed that the majority of teachers were in 'stuck' schools rather than 'moving' schools. Teachers from stuck schools held no goals for parent participation while teachers in moving schools 'focused their efforts on involving parents with academic content, thereby bridging the learning chasm between home and school' (Rosenholtz 1989, p. 152).

In another study, Becker (1981) surveyed 3700 primary school teachers and 600 principals and concluded that 'very few appear to devote any systematic effort to making sure that parental involvement at home accomplishes particular learning goals in a particular way' (Becker 1981, p. 22). Some organisations, particularly teachers' unions, have indicated from time to time that parents and community members should not be active participants and they have reacted very strongly against what they perceive to be a reduction in professional responsibilities of their teacher members.

Other writers have claimed that parent participation in schools is unlikely to succeed in Australia because it is a 'top-down' initiative by education systems. For example, Blackmore (1986) maintains that local participation by parents is primarily an organisational solution by state governments to the problems of managing large and increasingly unwieldy bureaucracies. Watt (1989) argues that it has been convenient for policy makers to use democratic concerns to justify economically driven education reform.

Mention should also be made of the view that parents are being increasingly perceived by governments to be 'consumer-citizens' (Woods 1988). That is, parents operate largely as individual consumers in making decisions about schooling and schooling practices for their children. They rarely share school-related interests with other parents or they may lack the opportunity to do so:

> They do not constitute a monolithic group. Individualism and difference (in priorities, preference and philosophy) characterise the consumer-citizenry. (Woods 1988, p. 328)

17.5 | A PARENT PARTICIPATION CONTINUUM

Various accounts in the educational literature refer to 'tapping parent power' and 'effective parent participation in schooling'. A number of accounts have been written by individual enthusiasts or vested interest groups and so their laudatory comments are not surprising – for example, Morris (1992), Gamage (1992), Meadows (1993) and Scherer (1998). To provide a balanced picture it is useful to distinguish between the different activities or roles that might be undertaken by parents and depict them on a continuum (see Table 17.1). The activities range from 'one-way information giving' to 'interactive partnerships' and there are a myriad of possible positions in between these two extremes of passive and active.

In the first column of the continuum of Table 17.1, the examples simply illustrate information giving; this could include notices, information about homework and perhaps details about the follow-up computer-based exercises that students are expected to complete.

The examples listed in the second column of the continuum of Table 17.1 are 'reporting progress' to parents. Variations of this category can include parent–teacher conferences. These face-to-face meetings can be most satisfying to the parent and to the teacher; however, few parents tend to take advantage of this opportunity because of their busy daily schedule or their reticence about appearing personally at the school (MacLure & Walker 1998). Teachers will often complain that the parents they really need to meet to discuss urgent student problems do not come to parent–teacher conferences.

Home–school notebooks are another interesting variation whereby a parent and a teacher correspond with each other in a notebook that is sent regularly between the two participants. It requires, of course, a substantial commitment of time by both parties and a willingness to maintain a regular schedule. Yet it does have the potential of keeping contact between the teacher and parents and is a reasonably effective and time-saving alternative to face-to-face meetings.

TABLE 17.1 Continuum of parent participation

One-way information giving	Reporting progress	Special events	Sharing of ideas	Parent assistance at school in non-instruction	Parent assistance at school in instruction	Governance issues	Interactive partnerships
• Notices sent home • Posters	• Home–school notebooks • Call-in times • Newsletters • Telephone calls	• Picnics • Art shows • Concerts • Open days • Tuckshops • Working bees	• Seminars • Classroom observation days • Informal	• Playground • Assistance on excursions • Liaison discussions • Organising sports days • Preparing art material	• Guest speakers • Leaders on school groups • Teaching with local business	• Chairing sub-committees • Members of school council	• Specific parent–teacher working groups

In addition, teachers are likely to request parents to be involved in a number of learning activities with their children at home (for example, giving reading assistance and listening to reading, and home tutoring in other subjects). Research studies have demonstrated that teacher requests to parents for assistance are likely to be far more effective if individualised instruction or training is provided and if there are mechanisms for monitoring parents' and children's progress in the home instruction (Fullan 1991; Finn 1998).

Special events for parents are depicted in the third column of Table 17.1. These can take various forms including parent evenings, open days, concerts and plays. Such events enable teachers to demonstrate certain special skills (dance routines, art work) that students have achieved, but they also provide an opportunity for teachers and parents to interact socially. Special occasions like these can enable a positive rapport to be developed between individual parents and a teacher. It can also be a useful occasion for teachers to seek out the respective strengths and interests of parents and to encourage them to be more actively involved (Hoover-Dempsey *et al.* 2005).

Fundraising activities have also been included under 'special events', although some parents might prefer to describe them as 'special chores'! Resources are always scarce in any school – funds are always needed to purchase additional library books or sporting equipment or microcomputers. Parents are usually very willing to be involved in fundraising activities such as school fetes, jumble sales, cake stalls and managing a school canteen if they can see that the funds generated will provide additional resources that will benefit their children. However, it is very limited if this is the only contact that parents have with their school. Fortunately, the availability of federal funds in the form of direct grants to schools rather than subsidy schemes has to some extent reduced the need for parent organisations to devote most of their energies to fundraising.

Sharing of ideas, as indicated in the fourth column in Table 17.1, typically takes the form of informal discussions and special seminars and workshops (Gorman & Balter 1997). The seminars in particular, if held on the weekends or in the evenings, can be valuable occasions for parents and school staff to share ideas about school goals, values analysis, or particular topics such as sex education or mathematics skills.

Funding by the Commonwealth Government enables education systems from time to time to fund special seminars. For example, funds from the Values Education for Australian Schooling Project (2005) enable good practice schools to run seminars. ACSSO (2009) has developed a very useful website listing articles that could be used for parent seminars. The use and reporting of profiles and citizen education projects (Discovering Democracy projects) are also providing opportunities for communication with and inputs from parents in some state systems (such as Civics and Citizenship, see Department of Education, Employment and Work Relations 2009).

Parents can be involved in assisting school staff with a number of non-instructional activities. At the primary school level in particular, parents are in considerable demand to assist as additional supervisors for excursions and visits. If handled sensitively by the school principals, developing a group of volunteer parents for these activities can establish strong links between them and their school.

More and more, parents are being sought to assist school staff with a number of instructional activities. To a certain extent, changes in employment patterns due to global financial crises have led to early retirement and redundancy packages and enabled parents to become available and willing to take on some of these tasks.

In the junior primary school, parents are often sought to assist with reading and miming stories to small groups of children and also to assist with various art and craft activities. As noted by Comer (2005), it is important to give parent volunteers meaningful tasks that they are capable of accomplishing and to place them with compatible staff members. Parents possess a wide range of specialist skills that can be a welcome and varied addition to the school curriculum (Hoover-Dempsey *et al.* 2005).

'Governance activities' is the seventh column in Table 17.1. Governance activities have had a chequered history in Australia since the 1980s. The ACT, Victoria and South Australia took the lead in innovative developments of school councils in the 1970s. Various problems and tensions emerged in Victoria in the late 1970s, largely due to concerns raised by high school principals, and as a result new guidelines for school councils were produced in that state in the 1980s. More recently, it appears that Victorian school councils have been operating very effectively. A research study by the Victorian Council of School Organisations (2005) concluded that councils were generally working well and had active, committed members. However, it did acknowledge that councils tended to concentrate mainly on traditional roles.

New South Wales in particular undertook a concerted effort to initiate school councils, beginning in 1991. The Federation of Parents' and Citizens' Associations of New South Wales reports indicate that councils are very active and committed and have been successful in lobbying the Department of Education and Training for additional funds.

School councils and boards are now in operation in all states and territories, but their functions and responsibilities vary considerably. They have the potential to be the ideal vehicle for teachers and parents to work together. Many of the school boards make major decisions about staffing, school buildings, resources and curriculum for their school.

No outstandingly successful prototype for school councils has yet been found. Various combinations of membership, functions and legal status have been initiated, but even in the same state system initial versions have been found to be unsuitable and different versions have replaced them.

17.6 | INTENDED PRACTICES AND ACTUAL OUTCOMES

To date, there have been few accounts in the Australian literature about how parents operate within school communities. Therefore the percentage of parents operating at different points on the continuum depicted in Table 17.1 is not known.

There have been some accounts of successful governance by school councils (Gamage 1993; Knight 1995) but they are relatively few in number. Some parents maintain social networks among other parents that can lead to very active participation at a local school (Sheldon 2002). It may be that only small numbers of parents are involved in the other categories listed in Table 17.1.

Beagley's (1997) study of parent involvement at a rural secondary school in Victoria revealed little participation, even though the structures were in place. The school has an elected school council with half of its members being parents or community members, as required by government policies. Yet the:

> nature of parents' involvement was passive, reactive and firmly rooted in the culture of traditional authority structures of State education. The School Council was seen by most of its parent participants as bogged down in administratia and controlled by the imperatives of the education bureaucracy and the teaching professionals (p. 9).

By contrast, McGilp and Michael's (1994) study of Pennycoe school, also in Victoria, revealed a strong level of participation by parents. Parents' participation was further heightened by a year-long arts project for the Year 4 children. Sets of parents were encouraged to offer instruction in a variety of activities including art, music, craft and dance.

The problem of participation is multifaceted, and the blame does not lie solely with any one group.

YOUR TURN

To what extent should it be a requirement for teachers to keep in frequent contact with parents? Aren't there many gains if teachers and parents work together in assisting the progress of individual students?

It is true that there are difficulties for parents, many of whom venture into the school environment with various anxieties, are considerably overwhelmed and are often poorly informed about typical school activities.

According to Power and Clark (2000), the problems that parents experience are not imaginary. 'Their sense of frustration, and often humiliation, of consultations with teachers is genuinely felt' (p. 44).

An area of major concern is Aboriginal parents and the extent to which their views and concerns are acted upon by school administrators. McInerney's (1989) study noted that Aboriginal parents (despite negative media portrayals) hold positive attitudes towards education. A typical Aboriginal response was 'Without proper schooling our children have no future' (p. 47). Yet these parents were also concerned about negative consequences of attending school, such as:

- My child receives no praise or support from school.
- My child is ridiculed by others.
- Even if my child does well at school he still can't get work.

McTaggart (1984, p. 12) notes that:

> Parents' knowledge of what goes on in schools tends to be restricted to the treatment of educational problems given by the media ... The images are both incomplete and confrontationist.

For parents of lower socio-economic backgrounds, the problem is especially severe (Wadsworth & Remaley 2007). They often perceive the school council to be an appendage of the principal, espousing traditional middle-class values. They often consider that the problems of their immediate neighbourhood are not translated into programs at the school. These parents need special encouragement and support before they will become regular participants in the school community. Andrews (1985, p. 30) maintains that the typical response from such parents tends to be: 'Every other time I've complained or spoken out too much, my kid has been picked on', or 'It doesn't affect my kid, she/he is doing OK'.

Teachers' language to the lay person can be almost incomprehensible. Not surprisingly, teachers receive new training in the academic disciplines and theory building of various kinds, and as a result of interaction with their peers establish their education jargon. This is particularly evident when teachers are asked to explain to parents why a child is not coping with a subject. In many cases, teachers use technical terms that lay people simply cannot understand. MacLure and Walker (1998) contend that the discourse between teachers and parents is rather like the discourse between doctors and patients. The teacher is in control, chooses the topics of discussion and dominates the interaction.

Perhaps all stakeholder groups are to blame for building up their unique set of language modes, norms and expectations. Parents can certainly build up their barriers around their family life, interests and ambitions (Kenway, Alderson & Grundy 1987). These barriers take a considerable amount of time and goodwill to break down. Boomer (1985, p. 1) refers to this as a kind of:

> educational apartheid ... they develop their own special forms of protection; an array of the equivalent of moats, barricades, deflection and passwords.

A recent major review of parent involvement by Pomerantz *et al*. (2007) makes some interesting distinctions. They distinguish between parents' school-based involvement (for example being present at general school meetings) and parents' home-based involvement (for example, assisting children with their homework). School-based involvement may be relatively low (for example, lower among the less educated) but home-based involvement can be very high in motivating children, and engaging them in intellectual activities (for example, reading books with children).

Pomerantz *et al*. (2007) offer further insights in that they conclude that parents who are naturally involved in children's academic lives are likely to be more influential than parents who are induced to be involved (for example, intervention programs to encourage greater parent involvement) (p. 398).

 Reflect upon the distinction made between parents' school-based involvement and parents' home-based involvement. How important are these involvements at different levels of schooling?

17.7 | TRAINING NEEDS FOR PARENTS

Cooper and Christie (2005) contend that parents need to be empowered – they need to be given the opportunity to articulate their own needs. Although some parents, as a result of their schooling and professional activities, are highly articulate, enthusiastic and very capable of participating in school decision making, there are many who are not (McGilp & Michael 1994; Sheldon 2002). The majority of parents do need assistance in such matters as knowledge of the educational system and interpersonal and communication skills (Zady, Portes & Del Castillo 1998).

Many parents do not have a clear idea of the education system in which their local school operates (Hughes & Greenhough 1998). They need information about the various levels of the hierarchy and the respective powers and functions of head office, regions and individual school principals. In particular, parents need to know the kinds of activities that a principal and their staff can initiate and maintain at a local school level, and an awareness of the constraints and monitoring procedures used by head office officials.

Another basic area is knowledge about the rights of parents in terms of schooling for their children. In many state and territory systems there is little specific detail provided in official regulations. In Victoria the rights and responsibilities of parents are established by law. The list of rights included in Figure 17.3 is an eclectic listing of rights proposed by various parent organisations. Andrews (1985) argues that parents in each local school community must lobby vigorously to ensure

FIGURE 17.3 A proposed list of parents' rights

The right to appeal:
- to be able to appeal against decisions that are considered to be unsatisfactory
- to be informed of their lines of appeal to impartial arbitration.

The right to be informed and consulted:
- to be given information about school services, procedures and rules and to be informed about the changes
- to have access to professional interpretation of records and files
- to visit and observe any programs involving their child and to have access to those working with their child
- to have knowledge of the curriculum, how it is being taught and by whom.

The right to influence:
- to make use of the democratic processes, including the right to lobby and to be represented on decision-making bodies
- to question the educational policy of their local schools
- to have a say in the running of the school and the teaching
- to participate in classroom activities.

The right to have values supported and acknowledged:
- to discuss values implicit in programs
- to insist that the teaching of the school is not in conflict with the values of people at home
- to expect the school to reinforce the broad cultural experiences and aspirations of the family and the society.

The right to staff/facilities:
- to expect that schools are provided with sufficient competent experienced teachers, ancillary and support staff
- to expect that the class size will be adjusted to suit specific needs
- to expect special services for children with handicaps, limitations, disabilities or exceptional talents.

Source: Based on Andrews 1985; WACSSO 1986.

that their particular list of parent rights is accepted and incorporated into a specific local school policy document.

Dependent upon the energies and successes of parents in a local school community, school policy documents might include comprehensive details about parent rights. Andrews (1985) suggests that checklists can be used, such as the example included in Figure 17.4, to provide a basis for further parent lobbying.

Even though these measures might appear a little too strong for some, most educators would concur, as a minimum, that parents have the right to be provided with information about such matters as the academic progress of their children; the major purposes of teaching programs; the methods used to teach particular skills; the methods used for assessing students; and policies for the teaching of controversial subjects (for example, sex education).

However, training needs for many parents are most evident in the areas of interpersonal and communication skills (MacLure & Walker 1998). Experienced parent participants need to be able to break down the apathy of other parents and seek out their support by informal home visits, telephone calls and parent meetings. They have to be able to develop and demonstrate empathy for the needs of the apathetic or uninvolved parent and be able to devise ways of gradually wearing down that person's resistance. They have to be able to engage parents within the parent network (Barton *et al.* 2004).

Parent drop-in centres are becoming more widespread in schools as principals realise that the provision of a meeting place for parents is a valuable strategy for getting them more involved in

FIGURE 17.4 A checklist for judging the comprehensiveness of your local school policy

How well does your school policy cover the following areas?	Not at all	Poorly	Reasonably well	Well
1 Its purpose.				
2 The profile of the school, neighbourhood and students.				
3 The general aims of education.				
4 The school's specific aims and objectives.				
5 An overview of arrangements for implementing the curriculum, including: • content areas • grouping of children • selection of curriculum activities • materials, equipment and environment.				
6 School organisation, including: • communication channels • staff responsibilities • the decision-making structure • administration rules and procedures • the school policy.				
7 Evaluation of: • children's progress • the curriculum • the school organisation • the school policy.				
8 School–community relations.				
9 Action to be taken.				
10 Use of jargon.				
11 Clarity and quality of presentation.				

Source: Based on Andrews 1985, p. 76.

school activities. A drop-in centre can enable parents to interact socially and discuss various matters relating to their school community. In so doing, it may enable many parents to increase their level of confidence and skills in communicating with other adults.

Special provisions need to be made to assist parents with language difficulties. Those staff with second-language expertise can be used on home visits to encourage these parents to support school affairs (Colombo 2004). Community liaison officers can also be used with good effect to maintain regular home visits to parents. Migrant advisory services are sometimes available to offer assistance. Information booklets about the school, printed in several languages, can also be a useful measure to attract the interest of parents of migrant families.

The building up of positive attitudes about school participation among parents is a time-consuming process and requires the concentrated efforts of many participants, including teachers, liaison officers from various departments, and experienced, supportive parents and friends (Griffith 1997; Howard 2007).

Mattingly *et al.* (2002) contend that many of the parent involvement programs used in the US have had limited success in changing parent behaviour because they fail to take account of the demographic and socio-economic characteristics of families that participate in the programs.

17.8 | TRAINING NEEDS FOR TEACHERS

The focus of training for many teachers revolves around learning about and demonstrating competence in planning and executing student lessons. Few pre-service courses focus on the role of parents in the school community, especially in terms of techniques for communicating effectively with parents. As a result, some teachers tend to make minimal use of parent assistance or, in some instances, actively resist communicating with parents (Fullan 1991). According to Rich (1998), if parents were given the opportunity to rate their child's teacher, the ratings might be very low indeed. She argues that many would score low marks about the extent to which they know and care about their children and their willingness to communicate with parents.

The extent to which teachers communicate regularly with parents can vary considerably between rural and urban centres. Teachers posted to rural schools have little choice but to be closely involved in the local community and to be in regular contact with parents in various social, cultural and sporting activities. In urban schools there is less opportunity for interaction and there may be difficulties for some teachers in understanding and empathising with the priorities and values of parents representing low socio-economic levels.

Bauch and Goldring (2000) and Guastello (2004) contend that a school that has a caring atmosphere has the greatest influence on positive relationships between teachers and parents.

Hiatt-Michael (2000) argues that beginning teachers need pre-service training modules in parent involvement.

Lasky (2000) asserts that emotionality is a major factor in teacher–parent relationships. She argues that emotions are not solely internal, personal phenomena but are also social in nature. Consequently, any training of teachers must focus on the deep-seated emotions that can cause limited interactions between a teacher and parents (Westergard 2007).

Pettit (1985) raises some interesting questions in Figure 17.5 that could be useful for teachers to reflect upon. It is important for all teachers to consider how accessible they are to parents and to revise, if necessary, the strategies they do use or should use, to increase their level of rapport with parents.

The principal can play a major role in a school by encouraging teachers to seek out parental help in their classrooms. The principal may need to use the example of several outstanding teachers on the staff to show how parents can become involved in various ways such as providing clerical support staff and teaching help in individual classrooms. Once a few teachers get involved in this way, it is likely that others on the staff will follow. One of the purposes of this involvement with parents is, of course, to give teachers the opportunity to work alongside them and gain a better understanding of parents' interests and motivations.

The procedures and examples of possible activities listed in Figure 17.6 provide some helpful ways of establishing higher levels of teacher support for parent involvement at a school.

FIGURE 17.5 Parent participation: issues for teachers to reflect upon

1 Am I, as a teacher, prepared to consider or reconsider the idea of parents participating with me and the possible benefits that may accrue? If I am not, does that mean that I consider parents have no rights or, if they have, that I am not prepared to acknowledge them?
2 Am I self-sufficient as a teacher or would I be more effective if I used the skills that parents and other people have and arranged my time to make this possible?
3 How accessible am I to parents?
4 Do I and can I create the best conditions for talking to parents?
5 Do I find reporting to parents useful to me? Do I ever wonder how useful it is to them?
6 If parents do not respond to personal invitations, do I follow up with further invitations?
7 Do I try to explain to parents what I am trying to achieve and to ask for their help?
8 If the help of parents and others is not accepted or acknowledged at my school, do I try to do anything about changing this situation?

Source: Based on Pettit 1985, pp. 53–5.

FIGURE 17.6 Some procedures and examples for involving parent volunteers in classrooms

Some precautions:
1 The principal should interview each prospective volunteer as if the position was for a paid job.
2 Each parent volunteer should be briefed about the responsibilities of the job, including ethical considerations.
3 Teachers on staff should be thoroughly briefed on the role of volunteer parents and their potential benefit to the school.
4 Each volunteer should be encouraged to develop or expand their skills on the job.
5 The value of the contribution made by individual volunteers should be duly acknowledged on all possible occasions.

Some examples of activities undertaken by parent volunteers:
1 Playing a musical instrument in assemblies or lessons.
2 Stamping and issuing textbooks.
3 Making drama sets and costumes.
4 Typing and duplicating stencils.
5 Teaching an approved sport or hobby.
6 Helping in preparing and distributing school newsletters.
7 Making tapes for listening posts.

Source: Based on Jones and Pettit 1984; Beacham and Hoadley 1985.

17.9 | SCHOOL COUNCILS

School councils in most states and territories are an important element of schooling. Although the composition and powers of school councils vary across the states, the membership typically consists of the principal and representatives of the staff, parents, the community and students (in the case of middle and secondary schools).

'Alternative' schools have a major commitment to a participative democratic process, and most of them operate some kind of school council. These alternative schools have typically very small enrolments and so it is feasible for all parents, teachers and students to meet regularly and make decisions jointly about all major school issues including the curriculum, deployment of staff and the use of resources. For a number of years, many small parish schools operating within Catholic education systems have also maintained their own local boards of management, and these have had independent control over staff appointments, school buildings and finances (including the setting of school fees).

In some cases school councils can be radically powerful and can bring about rapid change (Shaw & Swingler 2005). Gamage's (1993, p. 102) studies reveal that 'councils have become effective and efficient organisations, while the principals are highly satisfied and totally committed to the collaborative form of governance adopted in terms of the school council system'.

La Rocque and Coleman's (1989) study of school councils in British Colombia and Hatch's (1998) study of Alliance Schools in the US conclude that school councils can make a difference. School council members can develop a clear sense of what they want to accomplish and engage in activities to bring about these ends.

Harold (1997) describes the Boards of Trustees in New Zealand and notes that they have had a pivotal role in developing partnerships between teachers and parents. Each board consists of five elected parent representatives; an elected student representative (for schools with secondary students); the principal; and an elected staff representative. Clearly, this structure allows much wider powers of decision to be given directly to parents. Harold concludes that Boards of Trustees are operating successfully in the majority of schools.

However, as noted by Fullan (1991), how to increase and improve the effectiveness of school councils is an unstudied problem. There are still many unanswered issues and problems, and some of these are listed in Figure 17.7.

Lutz (1980) questions whether school councils really practise democratic decision making. He argues that school council participation of parents from a local school community is very limited and sporadic; that few council members are closely involved in decision making, and that few issues are ever made public and widely debated. It is certainly evident that for large schools it is extremely difficult for school board members to represent more than a few of the community interests (Chan & Chui 1997). Many of the disadvantaged community groups are never represented. Yet it might be argued that democracy means the freedom to participate or not to participate and that if individuals and groups feel strongly enough about an issue then they will participate vigorously.

Questions might also be raised whether school councils actually reduce conflicts between various interest groups or heighten the conflicts still more (see Figure 17.7). For example, Knight (1995) highlights some of the conflicts between teacher and parent members in Victoria. Is it possible that parent

FIGURE 17.7 Problems and issues for school councils

1. Do councils have real power if their control over finances is limited?
2. Are school councils really able to practise democratic decision making?
3. Is an adequate supply of dedicated and well-informed parents and community members available to fill school council positions?
4. Does the size of a school influence the effectiveness of school councils?
5. How can school council members understand and represent all sections of a local community if they tend to be better educated and more affluent than the majority of local citizens?
6. Will school councils ever be able to represent effectively such disadvantaged groups as migrants, the unskilled, the unemployed and low-income earners?
7. Do school councils really provide a structure for school principal, teachers and parents to coexist harmoniously?
8. Do school councils in the Australian context ever get complete control over decision making?

priorities (such as school discipline, and literacy and numeracy) are likely to be different from the priorities expressed by teachers (for example, providing a caring atmosphere and building student self-esteem)?

Finally, questions might also be raised about whether school councils in state education systems can ever anticipate becoming fully independent from head office policies and requirements. Recent accountability measures introduced into a number of education systems would seem to indicate that centralist requirements are increasing rather than decreasing (see for example, Government of South Australia 2008).

CONCLUDING COMMENTS

There are promising developments and opportunities for involving parents more effectively in classrooms and schools. Outcomes-based assessment is providing a common language for teachers and parents and is improving communication channels (Spady 1994; Grundy & Bonser 1997a). Moves to devolution in state and territory education systems over the last two decades have provided the opportunities for greater parent participation. However, these developments have not been without their setbacks, including recentralising initiatives associated with economic rationalism and corporate management demands.

KEY ISSUES RAISED IN THIS CHAPTER

1. There is agreement that parents potentially have a major role to play in schools, but there are many difficulties in nurturing a collaborative relationship between parents and teachers.
2. Historically in Australia parent and community participation in schools has not been a dominant pattern.
3. There are powerful pedagogical reasons why parents should be participants in schools but also powerful practical reasons why their participation should be limited.
4. Parents can have school-based involvement and home-based involvement. Both have their advantages.
5. Parents and teachers need training on techniques for communicating more effectively with each other.

REFLECTIONS AND ISSUES

1. Students and parents from diverse economic and cultural backgrounds all value education and look to schools as the key to preparing young people for their futures. What more should schools do to achieve this?
2. Fullan (1991) argues that parent participation at the school and classroom level is a fundamental mission of an effective school. Present arguments for and against this statement.
3. Some school council members complain that they suffer from a lack of direction, the feeling of being a rubber stamp, and parent and staff apathy. How might some of these problems be resolved?
4. Do you consider that schools are effective in communities where there are students from diverse backgrounds? What do you think needs to be done to confront issues of social dominance and social justice?
5. Stevenson (1998) contends that parents want to:
   - feel confident that their children will be happy
   - trust teachers
   - share their insights about their children with the teacher.

Have you experienced parents who share these goals? What steps can you take to bring about a more productive partnership with parents?
6 Do you consider that the notion of partnership between teachers and parents, reflecting equality and the complementary sharing of responsibilities, is unrealistic? Give reasons for your stance.
7 Are parents or teachers mainly responsible for creating student interest in learning? Explain, giving reasons.
8 MacLure and Walker (1998) contend that many of the meetings between parents and teachers are ceremonial, where both parties enact ritual performances of interest and concern. In your experience, is this a realistic assessment? How can these meetings be used more successfully for both parties?
9 To what extent do you consider that computer technology (especially email) enables teachers and parents to connect more successfully with each other?
10 Hughes and Greenhough (1998) argue that the knowledge bases of parents and teachers is one of 'difference and diversity' rather than 'superiority and deficit'. If this is the case, how might this affect communications between teachers and parents?
11 Parental involvement in schools not only improves teaching and learning, it can also transform families' lives (Comer 2005). Explain situations when this might occur. What are some limiting factors?
12 Establishing true partnerships with parents entails educators acknowledging and validating parents' views and ultimately sharing power (Cooper & Christie 2005). Discuss.
13 Some writers argue that school–community relations need to be open to constant scrutiny, nurture, refreshment and reinvigoration. What specific actions would you think might achieve this goal?

Special references

Cooper, C & Christie, CA (2005) 'Evaluating parent empowerment: A look at the potential of social justice evaluation in education', *Teachers College Record*, 107(10):2248–74.
Epstein, JL & Salinas, KC (2004) 'Partnering with families and communities', *Educational Leadership*, 61(8):12–19.
Katyal, KR & Evers, CW (2007) 'Parents – partners or clients? A reconceptualization of home–school interactions', *Teaching Education*, 18(1):61–76.
Mattingly, D, Prislin, R, McKenzie, T, Rodriquez, J & Kayzar, B (2002) 'Evaluating evaluations: The case of parent involvement programs', *Review of Educational Research*, 72(4):549–76.
Pomerantz, EM Moorman, EA & Litwack, SD (2007) 'The how, whom and why of parents' involvement in children's academic lives: More is not always better', *Review of Educational Research*, 77(3):373–410.
Shaw, A & Swingler, D (2005) 'Shared values and beliefs: The basis for a new school community', *The Australian Educational Leader*, 27(2):10–15.
Wadsworth, D & Remaley, MH (2007) 'What families want', *Educational Leadership*, 64(6):23–7.

Web sources

For additional resources on working effectively with parents, please go to: www.pearson.com.au/myeducationlab.

18

ASSESSMENT AND REPORTING

18.1 | INTRODUCTION

As noted by Wiliam (2008) 'today's schools face unprecedented challenges in preparing students for the unpredictable demands of the future workplace' (p. 36). Various solutions have been considered such as sanctions, curriculum changes, increased use of technology and of course new forms of assessment.

Hargreaves, Earl and Schmidt (2002) argue that assessment-led reform is one of the most favoured strategies to promote higher standards and more powerful learning. However, one of the main problems is that assessment is about several things at once. It is about grading and about learning (Carless 2007). This causes major problems for teachers whereby they might value innovative assessment ideas but in practice what they do is far more limited (James & Pedder 2006).

Assessment can take many forms and certainly has a much wider scope than traditional forms of objective tests and essay tests. Tomlinson (2008b) emphasises the diverse forms that assessment can take – she emphasises informal assessment that occurs throughout the teaching of a unit and not just at the end. It provides feedback for students and teachers.

We should never forget that assessment can have a dramatic effect on the lives of students (Cunningham 1998).

Wherever possible, forms of assessment should be used that raise students' self-esteem – learning experiences are needed that enable students to create success criteria and to organise their individual targets (Clarke 2001). Some of the newer approaches to assessment such as 'assessment for learning' and 'authentic and performance assessment' examined in this chapter may be more inclusive and user-friendly for students than traditional approaches.

There are significant and deep-rooted differences in the assessment systems of different countries. Black and Wiliam's (2005) survey of systems used in the United Kingdom, France, Germany and the United States provides some fascinating differences:
- UK – there has been a deep distrust of teachers; many new, formal tests have been initiated and there is some school-based assessment. There is ongoing research on formative assessment (James 2008).
- France – a range of different assessment systems are used; teachers concentrate on formative assessment and pedagogy and all summative assessment is handled externally.

- Germany – Germany relies on national tests and teachers are trusted to make summative judgments.
- US – there has been an increase in testing for accountability purposes; there is rigid pacing of teaching to ensure that adequate progress is made to the standards in the *No Child Left Behind Act 2001* (US Department of Education 2002).

Cumming and Maxwell (2004) consider that assessment practices across Australian states and territories are very uneven. The new frameworks are now specifying student outcomes and there are some opportunities for teachers to collaborate on formative assessment.

It is evident, as noted by Black and Wiliam (2005), that 'assessment practices and initiatives are determined at least as much by culture and politics as it is by educational evidence and values' (p. 260).

 Does assessment get in the way of learning? Could it be the case that a teacher might spend so much time on assessing that there is insufficient time for student learning to take place?

18.2 | ASSESSMENT

'Assessment' is the term typically used to describe the activities undertaken by a teacher to obtain information about the knowledge, skills and attitudes of students. Activities can involve the collection of formal assessment data (for example, by the use of objective tests) or the use of informal data (for example, by the use of observation checklists). Teachers typically assign a grade or mark (numerical score, letter grade, descriptive ranking) for work undertaken by students such as a project or a written test. Some of the basic principles of assessment are listed in Figure 18.1.

FIGURE 18.1 Some basic principles of assessment

---

1. Assessment can only be based on samples of behaviour and therefore inaccuracies will always occur (Salvia & Ysseldyke 1998).
2. Assessment must communicate to teachers how to make instruction more effective.
3. Assessment is not done mainly to grade students but to promote instruction.
4. Assessment must be fair to all individuals and groups (Willingham & Cole 1997).
5. Assessment must measure a broad range of abilities (Darling-Hammond & Falk 1997).
6. Assessment results should be meaningful to all participants, students, teachers and parents (Wiggins 1994).

18.3 | REASONS FOR ASSESSMENT

Assessment is usually undertaken for the following reasons:
- diagnosis of learning and monitoring progress
- grading students
- predicting future achievements
- motivating students
- diagnosis of teaching.

Diagnosing learning that has occurred and monitoring progress are major reasons for assessment (Chase 1999). This information may be gleaned by a teacher asking questions of individual students or listening to student comments. The diagnosis should help each student understand their weaknesses and it also guides the teacher on where to direct their instructional energies.

In most cases, student grades are assigned to indicate achievement at the end of a unit or term, semester or year. Sufficient evidence needs to be collected by a teacher to enable the person to assign accurate grades. Generally, the more frequently and varied the assessments used, the more informed the teacher will be about the grades to assign to students.

Assessment can also be used to predict students' eligibility for selection in future courses. This is usually of importance at upper secondary school levels.

Assessment can often increase the motivation of students, even though the teacher may not consciously highlight it as an incentive to work hard! It depends on the individual learner, as some students will be highly motivated by an impending test whereas others may suffer excessive stress or be de-motivated (McMillan & Hearn 2008).

Assessment data can provide valuable diagnostic information for the teacher, including some reasons why lessons fly or flop (Eisner 1993). It may indicate, for example, that aspects of content or processes were not understood fully by students, or that the material presented was too difficult or too easy for a particular class.

Of course, it is also important to be mindful of the distorting effects of assessment (Gipps & Murphy 1994). Different forms of assessment will promote particular kinds of learning (such as rote learning) and downgrade other kinds, especially if they are difficult to measure (such as higher order thinking).

18.4 | ASSESSING FOR WHOM?

There are close links between reasons for assessment and their intended audiences. Possible audiences include:
- *Learners:* these should be the main audience, but typically they are not given a high priority. They are rarely involved in planning the assessment activities.
- *Teachers:* teachers need feedback about the effectiveness of their teaching. Student assessment data are being used increasingly as a data source for appraising teachers.
- *Parents:* parents want regular feedback. Media efforts to publicise school results and 'league tables' of schools has led to increased clamourings for assessment information.
- *Tertiary institutions:* universities and Technical and Further Education (TAFE) colleges require specific assessment information from applicants intending to enrol.
- *Employers:* employers are demanding more specific information, especially in terms of literacy and numeracy and key competencies.

18.5 | IMPORTANT EMPHASES IN ASSESSMENT

18.5.1 ICT developments in assessment

The widespread use of computers in schools is now well established. There has been a significant investment in educational information and communication technologies (ICT) around the world (Quellmalz & Kozma 2003). According to Ridgway and McCusker (2003), ICT 'is at the centre of a cultural vortex which is bringing about radical social change ... It has had a profound effect on the cultural practices associated with every academic discipline over the last 20 years' (p. 310).

ICT enables assessment of real-world problems and gives students and teachers more opportunities for feedback and reflection. Yet, according to Baker (2003), technology-enhanced assessment is still emerging even though development is rapid. Raikes and Harding (2003), with reference to our current 'horseless carriage stage' (p. 268), argue that there are still many barriers to overcome, namely:
- cost and expected return on investment
- establishing the equivalence of pencil and paper and computer test forms
- security
- coping with the diversity of ICT environments and cultures in schools and colleges
- software and hardware reliability, and resilience of the system in the face of breakdown (Raikes & Harding 2003, p. 270).

But the opportunities using ICT do look promising. Consider, for example, the coordinated ICT Assessment Framework, funded by the US National Science Foundation and using a working group of international experts in ICT from Chile, Finland, Norway, Singapore and the USA (Quellmalz & Kozma 2003). As illustrated in Figure 18.2, the ICT strategies and tools that are currently being used by many teachers are quite impressive.

ICT tools are many, including the Internet, word processors and data bases. These can be used to accomplish multiple ICT strategies, such as 'communicate' and 'critically evaluate': the knowledge being assessed can include content such as the fact that the lack of scratch workspace on mathematics tests can cause underachievement on some computer-based tests (Russell, Goldberg & O'Connor 2003).

Baker (2003) and Raikes and Harding (2003) note that an ongoing problem with ICT for assessment is the competitive branding and positioning of rival groups developing very expensive assessment initiatives. Baker (2003), for example, suggests that approaches are needed to 'appropriately and rigorously test and publicly report findings of competing strategies' (p. 422).

 Do you consider that the computer can provide better assessment of cognitive skills compared with traditional tests?

FIGURE 18.2 Coordinated ICT assessment framework

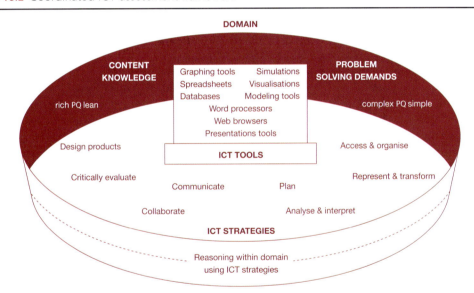

Source: Quellmalz and Kosma (2003), p. 392. Reprinted by permission of Taylor & Francis Group, <www.informaworld.com>

18.5.2 Assessment for learning

Over the last decade there has been major interest in a number of countries, but especially Scotland and England, the USA, Australia and Canada, in 'assessment for learning' or 'formative assessment'. One of the driving forces for this has been the seminal work of Black and Wiliam (1998) from the Assessment Reform Group in London. Subsequently, major projects have been directed by Mary James and David Pedder (2006) (Learning How to Learn Project) and Priestley (2005) in England, and Assessment is for Learning (AifL) in Scotland.

In Canada, Earl's (2005) work has been very influential. In California, the Classroom Assessment Project to Improve Teaching and Learning (CAPITAL), as outlined by Coffey, Sato and Thiebault (2005), attempts to analyse teachers' assessment practices, how they are shaped and how they are able to improve their day-to-day assessment efforts.

Baker (2007) describes another major project, CRESST POWERSOURCE, an international collaborative project which examines the use of multiple interim assessments of problem solving and explanation (formative assessment) in the teaching of middle school algebra.

It has been very evident to researchers that to encourage classroom teachers to use assessment for learning effectively is indeed very complex. Mary James, as reported in Marshall and Drummond (2006), notes the tension between the 'letter' and the 'spirit' of formative assessment. That is, many teachers use formative assessment practices superficially but do not integrate practices into their curriculum planning.

Hargreaves (2005) argues that there are various conceptions of assessment for learning, which she groups into six categories:

- monitoring students' performance against targets or objectives
- using assessment to inform next steps in teaching and learning
- teachers giving feedback for improvement
- learning about children's learning
- children taking some control of their own learning and assessment
- turning assessment into a learning event.

She concludes that these various definitions can be interpreted as two major categories for conceptions of learning: learning as attaining objectives; and learning as constructing knowledge. She notes that the majority of teachers still hold the measurement/objective conception, which is understandable in the light of a National Curriculum which has been operating in the UK since 1988.

Conceptually there are problems in treating formative assessment and summative assessment as separate entities. For example, Taras (2005) contends, after Scriven (1967), that 'all assessment begins with summative assessment (which is a judgment) and that formative assessment is in fact summative assessment plus feedback which is used by the learner' (p. 466).

Kennedy (2007) argues that modifications are needed to forms of summative assessment so that the two can co-exist more successfully. Negative wash-back effects of high-stakes summative assessment can greatly limit opportunities for formative assessment.

Pryor and Crossouard (2008) contend that there are contextual issues that need to be deconstructed in formative assessment – issues of power and learners' and teachers' identities that involves dialectical and sometimes conflictual processes. By this they mean that any interactions that occur between the teacher and students over assessment will not just be a neutral exchange but will involve issues of power and control. They consider that formative assessment interactions are rarely simple but will require the reduction of tensions, different priorities and perhaps even the talking through of perceived conflicts.

In terms of practicing assessment for learning, numerous researchers point to practical issues for teachers, such as Lee and Wiliam (2005); Coffey, Sato and Thiebault (2005); Brandom, Carmichael and Marshall (2005); Fisher and Frey (2007); Blanchard (2008); Brown and Hirschfeld (2008); and Priestley and Sime (2005). For example, Priestley and Sime (2005) concluded from their AifL study in Scotland that four factors for successfully engaging staff members are:

- proactive leadership
- professional trust in the capacity of teachers to drive change and adapt teaching
- the creation of space for collaboration between teachers
- the use of 'start-small' strategies.

Priestley and Sime (2005) argue that these four factors combine to 'stimulate high levels of socio-cultural interaction within a school' (p. 482).

 Have you tried to use formative assessment with a class? What plans did you make to do this? How successful were you?

18.6 | IMPORTANT CONCEPTS IN ASSESSMENT

18.6.1 Diagnostic/formative–summative

Looking first at *diagnostic assessment*: Obviously students come into classrooms with varying backgrounds and interests, so it is inefficient to start a new teaching unit without checking their knowledge and understandings. Some may lack the prerequisite skills needed to undertake the lessons required of them and, worse still, others may have certain negative attitudes to the topic that will prove a major difficulty unless the teacher is aware in advance of these emotional attitudes. On the other hand, if the students already have a number of skills or understandings that the teacher intended to teach them, their interest and enthusiasm would be reduced if the same activities were repeated. Diagnostic evaluation simply reminds teachers that they must start their instruction at the level the students have reached. What is more, the teacher needs to be continually aware of students' levels in their progress through the curriculum unit. In this sense, the teacher is undertaking diagnostic evaluation through all the stages of instruction.

Formative assessment provides data about instructional units in progress and students in action. The data help to develop or form the final curriculum product and help students adjust to their learning tasks through the feedback they receive (Chappuis & Chappuis 2008). Formative evaluation then is important because it provides data to enable 'on the spot' changes to be made where necessary. Students' learning activities can be refocused and redirected and the range and depth of the instructional activities of a curriculum can be revised in 'mid-stream' (Wiliam 2008; Brown & Hirschfeld 2008). It applies therefore to both course improvement and student growth, although some writers tend to concentrate only on the former (Pryor & Torrance 1996).

Clarke (2001) concentrates very much on the importance of formative assessment to bring about student growth. She cites Black and Wiliams' (1998) research findings that formative assessment strategies do raise standards of student achievement, especially for children of lower ability.

Summative assessment is the final goal of an educational activity. Eventually, teachers need to know the relative merits and demerits of a curriculum package. Also, they need to have collected appropriate information about the levels of achievement reached by students. Of course this information may be used in a diagnostic way as a preliminary to further activities, but it must be emphasised that summative evaluation provides the data from which decisions can be made.

Over recent years, related summative assessment terms have become widely used, such as *benchmarking* (the process of measuring standards of actual performance against those achieved by others with broadly similar characteristics) and *value-added* assessment (where raw scores from test results are adjusted to allow for the characteristics of the intake of the school: Clarke 1998). These forms of summative assessment usually involve 'high stakes' standards and the publication of results for parents and the community to make comparisons (see internal–external assessment details later in this chapter).

18.6.2 Informal–formal

Informal assessment is inevitable, ongoing and very useful. Informal observations of natural situations are especially valuable for gaining information about student interactions. The less obvious it is to students that they are being assessed, the more natural will be their behaviour.

Informal assessment is especially important in early childhood and lower primary classes. Teachers use various techniques such as observations, running records, anecdotal records and written notes to assess the development of the whole child (Carr 2001).

Sylva, Siraj-Blatchford and Taggart (2003) have developed an Early Childhood Environment Rating Scale which, although not directly measuring student assessment, does provide informal ratings on the quality of curriculum provision and pedagogy.

Formal assessment is planned and is often an obtrusive activity. Some questions about formal forms of assessment are raised in Figure 18.3. Thus any weekly tests and planned assignments could be categorised as formal assessments. There are a number of forms of informal and formal assessments that can be used (see Table 18.1).

TABLE 18.1 Commonly used assessment techniques

Techniques	Diagnostic	Formative	Summative
Informal observing and recording of student behaviour	Direct observation Anecdotal records *Case histories*	Direct observation *Anecdotal records* Case histories	Direct observation *Anecdotal records* Case histories
Informal collecting of information from students	Checklists Rating scales by teacher Unobtrusive techniques *Interest inventories* Rating scales by students Questionnaires Interviews *Sociograms* Self-reports	Checklists *Rating scales by teacher* *Unobtrusive techniques* Interest inventories Rating scales by students Questionnaires Interviews Sociograms *Self-reports*	Checklists Rating scales by teacher Unobtrusive techniques Interest inventories *Rating scales by students* *Questionnaires* *Interviews* Sociograms Self-reports
Analysis of student work examples	Individual and group projects Content analysis of workbook Logbooks and journals Portfolios	Individual and group projects Content analysis of workbook Logbooks and journals Portfolios	*Individual and group projects* *Content analysis of workbook* *Logbooks and journals* *Portfolios*
Testing of students	Objective tests Standardised tests Essay tests Semantic differentials *Attitude scales* *Simulation and role-plays* *Projective techniques*	Objective tests Standardised tests Essay tests Semantic differentials Attitude scales Simulation and role-plays Projective techniques	*Objective tests* *Standardised tests* *Essay tests* *Semantic differentials* Attitude scales Simulation and role-plays Projective techniques

Note: Italics refer to the optimal time to use a particular technique.

YOUR TURN

At a school where you are assigned to do practice teaching, use observational information to watch and listen to a small number of students.

- How do these students respond to questions?
- Do they seem interested in their work?
- Do they cooperate with one another?
- Reflect on what your data tells you about these students.

FIGURE 18.3 Some questions about formal forms of assessment

---
1 Can paper and pencil tests capture thinking and problem-solving skills?
2 Is too much teaching time used for testing? (Neill 1998)
3 To what extent do paper and pencil tests have gender or ethnic bias? (Harnisch & Mabry 1993)
4 What are the effects of stress and anxiety on test taking?
5 Do tests provide parents with understandable information about their children? (Orlich et al 1998)

18.6.3 Norm-referenced–criterion-referenced

Norm-referenced measures are used to compare students' performance in specific tests. These measures simply provide comparative age-based data on how well certain students perform in a test (for example, Maths or Reading). Of course, they are open to misinterpretation. Students who receive special coaching or good teaching are likely to outperform those students who do not have these opportunities. Norm-referenced measures can provide important evaluative data about the performance of students on specific tasks but do not tell us anything about an individual's potential or their attitude towards certain subjects.

As noted by Izard (2005), norm-referenced measures are only useful if details about the comparison groups are available. Quite often the comparison groups are dated, or do not match the test user's candidates in terms of age, curriculum undertaken or socio-economic background.

Criterion-referenced measures avoid the competitive elements of norm-referenced measures because information is obtained about students' performance in terms of their previous performances rather than in relation to the performances of others. Once the skill level for a particular task has been defined (the criterion), then it is presumed that a student will persevere until it is attained. The difficulty lies in defining learning activities in terms of tasks to be mastered. Certain subjects such as Mathematics and topics such as motor skills and mapping are particularly amenable to this approach, but it is more difficult to establish criterion-referenced tasks for 'creative writing' or 'art'.

Performance-based assessments have gained considerable support over recent years. They can be criterion- or standards-referenced, but are typically the former. In the US over 34 states use tests that include performance tasks (Heck & Crislip 2001). These performance tests require students to demonstrate their acquisition of problem solving and critical thinking (Yeh 2001) or writing skills (Heck & Crislip 2001). Some writers link these kinds of performance tests with constructivism – the theory that knowledge is constructed by individual human beings and not merely discovered (see, for example, von Glaserfield 1995; Phillips 1995).

The intention may be to develop criterion-referenced measures, but in many cases they finish up as norm-referenced measures. For example, Elliott and Chan (2002) contend that:

> in theory the assessment [for the National Curriculum in England and Wales] was supposed to be criterion-referenced and therefore linked to task specific standards of achievement. However, the standardised tests developed for each key stage have not been able to avoid a considerable element of norm-referencing and are too crude to inform teaching and learning. (p. 8)

 In classrooms you have visited have you observed students collaborating and helping each other on ways to improve their work? How can students be encouraged to do more of these self-assessments and cooperative activities?

18.6.4 Process–product

Most assessment involves making judgments about *products* such as an assignment, project or object. Products are often perceived to be the major priority of the course. Yet *processes* such as thinking skills, working cooperatively in groups, and problem solving are very important (Withers & McCurry 1990).

Payne (2003) contends that assessing processes such as interpersonal relationships and performances is important and that process and product are intimately related. He suggests that if:
- the steps involved in arriving at the product are indeterminate; and
- measuring the processes leading to the product is impractical

then the emphasis has to be on the product.

Wiggins (1998) considers that, although a number of practical techniques are available for assessing processes, this still requires the teacher to make judgments: Is the process observed/rated 'exemplary' or 'on course' or 'grounds for concern'?

However, various computer programs are now available whereby multiple process measures can be taken (Asp 2000; Cross 2006; Christophersen 2006; Lim & Chai 2008) (see also Chapter 2).

18.6.5 Learner judged–teacher judged

At most levels of schooling the *teacher* does the judging about standards. Typically individual teachers set and mark their tests and other forms of assessment. Rarely are *students* consulted or given responsibility for self-assessment.

Yet there are very promising developments if students are involved (Francis 2001; McMillan & Hearn 2008). Clarke (2001) contends that learners must ultimately be responsible for their learning. She states that the greatest impact on students is an overall rise in their self-esteem, as revealed by such student behaviours as:
- being able to say where they need help without any sense of failure
- beginning to set their own targets and goals
- being able to speak about their learning when they would not have done so before (Clarke 2001, p. 44).

Clarke (2001) also contends that learners' self-assessment also gives teachers greater insights into students' learning needs.

Munns and Woodward (2006) contend that there are strong theoretical and practical connections between student engagement and student self-assessment. Their study of primary school students in the Fair Go Project (action research into student engagement among low social-economic status students in Sydney's south-west) noted that students' reflections about their learning and the use of higher levels of thinking greatly improved their engagement.

McDonald and Boud (2003) undertook a study of ten high schools in Sydney where senior school students and their teachers were trained in the use of self-assessment. The experimental group achieved higher examination results than the control group. McDonald and Boud (2003) conclude that the 'use of self-assessment training as part of the curriculum provides a way of laying the foundation for the kinds of skills students will need as lifelong support after school' (p. 219).

 Would you agree that giving good feedback is one of the skills that a teacher needs to master? How effective do you consider you are in giving feedback that is both cognitive and motivational?

18.6.6 Internal–external

Internal assessment involves those directly participating in the teaching–learning process, usually classroom teachers. *External* assessors become involved when 'high-status' or 'high-stakes' assessments are to occur state-wide or nationally, typically at the completion of senior secondary schooling.

In the US high-stakes, standardised assessments are widely used and have been very popular over recent years in many states, because it is argued that they raise academic performances of students and contribute to their earning at least basic educational credentials (Schiller & Muller 2000).

However, there are many critics of high-stakes testing. Some of the major concerns include:
- Test scores are mainly used for sorting and ranking students; there are serious adverse effects on low-income and minority students (Casas & Meaghan 2001; Brennan et al. 2001).
- Tests divert valuable instructional time to preparing for testing (Froese-Germain 2001).

In Australia, with the exception of Queensland and the Australian Capital Territory, all states and territories use external assessments at Year 12. These are quite evidently high-stakes tests – they enjoy considerable public confidence and credibility, despite their limitations.

ACER was commissioned by the Commonwealth Government in 2005 to explore the feasibility of producing one high-stakes assessment for all states and territories. The report produced in 2006 by Masters, Forster and Tognolini (2006) recommended the creation of a new national certificate, the 'Australian Certificate of Education', but a change of government in 2007 caused this initiative to be delayed, if not abandoned.

International student assessment tests such as the Programme for International Student Assessment (PISA) and Trends in International Mathematics and Science Study (TIMSS) are closely monitored by governments and educational research agencies such as ACER. They are also clearly high stakes (for more details see Chapter 2).

 Look up details for Australian students on PISA. How does Australia rate with other countries in terms of scores in mathematics, reading literacy, science and problem solving? Can you have high quality (high-ranking scores) as well as high equity (small between or within school differentiation)?

There are other national tests which are having an impact on teachers and teaching methods. In 2008, the National Assessment Program, Literacy and Numeracy was expanded to include Year 9 as well as continuing with Years 3, 5 and 7. Both Woods (2007) and Wyatt-Smith (2008) argue that the promise of the National Plan (DEETYA 1998) to harness the power of assessment for diagnosis and learning improvement may not have been realised. Wyatt-Smith (2008) cites problems such as:
- political appeal rather than scientific evidence of fitness for purpose
- questions about the validity and quality of the tests themselves
- data access and analysis at the school level is very limited because teachers lack the technology skills.

Holland (2008) notes similar deficiencies with state tests developed in the USA to comply with the No Child Left Behind Legislation (2001). Some concerns include an unclear political context, problems associated with test construction and scoring, dishonest administration and test-taking activities and increasing reports of stress associated with test taking.

Although it is problematic whether these tests fairly and justly represent the diversity of Australian students, they are likely to be retained as a major, highly visible platform of centralised testing (Meadmore 2001).

Recent studies have highlighted some of the negative backwash effects of external summative assessments upon classroom teaching (Biggs 1998). Harlen (2005) argues that, if teachers ran their own internal summative assessments, this would largely overcome the problem. Yet there still remains the issue that teacher-developed tests are often lacking in reliability and validity.

The move in a number of countries, especially the US and the UK, to greatly expand their use of *standardised*, external tests poses dilemmas for teachers. Teachers have little choice but to spend considerable amounts of class time on preparation for the external tests. Klein, Zevenbergen and Brown (2006) and Volante (2006) note that this is causing many teachers to limit their use of authentic assessment tools such as portfolios. In Australia, similar emphases seem to be developing with the federal government mandating common standardised benchmarks for literacy and numeracy (Woods 2007). It is likely to put pressure on teachers in Australian schools and could narrow their modes of instruction and forms of assessment.

> **YOUR TURN**
>
> Imagine that you receive a telephone call from an angry parent who is very annoyed about the grade you have given her child for an assignment. A neighbour's child has received a much higher grade, also marked by you, even though the piece of work was much shorter and full of spelling errors. You have a meeting with the parent tomorrow in the principal's office. What will you say?

18.6.7 Inclusive–exclusive

The production of forms of assessment should, ideally, provide access to all learners and be *inclusive*, regardless of gender, ethnicity or disadvantage. Studies have indicated that in many cases assessment is far from inclusive but that it is *exclusive* (Susinos, Calvo & Rojas 2009; Hargreaves, Homer & Swinnerton 2008). Salvia and Ysseldyke (1998) cite examples where minority ethnic groups and females are not given equal opportunities. It is evident that a number of multiple choice tests tend to be biased against females (Gipps & Murphy 1994; Willingham & Cole 1997). Teachers' assessment of ethnic minority students can often be biased, as is reported by Cunningham (1998).

Cumming (2008) comments on some of the legal claims about assessment where inequity for different groups is being claimed. (See Chapter 2 for equity issues.)

Gipps (1994, p. 151) raises three fundamental questions about inclusivity:
1 Whose knowledge is taught?
2 Why is it taught in a particular way to this particular group?
3 How do we enable the histories and cultures of people of colour, and of women, to be taught in responsible and responsive ways?

Inclusivity also applies to students with special needs. There is a need for all students to have access to appropriate forms of assessment. Kopriva (1999) notes that there has been considerable interest in developing alternative assessments and alternative testing formats for students with special needs.

 In classes you have observed is there a gender difference in achievements of boys and girls in assessment tests in different subjects? Give examples.

18.6.8 Technicist–liberal/postmodernist

A number of writers argue that traditional forms of assessment are *technicist* and are used to identify and perpetuate the social hierarchy (Broadfoot 1979; Blackmore 1988). Many forms of assessment, especially traditional written examinations, concentrate on a narrow view of student achievement that emphasises the outcomes of the academic *curriculum*. Hargreaves, Earl and Schmidt (2002) contend that technological advances in assessment also have this narrow focus – using advanced computer skills to devise and refine valid forms of assessment.

The other option, according to Hargreaves, Earl and Schmidt (2002), is to consider the postmodern perspective and to highlight uncertainties and diversities. After all, 'human beings are not completely knowable and so no assessment process or system can therefore be fully comprehensive' (Hargreaves, Earl & Schmidt 2002, p. 83).

18.7 | COMMONLY USED ASSESSMENT TECHNIQUES

A number of assessment techniques are available to teachers and they can be used at various diagnostic, formative and summative stages. On the one hand, it is very desirable for teachers to use a variety of techniques to ensure that the multidimensionality of student performance is adequately explored

(Haney & Madus 1989). However, there is also the danger of over-assessing and collecting vast arrays of data that have limited use.

McMillan, Myran and Workman's (2002) research study of the assessment practices of over 900 primary school teachers concluded that they used direct observation as a major technique; they only tapped students' higher level thinking skills to a limited extent; and they placed greater importance on social behaviour than academic achievement.

Trepanier-Street, McNair and Donegan (2001) in their study of 300 lower primary and upper primary teachers discovered that lower primary grade teachers mainly used one-on-one assessment of specific skills, written observational notes, checklists, rating scales and portfolio information. Upper primary grade teachers used more teacher-made tests and published tests from textbooks and reading series.

The examples included in Table 18.1 are wide ranging and are repeated in all columns, depending on their applicability at diagnostic, formative and summative stages. They are presented in italics at the perceived optimal stage of use. Despite the range of informal techniques included in Table 18.1, it is likely that teachers still tend to use a number of the written tests, such as objective tests and essay tests.

Space precludes a detailed discussion of each of these techniques, but the examples given below provide brief descriptions and a reminder of their respective merits and demerits. After all, every teacher has to make judgments about which techniques to use from a wide selection.

18.7.1 Direct observation

At the pre-primary and lower primary levels, observation is an important tool to take account of the whole child within a broad educational framework. Although there are difficulties in developing and applying observation techniques, they have a range of applications. They can be used to study:
- group responsibility
- group participation
- attitudes towards subject matter
- specific elements of competence and skills.

The example in Figure 18.4 demonstrates how a planned observation of a small group of young children could be used to assess their social interaction and communication skills.

FIGURE 18.4 Planned observation for pre-primary students

Child's name:	Jackson
Focus:	Social interaction and communication skills
Task:	Collage task working with a partner
Mary:	I can see a circle.
Jackson:	I think it's a circle too.
Mary:	I have a circle. You have a square. I'm going to put my circle over there.
Jackson:	All right, I'll put my square over there.
Mary:	Where will I put this one?
Jackson:	It might go there.
Mary:	Do you want that coloured one?
Jackson:	No, you can have it.

Comment
The two children worked mainly in parallel with each other. Towards the end of the activity they began to help each other and to use language and negotiate deals with each other.

Merits
1. A teacher can gather information about the behaviour and the social, emotional and personal adjustment of individual students (Payne 2003).
2. Observation can be easily adapted to a variety of settings, and to tasks for students at all ages and educational levels (Athanasou & Lamprienou 2002).

Demerits
1. A teacher has to be careful not to draw inferences from a single incident.
2. Failure to record observations accurately can reduce the validity of a report.

18.7.2 Semantic differentials

The semantic differential is a technique that is ideally suited for use by the teacher and provides useful information about student attitudes, either as a single measurement or on a 'pre-/post-' basis. The semantic differential provides information about the intensity of a student's attitude by allocating a number for this intensity along the semantic space continuum.

In Figure 18.5, a semantic differential example is presented in which students' attitudes towards *forest clearing* are measured along a scale from good to bad, strong to weak and so on. The pairs of words are set out on opposing ends of a line so that it is possible to make a neutral response in the fourth space or to make responses in agreement to either word by marking the space anywhere from the middle to the end of each line. Each table can then be scored in terms of a key designed in advance by the teacher.

In the example given in Figure 18.5 the respondent was fairly strongly in agreement that forest clearing was *bad*, in agreement that forest clearing was *weak*, in full agreement that forest clearing was *ugly* and *sad*, mildly in agreement that forest clearing was *unwanted* and *familiar*, in full agreement that forest clearing was *expected*, and mildly in agreement that forest clearing was *fast*. The following marking key was used with this table:

good	1	....	bad
strong	7	....	weak
ugly	7	....	beautiful
happy	1	....	sad
wanted	1	....	unwanted
familiar	7	....	unfamiliar
expected	7	....	unexpected
fast	7	....	slow

On this basis the respondent's score per line was 6, 5, 7, 7, 5, 5, 7, 5, which gives a total of 47 out of 56 and it seemed that this student exhibited a negative attitude towards forest clearing.

FIGURE 18.5 Semantic differential example for secondary school students – forest clearing

	1	2	3	4	5	6	7	
good						X		bad
strong					X			weak
ugly	X							beautiful
happy						X		sad
wanted					X			unwanted
familiar			X					unfamiliar
expected	X							unexpected
fast			X					slow

The semantic differential instrument is very easy to construct, yet it provides meaningful information about student attitudes. Any pairs of word opposites can be used. The concepts, such as 'forest clearing', should be outlined by brief phrases or stated preferably by one word, but this is the only limitation.

Merits
1 The semantic differential provides a helpful measure of pupils' attitudes toward particular topics without asking them direct questions.
2 Research evidence has revealed that it is very reliable.

Demerits
1 Some pupils may not answer the semantic differential honestly.

18.8 | CURRENT TRENDS IN ASSESSMENT

18.8.1 Authentic assessment

'Authentic assessment' or, sometimes, 'the assessment of authentic learning' are two terms that were popularised in the 1990s and continue to be widely described in the assessment literature in the twenty-first century.

Marzano, Pickering and McTighe (1993) refer to the changing face of assessment and contend that the three factors responsible are: a changing emphasis from traditional objectives to exit outcomes; a move towards a holistic approach to teaching and learning based on a constructivist learning perspective; and a wide-ranging dissatisfaction with and criticism of traditional forms of assessing and reporting.

Alternative assessment is used to express a very different approach to assessment, largely diametrically opposed to traditional quantitative measurement of relatively low-level skills as illustrated by many standardised achievement tests.

Newmann and Wehlage (1993) define *authentic assessment* as the collection of assessment data about activities where students construct meaning and produce knowledge and suggest that these activities have value or meaning beyond success in school. Wiggins (1997) emphasises students doing assessment tasks in context.

Authentic assessment encompasses far more than what students learn as measured by standardised tests or even by ordinary teacher-made tests. Authenticity arises from assessing what is most important, not from assessing what is most convenient. Fundamentally, then, there is nothing new about authentic assessment as a reaction against narrowness in education and a return towards the kind of education that connects feeling, thinking and doing as advocated by John Dewey and other progressives early in the twentieth century.

 In your observations of classes have you noticed examples of authentic assessment provided by the teacher? How would you recognise whether it is authentic or not? Do students know when they are doing authentic tasks?

Applied to the curriculum, authentic assessment suggests that the curriculum must be directed at learning in the broadest possible sense; hence, the curriculum itself should be evaluated in terms of how well it contributes to students' deep understandings not only of subject matter but also of their own lives. In this sense, the popularisation of authentic assessment represents another manifestation of grassroots, bottom-up approaches to curriculum planning.

Fundamentally, authentic assessment is a way of capturing and somewhat formalising the myriad things that perceptive teachers have always considered – although often intuitively – about what is happening to their students (Gipps, McCallum & Hargreaves 2000). The advantages of formalising the process are in making it increasingly accessible to more and more teachers and in keeping it viable as an integral part of flexible curriculum planning and development against the inroads of centralised curriculum control. The basic danger in formalising the process is that, the more widely it is used, the more likely it is to be reduced to a formula co-opted by centralising influences and thus will lose much of its flexibility and value.

In authentic assessment, therefore, the tasks students undertake are more practical, realistic and challenging than traditional paper and pencil tests (Pryor & Torrance 1996). Students are engaged in more meaningful, context-bound activities, focusing their energies on 'challenging, performance-oriented tasks that require analysis, integration of knowledge, and invention' (Darling-Hammond, Ancess & Falk 1995, p. 2). Eisner (1993) states that the tasks of authentic assessment are 'more complex, more closely aligned with life than with individual performance measured in an antiseptic context using sanitised instruments that were untouched by human hands' (p. 224). Some general characteristics of authentic assessment are listed in Figure 18.6.

Although there are many enthusiastic supporters of authentic assessment (for example, Wiggins and McTighe 2005), there are many accounts of problems in implementing it. Franklin (2002) notes three major difficulties: parental unfamiliarity with the goals of authentic assessment; teacher preferences for traditional methods; and the greater amounts of time required to undertake authentic assessment.

Hargreaves, Earl and Schmidt (2002) also note three problems for teachers: knowing how to measure outcomes; in harmonising assessment expectations between home and school; and dealing with the issue of time and resources.

Hargreaves, Earl and Schmidt (2002) are also critical on the grounds that, from a post-modern perspective, authentic assessment is not knowable; it is contrived – schools are highly artificial places. Meir (1998) considers that 'much of what passes for authentic curriculum and authentic assessment is the jargon of contemporary pedagogy' (p. 598).

There are also concerns about the use of authentic assessment. Beck (1991) asserts that proponents of authentic assessment rarely present evidence in support of their claims. Terwilliger (1997) argues that the term 'authenticity' denigrates the importance of knowledge and basic skills as legitimate educational outcomes, despite substantial evidence to the contrary.

Darling-Hammond, Ancess and Falk (1995) contend that authentic assessment by itself will have limited impact unless fundamental school restructuring occurs and that this involves empowerment and shared decision making for teachers, parents and students.

18.8.2 Outcomes-based assessment

Outcomes-based education has impacted on many Western nations over the past few decades (Woods 2007). Various Commonwealth reports since the 1980s have emphasised high standard outcomes, efficiency and minimum standards in literacy and numeracy. The attempt to develop an outcomes-based, national school curriculum framework in the 1990s was a classic example of top-down engineering which inevitably had to falter, as described below.

An early and vocal exponent of outcomes-based education in the US was Spady. According to Spady (1993, p. ii): 'Outcome-based education means focusing and organising a school's entire

FIGURE 18.6 Some characteristics of authentic assessment

- Teachers collect evidence from multiple activities.
- Assessments reflect the tasks that students will encounter in the world outside schools.
- Assessments reveal how students go about solving problems as well as the solutions they formulate.
- Procedures for assessments and the contents of assessments are derived from students' everyday learning in schools.
- Assessments reflect local values, standards and control; they are not imposed externally.
- The tasks students are assessed on include more than one acceptable solution to each problem and more than one acceptable answer to each question.
- For each task, students are given clear criteria.
- Assessments require students to develop responses rather than select from predetermined options.

program and instructional efforts around the clearly defined outcomes we want all students to demonstrate when they leave school.' That is, the intended learning results are the start-up points in defining the system (Hansen 1989). A set of conditions are described that characterise real life and these are used to derive a set of culminatory role performances. Students are required to provide a culminating demonstration – the focus is on competence as well as content, but not on the time needed to reach this standard. Specifically, an outcome is an actual demonstration in an authentic context (Spady 1993, p. 4).

The major characteristics of outcomes-based assessment include:
- It is committed to success for all students – only successes are reported. Weaker students may only achieve a few outcomes; stronger students will achieve more outcomes.
- It is future oriented.
- It includes clearly defined and publicly derived 'exit outcomes'.
- Student assessment tasks are commonly used to assess the achievement of outcomes.
- It includes a variety of methods that assures students successful demonstration of all outcomes and provides more than one chance for students to be successful.
- It incorporates a criterion-referenced and consistently applied system of assessment, performance standards, credentialling and reporting.

An outcomes-based assessment approach, based on the traditional school subjects, was incorporated into the National Curriculum in the UK. For each of the subjects, outcomes (attainment targets) were devised for a set of key stages spanning primary and secondary schools.

As noted above, outcome statements were incorporated into the national profiles developed by the National Collaborative Curriculum Project in Australia (1991–93) (Marsh 1994a). Profiles were produced by teams of teachers for each of the eight learning areas, namely English, Mathematics, Science, Languages other than English, Studies of Society and Environment, the Arts, Health and Physical Education, and Technology.

Each profile consisted of *strands* or concepts that were divided into eight levels, which covered the compulsory years of schooling. The *level statement* provided a summary of what a student was expected to be able to do at the level; the *outcome statements* defined the absolutely essential elements of learning; the *pointers* showed in more detail what the outcome statements meant; and the *annotated work samples* consisted of a collection of pieces of student work to indicate appropriate standards to teachers (see also Chapter 9).

Major modifications to the national statements and profiles by states and territories occurred over the last decade. In many cases the number of outcomes per learning area were reduced; in Victoria, the number of levels was reduced to seven; and in some states, such as Western Australia, cross-curricular outcomes were strengthened (Holt 1997). New conceptualisations were developed in a number of states, including the New Basics in Queensland, Essential Learning in Tasmania and the Victorian Essential Learning Standards.

 To what extent do you consider that the outcomes-based approaches to assessment have been excessively time-consuming and not sufficiently competitive, which has led to a 'dumbing down' of standards (Berlach & McNaught 2007)?

It should be noted that the term 'standards' has replaced the term 'outcomes' in many countries. In the US, outcomes-based programs suffered a major decline in the mid-1990s, to be replaced by content standards and the higher levels of accountability. In Australia, the term 'outcomes' is still used in most states and territories but the major emphasis is now on standards and essential learnings.

For example, in Victoria, the Victorian Essential Learning Standards provide an interesting combination of disciplinary and interdisciplinary elements (see Table 18.2). The standards are clearly listed per level for each domain (subjects) and dimensions (outcomes).

By contrast, in Western Australia, the Curriculum Council's attempt to implement an outcomes-based course and assessment for senior secondary classes was contested by various education groups

TABLE 18.2 Victorian Essential Learning Standards

Standards by Domain Strand	Domain	Dimension
Physical, Personal & Social Learning	Health & Physical Education	Movement & physical activity
		Health knowledge & promotion
	Interpersonal Development	Building social relationships
		Working in teams
	Personal Learning	The individual learner
		Managing personal learning
	Civics & Citizenship	Civics knowledge & understanding
		Community engagement
Discipline-based Learning	The Arts	Creating & making
		Exploring & responding
	English	Reading
		Writing
		Speaking & listening
	Humanities	
	—Economics	Economics knowledge & understanding
		Economics reasoning & interpretation
	—Geography	Geographical knowledge & understanding
		Geospatial skills
	—History	Historical knowledge & understanding
		Historical reasoning & interpretation
	Languages Other Than English (LOTE)	Communicating in a language other than English
		Intercultural knowledge & language awareness
	Mathematics	Number
		Space
		Measurement, chance & data
		Structure
		Working mathematically
	Science	Science knowledge & understanding
		Science at work
Interdisciplinary Learning	Communication	Listening, viewing & responding
		Presenting
	Design, Creativity & Technology	Investigating & designing
		Producing
		Analysing & evaluating
	Information & Communications Technology (ICT)	ICT for visualising thinking
		ICT for creating
		ICT for communicating
	Thinking Processes	Reasoning, processing & inquiry
		Creativity
		Reflection, evaluation & metacognition

Source: Adapted from *Essential Learning Standards*, Victorian Curriculum and Assessment Authority, 2000.

and the daily newspaper (Berlach & McNaught 2007). This led in turn to attacks by the then Federal Education Minister and threats to withdraw funding (King & Banks 2006). The major arguments against the introduction of an outcomes-based approach to assessment in these senior secondary courses were that:
- the content is not clearly defined
- the reporting of student results is not sufficiently fine-grained for employers and tertiary institutions
- it represents a dumbing down of subjects
- outcomes are not appropriate in content-driven subjects such as Maths and Science.

More recently the Director General of the Ministry of Education, Sharyn O'Neill, announced that the use of outcome levels would cease in public schools (O'Neill 2009).

18.8.3 Performance assessment

Performance assessment is based on students demonstrating what they can do. According to the Ministry of Education, British Columbia (1994, p. 25), 'the term is used to describe approaches to assessment which value process as well as product'. Marzano, Pickering and McTighe (1993) and Wiggins and McTighe (2005) are more expansive in their definition of performance assessment in that it:
- refers to a variety of tasks and situations in which students are given opportunities to demonstrate their understanding and to thoughtfully apply knowledge, skills and habits of mind in a variety of contexts
- often occurs over time and results in a tangible product or observable performance
- encourages self-evaluation and revision
- sometimes involves students working with others
- requires judgment to score
- reveals degrees of proficiency based on established criteria
- makes public the scoring criteria
- requires active engagement between the teacher and the student
- needs to have formative feedback throughout the experience as an essential component.

Performance assessment has the potential to bring about major advances in teaching and learning. O'Neil (1992) contends that there are a number of likely dividends for teachers, students and policy makers.
- It will provide a more complete picture of students' abilities.
- It will involve teachers more in the assessment process and link it directly with teaching and learning.
- It will be an incentive for higher achievements by students.
- It is readily comprehended and appreciated by parents.

However, there are concerns about performance assessment and efforts to use it should be initiated cautiously with due regard for problems as they emerge. There are potential difficulties for performance assessments, including that:
- they may be far more expensive to use per student (Stecher & Klein 1997)
- on occasions they may require the use of special equipment
- they may be very time-demanding in an already crowded school timetable (Linn, Baker & Dunbar 1991)
- they may not be generally 'fair' to all students – there are technical questions of validity to consider (Cizek 1991)
- they may not be able to generalise from specific tasks to wider domains – there are concerns about transfer and generalisation
- they may not adequately serve the twin goals of improving classroom instruction and making teachers and schools accountable for student learning.

18.8.4 Examples of performance assessments

Assessment tasks

To achieve assessment of students on outcomes-based programs (strands, level statements and outcome statements), assessment tasks are acknowledged as a useful technique. Assessment tasks are concrete performance tasks designed to be part of regular classroom instruction. The 'authentic' nature of assessment tasks is important to teachers but especially to students – they need to recognise that various aspects of the typical school day can be incorporated as assessment tasks and that judgments based on them are likely to be far more meaningful than judgments based on external tests.

Assessment tasks will vary considerably in the length of time needed to complete them. Some can easily be accommodated in a single lesson or period, but others may extend over several weeks. It will depend on the activities being considered. Some may be more appropriate as brief, intense activities (for example, a role-play), while others may require extended time for exploratory investigation, analysis and presentations. Assessment tasks are likely to be mainly produced by individual teachers, but as students become more familiar with the activities they are likely to become willing and important planners and developers. In some classrooms, students are being given far more opportunities for self-assessment in regard to assessment tasks. By reflecting on their performances or products, students can understand criteria that need to be established and the goals they need to set themselves for further learning.

 Think about an assessment task you would like to develop for a particular class level and subject area. Consider the following rubrics – is it realistic? Does it require judgment and innovation? Does it require students to carry out an inquiry?

The opportunities for using ongoing teaching–learning activities as assessment tasks are many and varied. For example, Figure 18.7 provides 25 classroom activities that can be used most effectively.

Developing assessment tasks

A few pertinent assumptions and reminders may be worth considering.

Assumptions about creating assessment tasks:
- They must be meaningful to students.
- They must include explicit assessment criteria.
- Criteria will involve process as well as product.

FIGURE 18.7 Classroom activities that can be used for assessment

- Portfolios
- Journal writing
- Role-playing
- Imaginative writing
- Designing/presenting community projects
- Team interviewing
- Model building
- Surveys involving parents
- Dialogue diaries
- Mini-investigations
- Presenting position papers
- Reports based on reflective/critical thinking
- Individual and group projects
- Field trips
- Problem-solving tasks
- Concept mapping
- Induction/deduction tasks
- Panel discussions
- Dramatic enactments
- Computer simulations
- Flow charts
- Songs
- Collages
- Dances
- Plays

Questions to consider when designing assessment tasks:
- What knowledge, skills and attitudes will the students demonstrate?
- How will this activity enhance the curriculum taught in my class?
- Will I use formal or informal, structured or unstructured criteria for assessing the task?
- Will I design the assessment task single-handedly, work collaboratively on it with other teachers, or involve my students?
- What length of time will be available to complete the assessment task?
- What individual or group activities will be included?
- What materials and equipment will be needed?
- Will I assess the assessment task or will other teachers be involved, or will students do some self-assessment?
- How will the judgments be used for further teaching and learning?

The details provided about an assessment task should be enticing and inviting for the students. The format should be easy to follow. Most especially, the directions for successfully completing the task should be clear and achievable by a large majority of students. If the assessment task is based on ongoing classroom learning and the interests of the students, there should be no difficulty in producing tasks that are appealing and highly motivating to students.

The reality check comes with the criteria (rubrics) to be used to judge performance on the assessment task. Stating explicit criteria in advance should give most students sufficient notice about what will be expected of them. To ensure that a multidimensional approach is taken, it is important that the criteria include aspects relating to process (such as evidence of investigative skills) as well as product (such as presentation of models, charts, written materials). Self-assessment and peer assessment elements could be important aspects of many assessment tasks.

The example shown in Table 18.3 is based on 'Place and Space' and 'Investigation, Communication and Participation' strands from Studies of Society and Environment for students working within levels 3–8.

Merits of assessment task
1. Assessment tasks are concrete performance tasks that can be undertaken as part of regular classroom instruction.
2. They are meaningful to students.

Demerits of assessment task
1. They can be time-consuming to plan.
2. Devising the criteria (rubrics) can be difficult.

Portfolios

In the US, student portfolios developed as a major form of assessment in the mid-1990s largely due to the writings and acceptance of cognitive psychologists – for example, Resnick and Klopfer (1989) and the New Standards Project by Simmons and Resnick (1993).

The use of portfolios of student work has been central to the movement for authentic assessment. Their use has been based on the belief that what is most significant in any educational situation arises from the student's perception of that situation. Thus, authentic assessment emphasises individual-centred curricula, in which the teacher helps the student identify his or her interests and makes suggestions about how the student can deepen and broaden those interests in ways that lead to a wide variety of worthwhile and concomitant learnings.

Despite the teacher's help, however, authenticity requires the student to take responsibility for what is learned. Only in this way does learning become integrated with the rest of the student's life rather than remaining something apart, as an isolated lesson selected by someone else. Given the responsibility that students must take for their own learnings, it becomes incumbent upon them to demonstrate what they have learned and not simply to wait for their teachers to make these

TABLE 18.3 Sample assessment task

Title/level	Strand: Place and Space (Levels 3–8) Strand: Investigation, Communication and Participation (Levels 3–8), Studies of Society and Environment **Tourist brochure for City X (Australian city)**
Activity	Students will research details on any Australian city and create a brochure (equivalent to two pages of A4), demonstrating knowledge of features of places and research skills.
Preparation	The teacher will provide: • samples of commercial travel brochures • relevant maps and reference materials • sources to collect further information, experts to interview. The students will need to: (a) identify local tourist attractions (b) obtain basic information on physical and built features of chosen localities; determine how to obtain and collect information; who to contact; what will be possible within the time frame.
Time required	10–14 periods (3–4 weeks)
Directions for successfully completing the task	1 Choose an Australian city as a tourist attraction. 2 Determine the basic information needed to present the city as a desirable tourist destination. 3 Examine features included in professionally produced tourist brochures. 4 Plan out the sources to be used to collect further information and/or to interview persons. 5 Decide upon how key features will be selected and why they will have greatest appeal. 6 Consider ways of testing the appeal of chosen features. 7 In two pages, present the major features in an appealing format, making use of computer software if available.
Criteria to be used	• Brochure must contain up-to-date and accurate information about the city. • At least five interesting features need to be presented, using illustrations or written material. • Evidence of effective skills must be shown in investigating, collecting and analysing relevant material.
Variations and extensions	• Encourage students to use sophisticated computer software packages to illustrate/display features. • Encourage students with special needs to use predominantly drawings/illustrations in their brochures.

discoveries. Therefore, such use of student-initiated projects is an integral part of authentic assessment, and portfolios of student work are perhaps the most telling form of demonstration.

The idea of a portfolio is derived from the world of art. Artists create collections of their work that display much about themselves both professionally and personally, ranging from their skills and abilities to their aesthetic and ethical sensibilities. Applied to education, the creation of portfolios suggests that what the student has learned is most authentically demonstrated by what the student creates over a period of time, not by tests given at specific times.

The teacher may initially suggest a topic or set a problem for the student to investigate at the beginning of a project, but the student makes the basic decisions about what to do and how. In carrying out their projects, students can also learn how to assess themselves. They may become increasingly reflective about both their work and themselves as they ponder over what to include in their portfolios and how it will demonstrate growth in their skills and understandings as their projects unfold.

 If you use portfolios to assess students' work what safeguards (rubrics) would you use to ensure that the samples of work included are valid and reliable?

In assessing the portfolios of their students, teachers can consider what the portfolios demonstrate about learnings in the broadest and deepest possible senses. For instance, teachers can consider the depth of students' understandings and their abilities to use evidence appropriately, to make connections among different ideas coherently and to develop their own points of view defensibly (Hay & Moss 2005).

Portfolios can include any number of things – not only finished work but also notes, drafts, preliminary models and plans, logs and other records; not only written work but also audiotapes, videotapes, CD-ROMs, photographs, three-dimensional creations and other artefacts. Students decide what to create and what to include in their portfolios; hence, the portfolios reveal not only what individual students have done but also the strategies they have used in making their decisions. Teachers therefore can assess not only the finished products that portfolios contain but also the processes students have followed in carrying out their projects. What kinds of decisions have been made? How wise have they been? Where have they led? What are the alternatives? There may be numerous opportunities as projects unfold for teachers to discuss these questions with students and thus to offer advice and constructive criticism. Much of the authenticity of assessing portfolios is in the opportunities they provide to both teachers and students for considering the development of interests, attitudes and values as well as skills and conventional academic learnings (Lyons 1999).

For all these reasons, the use of portfolios is consistent with constructivism. Schwager and Carlson (1995, p. 11) suggest:

> As a child grows he/she integrates information from the environment which results in the construction of personal theories or schemata about how the world works. As additional experiences and information are encountered, children 'fine-tune' and restructure their theories by elaboration and reorganisation of the cognitive structures they have created.

Advocacy of portfolios by cognitive psychologists and their use in well-known projects have also helped to build acceptance for them (Resnick & Klopfer 1989; Simmons & Resnick 1993), and teachers using portfolios have found that they provide both sensitive and credible evidence of student achievement to parents and the community.

Computer-assisted instruction enables students to do a variety of projects (individually or in groups) and these are useful inclusions in portfolios because they provide tangible evidence of a range of problem-solving skills. For example, Lifter and Adams (1997) claim that many of the eight levels of multiple intelligence are incorporated into computer software CD-ROMs. Eisner (1997) argues that computers can now create multimedia displays that capture meanings from alternative forms of data.

Niguidula (2005) contends that digital portfolios (multimedia collections of student work stored and reviewed in digital format) are especially useful as assessment tools.

Figure 18.8 lists some examples of what can be included in a portfolio, although in practice there is virtually no limit on what a portfolio might contain.

Students can be involved in planning portfolios and working out the minimum requirements. For example, a primary school teacher negotiated the following portfolio requirements with her class:
- a cover letter explaining the choices students made and describing themselves as learners
- a table of contents
- at least two samples related to their writing

- at least two samples related to their reading
- another piece of their own choosing.

Portfolios were graded on:
- how well the students compared the samples and explained why they were included
- the actual content (Was there enough? Was there too much?)
- neatness and organisation
- effort expended
- clarity and completeness of the cover letter (Case 1994, p. 46).

In a number of cases, teachers undertook individual interviews with students about their portfolios before awarding final grades.

An increasing number of teachers are exploring the use of portfolios as an important 'authentic' assessment tool because:
- students can reflect on what they have learnt (Calfee & Perfumo 1996)
- students do the selecting of what to include and have to justify their choices
- students value the opportunity to assemble their materials
- students can demonstrate what they have done and, by inference, what they are capable of doing (Salvia & Ysseldyke 1998)
- students have to demonstrate thinking and expressive skills
- it provides an equitable and sensitive portrait of what students know and are able to do
- it enables teachers to focus on important student outcomes
- it is a tangible way to display and celebrate students' achievements (McTighe 1997)
- it provides credible evidence of student achievement to parents and the community (Hebert 1998).

Many states mandate that school systems use portfolios as a part of student assessment (Hebert 1998). Once mandated, however, portfolios and their use are almost always subject to external controls far removed from individual classrooms, thereby potentially undermining the very authenticity for which student portfolios are valued in the first place. These external controls may be necessary to demonstrate the credibility of portfolios to the general public, but some educators have questioned whether the move to state level acceptance so quickly can be justified. For example, Herman and Winters (1994) note that:
- inter-rater agreement on portfolio assessments from state reports is very low
- portfolio grades have only moderate correlations with other forms of assessment (for example, a moderate correlation of .47 between writing portfolio scores and direct writing assessments)
- portfolios may not represent an individual student's work but the efforts of several supporting peers, teachers or parents
- for teachers, the time taken in choosing portfolio tasks, preparing portfolio lessons and assessing portfolios is burdensome

FIGURE 18.8 Examples of what a student portfolio might contain

- Essays
- Journals
- Summaries
- Records, such as daily logs
- Self-assessments, such as checklists and rating forms
- Experiments
- Demonstration of skills
- Rough drafts and finished products

- Research notes
- Team or group activities
- Creative works
- Major projects or products, such as dioramas, oral history collections, audiotapes and videotapes, photographs, charts, cards and timelines
- Tests
- Teacher comments

- there are major costs involved in staff training, development of portfolio specifications, administration of portfolio records and their storage.

Torrance and Pryor (1995), referring to 'authentic' assessment trials in the UK, also voice caveats about being too ambitious and over-enthusiastic about these approaches, because the additional responsibilities for teachers in busy classrooms will be enormous.

> **YOUR TURN**
>
> - Identify a performance task that would be suitable for your students. Develop a set of guidelines that will help students understand what is required.
> - Develop a detailed rubric that will be used to score students' performance on the task. What were some of the problems you experienced in developing the rubric?

Merits of portfolios
1. Students find producing portfolios meaningful and good for their self-esteem.
2. Students have to justify their choices.

Demerits of portfolios
1. It is very time-consuming to asses portfolios.
2. It is difficult to establish appropriate rubrics.

18.9 RECORD-KEEPING AND REPORTING

Record-keeping for many teachers may be perceived as a chore, but it is impossible to rely on one's memory for details about students' learning and achievements. Record-keeping is typically undertaken because:
- It helps teachers monitor the progress of individual students and to use it as a basis for planning future learning experiences – it serves a formative function.
- Parents require detailed reporting of their child's achievements at regular intervals.
- The information can be useful for placement of students in subsequent years.
- The information is required by the school or state system or nationally, as an accountability measure (Sutton 1992).

Record-keeping can be very time-consuming and it is often quite instructive to reflect upon the range and type of record-keeping that is currently used. Some pertinent questions to ask about each item include:
- Why do this?
- Who is it for?
- Does it really match up with the original purpose?
- What happens to the data collected and recorded?
- Who actually uses it and for what purpose?
- Could it be organised more rationally to save time and effort?
- Would computer-records assist?

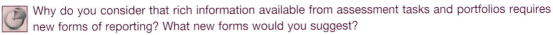
Why do you consider that rich information available from assessment tasks and portfolios requires new forms of reporting? What new forms would you suggest?

Of the records normally kept by a teacher (such as test records, subject records, samples of students' work, diagnostic information about each student, daily lesson notes and anecdotal records), the format of record or mark books has changed dramatically as a result of outcomes-based approaches.

The development of national statements and profiles in Australia, although aborted by the states in 1993, did lead to the creation of a common language relating to key learning areas, outcome statements and levels. Although it might be argued that this was a positive development and a means of reducing differences between the states, it has in turn created an increased workload for teachers. What information does a teacher record about each student – their success on outcome statements, or on specific strands and sub-strands, or on achieving a level?

Clearly the workload for teachers would be overwhelming if students were assessed on outcome statements for, say, 1 or 2 levels commensurate with the age group or ability of the students – this could represent 5–10 separate assessments and records. Alternatively, if assessments were only made of achieving a level (for example, assessing whether a student is at level 4 or 5), then this might provide insufficient information.

There is also the matter of how frequently the assessment and reporting is to occur. Most states and territories are working on the basis of assessing and reporting only once per year on the profiles with traditional assessments being used more frequently, such as once per term or once per semester. Many states and territories have now moved to requiring teachers to record reduced amounts of information.

The use of the profiles to date reveals that computer programs are essential to cope with the onerous task of recording assessment data from the profiles. Some software that has proved very popular includes CSI Profiles, DUX and KIDMAP (McLean & Wilson 1995; NSW Department of Education 2008b).

The ACER (Australian Council for Educational Research) and commercial publishers have taken the initiative in preparing assessment materials based on the profiles and for which easy-to-use computer programs have been developed. For example, the DART package (Forster 1994) was produced to assist teachers of upper primary and lower secondary classes to assess the strands of the English profile (viewing, reading, listening, speaking and writing). Assessment tasks were produced that enable teachers to observe students' use of particular skills in context. For example, Figure 18.9 depicts developmental skills and understandings in reading that are directly linked to the outcome statements and pointers. The number of achieved skills and understandings in the first column in Figure 18.9 can be matched to profile levels in the second column. A computer program is available that will readily produce a report for each student on each of the five strands in the English profile.

The DART range has been increased to include a similar array of assessment tasks that address the student outcomes in upper primary and junior secondary Mathematics, namely outcomes associated with the strands of number, measurement, space, chance and data. There are also other ACER packages that are aligned to the National Profile levels such as the Progressive Achievement Tests in Mathematics (King 1998) and iAchieve (ACER 2004; 2008).

Informative assessment booklets have also been published by the ACER on a range of topics including 'Portfolios' and 'Understanding Developmental Assessment' (Assessment Resource Kit (ARK), ACER 1996).

It is anticipated that many more innovatory packages will become available in the near future to assist teachers with the task of assessing and recording students' achievements on the profiles (Forster 2005). This will be essential, otherwise teachers will be devoting so much of their daily time to assessing, recording and reporting that their time for teaching will be greatly reduced.

18.9.1 Trends in reporting

Parents have a major role in schools and they have a right to receive regular school reports about the achievements of their children. However, because all parents have experienced schooling in the past, they have expectations about the format of reports and what they consider to be the highest priorities in reporting. There can also be a considerable generation gap between parents' experiences at school and current education provisions.

FIGURE 18.9 ACER – Record of a student's level of performance on the Reading strand, English Profile Form A

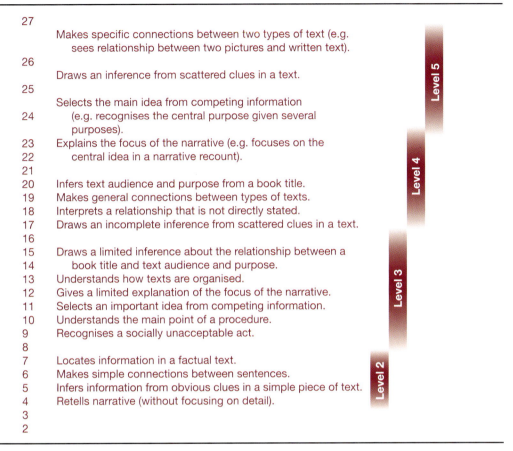

Source: M. Forster et al. 1994, *DART English Manual*, p. 41, reproduced by permission of the Australian Council for Educational Research.

The new and more complex forms of assessment clearly demand new forms of reporting (Wiggins 1998). Yet changes to reporting are not welcomed by parents if they create, in turn, further anxieties for them. Most educators agree about basic principles of reporting, namely:
- The process of communication must be fair, timely, confidential and clear (Loyd & Loyd 1997).
- The basis for comparing students' performance must be made known and be credible.
- The relative weight attached to categories that make up the final grade must be made explicit and kept uniform across students and teachers.
- Any summary judgments made in the report must be supported by data (Wiggins 1998).

A number of schools are now changing the type of communication they send to parents. The mailing to the parents of a single-sheet report form once a term or once a semester as the only form of communication has changed drastically. Schools now use:
- a variety of written reports
- parent–teacher meetings and interviews
- parent information evenings
- leaflets to explain new curriculum or assessment procedures
- newsletters.

The grades used on student reports are also changing, although residual approaches still occur. Quantitative scores out of 10 or 100 (percentage) for each school subject are deceptively simple. Sutton (1992) offers the caveat that the use of numbers has never been and never will be sufficient to describe the learning and development of students.

Letter grades can provide a guide to student achievement, but they abstract a great deal of information into a single symbol (Wiggins 1998). Further, the cut-off between grade categories is always arbitrary.

Narrative and descriptive accounts are popular with some teachers. These qualitative accounts certainly provide a more complete picture for parents, but they are time-consuming for teachers to prepare. A tendency, especially with word-processing packages, has been to standardise descriptive accounts into concise sentences that can then be selected from an 'item bank' and used in various subjects. This may be the solution to the time pressures of qualitative accounts, but it also reduces their impact and usefulness for parents.

Checklists of learning outcomes can be brief or very detailed and complicated. In many cases, checklists are difficult for parents to interpret without detailed explanations.

The directive by the Commonwealth Government, reluctantly agreed upon by the states because of the funding stipulations, might well be perceived by many educators to be a retrograde step in reporting student's achievements.

All education systems in Australia must use an A to E grading system for all key learning areas and a child's achievement must be reported relative to the child's peer group in the school by quartile bands. Izard (2005) refers to this Commonwealth initiative as the reintroduction of 'meaningless comparative letter grades' (p. 6). Moss and Godinho (2007) describe the action 'as being politically coerced into a reductionist and technical solution' (p. 4).

This directive could signal a change to more traditional forms of assessment and lead to further reductions in authentic assessment in Australia. As concluded by Moss and Godinho (2007) 'there is in a Australia a populist allegiance to twentieth-century post-war nostalgia and a numbing reproduction of the least effective learning practices when letter-grade reporting is adopted' (p. 16).

18.10 | NEW DEVELOPMENTS IN ASSESSMENT AND REPORTING

Two major factors are currently driving assessment in many countries: the emphasis on performance assessment and the priority given to standards and accountability.

Recent efforts to develop a comprehensive picture of student learning have involved systematically combining multiple choice formats and performance formats. Performance assessment formats have been used very successfully for writing (Heck & Crislip 2001). To date, performance assessments in writing have been well received by schools because they provide a relatively fair assessment and the learning tasks are directly related to classroom instruction (Supovitz & Brennan 1997; Baldwin 2004).

There are many other developments that are likely to make assessment more flexible and tailored to the needs of students and teachers. Consider the following:

- Computer adaptive testing (CAT) – CAT customises the assessment process so that the computer determines which level of questions to pose to the student – if a student answers a question correctly then he/she receives a more difficult item. Although expensive to develop at present, more customised versions are likely to be developed.
- Large-scale testing can now be done at computerised testing centres – students take their test online and receive their scores instantaneously.
- In the classroom (or at home) students can download specific assessment programs and then transmit them to the teacher or computer for scoring.
- Technology allows a variety of test-and-response formats using the computer's video and audio capabilities. Students will be able to answer orally or by constructing answers on the screen. Computer software will be able to translate items into many languages.

- Automated essay grading has made major advances, and prototypes are now available for use on a standard Windows PC and just using a single model answer (Williams 2001).
- Plagiarism and cheating by students are being thwarted by using software programs that screen student-written papers against databases of online resources (ASCD 2005, 5 December).
- Much of the paper testing we do today will become an anachronism. As students come to do the majority of their learning with technology, they will want the medium of assessment also to be technology (Bennett 2002).

E-assessments promise access to new content, immediate and automatic scoring and cheaper to deliver. Would you use them? Why or why not?

CONCLUDING COMMENTS

Assessment of students is a constant part of life in schools and very important element. Although some forms of assessment have stood the test of time and are still used widely (for example, external examinations), there have been enormous pressures over recent decades to widen the range of assessments and procedures.

It is likely that norm-referenced assessment will decrease as accountability focuses more on what students actually know and can do (Asp 2000). Performance assessment is likely to become far more prominent both in classrooms and for high-stakes testing. Electronic assessment will be integrated into the educational process along with online delivery of instruction.

KEY ISSUES RAISED IN THIS CHAPTER

1. Assessment-led reform is likely to continue as a major trend in all countries.
2. ICT assessment enables students to be assessed on wide-ranging content areas and real-world problems.
3. Assessment for learning (formative assessment) is currently being researched and promoted in many countries.
4. National assessment tests in literacy and numeracy in Australia may be useful but there are many caveats about their design and the impact upon teachers.
5. Performance assessment continues to be widely practiced in many countries especially through the use of assessment tasks and portfolios.
6. Outcomes-based assessment in Australia has largely been overtaken by standards and essential learnings.

REFLECTIONS AND ISSUES

1. Some educators argue that almost all kinds of traditional forms of assessment can be adapted for e-assessment. However are there some contexts where paper and pencil tests are still more suitable?
2. According to Wiliam (2006) 'only learners create learning, and so, when we look at the role that assessment plays in promoting learning, the crucial feature is not the validity of the assessment, or its reliability, but its impact on the student' (p. 2). Discuss.
3. Monitoring education systems from an output perspective is one of the major reasons for PISA and TIMSS. Yet PISA largely uses paper and pencil tests and does not use

computer-based testing. In so doing is PISA not tapping students' knowledge of real-life problems and issues?
4. To what extent is it possible to get students involved in self-assessment, peer assessment and deep learning?
5. With reference to a specific group of students, reflect on the assessment techniques you typically use. Why do you use these? Which others might you use in the future? Which ones would you not use? Give reasons.
6. 'Assessments should reflect on tasks students will encounter in the world outside schools and not merely those limited to the schools themselves' (Eisner 1993, p. 226). How might this be done? Give details of techniques you would use to achieve this end.
7. How can assessment help a student to learn? What information or feedback do they need to have, when and how? Describe an assessment technique that illustrates how assessment can help a student.
8. Some might argue that teachers' marking and grading practices tend to emphasise competition rather than personal improvement. What can be done to bring about more personal improvement in students?
9. 'Technology opens up new design choices for assessment so there is great importance on making these wisely. When attention is focused on technology at the expense of thinking through the assessment argument, worse assessment can actually result' (Mislevy 2002, p. 27). Do we need to be careful about over-enthusiasm in using technology? Discuss.
10. 'Technology is becoming a medium for learning and work ... as schools integrate technology into the curriculum, the method of assessment should reflect the tools employed in thinking and learning' (Bennett 2002, p. 8). Discuss.

Special references

Brady, L & Kennedy, K (2008) *Celebrating Student Achievement: Assessment and Reporting*, 3rd edn, Pearson Education, Sydney.
Carr, M (2001) *Assessment in Early Childhood Settings*, Sage, Thousand Oaks, CA.
Harlen, W (2007) *Assessment of Learning*, Sage, Thousand Oaks, CA.
Hay, T & Moss, J (2005) (eds) *Portfolios, Performance and Authenticity*, Pearson Education, Sydney.
Johnson, RL Penny, JA & Gordon, B (2009) *Assessing Performance*, Guilford Press, New York.
Klenowski, V (2002) *Developing Portfolios for Learning and Assessment*, Routledge Falmer, London.
Wiggins, G (1998) *Educative Assessment*, Jossey-Bass, San Francisco.
Wright, RJ (2008) *Educational Assessment*, Sage, Thousand Oaks, CA.

Web sources

For additional resources on assessment and reporting, please go to:
www.pearson.com.au/myeducationlab.

PART 5
THE TEACHING PROFESSION

Taking it to the Classroom
www.pearson.com.au/myeducationlab

Number of years teaching: 2 years
Year level teaching now: Year 1

First day of teaching memories:

I remember on my first day of school here [Melbourne Girls Grammar] I was so nervous. I actually grabbed the wrong child to take into my classroom! So, that sticks out clearly. The other memory that sticks out really clearly is the student that walked in and she had the biggest smile and her parents said to me, 'She's ready for Year 1', and I thought that was just beautiful.

Roshan Lee
Melbourne Girls Grammar

- chapter 19   Professional and cultural dimensions of teaching
- chapter 20   Ethical and legal issues in teaching
- chapter 21   Teacher competencies and standards

19
PROFESSIONAL AND CULTURAL DIMENSIONS OF TEACHING

19.1 | INTRODUCTION

The characteristics of a profession, at first glance, may appear to be clear-cut; however, this is far from true. In terms of the teaching profession it is even more problematic (Darling-Hammond 2006; Caldwell & Harris 2008). Strictly speaking, teachers do not control their own entry or stipulate the qualifications of teachers – two fundamental criteria of a profession – and so it might be argued that teaching is not a profession. Yet, it satisfies the other criteria of a profession – commitment to intellectual activities and the command of a body of specialised knowledge – very well.

Teachers acquire their professional skills within a specific context, the school. The school culture affects, and is affected by, the actions of teachers. Principals and school leaders attempt to mould the school culture according to specific goals. However, school cultures also have a unique resilience and changes do not come easily.

In this chapter we will examine some of the tangible and intangible elements of the culture of the school and how teachers interact with it.

19.2 | PROFESSION – MEANINGS AND INTERPRETATIONS

The use of the term 'profession' has its origins in Europe where it was used synonymously with the term 'occupation'. During the eighteenth century differences of status were accorded to certain occupations – such as the Anglican clergy, barristers and physicians – and these were known as the 'learned' or 'liberal' professions, largely because their practitioners would have studied Latin and normally were graduates of Oxford or Cambridge Universities (Perkin 1987, p. 13). According to Perkin, the terms 'learned' and 'liberal' were jettisoned over the intervening centuries, leaving us now with the multiple confusions and ambiguities of the term 'profession'.

Census publications use the words 'profession' and 'occupation' interchangeably. The term 'teaching profession' is widely used, yet it is unclear whether it is widely accepted by the general public.

Ryan and Cooper (2008) argue that it is the very nobility of the teacher's work that is evidence of its status as a profession. Teachers pass on to the young key skills that they need. Further, teachers have an enormous amount of independence and personal control within their respective classrooms. But is teaching a comparable profession with other professions such as law or medicine? If not, what criteria could be used to show the distinction? Lester (2007) suggests that perhaps teaching is a 'secondary profession' and law and medicine are 'primary professions'.

One way of trying to resolve such issues is to examine criteria that have been proposed to characterise a profession. Apart from the commonality of many of the criteria listed in the three classifications in Figure 19.1, it is instructive to reflect on how these criteria might be interpreted.

Using the Travers and Reborc (1990) core criteria as a basis for further discussion, the first criterion of 'a lifelong career commitment' is certainly problematic in Australia in the twenty-first century. Although it might have been assumed, especially in earlier decades, that teaching was a lifetime occupation, this is far from the case now. In addition to the effects of boom periods, which can attract many teachers into more remunerative positions in private industry (such as the current mining boom in northern Western Australia), a widespread state of concern and low morale among teachers is creating considerable movement out of teaching. This aspect is discussed in more detail later in this chapter in section 19.6 'Career structures'.

Few would deny that 'social service' is an important criterion for teachers, as many prospective teachers enter teaching for altruistic reasons. The desire to facilitate the growth and development of children is a very strong motivating factor. As noted by Stake (1987, p. 58), 'we deliberately try to change them and seldom exactly as they would change themselves. We interfere with their lives convinced we are helping them to something better.' All the more reason for teachers to be high level professionals if we are involved in such sensitive change processes with so many individuals over a lifetime career.

The criterion of 'intellectual techniques and activities' is a major focus of teaching, since most classroom activities are predominantly thinking activities.

The last two criteria in Figure 19.1 – 'code of ethics' and 'independent judgment relative to professional performance' – appear to be indicative of intentions rather than actual practice. The creation of the Australian Teaching Council in 1994 was an endeavour to develop national level standards and to define and establish independent judgments about the professional rights and obligations of teachers, even though it was disestablished two years later. The National Institute for Quality Teaching and School Leadership (NIQTSL) was established in 2004 to provide the opportunity to advance teacher quality and status. It is too early to judge whether it will be successful in terms of the above criteria (see also Chapter 21).

The major difficulty is that teachers are legally and financially dependent upon education system employers. It is the employers who assess professional performance and establish the activities of their employees. Thus, it is the employers who are largely involved in defining for teachers what it means to be a professional. Whether they have a legitimate right to do so is problematic (Lawton 2005). Further, Woods (2000) contends that employers are increasingly defining the teacher professional in performance terms – nearer to the innovative, enterprising, competitive entrepreneur of the private sector.

Not surprisingly, some authors argue that teaching is more like a skilled trade than a learned profession. For example, Connell (1985, p. 176) noted in his research on teachers that many do not think of teaching as a profession at all: 'it is a job, not a calling, with fixed limits of time and emotional involvement'. Apple and Aasen (2003) are also pessimistic about endeavours to improve teaching as a profession given the recent attacks on the working conditions and autonomy of teachers in many Western countries. Doring (1994) and Goodson (2005) contend that there has been a gradual erosion of the teaching profession in the United Kingdom since the introduction of the National Curriculum.

 Do you consider that teaching is a profession and much more than a skilled trade? Consider points for and against this statement.

FIGURE 19.1 Characteristics of a profession – three perspectives

1 A profession:
- involves activities, essentially intellectual
- commands a body of specialised knowledge
- requires extended professional preparation
- demands continuous in-service growth
- affords a life career and permanent membership
- sets up its own standards
- exalts service above personal gain
- has a strong, closely knit, professional organisation.

(Stinnett & Huggett 1963, p. 57)

2 A profession:
- gives a specialised, unique service that is essential to society
- possesses intellectual techniques
- offers a long period of training and professional socialisation
- enjoys a high degree of growth and individual professional autonomy
- exercises its own means of social control through the enforcement of a code of ethics
- commands a high level of commitment in which work and leisure hours are not easily demarcated
- offers a lifetime calling within a career structure
- encourages the pursuit of research, the diffusion of knowledge and in-service training.

(Purvis 1973, p. 57)

3 A profession involves:
- a lifelong career commitment
- social service
- intellectual techniques and activities
- a code of ethics
- independent judgement relative to professional performance.

(Travers & Reborc 1990, p. 11)

19.3 | PROFESSIONALISATION AND PROFESSIONAL DEVELOPMENT

Professionalisation is the process whereby members of a profession increasingly aspire to meet the criteria of their group (Johnson & Maclean 2008). That is, in terms of each of the criteria listed in Figure 19.1, such as career commitment and provision of social service, it is necessary for members to aspire to higher standards. The more successful members become in achieving and raising the standards of their criteria, the greater the opportunity for increased status (Gold & Evans 1998; Shulman 2007).

Professional development is the process whereby members go about improving their competencies (Wayne et al. 2008). According to Marginson (1993), professional development is the process of growth in competence and maturity through which teachers add range, depth and quality to their performance of their professional tasks. Given a supportive environment, and personal commitment by members, professional development can be maximised (Goodrum 2007).

Ingvarson (2002a) contends that professional learning for teachers in the twenty-first century must be based on three main principles, namely:
- Professional development content should focus on what students are to learn and how to address the different problems students may have in learning the material.
- Professional development should be based on analyses of the differences between (a) actual student performance and (b) goals and standards for student learning.

- Professional development should involve teachers in the identification of what they need to learn and in the development of the learning experiences in which they will be involved (p. 7).

McDiarmid (1995) focuses more on the needs of teachers in considering professional development. He advocates the need for colleagues to work together and the establishing of a larger learning community. Above all, he argues that professional development must be redefined as a central part of teaching and that policy makers and the general public must realise that this is an essential initiative.

Darling-Hammond (2006) also notes that many policy makers and lay people have a lack of understanding about the need for professional development.

It is difficult to judge whether professionalisation efforts over the last decade have raised the professional status of teachers or not. If consideration is given to the longer period of initial training, now based wholly in universities, and the graduate entry level for all new teachers, it might be conjectured that the general public might accord the teaching profession a higher status. This is certainly the stance taken by Lovat and McLeod 2006. Yet the pressing demands on teachers for accountability and quality teaching, as well as media publicity given to adverse results, could indicate that many groups are dissatisfied with teaching as a profession.

Spaull (1997) and Brown *et al.* (1996) contend that in some states, especially Victoria, there has been a de-professionalisation of teaching because of managerial interventions which have led to an erosion of teachers' rights and conditions of employment.

The prevailing economic rationalism is also working adversely on teacher professionalism because of its emphasis on information and skills in a narrow technical sense, to the exclusion of liberalism (Reid & Thomson 2003; Kennedy 2009).

Whitty (1994) argues that teaching is being de-professionalised by the emphasis on teacher competencies and craft skills rather than professional understanding. In a later paper, Whitty (2006) argues for a democratic professionalism that would attempt to demystify professional work and build alliances between teachers and a wide range of other stakeholders.

It should be noted that, if professional development activities for teachers are largely school-focused rather than university-based, this could lead to government initiatives to reduce initial training and generally lead to a lowering of the professional status of teachers. Lifelong career commitment is an important criterion for the profession (see Figure 19.1), but only if theoretical and practical elements are both pursued vigorously in professional development programs (Firestone 1993; Korthagen 2004).

> **YOUR TURN**
>
> As a beginning teacher, have you reflected on the professional competencies you currently have?
> - Try to list them and justify your choice.
> - Are there other professional competencies you are keen to develop?

19.4 | PROFESSIONS – LESSONS FROM HISTORY

Perkin (1987, pp. 14–16) has analysed the growth of professions over the centuries and has noted some interesting patterns:
- Groups aggressively carve out a niche for their respective organisations to give themselves the status, remuneration and security they feel entitled to whether they satisfy the criteria of professions or not.

- Success depends mainly on the resources that each group can mobilise. The main resource they can offer is the quality of their service to the public.
- Each profession uses its rhetoric and persuasion to 'sell' the quality of its service.
- Groups that control access to a scarce resource (such as medicine) do not need to be well organised. Other groups (for example, accountants) rely on strong organisation of knowledge, control of training and entry and publicity to ensure their status.

Perkin (1987) argues that teachers have not been very successful in raising the status of their profession. Until the late Victorian age in England, most teachers were clergymen or their dependents and as a result were accorded relatively low status. The reasons for the limited success of the teaching profession in the eighteenth century seem to be just as relevant in the twenty-first century:

- low status
- inability to control their own selection, training and qualification
- divided and ineffective organisation
- state interference and control
- low remuneration.

 What do your friends and family have to say about the status of teaching? What reasons do they give for having either a high opinion or a low opinion of teaching as a profession?

It is unfortunate but true that many members of the community believe that 'anyone' can teach. Unqualified teachers continue to be appointed to some non-government schools and to many universities. The service of teachers is little valued compared with professional services for medical treatment, legal advice or tax avoidance! Teaching has been cheap or free for so long that this continues to be the public's expectation of the profession.

Teaching as a profession can also be perceived differently across countries. Webb *et al.* (2004) compared conceptions of teacher professionalism in England and Finland. They concluded that in England teacher professionalism is associated with a drive to raise standards and with 'commercialised professionalism', while in Finland the major focus for teacher professionalism is on 'teacher empowerment'.

Sachs' (1997) study of teacher professionalism in Australia concludes that award restructuring and school reform in the late 1980s and early 1990s provided the political and professional conditions for public debate about teacher professionalism and its enactment within educational institutions. She cites two national Australian projects, the National Schools Network and the Innovative Links between Schools and Universities, as 'exemplars of how teachers both individually and collectively have been actively reclaiming the agenda for teacher professionalism in Australia' (p. 276).

Perkin (1987) argues that competing teacher organisations have not helped the profession because of their in-fighting. Primary school teachers in some states are segregated from secondary school teacher organisations.

As noted above, a major reason for the weakness of the teaching profession (Woods 2000; Whitty 2006) is the power of the monopolistic employer, the state. It controls 70–75 per cent of schools in each state and territory and influences all non-government systems in terms of curriculum and assessment. Within state schools, the state controls the remuneration and conditions of service of teachers.

19.5 | THE AUSTRALIAN TEACHING PROFESSION

The careers of Australian teachers can be described and analysed in various ways. In terms of basic statistics it should be noted that the number of teachers in Australian schools has nearly doubled over the last two decades and that teachers constitute 29 per cent of those individuals classified by the Australian Bureau of Statistics as being in a 'professional' occupation.

The earnings of full-time teachers have increased over recent years largely due to industrial action and strong representations by teachers' unions. The majority in 2007 earned between $50 000 and $60 000 (24% primary; 21% secondary) and between $70 000 and $80 000 (35% primary; 36% secondary) (McKenzie *et al.* 2008).

The proportion of teachers teaching in Catholic and independent schools rather than government schools continues to increase, especially at secondary level. Statistics in 2002 (ISCA 2002) revealed that 17% of all primary teachers taught in Catholic schools; 10% of all primary teachers in independent schools, and 73% of all teachers taught in government schools.

The emphasis at the secondary school level is even more marked. Of all secondary teachers, 20% taught in Catholic schools and 17% in independent schools, whereas only 63% of secondary teachers taught in government schools. Figures for 2010, if available, would be likely to show an even greater swing toward Catholic and independent schools. Within each education system it is evident that females predominate in primary schools whereas at the secondary level the proportion of female teachers is only slightly higher (see Table 19.1).

 Why do you consider the number of teachers wanting to teach in non-government schools keeps increasing? Do you think that there will ever be more teachers in non-government than government schools?

Also it should be noted that the breakdown of full-time and part-time teaching positions in 2007 revealed that there were 25% part-time female primary school teachers (compared with 9% part-time male teachers) and 22% part-time female secondary school teachers (compared with 7% part-time male teachers).

Teachers at both primary and secondary schools clearly work long hours each week on school-related activities. McKenzie *et al.* (2008) found that in 2007, 70% of primary school teachers and 71% of secondary school teachers worked between 41 and 60 hours per week.

 Did you anticipate the high number of hours teachers work on school-related activities each week? What activities would these be? Should support staff be employed to assist with time-consuming, non-teaching tasks?

TABLE 19.1 Proportions of female and male teachers

	Females %	**Males** %	**Missing data** %	
Primary teachers				
Government	80	20	1	100
Catholic	80	20	1	100
Independent	80	20	1	100
	79	20	1	100
Secondary teachers				
Government	57	43	1	100
Catholic	56	44	1	100
Independent	56	44	1	100
	56	43	1	100

Source: McKenzie et al. (2008) 'Staff in Australia's Schools Survey, 2007'. Copyright Commonwealth of Australia, reproduced by permission.

McKenzie et al. (2008) note that school teaching is one of the most female-intensive professional occupations in Australia and the degree of feminisation appears to be increasing. Yet it is also the case that, despite schools being highly feminised workplaces, a disproportionate percentage of principalships are held by males (Collard 2000). Whitehead's (2001) study of middle schooling in Australia also concludes that male teachers still predominate as administrators and the male hierarchy continues to prevail in many schools.

Teachers progress through four major promotional levels from entry into teaching to the position of school principal. The opportunities for promotion are typically based on qualifications, seniority and length of service and, in some situations, assessments of merit. Recent surveys reveal a slowing down of promotional opportunities due to the ageing of the teaching population and reduced resignation rates.

The global economic crisis commencing in 2008 may have caused a number of older teachers to delay their retirement plans. Younger teachers who had previously considered moving to other careers might have also reconsidered this option in the light of the global economic crisis. McKenzie et al. (2008) discovered that in 2007 the number of males and females who planned to leave teaching was still considerable.

Teaching is becoming more specialised in secondary schools and there is also an increase in the number of subject specialists in primary schools in subjects such as Art, Music, Physical Education and Languages.

McKenzie et al. (2008) assert that teachers are now better qualified, more experienced and work in schools that are far better resourced.

There can, however, be variations in different education systems and between rural and urban schools. Independent schools have become increasingly popular over recent decades (see Table 19.1). These schools offer a traditional form of education, usually with a religious affiliation, and parents pay considerable fees for the privilege of sending their children to these institutions. The schools vary enormously in levels of prestige but all operate as a community with well-articulated goals. Career opportunities in independent schools are relatively limited, but there are often other incentives such as merit pay linked to 'senior teacher' awards and related positions of responsibility.

Catholic education systems in all states and territories expanded rapidly during the 1970s as a result of Commonwealth government funding. This also necessitated the development of centralised administrative structures, Catholic Education Commissions, to coordinate, plan and manage a wide range of educational services. Teachers in Catholic schools are typically selected on their vocational commitment to teaching and to deeply felt, personal, professional and spiritual values (Christie & Smith 1991). Salaries of teachers have tended to be lower than for government school counterparts, but more adequate funding over recent years has enabled a higher level of comparability.

The distribution of teachers across Australia largely mirrors the distribution of the total population (see Table 19.2). In 2007, 72% of the primary school teachers were teaching in metropolitan centres and 28% in provincial and remote areas. Secondary school teachers mirrored similar figures, 68% teaching in metropolitan centres and 32% teaching in provincial and remote areas.

TABLE 19.2 Geographic location of teachers

School location	Primary	Secondary
Metropolitan	72	68
Provincial	24	30
Remote	4	2
	100	100

Source: McKenzie et al. (2008) 'Staff in Australia's Schools Survey, 2007'. Copyright Commonwealth of Australia, reproduced by permission.

Rural teachers are generally highly valued by their local community. They are accorded considerable status because of their economic and social contributions to rural life, but this in turn can place considerable pressures on rural teachers and their respective families (Dinham & Scott 2000). Although many teachers appreciate rural life, it does have its problems – especially the conflicting pressures of focusing on local perspectives and the rural heritage, but not to such an extent that rural children's life chances in metropolitan locations are diminished.

Teaching in the twenty-first century is complex for teachers (Ingvarson 2002b; Darling-Hammond 2006; Caldwell & Harris 2008) because they will have to manage a multiplicity of roles, including:
- balancing pressures for more academic rigour while also preparing students for an active and socially responsible role in society
- managing and using various technologies including the Internet, CD-ROMs and subsequent, inevitable refinements.

Dinham and Scott (2000) refer to a research study of teachers in New South Wales in the 1990s in which teachers were requested to list some of their major satisfactions and dissatisfactions about teaching (see Table 19.3). In a later study covering samples of teachers in Australia, the United Kingdom and the United States, Dinham and Scott (2000) concluded that there are three broad domains of teacher satisfaction:
- the 'core' business of teaching (centred on student achievement, teacher efficacy and personal and professional self-growth)
- extrinsic aspects of teaching (status of teachers, educational change)
- a central domain of satisfaction factors (including conditions of work), which varied from school to school.

Dissatisfaction factors were noted as being:
- amount and nature of educational change and restructuring
- media and public criticism of teachers and schools
- status of teachers.

The 2007 study of Australia's schools by McKenzie *et al.* (2008) revealed that primary school teachers were satisfied with most aspects of their job except the 'amount of non-teaching work expected to do' and 'the value society places on teachers' work' (Table 19.4). For secondary school teachers there were a number of dissatisfactions relating to the amount of non-teaching work, the salary level, and the value society places on non-teaching work (Table 19.5).

Caldwell and Harris (2008) argue that teaching has become very different. It is necessary to redefine the core work of teachers and free up their role for undertaking other professional duties. Hatch, White and Faigenbaum (2005) assert that teachers can demonstrate expertise, credibility and influence in school activities regardless of the formal positions they hold. Teachers will need to have global perspectives and skills (Bates 1998).

TABLE 19.3 Sources of satisfaction and dissatisfaction for teachers

Sources of teacher satisfaction	Sources of teacher dissatisfaction
- student achievement and thus teacher accomplishment - changing student behaviour and attitudes - recognition from others (parents, teachers, superiors) - self growth and the mastering of subject content and teaching skills - good relationships with students, parents and other teachers	- relationship with superiors and employers - the standing of teachers in society - system level changes - promotional procedures - changes to school responsibilities and management - unwanted transfers to undesirable locations

TABLE 19.4 Primary teachers' job satisfaction

How satisfied are you with the following aspects of your job?	Very satisfied %	Satisfied %	Dissatisfied %	Very dissatisfied %	Unsure %	Missing %	%
Your working relationships with your colleagues	38	48	5	1	<0.5	8	100
Your working relationships with your principal	32	48	8	4	1	8	100
Your working relationships with parents/guardians	28	58	4	1	1	8	100
What you are currently accomplishing with students	24	58	9	1	1	8	100
The amount of teaching you are expected to do	23	57	8	4	<0.5	8	100
Your freedom to decide how to do your job	23	51	14	5	1	8	100
Your opportunities for professional learning	19	51	16	5	1	8	100
The resources at your school	16	48	22	6	<0.5	8	100
Student behaviour	11	50	21	10	<0.5	8	100
Your opportunities for career advancement	10	56	15	6	6	8	100
Feedback on your performance	9	56	19	6	2	8	100
The balance between working time and private life	8	43	27	14	1	8	100
The amount of non-teaching work expected to do	7	32	31	20	1	8	100
Your salary	6	46	28	11	1	8	100
The value society places on teachers' work	3	26	39	23	2	8	100
Overall, how satisfied are you with your current job?	*20*	*58*	*10*	*3*	*1*	*8*	*100*

Source: McKenzie et al. (2008) 'Staff in Australia's Schools Survey, 2007'. Copyright Commonwealth of Australia, reproduced by permission.

YOUR TURN

- At this stage of your training, what do you consider are the most satisfactory elements of teaching? Why?
- Are there other aspects of teaching that you have experienced which you don't find satisfying? Describe these aspects and explain why you feel this way.

TABLE 19.5 Secondary teachers' job satisfaction

How satisfied are you with the following aspects of your job?	Very satisfied %	Satisfied %	Dissatisfied %	Very dissatisfied %	Unsure %	Missing %	%
Your working relationships with your colleagues	36	51	5	1	<0.5	6	100
Your working relationship with your principal	28	51	9	4	2	6	100
Your freedom to decide how to do your job	23	55	10	6	1	6	100
Your working relationships with parents/guardians	20	66	6	1	2	6	100
What you are currently accomplishing with students	19	59	13	2	1	6	100
Your opportunities for professional learning	19	51	18	6	1	6	100
The resources at your school	13	48	24	9	1	6	100
Your opportunities for career advancement	11	54	16	8	4	6	100
Student behaviour	11	47	23	12	1	6	100
The balance between working time and private life	9	46	26	12	1	6	100
Feedback on your performance	8	58	20	6	3	6	100
The amount of non-teaching work expected to do	7	37	29	20	1	6	100
Your salary	5	44	31	14	1	6	100
The value society places on teachers' work	3	25	39	26	2	6	100
The amount of teaching you are expected to do	20	59	12	3	1	6	100
Overall, how satisfied are you with your current job?	*18*	*60*	*12*	*3*	*2*	*6*	*100*

Source: McKenzie et al. (2008) 'Staff in Australia's Schools Survey, 2007'. Copyright Commonwealth of Australia, reproduced by permission.

19.6 | CAREER STRUCTURES

Studies of teachers' lives provide illuminating information about expectations, motivations and frustrations of teaching and, in so doing, provide some insights into the reasons for the relatively low status of teaching as a profession. Using the logic of administrators, a teacher's career is defined by six variables: 'entry, progression along an incremental salary scale, transfer to one or more differing locations, taking leave, promotion to an administrative position, and resignation or retirement' (Schools Council 1990, p. 104).

Herein lies the problem. For many teachers their career future is featureless, lacking in challenges, and just more of the same. Research studies of life histories of teachers (for example, Huberman

1989; Goodson 2001; Kelchtermans & Vandenberghe 1994) indicate that many teachers follow well-defined patterns of behaviour – although there is initial excitement and experimentation, this is superseded by boredom and negative attitudes (see also Chapter 21).

The patterns depicted in Figure 19.2 are based on research studies examined by the Schools Council (1990). Although caveats should be noted about the patterns not applying in all cases and the effects of other external factors (such as the economic climate and political initiatives), the consistency of their appearance in research studies is very marked.

The career entry phase is very much a case of withstanding reality shock – trying to survive the complexity of the first year of teaching (Cruickshank, Jenkins & Metcalf 2009; Rieg, Paquette & Chen 2007). In terms of the American teaching year, which commences in September, Kevin Ryan's (1970) book title *Don't Smile Until Christmas* conjures up a very poignant position for newly appointed teachers. Surviving day one is often the most urgent goal! (Salvo *et al.* 2005). Yet there is also an exciting discovery element in trying out teaching ideas with one's own students and classroom.

 Beginning career burnout is perceived to be a major problem. How might workloads and support for beginning teachers be adjusted to reduce burnout from happening?

FIGURE 19.2 Lifecycle phases

Career entry (First year of teaching)
- reality shock, trial and error
- discovery – enthusiasm, learning

Stabilisation (2–5 years of teaching)
- firming up on teaching as a career
- more instruction-centred
- greater self-confidence
- more flexibility in classroom management
- fewer discipline problems
- assertions of independence

Diversification and change (5–15 years of teaching)
- experimentation to increase effectiveness
- quest for new challenges
- willingness to take up new responsibilities

Stocktaking (12–20 years of teaching)
- boredom with the routines of teaching
- consideration of career shifts

Serenity (15–30 years of teaching)
- reduced career ambition
- high levels of self-sufficiency and confidence
- increased distance from students

Conservatism (30–40 years of teaching)
- negative attitudes about students
- negative attitudes about fellow teachers and administrators
- cynicism about reform efforts

Disengagement (34–45 years of teaching)
- channelling of energies to outside pursuits
- preparation for retirement.

Source: Based on Schools Council 1990.

The time spent in each of the phases is, of course, problematic and for some teachers the time period may be quite considerable. As noted by Kelchtermans and Vandenberghe (1994), the research on lifecycle phases does not answer the question of movement or transition from one phase to the next. Is the transition gradual or is it discontinuous and disruptive? Do teachers experience critical incidents – key events – that lead a teacher into another phase?

For some newly appointed teachers, critical incidents occur that heighten their frustration and dissatisfaction to the extent that they decide that a teaching career is not for them (Cruickshank, Jenkins & Metcalf 2009; Martinez 2004). The vast majority, however, appear to progress to a 'stabilisation' phase.

The stabilisation phase is a critical one for many teachers, in that decisions are usually made at this point about whether they will continue in the profession or not (and for many this will mean a commitment for the next 40 or more years). Those teachers with special skills, and therefore with marketable qualities for other careers, have greatest difficulty in deciding on teaching or not teaching.

A teacher in this phase, notwithstanding decisions about career choice, now begins to grow in self-confidence, demonstrates more effective classroom management skills and experiences less discipline problems with students (Mok 2005).

Although the research literature is quite unequivocal about these first two phases, the other phases as listed in Figure 19.2 are less consistent. For many, the 'diversification and change' phase is experienced between 5 and 15 years of teaching. It is an exciting, challenging phase during which a teacher becomes engrossed in numerous trials and experiments.

By contrast, the next phase – 'stocktaking' – is one of uncertainty and perhaps exhaustion or cynicism. Teachers going through this phase after approximately 12–20 years of teaching are experiencing serious self-doubts about whether they are in the right occupation.

Matters appear to be rationalised by the next phase, 'serenity', at which time teachers have established more modest goals for themselves and are less concerned about their performance compared with that of their peers. For some teachers this is reflected in a lack of interest in new programs and changes and more of a desire to follow the existing routines.

The 'conservatism' phase is largely negative with considerable criticism of, if not antipathy towards, school procedures, other staff and students. This leads inexorably to a final phase of 'disengagement', where a teacher's energies are channelled more and more into outside pursuits and preparation for retirement.

 At different stages of a teaching career, a teacher can enjoy, love, get excited about, become emotionally drained by and develop chronic stress about teaching. What triggers the positive and the negative feelings about teaching? How do you think you will cope with these feelings over the years?

Although the phases may vary considerably between education systems and according to gender, they do reveal major career issues that are likely to have had, and continue to have, deleterious effects on teaching as a profession. For example, the relatively low status of teaching as a profession acts against attracting many high calibre applicants into teaching; of those who do enter, many become frustrated and leave after the career entry phase.

How to make a teaching career more rewarding and attractive is a very important issue (Wise 2001; Cochran-Smith 2006). Some ongoing solutions that have been discussed include:
- increasing teachers' salaries
- using wider selection methods than a tertiary entrance score to select teacher education students (for example, interviews to judge applicants' interpersonal skills)
- recognition awards for exemplary teaching
- merit pay (such as the senior teacher scale) for exemplary performances
- recognition of career milestones
- leave without pay after five years for professional refreshment

- paid study leave
- generous maternity leave
- secondments to or exchanges with the public service or industry
- regular and frequent opportunities for professional development.

The Schools Council (1990) argues that if a number of these incentives were built into a teacher's career structure, many of the undesirable attitudes and behaviours described above could be greatly reduced. For example, they assert that at the 'career entry' phase teachers need mentor support by an experienced teacher and a lower than normal teaching load. At the 'stabilisation' phase they contend that teachers should be encouraged to apply for particular positions of responsibility within their respective schools and to have sizeable periods of professional development. At the 'diversification and change' phase, teachers should have available to them leave without pay for one school year.

The National Conference on Quality Teaching in 2001 reaffirmed the need for incentives for teachers – to recognise, celebrate and reward the quality of the work that teachers do. The teaching force needs to be involved in the career continuum of improvement and transformation (Commonwealth Department of Employment, Training and Youth Affairs 2001).

Ingvarson (2002b) argues that improvements in teaching careers in Australia are dependent upon the development of a standards-based professional learning system (see also Chapter 21).

19.7 | CONTINUING ISSUES FOR THE TEACHING PROFESSION

Over recent years the teaching profession has been given considerable attention by politicians and the media. Inevitably, reactions have been both positive and negative. According to an OECD (Organisation for Economic Cooperation and Development 1990) report, some major reasons for the spotlight on teachers include:

- a profound dissatisfaction within the teaching profession in many countries and a deterioration in industrial relations between teachers and their employing authorities
- intense pressures on teachers to be accountable
- pursuit of quality as a general priority
- problems of teacher unemployment
- problems of adequate resources.

Whether the teaching profession is increasing in status and quality is uncertain. There is no question that the training of teachers has changed in terms of length of training and the increased rigour resulting from university-based training. Whether the quality of graduates is now higher is a more subjective matter and depends on priorities over school- or university-based training, the emphasis on foundation disciplines, and the opportunities for specialist training in areas such as special education and multicultural studies (Ashenden 1994; Caldwell & Harris 2008).

In particular, there are a number of issues that are of major concern to the teaching profession and these are addressed briefly below. They include:

- ageing of teachers
- women in teaching and the feminisation of teaching
- class relations
- empowerment
- teacher morale.

19.7.1 Ageing of teachers

Numerous statements in the media indicate that there is a 'greying' of the teaching force and that this is a source of concern (for example, NSW Dept of Education and Training Auditing Office 2008). For many OECD countries the average age of teachers is increasing, although it is argued that the base period for comparison (the mid-1970s) was an artificially low starting point. Further, in some

TABLE 19.6 Proportions of male and female teachers by age

Age band	Primary teachers			Secondary teachers		
	Male %	Female %	Persons %	Male %	Female %	Persons %
21–25	4	6	6	2	7	5
26–30	14	12	12	7	13	11
31–35	12	10	10	10	9	10
36–40	11	10	11	11	11	11
41–45	11	12	12	13	14	14
46–50	17	18	17	17	17	16
51–55	19	19	19	21	17	19
56–60	10	8	9	13	10	11
61–65	2	3	3	3	3	3
66+	<0.5	<0.5	<0.5	1	<0.5	1
Missing data	2	1	2	1	1	1
	100	100	100	100	100	100
Average age	43	43	43	46	43	44

Source: McKenzie et al. (2008) 'Staff in Australia's Schools Survey, 2007'. Copyright Commonwealth of Australia, reproduced by permission.

countries there are major differences between males and females, with females being older on average than males. McMahon (2000) notes that in the UK in 1998, 60 per cent of teachers in England and Wales were aged 40 or over and 19 per cent were 50 or over. She also notes that there are increasing problems of recruitment into teaching in the UK – it is widely recognised as a high stress profession.

With reference to Australia, similar percentages are evident for 2007, as listed in Table 19.6. In summary, 59 percent of male primary school teachers and 67 percent of male secondary school teachers were aged 40 or over. The comparable figures for female teachers were 60 percent and 61 percent. Mayer (2006) notes that the teacher workforce in Australia is generally older than the rest of the professional workforce, with the highest proportion of teachers aged in their middle to late forties. She argues that we should analyse very carefully the aspirations and career expectations of the 'Generation X' or 'GenXers' (born between 1965 and 1979–80) and compare them with those of the 'Baby Boomers' (born from around the mid-1940s to the mid-1960s). Mayer's review of relevant literature on GenXers concludes that they are more likely to:
- prioritise family and personal values over high income
- have little loyalty to just one organisation
- take a non-linear path from education into work
- be sceptical of the status quo and authority
- seek flexible work practices
- seek the opportunity to learn (Mayer 2006, p. 67).

Mayer (2006) contends that policies for teacher employment and career opportunities should take note of GenXer preferences, especially with regard to giving new teachers opportunities to use their knowledge and skills and to allow more flexible work practices (Lacey & Gronn 2007). In particular, Mayer (2006) concludes that 'rigid standards and accountability practices seem at odds with the personal autonomy and input to decision making that young generations of workers seek' (p. 68).

Richardson and Watt (2006) in their large-scale Australian study also conclude that policy makers should not focus on a limited number of values for teacher education programs but must consider social utility values (opportunities to shape the future and enhance social equity) as well as personal utility values (time for family, job transferability). Hodkinson and Hodkinson's (2005) study of secondary school teachers in the UK concluded that the current policy approaches in the UK are 'over-focused on the acquisition of measurable learning outcomes, short-term gains and priorities that are external to the teachers' (p. 109).

19.7.2 Women in teaching and the feminisation of teaching

Various writers, such as Apple and Aasen (2003), Connell (1985) and Cavanagh (2005), provide convincing arguments about the direct and indirect sex discrimination that occurs in teaching and especially the under-representation of women in management roles (Whitehead 2001).

The feminisation of the teaching profession is not a recent phenomenon – it can be traced back to mass education in the 1800s. So, is it really a problem to have mainly females teaching primary school students?

Women clearly predominate in numbers at the pre-primary and primary school teaching levels (teaching is feminised at these levels), but at the secondary school level numbers are more evenly balanced (Capel, Leask & Turner 1997). In terms of leadership posts, women are markedly under-represented as principals in many OECD countries (Collard 2000). If anything, the trend is for female representation to be deteriorating. There are considerable pressures on women seeking management positions, such as family considerations and a negative stereotyping of leadership, compared with males (Yates 1998).

The number of females in teaching compared with males has brought about recent media attention to issues such as desirable gender balance and boys' underachievement due to a lack of male teachers.

Reports on these issues provide divergent findings. For example a Parliament of the Government of Australia Report (2002) concluded that the lower levels of academic engagement and achievement among boys reflected the reduced status and loss of confidence of males in the post-feminist era and recommended measures to counter male disaffection from school. Various Australian researchers such as Lingard (2003) and Mills, Martino and Lingard (2007) have disputed these findings.

Carrington and McPhee's (2008) study of 30 primary school teachers in the UK concluded that these teachers welcomed measures to increase the number of male teachers in primary schools to provide 'ethical templates' for the children in their care. Yet a study by Carrington *et al.* (2007) of 300 primary school students noted that their perception of a teacher's gender was largely immaterial to them. Yet another study by Carrington, Tymms and Merrell (2008) of 11-year-old students concluded that a matching of male teachers with classes of boys and female teachers with classes of girls had no discernible impact on either boys' or girls' attainment or on their respective attitudes to schools. Interestingly, male and female students taught by women were more inclined to show positive attitudes towards school than their peers taught by men.

It is perhaps sobering to note that a study by Cushman (2006) of New Zealand primary school principals revealed that although they were aware of media attention about employing more males, they considered their major commitment was to employ the best person for the job.

Clearly great care needs to be taken in making sweeping generalisations about the need for additional male teachers, matching boys' classes with male teachers (and girls' classes with female teachers) and the need to implement measures to overcome male students' underachievement in schools. Far more representative evidence is needed and 'sensational' media reports should be viewed with caution.

19.7.3 Class relations

Teachers are involved inexorably in class relations, but the patterns are complex (Rest 2000). As noted by Goodson (2005) and Lingard (2003), it is not a simple relationship whereby teachers as purported members of the new middle class are agents of social reproduction and bring about the ideological subordination of the working class. There are all kinds of class relations, such as relations with employers (the school principal as head of a small corporation in elite private schools); supporting working class students in coping with the academic curriculum and the personal conflicts this creates for individual teachers; and competition between schools and problems relating to availability of resources.

Ozga and Lawn (1981) assert that the teaching profession should not be viewed as a collaborator with the state. In terms of school education the state does provide schooling and compels the attendance of students. Yet teachers do not necessarily sustain all the explicit and implicit requirements established by the state. There are increasing tendencies for them to interact with other unionised groups of workers on matters of concern such as economic inequality and social justice. Teachers' social relationships are very significant in a school and in the wider community and class is a major issue (Cohen, Manion & Morrison 2004). According to Seddon (1991), teachers' work is very vulnerable because employers, using class and gender priorities, are bringing about a deskilling of teachers via basic skills testing and computer-assisted learning programs.

19.7.4 Empowerment

The term *teacher empowerment* has various meanings associated with it in the education literature. *Empowerment* of teachers (and students) occurs when they have opportunities to create meaning in their respective schools – to try out new approaches, to problem solve (Maeroff 1988; Marks & Louis 1997; Howes *et al.* 2005).

As portrayed by Webb *et al.* (2004), teachers in Finland are empowered – they have autonomy and a commitment to enable students to become active, independent learners. By contrast, *disempowered* teachers are those who teach defensively and control knowledge in order to control students. In these situations schooling becomes an empty ritual, unrelated to personal or cultural knowledge.

Teacher empowerment is a key element in schools. If teachers believe that their knowledge of teaching and learning matters and is considered a valuable factor in classroom making, they will progress markedly.

 Do you think teacher empowerment is important? Give an example of where you have seen a teacher demonstrate empowerment in their school.

Cochran-Smith (2006) contends that a number of teachers in the US have become so traumatised by the current education regime of test scores and the threats to their life-term employment that they teach defensively and don't go beyond teaching to the tests.

Post-structuralists argue that teachers and other workers operate in contexts of uncertainty and that the constraining rules of management just add to feelings of contradiction and despair (Day & Roberts-Holmes 1998; Achinstein & Ogawa 2006).

Some writers argue that the teaching profession is becoming steadily disempowered (Apple 1986) because of the encroachment of technical control procedures into the curriculum in schools. Bigum (1997) and Pagnucci (1998) argue that teachers are being controlled to a large measure by the computers introduced into schools. Others such as Green (1988) argue that teacher and student empowerment, jointly developed, is the important goal. The negotiation process between a teacher and his or her students empowers both groups as they share commitments and make decisions about class activities.

19.7.5 Teacher morale

The 1990s was a period when teacher morale in many countries was at a very low level. Hargreaves (1994, p. 6) refers to teachers in the UK, where the rampant and remorseless change had been imposed from above and was becoming a pressing and immediate feature of teachers' working lives. He adds that:

> it is extreme in the disrespect and disregard that reformers have shown for teachers themselves. In the political rush to bring about reform, teachers' voices have been largely neglected, their opinions overridden, and their concerns dismissed.

Woods (1990b, p. 207) is equally vociferous in his condemnation of events in the UK:

> The last five years have seen a pronounced decline in teacher morale ... the loss of salary negotiating rights, the imposition of conditions of service, weakening control, greater direction and increased demands on the service.

There is concern in Australia that teacher morale is at a very low level (Harris & Marsh 2005). They refer to the decline in teachers' morale, with many teachers feeling blocked and frustrated by their choice of career. Proudford (1998) contends that teachers are becoming alienated because of educational policy changes imposed from above. Teachers' work is becoming increasingly intensified and accompanied by heightened expectations and increased accountability.

The national collaborative curriculum project, overseen by senior politicians and bureaucrats during 1989–93, was a classic example of top-down change with minimal involvement of teachers and teacher groups and a blatant attempt by the Commonwealth Government to usurp power from the states and territories (Marsh 1994a). Other Commonwealth initiatives have followed in quick succession such as the Discovering Democracy project, Statements of Learning, History Summit, national testing and reporting of literacy and numeracy, and an A–E reporting of student results for all schools (see Chapter 2). It can be argued that all of these initiatives have been top-down and put additional workloads and stress upon teachers (Wyatt-Smith 2008; Woods 2007). The current 'Education Revolution', a National Curriculum being developed by the National Curriculum Board (renamed ACARA), has publicly stated that it will maximise teacher consultation; however, the processes to date seem to be very top-down. These Commonwealth measures, requiring compliance by states and territories, are in turn bringing about further teacher anxiety and concerns.

 Concerns about teacher morale are basically concerns about deterioration and de-professionalisation and requirements for intensification of effort in diverse activities. Is it getting better or worse? How do teachers feel about these changes? How does change affect them?

Duke (1984, p. 120) suggests that low teacher morale is symptomatic of a more deep-seated malaise and that teaching is an imperilled profession. He poses the following question and solution:

> Given the variety of threats and the particularly precarious position of segments of the profession, a reasonable question to ask may be, 'should the teaching profession be allowed to deteriorate further and possibly die?' Euthanasia may well be the best prescription if teachers no longer are able to fulfil the vital functions expected of them.

YOUR TURN

- Do you consider that workload is the biggest problem you will face as a teacher?
- Will the responsibilities of teaching have positive or negative effects on your personal and family life?
- Are the pressures of teaching any different from those of other professions? Give reasons.

19.8 | SCHOOL CULTURE AND TEACHING

Of course, teachers do not acquire their professional skills in a vacuum – the context of each school is very different and as a consequence all kinds of adjustments are needed to be made by teachers.

It is very clear that teachers entering the profession of teaching are faced with various tangible and intangible elements that comprise the school culture. Some elements may appear to be familiar, but this is often without foundation. The process of learning the culture is involved and tortuous. The task is especially difficult because each school is unique and the school student population is unique (Glover & Coleman 2005).

19.9 | CULTURE

Various writers, ranging from anthropologists to educationalists to artists, provide interpretations of the term 'culture' – it is a very ambiguous term.

Deal (1990, p. 132) notes that 'culture is a concept that captures the subtle, elusive, intangible, largely unconscious force that shapes a society or a workplace' – yet he prefers more commonsense definitions such as 'the way we do things around here' or 'what keeps the herd moving roughly west' (Deal & Kennedy 1982, p. 5).

Giroux (1981, p. 27) believes the term 'culture' is often used as an apology for the status quo. He considers that:

> it is more appropriate to view culture as a number of divergent instances in which power is used unequally to produce different meanings and practices, which in the final analysis reproduces a particular kind of society that functions in the interest of a dominant class. Thus it is more appropriate to speak of cultures, rather than culture.

Beare, Caldwell and Millikan (1991) provide a wider understanding of the term by concentrating on some of the tangible and intangible characteristics of culture:
- the underlying philosophy espoused by leaders and members
- the ways in which that philosophy is translated into an operational mission
- the value sets of leaders and others
- the metaphors that serve as frameworks for thinking and action
- the sagas, myths, stories, folk heroes and celebrations.

19.10 | SCHOOL CULTURE

The school is a place where students of diverse interests, backgrounds, experiences, expectations and needs congregate (Jackson 1997). Each school culture is unique, yet it is possible to generalise about school cultures – they are one of the key cultural entities in modern society (Nuthall 2005). Just as a culture can be described from an anthropological and aesthetic standpoint, it is possible to make similar linkages with a 'school culture'. Beare, Caldwell and Millikan (1991) suggest that some of the unique *anthropological* aspects of a school culture include:
- a unique mixing of ethnicity, values, experiences, skills and aspirations
- special rituals and ceremonies
- a unique history of achievements and traditions
- a unique socio-economic and geographic location.

Further, they consider that some aesthetic aspects of a school culture include:
- breadth, content and emphases of school subjects
- expressive and artistic skills of personnel
- cultural support with communities.

School cultures are always evolving and never static. Lucas and Valentine (2002) argue that principals and teacher leaders can have major impacts on school cultures – transforming a student culture into one that is 'characterised by vision, collegiality, trust, values, broad member participation, positive personal and organisational growth, empowerment, and continuous innovation' (p. 24).

A school culture can be well integrated in terms of its philosophy and mission or it can be disjointed. Cavanagh and Dellar (1998) refer to the cultures of individual classrooms, which may be very different from the overall school culture.

> **YOUR TURN**
>
> Think about a school you have visited or taught at where there is a very positive school culture – perhaps even transformational!
> - What are the forces that seem to be driving this school?
> - Has the positive school culture emerged suddenly or has it built up over a period of time? Give details.

Beare, Caldwell and Millikan (1991) consider that it is desirable for purposes of analysis to distinguish between 'inner space' characteristics of school culture such as values, philosophy and ideology, and 'outer space' characteristics such as conceptual, behavioural and visual manifestations (for example, metaphors, rules and regulations and uniforms). Figure 19.3 depicts the inner and outer spaces. The broken circle indicates that the inner (intangible) and outer (tangible) elements are constantly interacting. The large broken ellipse indicates that there is a constant interchange between the school and its wider community.

The inner space elements typically drive the school culture. Although intangible, 'value sets' of school personnel are often the basis for behaviour. Some schools have been formed to follow a particular 'philosophy' (for example, Montessori and Rudolph Steiner schools), but the majority have less focused philosophies. 'Ideologies' (for example, relating to student needs or teacher empowerment) are well developed in some schools.

However, it is the outer space elements that are more obvious to participants (see Figure 19.3). The conceptual and verbal manifestations may be spoken about openly or issued as written statements of policy. They include statements about school missions, goals, aims and objectives, and curriculum documents pertaining to specific subjects (Cavanagh & MacNeil 2002).

Metaphors are often used by school leaders and others to affirm a particular image of a school, which can be positive or negative (Joseph, Mikel & Windschitl 2002). Hargreaves' (1994) study of metaphors used to describe schools provides a most revealing list (Figure 19.4); many of them are far from positive!

Stories about a school (including 'half-truths' and fictitious accounts) help to develop a school culture. So do the heroic figures – that is, the official and unofficial leaders. As noted by Beare, Caldwell and Millikan (1991), they help to build the emotional bonds that hold the tribe together and, in so doing, they emphasise the closeness of community and the uniqueness of belonging.

The *visual* manifestations of a school culture are many (see Figure 19.3). They include the buildings and grounds – the general appearance and quality of the building, the friendliness of the reception area, the standard of the furnishings. The human possessions are the staff – their personalities, creativity and team activities. For example, some schools build up major staff strengths in particular subject areas.

Then there are the artefacts and memorabilia. Many schools have entrance halls to display their sporting trophies, artwork and honour boards. Where schools require students to wear a school uniform, this can be a powerful way of maintaining a school identity. School magazines and newsletters can also be used to affirm and celebrate particular aspects of the school culture.

FIGURE 19.3 A framework for analysing school culture

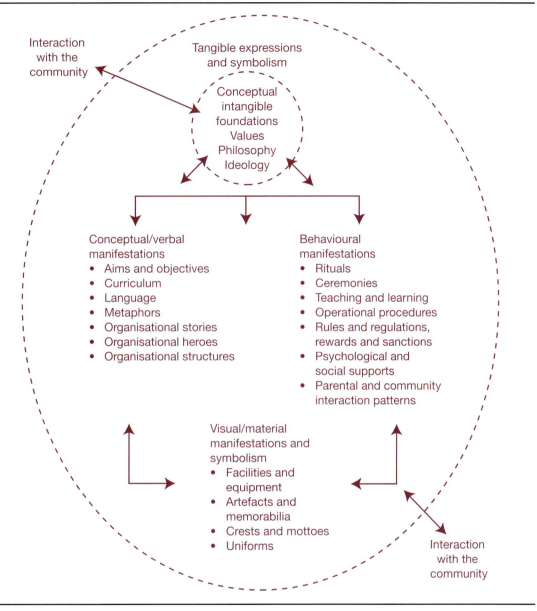

Source: Beare, Caldwell and Millikan, Creating an Excellent School, 1991, Taylor and Francis Books Ltd.

The *behavioural* manifestations are the everyday activities and meetings that occur. The routines designed for a school have been worked out pragmatically as the best fit for getting certain ends achieved. The particular configuration for periods, lunch breaks and allocations of subjects ensures that behaviours of students will occur in accordance with these routines. In addition, special school assemblies and sporting events occur regularly to support the school culture. From time to time sanctions may need to be applied to individual students, and given public airings, to ensure that the school ethos is maintained.

FIGURE 19.4 Metaphors associated with schools

- Assembly-line operation
- Ticking clock
- Garden
- Mirror of society
- Museum
- Factory
- Supermarket
- Rubik's cube
- Shopping centre
- Happy family
- Ant farm
- Warehouse
- Cross-stitch quilt
- Prison

Source: Based on Hargreaves 1994.

19.10.1 School culture and leadership

Leadership is closely linked to the school culture. Transformational leadership by the principal and teacher leaders attempts to widen the decision making within the school culture and to seek school-based solutions to challenges (Geijsel *et al.* 2002). A school culture is a positive one when it promotes dialogue, interaction and collaboration. It is less than positive if it is bureaucratic, top-down and driven by test results.

 Reflect on this statement. Have you visited schools where the school culture is very positive?

The principal is the primary source in identifying and articulating a vision for the school, but he or she will need a wider leadership team to modify the culture of the school (Heng & Marsh 2009). However, it is also the case that school leaders have to withstand pressures from external sources, in terms of market forces. Thus they are also the gatekeepers of the school culture and need to have the resilience to maintain it intact (Woods 2000).

19.10.2 School culture and beginning teachers

Newly appointed teachers have a variety of needs when they first enter their schools (Rieg, Paquette & Chen 2007). Quite often their first encounters with the school staff can be disappointing because the established staff act with indifference and a lack of support (Moore, Johnson & Kardoe 2002). The fortunate few are welcomed into the school culture and given professional support. In some schools, mentor support is provided and experienced teachers engage them in developmental cycles of planning, teaching and reflecting (Lucas 1999).

Moore, Johnson and Kardoe (2002) refer to some of the typical, unhelpful cultures that beginning teachers can experience – the 'veteran-oriented professional cultures', where the modes and norms of professional practice are determined by and aimed at serving veteran faculty members; and the 'novice-oriented professional cultures', where the youth, inexperience and high turnover of staff cause poor levels of organisation.

It is critical that schools be more welcoming to new teachers entering the profession so that the attrition rate of teachers can be lowered and long-term professional growth can be promoted (Goddard & Goddard 2006). As noted by Peske *et al.* (2001), many new teachers approach teaching tentatively or conditionally. Most anticipate having multiple careers over the course of their lives – long-term career teachers are now outnumbered by short-term teachers.

19.11 SCHOOL CULTURE AND SCHOOLING OVER THE DECADES

It might be anticipated that, because of changing student attitudes and backgrounds, changes in teaching backgrounds and interests and changing contexts and technology, schools would also vary considerably over the decades. This does not appear to be the case. Studies of teachers and schools over the decades by Kliebard (1986), Cuban (1983) and Nuthall (2005) reveal that there has been a remarkable stability in schooling. For example, Cuban (1983, p. 175) concludes that:

> a dominant core of teaching practices has endured since the turn of the century in both elementary and high school classrooms. These practices (teaching the whole group, reliance upon a textbook, rows of desks, question–answer framework for carrying on dialogue etc.) persisted over time, in different settings, in spite of changes in teacher education and the knowledge that students bring to school and major social and cultural movements.

Furthermore, the relative stability of schooling has been evident in most Western countries, including Australia, Canada, the UK and the US. A closer analysis of school culture over particular time periods could be instructive in isolating what are the critical factors for endurance or change.

19.11.1 The 1960s

Dan Lortie's major account of teaching, based on in-depth studies of primary school classrooms in the 1960s in the US, is described in this section. It is a thoughtful snapshot of primary school culture, but cannot be used to generalise beyond its specific context.

Dan Lortie undertook teacher interviews for a book on teaching in the 1960s, but it was not published until 1975. *Schoolteacher* is a sociological study of 94 teachers selected at random from 13 schools (representing a socio-economic range) including six primary schools, five junior high schools and two senior secondary schools. It has become a classic over the years because of its insights about teaching.

Lortie (1975, p. 59) uses comparisons with other occupations to gain understandings about teachers. He asserts that teachers receive very little training to become teachers:

- Practice teaching is short and comparatively casual compared with crafts, professions and highly skilled trades.
- The induction system for teachers is not well developed – 'there is an abruptness with which full responsibility is assumed.'
- Being a student at school is like serving an apprenticeship in teaching – students observe teachers over periods of up to 16 years, but what they learn is imitative; they never find out teachers' intentions and their personal reflections.
- Because of their isolation, beginning teachers frequently have to solve their own problems. Teachers adopt ideas from peers on a highly selective basis – they adopt them if it suits their way of doing things.

Teaching, according to Lortie (1975), is relatively *career-less* – that is, there are few stages and little opportunity for career moves upwards. The high proportion of females teaching in primary schools complicates the picture. Writing in the 1960s, Lortie asserts that the gentle incline of teaching with few stages suits the aspirations of women who will predominantly have marriage and child-bearing plans that will take them in and out of teaching. Whether this is the case in the twenty-first century for female teachers is a lot less certain.

 Do Dan Lortie's (1975) descriptions of classrooms in the 1960s still have relevance today? For example, do you consider teaching is relatively career-less with few stages and little opportunity for career moves upwards?

Lortie (1975) argues that teachers have a present-oriented view of rewards and their main satisfactions come from psychic rewards in their work – the enjoyment of teaching difficult concepts to a low ability student, for example. These *psychic rewards* are largely private (between the teacher and the student). Teachers take pride in their teaching successes with individual students, but behind closed doors within the cellular organisation of schools.

Compared with other occupations, teachers have *endemic uncertainties*. The work processes in teaching are difficult to measure. There is ambiguity about when to assess: 'teachers work with inherently changeful materials' (Lortie 1975, p. 136). Teachers never really know whether their teaching has had a lasting effect upon students or not.

Teachers, according to Lortie, are more interested in classroom demands than organisational matters. They have little interest in school-wide activities. High points for teachers are when they 'get through' to students and when they finish their teaching tasks.

Lortie's (1975) book, and that by Jackson (1968), provides memorable metaphors and insights about teaching and about the school culture in the 1960s in the US. Teacher individualism, presentism, psychic rewards and student delay, denial, interruption and social distraction provide powerful images of teaching in that decade.

19.11.2 The twenty-first century (2010 and beyond)

Although it could be interesting to trace developments in school cultures over each decade since the 1960s, the differences between the 1960s and 2010 will be highlighted.

Teachers in the twenty-first century are being confronted with a range of complex challenges, as individuals and as members of the wider professional community (Johnson & Maclean 2008). According to Glatthorn *et al.* 2008; Cruickshank, Jenkins & Metcalf 2009; Orlich *et al.* 2009, there are multiple reforms occurring in the US in terms of:

- subject matter teaching (outcome standards, pedagogy)
- equity reforms
- widespread uses of new forms of student assessment
- restructuring of schools
- professional development initiatives for teachers (Ryan & Cooper 2008; Cruickshank, Jenkins & Metcalf 2009).

The *internationalisation* of issues is such that many of these same reforms and initiatives are also occurring in Australia. For example, consider the following reforms:

- Restructuring of education systems: an increase in the power of political figures, especially the Minister for Education; a reduced role for the Director-General (CEO); and a greater influence of pressure groups.
- More rigorous attempts by the Commonwealth Government, linked to Education Acts and funding, to take over responsibilities from state and territory education systems.
- National assessment and reporting of student literacy and numeracy in Years 3, 5, 7 and 9 and creation of 'league tables' of schools' achievements.
- Creation of a National Curriculum for all students in English, Mathematics, Science and History with other subjects to follow.
- Devolution of responsibility to schools: a greater level of parent participation.
- Changes to the career structure for teachers: development of the 'Advanced Skills Teacher' (AST) category; greater degree of specification of working conditions.
- Increased use of fixed-term contracts for principals and teachers.
- Increased use of computer technology for administration and management of schools and as a mode of instruction.
- Changes to the curriculum in Years 11 and 12 to accommodate students' needs for a greater vocational emphasis.
- Increased attention to the use of middle schools to address the special needs of young adolescents.
- Increased measures to obtain accountability of teachers and schools.

19.11.3 Commonwealth–state relationships

The last few years in Australia have witnessed a much stronger determination by the Commonwealth Government to wrest control of education from the states. Unlike the 1960s, when state and territory education systems had little 'interference' from the Commonwealth, fifty years later there have been very different power relationships emerging.

There is now considerable evidence of 'hard policy' (legislation with delivery requirements linked to funding or non-funding). For example in 2003 all Ministers of Education agreed at a MCEETYA meeting that Statements of Learning would be developed in English, Mathematics, Science and Civics and Citizenship, Information and Communications Technologies. All states and territories are to develop essential knowledge, skills and understandings in these areas and year levels 3, 5, 7 and 9 will be subjected to national tests. Although to date not all of these tests have been developed or implemented, this is a classic example of 'hard policy' and a stepping-up of demands by the Commonwealth Government.

Tests for literacy and numeracy have evolved from state tests to national tests and now cover a wider range of students. The National Assessment Program now includes students from Years 3, 5, 7 and 9. Results are now widely distributed and are subject to various media reports and interpretations. Yet specialists in the area of literacy, such as Woods (2007) and Wyatt-Smith (2008), contend that the tests have political appeal rather than value for diagnosis and learning improvement.

The planning of a National Curriculum in 2008 is another example of hard policy. Non-government schools are required under the *Schools Assistance Bill 2008* to implement the new National Curriculum if they are to receive funding from the Commonwealth (Kennedy 2009). It is highly likely that the new curriculum body, the Australian Curriculum, Assessment and Reporting Authority (ACARA) will enforce requirements upon government schools when the new curricula are completed in 2010.

19.11.4 Equity issues and international rankings

Large-scale comparative tests in Science, Mathematics and literacy such as PISA (Program for International Student Assessment) and TIMMS (Trends in International Mathematics and Science Study) are certainly very important in the twenty-first century and were not done in the 1960s. The data on OECD countries using PISA and TIMMS is scrutinised very carefully by education leaders because it ranks countries on their performance in listed subjects (Griffiths 2009). The PISA data also provides performance differences between schools and an index of social background. As indicated in Chapter 2, Australian schools do not score well on equity. The relationship between social background and achievement is much stronger in Australia. This means that disadvantaged students have less opportunity to maximise their potential.

The levels of disadvantage are very pronounced when it comes to Indigenous students. As described in Chapter 2, the educational outcomes of Indigenous Australians have improved a little over recent decades but there is still no parity with non-Indigenous Australians (MCEETYA 2006a). Some of the ongoing education equity issues include the number of Indigenous students who 'drop out' before Year 10; few remain at school to complete Years 11 and 12; few gain entry into university or its vocational equivalent; and limited school options and life choices perpetuate intergenerational cycles of social and economic disadvantage.

There have been many attempts in the past to break down this disparity. The Rudd government's 'Education Revolution', announced in 2007, is aiming to improve equity issues for Indigenous students by establishing early childhood education (a two-year high-quality program for all Indigenous children aged 0–5 years); school and community educational partnerships; school leadership; quality teaching; and pathways to training, employment and higher education.

19.11.5 Assessment developments

Assessment developments have been very marked over the intervening 50 years. Formative assessment, or assessment for learning, is now being practiced by many teachers, even though there is the ever-looming presence of summative assessments (Blanchard 2008).

The other major development has been the use of ICT tools for both formative and summative assessment and for assessing standards. Student learning can now be systematically assessed by multiple choice formats and performance formats. For example, performance assessment formats have been used very successfully for writing (Graham & George 1992). Other developments include computer adaptive testing (CAT), which customises the assessment process so that the computer determines which level of questions to pose to the student (Badge *et al.* 2008). Also technology allows a variety of test-and-response formats using the computer's video and audio capabilities. Students can answer orally or by constructing answers on the screen. Automated essay gradings are now available for use on a standard computer (Wiliam 2008).

19.11.6 Conditions for teachers

Recent accounts by educators indicate that conditions for teachers are far from optimal and may be deteriorating (McCulloch 1998; Hargreaves & Fullan 1998).

Conditions for teachers in the UK in particular appear to be extremely depressing. Woods and Jeffrey (2002) assert that primary school teachers in UK schools now have to adopt a radical change of identity. Their previous set of values centring around 'holism, person-centredness and warm and caring relationships' (p. 92) has been replaced by emphasis on 'teacher competencies such as subject expertise, coordination, collaboration, management and supervision' (p. 95). According to Woods and Jeffrey (2002), primary school teachers' self-esteem has been attacked – their identities have now been defined in terms of performativity and audit accountability.

McMahon (2000) notes that the ambitious reforms program in the UK, with its emphasis on managerialism and a drive to raise standards, has resulted in higher levels of teacher stress:

> There is zero tolerance of underachievement. The consequences for schools and individual teachers judged to be underperforming are severe: schools failing are put into special measures; inspectors report on the competence of individual teachers; if a school cannot demonstrate improvement it faces closure, a teacher who fails to improve faces disciplinary measures and possible dismissal. (p. 2)

Little wonder that teacher stress is high and there are increasing numbers of teachers suffering burn-out and low morale (Brown, Ralph & Brember 2002; McPhee, Forde & Skelton 2002).

There are similar concerns voiced about teachers' work in the US. For example, Joseph, Mikel and Windschitl (2002) contend that, because of the standards movement in the US that now dominates the educational agenda, the work of teachers is becoming more routinised; teachers are being pressured to use methods of direct instruction to ensure that their students score highly on the standardised achievement tests.

The situation for Australian teachers is less clear. Few comprehensive reports are available. Yet there are ominous warning signs of teachers refocusing their teaching to ensure good results on the National Benchmarks (Wyatt-Smith & Campbell 2002) and increased demands on principals and teachers to achieve high performance standards for their respective schools (Cole 2007).

> **YOUR TURN**
>
> Examine some education policy documents about reforms and school developments.
> - Do they provide an accurate picture of what is happening in schools or what should happen?
> - If it is the latter, what is the likelihood that these reforms will occur?

For example, Angus & Olney (2009) in their study concluded that primary school principals expressed concerns about the large number of requirements expected of them. They were concerned especially by how they could target their resources to reduce the number of students failing to meet the national literacy and numeracy minimum standards. There will be even further demands upon them when the new National Curriculum is released in 2010.

Further, there are massive shortages of teachers in Science, Technology and Mathematics. This has led recently to a Commonwealth Review with the goal of developing a culture of innovation in Australian schools in general and specifically to consider ways of attracting knowledgeable graduates into teaching from the fields of Science, Technology and Mathematics (Committee for the Review of Teaching and Teacher Education 2002).

CONCLUDING COMMENTS

The analysis of two time periods, the 1960s and 2010, indicates that there has been an escalation and intensity of issues for teachers and that further stresses may be imminent for teachers in Australian schools. Yet 'some of the announcements of the death of the old order are premature; like Tom Sawyer, the deceased has a way of showing up at the funeral' (Lortie 1975, p. 217). It could be instructive to examine some of the imminent changes that Lortie forecast in the 1960s as a means of examining the extent to which a school culture does become modified over time.

Lortie (1975) asserted in the 1960s that change was inescapable. There was a burgeoning of institutions involved in various aspects of education. Schools were experimenting with different timetables, deployment of staff and learning styles. Yet these increased possibilities for variety and pluralism did not amount to much – the only revolution that occurred was in people's expectations and not in practice. Furthermore, Lortie argued that school systems used various tactics to deflect change pressures such as:
- having a few showplace schools but resisting widespread adoption
- having powerful rhetoric on an innovation but leaving current practices intact.

Lortie predicted that with the proliferation of options teachers would have to be more adaptive – there would be pressures on them to be more innovative. New techniques could involve new specialists entering the school culture unless teachers were willing to adapt and experiment – teachers might 'find themselves "encroached" upon by people with widely different orientations and commitments'. This is already occurring with the increased number of support teachers and paraprofessionals (for example, ICT technicians) with no corresponding increases in numbers of trained teachers (Allen 2002b) and the hiring of non-teacher-trained graduates.

Lortie also predicted that teachers would receive less 'ritual pity' from the general public in the future. 'It was conventional to lament their low pay and refer to them as "dedicated" … and in so doing teachers were exempted from high performance expectations and rigorous public scrutiny' (Lortie 1975, p. 221). The more teachers become involved in school-level decision making in the future, the more they will become potentially culpable for school system practices (Lortie 1975, p. 222). Public disaffection will create more and more demands for accountability.

These examples of predictions made by Lortie in the 1960s reveal that school personnel have become very adroit over the years in resisting change and will continue to demonstrate these skills. Yet innovations in the future may require vastly different and more specialised work practices for teachers. They will have to be extremely flexible and adaptive to cope with these changes. Lortie's predictions about reduced 'ritual pity' for teachers was patently obvious in the 1960s – but now in the twenty-first century more demanding accountability measures for teachers have definitely arrived (Kearney & Arnold 1994; Caldwell 1998; Zyngier 2009).

All kinds of scenarios are being introduced as possibilities in the third millennium, including:
- 'School in a box' – traditional schools will disappear and teachers will have their multimedia computers and will establish their own cottage schools based on the new tools and systems (Mecklenburger 1996; Australian Education Union 2006).

- Social movements (including class, race and gender politics) will affect what is taught in the twenty-first century (Slaughter 1997).
- New school structures will emerge such as schools for children 0–8 where the emphasis will be on total development operating on an ungraded basis (Collins 1992).

It is important that the predicted scenarios for the new millennium are more than mere castles in the air and better than futures cast in our own image. It is seductive to see the twenty-first century as a blank canvas. We should use our experiences in the nineteenth and twentieth centuries as a valuable basis for planning what we want for the twenty-first (Hargreaves & Evans 1997).

KEY ISSUES RAISED IN THIS CHAPTER

1. There are various ideas about whether teaching is, or is not, a profession.
2. Professionalisation is the process whereby members of a profession aspire to meet criteria of their group.
3. Professional development is where members go about improving their competencies.
4. Statistics on Australian teachers provide unique characteristics about gender balance, metropolitan/rural distribution of teachers, and the number of government and non-government schools.
5. Life histories of teachers reveal consistent phases from career entry to disengagement.
6. Some major issues for the teaching profession are the ageing of teachers; feminisation of teaching, class relations, empowerment and teacher morale.
7. School cultures are constantly evolving – they can be well integrated or disjointed.
8. The stability of schooling over the decades is evident by comparing the 1960s with 2010 and beyond.

REFLECTIONS AND ISSUES

1. Do you consider that the teaching profession is little valued compared with other professions? Select four or five key characteristics of the teaching profession and compare these with key features of one other profession, such as accounting.
2. In many countries teaching has been identified as one of the most stressful occupations. What are the major factors causing stress for teachers? Are there ways of reducing these stress levels?
3. How would you describe the school culture at the school you currently work in or at a school you know well? Whose interests are being served? How did it come to be that way? To what extent has it changed over recent years?
4. Lortie argues that conservatism, individualism and presentism are the key features of the teaching culture. Explain. Did it ever apply in Australia? Does it still apply?
5. Many educators conclude that the demands on schools are becoming more complex and teachers' roles are changing. They cite developments such as closer integration of pre-school and early primary education, the role of middle schooling, an increase in the school-leaving age and new curriculum emphasis, including vocational education and training. Comment on these listed developments. What practical activities are schools doing to develop them?
6. The variety in backgrounds of today's new teachers increases the importance of providing useful and sustained professional development at the school site. Why are teachers coming from a greater variety of backgrounds? Can school staff provide the professional development needed? Give examples of the types of professional development needed.
7. It is argued that teachers now have to meet the demands of more diverse student populations, higher expectations of schools and expanding fields of knowledge. Discuss.

8 There is evidence that schools (especially government schools) are in decay because of the widening gap between high-performing and low-performing students and a failure to meet expectations in the national goals of schooling (Caldwell 2003). Is this a realistic summary of Australian schools in 2010? Give reasons.
9 Will the first few decades of the twenty-first century witness the de-professionalisation of teaching as teachers crumble under multiple pressures and intensified work demands (Hargreaves & Fullan 2000)? Is this likely in Australia? Discuss.
10 How is devolution occurring in your state or territory? To what extent is it affecting teacher roles and the school culture? How have teachers adapted to these changes?
11 High-quality induction and professional development programs are needed for newly appointed teachers if we are to recruit and retain strong teachers in the next decade. Give reasons for this position.
12 Do you consider that new partnerships with groups and institutions beyond the school will open up to share some of the current responsibilities of teachers?

Special references

Apple, M & Aasen, P (2003) *The State and the Politics of Knowledge*, Routledge, London.
Caldwell, BJ & Harris, J (2008) *Why Not the Best Schools?* ACER, Melbourne.
Darling-Hammond, L (2006) *Powerful Teacher Education, Lessons from Exemplary Programs*, Teachers College Press, New York.
Fullan, M, Hill, P & Crevola, C (2006) *Break Through*, Corwin Press, San Francisco.
Hargreaves, A (2003) *Teaching in the Knowledge Society*, Teachers College Press, New York.
Johnson, D & Maclean, R (2008) *Teaching: Professionalisation, Development and Leadership*, Springer, London.

Web sources

For additional resources on professional and cultural dimensions of teaching, please go to: www.pearson.com.au/myeducationlab.

20

ETHICAL AND LEGAL ISSUES IN TEACHING

20.1 | INTRODUCTION

As if the imparting of knowledge and skills were not in itself a very exacting process, it is also essential that teachers adopt sound ethical standards in their classrooms. Teachers are required to make ethical decisions every day about students with whom they will engage, for how long and for what purpose. A teacher's time is very limited and so some students will gain and others will not receive this attention.

Students' rights and teachers' rights need to be examined carefully. Not only are there ethical considerations, but also there has been an increasing trend over recent years for the legal testing of student rights in various court cases.

20.2 | THE ETHICS OF TEACHING

The various missions of schools are to foster intellectual, social and personal development of students. Typically we tend to dwell on the intellectual mission – the passing on of specific knowledge and skills. However, another equally important mission is character education (Freakley & Burgh 2002). According to Chiarelott, Davidson and Ryan (1994, p. 170), another mission of schools 'is to ensure that the young acquire the ethical standards and enduring moral habits they will need to manage their own lives and contribute to the common good'.

Brock (1998) suggests that there are two fundamental questions to be addressed when considering ethics and professional teaching standards:
- What ought one do?
- What must one not do?

He suggests that the second question is the easier task because most education systems explicitly proscribe teacher behaviour that is patently unethical (for example, sexual relationships with students). Brock (1998) insists that the first question is far more difficult to answer because teachers face choosing between two or more 'right' answers. He quotes from Kidder (1996) that some of the genuine dilemmas that teachers face include:
- truth versus loyalty
- individual versus community

- short-term versus long-term
- justice versus mercy.

The character education mission of schools is no recent fad. Many early philosophers such as Socrates, Plato and Aristotle gave a high priority to this goal of education, maintaining that it required a lifetime of personal effort. Codes of education in most countries explicitly require teachers to teach the values associated with good citizenship, without violating the ethical views of individual groups (see also Chapter 16).

> **YOUR TURN**
>
> You have asked to see a parent over a problem with a child's behaviour. The next day the child shows signs of distress and fright and promises with tears not to do it again. Have you inadvertently caused this distress, perhaps even caused physical abuse of the child by the parent? What action should you take in future?

Various authors have attempted to isolate principles that teachers might adopt to provide sound ethical standards in classrooms. As noted by Oser, Dick and Patry (1992, p. 111), the successful teacher is one who concentrates not only on didactic or content matters but also on moral engagement because this will 'enhance the student's academic motivation as well as the societal relevance of his or her teaching, because the students will have learned to take responsibility for their actions'.

Ideally, students and a teacher in a classroom communicate with equal rights and without constraints of any kind. This of course rarely, if ever, happens. A teacher can provide caring and responsible behaviour but the opportunities for students to take responsibility and to participate in thinking, deciding and acting may be far from ideal.

Table 20.1 depicts five hypothetical levels of decision making ranging from open decision making (ideal) to avoidance (lowest rating). Most would agree that the first situation of open decision making should be the goal in all classrooms. In the second situation (limited decision making) the interests and viewpoints of students are taken into consideration but actual decisions are made by the teacher. The third situation (decision making by the teacher) is all about unilateral decision making that can be done quickly, efficiently and unobtrusively. Perhaps it is the wish of the teacher to minimise disturbances within a classroom, or it could reflect a fear of professional failure or a conviction that a teacher is supposed to lead. In the fourth situation (security seeking) a teacher delegates ethical issues to other persons or authorities such as the school principal. Perhaps this is done out of a teacher's

TABLE 20.1 Types of ethical decision making

Levels of decision making	Participation by students	Presumes reasoning competence of students	Commitment to a solution
Open decision making	Yes	Yes	Yes
Limited decision making	Yes	Yes	Yes
Decision making by teacher	No	No	Yes
Security seeking	No	No	Yes
Avoidance	No	No	No

fear of losing control, or perhaps out of deference to the hierarchical power structures operating in schools. In the fifth situation (avoidance) the teacher tries to avoid any discussion of, or action on, a specific ethical problem. The priorities of subject matter are usually given as the reasons for avoiding these discussions, but it may also be due to teacher beliefs that their students are not capable of considering ethical issues.

20.3 | TEACHING AS A MORAL CRAFT

The five levels of decision making described above provide some insights into the extent to which teachers may want to communicate with students, openly and with equal rights. However, it is necessary to remember the enormous pressures on a teacher's time (Hargreaves & Fullan 1998). According to Shulman (1983, p. 497):

> Teaching is impossible. If we simply add together all that is expected of a typical teacher and take note of the circumstances under which those activities are to be carried out, the sum makes greater demands than any individual can possibly fulfil. Yet teachers teach … We therefore confront two questions. What makes teaching impossible in principle? How is the impossible rendered possible in practice?

Teachers make moral decisions in their daily teaching when they decide to whom and where to give their attention, for how long, and using which strategies. The teacher is continually making trade-offs among competing demands but is guided by his or her moral values. What a teacher does each day is guided by the things that he or she values, the things he or she wants to achieve through teaching (Fullan & Hargreaves 1991).

> **YOUR TURN**
> - What do you value most from the students you teach? For example, is it that you want your students to be truthful?
> - Do you think your values are achievable in the classroom? Beyond the classroom?

The values teachers use are likely to be similar in terms of broad concerns. For example, Damon (1992) suggests that they typically include:
- fairness – being even-handed in dealing with different students
- power or control in limited situations – having authority over students in only a limited, specified range of activities and not over-extending their authority
- truthfulness – honest communication rather than the 'shading' of the truth. Dishonest communications weaken the trust relationship between the teacher and his or her students.

Freakley and Burgh (2002) suggest a similar list which includes:
- Fairness – this involves equity, impartiality, lack of bias, equality and justice
- Rights – we are entitled to various rights
- Privileges – are advantages or favours enjoyed by certain persons to act in certain ways
- Duties and obligations – duties are requirements that operate regardless of a person's consent; obligations are undertakings entered into by persons.

Quite frequently, teachers develop their moral craft in isolation. As noted by Richardson (1991), the general isolation of teachers is a continuing source of strain and limits the range of professional response to educational challenges. Few, if any, other occupations place such faith in the organisational unit of the solitary professional. It can be argued that teachers can develop their values uninhibited by other teachers and that this is a benefit. For some teachers, it might be less stressful to explore different value stances with students without being under the critical eye of their fellow teachers. Yet most professionals welcome the opportunity of sharing ideas and techniques with their peers – it enables them to clarify points and to reassess some assumptions that may not have been fully considered.

Whether teachers develop their moral craft in isolation or not, their impact on a class of students over a term, semester or year can be considerable (Weissbourd 2003). The teacher's style will reveal all kinds of moral influence on the students – it occurs in an indirect and unpredictable way, but it is enduring (Hansen 1993).

20.4 | ETHICAL RELATIONSHIPS BETWEEN THE TEACHER AND THE EDUCATION SYSTEM

In most education systems there are regulations and requirements that inhibit how teachers can develop their values with their classes of students, even though what a teacher does 'behind the classroom door' may not be closely scrutinised.

Recent court cases and public hearings in the United States illustrate how external factors can be very inhibiting. A school board in Pennsylvania in 2005 required 'intelligent design' (a religion-based interpretation of creation) to be taught by all biology teachers as an alternative to the theory of evolution (ASCD 2005, 29 September). Proponents of intelligent design argue that there are gaps in Darwin's theory of evolution and that those gaps are best filled by recognising the role of an intelligent agent in life's origin. The chief proponents of intelligent design are Christian fundamentalists and conservative political organisations. Opponents of intelligent design are largely scientists and science teachers who scoff at the notion that intelligent design is a new scientific theory – it is just a repackaging of creationism (Johnson 2008).

There are clearly some major value issues here that could greatly inhibit what classroom teachers can teach. Subsequently, there have been numerous court challenges in Pennsylvania and in other states (ASCD 2006, 18 March). A US District Judge ruled in December 2005 that teaching intelligent design as an alternative to the theory of evolution is unconstitutional (ASCD 2005, 21 December). However, the debate continues.

It has even been raised in Australia, where a coalition of 70 000 scientists, teachers and academics were signatories to an open letter to the federal Education Minister urging the government and educators to stop the teaching of intelligent design as science (ASCD 2005, 25 October). Brendan Nelson, the federal Education Minister at the time, did not heed their advice and backed the teaching of intelligent design alongside evolution, if parents wished it (*The Age* 29 October 2005).

 Why is the issue of creationism versus evolution still such a major issue in the science curriculum?

Another example of teachers being restricted is the case of a reading and writing studio course. This course was developed by teachers in Baltimore, US. Their purpose was to use popular teen magazines and to de-emphasise grammar (ASCD 2006, 10 February). Subsequently, the head of the Baltimore School District announced that the studio course would be dropped because it failed to prepare middle school students for state examinations.

As noted in Chapter 16, there is likely to be considerable controversy for teachers over issues dealing with gay rights. As a specific example of this, in 2006 in California the Senate passed a bill that will require schools to teach students about the historical contributions of gay people and buy textbooks that accurately portray the 'sexual diversity' of the nation (ASCD 2006, 8 April).

20.5 | ETHICAL RELATIONSHIPS BETWEEN THE TEACHER AND THE PRINCIPAL

The teacher may have a panoply of well-developed values and purposes, but the opportunities to carry them out may be limited because of directives and judgments made by the school principal. Principals 'are gatekeepers par excellence to preferred ends' (Sykes, Measor & Woods 1985, p. 232). If they have particular values about which they feel strongly, then these will predominate over any teacher views (Dempster 2008). As noted by Davies and Brighouse (2008), it is all very well for a principal to be passionate about particular topics but he/she needs to have a coherent approach for dealing with teachers in ethical ways – passionate leadership without ethics is blind.

Some authors, such as Imber (1983), argue that teachers have ethical rights pertaining to involvement in the decision-making process of a school. 'They should have the right to collaborate on decisions that relate to the utilisation of their own labour' (Imber 1983, p. 39).

 How can teachers with passionate ideas for change in a school persuade others? What might be some of the obstacles? In particular what strategies might be used to gain maximum support from the principal?

20.6 | ETHICAL RELATIONSHIPS BETWEEN TEACHER AND STUDENTS

The classroom teacher has every opportunity to develop emotional bonds with his/her students. The teacher needs to find ways to let each student know that he or she is respected and acknowledged as an individual (Konza, Grainger & Bradshaw 2001).

Ethical relationships revolve around respect between teacher and student. According to Lickona (1988), teachers can promote higher levels of student morality and character by:
- serving as role models who are always respectful and caring of others and who intervene as necessary to get students to be respectful and caring
- creating a family or community atmosphere in the class so that all students feel worthwhile and care about one another
- encouraging students to hold high academic and behavioural standards in order to teach the value of work as a way to develop oneself and contribute to a community.

Emmer and Gerwells (2006) contend that teachers need to respond with empathy to students to show that they are accepting of the students' perspective. Empathetic respondents keep the lines of communication open so that problems can be understood and resolved within a framework of respect.

Rothstein and Jacobsen (2009) suggest that with schools concentrating on raising maths and literacy scores over the last decade there has been a significant reduction in the teacher time devoted to social responsibility toward their students. They contend that it is essential for teachers to support students' spiritual, moral, social and cultural development as well as concentrating on a narrow curriculum devoted to raising test scores in maths and literacy.

 Should schools be accountable for the social and emotional development of students as well as academic performance?

20.7 | ETHICAL RELATIONSHIPS BETWEEN A SCHOOL AND PRIVATE INDUSTRY

In a period of privatisation and corporate sponsorship, schools are becoming increasingly involved in sponsorship arrangements which create additional ethical tensions. To a certain extent schools have always been involved in seeking sponsorship support from the local community – for example, local firms advertising in the school magazine or paying for the printing of a program for a school sporting event. In recent years the opportunities and necessity for sponsorship have widened considerably. It is no longer a matter of gaining sponsorship to acquire resources or to supplement ongoing minor expenditure. For some schools it is rapidly becoming their life-blood (Skildum-Reid 1999; Cook & Barker 2001; Molnar 2005).

Molnar (2008) cites data from the 'Commercialism in Education Research Unit' at Arizona State University to demonstrate how pervasive commercial activities have become in schools and the rapidity of their growth. Notwithstanding, he also points out that the activities of corporations are difficult to determine as the 'gloss of charity tends to obscure what corporations get out of these connections' (Molnar 2008, p. 210).

It can be seen from Table 20.2 that private industry in the US has very close ties with many individual schools and school districts and that the collaboration is growing yearly. Of course there has been resistance to some commercial activities, especially the sale of junk food and soft drinks which are clearly linked to obesity and poor health in youth. There are ethical matters to consider also. Surely it is indefensible to allow corporations to direct millions of dollars of sophisticated advertising at children.

TABLE 20.2 Categories of commercial activity in schools in the US

Categories	Examples of firms	Percentage change from 2002–2003
1 **Sponsorship of programs and activities** • Provide awards, books and computers • Fund academic competitions	• Shell Oil • General Electric	+ 1
2 **Exclusive agreements** • Exclusive agreements to sell products in school grounds and to exclude competitors	• Coca Cola • Manufacturers of sweets and snacks	+ 65
3 **Incentive programs** • Incentives to students to achieve goals	• Pizza Hut's national reading incentive program • Scholastic – essay contest • National Basketball Association for a reading program	+ 8
4 **Appropriation of space** • Using school property to promote individual corporations	• Naming rights for schools and school facilities, for example Rust-Oleum paid $100 000 naming rights for a high school stadium • Apple computers	+ 300
5 **Sponsored educational materials** • Curriculum materials produced by or for an outside corporation	• Proctor and Gamble • Campbell soups	+ 400
6 **Electronic marketing** • Provision of free television equipment, web portals, cable television	• Channel One (free to schools if students watch 12 minutes of news and 2 minutes of commercials each day) • Cable in the Classroom • Futures for Kids	+ 11
7 **Fundraising** • Fundraising to cover operational costs of schools and extracurricular expenses	• Grocery chains such as Tyson Foods • Safeway supermarket chain • Target	+ 17

As noted in Table 20.2, the various tactics used by corporations are increasing rapidly – presumably because their advertising at children is working. As noted by Molnar (2008) 'commercialism in schools is a complex phenomenon that reflects powerful economic, social, cultural and political forces' (p. 214).

 How do you react to the statements that marketing that takes place in school grounds is immoral and destructive?

There are other wider links between private companies and education in the US. Other developments include the Educational Management Organisations (EMOs) – private companies that manage schools for profit. Furtwengler (1998) notes that two EMOs in the US are operating government schools in Arizona and Minnesota under contract.

Then there is the growth of charter schools. In many US states charters to run a public school are granted to groups of parents or teachers, or business organisations. In 2004 charter laws were in place in 40 states and national enrolments had swelled to some 685 000 students (Hoxby 2004). The growth of these charter schools has been due, in part at least, to the belief that a market-driven organisation will outperform a traditional bureaucratic model.

Commercial firms have moved rapidly into the field of testing. For example, an ASCD Smart Brief (2006, 18 March) notes that Harcourt Assessment has a $44 million contract with the state of Illinois to produce and administer Standards Achievement Tests.

The relationships between private industry and education in Australia might appear to be less advanced than in the US but without regular monitoring of data, such as that provided by the University of Arizona, it is difficult to know the true situation.

Partnerships and sponsorships with private industry and education systems do occur. For example, in Victoria the Board of Studies negotiated a partnership with McDonald's whereby part-time workers at McDonald's earned credit toward a Certificate II in Food Retailing, units that counted towards the Victorian Certificate of Education (VCE). This was discontinued in 2003 in favour of part-time apprenticeships (Sutton 2009).

In a number of education systems, incentive arrangements between major retailers and schools have been negotiated whereby certain levels of local purchases enable schools to obtain computers as 'rewards'.

Caution is obviously needed in considering sponsorships and partnerships in Australia. French (1992) argues that long-term sponsorships at system and school level should be the goal, but this requires major commitment from all players. The choice of companies to approach must be carefully discussed, making sure that links with particular firms do not compromise the integrity of the school or system and the goals that it upholds (Hargreaves & Fullan 1998). For example, there would be major ethical difficulties in establishing links with a cigarette manufacturer, a brewery, or companies producing unhealthy foods. Some moderate possible sponsorship arrangements are included in Figure 20.1.

Obtaining sponsorship necessitates convincing specific firms that your school has something to offer, which may involve further difficult, ethical decisions (Skildum-Reid 1999; Vining 2000). Some relevant questions might include:
- Is your school innovative?
- Does your school have a particular philosophy or mission that would be attractive to particular firms?
- Do you have site facilities that are special or attractive?
- Does your school have a local or national reputation in areas such as sports, art, music, technology or special needs?

Many private schools may have many of these attributes, but this would not be the case with government schools.

A newspaper article in one Australian state published a statement by the State Minister for Education that 'public schools need to market themselves better if they wanted to stop the trend towards parents choosing private schools for their children' (Strutt, *West Australian* 26 February 2006, p. 11).

Ethical issues emerge when staff and the school principal consider their school mission and the extent to which they want to redirect it to make it more conducive to sponsorship interests. Perhaps a number of staff will reject outright any such suggestions. Would any such redirections reduce the quality of the teaching and the ultimate learning benefits for students? What controls or checks would be needed? There would be myriad issues to discuss in sorting out some of these ethical matters.

Yet in the short term (and the long term), carefully planned sponsorship arrangements might be helpful to staff and students and the overall quality of the teaching–learning program. For example, some of the forms of sponsorship included in Figure 20.2 might be quite acceptable to staff and the local school community, with obvious financial gains for the school.

FIGURE 20.1 Some possible sponsorship arrangements

- Money for a specific piece of equipment
- Funds to defray cost of trips, leaflets or other school publications
- Help to stage events in school (plays, conferences, special visitors or guests)
- The purchase of specific books for specific courses
- Help to buy a new school minibus
- Sponsoring a student (or member of staff) on a course
- Equipping classrooms or specific areas of the school with carpets, blinds, furniture or equipment
- Help to fund a new course or pilot project
- A contribution to prizes for Speech Day/Awards Day
- Giving time and expertise in the classroom or on wider curriculum projects
- Encouraging companies to advertise themselves at public functions for which the school would charge (careers conventions, for example)
- Encouraging closer liaison with the school by means of work experience placements

Source: Adapted from L French, 'Marketing and public relations for schools', in J Donnelly (ed.), The School Management Handbook*, 1992, Kogan Page, London, pp. 135 and 136.*

FIGURE 20.2 What a school can offer a potential sponsor

- Carrying the company's name (on a minibus, a suite of rooms, programs etc.)
- Putting school building grounds at their disposal for social or training purposes (sports grounds, meeting rooms, conference facilities or short-course provision)
- Publicity for both organisations in the press, radio or television
- Providing work experience for students where appropriate
- Providing future employees for the company
- Being part of their industry–school program (if they have one)
- Offering to undertake research projects for the company (e.g. an upper school student project)
- Offering help for which you have facilities (loaning of multimedia material, printing facilities, loan of minibus for weekend/holiday use or catering)

Source: Adapted from L French, 'Marketing and public relations for schools', in J Donnelly (ed.), The School Management Handbook*, 1992, Kogan Page, London, pp. 135 and 136.*

YOUR TURN

What types of sponsorship, if any, do you consider are acceptable for a school? Consider how any of these arrangements might help or hinder your teaching.

20.8 | LEGAL ISSUES IN TEACHING

Education and the law has not been a contentious issue in Australia until recent decades. If comparisons are made with the amount of litigation on educational matters in the US, the number of cases in Australia is infinitesimally low!

Birch and Richter (1990) contend that the number of school law cases in Australia is low because of three main factors, namely:

1. The comparative ignorance of participants (especially parents and students) of their legal rights.
2. The prohibitive legal and personal costs associated with the taking of action.
3. The absence of entrenched rights for Australian citizens in national or state constitutions.

Each of the states has Education Acts and there are Education Ordinances for the federal territories (enacted laws). For each of these Acts and Ordinances there are regulations – usually in loose-leaf form and subject to regular amendments.

In addition, case law is very significant, comprising decisions made by judicial and quasi-judicial organisations. As noted by Birch and Richter (1990, p. 140), 'case law may interpret enacted law to correct the unlawful practices engaged in custom law or "make" law in the sense that the courts determine what the law is in an area such as torts (the law involving the wrong doing by one person to another), for which there is little or no enacted law'.

Recent examples indicate that the number of litigations is rising in Australia because, increasingly, individuals will challenge if they feel disaffected or disadvantaged by the education system. Stewart (2005) notes that there has been a dramatic increase in both case and statute law over the last decade and there are now many instances of 'students, or their parents, or other persons seeking legal redress for alleged harms incurred in school settings' (p. 130).

20.9 | RIGHTS OF TEACHERS

Teachers, like any other workers, do a job where tasks to be performed are defined. Further, all workers are subjected to some form of oversight mechanism whereby incumbents are monitored for their performance of these tasks.

Mitchell and Kerchner (1983) suggest that jobs can have tasks planned (for example, automobile assembly) or adaptive, where workers have to accommodate unexpected elements (for example, firefighters). Monitoring of tasks can also be by direct oversight (as with assembly line workers) or indirect (as with architects). They contend that it is possible to produce a matrix to illustrate these categories (see Table 20.3) and that teachers belong to the 'profession' category. It is interesting to note that teachers are required to be responsible for activities and that malpractice is a basis for some kind of reprimand, including lawsuits.

Teachers' rights are clearly a difficult balancing act. On the one hand they have the freedom to exercise personal rights, but they are also obligated to support the welfare of schools and students (see also Chapter 19).

 Reflect on what you consider are your personal rights. To what extent do these personal rights support or differ from school responsibilities?

TABLE 20.3 Matrix of task structures

	Direct inspection	Indirect monitoring
Preplanned tasks	Labour (loyalty/insubordination)	Craft (precision/incompetence)
Adaptive tasks	Art (sensitivity/frivolousness)	Profession (responsibility/malpractice)

As noted above, there have been numerous court actions against teachers in the US, and cases are increasing in number in Australia over recent years (religious teaching 1976, New South Wales; corporal punishment 1959, Queensland; teacher negligence 1977, Queensland; and system negligence 1982, High Court; cited in Birch and Richter 1990).

Some issues that often arise in the courts include those noted below.

20.9.1 Academic freedom

This is interpreted in terms of freedom to teach and freedom to learn. It deals mainly with issues in the classroom and the teachers' and students' rights to discuss ideas and read material of their choosing (Ryan & Cooper 2008). Conflicts often arise when controversial issues are discussed in classrooms, such as sexual mores or abortion (ASCD 2005, 30 August). Political controversies can also be a point of tension.

Major sources of legal controversy are particular books that contain offensive passages or sexually explicit material. Many education systems have committees to monitor and classify printed materials. In a number of cases, written material is excluded because of unacceptable content about such areas as racial implications, religious debasement, family life and sex education.

Middleton (1994) describes her membership of the Indecent Publication Tribunal in New Zealand and notes the tension between, on the one hand, protecting students from explicit materials and exploitation and on the other, fostering liberty for individuals and freedom of expression.

Palfreyman (2007) highlights the extent to which the law protects individual teachers' right to express their views and opinions freely without fear of reprisal. He concludes that in some countries academic freedom can be threatened by government anti-terror legislation but more insidious pressures are likely to come from social and religious conservatism.

 Anti-terror legislation is now in place in Australia at federal and state levels. Persons convicted to date have been involved in training with terrorist organisations and producing books to incite, but it is conceivable that in the future teachers might be accused of being involved in various ways. What safeguards should you take as a teacher to prevent accusations of involvement?

20.9.2 Employment discrimination

Teachers are subjected to various layers of regulation including *state education statutes* (determining, for example, finances allocated to schooling sectors); *parliamentary regulations* (which may state curriculum requirements); *administrative instructions* (including those covering leave provisions, copyright restrictions); and *school rules* (such as school procedures and codes of conduct). These various laws and regulations impact heavily on teacher behaviour and to a large extent limit opportunities for reform (Angus 1998).

Employment arrangements for teachers now vary considerably between and within systems due to the emergence of contract positions, fewer opportunities for tenure, and school council powers to hire and dismiss staff (Education Victoria 1998).

Recent Equal Opportunity Acts in Australia at federal and state levels have to some extent reduced discrimination based on race, sex and age.

20.9.3 Freedom of speech

Teachers are generally permitted to speak and write freely on a range of topics, but there are often state government regulations that prevent topics relating to working conditions being discussed.

20.9.4 Copying of published materials

Copyright law is designed to give authors the right to own their creative works (Fischer, Schimmel & Kelly 2008).

It can affect teachers in terms of copyright of their own creative works, but mainly it applies to 'fair use' in making copies of other authors' copyrighted work. There are a range of categories that might be included under 'fair use' applying to books and papers, music, television programs, CDs, DVDs, videotapes and computer software.

Copyright laws are now well established in Australia and there are specific rules relating to the nature of the material, the audiences and the permitted number of copies that can be made. Recent court actions against several universities and schools indicate that this issue will remain a major one in the foreseeable future.

20.9.5 Defamation

Teachers have access to a wide range of personal and academic data about individual students. Although these data may be communicated to other teachers and administrators, the information is privileged.

If statements are made 'which expose another person to hatred, shame, disgrace, contempt or ridicule they are defamatory' (Fischer, Schimmel & Kelly 2008, p. 113). If the statements are spoken they are called 'slander'. If the statements are written they are called 'libel'.

There have been legal cases where students and their parents have sued for defamation when privileged information has been communicated to outside parties.

20.9.6 Negligence

A school and its teachers must ensure a safe educational environment for its students. Professionals are generally being held more accountable for their actions and litigation is becoming more prevalent.

Teachers basically have three main responsibilities, according to Travers and Reborc (1990). These are to:
- adequately supervise their students
- provide proper instruction
- maintain the safety of the students while under their supervision.

According to Newnham (2000), parents and students are more willing nowadays to pursue their rights through the process of litigation to recover compensation. She states that 'litigation may follow breaches of the *Education Act*, negligence, breach of contract, defamation, assault and educational malpractice' (p. 52).

Negligence is defined in terms of:
- duty of care – to avoid acts that would be likely to injure another person (the plaintiff sues the teacher and/or the school authority as the defendant)
- foreseeability – if the consequences of the act are likely, then the teacher or the school authority is liable
- breach of duty – the standard of care of a teacher is that of a reasonable parent
- causation – the plaintiff must show a sufficiently close connection between the breach of duty and the damage.

Although this list may appear to be very daunting to teachers and especially beginning teachers, Newnham (2000) is more cheerful when she notes that a plaintiff must prove all elements of negligence in order to successfully sue for negligence.

Notwithstanding, teachers and schools need to be aware of their legal responsibilities to students. Varnham (2001) also notes that school managers and trustees need to be very aware of a school's responsibility in respect of teacher misconduct towards students. Thus, if fighting occurs in a classroom and a student is injured due to insufficient teacher supervision, the teacher may well be liable.

As noted by Brown and Munn (2008), school violence has increased dramatically and this puts considerable strain on teachers. Even though it might be argued that school violence is a social problem and reflects a lack of social cohesion, it still behoves teachers to be wary of accusations that might be levelled at them over supervision responsibilities and duty of care.

Other legal cases have resulted when injuries and even death occurred for particular students while on a school excursion, such as visits to the zoo, camping excursions and Duke of Edinburgh Award activities (Tronc 2002; Parry & Clarke 2004; Han & Akiba 2005).

Injury claims from students involved in unpaid work experience or work placements are a major concern for many high schools. There have been instances where individual schools and systems have not had sufficient insurance cover for payment of compensation due to student injuries or damage to employers' equipment (Cumming 1998).

The provision of proper instruction has appeared as a legal issue in recent years, especially with regard to Special Education students. In competitive times where schools are actively marketing the advantages of one school over another, it can lead to litigation if parents have evidence to demonstrate that a school has failed to deliver a product or service (Mawdsley & Cumming 2008).

Not necessarily leading to litigation yet, but a possible reason for further investigation, are schools that provide 'freebies' to students in a bid to boost student enrolment and to prevent the school being shut down. For example, secondary students enrolling at Hong Kong secondary schools will receive free textbooks, free lunch for a year, one set of free summer and winter uniforms and HK$600 in book subsidies (*The Standard*, 10 July 2009, p. 1).

The checklist in Figure 20.3 is a useful reminder of particular situations that have led to legal action in the United Kingdom.

FIGURE 20.3 Checklist of situations that impose a duty of care

- Supervision of children
    - before the start of the school day
    - during breaks
    - over lunch
    - after the end of the school day and at 'after-school' clubs
    - in lessons and within the classroom
    - in laboratories
    - in workshops
    - on school transport
    - on out-of-school activities (cultural and recreational days out, field trips, activity centres, trips abroad and foreign exchanges)
- Sports and games
- Safety of the school premises
    - the duty of care for students, and indeed for staff or even for trespassers (including children out of school hours, over the weekend and during school holidays)
- Security of the school
    - parental access
    - intruders
- Administering medicines and first aid

20.9.7 Discipline

Corporal punishment is used very infrequently now in most school systems throughout Australia. Alternatives now used are chiefly exclusion from classes, detentions and suspension from schools. Yet there are still provisions in the Criminal Code, according to Birch and Richter (1990), that empower teachers to administer punishment, including corporal punishment in some circumstances. Teachers in the private school sector continue the practice of corporal punishment in some instances.

> **YOUR TURN**
>
> You have made arrangements for your Year 6 class to visit the city zoo.
> - What duty of care arrangements must you consider?
> - Consider the extra adults who may be needed to provide adequate duty of care. What will be their responsibilities?
> - What are your responsibilities?

20.10 | RIGHTS OF STUDENTS

Papers are published from time to time on specific examples of student rights. Examples are given below.

20.10.1 Discipline and punishment, exclusion from school

Osler (2000) examines children's rights with regard to *discipline and punishment*. She argues that schools need to follow the United Nations Convention on the Rights of the Child in formulating an overall management strategy and not merely respond to situations in an ad hoc way.

Tronc (2002) notes that corporal punishment is still an available option legally in some non-government schools but the legal position in some states, such as Queensland, appears to include inconsistencies.

Exclusion from school is another important element relating to the rights of students. Munn et al. (2001) argue that exclusion from school has serious consequences for young people in Scotland and England. It can reduce their opportunities to gain educational qualifications and it can adversely influence a young person's self-esteem. They provide evidence from schools in Scotland that the number of children excluded from school is a cause for concern. They contend that schools must seriously examine their ethos and staff beliefs if exclusions are to be minimised.

Partington's (2001) study of Years 8–10 in government schools in Western Australia noted that suspensions of students from school increased from 2500 in 1993 to 17 000 in 1999. He concluded from his research that many schools issued unjustified suspensions which were in breach of policies that espouse equity, fairness and communication.

MacLeod (2007) and Hayden and Blaya (2008) note that exclusion from school inevitably leads to early 'drop outs' from education and training. Exclusions from school can reinforce in the minds of students their dissatisfaction with the content of the mainstream curriculum.

20.10.2 Privacy: searches, confiscations and drug testing

Searches and confiscations is another major issue, particularly with regard to the number of cases of students possessing weapons and illegal drugs. Ehlenberger (2002) notes that school officials need only reasonable suspicion to search students in public schools, but sworn law enforcement officials normally must have probable cause to search students. She contends that 'the best search policies are developed by school boards who work collaboratively with local law enforcement officials, local judges and attorneys, school staff and community members' (p. 35).

To strip search or not to strip search is a perplexing issue facing school leaders. 'Since this type of search is the most intrusive of all searches, reasonable cause must be established prior to the search' (Essex 2005, p. 109). Although leaders might have suspicions about a student carrying drugs and want to organise a strip search, they run the risk of inviting significant legal challenges.

Drug use and abuse are of considerable concern in many schools. As noted above, there are limits on the authority of school officials to search students. The drug testing of students is an extension of the issue. According to Russo (2001), the courts in the US have indicated that they will uphold drug testing in schools only if it is based on individualised suspicion or where it is carried out randomly for students, such as those in extracurricular activities.

Although there is little comparative information about Australian students, statistics on drug use in the US are disturbing. In 2001, 15 per cent of 8th graders, 33 per cent of 10th graders and 37 per cent of 12th graders had used marijuana in the past year, while 10 per cent, 17 per cent and 20 per cent respectively had used an illicit drug other than marijuana in the same period (Johnston, O'Malley & Backman 2002). Further, the National Centre for Education Statistics (2001) stated that, in 1997 and 1999, 30–32 per cent of students reported someone offering, selling or giving them an illegal drug on school property.

Schools have to juggle the multiple priorities of academic standards and a safe and drug-free school environment (Yamaguchi; O'Malley & Johnston 2004). School principals have increasingly resorted to school searches for drugs when they have reasonable suspicion about a group of students. Yet these school searches are highly expensive to undertake and there may be potential negative effects on school climate (Hyman & Perone 1998).

There are other issues such as which groups have access to drug tests of students which are carried out confidentially. Should it be social workers and/or parents and/or schools? (Lam & Lee 2009).

20.10.3 Property

Lost property is another vexatious issue that has legal implications, especially with the widespread use by students of mobile phones, laptop computers and tablet computers. According to Monterosso (2002), new legislation in Western Australia requires the school principal to follow strict procedures including taking possession of the lost items; undertaking reasonable steps to establish the rightful owner's identity; if the owner cannot be located, placing advertisements in local newspapers for items valued at more than $100; and after a two-week period if the identity of the owner is not discovered, arranging for the property to be sold or given away.

20.10.4 Use of camera/video phones in schools

The emergence of mobile phones with built-in digital cameras is creating legal and ethical concerns for school systems throughout the world. Users of such phones can instantly email, print or post pictures to other mobiles or websites (Parry 2005).

In Australia, Britain, the US and Canada, local authorities and schools have introduced outright bans. There have been incidents such as the Singaporean student who took a three-minute video clip of an emotionally overwrought teacher berating another student in front of the class and then posted it on the Internet (Parry 2005).

The use of camera phones raises a basic problem of invasion of privacy. Yet if a school bans the use of camera phones, parents and students could well object because the phone was probably purchased for convenience and security reasons.

This is a classic case of deciding upon issues of privacy versus students' rights to own and use a camera phone. As noted by Parry (2005), this is one of the many instances where developments in technology have outpaced laws and regulation. Of course, there may be other technological advances about to be launched that will create new ethical and legal challenges.

20.10.5 Wearing the hijab or jilbab

Wearing the hijab or jilbab is another very complex issue revolving around such matters as individual religious convictions and the need for modesty; school uniform and the authority of the school; and discrimination against women and girls. Blair and Aps (2005) contend that laws on the protection of human rights and the overcoming of racial discrimination in many countries need to be rationalised to provide consistency.

Smith (2007) notes that the European Union might be brought into legal cases that have surfaced in France, Belgium, Germany and the UK and that human rights challenges could possibly be successful.

As an example, a Shiite Muslim student attending a Sydney girls' high school fought a two-month battle for the right to wear a mantoo (an ankle-length religious coat). Her principal had earlier given her detention for breaching the school's dress code. The state Premier finally publicly supported the student's action and this ended the media furore. However, it did not resolve issues about the implementation of the government's uniform policy (*Sydney Morning Herald* 18 May 2005).

Wake and Sangster (2008) refer to a case in the UK where a school principal banned a 14-year-old school girl from wearing a Kara (plain steel bangle with significance for the Sikh religion) because it contravened the school dress code. Although it might be construed that this was unjustified racial and religious discrimination, appeals by the parents of the girl were not successful.

20.10.6 Student rights regarding graduation

There have been ongoing appeals in the US over graduation opportunities and errors that have proved to be embarrassing if not financially draining for schools. For example, in California a group of 10 students and their parents appealed to a San Francisco Superior Court to suspend use of scores as a determinant of graduation (ASCD 2006, 10 February).

In New York a senior student filed a class-action suit against the College Board claiming that he was unfairly assessed. He sought damages and a refund of test fees (ASCD 2006, 11 April).

20.10.7 Bullying

Bullock (2002) defines bullying or victimisation as the repeated exposure over time to negative actions on the part of one or more others. That is, bullying is not just physical assault. It can also include name-calling and teasing, hitting, kicking and isolation (Garbarino & deLara 2003). According to research undertaken by Sweeting and West (2001) and Cooper and Snell (2003), bullying may begin with labelling but once begun it is hard to stop.

Cyber-bullying (as described in Chapter 13) is a growing version of bullying. Varjas, Hendrick and Meyers (2009) contend that cyber-bullying occurs relatively independently from school-based bullying (physical and verbal bullying) and is even more difficult to address.

Most educators agree that bullying at schools is closely linked to family characteristics (Holt, Kantor & Finkelhor 2009) and especially to domestic violence at home (Georgiou 2009). Lambert, Scourfield, Smalley and Jones (2008) contend that school-based prevention initiatives such as clear policies on bullying can lead to a reduction in bullying. Yet they also admit that school policies can only have very limited impact on home circumstances where there are frequent occurrences of conflict and violence.

The Children's Court in each state currently deals with restraining orders served on students who have been found to be bullying other students. This is a growing problem and the number of restraining orders issued each month is increasing (Rigby 1996).

Stein (1999) contends that bullying in early grades is closely related to sexual harassment in later grades. She provides a wealth of data to support her stance that sexual harassment is a problem in schools. Stein argues that school officials are not familiar with the signs and existence of sexual harassment in schools and, furthermore, they have no policies to deal with the problem.

Sears (1999) argues that adolescents who 'have come out' about their sexual preferences are very frequently bullied in schools. The bullying can range from casual verbal abuse and ridicule to serious physical attacks.

20.10.8 Protection from paedophiles

There has been growing public awareness of the existence of paedophiles, and child sex abuse, and this has of course created considerable anxiety for children and their parents.

Hinkelman and Bruno (2008) note that primary school teachers have special responsibilities because the majority of sexually abused youth are often victims between the ages of 8 and 12 years. They contend that primary school teachers need to be aware of children who have regular physical complaints (for example, headaches and stomach sickness) and have academic difficulties (for example, lower achievement scores and lower performance on memory tasks). Walsh and Farrell (2008) in their study of early childhood teachers in Australia also concluded that teachers needed more specialist knowledge for dealing capably with cases of child abuse and neglect.

Gibson (2009) notes that reports of child sex abuse in Western Australia has soared by 80 per cent since mandatory reporting laws began on 1 January 2009. Police clearances are now mandatory for teachers prior to entering the teaching service, but this has not prevented a number of teachers across all states and territories being charged by the federal police for dealing in child pornography and abusing children. The vetting of teachers who wish to work with children is a complex matter and the categories and exclusions are complex, according to Gillespie (2007). Also, arguments can be raised about whether a restorative justice approach directed toward healing and reconciliation, rather than a severe retributive, punitive criminal justice system might be more suitable in at least some cases (Monterosso 2007).

However it should be noted that students do not only risk being sexually assaulted by teachers. Dunford (2006) contends that students are at greater risk of sexual assaults from other students than from teachers.

Clearly, the Internet has allowed pornography to flourish. It has also been the source used by federal police to search out and charge potential paedophiles for illegal behaviours. There are various parent and public action groups against paedophiles. For example, <www.kidscope.org.uk/parents/paedophiles.shtml> provides valuable information on:

- who are paedophiles?
- what paedophiles typically say when they approach children
- what parents can do
- what to tell your children
- if children get lost
- if children travel alone
- children having access to a mobile phone
- what if something happens? (if approached, children should make a fuss).

20.11 | ENFORCEMENT OF RIGHTS

20.11.1 Court cases and the provision of legal advice

Many of the court cases in the US have involved consideration of excessive punishment, through corporal punishment, assault and battery, negligence, suspension, search and seizure, defamation and rights to privacy, and away-from-school injuries.

A number of court cases are now occurring in Australia (see section 20.8 above). The National Children's and Youth Law Centre was established in 1993 with a three-year seeding grant from the Australian Youth Foundation to be an advocate for children and young people. During this period it published and widely distributed *Know Your Rights at School* (National Children's and Youth Law Centre 1994). This included detailed information sheets, and special editions were produced for each state and territory's government schools. NCYLC authors of each special edition stress that specific information only applies to that state.

The NCYLC provides information online, termed *Lawstuff* <www.lawstuff.org.au>. The Centre has developed a national profile among children and young people and is recognised as one of a few peak national bodies advocating for children and young people. For example, *Lawstuff* includes information on a range of topics including bullying, leaving home, mobile phones, sexual harassment, tattoos and piercings (Lawstuff 2009).

Some details and extracts from <www.lawstuff.org.au> 'School' (2010) NCYLC information sheets follow.

20.11.2 Discipline and punishment

The information sheet on discipline and punishment lists the methods that schools typically use to enforce school rules, namely:
- praise and reward
- education
- taking away privileges
- time out from class
- involving the student's parents
- shaming
- detention or extra work.

The document states that there should be a discipline policy drawn up by the school decision-making group, that students and parents should have real input into the policy, and that it is the school principal's responsibility to ensure that students have full information about the discipline policy.

The remaining segments of this information sheet have a question-and-answer format, including the following:

(Q) Can I be grounded or stopped from going on a school visit?

(A) A school can restrict or prohibit a student's participation in a school activity or activities if you break the school rules. However you cannot be denied teaching materials or the opportunity to fulfil course requirements or assessments, including the opportunity to attend a field trip during school hours that is part of your education. You cannot be excluded from school activities such as a school prize-giving, or parents' evening.

A school cannot block you from attending a school activity that is part of your essential educational program if you do not have the correct school uniform on. You can be blocked from attending an activity due to incorrect uniform only if you will be representing your school. If you are to be stopped from attending a school activity, your parents must be consulted.

You could be grounded from school socials or sports or cultural activities outside school hours, or from non-educational activities during school hours. However, the school cannot ban you from a private party organised by other students or parents. Nor is the school responsible for your behaviour at such private social functions.

A teacher or the school principal can order you to leave a class or wait in a particular place for a short period if your behaviour is disrupting the class. If you are out of class for a longer period, for example for more than one school period, you should be supervised and given school work to do.

(Q) Can a teacher ridicule or humiliate me?

(A) No. A teacher may criticise your work or your behaviour, but the United Nations Convention on the Rights of the Child (CROC) states that school discipline must be consistent with a student's human dignity. Teachers should not treat you with ridicule or make offensive personal remarks. Any comments which put you down because of your sex, race, culture or disability may amount to unlawful discrimination. Teachers, as well as students, should not engage in bullying behaviour. That is any offensive or aggressive behaviour, which can be physical, social or emotional, that is repeated over time. Such conduct is likely to be in breach of the teachers' code of conduct and also school policies.

Teachers must avoid giving any degrading or injurious punishment. You should not be made to stand in one position for more than a short period or be given an unpleasant job such as cleaning out the toilets. But if you drop litter in the class or playground the school may make you tidy the classroom or collect rubbish. You can be made to clean up your graffiti.

Remember, when you treat teachers and other school staff with courtesy and respect, they are more likely to treat you in the same way.

(Q) What are my rights if I am put on detention?

(A) A teacher can hold you back after school if you break the school rules but not for an inability to learn. You should not be given detention because you are a slow learner or having difficulties with your work.

Before the school can keep you back, they must obtain your parent's or caretaker's consent and make sure that there is an arrangement to get you home from school. If there is no alternative arrangement to get home, the school should not keep you back. Teachers should not make you attend detention outside the school grounds.

You should not be left alone for long periods of time during a detention. You should be given meaningful work to do, not humiliating tasks like writing 100 times 'I am a stupid person'.

(Q) Can teachers or the principal use the strap or cane?

(A) No! The cane, the strap, or any other form of corporal punishment is forbidden in all government schools. It is up to the Principal how students will be disciplined at your school but they cannot include forms of physical punishment.

However, school teachers can use reasonable force to control a student under their care. This is usually as a last resort and used in situations where a student is harming themselves or is a safety risk to other students.

(Q) What if I think a punishment is unfair?

(A) The school principal and your teachers have the legal power to enforce standards of behaviour to help the school carry out its responsibility to educate students.

If a punishment is serious (such as suspension from school) the school has to take great care to make sure that the facts are investigated properly and that the student and the parents have a chance to give their point of view. In some cases the courts have overruled decisions of a teacher or school principal where the student was not given a fair hearing.

If you feel you have been unfairly treated or are about to be punished unreasonably there are things you could do.

- If the teacher has given the punishment, ask to see the year advisor or school principal and give your point of view.
- Ask your parents or carers for support and get them to take the matter up with the school principal, the school counsellor or school decision-making group.
- Get support from your student representative on the school decision-making group or from a youth group, cultural group or legal advice agency.

It is always a good idea to write out your version of what happened. You could ask someone else to write it down as you tell it. If there are arguments over what was done and said it will help if the facts are written down as soon as possible.

Source: <www.lawstuff.org.au>, *School – Discipline and Punishment*, 2010.

20.11.3 Searches and confiscations

This information sheet states that students have the same legal protection of their property as anyone else:

Australian law protects the rights of people to their own property and to enjoy the use of their property. If you own something then it is against the law for anyone to take it from you against your wishes, to refuse to return it if you ask, or to deliberately damage it.

Schools can make reasonable rules about what you can and cannot bring to school. They can ban anything that is illegal or dangerous or is likely to cause disruption to the smooth running of the school and the education of other students.

The remaining segments of the information sheet continue the question-and-answer format, including the following:

(Q) What can I take to school?

(A) You can take anything to school unless it is:
- *dangerous or illegal*: such as drugs, guns, knives or other items such as knuckle dusters or irritant sprays
- *forbidden by school rules*: a principal can forbid an item being taken to school to ensure the safety and welfare of persons on the school's premises (items likely to include cigarettes, certain items of jewellery and matches)
- *likely to cause disruption to the school*: a principal can prohibit an item being taken to school to maintain good order on the school premises (such as stereos, a pet snake or a noisy whistle or toy).

However, if you take valuable items to school they are your responsibility and you cannot expect the school to compensate you if they are lost or stolen. A school staff member or the school office may agree to look after it for you.

(Q) Do teachers have a right to search me or my school bag?

(A) Teachers have no right to search you or your school bag unless you agree. If you have nothing to hide, it may be easier to agree to a search, but you do not have to. However it may be part of the teacher's authority to maintain order and discipline to conduct a search of a student in a serious matter. Any such search should be undertaken only when necessary for the prevention of harm and where no other response is possible. Even then, it should be undertaken sensitively, in private, with an independent witness, and a search of a female student should not be undertaken by a male teacher.

(Q) If I do not agree can a teacher search me by force?

(A) No. Teachers have no right to use physical force on you to carry out a search of your clothing, pockets or your bag except when there is a threat to the safety of other students. It is an assault and a criminal offence if a teacher searches you, or grabs your school bag or clothing without your permission. But a teacher can ask you to open up your bag or empty out your pockets. Desks are school property and teachers can look inside even if you object. Lockers may be searched for the same reason, if it was provided to you for free or you paid a refundable deposit. If you paid a non-refundable deposit, then the school cannot search your locker, unless you signed a contract allowing this.

Searching students should generally be done by the police who are authorised to conduct such searches. If the school calls the police they may, in certain circumstances, perform a search without a warrant. The police can only do this if there are facts to support a reasonable suspicion that you have something that may be a weapon, drugs, stolen goods or evidence of a crime.

(Q) If the school gets permission from my parents or carer to search me must I let them?

(A) You can decide for yourself whether to let a teacher search you or your bag. Your parents cannot give permission on your behalf unless you are so young that you cannot make your own decision. Teachers should get your permission before any search is carried out.

(Q) Can the school confiscate clothing or personal property without my consent?

(A) Teachers cannot take any of your personal property from you unless you agree. Teachers cannot force you to hand over non-uniform clothing or jewellery. But teachers do have the authority to control and manage the classroom, and you may be disciplined if you do not agree. If you agree to hand it over to a teacher, it should be returned to you at the end of the day.

There are exceptions to this general rule. A teacher who thinks that an item of property is a serious threat to your safety or the safety of other students is entitled to confiscate it. If you have dangerous weapons, drugs, alcohol, cigarettes, fireworks, jewellery with sharp edges, stolen property or indecent literature at school you can be required to hand them to a teacher. Any drugs, weapons or stolen property you have on you may be handed to the police. Other items should be handed back to you or your parents as soon as possible, usually at the end of the day.

(Q) What if a teacher takes something of mine and does not give it back?

(A) A teacher who confiscates something of yours must look after it, keep it safely and take care to ensure it is not damaged. If the teacher loses or damages your property, you can ask the teacher to replace it or pay you the value of the item. A teacher does not have to return an item if it is in police custody.

(Q) What about mobile phones and iPods?

(A) The school may prohibit mobile phones or other electronic devices at school or set conditions on their use. An example of such a condition would be not using the phone during class times. These rules would be in place to ensure that other students do not have their education disrupted. You may face disciplinary action if you break these rules and may be asked to hand your electronic device in.

Where the item's use contravenes the school's 'Acceptable Use Policy', they may be confiscated by school staff. They should be returned at the end of the school day.

(Q) Do teachers or the school have any special powers to search for drugs?

(A) No. The only people who have special powers to search for illegal drugs are the police. This means that if a teacher wants to search you for drugs you can refuse. They cannot order or force you to agree to the search.

(Q) Can teachers call the police to come to the school to carry out a search?

(A) Yes. The school can ask the police to the school to search you if the school believes you have drugs. The school must tell your parents or carer and ask them to come to school to be with you when you are searched or questioned.

A police officer who has a search warrant or reasonable grounds for thinking that you have drugs on you has the authority to search you or your bag without your consent. Not agreeing to a police search could lead to your arrest.

Source: <www.lawstuff.org.au>, *School – Searches and Confiscations*, 2010. <end Q>

20.11.4 Exclusion from school

Every Australian child has a right to be educated at a government school. This is a basic human right and is recognised throughout Australia and internationally through the United Nations Convention on the Rights of the Child (CROC). Exclusion from a school should be a last resort only.

Suspensions and expulsions are strategies within the student welfare policy and discipline code of the school. These strategies will be implemented in cases of unacceptable behaviour, where it will be in the best interests of the school community and/or the student involved, for the student to be removed from the school for a period of time or completely. Schools and the relevant Department of Education must act fairly when considering whether to suspend or expel the student.

(Q) Can I be suspended from school?

(A) A school principal can suspend any student for a breach of the school rules and after other efforts to control the behaviour of the student have failed. Suspensions should be for the shortest time necessary. Before you are suspended the principal must provide notice to you and your parents about the length of time, and reasons for the proposed suspension, and provide you with an opportunity to comment. For a serious breach of school rules a principal can suspend a student immediately. But soon after the suspension has taken place, the same notice must be provided to the student and the parents about the suspension. A suspended student must be given opportunities to fulfil their course requirements and assessments. In some cases, a conference with your parents or carers and the principal will be arranged which may result in a behaviour improvement plan being prepared. A formal appeal process may also be available, depending on the length of the suspension and the procedures in place in each particular state.

(Q) Can the school send me home if I misbehave or if I break school rules?

(A) You cannot be sent home for not being in school uniform or for breaking other school rules. You are entitled to be at school during school hours unless you have been suspended by the principal. However, the school may contact your parents and ask that you be taken home.

(Q) When can a student be expelled from school?

(A) A student can be expelled from school when there has been a serious breach of the school rules, such as behaviour that threatens the safety of a person on the school premises, or is likely to cause damage to property, or has seriously disrupted the education of other students. The behaviour leading to a recommendation of expulsion can be either a serious one-off incident or a pattern of behaviour. A student who is older than the school leaving age may also be expelled if they have shown unsatisfactory participation in school activities.

(Q) What is an expulsion?

(A) An expulsion (in some states known as exclusion) means you have to leave your school. In most stages, the principal only has the power to recommend expulsion. Only the principal's supervisor can expel you. A school must send a written notice to the student and their parents of the recommendation to expel and explaining the reasons. The student is placed on suspension until a decision is made and should be given school work to do in that time.

You and parents must be given the chance to explain your side of the story and any special circumstances that support your argument that you should not be expelled.

If you are expelled, you and your parents must be notified of the right to appeal. There are appeal procedures set by the Department of Education in each state. The Department of Education must assist you to enrol in an alternative school.

(Q) What arguments can I put forward in the appeal?

(A) You and your parents should go through any incident reports or school counsellor reports carefully and, if there is anything that you think is incorrect or exaggerated, you should write out your version of what happened and the reasons why you think the expulsion would be unfair. Take along any good school reports or character references you can get. Ask a sympathetic teacher or school psychologist to support you.

Arguments against expulsion:

- you have not done what the school says you have done
- you disagree with what is said to have happened and feel you should be given the benefit of the doubt

- the principal has not raised the matter with you or your parents before and they have not had the opportunity to deal with the problem
- the reasons for expulsion have not been proved
- you are being dealt with more harshly than other students who have misbehaved in the same way
- the discipline policies of the school or the Department of Education are not being followed
- the complaints against you are all from one teacher or staff member and are exaggerated – other teachers are satisfied with your behaviour
- your misbehaviour is not serious enough to justify expulsion
- other methods of discipline should be tried before expelling you
- your general behaviour in the school and at home causes no problems
- you should be given credit for your positive contributions to the school and not be judged on one or two incidents
- your behaviour was caused by cross-cultural misunderstandings or discrimination
- you and your family's personal circumstances deserve sympathy and you should be given another chance
- since the incident, your family has taken control of the situation and further misbehaviour is unlikely
- you should be offered counselling to deal with the cause of the problem rather than being expelled from school.

(Q) What can you do if you have been unfairly expelled?

(A)
- You can ask the Minister for Education to reconsider the decision.
- Ask a community legal centre or the National Children's and Youth Law Centre for advice and support.
- If you have been discriminated against because of your race, sex, political or religious beliefs, age or disability you can complain to the Australian Human Rights Commission or Anti Discrimination authority in your state.
- If you have not been given a fair hearing or if the legal grounds for expulsion have not been proved you can complain to the Ombudsman.
- You might be able to challenge the decision through the courts. You will need a lawyer to represent you but you might be granted legal aid.

<source> Source: <www.lawstuff.org.au>, *School – Suspensions and Expulsions*, 2010.

Source: National Children's and Youth Law Centre. Check out our website <www.lawstuff.org.au>.

The information sheets provided by NCYLC certainly highlight the rights of students and are providing a valuable service to students and parents (and teachers). The NCYLC online information website *Lawstuff* is designed to provide legal advice to under-18-year-olds. It allows students privacy in finding out about a range of legal rights. The site also has an email function called 'Lawmail' where students can get legal advice on specific problems.

CONCLUDING COMMENTS

There are a number of ethical matters relating to teacher–student, teacher–principal and teacher–community relationships. There are concerns that need to be reflected upon and discussed widely by school personnel. Legal issues are becoming more prevalent in Australia over recent years. As participants in the education system become more aware of their rights, the number of court actions is likely to increase markedly.

KEY ISSUES RAISED IN THIS CHAPTER

1. As well as intellectual development students need to acquire ethical standards and enduring moral habits.
2. In their daily teaching, teachers make trade-offs among competing demands but are guided by their moral values.
3. In all education systems there are regulations and requirements that affect how teachers can develop their values with their classes of students.
4. A teacher may have a panoply of well-developed values and purposes but these may be limited by the judgments of the principal.
5. Ethical relationships revolve around respect between teacher and student.
6. Schools are becoming increasingly involved in sponsorship arrangements, which create ethical tensions. Some critics argue that these arrangements are immoral and destructive.
7. A number of issues can arise over teachers' rights, especially academic freedom, defamation, negligence and discipline.
8. The rights of students also raises a number of issues especially the use of mobile phones with cameras, discipline and punishment, searches and confiscations.

REFLECTIONS AND ISSUES

1. The National Education Association in the USA has three sources of ethical ideals, namely ethics of inquiry (freedom to learn); a civic ethics (public conduct of citizens); and an ideal of professionalism (working with others to create, support and maintain challenging learning environments for all). Reflect on these ideals with regard to education in Australia. Discuss.
2. Before establishing a partnership with business, school personnel need to be sure of some fundamental points:
   - Will it serve the interests of all students?
   - Will the partnership be genuinely reciprocal?
   - Is the business or company socially responsible?

   Do you agree with Hargreaves and Fullan (1998) that these are important principles? Are there other issues to consider? Discuss.
3. What is your definition of academic freedom? How does this affect what controversial issues you might teach in your classroom? What restrictions are likely to be imposed on what you teach and by whom?
4. A high school administrator acting on information from a student conducts a search of a student locker and seizes some drugs. What are the rights of the teacher and the student whose locker was searched? What are the likely legal implications?
5. You observe a student of your school using obscene language and offensive behaviour at the local shopping centre. Do you discipline the student on the spot, refer the matter to the principal the next day, or do nothing? Give reasons for your stance.
6. Teachers and counsellors in a school must create an environment of open communication and develop school-based programs to increase school personnel's knowledge of abuse and understanding of its effects on student victims. Discuss points for and against this statement.

Special references

Fischer, L, Schimmel, D & Kelly, C (2008) *Teachers and the Law*, 4th edn, Longman, New York.
Imber, M & Van Geel, T (2004) *A Teacher's Guide to Education Law*, McGraw Hill, Hightstown, New Jersey.
Ryan, K & Cooper, JM (2008) *Those Who Can, Teach*, 9th edn, Houghton Mifflin, Boston.
Strike, K & Soltis, J (2004) *The Ethics of Teaching*, 4th edn, Teachers College Press, New York.
Urban, H (2004) *Positive Words, Powerful Results: Simple Ways to Honour, Affirm and Celebrate Life*, Fireside, New York.

Web sources

For additional resources on ethical and legal issues in teaching, please go to:
www.pearson.com.au/myeducationlab.

21
TEACHER COMPETENCIES AND STANDARDS

21.1 | INTRODUCTION

Devising standards for teaching is a laudable task, but one that has resulted in many disagreements and dead ends. Few would deny that teachers must set high standards, and as professionals they need to have professional standards that are publicly available. The difficulty arises in determining which standards should be applied and how they will be evaluated (McInerney, Van Etten & Dowson 2007; Ingvarson & Rowe 2007).

Hoban (2004) argues that it is nonsensical to talk about the 'best' standards because programs will 'vary according to the goals, course content, beliefs of the teacher educators, students and teachers, as well as the social–cultural contexts of schools involved' (p. 117).

It is widely recognised that the role of the teacher is probably more complex than it has ever been and now requires an unprecedented range of skills and knowledge (House of Representatives Inquiry into Teacher Education 2005). So how do we translate these skills into specific standards?

Louden (2000) contends that the first wave of professional standards for teachers in the 1990s was largely competency-based. A second wave has emerged: the standards appear to be higher than the first wave and they contain subject-specific sets of professional standards.

The House of Representatives Standing Committee on Education and Vocational Training's Inquiry into Teacher Education (2005) was wide-ranging in its Terms of Reference. It examined the preparation of primary and secondary teaching graduates and their ability to be able to:
- teach literacy and numeracy
- teach vocational education courses
- effectively manage classrooms
- successfully use information technology
- deal with bullying and disruptive students and dysfunctional families
- deal with children with special needs or disabilities
- achieve accreditation
- deal with senior staff, fellow teachers, school boards, education authorities, parents, community groups and other related government departments (p. 1).

> **YOUR TURN**
>
> How realistic is this list for pre-service teachers? What support will be needed to enable pre-service teachers to attain these competencies?

21.2 | QUALITY OF TEACHING – NATIONAL INQUIRIES AND PROGRAMS

Quality teachers are needed more than ever to assist students with their learning (Chauncey 2005). A positive teaching–learning relationship between the teacher and students is crucial at a time when 'increasing family breakdown, social and economic change and the uncertainties of the "risk" society have made more and more children in schools "casualties of change"' (Eckersley 1995).

Owen, Kos & McKenzie (2008) conclude from their survey that quality teachers are needed for:
- early childhood education
- Indigenous education
- vocational education and training
- middle years of schooling
- diverse and special needs among students.

These needs are complicated by ever-increasing quality assurance and public accountability demands (Dymoke & Harrison 2006; Cochran-Smith 2005). Education is largely taxpayer funded and increasingly market driven. As a consequence there has been a constant flow of reports and inquiries into teacher education over the decades to monitor or reform teaching and to attempt to achieve higher teaching standards (Darling-Hammond 2006). The reports have examined both the quality of teachers entering the profession (pre-service) and practising teachers (in-service) (Collinson 1999).

These major national inquiries into education (see Table 21.1) have, in many cases, caused new programs and services to be developed.

It is not possible to provide details of all these national inquiries, but several important ones are described.

 Have successive inquiries built on previous ones in terms of refinement? Read up about one of the inquiries listed in Table 21.1.

In 1973 the newly elected Labor government established a 'blue ribbon' committee of 11, chaired by Professor Peter Karmel, to inquire into education in Australian schools. The Karmel Committee (Karmel 1973) recommended seven major programs that were urgently needed to overcome gross inequalities in education. The Karmel Report recommendations were accepted in full by the federal government, and immediate steps were taken to provide a structure to implement them. By Act of Parliament, the Schools Commission was established in 1973 and given wide terms of reference.

The Schools Commission, through its Professional Development Program during the period 1974–77, provided substantial funding for a variety of in-service activities. The amount declined subsequently and all funding was discontinued in 1987.

A major program for improving education for youth, under the direction of the Commonwealth Schools Commission, was the Participation and Equity program (1984–87). This program promoted school improvement projects in the areas of teacher–student–parent interaction, curriculum, school structure and organisation by providing grants to the states and to designated 'target schools'.

The Australian Council of Trade Unions (ACTU) produced policy statements in its *Australia Reconstructed* (1987), in which it argued for skills in communications and numeracy and a common curriculum for all students. Award restructuring principles were subsequently negotiated with the federal government and this led to a national training agenda, an Australian Standards Framework with occupational competence defined in terms of an eight-step scale.

TABLE 21.1 Review of major national inquiries into education

Date	Title of committee	Major recommendations
1973	*Schools in Australia* (Karmel Committee)	Establish Schools Commission (especially Professional Development program 1974–87). Participation and Equity program 1984–87.
1980	*National Inquiry into Teacher Education* (Auchmuty Committee)	Core of studies and list of skills and knowledge for pre-service teachers.
1987	*Australia Reconstructed* (Australian Council of Trade Unions) *Skills for Australia* (Dawkins, DEET policy)	Skills in literacy and numeracy, common curriculum. Improving initial and ongoing training of teachers.
1990	*Teacher Education in Australia* (Ebbeck Committee)	Models of teacher preparation for early childhood, primary and secondary pre-service teachers.
1990	*Australia's Teachers: An Agenda for the Next Decade* (Schools Council, NBEET)	Report on problems faced by teachers.
1992	*Improving Australia's Schools* (National Industry Education Forum)	Performance appraisals of teachers and linkages with industry.
1996	*National Project on the Quality of Teaching and Learning* (NPQTL)	National Competency Framework for Beginning Teachers.
1998	*National Standards and Guidelines for Initial Teacher Education* (Australian Council of Deans of Education)	Draft standards and guidelines for initial teacher education.
1998	*A Class Act: Inquiry into the Status of the Teaching Profession* (Senate Employment, Education and Training References Committee)	The need to reorganise and assess teaching knowledge and skills.
1998	NSW Ministerial Advisory Council on the Quality of Teaching	The need to contextualise.
2003	Inquiry into the Suitability of Pre-service Training Courses (Victorian Education and Training Committee)	To investigate concerns about the quality and relevance of pre-service teacher education.
2005	*Knowing our Business: The role of education in the University* (Australian Council of Deans of Education)	Greater resources needed for Education as a specialist field.
2005	Inquiry into Teacher Education (House of Representatives Standing Committee on Education and Vocational Training, Commonwealth)	To ascertain the preparedness of graduates to meet current and future demands of teaching.

The Australian Education Council commissioned a report, *Teacher Education in Australia*, chaired by F Ebbeck. This report, released in 1990, recommended models of teacher preparation for early childhood, primary and secondary pre-service teachers. The first degree was to be complemented by a Bachelor of Education degree undertaken part-time by the pre-service teacher while employed half-time as an assistant teacher. As noted by Seddon (1995), this proposal would enable teachers to complete double degrees with the equivalent of four years' training.

The establishing of the National Project on the Quality of Teaching and Learning (NPQTL) was a major initiative in 1996. Representatives from federal and state governments, employers and unions became engaged in a number of major issues about teaching including:
- work organisation
- professional preparation and career development
- professional issues.

The standards of beginning teachers were given close attention, especially the use of competency-based standards.

The Report by the Senate Employment, Education and Training References Committee in 1998, in *A Class Act: Inquiry into the Status of the Teaching Profession*, concluded that it was essential to assess and recognise advanced teaching knowledge and skills and that teachers should operate their own system to certify teachers who attained the appropriate standards (Abbott-Chapman, Hughes & Williamson 2001). As indicated below, this matter is currently being discussed but is not yet resolved.

The Mayer Committee, established in 1992 to examine generic, work-related competencies identified by the Finn Committee report (Finn 1991), produced a set of seven generic competencies, complete with three standards for each.

A national agency that has highlighted competencies in education has been the National Office for Overseas Skills Recognition (NOOSR), currently an office within Australian Education International. Although the focus by NOOSR was initially on providing a competency-based approach to assessing the qualifications of skilled immigrants, it works on a wider front and supports professions wanting to reconceptualise their curriculum for continuing education in terms of competency-based standards. It was inevitable that the teaching profession would also be pressed to become involved.

A National Competency Framework for Beginning Teachers was produced by NPQTL in 1996 and distributed widely to universities.

The Australian Council of Deans of Education (ACDE) worked with other agencies in 1996 to develop a set of draft standards and guidelines for initial teacher education. Over a two-year period ACDE consulted widely with key stakeholder groups prior to publishing its report in 1998. It was seen as a first in teacher education – 'the first serious attempt to articulate a comprehensive national planning statement aimed at ensuring the quality of our new teachers and the learning they facilitate' (ACDE 1998, p. 2).

The set of generic standards for pre-service teachers (see Figure 21.1) was positively received by the Ministerial Council on Education, Employment, Training and Youth Affairs (MCEETYA) and it was recommended that all states and territories examine the report. A number of states accepted the recommendation that all initial teacher education programs should be four years in duration. A number of university pre-service program officers have incorporated the desired standards and attributes into their respective programs.

However, despite these pressures, teacher education has still remained relatively impervious to national reports, largely because pre-service teacher education occurs solely within the higher education sector (Kennedy 1994).

YOUR TURN

- Why do you think there have been so many inquiries and reports into education and teachers? Is it because there are major problems or deficiencies? Is it because educating children is so complex that there are many different points of view?
- Have there been any short- or long-term implementations or follow-ups to any of the reviews listed in Table 21.1?

FIGURE 21.1 National standards and guidelines for initial teacher education

Desired graduate attributes

1. General professional attributes
   Example – an understanding and commitment to maintain the highest professional and ethical standards
2. Duty of care, health and safety
   Example – acquired knowledge of statutory requirements and skills of identification
3. Students and their communities
   Example – general knowledge and understanding of human growth and development
4. Indigenous education
   Example – developed knowledge, understandings to effectively teach Indigenous students
5. Content studies
   Example – have developed an understanding to an appropriate level of areas they are prepared to teach
6. Curriculum
   Example – gained a knowledge of relevant curriculum documents and resources
7. Literacy
   Example – have high levels of competence in literacy and linguistic awareness
8. Numeracy
   Example – should be adequately and confidently numerate
9. Teaching and learning
   Example – have a sound and adequate knowledge of all aspects of learning processes
10. Relationships with learners and behaviour management
    Example – able to build positive relationships with learners and to encourage student behaviour which promotes learning
11. Technology
    Example – have an understanding of an ability to use appropriate technologies, particularly information technology
12. Assessment and evaluation
    Example – have the knowledge and ability to use appropriate technologies, particularly information technology
13. Working with others
    Example – have the interpersonal skills to cooperate effectively with professional colleagues
14. Working in schools and systems
    Example – have an understanding of a range of teacher roles inside and outside the classroom and their interrelationships.

Source: Australian Council of Deans of Education (ACDE) (1998), *Preparing a Profession, reproduced by permission of* ACDE, Adelaide, p. 8.

21.3 | COMPETENCY-BASED TEACHING

Competency-based approaches (CBT) to teaching in Australia were highlighted in the 1990s. They are still widely used in teacher education in the vocational education sector, in adult learning and second language learning and online learning (Murray 2009; Chew & Seow 2007).

For primary and secondary schools in the twenty-first century there has been a movement away from competency-based approaches because they are now considered to be too atomistic, too regulative and too aligned to outcomes-based approaches (Fullerton & Clements 2002).

Nevertheless it is important to understand how and why competencies have been developed and their value in certain contexts. The language used by exponents of this approach is specialised and it is important to appreciate the specific meanings given to terms.

A *competent professional* has the attributes necessary for job performance to the appropriate standards (Gonczi, Hager & Oliver 1990). That is, the professional possesses a set of relevant *attributes* such as knowledge, abilities, skills and attitudes. These attributes jointly underlie competence and are often referred to as competencies. It is necessary to use the term 'attributes' because competence is an *intangible construct* – it cannot be observed directly. Some attributes that underlie professional competence may be readily recognisable while others may be difficult to recognise. According to Butler (1990, p. 2) 'attributes can include specialised knowledge, cognitive skills, technical skills, interpersonal skills, traits (such as personal energy levels and certain personality types) and, finally, attitudes that elicit desired behaviour patterns'. A requirement, of course, is to test whether the attributes believed to underlie competence are present and at an appropriate level in individuals.

Performance is another major element in testing competence – this typically refers to performance of a role or set of tasks.

There are a number of roles within a profession (for example, surveyor, educational administrator), and roles typically comprise a wide range of tasks and even sub-tasks. Gonczi, Hager and Oliver (1990) list the following tasks for two professionals – an engineer and a pharmacist.

- A general task: A competent engineer is required to produce a mathematical model to predict the life of a cylindrical shaft under variable conditions.
- A specific task: A competent pharmacist is required to maintain a system of recording all dispensed prescriptions.

Rather than focusing on performance in tasks, another alternative is to examine performance within a domain (as an area of professional practice which requires a high degree of professional performance). Domains in teaching could include face-to-face instruction, planning and preparing for instruction and school-wide policy planning.

The final element to consider under competence is the matter of *standards*. Appropriate standards are usually defined in terms of *minimum standards* to demonstrate competence for a role or task or domain and this will involve establishing certain criteria to make this judgment. For example, Heywood, Gonczi and Hager (1992, p. 37) cite the following example from Veterinary Science:

> 'Element of Competency'
>
> Provide first-aid and implement emergency veterinary care.
>
> Performance Criteria:
> - problems requiring urgent attention are identified and ranked in order of importance
> - options for care and treatment are identified and evaluated
> - emergency treatment is tenable and timely
> - suffering is alleviated in a manner consistent with the circumstances
> - veterinary care is consistent with prevailing ethical and legal constraints.

Competency standards for teachers are typically generic in nature, they define knowledge, skills and abilities to apply to all teachers across all sectors, developmental levels and sites. Is this feasible? What are some problems with this approach?

In summary, competency-based standards provide a different focus for professions such as teaching. For teachers (pre-service and in-service) they provide more specific criteria for appraising or assessing standards of teaching. The use of competency-based standards emphasises:
- performance – this can be observed
- key professional tasks or elements – attributes of the person and performance on the tasks and elements are assessed

- that standards can be established at various levels such as entry level (pre-service), experienced teacher and senior teacher
- standards that embody the ability to transfer and apply skills and knowledge to new situations and environments
- that teachers' competence is judged against pre-established performance standards
- that some methods that could be used to provide evidence on which to infer competence include
  - direct observation of work activities
  - skills tests
  - projects
  - log books or diaries
  - portfolios.

As indicated earlier, competency-based standards for students are being used at post-compulsory levels. Nationally developed TAFE modules and employment-focused courses (such as Work Studies) are having an impact on the teaching of Years 11 and 12 (post-compulsory students). Whether these developments will put further pressure on using competencies in the higher education sector is debatable. Hinton (1997) argues that the core work of teachers needs to be carefully examined and redefined, but stops short of recommending a competency-based approach.

> **YOUR TURN**
>
> Let's take a major element of teaching: assessment of students.
> - What teacher competencies would you consider are essential ones for pre-service teachers to achieve? For example, would you include: 'uses both formative and summative assessment strategies'? Or 'implements a variety of assessment tools'?
> - How many should be on the list – a dozen or more? Would a pre-service teacher be required to demonstrate an adequate standard of performance for each?

21.4 | ADVANTAGES AND DISADVANTAGES OF COMPETENCY-BASED TEACHING

Teachers traditionally receive a credential (degree or diploma) and use references or testimonials to affirm their competence as teachers. Whether this is the best way of demonstrating professional competence is problematic. Burrow (1993) goes further and suggests that the dominant paradigm of teaching is outmoded and needs drastic changes (for example, outmoded practices include streaming, control of the learning process by the teacher, an uneven reward structure based on competition, and hierarchical school organisation). Whether a competency-based approach can alleviate all these 'ills' is also problematic.

A range of arguments have been published both for and against the use of competency-based teaching. It is difficult to separate dogma and rhetoric from well-balanced reasons. However, it would appear that the purported *advantages* of competency-based teaching (CBT) include the following:
- It supports other training developments in Australia (for example the training reform agenda) to produce high-quality professionals.
- It assists professionals to obtain positions in different Australian states (through national registrations).
- It provides explicit statements of what people need to be able to practise successfully as a professional.

- It provides impartial benchmarks for professional workers arriving from overseas.
- It improves equity by providing due recognition for disadvantaged groups.
- It facilitates the design and assessment of pre-service and in-service teacher education programs.
- It facilitates articulation of pathways into the teaching profession.
- It facilitates linkages between professional practice and the underlying disciplines.
- It is an effective way of demonstrating quality and accountability to the general public.
- It facilitates the development of transferable generic skills.

There is no question that some *major national and state groups are currently supportive of competency-based standards* applied to training, including professional training. They include the National Centre for Vocational Education Research and the Australian Institute of Training and Development.

The National Institute for Quality Teaching and School Leadership, established in 2004, set up working parties to examine standards which may include competencies. It has been renamed 'Teaching Australia' and its current activities are described later in this chapter. The Australian working population is certainly more mobile than in previous decades. The 'different railway gauge' mentality can no longer operate in the twenty-first century (Nelson 2002). Differences in terms of registration and entry qualifications in the various states and territories can no longer be tolerated and perhaps *national registrations* should have occurred much earlier. The use of competency-based teaching (CBT) is a means of providing clear guidelines that can apply across all states and territories and promote greater mobility of workers, especially professional workers. CBT streamlines the entry and exit points in a profession and provides a greater articulation of the different career levels within each profession.

Gonczi, Hager and Oliver (1990) argue that CBT approaches are especially useful in times of labour shortage and, in particular, major shortages in particular professions. By having a CBT approach that facilitates the recognition of skills, shortages can be reduced and professional workers can be attracted to locations of need.

The emphasis of CBT on *explicit statements* about standards may in fact be a major step forward for the teaching profession. Burrow (1993, p. 111) argues that the profession is mature enough to demystify the nature of the work of teachers:

> to define and promote its richness and complexity, and hence to establish the standards by which we can guarantee our students quality assurance.

Perhaps it is highly desirable for all professions to *develop* and own their competencies.

Heywood, Gonczi and Hager (1992) assert that each profession should periodically examine its professional values and overall capacities and, in so doing, assess its position in the community and its relations with other professions. It is quite possible that, if the teaching profession developed a CBT approach, it would raise its community image. Further, CBT provides a common ground and a common language for providers, for registering authorities and for the profession: 'they enable the relative roles of the providers and profession to become clearer in a mutually cooperative environment' (Heywood, Gonczi & Hager 1992, p. 18).

A CBT approach, it is argued, provides *impartial benchmarks* for professionals and especially overseas-trained professionals. Over the decades there have been great difficulties in analysing and ranking qualifications received by professionals in overseas countries. The establishment of the National Office of Overseas Skills Recognition (NOOSR) in 1990 has led in turn to an encouragement of a CBT approach in many professions – over 80 per cent of the regulated professions (including architecture, nursing and veterinary science) and an increasing number of the non-regulated professions (such as accountancy and agricultural sciences). The teaching profession, as a non-regulated profession, continues to explore CBT, especially for TAFE teachers.

It is very evident that a CBT approach has the potential to assist *disadvantaged groups* whose skills may not currently receive due recognition. A CBT approach emphasises the performance of skills carried out in objective situations with less emphasis given to the testing of knowledge. Milligan (1994) argues that women's positions in the school sector workforce could be greatly enhanced by a CBT approach in terms of merit-based criteria for initial appointments, promotion and professional development.

It is possible that a CBT approach can contribute positively to the *planning* of professional courses. This can be considered in terms of the planning framework or rationale; the design of specific units and the pedagogy used to teach them; and the type of assessment used for certification and accreditation purposes.

In terms of the teaching profession, it is uncertain whether these three elements of planning are acceptable to the majority of educators. For example, some educators (for example, Cairns 1992) object to the framework of a CBT approach but could entertain a CBT approach to some assessment elements of a pre-service teacher education program. Other educators (for example, Crawford & Deer 1991) argue that a pedagogy where students actively construct knowledge is crucial for teacher education programs and is integral to a holistic competencies approach, yet they might object to an assessment format based largely on competencies.

A detailing of the competencies to be developed in pre-service teacher education programs facilitates opportunities for applicants to enter programs from an increased range of areas including school leavers, TAFE and mature age students who have access to recognition of prior learning (RPL) credit. By having explicit details it enables a greater *articulation of pathways* from these various sources.

Some studies undertaken on teacher competencies and teacher education indicate that they have the potential to provide *improved linkages* between professional practice and the underlying disciplines. For example, Preston and Kennedy (1994) in their study of 11 teacher education courses in Australia concluded that a CBT approach had the potential to provide a higher level of integration between the practicum and curriculum and instruction, and foundation and discipline subjects.

It is quite possible that a CBT approach communicates more effectively to the wider community and helps to establish *accountability* standards. For example, in New South Wales in 1994 the then Minister for School Education established a committee to develop competency standards for teachers in that state 'to show the public that the government was ensuring standards and therefore quality and value for money' (Walker 1994, p. 2). This report, *Desirable Attributes of Beginning Teachers*, was published by the Ministerial Advisory Council on Teacher Education and Quality of Teaching in 1994, and in 1996 the Standards Council of the Teaching Profession published *Professional Standards for Teachers* in Victoria.

Studies such as the Mayer Committee report (Mayer 1992) highlight the importance of transferable generic skills for employment and schooling, and ones that are genuinely inclusive for males and females (Ruby 1992). Writings by educators such as Moses and Trigwell (1993) indicate that generic skills need to be carefully planned and incorporated into skill-based or technical subject units. The CBT approach provides for a comprehensive process ensuring that the generic skills are included and assessed.

Despite this long list of purported *advantages* of competency-based standards, there is an equally long list of purported *disadvantages*. In summary, purported *disadvantages* include:
- competency-based standards produce a levelling down to minimum standards
- they devalue the wider goals of teacher education programs
- the emphasis on standardisation and uniformity is a threat to the autonomy of teacher education programs
- performance-based approaches have been tried in the past (performance-based teacher education in the 1960s) and proved to be a failure
- in teacher education there can be no absolute levels
- generic competencies are a fallacy
- it is undesirable to have a total system-wide national approach based on competencies across schools, TAFE and higher education with one orientation and embedded beliefs and practices.

CBT favours a limited building block, rather than an organic approach to learning – reductionism as opposed to holism (Nunan 2001). Is this a fair description of what happens with CBT planning?

Some educators argue that CBT approaches are undesirable because they prescribe only *minimum standards* and therefore discourage excellence. They reduce standards to the lowest common denominator. Some CBT approaches, such as the Mayer key competencies, do prescribe three levels from minimum to maximum competence but it is true that many CBT approaches, and for that matter mastery approaches, concentrate on a minimum standard. However, Hager (1994) argues that this is no different from traditional examinations, which are also based on minimum marks for gaining a pass.

Lally and Myhill (1994) and Walker (1994) argue that the goals of many professional courses undertaken at universities (including pre-service teacher education) involve scholarly work, including:
- fostering student development as a whole person
- teaching an existing body of knowledge but also creating new forms of that knowledge both in product and process
- developing students as critical thinkers.

That is, they consider there are much *wider goals* of university programs beyond what might be developed using a CBT approach.

 A narrow competency-based approach to teacher education is dangerous in its failure to capture essential elements of what a teacher can know and judge (Murray 2009). If this is the case what are the alternatives?

Educators have also criticised the CBT approach for its emphasis on *standardisation and uniformity*. For example, Heywood, Gonzci and Hager (1992, p. 44), in their guide to developing competency standards for professions, are prescriptive in their statement that:

> This is the basic format, which may need to be adapted to suit the needs of a particular profession. Such adaptations are likely to be by way of elaboration and fine tuning, not by major departures from the basic format which is a suitable starting point for all occupations.

Thompson (1989) is also quite prescriptive when he states that a competency-based system must contain:
- competencies or duties to be attained and which are clearly stated as performance objectives
- programs that should be modularised, containing self-instructional activities
- programs which in themselves should contain a variety of learning resources.

Cairns (1992) argues that CBT is merely historical repetition – a retrogression to the *performance-based teacher education* (PBTE) models of the 1960s. He asserts that the recent initiatives in Australia are clearly the product of the government, employers and trade unions and the CBT applications in management and training. He is especially critical of the fact that the traditional education sector – academics and teachers – has not had a major involvement in the debate:

> First, it appears that there has been a deliberate and conscious effort to capture the high ground by excluding these elements of the education industry until most of the apparatus and policy was in place, and secondly, the teachers and teacher educators in particular as a sub-set of the education academics have a long and not too enamoured experience of competency-based education. (Cairns 1992, p. 10)

Walker (1994) takes a more moderate stance. He reiterates that the competency-based approaches in the 1960s and early 1970s were failures, based on the psychology of behaviourism and breaking down a teacher's performance into discrete, observable items of behaviour. However, he contends that there are misconceptions about current CBT approaches. They are more holistic and have a broader, professional approach than the earlier PBTE versions. Notwithstanding, 'behaviourism still prevails in technical and vocational education, throughout TAFE, and is the framework adopted by the National Training Board' (Walker 1994, p. 6).

Unlike many trade jobs where *absolute standards* are required (for example, to measure the diameter of a wire), it is not possible or valid to describe professional competence in terms of skills checklists and specific absolute standards. This is especially the case in teacher education (Australian Council of Deans of Education 2001).

In the professions there are many personal qualities relating to professional competence that are difficult to measure, such as managerial skills, leadership abilities, interpersonal effectiveness, empathy, initiative and problem-solving ability (Masters & McCurry 1990; Van den Berg 2002).

Gonczi, Hager and Oliver (1990) agree that professional work does not lend itself to absolute standards and that it is clearly inappropriate to try to use absolute standards to rate the interpersonal competence of a lawyer or the capacity of a doctor to cure a patient's ailment. Yet they argue that it does not follow that professional standards need be arbitrary or capricious. They contend that there will be different levels of professional competence and each profession must arrive at a suitable standard based on:

- direct observation of what is achievable in actual practical situations
- maintaining a standard high enough to ensure public confidence
- maintaining a standard that provides equity to all intending aspirants and does not exclude particular groups.

Although many professionals support the idea of *generic competencies*, such as problem-solving and communication skills, it is difficult to apply them to specific training programs such as teacher education programs. Barrow (1990) argues that generic competencies are a fallacy and he has grave reservations about the universality of generic constructs. Bartlett (1992) maintains that, because generic competencies depend on a range of contexts and specific forms of actions, they have limited application. Yet generic competencies are embedded in many teaching programs, and perhaps greater attention needs to be given to explicating the connections and providing visibility to them through appropriate assessments (Marsh 1995).

 Workers of the future will require skills and sensibilities that are significantly different from those of the past (Australian Council of Deans of Education 2001). Can a competency-based approach address these future issues?

21.5 | STANDARDS FOR TEACHING

The work done by the National Project on the Quality of Teaching and Learning (NPQTL) was significant even though the long-term impact was minimal. The NPQTL was a three-year tripartite project with membership drawn from government and non-government school authorities, teacher unions, the Commonwealth Government and the Australian Council of Trade Unions (ACTU). The NPQTL was concerned about barriers and impediments to improving the quality of teaching and considered that the development of national competency standards would greatly assist in alleviating these barriers.

In the first instance the NPQTL concentrated on the production of national competency standards (NCSs) for beginning teachers, based on an integrated approach which incorporated performance (of a set of tasks) and attributes (knowledge, skills and attitudes) into a single framework.

Three project teams were commissioned to develop competency standards. Five areas of competence were produced for the NPQTL framework and for each area elements, case study examples, and indicators of effective practice were produced. The five areas of competence were:

1. Using and developing professional knowledge and values
2. Communicating, interacting and working with students and others
3. Planning and managing the teaching and learning process
4. Monitoring and assessing student progress and learning outcomes
5. Reflecting, evaluating and planning for continuous improvement.

A sample area (competence number 4) is depicted in Table 21.2.

TABLE 21.2 Sample area of competence developed by NPQTL

Area of Competence 4: Monitoring and Assessment Student Progress and Learning Outcomes

The primary purpose of assessment is to monitor progress in students' learning and to measure students' achievement against learning objectives. Teachers need to be able to devise assessment strategies which are closely related to learning objectives, reflect the nature of students' programs of work and provide feedback on progress. Monitoring progress is an important part of the learning process and enables teachers, students and parents to contribute to ongoing learning.

Elements	Some indicators of effective practice for this element
(i) The teacher knows the educational basis and role of assessment in teaching	The teacher: – justifies assessment processes and strategies in terms of planned student learning outcomes – uses assessment procedures consistent with content and process goals – values collaborative approaches with parents and others in assessing students' progress – plans and conducts assessment in accordance with school policies – is aware of ethical and legal issues relating to the collection and use of assessment data.
(ii) The teacher uses assessment strategies that take account of the relationships between teaching, learning and assessment	The teacher: – knows and uses a range of assessment strategies to build an holistic picture of individual student learning – uses assessment procedures consistent with content and process goals – plans an assessment program as part of the teaching and learning program – uses assessment to inform future planning – encourages student self- or peer-assessment where appropriate.
(iii) The teacher monitors student progress and provides feedback on progress	The teacher: – observes and responds to patterns of student learning behaviour – draws on a range of information sources in assessing individual student performance – provides consistent and timely feedback to students and parents – assesses to check progress, identify specific learning difficulties and indicate achievement – uses monitoring and assessment activities to enhance the self-esteem of students – maintains student achievement records in accordance with school policies.
(iv) The teacher maintains records of student progress	The teacher: – designs a recording system of appropriate detail and utility – records assessment outcomes accurately and consistently – adheres to principles of confidentiality.
(v) The teacher reports on student progress to parents and others responsible for the care of students	The teacher: – provides detailed, accurate and comprehensible reports on progress – uses assessment and reporting procedures consistent with school policies – prepares information to meet certification requirements.

Source: Draft Competency Framework for Teaching, National Project on the Quality of Teaching and Learning (1993), p. 25. Copyright Commonwealth of Australia, reproduced by permission.

However, the take up of these competency standards was limited and certainly did not achieve national significance. A pilot study undertaken by Preston and Kennedy (1994) revealed that the NPQTL competencies did have some potential for pre-service teacher education, namely:
- as a common framework for collaboration between university staff, school staff and student teachers
- as a guide for the organisation of school experience – to ensure specific activities are built into the practicum
- as a framework for student teacher reflection, self-assessment and planning
- as a framework for the assessment of student teachers.

However, the authors also issued a number of caveats:
- the language used to describe competencies is not inclusive
- the competencies represent a particular view of teachers' work and the teaching profession and this view is likely to be contested
- the competencies focus on beginning teachers rather than on the career needs of a professional
- the competencies do not address how beginning teachers can best be provided with access to the knowledge base of teaching (Kennedy & Preston 1994, p. 5).

Other educators criticised the NPQTL competencies for being too strongly influenced by outcomes-based education – an atomisation approach (Fullerton & Clements 2002). They argued that it is inappropriate for the same generic approach to be used in schools with very different settings.

A number of universities are continuing to explore new approaches to pre-service teacher education, including a school-based focus (as a consortium with local schools), graduate programs such as problem-based Master of Teaching programs, and competency-based Bachelor of Education programs (see Australian Council of Deans of Education 2005).

At the state level, standards frameworks were also produced by specialist groups such as the Centre for Leadership and Teaching Excellence (2008) in Queensland and the Victorian Institute of Teaching (2009) in Victoria. These specialist groups are linked to teacher education or registration bodies, as is depicted in Figure 21.2. However, it should be noted that the registration boards simply enforce minimum requirements for registration and not standards.

Louden (2000) contends that these standards frameworks developed in the 1990s all cover common ground, including teaching, learning, assessment, communication with stakeholders and professional learning. Some of the frameworks set levels of performance for beginning and experienced teachers and include indicators. Notwithstanding, Louden (2000) argues that these sets of standards frameworks represent a first wave, and asserts that they are deficient in specific areas, namely:
- *Long list of duties* – 'the division of teaching into so many dimensions, elements and indicators conflicts with teachers' practical sense that teaching is a holistic task' (Louden 2000, p. 124).
- *Opaque language* – includes a lot of educational jargon that is obscure. 'It also describes a field of knowledge as if it were unproblematic' (Louden 2000, p. 124).
- *Generic skills* – the standards are expected to apply equally to all subject areas and to teachers of children of all ages. 'The standards inevitably leave out the subject specific knowledge and skills that make most sense to teachers' (Louden 2000, p. 125).
- *Decontextualised performances* – different teaching contexts greatly affect whether or not a teacher will reach a particular standard.
- *Expanded duties* – many of these frameworks include duties 'which extend well beyond the core of teachers' classroom work' (Louden 2000, p. 126). There could be major differences between teachers' conceptions of their work and system expectations.

FIGURE 21.2 State level boards of teacher education and registration, listed by year of commencement

Queensland	1971	Board of Teacher Education
	1989	Board of Teacher Registration
South Australia	1976	Teachers Registration Board
Tasmania	2000	Teachers Registration Act
Victoria	2001	Victorian Institute of Teaching Act
Western Australia	2002	College of Teaching Act
Northern Territory	2004	Teachers Registration Board Act

> **YOUR TURN**
>
> What happens to teacher standards and competencies when they have been developed? Are they incorporated into course outlines? Are pre-service teachers assessed on these standards? Discuss possible disjunctions between intended uses and actual uses.

Louden (2000) contends that we are now experiencing a second wave of standards frameworks, largely due to efforts by the largest teacher professional associations. Three standards development projects for Science, Mathematics and English have been completed through funding assistance from the Australian Research Council. They are subject-specific sets of professional standards, and to a large extent appear to overcome many of the deficiencies of the 'first wave' described above.

21.6 | STANDARDS FOR TEACHING MATHEMATICS

The Standards for Excellence in Teaching Mathematics in Australian Schools were adopted by the Australian Association of Mathematics Teaching (AAMT) in 2002 and an updated version was produced in 2006. The standards consist of:
- Professional knowledge
- Professional attributes
- Professional practice (see Figure 21.3).

FIGURE 21.3 Standards for Excellence in Teaching Mathematics in Australian Schools

Domain 1 Professional Knowledge
    1.1 Knowledge of students
    1.2 Knowledge of mathematics
    1.3 Knowledge of students' learning of mathematics

Domain 2 Professional Attributes
    2.1 Personal attributes
    2.2 Personal professional development
    2.3 Community responsibilities

Domain 3 Professional Practice
    3.1 The learning environment
    3.2 Planning for learning
    3.3 Teaching in action
    3.4 Assessment

Since 2005, AAMT has awarded the credential 'Highly Accomplished Teacher of Mathematics' (HAToM) to those teachers who are assessed on the AAMT standards. The assessment involves the use of responses to simulated teaching decisions; portfolio; and interview. Professional learning programs (PLUMS 2006) have also been developed and have been funded by Teaching Australia.

21.7 | STANDARDS FOR TEACHING ENGLISH

The English and Literacy standards were produced jointly by the Australian Association for the Teaching of English and the Australian Literacy Educators' Association (Hayes 2006). The Standards for Teachers of English Language and Literacy in Australia (STELLA) include the core standards listed in Figure 21.4. A range of teaching resources for assisting with the standards are now available.

FIGURE 21.4 Standards for teachers of English Language and Literacy in Australia (STELLA)

1 **Professional Knowledge**
 1.1 Teachers know their students
 1.2 Teachers know their subject
 1.3 Teachers know how students learn to be powerfully literate

2 **Professional Practice**
 2.1 Teachers plan for effective learning
 2.2 Teachers create and maintain a challenging learning environment
 2.3 Teachers assess and review student learning and plan for future learning

3 **Professional Engagement**
 3.1 Teachers demonstrate commitment
 3.2 Teachers continue to learn
 3.3 Teachers are active members of the professional and wider community

21.8 | STANDARDS FOR TEACHING SCIENCE

The Australian Science Teachers Association (ASTA) produced national Professional Standards for Highly Accomplished Teachers of Science in 2007 (see Figure 21.5), having produced a set of National Professional Standards in 2002. It is also producing National Professional Standards for Accomplished Primary Teaching in 2009.

Their standards are very similar to those of Mathematics in that their categories include professional knowledge, professional practice and professional attributes. However, the rationale for standards in teaching Science is expressed a little more eloquently:

> Highly accomplished teachers of science do not just communicate information; they educate minds …

Highly accomplished teachers of Science can model the values and habits of mind inherent in what it means to do Science (Australian Science Teachers Association 2002, p. 5).

YOUR TURN

If each subject discipline develops its own rigorous set of standards (as has happened in Australia for English, Mathematics and Science), what is the cumulative impact on students and teachers? Will it cause an unreasonable and unrealistic load? What are the alternatives?

FIGURE 21.5 Professional Standards for Highly Accomplished Teachers of Science (ASTA)

A. PROFESSIONAL KNOWLEDGE

Highly accomplished teachers of Science have an extensive knowledge of science, science education and students.

1. They have a broad and current knowledge of science and science curricula, related to the nature of their teaching responsibilities.
2. They have a broad and current knowledge of teaching, learning and assessment in science.
3. They know their students well and they understand the influence of cultural, developmental, gender and other contextual factors on their students' learning in science.

B. PROFESSIONAL PRACTICE

Highly accomplished teachers of Science work with their students to achieve high quality learning outcomes in science.

4. They design coherent learning programs appropriate for their students' needs and interests.
5. They create and maintain intellectually challenging, emotionally supportive and physically safe learning environments.
6. They engage students in generating, constructing and testing scientific knowledge by collecting, analysing and evaluating evidence.
7. They continually look for and implement ways to extend students' understanding of the major ideas of science.
8. They develop in students the confidence and ability to use scientific knowledge and processes to make informed decisions.
9. They use a wide variety of strategies, coherent with learning goals, to monitor and assess students' learning and provide effective feedback.

C. PROFESSIONAL ATTRIBUTES

Highly accomplished teachers of Science are reflective, committed to improvement and active members of their professional community.

10. They analyse, evaluate and refine their teaching practice to improve student learning.
11. They work collegially, within their school community and wider professional communities to improve the quality and effectiveness of science education.

Source: Adapted from <www.teachingaustralia.edu.au>.

21.9 | 'TEACHING AUSTRALIA' AND THE NATIONAL INSTITUTE FOR TEACHING AND SCHOOL LEADERSHIP

Teaching Australia is currently working with other professional associations to develop specialist standards. These include:
- Accomplished early childhood teaching (being developed by Early Childhood Australia)
- Accomplished principals (being developed by Principals Australia)
- National professional standards for primary teachers (being co-developed by several professional associations including the Australian Science Teachers Association, the Australian Federation of Societies for Studies of Society and Environment, and the Australian Association of Mathematics Teachers) (<www.teachingaustralia.edu.au/ta/go/home/op/edit/pid/526> extracted 28 July 2009).

In September 2009, the Ministerial Council for Education, Early Childhood Development and Youth Affairs (MCEECDYA) agreed upon the establishment of the Australian Institute for Teaching and School Leadership to take responsibility for the development of rigorous national standards and high-quality professional development for teachers.

Ingvarson (1998) suggests that these Australian projects gained valuable insights from standards-based systems in the United States such as the National Board for Professional Teaching Standards (NBPTS) and the Interstate New Teachers Assessment Standards Consortium (INTASC).

The National Board for Professional Teaching Standards (NBPTS) in particular has been very successful in the US. 'It is an independent professional body with the sole function of providing a national system for recognising and valuing the knowledge and skill of "highly accomplished" teachers' (Ingvarson 1998, p. 3). Twelve certification fields are available currently and they will eventually cover 30 fields. Teachers who request to be certified have to submit a portfolio of work examples and complete exercises at an assessment centre.

The mission of the NBPTS is to advance the quality of teaching and learning by:
- maintaining high and rigorous standards for what accomplished teachers should know and be able to do
- providing a national voluntary system certifying teachers who meet these standards
- integrating National Board Certification in American education and capitalising on the expertise of National Board Certified Teachers (NBPTS 2009).

Yet, others are critical of these highly centralised performance assessment programs – 'this is the domain of assessment centres and trained assessors, assessment instruments and assessment processes that are validated and publicly displayed as icons of objectivity' (Emmett 2002 p. 5).

Attempts at the creation of general teaching standards for the Australian teaching profession were very protracted. After a national discussion paper (September 2000), a national summit (April 2001) and a national meeting (April 2002), a National Institute for Quality Teaching and School Leadership was announced by the federal Minister in July 2003. It was later renamed 'Teaching Australia' (2006).

Unlike the situation in the US, where private organisations have developed teacher standards and teachers have the choice to submit for assessment and accreditation, in Australia the federal government seems determined to manage the process but continues to prevaricate about how to proceed.

A major problem for teachers and administrators is to get agreement on how the standards will be used, for example whether they are subject-specific standards (such as those devised for English, Mathematics and Science) or generic teacher standards. The Teacher Standards, Quality and Professionalism National Reference Group (TQELT) (2002) lists the following uses for standards:
- as a framework and guide for teacher education (pre-service) and continuous professional learning (in-service)
- to enable teachers and administrators to reflect on and assess professional teaching practice
- to recognise and certify teachers who have attained standards for highly accomplished professional practice.

To provide a concluding balance to the discussion, it should be noted that there are many critics of both subject-specific and generic teacher standards. For example, Verloop, Van Driel and Meijer (2001) argue that standards which are largely based on teacher knowledge, with its well-established and rigid routines of the profession, do not provide teachers with the total perspective. They tend to dismiss propositional knowledge and formal theory, which have to be an integral component of teachers' knowledge and values.

Nasir, Hand & Taylor (2008) provide a timely reminder that there is 'domain knowledge' (such as in the standards listed above for English, Mathematics and Science) but also 'cultural knowledge' which is knowledge derived from settings outside of school and must not be ignored.

Cochran-Smith (2001b) takes a similar stance when she contends that the standards recently developed only emphasise narrow views of teaching and learning. Missing, in her opinion, are the dilemmas that teachers face as change agents, and the need to challenge current arrangements of schools and classroom practices.

Meadmore (2004) contends that the new 'performativity' agenda has forced teachers to be more efficient, effective, and accountable and subject to surveillance by others. Broadfoot (2002) suggests that we may be 'in danger of unwittingly unleashing a Frankenstein's monster' (p. 143).

Burnett and Meacham (2002) contend that the current standards developed in Australia, produced largely by professional peers, 'gives a one-sided view that may focus on staff development rather than accountability' (p. 143).

Yet Emmett (2002) contends that personal goal setting and self-appraisal is most important. He concludes that:

> finding some balance between an assessment process that is viewed as an intrusion on the professionalism of teachers and their practice and one that allows for a consistency in judgment of the capabilities of teachers in demonstrating their professional competence is the key to the usefulness of standards of professional practice. (p. 5)

CONCLUDING COMMENTS

Professional standards for teaching continue to be a major focus in the twenty-first century. The generic competency-based standards developed in the 1990s have largely been overtaken now in 2010 by new developments – largely subject-specific standards. The National Board for Professional Teaching Standards in the US has been extremely successful and this has led major subject associations in Australia to develop subject-specific standards. Attempts to develop general teacher standards are continuing, but impediments keep arising due to political factors and rivalry between states.

KEY ISSUES RAISED IN THIS CHAPTER

1. Teachers must set high standards and as professionals they need to have professional standards which are publicly available.
2. Quality teachers are needed more than ever to assist students with their learning.
3. Over the decades there have been many inquiries into teacher education with seemingly limited impact.
4. Competency-based approaches to teaching were promoted heavily in the 1990s but in the last decades they have been discontinued in favour of standards.
5. Standards for Teaching in Australia were developed initially by three major professional associations, AAMT, ASTA and STELLA.
6. Teaching Australia, the national standards body, has been encouraging the development of additional standards in early childhood education and primary teaching.

REFLECTIONS AND ISSUES

1. What are beginning teachers' conceptions of competence? Is it a sound knowledge base, or effective classroom management? Do you agree with these two? What others would you add?
2. For initial teacher education programs is it possible to develop sufficient content knowledge and pedagogical knowledge to become a quality teacher?
3. What do the voices of students have to say about quality teaching and teacher standards from the lived world of their learning experiences (Scanlon 2004)? Is this an important source? How might this information be obtained?
4. Why is it important to have national teacher standards? Is it possible to have national standards that cater for local contexts and issues?

5. Who wants to measure teacher quality? Is it politicians, school administrators, professional teaching associations or individual teachers? What are the arguments advanced by each of these groups?
6. How will teachers' standards be used as tools for action? Will it be for professional learning or accountability?
7. 'Teaching Australia' is promoting a series of subject-specific national professional standards, such as in English, Mathematics and Science and for primary teachers and early childhood. Yet specialists such as Ingvarson & Rowe (2007) contend that teachers as a profession must work harder on defining, evaluating and certifying high-quality teaching. Do you have any solutions to this problem? What are some of the ongoing problems?
8. Why is it that only a few able graduates choose to do teaching? Is it mainly extrinsic factors such as problems with remuneration, workload, employment conditions and status? Discuss.
9. There are some basic questions about teacher standards. Consider the following:
   - What is good teaching?
   - What should teachers know and be able to do?
   - What evidence about teaching needs to be collected? By whom? When?
   - How is teacher performance to be judged?
   - Where do we set the standard for good teaching?

   Reflect on these questions and give your responses to any two that are of special interest to you.

Special references

Australian Curriculum Studies Association (2005) *Quality Teachers: Quality Teaching*, ACSA, Canberra.
Cochran-Smith, M (2005) 'The new teacher education: for better or for worse', *Educational Researcher*, 34(7):3–17.
Cosgrove, F (2007) Standards of professional practice: supporting effective teacher learning in Victoria, Occasional Paper no. 100, CSE, Melbourne.
Darling-Hammond, L (2006) *Powerful Teacher Education: Lessons from Exemplary Programs*, Teachers College Press, New York.
Dinham, S Ingvarson, L & Kleinhenz, E (2008) 'Investing in teacher quality', *EQ Australia*, Spring, pp. 4–5.
Green, H (2004) *Professional Standards for Teachers and School Leaders*, Routledge, London.
Hayes, T (2006) 'Professional teaching associations and professional standards: Embedding standards in the "discourse of the profession"', Teaching Australia, Canberra.
McInerney, DM Van Etten, S & Dowson, M (2007) *Standards in Education*, Information Age Publishing, London.

Web sources

For additional resources on teacher competencies and standards, please go to:
www.pearson.com.au/myeducationlab.

BIBLIOGRAPHY

A

Abate, V (1994) *Computer Graphics: A Visual Communication*, Longman Cheshire, Melbourne.

Abbott-Chapman, J, Hughes, P & Williamson, J (2001) 'Teachers' perceptions of classroom competencies over a decade of change', *Asia-Pacific Journal of Teacher Education*, 29(2):171–85.

Accelerated Christian Education (see ACE).

ACDE (1998) 'Preparing a profession', ACDE, Canberra.

ACDE (2001) *New Learning: A Charter for Australian Education*, ACDE, Canberra.

ACDE (2005) Teaching Tomorrow's Teachers, ACDE submission to the House of Representatives, Inquiry into Teacher Education, ACDE, Canberra, Victorian Institute of Teaching (2001).

ACE (Accelerated Christian Education) (2008) *Curriculum*, <www.schooloftomorrow.com/curriculum/Default.aspx> extracted 22 October 2008.

ACER (1996) Assessment resource kit, ACER, Melbourne.

ACER (2004) Online assessment program aids learning in the home, *ACER* Winter:9–10.

ACER (2008) KIDMAP program, ACER, Melbourne.

Achinstein, B & Ogawa, R (2006) '(In) fidelity: What the resistance of new teachers reveals about professional principles and prescriptive educational policies', *Harvard Educational Review*, 76(1):30–61.

ACSA (1996) 'From alienation to engagement: Opportunities for reform in the middle years of schooling', (Vols 1, 2 & 3) Australian Curriculum Studies Association, Canberra.

ACSA (2005) *Quality Teachers: Quality Teaching*, ACSA, Canberra.

ACSSO (Australian Council of State School Organisations) (2009) Values in education, <www.valuesineducation.org/au/links.htm> extracted 12 April 2009.

ACTU (Australian Council of Trade Unions) (1987) *Australia Reconstructed*, AGPS, Canberra.

Adams, ME (1997) *Integrating Technology into the Curriculum*, Hawker Brownlow, Melbourne.

AEC (1993) *National Action Plan for the Education of Girls 1993–97*, Curriculum Corporation, Melbourne.

AEU (2006) *Educational Leadership and Teaching for the 21st Century: A Desirable Scenario*, Australian Education Union, Melbourne.

AEU (2009) *Public Education for our Future*, Autumn (5):1–5.

Aiken, WM (1942) *The Story of the Eight-Year Study*, Harper, New York.

Ailwood, J (2003) 'A national approach to gender equity policy in Australia: Another ending, another opening', *International Journal of Inclusive Education*, 8(1):3–15.

Ainley, J (2000) 'Learning with Laptops', *ACER Research Developments*, Autumn, 8–9.

Aitken, G (1999) 'The challenge to order', *English in Aotearoa*, December:1–14.

Alberty, H (1953) 'Designing programmes to meet the common needs of youth'. In NV Henry (ed), *Adapting the Secondary School Programme to the Needs of Youth*, University of Chicago, Chicago.

Albion, PR (1996) 'Student-teachers' use of computers during teaching practice in primary classrooms', *Asia-Pacific Journal of Teacher Education*, 24(1):63–75.

Alderman, MK (1990) 'Motivation for at-risk students', *Educational Leadership*, 48(1):27–30.

Allen, D & Fraser, BJ (2007) 'Parent and student perceptions of classroom learning environment and its association with student outcomes', *Learning Environments Research*, 10:67–82.

Allen, R (2002a) 'Collaborative curriculum planning', *Education Update*, 44(3):1–6.

Allen, R (2002b) 'Teachers and paraeducators: Defining roles in an age of accountability', *Education Update*, 44(7):1–7.

Allen, R (2007) 'Green schools: Thinking outside the schoolroom box', *Education Update*, 49(11):1–8.

Allen, RH (2010) *High-impact Teaching Strategies for the 'XYZ' Era of Education*, Allyn and Bacon, Boston.

Allodi, MW (2007) 'Assessing the quality of learning environments in Swedish schools: Development and analysis of a theory-based instrument', *Learning Environments Research*, 10(3):157–75.

Alonso, F Manrique, D Vines, JM (2009) 'A moderate constructionist e-learning instructional model evaluated on computer specialists', *Computers and Education*, 53(1):57–65.

Altbach, PG (1987) 'Textbooks in comparative context'. In RM Thomas & VN Kobayashi (eds), *Educational Technology – Its Creation, Development and Cross-cultural Transfer*, Pergamon, Oxford.

Amidon, P (1971) *Nonverbal Interaction Analysis*, Amidon & Associates, Minneapolis.

Amundson, KJ (1991) *Teaching Values and Ethics*, AASA, Arlington, Virginia.

Anderson, A, Hattie, J, & Hamilton, RJ (2005) 'Focus of control, self-efficacy, and motivation in different

schools: Is moderation the key to success?', *Educational Psychology*, 25(5):517–35.
Anderson, J & Alagurnalai, S (1997) 'HTML: The next language of communication for information technology in open learning', *Unicorn*, 23(3):11–20.
Anderson, KL (2001) 'Voicing concern about noisy classrooms', *Educational Leadership*, 58(7):77–81.
Anderson, LW & Sosniak, LA (1994) (eds) *Bloom's Taxonomy: A Forty-year Retrospective, Ninety-third Yearbook of the National Society for the Study of Education*, University of Chicago Press, Chicago.
Anderson-Inman, LA & Horney, M (1993) Profiles of hypertext readers: Results from the Electro Text Project, Paper presented at the Annual Conference of the American Educational Research Association, Atlanta.
Andrade, J Area, J Garua, R Rodriguez, S Sevane, M & Suarez, S (2008) 'Guidelines for the development of e-learning systems by means of proactive questions', *Computers and Education*, 51(4):1510–22.
Andrews, G (1985) *The Parent Action Manual*, Schools Community Interaction Trust, Melbourne.
Andrich, D (2006) A report to the Curriculum Council of Western Australia regarding assessment for tertiary selection, <www.platowa.com/Official_word> extracted 14 November 2008.
Angus, M (1990) 'Making better schools: Devolution the second time around', Paper presented at the Annual Conference of the American Educational Research Association, Boston.
Angus, M (1998) *The Rules of School Reform*, Falmer, London.
Angus, M & Ainley, J (2007) *Study into the resourcing of Australian primary schools (SRAPS)*, Australian Primary Principals Association, Canberra.
Angus, M. & Olney, H. (2009) 'How can low SES schools most effectively target their resources?' *Targeting Resources in Primary Schools*, Australian Primary Principals Association, Melbourne.
Angus, M Olney, H Ainley, J & Caldwell, B (2004) *The Sufficiency of Resources for Australian Primary Schools*, Department of Education, Employment and Workplace Relations, Canberra.
Angus, M Olney, H Selleck, R Ainley, J Burke, G Caldwell, B & Spinks, J (1999) *Resourcing Australian Primary Schools: A Historical Perspective*, Department of Education, Science and Training, Canberra.
Annetta, L Minogue, J Holmes, S Cheng, MT (2009) 'Investigating the impact of video games on high school students' engagement and learning about genetics', *Computers and Education*, 52(1):74–85.
Anyon, J (2005) *Radical Possibilities: Public Policy, Urban Education and a New Social Movement*, Routledge, New York.
Apple, M & Aasen, P (2003) *The State and the Politics of Knowledge*, Routledge, London.
Apple, MW (1986) *Teachers and Texts*, Routledge & Kegan Paul, New York.
Arends, RI (2009) *Learning to Teach*, 8th edn, McGraw Hill, New York.

Armstrong, T (2000) *Multiple Intelligences in the Classroom*, ASCD, Alexandria, Virginia.
Aronson, E, Beaney, N, Stephen, C, Sikes, J & Snapp, M (1978) *The Jigsaw Classroom*, Sage, Beverley Hills, California.
Aronson, J (2004) 'The threat of stereotype', *Educational Leadership*, 62(3):14–20.
Arthur, M Gordon, C & Butterfield, N (2003) *Classroom Management*, Thomson, Melbourne.
Arthur-Kelly, M Lyons, G Butterfield N & Gordon, C (2006) *Classroom Management*, Thomson, Melbourne.
ASCD (2004) September 7: 'NCLB's testing of core subjects is causing schools to cut back on arts offerings', *Smart Brief*, ASCD, Virginia, <www.smartbrief.com/news/ascd/archive>.
ASCD (2005) August 30: 'Sexual mores in schools', *Smart Brief*, ASCD, Virginia.
ASCD (2005) December 21: 'Judge rules against Intelligent Design in landmark Pennsylvania case', *Smart Brief*, ASCD, Virginia.
ASCD (2005) December 5: 'Software programs to screen plagiarism', *Smart Brief*, ASCD, Virginia.
ASCD (2005) October 21: 'Blogging to hone grammar and creative writing skills', *Smart Brief*, ASCD, Virginia.
ASCD (2005) October 25: 'Critics of teaching Intelligent Design in Australia', *Smart Brief*, ASCD, Virginia.
ASCD (2005) October 27: 'Parental involvement', *Smart Brief*, ASCD, Virginia.
ASCD (2005) September 29: 'Teaching Intelligent Design theory is not illegal', *Smart Brief*, ASCD, Virginia.
ASCD (2006) April 11: 'Class action suit', *Smart Brief*, ASCD, Virginia.
ASCD (2006) April 8: 'Controversial Californian Bill', *Smart Brief*, ASCD, Virginia.
ASCD (2006) February 14: 'Taking advantage of NCLB free tutoring', ASCD *Smart Brief*, ASCD, Virginia.
ASCD (2006) February 10: 'Baltimore schools CEO drops controversial Studio Course', *Smart Brief*, ASCD, Virginia.
ASCD (2006) March 18: 'Illinois standards achievement tests', *Smart Brief*, ASCD, Virginia.
ASCD (2006) May 13: 'California Senate supports teaching of gay's contributions', *Smart Brief*, ASCD, Virginia.
ASCD (2006) May 17: 'British Government to study need to teach national values', *Smart Brief*, ASCD, Virginia.
ASCD (2006) May: 'Social science textbooks and references to lesbians, gays, bisexuals', *Smart Brief*, ASCD, Virginia.
Ashenden, D (1994) 'Two views of Australian schooling', *EQ Australia*, Summer (4):5–7.
Asp, E (2000) 'Assessment in education: Where have we been? Where are we headed?'. In RS Brandt (ed.) *Education in a New Era*, ASCD, Alexandria, Virginia.
Aspin, D (2003) 'Actions speak louder', *EQ Australia*, 4(1):6–8.

Association for Supervision and Curriculum Development (see ASCD)
ASTA (2002) *National Professional Standards for Highly Accomplished Teachers of Science*, ASTA, Melbourne.
Athanasou, J & Lamprienou, T (2002) *A Teacher's Guide to Assessment*, Social Science Press, Sydney.
Atkins, MJ (1993) 'Evaluating interactive technologies for learning', *Journal of Curriculum Studies*, 25(4):333–42.
Australian Council for Educational Research (see ACER)
Australian Council of Deans of Education (see ACDE)
Australian Curriculum Studies Association (see ACSA)
Australian Education Council (see AEC)
Australian Education Union (see AEU)
Australian Science Teachers Association (see ASTA)
Aveling, N (2002) 'Student teachers' resistance to exploring racism: Reflections on "doing" border pedagogy', *Asia-Pacific Journal of Teacher Education*, 30(2):119–29.
Ayers, W (1993) *To Teach: The Journey of a Teacher*, Teachers College Press, New York.

B

Babb, KA & Ross, C (2009) 'The timing of online lecture slide availability and its effect on attendance, participation and exam performance', *Computers and Education*, 52(4):868–81.
Back Pack Net Centre (2005) Classroom of the Future. <www.backpack.com.sg/faq.html>.
Badge, JL Dawson, E Cann, AJ & Scott, J (2008) 'Assessing the accessibility of online learning' *Innovations in Education and Teaching International*, 45(2):103–113.
Bagshaw, B (2005) *Sydney Olympic Park: The Olympic Movement, Education and Social Change*, Sydney Olympic Park, Sydney.
Baker, EL (2003) 'Reflections on technology-enhanced assessment', *Assessment in Education*, 10(3):421–4.
Baker, EL (2007) 'Presidential address: The end(s) of testing', *Educational Researcher*, 36(6):309–17.
Bakker, HE & Piper, JB (1994) 'California provides technology evaluations to teachers', *Educational Leadership*, 51(7):67–8.
Baldwin, D (2004) 'A guide to standardised writing assessment', *Educational Leadership*, 62(2):72–5.
Ball, DL & Cohen, DK (1996) 'Reform by the book: What is – or might be – the role of curriculum materials in teacher learning and instructional reform?', *Educational Researcher*, 25(9):6–8.
Banks, JA (1973) (ed.) *Teaching Ethnic Studies*, Forty Third Year Book, National Council for the Social Studies, Washington DC.
Banks, JA & Banks, CA (2008) *Teaching Strategies for the Social Studies*, Longman, New York.
Banks, R (2004) *Middle School*, Clearinghouse on Early Education and Parenting, <ceep.crc.uiuc.edu/poptopics/middle.html>.
Barab, SA & Roth, WM (2006) 'Curriculum–based ecosystems: Supporting knowledge from an ecological perspective, *Education Researcher*, 35(5):3–13.
Barratt, R (1998) Shaping middle schooling in Australia: A report of the National Middle Schooling Project, Australian Curriculum Studies Association, Canberra.
Barrow, R (1984) *Give Teaching Back to Teachers*, Althouse Press, London, Ontario.
Barrow, R (1990) *Understanding Skills: Thinking, Feeling and Caring*, Althouse Press, Ontario.
Barry, K & King, L (1998) *Beginning Teaching & Beyond*, 3rd edn, Social Science Press, Katoomba.
Barry, K, King, L, Pitts-Hill, K & Zehnder, S (1998) An investigation into student use of a heuristic in a series of cooperative learning problem solving lessons, Paper presented at the Annual Conference of the American Educational Research Association, San Diego.
Bartky, SL (1996) 'The pedagogy of shame'. In C Luke (ed.), *Feminisms and Pedagogies of Everyday Life*, State University of New York Press, New York.
Bartlett, L (1992) Vision and revision: A competency-based scheme for the teaching profession, Paper presented at the Australian Teacher Education Conference, Ballina, NSW.
Barton, AC Drake, C Perez, J St Louis, K & George, M (2004) 'Ecologies of parental engagement in urban education', *Educational Researcher*, 33(4):3–12.
Barton, PE (2004), 'Why does the gap persist?', *Educational Leadership*, 62(3):8–13.
Bates, R (1998) 'Preparing teachers to teach in the year 2007', *Unicorn*, 23(2):39–48.
Bauch, PA & Goldring, EB (2000) 'Teacher work context and parent involvement in urban high schools of choice', *Educational Research and Evaluation*, 6(1):1–23.
BBC (2007) 'Doubts over hi-tech white boards', 30 January 2007, <news.bbc.co.uk/1/hi/education/6309691.stm> extracted 23 April 2009.
Beagley, D (1997) Enabling effective parent participation, Paper presented at the Biennial Conference of the Australian Curriculum Studies Association, Sydney.
Beane, J & Lipka, R (2006), 'Guess again: Will changing the grades save middle-level education?', *Educational Leadership*, 63(7):26–32.
Bear, GG & Richards, HC (1981) 'Moral reasoning and conduct problems in the classroom', *Journal of Educational Psychology*, 73:644–70.
Beare, H Caldwell, BJ & Millikan, RH (1991) *Creating an Excellent School*, Routledge, London.
Beatty, I (2004) 'Transforming student learning with classroom communication systems', *Educause Centre for Applied Research*, February, (3):1–12.
Beck, MD (1991) 'Authentic Assessment' for large scale accountability purposes: Balancing the rhetoric, Paper presented at the Annual Conference of the American Educational Research Association, Chicago.
Becker, H (1981) Teacher practices of parent involvement at home – a statewide survey, Paper presented at the Annual Conference of the American Educational Research Association, Chicago.

Becker, HJ (1998) 'Running to catch a moving train: Schools and information technologies', *Theory into Practice*, 37(1):20–30.

Becker, J & Varelas, M (2001) 'Piaget's early theory of the role of language in intellectual development: A comment on De Vries's account of Piaget's Social Theory', *Educational Researcher*, 30(6):22–4.

Bell, PA Fisher, JD & Loomis, RJ (1976) *Environmental Psychology*, WB Saunders, Philadelphia.

Bellack, A (1964) 'The structure of knowledge and the structure of the Curriculum'. In D Huebner (ed.), *A Reassessment of the Curriculum*, Teachers College Press, New York.

Benjamin, J Bessant, J & Watts, R (1997) *Making Groups Work*, Allen & Unwin, Sydney.

Bennett, N Desforges, C Cockburn, A & Wilkinson, E (1984) *The Quality of Pupil Learning Experiences*, Lawrence Erlbaum, London.

Bennett, RE (2002) 'Inexorable and inevitable: The continuing story of technology and assessment', *Journal of Technology, Learning and Assessment*, 1(1):2–23.

Bennett, SN (1981) 'Time and space: Curriculum allocation and pupil involvement in British open-space schools', *The Elementary School Journal*, 82(1):18–26.

Berge, ZL & Collins, MP (1995) *Computer Mediated Communication and the Online Classroom*, Collins, London.

Berger, KS (2000) *The Developing Person through Childhood and Adolescence*, 2nd edn, Worth Publishers, New York.

Berger, KS (2006) *The Developing Person through Childhood and Adolescence*, 7th edn, Worth Publishers, New York.

Berkowitz, MW (1998) Educating for character and democracy: A practical introduction, Paper presented at the Participaccion Ciudadana, Bogota, Colombia.

Berlach, RG (2004) Outcomes-based education and the death of knowledge, Paper presented at the Australian Association for Research in Education Conference, Melbourne.

Berlach, RG & McNaught, K (2007) 'Outcomes based education? Rethinking the provision of compulsory education in Western Australia', *Issues in Educational Research*, 17(1):1–11.

Betts, F (1994) 'On the birth of the communication age: A conversation with David Thornburg', *Educational Leadership*, 51(7):20–3.

Beyer, LE (1997) 'The moral contours of teacher education', *Journal of Teacher Education*, 48(4):245–54.

Biddle, BJ & Berliner, DC (2002) 'Small class size and its effects', *Educational Leadership*, 59(5):12–23.

Biggs, J (1998) 'Assessment and classroom learning: A role for summative assessment?', *Assessment in Education: Principles, Policy and Practice*, 5(1):1–16.

Bigum, C (1997) 'Teachers and computers: In control or being controlled', *Australian Journal of Education*, 41(3):247–62.

Birch, JK & Richter, I (1990) (eds) *Comparative School Law*, Pergamon Press, London.

Bitter, GG & Pierson, ME (2005) *Using Technology in the Classroom*, 6th edn, Pearson/Allyn & Bacon, Boston.

Black, P & Wiliam, D (1998) 'Inside the black box: Raising standards through classroom assessment', *Phi Delta Kappan*, 80(2):139–48.

Black, P & Wiliam, D (2005) 'Lessons from around the world: How policies, politics and cultures constrain and afford assessment practices', *The Curriculum Journal*, 16(2):249–61.

Black, P Swann, J & Wiliam, D (2006) 'School pupils' beliefs about learning', *Research Papers in Education*, 21(2):151–70.

Black, R (2006) *Equity and Excellence: Where Do We Stand?* An Education Foundation Fact Sheet, Education Foundation, Melbourne.

Black, R Stokes, H & Turnbull (2010) 'Reimagining learning for schools in disadvantaged areas', *Curriculum Perspectives* (in press).

Blackmore, J (1986) 'Tensions to be resolved in participation and school-based decision-making', *Educational Administration Review*, 4(l):19–68.

Blackmore, J (1988) *Assessment and Accountability*, Deakin University Press, Geelong.

Blackmore, J (1999) 'Privatising the public: The shifts in priorities in self-managing schools away from public education and social justice', *Curriculum Perspectives*, 19(1):68–75.

Blain, J (2001) (ed.) *Developing Cross-curricular Learning in Museums and Galleries*, Trentham Books, Stoke-on-Trent.

Blair, A & Aps, W (2005) 'What not to wear and other stories: Addressing religious diversity in schools', *Education and the Law*, 17(1):1–22.

Blanchard, J (2008) 'Learning awareness: Constructing formative assessment in the classroom, in the school and across schools', *The Curriculum Journal*, 19(3):137–150.

Blatchford, P (2003) *The Class Size Debate: Is Small Better?* Open University Press, Maidenhead.

Blatchford, P Moriarty, V Eamonds, S & Martin, C (2002) 'Relationships between class size and teaching: A multimethod analysis of English infant schools', *American Educational Research Journal*, 39(1):101–32.

Bloom, BS (1968) 'Learning for mastery', *Evaluation Comment* 1(2):3–9.

Bloom, BS, Engelhart, MD, Frost, EJ, Hill, WH & Krathwohl, DR (1956) *Taxonomy of Educational Objectives, Handbook 1: Cognitive Domain*, David McKay, New York.

Bloom, R & Bourdon, L (1980) 'Types and frequencies of teachers' written instructional feedback', *Journal of Educational Research*, 74(1):13–14.

Blyth, A (2002) 'Outcomes, standards and benchmarks', *Curriculum Perspectives*, 22(3):13–22.

Board of Studies, NSW (2006) *Personal Development, Health and Physical Education K–6*, Board of Studies, Sydney.

Board of Studies, Victoria (1995) *Studies of Society and Environment, Curriculum and Standards Framework*, Board of Studies, Melbourne.

Boomer, G (1985) Long division: A consideration of participation, equality and brain power in Australian Education, Paper presented at the Australian Council for State School Organisations Annual Conference, Launceston, Tasmania.

Boon, TL & Yong, KM (2006) 'Computer-associated remediation in Mathematics', *Celebrating Learning through Active Research*, Ministry of Education, Singapore.

Borich, GD & Tombari, ML (1997) *Educational Psychology*, 2nd edn, Longman, New York.

Boston, K (1993) Circular letter to CURASS members, 5 July 1993.

Bottini, M & Grossman, S (2005) 'Centre-based teaching and children's learning', *Childhood Education*, 81(5):274–7.

Bottoms, G (2007) 'Treat all students like the "best" students', *Educational Leadership*, 65(5):20–25.

Boutte, GS (2002) 'The critical literacy process: Guidelines for examining books', *Childhood Education*, Spring:147–52.

Bowker, R & Tearle, P (2007) 'Gardening as a learning environment: A study of children's perceptions and understanding of school gardens as part of an international project', *Learning Environments*, 10(2):83–100.

Bowles, D (1980) *School–community Relations, Community Support, and Student Achievement: A Summary of Findings*, University of Wisconsin, Madison.

Boyd, WL (1990) 'Balancing competing values in school reform: International efforts in restructuring education systems'. In JD Chapman & JF Dunstan (eds), *Democracy & Bureaucracy*, Falmer, London.

Boyes, MC & Chandler, M (1992) 'Cognitive development, epistemic doubt, and identifying formation in adolescence', *Journal of Youth and Adolescence*, 21:277–304.

Boynton, M & Boynton, C (2005) *The Educator's Guide to Preventing and Solving Discipline Problems*, ASCD, Alexandria, Virginia.

Brady, L & Kennedy, K (2010) *Curriculum Construction*, 4th edn, Pearson, Sydney.

Brady, L & Kennedy, K (2008) *Celebrating Student Achievement: Assessment and Reporting*, 3rd edn, Pearson Education, Sydney.

Brady, L (1996) 'Outcome-based education: A critique', *The Curriculum Journal*, 7(1):5–16.

Brandom, A Carmichael, P & Marshall, B (2005) 'Learning about assessment for learning: A framework for discourse about classrooms', *Teacher Development*, 9(2):201–14.

Brandt, RS & Perkins, DN (2000) 'The evolving science of learning'. In RS Brandt, *Education in a New Era*, ASCD, Alexandria, Virginia.

Brennan, C (1998) 'Why it isn't being implemented? Race, racism and indigenous education'. In G Partington (ed.), *Perspectives on Aboriginal and Torres Strait Islander Education*, Social Science Press, Sydney.

Brennan, RT Kim, J Wenz-Gross, M & Siperstein, GN (2001) 'The relative equitability of high-stakes testing versus teacher-assigned grades: An analysis of the Massachusetts Comprehensive Assessment System (MCAS)', *Harvard Educational Review*, 71(2):173–212.

Brighouse, T (1995) Foreword, in J Moyles *Beginning Teaching: Beginning Learning*, Open University Press, Buckingham.

Broadfoot, P (1979) *Assessment, Schools and Society*, Methuen, London.

Broadfoot, P (2002) Editorial 'Beware the consequences of assessment!', *Assessment in Education*, 9(3):5–7.

Brock, P (1998) *The Ethics of the Teaching Profession Standards*, NSW Department of Education and Training, Sydney.

Bronzaft, AL & McCarthy, DP (1975), 'The effect of elevated train noise on reading ability', *Environment and Behaviour*, 7(4):21–7.

Brookfield, SD (1995) *Becoming a Critically Reflective Teacher*, Jossey-Bass, San Francisco.

Brooks, DW (1997) *Web-Teaching*, Plenum, New York.

Brophy, J (1981) 'Teacher praise: A functional analysis', *Review of Educational Research*, 51(1):5–32.

Broudy, HS & Palmer, JR (1965) *Exemplars of Teaching Methods*, Rand McNally, Chicago.

Brown, GT & Hirschfeld, GH (2008) 'Students' conceptions of assessment: Links to outcomes', *Assessment in Education: Principles, Policies and Practice*, 15(1):3–17.

Brown, J & Munn, P (2008) 'School violence as a social problem: Charting the rise of the problem and the emerging specialist field', *International Studies in Sociology of Education*, 18(3/4):19–230.

Brown, L Seddon, T Angus, L & Rushbrook, P (1996) 'Professional practice in education in an era of contractualism: Possibilities, problems and paradoxes', *Australian Journal of Education*, 40(3):311–27.

Brown, M (2009) *Foundation Blocks: Personal, Social and Emotional Development*, Curriculum Corporation, Melbourne.

Brown, M Ralph, S & Brember, I (2002) 'Change-linked work-related stress in British teachers', *Research in Education*, 67):1–12.

Brummelhuis, A & Plomp, T (1994). 'Computers in primary and secondary education: The interest of an individual teacher or a school policy', *Computers in Education*, 22(4):291–9.

Bruner, JS (1966) *Toward a Theory of Instruction*, Harvard University Press, Cambridge.

Buckingham, J (2000) 'The truth about private schools in Australia', *Issue Analysis*, 13(1):1–3.

Budin, H (1999) 'The computer enters the classroom', *Teachers College Record*, 100(3):656–70.

Bull & Solity, *Classroom Management: Principles to Practice*, 1987, Taylor and Francis Books Ltd.

Bullivant, BM (1973) (ed.) *Educating the Immigrant Child*, Angus and Robertson, Sydney.

Bullock, JR (2002), 'Bullying among children', *Childhood Education*, Spring:130–3.

Burn, K Hagger, H Mutton, T & Everton, T (2000) 'Beyond concerns with self: The sophisticated thinking of beginning teachers', *Journal of Education for Teaching*, 26(3):259–78.

Burnett, PC & Meacham, D (2002) 'Measuring the quality of teaching in elementary school classrooms', *Asia-Pacific Journal of Teacher Education*, 30(2):141–54.

Burns, C & Myhill, D (2004) 'Interactive or inactive? A consideration of the nature of interaction in whole class teaching', *Cambridge Journal of Education*, 34(1):35–50.

Burns, RB & Mason, DA (2002) 'Class composition and student achievement in elementary schools', *American Educational Research Journal*, 39(1):207–33.

Burrow, S (1993) 'National competency standards for the teaching profession: A chance to define the future of schooling or a reaffirmation of the past?'. In C Collins (ed.), *Competencies*, ACE, Canberra.

Butin, R (2003) 'Of what use is it? Multiple conceptualisations of service learning within education', *Teachers College Record*, 105(9):1674–92.

Butler, J (1990) *Gender Trouble: Feminism and the Subversion of Identity*, Routledge, New York.

Buzzelli, C & Johnston, B (2001) 'Authority, power and morality in classroom discourse', *Teaching and Teacher Education*, 17(1):873–84.

C

Caffyn, RE (1989) 'Attitudes of British secondary school teachers and pupils to rewards and punishments', *Educational Research*, 31(3):210–20.

Cain, G & Herod, J (2002) *Multivariable Calculus*, Georgia Technological University, Athens.

Cairns, L (1992) 'Competency-based education: Nostradamus's nostrum?' *Journal of Teaching Practice*, 12(1):1–31.

Caldwell, BJ (1997) 'The impact of self-management and self government on professional cultures of teaching: A strategic analysis for the twenty-first century'. In A Hargreaves & R Evans (eds), *Beyond Educational Reform*, Open University Press, Buckingham.

Caldwell, BJ (1998) Strategic leadership, resource management and effective school reform, Paper presented at the Annual Conference of the American Educational Research Association, San Diego.

Caldwell, BJ (2003) A new vision for public schools in Australia, Paper presented at the Economic and Social Outlook Conference of the Melbourne Institute, University of Melbourne.

Caldwell, BJ (2006) 'Give us the power to transform', <www.theage.com.au/news/education-news/give-us-the-power-to-transform/2006> extracted 14 January 2010.

Caldwell, BJ & Harris, J (2008) *Why Not the Best Schools?* ACER, Melbourne.

Caldwell, BJ & Spinks, JM (1993) *Leading the Self-Managing School*, Falmer, London.

Caldwell, BJ & Spinks, JM (1998), *Beyond the Self-Managing School*, Falmer, London.

Calfee, R & Perfumo, P (1996) (eds) *Writing Portfolios in the Classroom*, Lawrence Erlbaum, Mahwah, New Jersey.

Calfee, RC & Chambliss, MJ (1988) The structure of social studies textbooks: Where is the design?, Paper presented at the Annual Conference of the American Educational Research Association, New Orleans.

Cameron, J (2001) 'Negative effects of reward on intrinsic motivation – a limited phenomenon', *Review of Educational Research*, 71(1):29–42.

Campbell, E (2001) Moral lessons: The ethical role of teachers, Paper presented at the Annual Conference of the American Educational Research Association, Chicago.

Campbell, E (2006) 'Curricular and professional authority in schools', *Curriculum Inquiry*, 36(2):111–18.

Cangelosi, JS (1992) *Systematic Teaching Strategies*, Longman, Melbourne.

Canter, L & Canter, M (1992) *Assertive Discipline: Positive Behaviour Management for Today's Classroom*, 2nd edn, Canter and Associates, Santa Monica.

Capel, S Leask, M & Turner, T (1997) *Starting to Teach in the Secondary School*, Routledge, London.

Carey, P (2006) 'From instructor to constructor', *EQ*, Winter:15–16.

Carless, D (2007) 'Learning-oriented assessment: Conceptual bases and practical implications', *Innovations in Education and Teaching International*, 44(1).57–66.

Carr, M (2001) *Assessment in Early Childhood Settings*, Sage, Thousand Oaks, CA.

Carrington, B & McPhee, A (2008) 'Boys' "underachievement" and the feminization of teaching', *Journal of Education for Teaching*, 34(2):109–20.

Carrington, B Francis, B Hutchings, M Shelton, C Read, B & Hall, I (2007) 'Does the gender of the teacher really matter? Seven to eight-year-olds' accounts of their interactions with their teachers', *Educational Studies*, 33(4):397–413.

Carrington, B Tymms, P & Merrell, C (2008) 'Role models, school improvement and the "gender gap" – do men bring out the best in boys and women the best in girls?' *British Educational Research Journal*, 23(3):315–27.

Carrington, V (2004) 'Mid-term review: The middle years of schooling', *Curriculum Perspectives*, 24(1):30–41.

Carter, D Ditchburn, G & Bennett, G (1999) 'Implementing the Discovering Democracy School Materials Project in Western Australia: A question of fit', *Curriculum Perspectives*, 19(3):53–6.

Casas, FR & Meaghan, DE (2001) 'Renewing the debate over the use of standardised testing in the evaluation of learning and teaching', *Interchange*, 32(2):147–81.

Case, R (1985) *Intellectual Development: Birth to Adulthood*, Academic Press, Orlando.

Case, SH (1994) 'Will mandating portfolios undermine their value?', *Educational Leadership*, 52(2):46–7.

Cavanagh, R & MacNeil, N (2002) 'School visioning: Developing a culture for shared creativity', *The Practising Administrator*, 3(1):15–18.

Cavanagh, RF & Dellar, G (1998) The development, maintenance and transformation of school culture, Paper presented at the Annual Conference of the American Educational Research Association, San Diego.

Cavanagh, SL (2005) 'Female–teacher gender and sexuality in twentieth-century Ontario, Canada', *History of Education Quarterly*, 45(2):247–76.

Cavarretta, J (1998) 'Parents are a school's best friend', *Educational Leadership*, 55(8):12–15.

Cawelti, G (2003) 'Lessons from research that changed education', *Educational Leadership*, 60(5):2–9.

Central Advisory Council for Education (1967) *Children and their Primary Schools*, Report of the Central Advisory Council for Education, Vols. 1 & 2, HMSO, London.

Centre for Leadership and Teaching Excellence (2008) in Queensland, <www.clte.com.au/index.php?option+=com_content&task=view&id=44&Itemid=70>.

Chadbourne, R & Quin, R (1989) 'Has restructuring left high school teachers professionally stranded?', *Australian Journal of Teacher Education*, 14(2):9–20.

Chai, P (2005) 'Teach less, learn more', *Voices from our Teachers*, Ministry of Education, Singapore.

Chambliss, MJ Calfee, RC & Wong, I (1990) Structure and content in science textbooks: Where is the design? Paper presented at the Annual Conference of the American Educational Research Association, Boston.

Chan, B & Chui, HS (1997) 'Parental participation in school councils in Victoria, Australia', *International Journal of Educational Management*, 11(3):102–10.

Chan, KW (2004) *Teaching Strategies and Classroom Organisation*, Hong Kong Institute of Education, Hong Kong.

Chang, K Chen, YL Lin, HY & Sung, YT (2008) 'Effects of learning support in simulation-based physics learning', *Computers and Education*, 51(4):1486–98.

Chapin, JR & Messick, RG (1999) *Elementary Social Studies*, 2nd edn, Longman, New York.

Chapman, J (1990) 'School based decision making and management: Implications for school personnel'. In J Chapman (ed.), *School Based Decision Making and Management*, Falmer, London.

Chappuis & Chappuis (2008) 'The best value in formative assessment', *Education Leadership*, 65(4):14–19.

Charles, CM (2004) *Building Classroom Discipline*, 7th edn, Longman, New York.

Chase, CI (1999) *Contemporary Assessment for Educators*, Longman, New York.

Chauncey, C (2005) *Recruiting, Retraining and Supporting Highly Qualified Teachers*, Harvard Education Press, Cambridge, Mass.

Checkley, K (2006) 'Teaching, the second time around', *Education Update*, 48(3):1–8.

Chew, LC & Seow, A (2007) 'Actual competencies of teachers for on-line testing', *Pacific-Asian Education*, 19(1):90–103.

Chiarelott, L Davidson, L & Ryan, K (1994) *Lenses on Teaching*, Harcourt Brace, Fort Worth.

Chokshi, S & Fernandez, C (2004) 'Challenges to importing Japanese lesson study: Concerns, misconceptions and nuances', *Phi Delta Kappan*, 85(7):520–5.

Christensen, A & Green, L (1982) *Trash to Treasures*, Libraries Unlimited, Littleton, Colorado.

Christie, D & Smith, P (1991) 'Teachers' careers in Catholic schools'. In R. Maclean & P. McKenzie (eds), *Australian Teachers' Careers*, ACER, Melbourne.

Christophersen, P (2006) 'Unlocking creativity with ICT', *EQ*, Winter:11–14.

Chubbuck, S Clift, RT Allard, J & Quinlan, J (2001) 'Playing it safe as a novice teacher', *Journal of Teacher Education*, 52(5):365–76.

Churchill, D & Churchill, N (2007) 'Educational affordances of PDAs: A study of a teacher's exploration of this technology', *Computers and Education*, 50(4):1439–50.

Civics Expert Group (1994) *Whereas the People . . . Civics and Citizenship Education*, AGPS, Canberra.

Cizek, G (1991) 'Innovation or enervation', *Phi Delta Kappan*, 72(9):695–9.

Clandinin, DJ & Connelly, FM (1991) 'Narrative and story in practice and research'. In D Schon (ed.), *Case Studies of Reflective Practice*, Teachers College Press, New York.

Clarke, S (1998) *Targeting Assessment in the Primary Classroom*, Hodder & Stoughton, London.

Clarke, S (2001) *Unlocking Formative Assessment*, Hodder & Stoughton, London.

COAG (2007) *The Future of Schooling in Australia*, COAG, Canberra.

Cobington, M (1984) 'The self-worth theory of achievement motivation: Findings and implications', *Elementary School Journal*, 85:5–20.

Cochran-Smith, M (2001b) 'Higher standards for prospective teachers: What's missing from the discourse?', *Journal of Teacher Education*, 52(3):179–81.

Cochran-Smith, M (2005) 'The new teacher education: for better or for worse', *Educational Researcher*, 34(7):3–17.

Cochran-Smith, M (2006) 'Ten promising trends (and three big worries)', *Educational Leadership*, 63(6):20–5.

Coffey, J Sato, M & Thiebault, M (2005) 'Classroom assessment: Up close and personal'. *Teacher Development*, 9(2):169–84.

Cohen, L Manion, L & Morrison, K (2004) *A Guide to Teaching Practice*, 7th edn, Routledge, London.

Cohen, S Krantz, D Evans, GW & Stokes, D (1979) 'Community noise and children: Cognitive, motivational and physiological effects'. In J Tobias (ed.), *The Proceedings of the Third International Congress on Noise as a Public Health Problem*, American Speech and Hearing Association, Washington DC.

Coiro, J (2005) 'Making sense of online text', *Educational Leadership*, 63(2):30–35.

Coladarci, T & Gage, N (1984) 'Effects of a minimal intervention on teacher behaviour and student achievement', *American Educational Research Journal*, 21(3):539–55.

Cole, P (2007) 'Give them all a chance', *EQ Australia*, Spring:13–14.

Cole, P (2008) 'Proposals for better aligning curriculum arrangements with the goals of schooling: 21st century curriculum paper', ACSA, Canberra.

Cole, PG & Chan, LKS (1994) *Teaching Principles and Practice*, 2nd edn, Prentice Hall, New York.

Collard, JL (2000) Organisational culture and principal gender, Paper presented at the Annual Conference of the American Educational Research Association, New Orleans.

Collins, K (1992) 'Primary schools in the twenty-first century', *EQ* 8:20–2.

Collinson, V (1999) 'Redefining teacher excellence', *Theory into Practice*, 38(1):4–11.

Colombo, MW (2004) 'Family literacy nights – and other home-school connections', *Educational Leadership*, 61(8):48–51.

Comer, JP (2005) 'The rewards of parent participation', *Educational Leadership*, 62(6):38–43.

Committee for the Review of Teaching and Teacher Education (2002) Strategies to attract and retain teachers of science, technology and mathematics, Discussion paper, Commonwealth Department of Education, Science & Training, Canberra.

Commonwealth Department of Education, Science and Training (2001) *Making Better Connections*, Commonwealth Department of Education, Science and Training, Canberra.

Commonwealth Department of Employment, Training and Youth Affairs (2001) Improvement or transformation, National Conference on Quality Teaching, Melbourne.

Commonwealth of Australia (1973) *Schools Commission Act*, Commonwealth of Australia, Canberra.

Commonwealth of Australia (1998) *Senate Report*, Canberra.

Commonwealth of Australia (2008) *Schools Assistance Bill (2008)* 12 December, <www.comlaw.gov.au/ComLaw/Legislation/Bills1.nsf/0/64EA2130969C3B5FCA2574CE0010AF70/$file/R3069B.pdf> extracted 3 January 2009.

Connell, R (2009) 'Fixing disadvantage in education', *EQ Australia*, Autumn:7–8.

Connell, RW (1985) *Teachers' Work*, Allen & Unwin, Sydney.

Connolly, P & Maicher, K (2005) Work in progress – computer-based instruction and web-based tutorials: Effectiveness and applications, Paper presented at the 35th Education Conference, Indianapolis.

Conran, P (1989) *School Superintendents' Complete Handbook*, Prentice Hall, Englewood Cliffs, New Jersey.

Cook, P & Barker, S (2001) 'Reinventing your school: A positive approach to marketing public schools', *The Practising Administrator*, 23(2):20–5.

Cooke, BL & Nicholson, A (1992) *Group Work in the Classroom*, Longman, Hong Kong.

Cooper, C & Christie, CA (2005) 'Evaluating parent empowerment', *Teachers College Record*, 107(10):2248–74.

Cooper, D & Snell, J (2003) 'Bullying – not just a kid thing', *Educational Leadership*, 60(6):22–5.

Cooper, I (1982) 'The maintenance of order and use of space in primary school buildings', *British Journal of Sociology of Education*, 3(3):14–23.

Cooper, P & Simonds, CJ (2002) *Communication for the Classroom Teacher*, Allyn & Bacon, Boston.

Cosgrove, F (2007) Standards of professional practice: Supporting effective teacher learning in Victoria, Occasional Paper no. 100, CSE, Melbourne.

Costa, AL (2008) 'The thought filled curriculum', *Educational Leadership*, 65(5):20–25.

Cotton, K (2000) *Classroom Questioning*, North West Regional Educational Laboratory, Oregon.

Council of Australian Governments (see COAG)

Cowley, S (2001) *Getting the Buggers to Behave*, Continuum Press, London.

Cox, AJ (2006) *Boys of Few Words*, Guilford Press, New York.

Cox, B (2004) 'Studying values, controversial issues and religions'. In C. Marsh (ed.), *Teaching Studies of Society and Environment*, 4th edn, Pearson Education Australia, Sydney.

Cradler, J & Bridgforth, E (2004) Effective site level planning for technology integration, <www.wested.org/techpolicy/planning.html>.

Crain W (2005) *Theories of Development*, 5th edn, Prentice Hall, Upper Saddle River, New Jersey.

Crandell, C (1995) 'Speech perception in specific populations'. In C Crandell, J Smaldino & C Flexer (eds), *Sound Field FM Amplification*, Singular Publishing, San Diego, California.

Crawford, K & Deer, CE (1991) Do we practice what we preach? – Putting policy into practice in teacher education, Paper presented at the Annual Conference of the Australian Teacher Education Association, Melbourne.

Creative Curriculum Net (2006) Teaching strategies: Dynamic curriculum, assessment and training for early childhood education, <www.teachingstrategies.com/pages/page.cfm?pageid=204>.

Crittenden, B (1981) *Education for Rational Understanding*, ACER, Melbourne.

Cross, M (2006) 'Breaking down class barriers', *The Guardian*, 19 January:6.

Cruickshank, D Jenkins, D & Metcalf, K (2009), *The Act of Teaching*, 5th edn, McGraw Hill, Boston.

Cuban, L (1983) 'How did teachers teach, 1890–1980?' *Theory into Practice*, 22(3):159–65.

Cuban, L (1993) *How Teachers Taught: Constancy and Change in American Classrooms 1890–1990*, Longman, New York.

Cuban, L (2004) 'Whatever happened to the Open Classroom?', *Education Next*, 4(2):3–14.

Cullingford, C (2006) 'Children's own vision of schooling', *Education 3–13*, 34(3):211–21.

Cumming, J (1998) (ed.) *Outcome-Based Education: Ideas for Professional Development*, ACSA, Canberra.

Cumming, JJ (2008) Legal and educational perspectives of equity in assessment, *Assessment in Education: Principles, Policies and Practice*, 15(2):123–35.

Cumming, JJ & Maxwell, GS (2004) 'Assessment in Australian schools: Current practices and trends', *Assessment in Education*, 11(1):89–108.

Cummings, R Dyas, L Maddux, CD & Kochman, A (2001) 'Principled moral reasoning and behavior of preservice teacher education students', *American Educational Research Journal*, 38(1):143–58.

Cummins, J Bismilla, V Chow, P Cohen, S Giampapa, F Leoni, L Sandhu, P & Sastri, P (2005) 'Affirming identity in multilingual classrooms', *Educational Leadership*, 63(1):38–43.

Cunningham, GK (1998) *Assessment in the Classroom*, Falmer, London.

Curriculum and Standards Framework (2002) *My Home*, CSF, Melbourne.

Curriculum Corporation (2004) *Values Education in Action: Case Studies from 12 Values Education Schools for the National Values Education Forum*, Curriculum Corporation, Melbourne.

Curriculum Corporation (2005) *National Framework for Values Education in Australian Schools*, Curriculum Corporation, Melbourne.

Curriculum Corporation (2006) *Statements of Learning for Civics and Citizenship*, Curriculum Corporation, Melbourne.

Curriculum Corporation (2009) *Building Values across the Whole School*, Curriculum Corporation, Melbourne.

Cushman, P (2006) Gender balance desirability and the favouring of male applicants for primary school teaching positions, *Pacific-Asian Education*, 18(2): 37–50.

D

Damon, W (1992) 'Teaching as a moral craft and developmental expedition'. In F Oser, A Dick & JL Patry (eds), *Effective and Responsible Teaching*, Jossey-Bass, San Francisco.

Daniels, H (2007) *Vygotsky and Research*, Routledge, London.

Danielson, C (2002) *Enhancing Student Achievement* ASCD, Alexandria, Virginia.

Darling-Hammond, L (1994) 'Performance-based assessment and educational equity', *Harvard Educational Review*, 64(1):5–30.

Darling-Hammond, L (2006) *Powerful Teacher Education, Lessons from Exemplary Programs*, Teachers College Press, New York.

Darling-Hammond, L Ancess, J & Falk, B (1995) *Authentic Assessment in Action*, Teachers College Press, New York.

Das, E & Rahimah, A (2006) 'Use of animated power point lectures', *Journal of Vocational Education and Training*, 7(2): 23–37.

Davidson, AJ Rowland, ML & Sherry, MF (1982) *Strategies and Methods: A Guide for Teachers of the Social Sciences*, Victorian Commercial Teachers Association, Melbourne.

Davies, B (2007) *Developing Sustainable Leadership*, Sage, London.

Davies, B (2009) *Essentials of School Leadership*, Sage, London.

Davies, B & Brighouse, T (2008) *Passionate Leadership in Education*, Sage Publications, London.

Davies, B & Ellison, L (2000) Site-based management – myths and realities, Paper presented at the Annual Conference of the American Educational Research Association, New Orleans.

Davies, J Hallam, S & Ireson, J (2003) 'Ability groupings in the primary school: Issues arising from practice', *Research Papers in Education*, 18(1):45–60.

Davies, P & Dunnill, R (2008) '"Learning Study" as a model of collaborative practive in initial teacher education', *Journal of Education for Teaching*, 34(1):3–16.

Davis, D & Sorelli, J (1995) *Mastery Learning in Public Schools*, <www.chiron.valdosta.edu/whuitt/files/mastlear.html>, extracted 22 October 2008.

Davis, EA & Krajcik, JS (2005) 'Designing educative curriculum materials to promote teacher learning', *Educational Researcher*, 34(3):3–14.

Davis, JC & Palmer, J (1992) 'A strategy for using children's literature to extend the social studies curriculum', *The Social Studies*, 81(2):125–8.

Dawkins, J (1988) *Strengthening Australia's Schools*, Minister for Employment, Education and Training, Canberra.

Day, C (2000) *The Life and Work of Teachers*, Routledge, London.

Day, C & Roberts-Holmes, G (1998) The best of times, the worst of times: Stories of change and professional development in England, Paper presented at the Annual Conference of the American Educational Research Association, San Diego.

de Castell, S (2000) 'Literacies, technologies and the future of the library in the "information age"', *Journal of Curriculum Studies*, 32(3):359–76.

De Kock, A Sleegers, P & Voeten, M (2004) 'New learning and the classification of learning environments in secondary education', *Review of Educational Research*, 74(2):141–70.

de Leng, BA Dolmana, D Jobsia, R Muijtjena, M & Van der Vieuten, C (2008) 'Exploration of an e-learning model to foster critical thinking on basic science concepts during work placements', *Computers and Education*, 53(1):1–13.

De Leo, J (2003) 'Making children whole', *EQ Australia*, Summer (4):10–11.

De Vaney, A (1998) 'Educational technology', *Theory into Practice*, 37(1):2–3.

De Vries, R (1997) 'Piaget's social theory', *Educational Researcher*, 26(2):4–17.

De Vries, R & Zan, B (1994) *Moral Classrooms, Moral Children: Creating a Constructivist Atmosphere in Early Education*, Teachers College Press, New York.

Deal, T (1985) 'The symbolism of effective schools', *Elementary School Journal*, 85(5):601–34.

Deal, TE (1990) 'Healing our schools: Restoring the heart'. In A Lieberman (ed.), *Schools as Collaborative Cultures: Creating the Future Now*, Falmer, London.

Deal, TE & Kennedy, AA (1982) *Corporate Cultures: The Rites and Rituals of Corporate Life*, Addison-Wesley, Reading, Massachusetts.

Deci, EL Koestner, R & Ryan, RM (2001) 'Extrinsic rewards and intrinsic motivation in education: Reconsidered once again', *Review of Educational Research*, 71(1):1–28.

Dede, C (1998) (ed.) *Learning with Technology: ASCD Yearbook 1998*, ASCD, Virginia.

DEET (1984) *Participation and Equity Program (1984–87)*, DEET, Canberra.

DEETYA (1998) *Literacy for All: The Challenge for Australian Schools, Commonwealth Literacy Policies for Australian Schools*, Australian Schooling Monograph Series No. 1, Canberra.

Delfabbro, P Winefield, T Trainor, S Dollard, M Anderson, S Metzer, J & Hammarstron, A (2006) 'Peer and teacher bullying/victimization of South Australian secondary school students: Prevalence and psychological profiles', *British Journal of Educational Psychology*, 76(2):71–90.

Dembo, MH (1991) *Applying Educational Psychology in the Classroom*, 4th edn, Longman, New York.

Dempster, N (2008) 'Leadership for Learning: Some ethical connections'. In J Macbeath & YC Cheng (eds) *Leadership for Learning*, Sense Publishers, Rotterdam.

Department of Education and Science (1975) *Acoustics in Educational Buildings*, HMSO, London.

Department of Education and Training (2006a) *Pathways to Excellence: Kindergartens and Pre-Schools*, Department of Education and Training, Perth.

Department of Education and Training (2006b) *Small Steps, Giant Leaps Forward*, Department of Education and Training, Perth.

Department of Education, Employment and Workplace Relations (2008) 'The Adelaide declaration on national goals for schooling in the 21st century', Adelaide Declaration (1999).

Department of Education, Employment and Workplace, Relations (2009) 'Civics and Citizenship education', <www.civicsandcitizenship.edu.au/cce/> extracted 12 April 2009.

Department of Employment, Education, Training and Youth Affairs (see DEETYA)

Department of Education, Science and Training (2005) *National Framework for Values Education in Australian Schools*, Department of Education, Science and Training (DEST), Canberra.

Devine, S (2009) What is moral education?, Unpublished paper, School of Education, University of Northampton.

Dewey, J (1916) *Democracy and Education*, Macmillan, New York.

Dewey, J (1938) *Experience and Education*, Collier, New York.

Dillman, R (2006) Tutorial: *The Communication Process*, HFCL, New York.

Dillon, JT (1994) *Using Discussion in Classrooms*, Open University Press, Buckingham.

Dimmock, C (1990) 'Managing for quality and accountability in Western Australian education', *Educational Review*, 42(2):197–206.

Dimmock, C & Hattie, J (1994) 'Principals' and teachers' reactions to school restructuring', *Australian Journal of Education*, 38(1):36–55.

Dimmock, C & O'Donoghue, TA (1997) *Innovative School Principals and Restructuring*, Routledge, London.

Dinham, S & Scott, C (2000) Teachers' work and the growing influence of societal expectations and pressures, Paper presented at the Annual Conference of the American Educational Research Association, New Orleans.

Dinham, S Ingvarson, L & Kleinhenz, E (2008) 'Investing in teacher quality', *EQ Australia*, Spring:4–5.

Dinkelman, T (2001) 'Service learning in student teaching: "What's social studies for?"', *Theory and Research in Social Education*, 29(4):617–39.

Dockett, S & Perry, B (2005) 'Starting school in Australia', *Early Years*, 25(3):271–82.

Dockrell, JE & Shield, BM (2006) 'Acoustic barriers in classrooms: The impact of noise on performance in the classroom', *British Educational Research Journal*, 32(3):509–25.

Dodd, AW (1998) 'What can educators learn from parents who oppose curricular and classroom practices?', *Journal of Curriculum Studies*, 30(4):461–78.

Dodge, DT Colker, LJ & Heroman, C (2002) *The Creative Curriculum for Early Childhood*, 4th edn, Teaching Strategies, Washington DC.

Doherty, WJ & Needle, RN (1991) 'Psychological adjustment and substance use among adolescents before and after a parental divorce', *Child Development*, 62):328–37.

Donnelly, K (2002) 'A review of New Zealand's school curriculum', *Education Forum*, October 2002:1–69.

Donnelly, K (2007) Australia's adoption of outcomes based education – education panacea or failed experiment?, Unpublished paper.

Doring, A (1994) 'Teacher training in England: Is the profession being undermined?', *Unicorn*, 20(3):46–53.

Dorman, JP Adams, J & Ferguson, J (2002) 'A Cross-national investigation of students' perceptions of mathematics classroom environment and academic efficacy in secondary schools', American Educational Research Association, New Orleans.

Dryfoos, J (2000) 'The mind–body building equation', *Educational Leadership*, 57(6):14–17.

Dryfoos, J (2004) *Evaluation of Community Schools: An Early Look*, <www.communityschools.org/evaluation/evalbrieffinal.html>.

Duke, DL (1984) *The Imperiled Profession*, SUNY Press, Albany, New York.

Dunford, J (2006) 'Children at greater sex assault risk from other pupils', *Times Educational Supplement*, 20 January:5.

Dunkin, MJ (1987) 'Teacher's sex'. In MJ Dunkin (ed.) *International Encyclopaedia of Teaching and Teacher Education*, Pergamon Press, Oxford.

Dunn, R (1990) 'Rita Dunn answers questions on learning styles', *Educational Leadership*, 48(15):15–19.

Dunn, R Beaudry, JS & Klavas, A (1989) 'Survey of research on learning styles', *Educational Leadership*, 46(6):50–8.

Dunn, RE (2002) 'Growing good citizens with a world-centred curriculum', *Educational Leadership*, 60(2):10–13.

Dusseldorp Skills Forums (2005) *How Young People are Faring: Key Indicators*, Dusseldorp Skills Forum, Melbourne.

Dweck, C & Elliott, S (1983) 'Achievement motivation'. In P Mussen (ed.), *Handbook of Child Psychology: 4, Socialization, Personality and Social Development*, Wiley, New York.

Dymoke, S & Harrison, JK (2006) 'Professional development and the beginning teacher: Issues of teacher autonomy and institutional conformity in the performance review process', *Journal of Education for Teaching*, 32(1):71–92.

Dynan, M (1980) *Do Schools Care? Co-operative Research Project*, 29, Education Department of Western Australia, Perth.

E

Earl, LM (2005) *Thinking about Purpose in Classroom Assessment*, ACSA, Canberra.

Ebbeck, M (1990) (chair) *The Standing of Teachers and Teaching, Ebbeck Report*, Report No. 6, AGPS, Canberra.

Eckerman, AK (1994) *One Classroom, Many Cultures*, Allen & Unwin, Sydney.

Eckersley, R (1995) 'Values and visions: Youth and the failure of modern western culture', *Youth Studies Australia*, 14(1):13–21.

Eckman, A (2001) 'Beyond bullying', ASCD *Education Update*, 43(6):1–3.

Education Department, Western Australia (1907) *Annual Report*, Government Printer, Perth.

Education Department, Western Australia (1909) *Annual Report*, Government Printer, Perth.

Education Queensland (2000) *New Basics Project: Technical Paper*, Education Queensland, Brisbane.

Education Queensland (2008) Toowoomba Curriculum Exchange Outcomes Based Education, <www.teachers.ash.org.au/bce/obe.htm> extracted 22 October 2008.

Education Victoria (1998) *Schools of the Third Millennium: Self-Governing Schools*, Education Victoria, Melbourne.

Edwards, BW (2006) 'Environmental design and educational performance', *Research in Education*, 76(3):14–32.

Edwards, CH & Watts, V (2004) *Classroom Discipline and Management: An Australasian Perspective*, John Wiley, Brisbane.

Edwards, E (1985) *Teenagers, Alcohol and Road Safety*, Road Traffic Authority, Melbourne.

Ehlenberger, KR (2002) 'The right to search students', *Educational Leadership*, 59(4):31–5.

Ehman, LH (1977) Social studies instructional factors causing change in high school students' sociopolitical attitudes over a two year period, Paper presented at the Annual Conference of the American Educational Research Association, New York.

Eisner, EW (1979) *The Educational Imagination*, McMillan, New York.

Eisner, EW (1993) 'Reshaping assessment in education: Some criteria in search of practice', *Journal of Curriculum Studies*, 25(3):219–33.

Eisner, EW (1997) 'The promise and perils of alternative forms of data representation', *Educational Researcher*, 26(6):4–9.

Eisner, EW (2005) 'Back to whole', *Educational Leadership*, 63(1):14–19.

Elliott, J & Chan, KK (2002) Curriculum reform east and west: Global trends and local contexts, Unpublished paper, University of East Anglia.

Ellis, AK & Fouts, JT (1997) *Research on Educational Innovations, Eye on Education*, Princeton Junction, New Jersey.

Ellis, D (2003) 'Storefront: a school in a shopping mall', *EQ Australia*, Spring (3):38–9.

Eltis, K (Chair) (1995) *Focusing on Learning: Report of the Review of Outcomes and Profiles in NSW Schooling*, NSW Department of Training and Education Coordination, Sydney.

Emmer, ET & Gerwells, MC (1998) Teachers' views and uses of cooperative learning, Paper presented at the Annual Conference of the American Educational Research Association, San Diego.

Emmer, ET & Gerwells, MC (2006) *Classroom Management for Secondary Teachers*, 7th edn, Allyn & Bacon, Boston.

Emmer, ET Evertson, CM & Worsham, ME (2008) *Classroom Management for Secondary Teachers*, 6th edn, Allyn & Bacon, Boston.

Emmett, G (2002) The Victorian Institute of Teaching, Paper presented at the Annual Conference of the Australian Association for Research in Education, Brisbane.

Epstein, JL & Salinas, KC (2004) 'Partnering with families and communities', *Educational Leadership*, 61(8):12–19.

Erikson, A & Wintermute, M (1983) 'Students, structure, spaces: Activities in the building environment', *ERIC Research in Education*, ED233796, Washington DC.

Erikson, D (2007) Student perceptions of IWB's as a teaching and learning medium, Unpublished paper, Firbank Grammar School, Brighton, Victoria.

Essex, NL (2005) 'Student privacy rights involving strip searches', *Education and the Law*, 17(3):105–10.

Evertson, C & Harris, A (1999) *Support for Managing Learning-Centred Classrooms: The Classroom Organisation and Management Program*, Lawrence Erlbaum.

Eyers, V Cormack, P & Barratt, R (1992) *The Report of the Junior Secondary Review: The Education of Young Adolescents, 11–14*, Dept of Education, Training and Employment, Adelaide.

F

Fan, L & Kaeley, GS (1998) Textbooks use and teaching strategies: An empirical study, Paper presented at the Annual Conference of the American Educational Research Association, San Diego.

Fantini, M (1980) Community participation: Alternative patterns and their consequence on educational achievement, Paper presented at the Annual Conference of the American Educational Research Association, San Francisco.

Farrell, JP (2001) 'Can we really change the forms of formal schooling? And would it make a difference if we could?', *Curriculum Inquiry*, 31(4):389–94.

Feeney, A & Feeney, D (2002) *Bridging the Gap between the Haves and the Have Nots: The Role of Education in Overcoming the Increasing Distance between the Haves and the Have Nots*, World Education Fellowship Australian Council, Brisbane.

Fenstermacher, GD (2001) 'On the concept of manner and its visibility in teaching practice', *Journal of Curriculum Studies*, 33(6):639–54.

Fetterman, DM (1996) 'Videoconferencing on line: Enhancing communication over the Internet', *Educational Researcher*, 25(4):23–7.

Field, T (1980) 'Imaginative alternative use of learning spaces'. In M Poole (ed.), *Creativity across the Curriculum*, George Allen and Unwin, Sydney.

Fill, K & Ottewill, R (2006) 'Sink or swim: Taking advantage of developments in video streaming', *Innovations in Education and Teaching International*, 43(4):397–408.

Finch, L (1999) Discovering Democracy: The last of the Leviathans? *Curriculum Perspectives*, 19(3):63–6.

Finn, B (1991) (Chair) *Report of the Australian Education Council Review Committee, Young People's Participation in Post-compulsory Education and Training*, AEC, Melbourne.

Finn, JD (1998) 'Parental enagagement that makes a difference', *Educational Leadership*, 55(8):20–4.

Finn, JD Pannozzo, G & Achilles, C (2003) 'The "Whys" of class size: Student behaviour in small classes', *Review of Educational Research*, 73(3):321–68.

Firestone, WA (1993) 'Why "professionalizing" teaching is not enough', *Educational Leadership*, 50(6):6–11.

Fischer, L, Schimmel, D & Kelly, C (2008) *Teachers and the Law*, 4th edn, Longman, New York.

Fisher, D & Frey, N (2007) 'A tale of two middle schools: The difference in structure and instruction', *Journal of Adolescent and Adult Learning*, 51(2):204–11.

Fisher, DL & Fraser, BJ (1981) 'Validity and use of the "My Class Inventory"', *Science Education*, 65(2):145–56.

Fisher, DL & Khine, MS (2006) (eds) *Contemporary Approaches to Research on Learning Environments: World Views*, World Scientific, Singapore.

Fitzgerald, RT (1976) *Poverty and Education in Australia*, Commission of Inquiry into Poverty, AGPS, Canberra.

Flanders, N (1970) *Analysing Teacher Behaviour*, Addison-Wesley, Reading, Massachusetts.

Ford, N & Chen, SY (2001) 'Matching/mismatching revisited: An empirical study of learning and teaching styles', *British Journal of Educational Technology*, 32(1):5–22.

Ford, RW (2001) 'A Virtual Enrichment Program for primary students living in outback areas', *Australian Journal of Educational Technology*, 17(1):45–51.

Forlin, P & Forlin, C (1996) 'Legal frameworks for devolution in regular and special education', *Australian Journal of Education*, 40(2):177–89.

Forman, E (1992) 'Discourse, intersubjectivity, and the development of peer collaboration: A Vygotskian approach'. In L Winegar & J Valsiner (eds), *Children's Development Within Social Context*, 1):143–59, Erlbaum, Hillsdale, New Jersey.

Forster, EM (1924) *A Passage to India*, Edward Arnold, London.

Forster, M (1994) 'DART: Assisting teachers to use the English Profile in Assessing and Reporting'. In J Warhurst (ed.), *Teaching and Learning, Implementing the Profiles*, ACSA, Canberra.

Forster, M (2005) 'A new role for school reports', *EQ Australia*, Winter (2):16–17.

Forster, M & Anderson, P (2003) 'Can compassion be measured?', *EQ Australia*, Summer (4):12–13.

Forte, I & Schurr, S (1996) *Curriculum & Project Planner*, National Incentive Publications, Nashville.

Fowler, K & Manktelow, J (1995) Improve your communication skills, <www.mindtools.com> extracted 23 April 2009.

Fowler, S (2008) *Multisensory Rooms and Environments: Controlled Sensory Experiences for People with Profound and Multiple Disabilities*, Jessica Kingsley, Sydney.

Fox, CL & Boulton, M (2005) 'The social skills problems of victims of bullying: Self, peer and teacher perceptions', *British Journal of Educational Psychology*, 75:313–28.

Fraenkel, JR (1976) 'The Kohlberg Bandwagon: Some reservations', *Social Education*, 40(4):216–22.

Fraenkel, JR (1977) *How to Teach About Values: An Analytic Approach*, Prentice Hall, Englewood Cliffs, New Jersey.

Francis, D (2001) 'The challenge of involving students in the evaluation process', *Asia-Pacific Journal of Teacher Education*, 29(2):13–37.

Franek, M (2006) 'Foiling cyberbullies in the New Wild West', *Educational Leadership*, 63(4):39–43.

Franklin, J (2002) 'Assessing assessment: Are alternative methods making the grade?', *ASCD Curriculum Update*, Spring, 1–8.

Franklin, J (2004) 'How technology is transforming K–12 Arts classes', *Curriculum Update*, Spring:4–5.

Franklin, S (2006) 'VAKing out learning styles – why the notion of 'learning styles' is unhelpful to teacher', *Education 3–13*, 34(1):81–87.

Fraser, B & Ferguson, PD (1999) Classroom environment changes across the transition from elementary to high school: Sex and school size differences, Paper presented at the Annual Conference of the American Educational Research Association, Montreal.

Fraser, BJ & Goh, SC (2003) 'Classroom learning environments. In JP Keeves & R Watanabe (eds), *International Handbook of Education Research in the Asia-Pacific Region*, Kluwer, Dordrecht.

Fraser, BJ & Walberg, HJ (1991) (eds) *Educational Environments*, Pergamon, Oxford.

Fraser, BJ McRobbie, CJ & Fisher, DL (1996) Development, validation and use of personal and class forms of a new classroom environment instrument, Paper presented at the Annual Conference of the American Educational Research Association, New York.

Frawley, T (2005) 'Gender bias in the classroom', *Childhood Education*, Summer:221–7.

Freakley, M & Burgh, G (2002) *Engaging with Ethics*, Social Science Press, Sydney.

Freebody, P (2005) 'Learning objects are tracking well', *EQ Australia*, Spring (3):7–9.

Freeman, J (2007) 'How it feels to be a gifted and talented child', *The College of Teachers*, 57(4):7–15.

French, L (1992) 'Marketing and public relations for schools'. In J Donnelly (ed.), *The School Management Handbook*, Kogan Page, London.

Frid, S (2001) 'Supporting primary students' on-line learning in a virtual enrichment program', *Research in Education*, 66:9–27.

Froese-Germain, B (2001) 'Broadening the discourse on student assessment: Response to Casas and Meaghan', *Interchange*, 32(2):183–90.

Frymier, J (1977) *Annehurst Curriculum Classification System: A Practical Way to Individualise Instruction*, Kappa Delta Pi Press, Lafayette, Indiana.

Fuhrman, SH & Elmore, RF (2004) (eds) *Redesigning Accountability Systems for Education*, Teachers College Press, New York.

Fullan, M (2001) *Leading in a Culture of Change*, Jossey-Bass, San Francisco.

Fullan, M Hill, P & Crevola, C (2006) *Break Through*, Corwin Press, San Francisco.

Fullan, MG (1991) *The New Meaning of Educational Change*, Cassell, London.

Fullan, MG (1993) *Change Forces*, Falmer, London.

Fullan, MG & Hargreaves, A (1991) *Working Together for Your School*, ACEA, Melbourne.

Fuller, C & Stone, ME (1998) 'Teaching social studies to diverse learners', *The Social Studies*, 89(4):154–7.

Fullerton, T & Clements, MA (2002) The relevance of generic teacher competencies in the preparation of prospective teachers of Mathematics, Unpublished Paper, Faculty of Education, University of Newcastle.

Furtwengler, CB (1998) 'Heads up! The EMOs are coming', *Educational Leadership*, 56(2):44–7.

Futoran, GC Schofield, JW & Eurich-Fulmer, R (1995) 'The Internet as a K–12 educational resource: Emerging issues of information access and freedom', *Computers in Education*, 24(3):229–36.

G

Gage, J (2005) *How to use an Interactive Whiteboard*, David Fulton, London.

Gage, NL & Berliner, DC (1976) 'The psychology of teaching methods'. In NL Gage (ed.), *The Psychology of Teaching Methods*, University of Chicago Press, Chicago.

Gage, NL & Berliner, DC (1992) *Educational Psychology*, 5th edn, Houghton Mifflin, Boston.

Gage, NL & Berliner, DC (1998) *Educational Psychology*, 7th edn, Houghton Mifflin, Boston.

Gaither, M (2008) 'Why homeschooling happened', *Educational Horizons*, 86(4):226–37.

Galbreath, J (1997) 'The Internet, past, present and future', *Educational Technology*, 37(6):39–45.

Gale, T & Cross, R (2007) 'Nebulous gobbledegook: The politics of (re)learning how and what to teach in Australia'. In A Berry, A Clemens & A Kostogriz (eds), *Dimensions of Professional Learning: Professionalism, Practice and Identity*, Sense Publishers, Rotterdam:5–22.

Gall, MD (1981) *Handbook for Evaluating and Selecting Curriculum Materials*, Allyn & Bacon, Boston.

Gallagher, M Millar, R & Ellis, R (1996) 'The role of adolescent perceptions in personal and social education', *Journal of Curriculum Studies*, 28(5): 577–96.

Galotti, KM Kozberg, SF & Farmer, MC (1991) 'Gender and developmental differences in adolescents' conceptions of moral reasoning', *Journal of Youth and Adolescence*, 20:13–30.

Galton, M & MacBeath, J (2002) *A Life in Teaching? The Impact of Change on Primary Teachers' Working Lives*, National Union of Teachers, London.

Galton, M & Williamson, J (1992) *Group Work in the Primary Classroom*, Routledge, London.

Galton, M Simon, B & Croll, P (1980) *Inside the Primary Classroom*, Routledge & Kegan Paul, London.

Gamage, DT (1992) 'Challenges facing school councils', *Education Monitor*, 3(3):23–8.

Gamage, DT (1993) 'A review of community participation in school governance: An emerging culture in Australian education', *British Journal of Education Studies*, 41(2):134–63.

Garbarino, J & deLara, E (2003) 'Words can hurt forever', *Educational Leadership*, 60(6):18–21.

Gardner, H (1983) *Frames of Mind: The Theory of Multiple Intelligences*, Basic Books, New York.
Gardner, H (2006) *Changing Minds*, Harvard Business School Press, Boston.
Gardner, P (1997) *Managing Technology in the Middle School Classroom*, Hawker Brownlow, Melbourne.
Gargiulo RM (2008) *Special Education in Contemporary Society: An Introduction to Exceptionality*, 3rd edn, Sage, Los Angeles.
Garner, BK (2008) 'When Students Seem Stalled', *Educational Leadership*, 65(6):32–39.
Garner, R & Gillingham, M (1996) *Internet Communication in Six Classrooms*, Lawrence Erlbaum, New Jersey.
Gay, K (1986) *Ergonomics*, Enslow Publishers, Hillsdale, New Jersey.
Geijsel, F Sleegars, P Leithwood, K & Jantzi, D (2002) Transformational leadership effects on teachers' commitment and effort toward school reform, Paper presented at the Annual Conference of the American Educational Research Association, New Orleans.
George, CJ & McKinley, D (1974) *Urban Ecology*, McGraw-Hill, New York.
George, E (2006) 'Failing the future: Development objectives, human rights obligations and gender violence in schools'. In F Leach & C Mitchell (eds), *Combating Gender Violence in and around Schools*, Trentham Books, Stoke-on-Trent.
George, P Lawrence, G & Bushnell, D (1998) *Handbook for Middle School Teaching*, 2nd edn, Longman, New York.
Georgiou, SN (2009) 'Personal and material parameters of peer violence at school', *Journal of School Violence*, 8(2):100–19.
Gibbs, D & Krause, KL (2000) (eds) *Cyberlines*, James Nicholas, Albert Park, Victoria.
Gibbs, JC (1977) 'Kohlberg's stages of moral judgement: A consecutive critique', *Harvard Educational Review*, 47(1).
Gibson, D (2009) 'Child sex abuse reports soar', *West Australian*, July 11, p. 11.
Gibson, IW (2002) 'Leadership, Technology and Education: Achieving a balance in new school leader thinking and behaviour in preparation for twenty-first century global learning environments', *Journal of Information Technology for Teacher Education*, 11(3):315–34.
Gilbert, R (2004) 'Elements of values education', *The Social Educator*, 22(4):8–14.
Gilbert, R & Gilbert, P (1998) *Masculinity Goes to School*, Allen & Unwin, Sydney.
Gill, J & Reid, A (1999) Civics education: The state of play or the play of the state? *Curriculum Perspectives*, 19(3):31–40.
Gillard, J (2008a) Equity in the education revolution, Speech at the 6th Annual Higher Education Summit, Sydney, 3 April 2008, <www.mediacentre.dewr.gov.au/mediacentre/Gillard/Releases/EquityintheEduationRevolution.htm> extracted 13 October 2009.
Gillard, J (2008b) Delivering Australia's first national curriculum, Speech given to the ACOSS National Conference, Melbourne, 10 April 2008, <www.mediacentre.dewr.gov.au/mediacentre/gillard/releases/deliveringaustraliasfirstnationalcurriculum.htm> extracted 3 January 2009.
Gillespie, AA (2007) 'Barring teachers: the new vetting arrangements', *Education and the Law*, 19(1):1–18.
Gilligan, C & Attanucci, J (1988). 'Two moral orientations'. In C Gilligan, JV Ward & JM Taylor with B Bardige (eds), *Mapping the Moral Domain: A Contribution of Women's Thinking to Psychological Theory and Education* (pp. 73–86), Harvard University Press, Cambridge, Massachusetts.
Gilligan, C (1982) *In a Different Voice*, Harvard University Press, Cambridge.
Gipps, C & Murphy, P (1994) *A Fair Test? Assessment, Achievement and Equity*, Open University Press, Milton Keynes, Bucks.
Gipps, C McCallum, B & Hargreaves, E (2000) Classroom assessment and feedback strategies of 'expert' elementary teachers, Paper presented at the Annual Conference of the American Educational Research Association, New Orleans.
Gipps, CV (1994) *Beyond Testing*, Falmer, London.
Giroux, HA (1981) *Ideology, Culture and the Process of Schooling*, Falmer, London.
Giroux, HA (1988) *Teachers as Intellectuals*, Bergin and Garvey, Granby.
Gitlin, A & Ornstein, S (2007) 'A political humanist curriculum for the 21st century'. In A Ornstein,␣ EF Pajak & SB Ornstein (eds), *Contemporary Issues in Curriculum*, 4th edn, Pearson/Allyn & Bacon, Boston.
Givvin, KB Stipek, D Salmon, J & McGyvers, V (2001) 'In the eyes of the beholder: Students' and teachers' judgments of student motivation', *Teaching and Teacher Education*, 17, 321–31.
Glasser, W (1992) *The Quality School*, Harper-Collins, New York.
Glassman, M & Wang, Y (2004) 'On the interconnected nature of Vygotsky', *Educational Researcher*, 33(2): 19–21.
Glatthorn, AA & Fontana, J (2002) *Standards and Accountability: How Teachers See Them*, National Education Association, Washington DC.
Glatthorn, AA & Jailall, J (2000) 'Curriculum for the new millennium'. In RS Brandt (ed.), *Education in a New Era*, ASCD, Alexandria, Virginia.
Glatthorn, AA Whitehead, BM & Boschee, F (2008) *Curriculum Leadership: Strategies for Development and Implementation*, Sage, Thousand Oaks, CA.
Glover, D & Coleman, M (2005) 'School culture, climate and ethos: Interchangeable or distinctive concepts?', *Journal of Inservice Education*, 31(2): 251–71.
Goddard, R & Goddard, M (2006) 'Beginning teacher burnout in Queensland schools: Associations with serious intentions to leave', *Australian Educational Researcher*, 33(2):61–75.

Gold, A & Evans, J (1998) *Reflecting on School Management*, Falmer, London.

Goldsmith, LT & Mark, J (1999) 'What is a standards-based mathematics curriculum?', *Educational Leadership*, 57(3):40–5.

Gonczi, A Hager, P & Oliver, L (1990) *Establishing Competency-based Standards in the Professions*, NOOSR Research Paper No. 1, AGPS, Canberra.

Goodrum, D (2007) 'Becoming a better teacher', *EQ Australia*, Summer:6–7.

Goodson, I (1988) *The Making of Curriculum*, Lewes, Falmer, England.

Goodson, I (2001) 'Social histories of educational change', *Journal of Educational Change*, 2(1):1–31.

Goodson, I (2005) 'The exclusive pursuit of social inclusion', *Forum*, 47(2–3):7–16.

Goodson, IF & Marsh, CJ (1996) *Studying School Subjects*, Falmer, London.

Goodwin, P (2008) *Understanding Children's Books: A Guide for Education Professionals*, Sage, Thousand Oaks, CA.

Gore, J (1998) Revisiting values education: The role of civics and citizenship education, Paper presented at the Annual Conference of the Pacific Circle Consortium, Mexico.

Gorman, JC & Balter, L (1997) 'Culturally sensitive parent education: A critical review of quantitative research', *Review of Educational Research*, 67(3): 339–69.

Government of South Australia (2008) Governing, <www.decs.sa.gov.au/governance/banner.asp?navgrp=Local&id=27441&extra=?...> extracted 14 April 2009.

Goy, C (2000) 'Minimising alienation in the student learner', *The Practising Administrator* (2):12–13.

Grabe, M & Grabe, C (2000) *Integrating the Internet for Meaningful Learning*, Houghton Mifflin, Boston.

Graham, N & George, J (1992) *Marking Success*, Pembroke, London.

Grebennikov, L (2006) 'Preschool teachers' exposure to classroom noise', *International Journal of Early Years Education*, 14(1):35–44.

Grebennikov, L & Wiggins, M (2006) 'Psychological effects of classroom noise on early childhood teachers', *The Australian Education Researcher*, 33(3):35–53.

Gredler, ME (2007) 'Of cabbages and kings: Concepts and inferences curiously attributed to Lev Vygotsky' (commentary on McVee, Dunsmore & Gavelick, 2005), *Review of Education Research*, 77(2):233–8.

Green, B (1988) (ed.) *Metaphors and Meanings*, Australian Association for the Teaching of English, Perth.

Green, H (2004) *Professional Standards for Teachers and School Leaders*, Routledge, London.

Gregory, D (1997) Making multicultural connections through trade books, <www.mcps.k12.md.us/curriculum/socialstd/MBD/Books_Begin.html>.

Grey, D (2001) *The Internet in Schools*, 2nd edn, Continuum Press, London.

Grieshaber, S (2009) 'Equity and quality in the early years of schooling', *Curriculum Perspectives*, 29(1):91–97.

Griffin, P (1998) 'Outcomes and profiles: Changes in teachers' assessment practices', *Curriculum Perspectives*, 18(1):9–19.

Griffith, J (1997) 'Student and parent perceptions of school social environment: Are they group based?', *Elementary School Journal*, 98(2):135–50.

Griffiths, T (2009) Social justice, equity, schools and the curriculum, *Curriculum Perspectives*, 29(1):76–82.

Gronlund, NE (1981) *How to Write and Use Instructional Objectives*, 4th edn, Macmillan, New York.

Groundwater-Smith, S Cusworth, R & Dobbins, R (1998) *Teaching: Challenges and Dilemmas*, Harcourt Brace, Sydney.

Grundy, S & Bonser, S (1997a) 'Choosing to change: Teachers working with student-outcome statements', *Curriculum Perspectives*, 17(1):1–12.

Grundy, S & Bonser, S (1997b) 'In whose interests? Competing discourses in the policy and practice of school restructuring', *Australian Journal of Education*, 41(2):150–68.

Guastello, EF (2004) 'A village of learners', *Educational Leadership*, 61(8):79–83.

Gunter, PL Shores, RE Jack, SL Rasmussen, SK & Flowers, J (1995) 'On the move: Using teacher/student proximity to improve students' behaviour', *Teaching Exceptional Children*, 28(1):12–14.

Gurian, M & Stevens, K (2004) 'With boys and girls in mind', *Educational Leadership*, 62(3):21–7.

Guskey, TR & Pigott, TD (1988) 'Research on group-based mastery learning programs: A meta-analysis', *Journal of Educational Research*, 81(4):197–216.

H

Haan, N (1985) 'Processes of moral development: Cognitive or social disequilibrium?', *Developmental Psychology*, 21(4):996–1006.

Hachiya (1955) *The Agony of Hiroshima: The Journal of a Japanese Physician, August 6 – September 30, 1945.* W Wells (trans.), University of North Carolina Press, Chapel Hill.

Hackbarth, S (1997) 'Integrating web-based learning activities into school curriculum', *Educational Technology*, 37(3):59–71.

Hager, P (1994) 'Professional competence and education'. In F Crowther, B Caldwell, J Chapman, G Lakomski & D Ogilvie (eds), *The Workplace in Education*, Edward Arnold, Sydney.

Hahn C & Stout K (1994) *The Internet Complete Reference*, Osborne, McGraw-Hill, Berkeley.

Hahn, CL & Avery, PG (1985) 'Effect of value analysis discussions on students' political attitudes and reading comprehension', *Theory and Research in Social Education*, 13(2):47–60.

Halford, GS (1993) *Children's Understanding: The Development of Mental Models*, Lawrence Erlbaum, London.

Hall, BP (1973) *Value Clarification as Learning Process*, Paulist Press, New York.

Hall, RM (1995) The classroom climate: A chilly one for women? Project on the Status and Education of Women of the Association of American Colleges, WAAC, Washington DC.

Hall, T (2002) Differentiated instruction, Wakefield, MA: National Center on Accessing the General Curriculum, <www.cast.or/publications/ncac_diffinstruc.html> extracted 21 October 2008.

Hambel, S (2006) 'Deconstructing whiteness through education', *Curriculum Perspectives*, 26(1):1–11.

Hamberger, NM & Moore, RL (1997) 'From personal to professional values: Conversations about conflicts', *Journal of Teacher Education*, 48(4):301–10.

Hamilton, L & Stecher, B (2004) 'Responding effectively to test-based accountability', *Phi Delta Kappan*, 85(1):578–92.

Han, S & Akiba, M (2005) 'School liability for student injury from school violence: Comparison between South Korea and the USA', *Education and the Law*, 17(4):161–72.

Haney, W & Madus, G (1989) 'Searching for alternatives to standardised tests: Whys, whats and whethers', *Phi Delta Kappan*, May:683–7.

Hansen, DT (1993) 'The moral importance of the teacher's style', *Journal of Curriculum Studies*, 25(5):397–422.

Hansen, DT (1995) Teaching and the moral life of classrooms, *Journal for a Just and Caring Education*, 2(2):59–74.

Hansen, JM (1989) 'Outcome-based education: A smarter way to assess student learning', *Clearing House*, 63(4):172–4.

Hansen, S (1998) 'Preparing student teachers for curriculum-making', *Journal of Curriculum Studies*, 30(2):165–80.

Hansford, G (2000) 'Asynchronous and synchronous forms of instruction', *Australian Journal of Educational Technology*, 16(2):38–53.

Harcourt Trade Publishers (2006) Trade Books, <www.harcourtbooks.com/ChildrensBooks/teachertools.asp>.

Hardre PL & Sullivan DW (2007) 'Student differences and environmental perceptions: How they contribute to student motivation in rural high schools', *Learning and Individual Differences*, 10(3):41–50.

Hargreaves, A (1994) *Changing Teachers, Changing Times: Teachers' Work and Culture in the Post-modern Age*, Cassell, London.

Hargreaves, A (2003) *Teaching in the Knowledge Society*, Teachers College Press, New York.

Hargreaves, A & Evans, R (1997) (eds) *Beyond Educational Reform*, Open University Press, Buckingham.

Hargreaves, A & Fullan, M (1998) *What's Worth Fighting for Out There?*, Teachers College Press, New York.

Hargreaves, A & Fullan, M (2000) 'Mentoring in the new millennium', *Theory into Practice*, 39(1):1–55.

Hargreaves, A & Moore, S (1999) 'Getting into outcomes: The emotions of interpretation and implementation, *Curriculum Perspectives*, 19(3):1–10.

Hargreaves, A Earl, L & Schmidt, M (2002) 'Perspectives on alternative assessment reform', *American Educational Reform Journal*, 39(1):69–95.

Hargreaves, A Earl, L Moore, S & Manning, S (2001) *Learning to Change*, Jossey-Bass, San Francisco.

Hargreaves, DH (1972) *Interpersonal Relations and Education*, Routledge & Kegan Paul, London.

Hargreaves, DH & Hopkins, D (1991) *The Empowered School*, Cassell, London.

Hargreaves, DH & Hopkins, D (1994) *Development Planning for School Improvement*, Routledge, London.

Hargreaves, E (2005) 'Assessment for learning? Thinking outside the (black) box', *Cambridge Journal of Education*, 35(2):213–24.

Hargreaves, M Homer, M & Swinnerton, B (2008) 'A comparison of performance and attitudes in mathematics amongst the gifted: Are boys better at mathematics or do they just think they are?' *Assessment in Education: Principles, Policy and Practice*, 15(1):19–38.

Harlen, W (1994) *Evaluating Curriculum Materials*, SCRE Spotlights, Edinburgh, Scottish Council for Research in Education.

Harlen, W (2005) 'Teachers' summative practices and assessment for learning – tensions and synergies', *The Curriculum Journal*, 16(2):207–23.

Harlen, W (2007) *Assessment of Learning*, Sage, Thousand Oaks, CA.

Harman, G (1990) 'Democracy, bureaucracy and the politics of education'. In J Chapman & J Dunstan (eds), *Democrary & Bureaucracy: Tensions in Public Schooling*, Falmer, London.

Harmin, M (1994) *Inspiring Active Learning*, ASCD, Alexandria, Virginia.

Harold, B (1997) Negotiating partnerships between the home and school: a New Zealand perspective, Paper presented at the Biennial Conference of the Australian Curriculum Studies Association.

Harris, C (2005) 'The promise of cultural institutions: Learning SOSE beyond the classroom', *The Social Educator*, 24(1):44–9.

Harris, C & Marsh, CJ (2005) (eds) *Curriculum Developments in Australia: Promising Initiatives, Impasses and Dead-ends*, Openbook, Adelaide.

Harris, D & Bell, C (1990) *Evaluating and Assessing for Learning*, 2nd edn, Kogan Page, London.

Harris-Hart C (2009) The national history curriculum: Tragedy or triumph? Paper presented at the Biennial Australian Curriculum Studies Conference, Canberra, October 2–4.

Harrow, AJ (1972) *A Taxonomy of the Psychomotor Domain: A Guide for Developing Behavioural Objectives*, David McKay, New York.

Harshman, RE & Gray, CE (1983) 'A Rationale for Value Education', *Theory and Research in Social Education*, 11(3):45–66.

Hart, B & Risley, TR (1995) *Meaningful Differences in the Everyday Experience of Young American Children*, Paul H Brookes, Baltimore.

Hatch, T (1998) 'How community action contributes to achievement', *Educational Leadership*, 55(8):16–19.

Hatch, T White, M & Faigenbaum, D (2005) 'Expertise, credibility and influence: How teachers can influence policy, advance research and improve performance', *Teachers College Record*, 107(5):1004–35.

Hattie, J (2006) 'The paradox of reducing class size and improving learning outcomes', *International Journal of Educational Research*, 43(6):387–425.

Hattie, J & Fletcher, R (2005) 'Self esteem = success / pretensions: Assessing pretensions / importance in self-esteem.' In HW Marsh, RG Graven & D McInerney (eds), *International Advances in Self Research, Vol 1*, Information Age Publishing, Greenwich, CT.

Hay, P (2010) 'No one gets an OP of 1' (tentative title), *Curriculum Perspectives* (in press).

Hay, T & Moss, J (2005) (eds) *Portfolios, Performance and Authenticity*, Pearson Education, Sydney.

Haycock, K & Crawford, C (2008) 'Closing the teacher quality gap', *Educational Leadership*, 65(7):14–19.

Hayden, C & Blaya, C (2008) Lost in transition? A comparison of early "drop out" from education and training in England and France, *The International Journal of School Disaffection*, 6(1):19–24.

Haydon, G (1998) 'Between the common and the differentiated: Reflection on the work of the school curriculum and assessment authority on values education', *The Curriculum Journal*, 9(1):5–21.

Hayes, D (2006) *Primary Education: The Key Concepts*, Routledge, London.

Hayes, D (2008) *Foundations of Primary Teaching*, 4th edn, Routledge, London.

Hayes, D (2009) 'Co-opting the market in support of young people who are not well served by school: Service-based innovation in high poverty and high difference contexts', *Curriculum Perspectives*, 29(1).

Hayes, D & Chodkiewicz, A (2006) 'School-community links: Supporting learning in the middle years', *Research Papers in Education*, 21(1):3–18.

Hayes, M & Vivian, C (2008) 'What kind of place is secondary school?', *The Educational Forum*, 72(1):23–31.

Hayes, T (2006) 'Professional teaching associations and professional standards: Embedding standards in the "discourse of the profession"', *Teaching Australia*, Canberra.

Heaven, PCL (2001) *The Social Psychology of Adolescence*, Palgrave, London.

Hebert, EA (1998) 'Lessons learned about student portfolios', *Phi Delta Kappan*, 79(8).

Heck, RH & Crislip, M (2001) 'Direct and indirect writing assessments: Examining issues of equity and utility', *Educational Evaluation and Policy Analysis*, 23(3):275–92.

Hehir, T (2007) 'Confronting ableism', *Educational Leadership*, 64(5):8–15.

Helsing, D (2002) Developing a positive relationship to the uncertainties of teaching, Paper presented at the Annual Conference of the American Educational Research Association, New Orleans.

Helwig, C Turiel, E & Nucci, L (1997) Character education after the bandwagon has gone, Paper presented at the Annual Conference of the American Educational Research Association, Chicago.

Henderson, D Fisher, D & Fraser, B (1998) Learning environment, student attitudes and effects of student's sex and other science study in environmental science classes, Paper presented at the Annual Conference of the American Educational Research Association, San Diego.

Hendrick, J (2001) *The Whole Child*, 7th edn, Prentice Hall, Upper Saddle River, New Jersey.

Hendry, GD Heinrich, P Lyon, P Barratt, A Simpson, J Hyde, S Gonsalkorale, S Hyde, M & Mgaieth, S (2005) 'Helping students understand their learning styles: Effects on study self-efficacy, preference for group work and group climate', *Educational Psychology*, 25(4):395–407.

Heng, MA & Marsh, CJ (2009) 'Understanding middle leaders: A closer look at middle leadership in primary schools in Singapore', *Educational Studies*, 35(5):525–36.

Henniger, ML (2004) *The Teaching Experience*, Pearson, Merrill Prentice Hall, Columbus, Ohio.

Henry, SE (2001) 'What happens when we use Kohlberg?: His troubling functionalism and the potential of pragmatism in moral education', *Educational Theory*, 51(3):259–78.

Herman, JL & Winters, L (1994) 'Synthesis of research: Portfolio research: A slim collection', *Educational Leadership*, 52(2):48–55.

Herr, K & Arms, E (2004) 'Accountability and single sex schooling: A collision of reform agendas', *Educational Evaluation and Policy Analysis*, 26(4):78–95.

Hewitt, TW (2006) *Understanding and Shaping Curriculum*, Sage, Thousand Oaks, CA.

Heywood, L Gonczi, A & Hager, P (1992) *A Guide to Development of Competency Standards for Professions*, NOOSR Research Paper No. 7, AGPS, Canberra.

Hiatt, B (2006) 'New OBE hits trouble over uni entry marks', *West Australian*, 13 Sept., p. 5.

Hiatt, B (2008) 'Maths curriculum guru queries use of calculators', *West Australian*, 15 October p. 14.

Hiatt, B (2008) 'Spelling, grammar back at heart of new English', *West Australian*, 17 October p. 9.

Hiatt, B (2008) 'National plan to teach history from kindy', *West Australian*, 13 October p. 11.

Hiatt-Michael, D (2000) Parent involvement as a component of teacher education programs in California, Paper presented at the Annual Conference of the American Educational Research Association, New Orleans.

Hidi, S & Harackiewicz, JM (2000) 'Motivating the academically unmotivated: A critical issue for the 21st century', *Review of Educational Research*, 70(2):151–80.

Hiemstra, R & Sisco, B (1990) *Individualizing Instruction: Making Learning Personal, Empowering and Successful*, Jossey-Bass, San Francisco.

Hill, BV (1991) *Values Education in Australian Schools*, ACER, Melbourne.

Hill, BV (2003) 'Send reinforcements: We're going to teach values', *EQ Australia*, Summer(4):5–6.

Hill, R & Russell, V (1999) 'Systemic, whole-school reform of the middle years of schooling'. In R Bosker, B Creemers & S Stringfield (eds), *Enhancing Educational Excellence, Equity and Efficiency: Evidence from Evaluation of Systems and Schools in Change*, Kluwer, Dortrecht, Netherlands.

Hinkelman, L & Bruno, M (2008) 'Identification and reporting of child sexual abuse: The role of elementary school professionals', *The Elementary School Journal*, 108(5):376–91.

Hinton, F (1997) 'Winds of change: Teachers in the year 2007', *Unicorn*, 23(2):18–24.

Hirst, PH (1974) *Knowledge and the Curriculum*, Routledge and Kegan Paul, London.

Hlebowitsh, PS (1998) The burdens of the new curricularist, Paper presented at the Annual Conference of the American Educational Research Association, San Diego.

Hoban, GF (2004) 'Seeking quality in teacher education design: A four-dimensional approach', *Australian Journal of Education*, 48(2):117–33.

Hoban, P & Littlejohn, M (2009) 'History in a digital world', *The Social Educator*, 27(1):23–27.

Hobart Declaration (1989) (see MCEETYA 1989)

Hodkinson, H & Hodkinson, P (2005) 'Improving school teachers' workplace learning', *Research Papers in Education*, 20(2):109–31.

Hoek, DJ & Seegers, G (2005) 'Effects of instruction on verbal interactions during collaborative problem solving', *Learning Environment Research*, 8:19–39.

Hogan, D & Fearnley-Sander, M (1999) 'An education for heteronomy: A critique of the Discovering Democracy Project', *Curriculum Perspectives*, 19(3):57–62.

Holland, NE (2008) 'Refocusing educational assessments on teaching and learning, not politics', *The Educational Forum*, 72(3):215–26.

Holt Publishing (1972) *First Things: Values*, Holt, Chicago.

Holt Publishing (1974) *First Things: Social Reasoning*, Holt, Chicago.

Holt Publishing (1975) *Holt Social Studies Curriculum*, Holt, Chicago.

Holt, G (2005) *Access Program, Swan View Senior High School*, Vocational Education and Training, Perth.

Holt, J (1964) *How Children Fail*, Penguin, London.

Holt, J (1997) 'Statements and Profiles: Where are we now?', *EQ Australia*, Spring (3):15–17.

Holt, MK Kantor, GK & Finkelbor, T (2009) Parent/child concordance about bullying involvement and family characteristics related to bullying and peer victimization, *Journal of School Violence*, 8(1):42–63.

Holt, Rinehart & Winston (2006) One line store for 6–12 subjects, <www.hrw.com/>.

Holt-Reynolds, D (2000) 'What does the teacher do? Constructivist pedagogies and prospective teachers' beliefs about the role of a teacher', *Teaching and Teacher Education*, 16(1):21–32.

Hoover-Dempsey, KV Walker, J Sandler, HM Whetsel, D Green, C Wilkins, AS & Closson, K (2005) 'Why do parents become involved? Research findings and implications', *Elementary School Journal*, 106(2):105–25.

Hopkins, D (1989) 'Teacher research as a basis for staff development'. In MF Wideen & I Andrews (eds), *Staff Development for School Improvement*, Falmer, London.

Hopmann, S & Kunzli, T (1997). 'Close our schools! Against current trends in policy making, educational theory and curriculum studies', *Journal of Curriculum Studies*, 29(3):259–66.

Horowitz, P & Otto, D (1973) *The Teaching Effectiveness of an Alternative Teaching Facility*, (ERIC Document Reproduction Service No. ED083242) University of Alberta, Alberta.

House of Representatives Standing Committee on Education and Vocational Training (2005), *Inquiry into Teacher Education*, Commonwealth of Australia, Canberra.

Howard, GR (2007) 'As diversity grows, so must we', *Education Leadership*, 64(6):16–22.

Howes, A Booth, T Dyson, A & Frankham, J (2005) 'Teacher learning and the development of inclusive practices and policies: Framing and Context', *Research Papers in Education*, 20(2):133–48.

Hoxby, C (2004) 'Political jurisdictions in heterogeneous communities', *Journal of Political Economy*, 112(2):47–59.

Huberman, AM (1989) 'On teachers' careers: Once over lightly with a broad brush', *International Journal of Educational Research*, 13(4):78–93.

Hue, MT (2007) 'The relationships between school guidance and discipline: Critical contrasts in two Hong Kong secondary schools', *Educational Review*, 59(3):343–61.

Hughes, M & Greenhough, P (1998) Parents' and teachers' knowledge bases and instructional strategies, Paper presented at the Annual Conference of the American Educational Research Association, San Diego.

Hughes, P (2004) 'How do teachers influence people: A study of the effects of teachers on some prominent Australians', *Australian College of Education*, 33, Canberra.

Hunt, NP (1997) 'Using technology to prepare teachers for the twenty-first century', *Asia-Pacific Journal of Teacher Education*, 25(3):345–50.

Hunt, TC & Yarusso, LC (1979) Open education: Can it survive its critics? *Peabody Journal of Education*, 56(4):294–300.

Hyman, I & Perone, D (1998) The other side of school violence: Educator policies and practices that may contribute to student misbehaviour, *Journal of School Psychology*, 36:7–17.

I

Ikemotu, T (1995) What is values clarification? Moral issues, <www.hi-ho.ne.jp/taku77>.

Ikemotu, T (2006) *Policy Implementation and Learning*, Center for the Study of Teaching and Policy, University of Washington, Seattle.

Imber, M (1983) 'Increased decision making involvement for teachers: Ethical and practical considerations', *Journal of Educational Thought*, 17(1):36–41.

Imber, M & Van Geel, T (2004) *A Teacher's Guide to Education Law*, McGraw Hill, Hightstown, New Jersey.

Infantino, J & Little, E (2005) 'Students perceptions of classroom behaviour problems and the effectiveness of different disciplinary methods', *Educational Psychology*, 25(5):491–508.

Ingvarson, L (1998) 'Professional standards: A challenge for the AATE', *English in Australia*, 122:1–17.

Ingvarson, L (2002a) *Building a Learning Profession*, Paper No. 1, Commissioned Research Series, Australian College of Educators, Canberra.

Ingvarson, L (2002b) 'Strengthening the profession? A comparison of recent reforms in the UK and USA', ACER Policy Briefs Issue 2, ACER, Melbourne.

Ingvarson, L & Rowe, K (2007) Conceptualising and evaluating teacher quality, Paper presented at the Economics of Teacher Quality Conference, Australian National University, Canberra.

Izard, J (2005) Impediments to sound use of formative assessment (and actions we should take to improve assessment for learning), Paper presented at the Annual Conference of the Australian Association for Research in Education, Melbourne.

J

Jackson, JW (2002) 'Enhancing self-efficacy and learning performance', *Journal of Experimental Education*, 70(3):243–54.

Jackson, PW (1968) *Life in Classrooms*, Holt, Rinehart & Winston, New York.

Jackson, PW (1992) (ed.) *Handbook of Research on Curriculum*, Macmillan, New York.

Jackson, PW (1997) 'The daily grind'. In DJ Flinders & SJ Thornton (eds), *The Curriculum Studies Reader*, Routledge, New York.

James, M (2008) Assessment for learning: Research, policy and practice in the (dis) United Kingdom, Paper presented at the Hong Kong Institute of Education symposium, April.

James, M & Pedder, D (2006) 'Beyond method: Assessment and learning practices and values', *Curriculum Journal*, 17(2):109–38.

Jardine, DW (2006) 'Welcoming the old man home: Meditations on Jean Piaget, interpretation and the "nostalgia for the original"'. In DW Jardine, S Friesen & P Clifford, *Curriculum in Abundance*, Lawrence Erlbaum, Mahwah, New Jersey:73–86.

Jensen, RP (2004) 'Class sizes and academic performance at primary and secondary schools', Melbourne Institute of Applied Economic and Social Research, Melbourne.

Jensen, E (1998b) 'How Julie's brain learns', *Educational Leadership*, 56(3):41–5.

John, PD (2006) 'Lesson planning and the student teacher: Re-thinking the dominant model', *Journal of Curriculum Studies*, 38(4):483–98.

Johnson, D & Maclean, R (2008) *Teaching Professionalisation, Development and Leadership*, Springer, London.

Johnson, DW & Johnson RT (2009) 'An educational psychology success story: Social story: Social interdependence theory and cooperative learning', *Educational Researcher*, 38(5):365–79.

Johnson, DW Johnson, RT & Holubec, EJ (1994) *The New Circles of Learning: Co-operation in the Classroom and School*, ASCD, Alexandria, Virginia.

Johnson, P & Jan, LW (2003) A thinking–feeling approach to values education, *EQ Australia*, Summer (4):36–8.

Johnson, RL Penny, JA & Gordon, B (2009) *Assessing Performance*, Guilford Press, New York.

Johnson, VD (2008) 'A contemporary controversy in American education: Including Intelligent Design in the Science curriculum'. In BS Stern & ML Kysilka (eds) *Contemporary Readings in Curriculum*, Sage Publications, Thousand Oaks, CA.

Johnston, LD O'Malley, PM & Backman, JG (2002) Monitoring the Future: National survey results on drug use, 1975–2001. 1 secondary school students, National Institute of Drug Abuse, Bethesda, Maryland.

Johnston, R (2009) Nationhood, literacy and curriculum: Literate Australia, Paper presented at the Biennial Australian Curriculum Studies Conference, Canberra, October 2–4.

Johnston, S (1994) 'Resolving questions of "why" and "how" about the study of curriculum in teacher education programmes', *Journal of Curriculum Studies*, 26(5):525–40.

Jones, A & Moreland, J (2005) 'The importance of pedagogical content knowledge in assessment for learning practices: A case-study of a whole-school approach', *The Curriculum Journal*, 16(2):193–206.

Jones, BD (2002) 'Recommendations for implementing internet inquiry projects', *Journal of Educational Technology Systems*, 30(3):271–91.

Jones, SM & Dindie, K (2004) 'A meta-analytic perspective on sex equity in the classroom', *Review of Educational Research*, 74(4):443–72.

Jones, VF & Jones, LS (1998) *Comprehensive Classroom Management*, 5th edn, Allyn & Bacon, Boston.

Joseph, PB Mikel, E & Windschitl, M (2002) Reculturing curriculum: The struggle for curriculum leadership, Paper presented at the Annual Conference of the American Educational Research Association, New Orleans.

Joyce, B & Showers, B (1986) Invisible teaching skills: The orientation from theory-derived research on teaching and curriculum, Paper presented at the Annual Conference of the American Educational Research Association, San Francisco.

Joyce, B & Weil, M (1986) *Models of Teaching*, 3rd edn, Prentice Hall, Englewood Cliffs.

Judson, G (2006) 'Curriculum spaces: Situating educational research, theory and practice', *Journal of Educational Thought*, 40(3):229–45.

Jury, TW (2004) 'Online vs traditional classes: The difference is they are different', *Journal of Instruction Delivery Systems*, 18(2):20–3.

K

Kao, GY Lin, SS & Sun, CT (2008) 'Breaking concept boundaries to enhance creative potential: Using integrated concept maps for conceptual self-awareness', *Computers and Education*, 51(4):1718–28.

Karlsson, J (2007) 'Australian voices confront the education-for-boys backlash and normative discourse in education', *Pedagogy, Culture and Society*, 15(1):129–33.

Karmel, P (1973) (Chairperson) *Schools in Australia: Report of the Interim Committee of the Australian Schools Commission*, AGPS, Canberra.

Katyal, KR & Evers, CW (2007) 'Parents – partners of clients? A reconceptualization of home-school interactions', *Teaching Education*, 18(1):61–76.

Katz, LG (1994) 'The Project Approach', *ERIC Digest*, Eric Clearinghouse on Elementary and Early Childhood Education, April.

Katz, LG & Chard, SC (2000) *Engaging Children's Minds: The Project Approach*, 2nd edn, Ablex Publishing, Stamford, Connecticut.

Kazepides, AC (1977) 'The logic of values clarification', *Journal of Educational Thought*, 11(2):27–33.

Ke, F (2008) 'A case study of computer gaming for math: Engaged learning from game play', *Computers and Education*, 51(4):1609–20.

Keamy K & Nicholas H (2007) *Personalising Education: From Research to Policy and Practice*, Office for Education Policy and Innovation, Melbourne.

Kearney, CP & Arnold, ML (1994) 'Market driven schools', *Theory into Practice*, 33(2):112–17.

Keating, J & Lamb, S (2004) *Public Education and the Community: a Report to the Education Foundation*, Education Foundation, Melbourne.

Kebritchi, M & Hirumi, A (2008) 'Examining the pedagogical foundations of modern educational computer games', *Computers and Education*, 51(4):1729–43.

Keddie, A (2005) 'On fighting and football: Gender justice and theories of identity construction', *International Journal of Qualitative Studies in Education*, 18(4):425–44.

Keddie, A & Mills, M (2008) *Teaching Boys: Developing Classroom Practices that Work*, Allen & Unwin, Sydney.

Keeves, JP (1982) (Chairperson) *Education and Change in South Australia: Report of the Committee of Inquiry into Education in South Australia*, Government Printer, Adelaide.

Kelchtermans, G & Vandenberghe, R (1994) 'Teachers' professional development: A biographical perspective', *Journal of Curriculum Studies*, 26(1):45–62.

Kelly, AV (2009) *The Curriculum: Theory and Practice*, 6th edn, Sage, Los Angeles.

Kennedy, K (2009) 'The idea of a national curriculum in Australia: What do Susan Ryan, John Dawkins and Julia Gillard have in common?' *Curriculum Perspectives*, 29(1):1–14.

Kennedy, K & Hui, S (2003) Attitudes towards research: The case of curriculum leaders in Hong Kong. Paper presented at the Annual Conference of the Australian Association for Research in Education, Sydney.

Kennedy, KJ (1994) (ed.) *Reshaping Teacher Education: Faculty Renewal or Organisational Downsizing?*, ACSA, Canberra.

Kennedy, KJ (2001) 'Civics and citizenship education', In CJ Marsh (ed.) *Teaching Studies of Society and the Environment*, 3rd edn, Prentice Hall, Sydney.

Kennedy, KJ (2005) *Changing Schools for Changing Times*, Chinese University Press, Hong Kong.

Kennedy, KJ (2007) Barriers to innovative school practice: A socio-cultural framework for understanding assessment practices in Asia, Paper presented at the Redesigning Pedagogy – Culture, Understanding and Practice Conference, Singapore, May.

Kennedy, KJ (2008) 'Civics and citizenship education'. In CJ Marsh, *Studies of Society and Environment: Exploring the Teaching Possibilities*, Pearson, Sydney.

Kennedy, KJ & Preston, B (1994) Teacher competencies and teacher education: Progress report on a research project. Paper presented at the Annual Conference of the Australian Association for Research in Education, Newcastle.

Kenway, J (1997) 'Boys' education in the context of reform', *Curriculum Perspectives*, 17(1):57–60.

Kenway, J Alderson, A & Grundy, S (1987) *A Process Approach to Community Participation in Schooling: The Hamilton Project*, Murdoch University, Perth.

Kerin, R & Comber, B (2008) 'Assessing the risks and possibilities: Standardised literacy testing at Year 9', *Curriculum Perspectives*, 28(3):65–70.

Kerr, D (2000) *Achieving a World Class Curriculum in Australia*, IARTV seminar series, No. 96, IARTV, Melbourne.

Kerr, D (2006) Key developments in national curriculum work, Paper presented at the Australian Curriculum Studies Association Invitational Symposium, Melbourne, August.

Kesidou, S & Roseman, JE (2002) Project 2061, 'Analyses of middle school Science textbooks', *Journal of Research in Science Teaching*, 40:535–43.

Khan, BH (1997) *Web-Based Instruction*, Educational Technology Publications, Englewood Cliffs, New Jersey.

Kidder, R (1996) *How Good People Make Tough Choices: Resolving the Dilemmas of Ethical Living*, Simon and Schuster, New York.

Killen, R (2006) *Effective Teaching Strategies*, Thomson, Melbourne.

Kim, B Park, H & Baek, Y (2008) 'Not just fun, but serious strategies: Using metacognitive strategies in a game-based learning', *Computers and Education*, 52(4):800–10.

Kim, JS & Sunderman, GL (2005) 'Measuring academic proficiency under the *No Child Left Behind Act*: Implications for educational equity', *Educational Researcher*, 34(8):3–13.

King, JF (1998) Assessment at the chalkface, Paper presented at the Annual Conference of the International Congress of Applied Psychology, San Francisco.

King, R & Banks, A (2006) 'Abandon OBE or lose $1b in funding, Bishop tells Ravlich', *West Australian*, 10 October, p. 1.

King, SO & Robinson, CL (2008) '"Preety Lights" and Maths! Increasing student engagement and enhancing learning through the use of electronic voting systems', *Computers and Education*, 53(1):189–99.

Kipling, R (2002) *The Complete Verse*, Kyle Cathie Ltd, London.

Kirby, K (1991) 'Drop that pencil, flash that cursor', *Education Quarterly*, November (3):29–33.

Kirschner, PA Sweller, J & Clark, RE (2006) 'Why minimal guidance during instruction does not work: An analysis of the failure of Constructivist, Discovery, Problem-Based, Experimental and Inquiry-Based teaching', *Educational Psychologist*, 41(2):25–85.

Klein, AM Zevenbergen, A & Brown, N (2006) 'Managing standardised testing in today's schools', *Journal of Educational Thought*, 40(2):145–57.

Klenowski, V (2002) *Developing Portfolios for Learning and Assessment*, Routledge Falmer, London.

Kliebard, H (1986) *The Struggle for the American Curriculum 1893–1958*, Routledge and Kegan Paul, Boston.

Knight, J (2008) 'Supporting Trust and Foundation Schools', <www.trustandfoundationschools.org.uk/> extracted 14 April 2009.

Knight, T (1995) 'Parents, the community and school governance'. In C Evers & J Chapman (eds), *Educational Administration: An Australian Perspective*, Allen & Unwin, Sydney.

Knupfer, NN (1998) 'Gender visions across technology advertisements and the WWW: Implications for educational equity', *Theory into Practice*, 37(1):54–63.

Kohlberg, L (1966) 'Moral education in our schools', *School Review*, 74(1):62–8.

Kohlberg, L (1975) 'The cognitive-developmental approach to moral education', *Phi Delta Kappan*, 56(10):670–7.

Kohn, A (1996) *Beyond Discipline: From Compliance to Community*, ASCD, Alexandria, Virginia.

Kohn, A (1997) 'How not to teach values: A critical look at character education', *Phi Delta Kappan*, X(X):429–39.

Konstantopoulos, S (2008) 'Do small classes reduce the achievement gap between Low and High achievers? Evidence from project STAR', *Elementary School Journal*, 108(4):275–91.

Konza, D Grainger, J & Bradshaw, K (2001) *Classroom Management: A Survival Guide*, Social Science Press, Sydney.

Kopriva, R (1999) A conceptual framework for valid and comparable measurement, Paper presented at the Annual Conference of the American Educational Research Association, Montreal.

Korthagen, FA (2004) 'In search of the essence of a good teacher: Towards a more holistic approach in teacher education', *Teaching and Teacher Education*, 20:77–97.

Kostelnik, MJ Soderman, AK & Whiren, AP (2007) *Developmentally Appropriate Curriculum*, 4th edn, Pearson/Merrill/Prentice Hall, Columbus, Ohio.

Kougl, K (1997) *Communicating in the Classroom*, Waveland Press, Austin, Texas.

Kougl, K (2006) *Communicating in the Classroom*, Waveland, Chicago.

Kranz, C (2002) 'Schools restructure classrooms: Open spaces out of vogue', *Cincinati Enquirer*, November 12:4.

Krathwohl, DR Bloom, BS & Masia, BB (1956) *Taxonomy of Educational Objectives. Handbook II: Affective Domain*, David McKay, New York.

Krause, KL Bochner, S & Duchesne, S (2003) *Educational Psychology for Learning and Teaching*, Thomson, Melbourne.

Kreitzer, AE & Madaus, GF (1994) 'Empirical investigations of the hierarchial structure of the taxonomy'. In LW Anderson & LA Sosniak (eds), *Bloom's Taxonomy: A Forty-year Retrospective*, University of Chicago Press, Chicago.

Kuiper, E Volman, M & Terwel, J (2005) 'The Web as an information resource in K–12 Education', *Review of Educational Research*, 75(3):285–328.

Kulm, G & Grier, L (1998) *Project 2061 – Mathematics Curriculum Materials Analysis Scheme – Reliability Study*, American Association for the Advancement of Science, Washington DC.

L

La Rocque, L & Coleman, P (1989) 'Quality control: School accountability and district ethos'. In M Holmes, K Leithwood & D Musella (eds), *Educational Policy for Effective Schools*, OISE Press, Toronto.

Lacey, K & Gronn, P (2007) 'Letting go: Former principals reflect on their role exit', Seminar Series, Centre for Strategic Education, No. 163, Melbourne.

Ladbrooke, A (1997) *School Development Manual: A Practical Guide for School Improvement*, Pearson, Sydney.

Lally, M & Myhill, M (1994) *Teaching Quality: The Development of Valid Instruments of Assessment*, AGPS, Canberra.

Lam, A & Lee, A (2009) 'Row over who gets drug test results', *South China Morning Post*, July 10, p. 4.

Lambert, P Scourfield, J Smalley, N & Jones, R (2008) 'The social context of school bullying: Evidence

from a survey of children in South Wales', *Research Papers in Education*, 23(3):269–91.
Landsman, J (2004) 'Confronting the racism of low expectations', *Educational Leadership*, 62(3):28–33.
Landsman, J (2006) 'Bearers of hope', *Educational Leadership*, 63(5):26–33.
Lang, P & Hyde, N (1987) 'Pastoral care: Not making the same mistakes twice', *Curriculum Perspectives*, 7(2):1–11.
Lang, QC (ed.) (2006) *Engaging in Project Work*, McGraw Hill, Singapore.
Langrehr, J (1983) 'How do you select curriculum materials?' *Curriculum Perspectives*, 3(1):31–6.
Lareau, AP (1986) Perspectives on parents: A view from the classroom, Paper presented at the Annual Conference of the American Educational Research Association, San Francisco, California.
Lasky, S (2000) 'The cultural and emotional politics of teacher-parent interactions', *Teaching and Teacher Education*, 16:843–60.
Lasswell, HD (1948) 'Clarifier of public discussion', *Quarterly Journal of Speech*, 34(4):3–14.
Latham, G Blaise, M Dole, S Faulkner, J Lang, J & Malone, K (2006) *Learning to Teach: New Times, New Practices*, Oxford University Press, Melbourne.
Lau, J (2006) 'Cooperative learning motivates pupils to achieve better class test results for combined humanities', *Celebrating Learning through Action Research*, Ministry of Education, Singapore.
Lawstuff (2009) <www.lawstuff.org.au/about.asp> extracted 14 January 2010.
Lawton, D (1975) *Class Culture and the Curriculum*, Routledge and Kegan Paul, London.
Lawton, D (2005) *Education and Labour Party Ideologies: 1900–2001 and Beyond*, Routledge Falmer, London.
Leach, F & Mitchell, C (2006) *Combating Gender Violence in and around Schools*, Trentham Books, Stoke-on-Trent.
Leach, J & Moon, B (2008) *The Power of Pedagogy*, Sage, London.
Lee, C & Wiliam, D (2005) 'Studying changes in the practices of two teachers developing assessment for learning'. *Teacher Development*, 9(2):265–83.
Lee, CK & Yamping, F (2006) Lesson study and the power of continuous improvement – theorizing in light of a Singapore case, Paper presented at the 2nd Annual Conference on Learning Study, Hong Kong.
Lee, JS & Bowen, NK (2006) 'Parent involvement, cultural capital and the achievement gap among elementary school children', *American Educational Research Journal*, 43(2):193–216.
Lee, MM (2007) *Classroom Management: Models, Applications and Cases*, Pearson Education, Upper Saddle River, NJ.
Lee, V (1990) (ed.) *Children Learning in School*, Hodder & Stoughton, London.
Leicester, M Modgil, C & Modgil, S (2000) *Classroom Issues, Practice, Pedagogy and Curriculum*, Falmer, London.

Leigh, A & Ryan, C (2008) *How has School Productivity Changed in Australia?* Research School of Social Sciences, Australian National University, Canberra.
Lemin, M Potts, H & Welsford, P (1994) (eds) *Values Strategies for Classroom Teachers*, ACER, Melbourne.
Leming, JS (1981) 'Curricular effectiveness in moral-values education: A review of research', *Journal of Moral Education*, 10(3):16–27.
Leming, JS (1993) 'In search of effective character education', *Educational Leadership*, 51(3):63–71.
Lerner, D (1996) 'Intrinsic motivation in a longitudinal study', *Journal of Educational Psychology*, 93(1):15–20.
Lester, S (2007) On professions and being professional, <www.sld.demon.co.uk/profnal.pdf> extracted 19 July 2009.
Leung, CC (2006) 'Bulldoze ageing government schools, says expert', *The Age*, 5 July, p. 3.
Levine, M (2003) 'Celebrating diverse minds', *Educational Leadership*, 61(2):12–18.
Lewis, C Hurd, J & Perry R (2004) 'A deeper look at lesson study', *Educational Leadership*, 61(5):6–11.
Lewis, C Perry, R & Murata, A (2006) 'How should research contribute to instructional improvement: The case of lesson study', *Educational Researcher*, 35(3):3–14.
Lewis, R (2000) 'Classroom discipline and student responsibility', *Teaching and Teacher Education*, 17(3):307–19.
Li, DD & Lim, CP (2007) 'Scaffolding online historical inquiry tasks: A case of two secondary school classrooms', *Computers and Education*, 50(4):1394–1410.
Lickona, T (1988) 'Educating the moral child', *Principal*, 68:6–10.
Lieble, JA (1980) 'Guideline recommendations for the design of training facilities', *NSPI Journal*, 19:21–30.
Lifter, M & Adams, ME (1997) *Integrating Technology into the Curriculum*, Hawker Brownlow, Melbourne.
Lim, CP & Chai, CS (2008) Rethinking classroom-oriented instructional development models to mediate instructional planning in technology-enhanced learning environments, *Teaching and Teacher Education*, 24(8):2002–13.
Lingard, B (2003) 'Where to in gender policy in education after recuperative masculinity politics?' *International Journal of Inclusive Education*, 7(1):33–56.
Linn, RL Baker, EL & Dunbar, SB (1991) 'Complex performance-based assessment: Expectations and validation criteria', *Educational Researcher*, 20(8):15–21.
Little, E (2003) *Kids Behaving Badly: Teacher Strategies for Classroom Behaviour*, Pearson Prentice Hall, Sydney.
Little, E (2005) 'Secondary school teachers' perceptions of students' problem behaviours', *Educational Psychology*, 25(4):369–77.
Lo, ML (2007) 'Improving teaching and learning through a learning study', *Curriculum Perspectives*. 28(1):12–20.
Lo, ML & Pong, WY (2002) *Catering for Individual Differences*, INSTEP, University of Hong Kong Press.

Lo, ML Pong, WY & Pakey, CPM (2005) (eds) *For Each and Everyone: Catering for Individual Differences through Learning Studies*, Hong Kong University Press, Hong Kong.

Loader, D (1998) 'The empty principal', *The Professional Reading Guide*, 19(3):1–15.

Loader, D (1999) Redefining 'Public' in Education, *Curriculum Perspectives*, 19(1):53–7.

Loi, D & Dillon, P (2006) 'Adaptive educational environments as creative spaces', *Cambridge Journal of Education*, 36(3):363–81.

Lokan, J (1996) Competency-based approaches and literacy education, Paper presented at the Annual Conference of the American Educational Research Association, New York.

Lortie, DC (1975) *Schoolteacher*, University of Chicago Press, Chicago.

Lortie, DC (2002) *Schoolteacher*, 2nd edn, University of Chicago Press, Chicago.

Louden, W (2000) 'Standards for standards: The development of Australian professional standards for teaching', *Australian Journal of Education*, 44(2):118–34.

Louden, W (2006) *In Teachers' Hands: Effective Literacy Teaching Practices in the Early Years of Schooling*, Department of Education, Science and Training, Canberra.

Lovat, T & McLeod, J (2006) 'Fully professionalized teacher education: An Australian study in persistence', *Asia Pacific Journal of Teacher Education*, 34(3):287–300.

Lovat, T & Smith, D (1995) *Curriculum: Action on Reflection Revisited*, 3rd edn, Social Science Press, Wentworth Falls.

Lovat, T & Toomey, R (2007) (eds) *Values Education and Quality Teaching: The Double Helix Effect*, David Barlow Publishing, Sydney.

Lovat, TJ (2009a) Australian perspectives on values education: Research in philosophical, professional and curricular dimensions, <www.schools.nsw.edu.au/edu-leadership/prof-read/ethics/lovat.php>.

Lovat, TJ (2009b) Synergies and balance between values education and quality teaching, Paper presented at the Annual National Values Education Conference, Canberra.

Lovegrove, MN & Lewis, R (1991) (eds) *Classroom Discipline*, Longman Cheshire, Melbourne.

Loyd, BH & Loyd, DE (1997) 'Kindergarten through Grade 12 standards: A philosophy of grading'. In GD Phye (ed.), *Handbook of Classroom Assessment*, Academic Press, San Diego.

Lucas, CA (1999) 'Developing competent practitioners', *Educational Leadership*, 56(8):45–8.

Lucas, SE & Valentine, JW (2002) Transformational leadership: Principals, leadership teams, and school culture, Paper presented at the Annual Conference of the American Educational Research Association, New Orleans.

Lui, M & Read, WM (1994) 'The relationship between the learning strategies and learning styles in a hypermedia environment', *Computers in Human Behaviour*, 10(4):419–34.

Luik, P & Mikk, J (2007) 'What is important in electronic textbooks for students of different levels?', *Computers and Education*, 50(4):1483–94.

Luiselli, JK Putnam, RF Handler, M & Feinberg, A (2005) 'Whole-school positive behaviour support: Effects on student discipline problems and academic performance', *Education Psychology*, 25, Issues 2&3:183–98.

Luke, A Weir, K & Woods, A (2008) *Development of a Set of Principles to Guide a P–12 Syllabus Framework*, Queensland Studies Authority, Brisbane.

Luke, C (1995) Multimedia Multiliteracies, *Education Australia*, Autumn (30):14–17.

Lundin, T (2003) 'Preparing tomorrow's teachers to use technology', *Educational Technology Research & Development*, 51(1):39–40.

Lutz, FW (1980) 'Local school board decision-making: A political-anthropological analysis', *Education and Urban Society*, 12(4):17–29.

Lyons, N (1999) 'How portfolios can shape emerging practice', *Educational Leadership*, 56(8):630–66.

M

Macdonald, J Heap, N & Mason, R (2001) 'Have I learnt it? Evaluating skills for resource-based study using electronic resources', *British Journal of Educational Technology*, 32(4):419–33.

MacDonald, JB & Leeper, RR (1965) (eds) *Theories of Instruction*, Association for Supervision and Curriculum Development, Washington DC.

MacLeod, G (2007) Are we nearly there yet? Curriculum, relationships and disaffected pupils, *The International Journal of School Disaffection*, 5(1):29–36.

MacLure, M & Walker, B (1998) Disenchanted evenings: The social organisation of talk in parent teacher consultations in UK secondary schools, Paper presented at the Annual Conference of the American Educational Research Association, San Diego.

Maeroff, GI (1988) *The Empowerment of Teachers*, Teachers College Press, New York.

Mager, RF (1984) *Preparing Instructional Objectives*, 3rd edn, Lake Publishers, Belmont, California.

Mallory, ME (1989) 'Q-sort definition of ego identity status', *Journal of Youth and Adolescence*, 18:399–412.

Malone, BG Bonitz, DA & Rickett, M (1998) 'Teacher perceptions of disruptive behaviour: Maintaining instructional focus', *The Teacher Educator*, 7(4):21–35.

Mann, L (1997) 'The learning environment', ASCD *Education Update*, September:3–6.

Maple, T (2005) 'Beyond community helpers', *Childhood Education*, Spring:133–8.

Marcia, JE (1966) 'Development and validation of ego-identity status', *Journal of Personality and Social Psychology*, 3:551–8.

Marginson, S (1993) *Education and Public Policy in Australia*, Cambridge University Press, Cambridge.

Marks, GN & Cresswell, J (2005) 'State differences in achievement among secondary school students in Australia', *Australian Journal of Education*, 49(2): 141–51.

Marks, H (2000) 'Student engagement in instructional activity: Patterns in the elementary, middle and high school years', *American Educational Research Journal*, 37(1):153–84.

Marks, HM & Louis, KS (1997) 'Does teacher empowerment affect the classroom? The implications of teacher empowerment for instructional practice and student academic performance', *Educational Evaluation and Policy Analysis*, 19(3):245–75.

Marsh, CJ (1994a) *Producing a National Curriculum: Plans and Paranoia*, Allen & Unwin, Sydney.

Marsh, CJ (1994b) *Teaching Studies of Society and Environment*, Prentice Hall, Sydney.

Marsh, CJ (1995) An exploratory paper on foundation knowledge and the key competencies, Unpublished paper, DEET, Canberra.

Marsh, CJ (2004) *Key Concepts for Understanding Curriculum*, 3rd edn, Routledge Falmer, London.

Marsh, CJ (2009) *Key Concepts for Understanding Curriculum*, 4th edn, Routledge, London.

Marsh, CJ & Stafford, K (1988) *Curriculum: Australian Practices and Issues*, McGraw-Hill, Sydney.

Marsh, CJ & Willis, G (2007) *Curriculum: Alternative Approaches, Ongoing Issues*, 4th edn, Prentice Hall, Columbus, Ohio.

Marshall, B & Drummond, MJ (2006) 'How teachers engage with assessment for learning: Lessons from the classroom', *Research Papers in Education*, 21(2):133–49.

Martin, A & Marsh, H (2005) 'Motivating boys and motivating girls: Does teacher gender really make a difference?', *Australian Journal of Education*, 49(3):320–34.

Martinez, K (2004) 'Mentoring new teachers: Promise and problems in times of teacher shortage', *Australian Journal of Education*, 48(1):95–108.

Martino, W & Pallotta-Chierolli, M (2005), *Being Normal is the Only Way to Be: Boys and Girls Perspectives on School*, University of NSW Press, Sydney.

Marton, F & Booth, S (1997) *Learning and Awareness*, Lawrence Erlbaum, Mahwah, NJ.

Marzano, RJ Pickering, D & McTighe, J (1993) *Assessing Student Outcomes*, ASCD, Alexandria, Virginia.

Marzano, RJ Marzano, JS & Pickering, DJ (2003) *Classroom Management that Works*, ASCD, Alexandria, Virginia.

Maslow, AH (1954) *Motivation and Personality*, Harper & Row, New York.

Masters, GN & McCurry, D (1990) *Competency-based Assessment in the Professions*, NOOSR Research Paper No. 2, AGPS, Canberra.

Masters, GN Forster, M & Tognolini, J (2006) *Australian Certificate of Education: Exploring a Way Forward*, Department of Education, Employment and Workplace Relations, Canberra.

Matoba, M Crawford, KA & Arani, RS (2001) (eds) *Lesson Study: International Perspective on Policy and Practice*, Educational Science Publishing House, Beijing.

Matson, M & Smith, D (1987) *Bush Rescue*, Jacaranda Software, Brisbane.

Mattingly, D Prislin, R McKenzie, T Rodriguez, J & Kayzar, B (2002) 'Evaluating evaluations: The case of parent involvement programs', *Review of Educational Research*, 72(4):549–76.

Mawdsley, RD & Cumming, JJ (2008) Educational malpractice and setting damages for ineffective teaching: A comparison of legal principles in the USA, England and Australia, *Education and the Law*, 20(1):25–46.

May, N (1981) The teacher-as-researcher movement in Britain, Paper presented to the Annual Conference of the American Educational Research Association, Los Angeles.

Mayer, D (2006) 'The changing face of the Australian teaching profession: New generations and new ways of working and learning', *Asia-Pacific Journal of Teacher Education*, 34(1):57–71.

Mayer, E (1992) (Chairperson) *Employment-related Key Competencies for Post-compulsory Education and Training*, AGPS, Canberra.

McCaslin, M (2006) 'Student motivational dynamics in the era of school reform', *The Elementary School Journal* 106(3):482–9.

McCollow, J (2007) The stupid country: How Australia is dismantling public education, *Professional Magazine*, 22, November:32–33.

McCombs, BL Daniels, DH & Perry, KE (2008) 'Children's and teacher's perceptions of learner-centered practices and student motivation: Implications for early schooling', *Elementary School Journal*, 109(1):16–34.

McCormick, CB & Pressley, M (1997) *Educational Psychology*, Longman, New York.

McCulloch, G (1998) The national curriculum and the cultural politics of secondary schools in England and Wales, Paper presented at the Annual Conference of the American Educational Research Association, San Diego.

McCutcheon, G (1980) 'How do elementary school teachers plan? The nature of planning and influences on it', *Elementary School Journal*, 81(1):4–23.

McCutcheon, G (1997) 'Curriculum and the work of teachers'. In DJ Flinders & SJ Thornton (eds), *The Curriculum Studies Reader*, Routledge, New York.

McDevitt, TM & Ormrod, JE (2002) *Child Development and Education*, Merrill Prentice Hall, Columbus, Ohio.

McDiarmid, GW (1995) *Realising New Learning for all Students: A Framework for the Professional Development of Kentucky Teachers*, National Centre for Research on Teacher learning, East Lansing, Michigan.

McDonald, B & Boud, D (2003) 'The impact of self-assessment training on performance in external examinations', *Assessment in Education*, 10(2):209–20.

McDonald, F & Wilks, R (1994) A survey of 45 primary school teacher's self-perceived discipline styles: A pilot study, Unpublished paper, RMIT, Bundoora.

McDonald, H & Ingvarson, L (1997) 'Technology: A catalyst for educational change', *Journal of Curriculum Studies*, 29(5):513–27.

MCEETYA (1989) *The Hobart Declaration on National Goals for Schooling*, AEC, Canberra.

MCEETYA (1999) *The Adelaide Declaration on National Goals for Schooling in the 21st century*, MCEETYA, Canberra.

MCEETYA (2003) *Values Education Study*, MCEETYA, Canberra.

MCEETYA (2006a) *National Assessment Program – Years 6 and 10 Civics and Citizenship Report 2004*, Curriculum Corporation, Melbourne.

MCEETYA (2006b) *Australian Directions in Indigenous Education, 2005–2008*, AESOC Senior Officials Working Party on Indigenous Education, MCEETYA, Melbourne.

MCEETYA (2008) *Melbourne Declaration on Educational Goals for Young Australians*, MCEETYA, Canberra: full declaration available at <www.mceedya.edu.au>.

MCEETYA (2009) Reporting and Comparing School Performances, <www.appa.asn.au/index.php/appa-business/news-items/521-mceetya-paper-repo> extracted 2 May 2009.

McFarlane, AE & Jared, E (1994) 'Encouraging student teacher confidence in the use of information technology', *Computers in Education*, 22(1):155–60.

McGaw, B (2006) Achieving quality and equity in education, The Bob Hawke Prime Ministerial Centre, 3 August, <www.unisa.edu/au/hawkecentre/events/2006events/education_McGaw.asp> extracted 2 May 2009.

McGaw, B (2007) 'Achieving economic and social objectives', *Professional Magazine*, 22 November: 11–17.

McGhan, B (2005) The possible outcomes of outcome-based education, The Centre for Public School Renewal, <comnet.org/cpsr/essays/obe.htm>

McGilp, J & Michael, M (1994) *The Home-School Connection*, Eleanor Curtain Publishing, Armadale, NSW.

McGowan, WS (2005) '"Flexibility", community and making parents responsible', *Educational Philosophy and Theory*, 37(6):891–903.

McGrath, H (2003) 'New thinking on self-esteem', *EQ Australia*, Winter (2):16–17.

McInerney, DM (1989) 'Urban Aboriginal parents' views on education: A comparative analysis', *Journal of Intercultural Studies*, 10(2):43–65.

McInerney, DM (1991) 'Key determinants of motivation of non-traditional Aboriginal students in school settings: Recommendations for educational change', *Australian Journal of Education*, 35(2):154–74.

McInerney, DM & McInerney, V (2005) *Educational Psychology: Constructing Learning*, Pearson Education, Sydney.

McInerney, DM Van Etten, S & Dowson, M (2007) *Standards in Education*, Information Age Publishing, London.

McIntyre, D Pedder, D & Rudduck, J (2005) 'Pupil voice: Comfortable and uncomfortable learnings for teachers', *Research Papers in Education*, 20(2):149–68.

McKeachie, WJ & Kulick, JA (1975) 'Effective college teaching'. In FN Kerlinger (ed.), *Review of Research in Education*, 3, AERA, Washington DC.

McKenzie, P Kos, J Walker, M & Hong, J (2008) *Staff in Australia's Schools*, 2007, DEEWR, Canberra.

McLaughlin, M (2001) 'Community counts', *Educational Leadership*, 58(7):14–18.

McLean, K & Wilson, B (1995) 'The big picture', *Curriculum Perspectives*, 15(3):56–8.

McLeod, JH & Reynolds, R (2003) *Planning for Learning*, Social Science Press, Sydney.

McLeod, JH Reynolds, R & Weckert, C (2001) *Enriching Learning*, Social Science Press, Sydney.

McMahon, A (2000) Managing teacher stress to enhance pupil learning, Paper presented at the Annual Conference of the American Educational Research Association, New Orleans.

McMillan, J Myran, S & Workman, D (2002) 'Elementary teachers' classroom assessment and grading practices', *Journal of Educational Research*, 95(4):203–13.

McMillan, JH & Hearn, J (2008) Student self-assessment: The key to stronger student motivation and higher achievement, *Education Horizons*, 87(1):40–56.

McMurry, CA & McMurry, FM (1926) *The Method of the Recitation*, Macmillan, New York.

McNeil, JD (2003) *Curriculum: The Teachers Initiative*, 3rd edn, Merrill Prentice Hall, Columbus.

McPhee, A Forde, C & Skelton, F (2002) Teacher education in the UK in an era of performance management, Unpublished paper, University of Glasgow.

McQuillan, P (1994) 'Computers and pedagogy: The invisible presence', *Journal of Curriculum Studies*, 26(6):631–54.

McTaggart, R (1984) 'Action research and parent participation: Contradictions, concerns and consequences', *Curriculum Perspectives*, 4(2):7–14.

McTighe, J (1997) 'What happens between assessments?', *Educational Leadership*, 54(4):6–13.

Meadmore, D (2001) 'Uniformly testing diversity? National testing examined', *Asia–Pacific Journal of Teacher Education*, 29(1):19–30.

Meadmore, D (2004) 'The rise and rise of testing: How does this shape identity?'. In B Burnett, D Meadmore & G Tait (eds) *New Questions for Contemporary Teachers*, Pearson, Sydney.

Meadows, BJ (1993) 'Through the eyes of parents', *Educational Leadership*, 51(2):31–4.

Means, B (2000) 'Technology in America's schools: Before and after Y2K'. In RS Brandt (ed.), *Education in a New Era*, ASCD, Alexandria, Virginia.

Means, R (2001) 'Technology use in tomorrow's schools', *Education Leadership*, 58(4):57–61.

Mecklenburger, J (1996) 'Laptop primary, Internet high', *EQ Australia* (2):19–22.

Meere, P (1993) Towards reconceptualizing teacher education, Paper presented at the Australian Teacher Education Association Conference, Fremantle.

Meir, D (1998) 'Authenticity and educational change'. In A Hargreaves et al., *International Handbook of Educational Change*, Kluwer, Dordrecht, Netherlands.

Melton, J (2004) 'Online course presentation: Program issues to consider', *Journal of Instruction Delivery Systems*, 18(3):17–19.

Menges, RJ & Weimer, M (1996) *Teaching on Solid Ground*, Jossey-Bass, San Francisco.

Middleton, S (1994) 'Sex, drugs and bombs: Six years on the indecent publications tribunal', *Sites* Spring (29):18–44.

Milentijevic, I Ciric, V & Vojmovic, O (2007) 'Version control in project-based learning', *Computers and Education*, 50(4):1331–38.

Miles, MB & Ekholm, M (1985) 'What is school improvement?'. In WG Van Velzen et al. (eds), *Making School Improvement Work*, OECD, Leuven.

Millard, C (2003) ''Pie in the sky' or achievable outcome? *EQ Australia*, Winter (2):7–8.

Miller, PW (1981) *Nonverbal Communication*, National Educational Association, Washington DC.

Milligan, S (1994) *Women in the Teaching Profession*, AGPS, Canberra.

Mills, M (2006) 'Issues of masculinity and violence in Australian schools'. In F Leach & C Mitchell (eds) *Combating Gender Violence in and around Schools*, Trentham Books, Stoke-on-Trent.

Mills, M Martino, W & Lingard, B (2007) 'Getting boys' education "right": The Australian Government's Parliamentary Inquiry Report as an exemplary instance of recuperative masculinity politics', *British Journal of Sociology of Education*, 28(1):5–21.

MindMatters (2000) <www.mindmatters.edu.au/default.asp> extracted 14 January 2010.

Ministerial Council on Education, Employment, Training and Youth Affairs (see MCEETYA)

Ministry of Education, British Columbia (1994) *Performance Assessment*, Ministry of Education, Victoria, BC.

Ministry of Education, Singapore (2005) Closer Step to the Futuristic Classroom, <www.moe.gov.sg/corporate/contactonline/2005/Issue07/big_pic/bigpic.htm>.

Mislevy, RJ (2002) The roles of technology in the assessment argument, Paper presented at the Annual Conference of the American Educational Research Association, New Orleans.

Mitchell, DE & Kerchner, CT (1983) 'Labor relations and teacher policy'. In LS Shulman & G Sykes (eds), *Handbook of Teaching and Policy*, Longman, New York.

Mok, YF (2005) 'Teacher concerns and teacher life stages', *Research in Education*, 73, May:53–71.

Molnar, A (2000) 'Zap me! Linking schoolhouse and market place in a seamless web', *Phi Delta Kappan*, 81(8):601–603.

Molnar, A (2005) 'Ivy-covered malls and creeping commercialism', *Educational Leadership*, 62(5):74–9.

Molnar, A (2008) 'Cashing in on the classroom'. In BS Stern & ML Kysilka (eds) *Contemporary Readings in Curriculum*, Sage, Thousand Oaks, CA.

Monke, LW (2006) 'The overdominance of computers', *Educational Leadership*, 63(4):2–23.

Montalvo, GP Mansfield, EA & Miller, RB (2007) 'Liking or disliking the teacher: Student motivation, engagement and achievement', *Evaluation and Research in Education*, 20(3):144–58.

Monterosso, S (2002) 'Lost property and schools: Finders keepers?', *The Practising Administrator*, 24(3):22–3.

Monterosso, S (2007) Restorative Justice, Curtin University, School of Business Law, Working Paper Series, 7/1, February, 2007.

Moore, A (2004) *The Good Teacher*, Routledge Falmer, London.

Moore, Johnson, S & Kardoe, SM (2002) 'Keeping new teachers in mind', *Educational Leadership*, 59(6):12–17.

Moore, KD (2009a) *Classroom Teaching Skills*, 2nd edn, McGraw Hill, Boston.

Moore, KD (2009b) *Effective Instructional Strategies*, 2nd edn, Sage, Thousand Oaks, CA.

Moos, RH & Trickett, E (1974) *Classroom Environment Scale Manual*, Consulting Psychologist Press, Palo Alto.

Morris, W (1992) Parents and school governance, Paper presented at the Annual Conference of the Western Australian Primary Principals' Association, Perth.

Morrison, K & Ridley, K (1988) *Curriculum Planning and the Primary School*, Paul Chapman, London.

Mortimer, P Sammons, P Stoll, L Lewis, D & Ecob, R (1988) *School Matters: The Junior Years*, Open Books, London.

Moses, I & Trigwell, K (1993) *Teaching Quality and Quality of Learning in Professional Courses*, AGPS, Canberra.

Moss, P & Godinho, S (2007) 'Reforming curriculum and assessment practices: Implications for educating teachers in the A to E economy', *Curriculum Perspectives*, 27(3):12–29, 35–48.

Moyles, J (2007) (ed.) *Beginning Teaching: Beginning Learning*, 3rd edn, Open University Press, Buckingham.

Munn, P Cullen, M Johnstone, M & Lloyd, G (2001) 'Exclusion from school: A view from Scotland of policy & practice', *Research Papers in Education*, 16(1):23–42.

Munns, G & Woodward, H (2006) 'Student engagement and student self-assessment: The REAL framework'. *Assessment in Education*, 13(2):193–213.

Murphy, D & Rosenberg, B (1998) 'Recent research shows major benefits of small class size', *Educational Issues Policy Brief* 3, American Federation of Teachers, Washington DC.

Murphy, J (1991) *Restructuring Schools*, Cassell, London.

Murphy, P & Moon, B (1989) (eds) *Developments in Learning and Assessment*, Hodder & Stoughton, London.

Murray, J (2009) 'Teacher competencies in the post-method landscape: The limits of competency-based training in TESOL teacher education', *Teacher Competencies*, 24(1):1–15.

Myhill, D (2006) 'Talk, talk, talk: Teaching and learning in whole class discourse', *Research Papers in Education*, 21(1):19–41.

N

Nasir, NS Hand, V & Taylor, EV (2008) 'Culture and Mathematics in school: Boundaries between "cultural" and "domain", Knowledge in the mathematics classroom and beyond'. In GJ Kelly, A Luke & J Green (eds) *Review of Research in Education*, 32(1):241–67.

National Board of Professional Teaching Standards (NBPTS) (2009), <www.nbpts.org/>.

National Centre for Education Statistics (2001) Indicators of school crime and safety, US Department of Education, Washington DC.

National Children's and Youth Law Centre (see NCYLC)

National Council for the Social Studies (2006) Notable trade books for young people, <www.socialstudies.org/resources/notable>.

National Curriculum Board (see NCB)

National Project on the Quality of Teaching and Learning (1993) *Draft Competency Framework for Teaching*, NPQTL, Canberra.

National Science Resources Centre (1999) Learning Science by doing Science, <www.nsrconline.org/>.

National Science Teachers Association (2006) Outstanding Science trade books for students K–12, <www.nsta.org/ostbc>.

NCB (2008a) *National Curriculum Development paper*, NCB, June 2008, Melbourne.

NCB (2008b) *The Shape of the National Curriculum: A Proposal for Discussion*, NCB, Oct 2008, Melbourne.

NCB (2008c) *Initial Advice Papers: English; Mathematics; Science; History*, NCB, Oct 2008, Melbourne

NCB (2008d) *National Framing Papers: English; Mathematics; Science; History*, NCB, May 2008, Melbourne

NCB (2009a) *Shape of the Australian Curriculum: Mathematics*, NCB, May 2009, Melbourne.

NCB (2009b) *The Shape of the Australian Curriculum*, NCB, May 2009, Melbourne.

NCYLC (1994) *Know Your Rights at School*, NCYLC, Sydney.

NCYLC (2005) <www.ncylc.org.au> extracted 14 January 2010.

Nelson, B (2002) *Quality Teaching – a National Priority*, Report of a National Meeting of Professional Educators, Canberra ACE, Canberra.

Nelson, JL Palonsky, SB & McCarthy, MR (2004) *Critical Issues in Education: Dialogues and Dialectics*, McGraw Hill, Boston.

Nelson, MR (1992) *Children and Social Studies*, 2nd edn, Harcourt Brace Jovanovich, Philadelphia.

Ness, M (2001) 'Lessons of a first-year teacher', *Phi Delta Kappan*, 82(9):700–05.

Newhouse, P (1998) 'The impact of portable computers on classroom learning environments', *Australian Educational Computing*, 13(1):5–11.

Newmann, FM & Wehlage, GG (1993) 'Five standards of authentic instruction', *Educational Leadership*, 50(7):8–12.

Newnham, J (2000) 'When is a teacher or school liable in negligence?', *Australian Journal of Teacher Education*, 25(1):52–9.

Niguidula, D (2005) 'Documenting learning with digital portfolios', *Educational Leadership*, 63(3):44–7.

Noddings, N (1992) *The Challenge to Care in Schools: An Alternative Approach to Education*, Teachers College Press, New York.

Noddings, N (2008) 'All our students thinking', *Educational Leadership*, 65(5):8–13.

Nolen, JL (2003) 'Multiple intelligences in the classroom', *Education*. 124(1):115–19.

Norris, J (2008) 'Meeting curriculum challenges in special school: Embracing the early years curriculum', *Primary and Middle Years Educator*, 6(2):3–8.

North, CE (2008) 'What is all this talk about "Social Justice"? Mapping the terrain of Education's latest catchphrase', *Teachers College Record*, 110(6): 1182–1206.

Norton, P & Wiburg, KM (2003) *Teaching with Technology*, 2nd edn, Thomson/Wadsworth, Belmont, California.

NSW Board of Studies (2006), *NSW Primary Curriculum*, <www.boardofstudies.nsw.edu.au>.

NSW Dept of Education and Training (2008a) *Excellence and Innovation: Meeting the Diverse Needs of Students*, <www.det.nsw.edu.au/reviews/futuresproject/issuespapers/diverseneeds.htm>, extracted 21 October 2008.

NSW Dept of Education and Training (2008b) *New South Wales Government Charter for Equity in Education and Training*, <www.det.nsw> extracted 3 May 2009.

NSW Dept of Education and Training (2008c) *NSW Public Schools: Learning and Teaching: KIDMAP*, Dept of Education and Training, Sydney.

NSW Dept of Education and Training (2009) *Average Class Sizes – Reports and Statistics*, <www.det.nsw.edu.au/media/downloads/reports_stats/class_sizes.pdf>, extracted 30 March, 2009.

NSW Dept of Education and Training Auditing Office (2008) *Ageing Workforce – Teachers*, Audit Office of NSW, Sydney.

NSW Dept of School Education (1991) *Values Education in NSW Public Schools*, Dept of School Education, Sydney.

NSW Dept of School Education (2001) *Values of NSW Public Schools*, Dept of School Education, Sydney.

NSW Road Traffic Authority (2009), <www.rta.nsw.gov.au> extracted 14 January 2010.

NSW Traffic Authority (2005) *It's Smart to be Safe*, NSW Traffic Authority, Sydney.

Nucci, L (2008) Moral development and moral education: An overview, *Studies in Social & Moral Education*, University of Illinois, Chicago.

Nucci, L & Weber, E (1991) 'The domain approach to values education: From theory to practice'. In W Kurtines & J Gewirtz (eds), *Handbook of Moral Behaviour and Development*, McCutchan, Berkeley.

Nunan, D (2001) 'Teaching grammar in context'. In CN Candlin & N Mercer (eds) *English Language Teaching in its Social Context*, Routledge, London.

Nuthall, G (2005) 'The cultural myths and realities of classroom teaching and learning: A personal journey', *Teachers College Record*, 107(5):895–934.

Nyquist, EB (1976) 'The American no-fault morality', *Phi Delta Kappan*, 58(3):85–92.

O

O'Brien P & Goddard, R (2006) 'Beginning teachers: Easing the transition to the classroom', *The Australian Educational Leader*, (1):28–32.

O'Connor, C & Fernandez, S (2006) 'Race, class and disproportionality: Re-evaluating the relationship between poverty and special education placement', *Education Researcher*, 35(6):6–11.

O'Donoghue, T & O'Brien, S (1994) Recent trends in the literature on parental involvement in school decision-making, Unpublished paper, University of WA, Perth.

O'Neil, J (1992) 'Putting performance assessment to the test', *Educational Leadership*, 49(8):14–19.

O'Neil, J (1994) 'Aiming for new outcomes: The promise and the reality', *Educational Leadership*, 51(3):6–8.

O'Neill, S (2009) *Directors General Report*, WA DET, Perth.

O'Shea, MR (2005) *From Standards to Success*, ASCD, Alexandria, Virginia.

OECD (1990) *The Teacher Today*, OECD, Paris.

OECD (2005) *PISA*, Vol. 1, Analysis OECD, Paris.

OECD (2006) *Education at a Glance*, OECD Indicators 2006, Secretary General of the OECD, Paris, France.

Ohler, J (2006) 'The world of digital story telling', *Educational Leadership*, 63(4):44–7.

Oliva, PF (2008) *Developing the Curriculum*, 6th edn, Longman, New York.

Oliver, DW & Newman, FM (1967) *The Public Issue Series, Harvard Social Studies Project*, American Education Publications, Columbus, Ohio.

Organization for Economic Cooperation and Development (see OECD)

Orlich, DC Harder, RJ Callahan, RC & Gibson, HW (2009) *Teaching Strategies*, 9th edn, Wadsworth, Cengage learning, Boston.

Ornstein, A & Lasley, TJ (2004) *Strategies for Effective Teaching*, McGraw Hill, Chicago.

Ornstein, AC & Hunkins, FP (2003) *Curriculum: Foundations, Principles and Issues*, 4th edn, Pearson/Allyn & Bacon.

Oser, F Dick, A & Patry, JL (1992) (eds) *Effective and Responsible Teaching*, Jossey-Bass, San Francisco.

Osler, A (2000) 'Children's rights, responsibilities and understandings of school discipline', *Research Papers in Education*, 15(1):49–67.

Owen, S Kos, J & McKenzie, P (2008) *Teacher Workforce Data and Planning Processes in Australia*, DEEWR, Canberra.

Ozga, JT & Lawn, MA (1981) *Teachers Professionalism and Class*, Falmer, London.

Ozolins, J (2009) Creating public values: Schools as moral habitats, Paper presented at the Annual National Values Education Conference, Canberra.

P

Page, RN (1998) 'Moral aspects of curriculum: "Making kids care" about school knowledge', *Journal of Curriculum Studies*, 30(1):1–26.

Pagnucci, GS (1998) 'Crossing borders and talking tech: Educational challenges', *Theory into Practice*, 37(1):46–53.

Palfreyman, D (2007) 'Is academic freedom under threat in the UK and US higher education?', *Education and the Law*, 19(1):19–40.

Pang, MF & Marton, F (2003) 'Beyond "lesson study" – Comparing two ways of facilitating the grasp of economic concepts', *Instructional Science* 31(3): 175–94.

Papert, S (1996) *The Connected Family, Bridging the Digital Generation Gap*, Longstreet Press, Marietta, Georgia.

Parker, W & Hess, D (2001) 'Teaching with and for discussion', *Teaching and Teacher Education*, 17: 273–89.

Parliament of the Government of Australia Report (2002) *Senate Inquiry into Education*, Canberra.

Parry, G (2005) Camera/video phones in schools: Law and practice, *Education and the Law*, 17(3):73–85.

Parry, G & Clarke, L (2004) 'Risk assessment and geography teachers: A survey', *Education and the Law*, 16(2):128–30.

Partington, G (1998) (ed.) *Perspectives on Aboriginal and Torres Strait Islander Education*, Social Science Press, Katoomba.

Partington, G (2001) 'Student suspensions: The influence on students and their parents', *Australian Journal of Education*, 45(3):323–40.

Pascoe, S (2002) 'Values in education: An overview'. In S Pascoe (ed.), *Values in Education*, Australian College of Educators, Canberra.

Paske, GH (1986) 'The failure of indoctrination: A response to Wynne', *Educational Leadership*, 43(4):11–12.

Patthey-Chavez, GG (1998) Measuring participation, Paper presented at the Annual Conference of the American Educational Research Association, New York.

Payne, DA (2003*) Applied Educational Assessment*, 2nd edn, Wadsworth/Thomson, Belmont, California.

Payne, PG (2009) The 'great moral challenge' of social ecology for an 'education revolution', Paper presented at the Annual National Values Education Conference, Canberra.

Peha, JM (1995) 'How K–12 teachers are using computer networks', *Educational Leadership*, 53(2):18–25.

Penney, D & Walker, M (2007) 'Senior secondary schooling in WA: Transforming curriculum, lives and society?' *Curriculum Perspectives*, 27(3):22–35.

Perarsky, D (1980) 'Moral dilemmas and moral education', *Theory and Research in Social Education*, 8(1):1–8.

Perkin, H (1987) 'The teaching profession and the game of life'. In P Gordon, H Perkin, H Sockett & E Hoyle (eds), *Is Teaching a Profession?*, University of London Institute of Education, London.

Perkins-Gough, D, Lindfors, S & Ernst, D (2002) 'A curriculum for peace', *Educational Leadership*, 60(2):14–17.

Perkinson, HJ (1993). *Teachers Without Goals, Students Without Purposes*, McGraw-Hill, New York.

Perlstein, D (2000) 'Failing at kindness: Why fear of violence endangers children', *Educational Leadership*, 57(6):76–9.

Perrone, V (2000) *Lessons for New Teachers*, McGraw-Hill, Boston.

Perth Now (2007) 'Sorry day for English teaching, long overdue', Paul Murray, 12 November.

Peske, H Liu, E Moore Johnson, S Kaufman, D & Kardos, S (2001) 'The next generation of teachers: Changing conceptions of a career in teaching', *Phi Delta Kappan*, 83(4):304–11.

Peters, RS (1976). 'Why doesn't Lawrence Kohlberg do his homework?', *Phi Delta Kappan*, 56(10):678–9.

Petersen, P (1979) 'Direct instruction: Effective for what and for whom?', *Educational Leadership*, 37(4):46–8.

Petersen, P (1982) 'Issue: Should teachers be expected to learn and to use direct instruction?', *ASCD Update*, 24(5.

Pettit, D (1985) 'Too many cooks or not enough broths?', *School and Community News*, 9(1):17–23.

Phillips, DC (1995) 'The good, the bad, and the ugly: The many faces of constructivism', *Educational Researcher*, 24(7):5–12.

Pinar, WF (1999) (ed) *Contemporary Curriculum Discourses*, Peter Lang, New York.

Pinar, WF (2004) *What is curriculum theory?* Lawrence Erlbaum, Mahwah, NJ.

Piper, K (1976) *Evaluation in the Social Sciences for Secondary Schools: Teachers' Handbook*, AGPS, Canberra.

Piper, K (1997) *Riders in the Chariot: Curriculum Reform and the National Interest*, ACER, Melbourne.

Placier, M Walker, M & Foster, B (2002) Writing the 'Show-Me' Standards: Teacher Professionalism and Political Control in US State Curriculum Policy, *Curriculum Inquiry*, 32(3):281–310.

PLATOWA (Parents Against Outcomes Based Education, WA) (2008), homepage, extracted 21 October 2008.

Platt, R (2005) 'Standardised tests: Whose standards are we talking about?', *Phi Delta Kappan*, 85(5):381–5.

Plitt, B (2004) 'Teacher dilemmas in a time of standards and testing', *Phi Delta Kappan*, 85(10):745–9.

Podell, DM & Tournaki, N (2001) Can all teachers teach all students? Student characteristics and teacher tolerance, Paper presented at the Annual Conference of the American Educational Research Association, New Orleans.

Poi, HJ Harskamp, EG Suhre, C & Goedhart, MJ (2008) 'How indirect supportive digital help during and after solving physics problems can improve problem-solving abilities', *Computers and Education*, 53(1):34–50.

Pollard, A & Tann, S (1997) *Reflective Teaching in the Primary School*, 2nd edn, Cassell, London.

Pollard, K (2002) 'NSW: Class sizes, teacher quality targeted in budget', *AAP General News*, Australia:1–5.

Pomerantz, EM Moorman, EA & Litwack, SD (2007) 'The how, whom and why of parents' involvement in children's academic lives: More is not always better', *Review of Educational Research*, 77(3):373–410.

Poo, SP & Thye, LK (2006) 'Are e-lectures as effective as the normal lectures?', *Celebrating Learning through Action Research*, Ministry of Education, Singapore.

Poole, CH (2004) 'Plagiarism and the online student: What is happening and what can be done?', *Journal of Instruction Delivery Systems*, 18(2):11–14.

Popham, WJ (2005) Students' attitudes count, *Educational Leadership*, 62(5):84–5.

Portelli, JP (1987) 'Perspectives and imperatives on defining curriculum', *Journal of Curriculum and Supervision*, 2(4):354–67.

Postman, N & Weingartner, C (1987) *Teaching as a Subversive Activity*, Dell, New York.

Power, FC (1997) Understanding the character in character education, Paper presented at the Annual Conference of the American Educational Research Association, Chicago.

Power, J & Berlach, RG (2005) 'The teaching internship and outcomes-based education', *Change: Transformations in Education*, 8(2):76–90.

Power, S & Clark, A (2000) 'The right to know: Parents, school reports and parents' evenings', *Research Papers in Education*, 15(1):25–48.

Pratt, D (1980) *Curriculum: Design and Development*, Harcourt Brace Jovanovich, New York.

Preston, B & Kennedy, KJ (1994) Models of professional standards for beginning practitioners and their application to initial professional education, Paper presented at the Annual Conference of the Australian Association for Research in Education, Newcastle.

Price, LF (2005) 'The biology of risk taking', *Educational Leadership*, 62(7):22–7.

Priestley, M (2005) 'Making the most of the Curriculum Review: Some reflections on supporting and sustaining change in schools'. *Scottish Educational Review*, 37(1): 29–38.

Priestley, M & Sime, D (2005) 'Formative assessment for all: A whole-school approach to pedagogic change', *Curriculum Journal*, 16(2): 475–92.

Proshansky, HK Ittelson, WH & Rivlin, LG (1976) *Environmental Psychology: People and their Physical Settings*, Holt, Rinehart & Winston, New York.

Proudford, C (1998) 'Implementing educational policy change: Implications for teacher professionalism and professional empowerment', *Asia-Pacific Journal of Teacher Education*, 26(2):139–50.

Pryor, J & Crossouard, B (2008) A socio-cultural theorisation of formative assessment, *Oxford Review of Education*, 34(1):1–20.

Pryor, J & Torrance, H (1996) 'Teacher–pupil interaction in formative assessment: Assessing the work or protecting the child', *Curriculum Journal*, 7(2):205–26.

Purpel, D & Ryan, K (1976) (eds) *Moral Education: It Comes with the Territory*, McCutcheon, Berkeley, California.

Q

Quality of Education Review Committee chaired by P Karmel (1985) *Quality of Education Review*, Australian Government Printing Service, Canberra.

Quek, CL (2006) (ed.) *Engaging in Project Work*, McGraw Hill Education (Asia), Singapore.

Quellmalz, ES & Kozma, R (2003) 'Designing assessments of learning with technology', *Assessment in Education*, 10(3):391–408.

R

Raikes, N & Harding, R (2003) 'The horseless carriage stage; Replacing conventional measures', *Assessment in Education*, 10(3):267–77.

Ramos, SO & Yudko, E (2006) '"Hits" (not "Discussion Posts") predict student success in online courses: A double cross-validation study', *Computers and Education*, 50(4):1174–82.

Raths, L Harmin, M & Simon, SB (1966) *Values and Teaching: Working with Values in the Classroom*, Charles E Merrill, Columbus, Ohio.

Ravitch, D (2002) 'September 11: Seven lessons for schools', *Educational Leadership*, 60(2):6–9.

Ray, H (1992) *Summary of Mainstream Amplification Resource Room Study (MARRS) Adoption Data Validated in 1992*, Wabash and Ohio Special Education District, Norris City, Illinois.

Reay, D (1998) *Mothers' Involvement in their Children's Primary Schooling*, UCL Press, London.

Reed, DC (2009) *Following Kohlberg: Liberalism and the Practices of Democratic Community*, University of Chicago Press, Chicago.

Rees, NS & Johnson, K (2000) 'A lesson in smaller class sizes', *Heritage Views 2000* (online), <www.heritage.org/views/2000/ed053000.html>.

Reichman, J & Healey, W (1993) 'Learning disabilities and conductive hearing loss involving otitis media', *Journal of Learning Disabilities*, 16:272–8.

Reid, A (1998) (ed.) 'Going public', *Education Policy and Public Education in Australia*, ACSA, Canberra.

Reid, A (2005) 'The politics of National Curriculum Collaboration: How can Australia move beyond the railway gauge metaphor'. In C Harris & CJ Marsh (eds), *Curriculum Developments in Australia: Promising Initiatives, Impasses and Dead-ends*, Openbook, Adelaide.

Reid, A (2009) 'Is this a revolution? A critical analysis of the Rudd government's national education agenda', *Curriculum Perspectives*, 29(3):1–15.

Reid, D & Thomson, P (2003) (eds) *Rethinking Public Education: Towards a Public Curriculum*, Australian Curriculum Studies Association, Brisbane.

Reid, WA (1994) *Curriculum Planning as Deliberation*, University of Oslo, Report No. 11, Oslo.

Remboldt, C (1998) 'Making violence unacceptable', *Educational Leadership*, 56(1):32–8.

Render, G Padilla, J & Krank, H (1989) 'What research really shows about assertive discipline', *Educational Leadership*, 46(6):72–5.

Renshaw, P (1992) 'The reading apprenticeship of preschool children'. In J Cullen & J Williamson (eds), *The Early Years: Policy, Research and Practice*, Murdoch University, Perth.

Renzulli, JS (1982) 'Dear Mr & Mrs Copernicus: We regret to inform you . . .', *Gifted Child Quarterly*, 26:11–14.

Resnick, LB & Klopfer, LE (1989) (eds) *Toward the Thinking Curriculum: Current Cognitive Research*, ASCD, Alexandria, Virginia.

Rest, J (1975) 'The validity of tests of moral judgement'. In JR Meyer (ed.), *Values Education Theory/Practice/Problems/Prospects*, University Press, Waterloo, Ontario.

Rest, JR Narvalz, D Bebau, M & Thomas, S (1999a) *Postconventional Moral Thinking: A Neo-Kohlbergian Approach*, Lawrence Erlbaum, Mahwah, New Jersey.

Rest, JR Narvalz, D Bebau, M & Thomas, S (1999b) 'A neo-Kohlbergian approach: The DIT and Schema theory', *Educational Psychology Review*, 11:291–324.

Rest, R (2000) Author's introduction, 'The enduring dilemmas of class and colour in American education', *Harvard Educational Review*, 70(3): 257–65.

Rethinam, V Pyke, C & Lynch, C (2008) 'Using multi-level analysis to study the effectiveness of Science curriculum materials', *Evaluation and Research in Education*, 21(1):18–42.

Reynolds, D Creemers, B Nesselrodt, P Schaffer, E Stringfield, S & Teddlie, C (1994) *Advances in School Effectiveness Research and Practice*, Pergamon, Oxford.

Reynolds, P (2001) 'A dysfunction between personal, professional and societal values in preservice teacher education', *Australian Journal of Teacher Education*, 26(2):38–49.

Reynolds, RJ (2005) 'The education of Australian Aboriginal and Torres Strait Islander students', *Childhood Education*, Fall:31–5.

Rich, D (1998) 'What parents want from teachers', *Educational Leadership*, 55(8):37–9.

Richardson, PW & Watt, HM (2006) 'Who chooses teaching and why? Profiling characteristics and motivations across three Australian universities', *Asia-Pacific Journal of Teacher Education*, 34(1):27–56.

Richardson, R (1991) *Daring to be a Teacher*, Trentham Books, Stoke-on-Trent.

Richardson, W (2006) 'The educator's guide to the read/write web', *Educational Leadership*, 63(4):24–8.

Ridgway, J & McCusker, S (2003) 'Using computers to assess new educational goals', *Assessment in Education*, 10(3):309–28.

Rieg, SA Paquette, KR & Chen, Y (2007) 'Coping with stress: An investigation of novice teachers' stressors in the Elementary Classroom', *Education*, 128(2):211–226.

Rigby, K (1996) *Bullying in Schools and What to Do About it*, ACER, Melbourne.

Ripple Media (1998) *Convict Fleet to Dragon Boat*, CD-Rom, Ripple Media, Adelaide.

Rizvi, F Lingard, B & Lavia, J (2006) Postcolonialism and education: Negotiating a contested terrain, *Pedagogy, Culture and Society*, 14(3):249–62.

Roberts, WB (2006) *Bullying from Both Sides*, Corwin Press, Thousand Oaks, CA.

Roe, B.D., Ross, E.P. & Burns, P.C. (1989) Student Teaching and Field Experiences Handbook, Merrill, Columbus.

Roesner, L (1995) 'Changing the culture at Beacon Hill', *Educational Leadership*, 52(7):28–32.

Rogers, B (1992) *Supporting Teachers in the Workplace*, Jacarandah Press, Brisbane.

Rogers, CR (1969) *Freedom to Learn*, Charles E Merrill, Columbus, Ohio.

Rogers, S & Renard, L (1999) 'Relationship-driven teaching', *Educational Leadership*, 57(1):34–7.

Rolheiser, C Hundey, I & Gordon, K (1998) Educational citizenship: Enhancing social responsibility in a teacher education pilot, OISE/UT, Paper presented at the Annual Conference of the American Educational Research Association, San Diego.

Rooney, J (2006) 'Rekindling our energy for neglected children', *Educational Leadership*, 63(5):86–7.

Rosenholtz, SJ (1989) *Teachers' Workplace: The Social Organization of Schools*, Longman, New York.

Rosenholtz, SJ (1991) *Teacher's Workplace: The Social Organization of Schools*, Teachers College Press, New York.

Rosenshine, B (1986) 'Synthesis of research on explicit teaching', *Educational Leadership*, 43(7):60–9.

Rosenshine, B & Stevens, R (1986) 'Teaching functions'. In MC Wittrock (ed.), *Handbook of Research on Teaching*, Macmillan, New York.

Ross, RP (1982) The design of education environment: An expression of individual differences or evidence of the 'press toward synomorphy?', Paper presented at the Annual Conference of the American Educational Research Association, New York.

Roth WM & Lee YJ (2007) 'Vygotsky's neglected legacy: Cultural-Historical activity theory', *Review of Educational Research*, 77(2).

Rotherham, AJ & Willingham, D (2009) '21st century skills: The challenges ahead', *Educational Leadership*, 67(1):16–21.

Rothstein, R & Jacobsen, R (2009) 'Measuring social responsibility', *Educational Leadership*, 66(8):14–19.

Rubin, BC (2006) 'Tracking and detracking: Debates, evidence and best practice', *Theory into Practice*, 45(1):4–14.

Ruby, A (1992) 'If Freeman Butts calls, tell him we might be changing course —', *The Practising Administrator*, 14(4):4–7.

Rudd, K (2008) Media Release with the Deputy Prime Minister, 'First steps towards a National Curriculum', 30 January.

Rudner, LM & Boston, C (2003) 'Data warehousing: Beyond disaggregation', *Educational Leadership*, 60(5):62–65.

Russell, G & Bradley, G (1996) 'Computer anxiety and student teachers: Antecedent and intervention', *Asia-Pacific Journal of Teacher Education*, 24(3):245–57.

Russell, M Goldberg, A & O'Connor K (2003) 'Computer-based testing and validity: A look back into the future', *Assessment in Education*, 10(3):279–93.

Russo, CJ (2001) 'Recent developments in the USA: Drug testing of students', *Education and the Law*, 13(2):155–60.

Ryan (1970) *Don't smile until Christmas*, University of Chicago Press, Chicago.

Ryan, K (1993) 'Mining the values in the curriculum', *Educational Leadership*, 51(3):16–18.

Ryan, K & Cooper, JM (2008) *Those Who Can, Teach*, 9th edn, Houghton Mifflin, Boston.

Ryan, K Cooper, JM & Tauer S (2008) *Teaching for Student Learning: Becoming a Master Teacher*, Hougton Mifflin, Boston.

S

Sachs, J (1997) Reclaiming the agenda of teacher professionalism: An Australian experience, *Journal of Education for Teaching: International Research and Pedagogy*, 23(3):263–76.

Sadker, D & Silber, ES (2007) (eds) *Gender in the Classroom*, Lawrence Erlbaum, Mahwah, New Jersey.

Saklofske, D & Eysenck, S (1997) *Individual Differences in Children and Adolescents*, Transaction Publishers, London.

Salvia, J & Ysseldyke, JE (1998) *Assessment*, 7th edn, Houghton Mifflin, Boston.

Salvo, JC Kibble, L Furay, M & Sierra, E (2005) 'Surviving day one ... and beyond', *Educational Leadership*, 62(8):24–8.

Samples, B (1992) 'Using learning modalities to celebrate intelligence', *Educational Leadership*, 50(2):62–6.

Sanders, J & Nelson, SC (2004) 'Closing gender gaps in science', *Educational Leadership*, 62(3):74–7.

Santrock, JN (1976) 'Affect and facilitative self-control: Influence of ecological setting, cognition and social agent', *Journal of Educational Psychology*, 68(5):529–35.

Santrock, JN (2001) *Educational Psychology*, McGraw Hill, Boston.
Santrock, JN (2008) *Educational Psychology*, McGraw Hill, Boston.
Sarason, S (1993) *The Predictable Failure of Educational Reform*, Jossey-Bass, San Francisco.
Saskatoon Public Schools (2008) What are learning contracts?, <www.olc.spsd.sk.ca/DE/PD/instr/strats/learningcontracts/iindex.html>, extracted 21 October 2008.
Save Our Schools (2008) 'Social Equity in Education as a National Goal', <soscanberra.com/file_download/14> extracted 4 May 2009.
Savoy, A Proctor, RW & Salvendy, G (2008) 'Information retention from Power Point and traditional lectures', *Computers and Education*, 52(4):858–67.
Saye, J (1998) 'Creating time to develop student thinking', *Social Education*, 62(6):356–61.
Scalfino, L (2003) 'One school's values frameworks', *EQ Australia*, Summer (4):33–5.
Scanlon, L (2004) 'She just blends and just comes down to our level and communicates with us like we're people', *Change: Transformations in Education*, 7(1):93–108.
Scardamalia, M & Bereiter, C (2001) 'Knowledge building: Theory, pedagogy and technology'. In K Sawyer (ed) *Cambridge Handbook of the Learning Sciences*, Cambridge University Press, New York.
Scherer, M (1998) 'The shelter of each other: A conversation with Mary Pepper', *Educational Leadership*, 55(8):6–11.
Schiller, KS & Muller, C (2000) 'External examinations and accountability: Educational expectations and high school graduation', *American Journal of Education*, February (108):73–7.
Schirmer, BR & McGough, S (2005) 'Teaching reading to children who are deaf: Do the conclusions of the National Reading Panel apply?', *Review of Educational Research*, 75(1):83–117.
Schlaefi, A Rest, JR & Thomas, SJ (1985) 'Does moral education improve moral judgement? A meta-analysis of intervention studies using the Defining Issues Test', *Review of Educational Research*, 55(3):319–52.
Schmid, EC (2008) 'Potential pedagogical benefits and drawbacks of multimedia use in the English language classroom equipped with interactive whiteboard technology', *Computers and Education*, 52(4):992–8.
Schmoker, M (2003) 'First things first: Demystifying Data Analysis', *Educational Leadership*, 60(5):23–25.
Schmoker, M & Marzano, RJ (1999) 'Realizing the promise of standards-based education', *Educational Leadership*, 56(6):17–21.
Schneider, F & Gullans, C (1962) *Last Letters from Stalingrad*, Morrow, New York.
Schofield, JW & Davidson, AL (2000) Internet use and teacher change, Paper presented at the Annual Conference of the American Educational Research Association, New Orleans.

Schools Council (1990) *Australia's Teacher: An Agenda for the Next Decade*, AGPS, Canberra.
Schuster, JW Hemmeter, ML & Ault, MJ (2001) 'Instruction of students with moderate and severe disabilities in elementary classrooms', *Early Childhood Research Quarterly*, 16:329–41.
Schwager, MT & Carlson, JS (1995) Teacher perceptions in learning and assessment and their interrelationships, Unpublished paper, University of California, Riverside.
Schwartz, G (1996) 'The rhetoric of cyberspace and the real curriculum', *Journal of Curriculum and Supervision*, 12(1):76–84.
Scott, A (1999) *Learning Centres*, Kogan Page, London.
Scott, B (1989) *Schools Renewal: A Strategy to Revitalise Schools within the New South Wales State Education System*, NSW Education Portfolio, Sydney.
Scott, D (2008) 'Early childhood and community: Capacity building in early childhood networks'. In Robinson, G Eickelkamp, U Goddnow, J & Katz, I (eds) *Contexts of Child Development*, Darwin, Charles Darwin University.
Scott, K (1985) Missing developmental theories in moral education, Paper presented at the Annual Conference of the National Council for the Social Studies, Chicago.
Scriven, M (1983) 'Evaluation as a paradigm for educational research', *Australian Educational Research*, 10(3):5–18.
Sears, JT (1999) 'Teaching queerly: Some elementary propositions'. In WJ Letts & JT Sears (eds), *Queering Elementary Education*, Rowman and Littlefield, Lanham, MD.
Sebba, R (1986) *Architecture as Determining the Child's Place in the School*, ERIC Research in Education, ED284367, Washington DC.
Seddon, T (1991) 'Teachers' work: A perspective on schooling'. In R Maclean & P McKenzie (eds), *Australian Teachers' Careers*, ACER, Melbourne.
Seddon, T (1995) 'Managing the reform of teachers and their work: Perspectives, prospects and paradox'. In CW Evers & JD Chapman (eds), *Educational Administration*, Allen & Unwin, Sydney.
Seitsinger, AM (2005) 'Service-learning and standards-based instruction in middle schools', *Journal of Educational Research*, 99(1):19–30.
Sendag, S & Odabagi, HF (2009) 'Effects of an online problem based learning course on content knowledge acquisition and critical thinking skills', *Computers and Education*, 53(1):132–41.
Settelmaier, E (2002) Transforming the culture of science education: The promise of moral dilemma stories, Unpublished dissertation, Science and Mathematics Education Centre, Curtin University.
Shariff, S & Govin, R (2006) 'Cyber-hierarchies: A new arsenal of weapons for gendered violence in schools'. In F Leach & C Mitchell (eds) *Combating Gender Violence in and around Schools*, Trentham Books, Stoke-on-Trent.
Shaver, J (1985) 'Commitment to values and the study

of social problems in citizenship education', *Social Education*, 49(3):112–21.
Shaw, A & Swingler, D (2005) 'Shared values and beliefs: The basis for a new school community', *The Australian Educational Leader*, 27(2):10–15.
Sheldon, SB (2002) 'Parents' social networks and beliefs as predictors of parent involvement', *The Elementary School Journal*, 102(4):301–22.
Shelton, CM (2000) 'Portraits in emotional awareness', *Educational Leadership*, 58(1):30–3.
Sheridan, G (1985) 'The lies they teach our children', *The Weekend Australian*, February 2–3, 1985, p. 15.
Short, KG & Burke, C (1991) *Creating Curriculum*, Heinemann, Portsmouth.
Shulman, L (1983) *Handbook of Teaching and Policy*, Macmillan, Chicago.
Shulman, L (1986) 'Those who understand: Knowledge growth in teaching', *Educational Researcher*, 15(2): 4–14.
Shulman, L (1992) 'Ways of seeing, ways of knowing, ways of teaching, ways of learning about teaching', *Journal of Curriculum Studies*, 28, pp. 393–6.
Shulman, LS (2007) Practical wisdom in the service of professional practice, *Educational Researcher*, 36(9):560–3.
Silver, H Strong, R & Perini, M (1997) 'Integrating learning styles and multiple intelligences', *Educational Leadership*, 55(1):22–9.
Silver-Pacuilla, H & Fleischman, S (2006) Technology to help struggling students, *Educational Leadership*, 63(5):84–5.
Simkins, M Cole, K Tavalin, F & Mwans, B (2002) *Increasing Student Learning through Multimedia Projects*, ASCD, Alexandria, Virginia.
Simmons, W & Resnick, L (1993) 'Assessment as the catalyst of school reform', *Educational Leadership*, 50(5):11–15.
Simpson, L & Clancy, S (2005) 'Enhancing opportunities for Australian Aboriginal literacy learners in early childhood settings', *Childhood Education*, 15:327–32.
Sinclair, K & Hatton, N (1992) 'The motivating role'. In C Turney, N Hatton, K Laws, K Sinclair & D Smith (eds), *The Classroom Manager*, Allen & Unwin, Sydney.
Singer, AJ (2003) *Teaching to Learn, Learning to Teach*, Lawrence Erlbaum, Mahwah, New Jersey.
Singh, A Doyle, C Rose, A & Kennedy, W (1997) 'Reflective internship and the phobia of classroom management', *Australian Journal of Education*, 41(2):105–18.
Siozos, P Palaigeorgion, G Triantafyllakos, G & Despotakis, T (2008) 'Computer based testing using "digital ink": Participatory design of a Tablet PC based assessment application for secondary education', *Computers and Education*, 52(4):811–19.
Sireci SG (2005) Unlabelling the Disabled: A Perspective on Flagging Scores from Accommodated Test Administrations, *Educational Researcher*, 34(1):3–12.
Sireci, S Scarpati, SE & Li, S (2005) 'Test accommodation for students with disabilities: An analysis of the interaction hypothesis', *Review of Educational Research*, 75(4):457–90.
Skilbeck, M (1980) Core curriculum for a multicultural society, Unpublished paper, Curriculum Development Centre, Canberra.
Skildum-Reid, K (1999) 'Schools lose the plot on sponsorship', *Professional Marketing*, Dec/Jan, 2(25).
Slack, N & Norwich, B (2007) 'Evaluating the reliability and validity of a learning styles inventory: A classroom based study', *Educational Research*, 49(1):51–63.
Slater, B (1968) 'Effects of noise on pupil performance', *Journal of Educational Psychology*, 59(3):87–94.
Slaughter, S (1997) 'Class, race and gender and the construction of post-secondary curricula in the United States: Social movement, professionalization and political economic theories of curricula change', *Journal of Curriculum Studies*, 29(1):1–30.
Slavin, R (1995) 'Detracking and its detractors: Flawed evidence, flawed values', *Phi Delta Kappan*, 77(1):220–1.
Slavin, RE (1978) 'Student teams and achievement divisions', *Journal of Research and Development in Education*, 12:39–49.
Slavin, RE (1987) 'Mastery learning reconsidered', *Review of Educational Research*, 57(2):175–213.
Slavin, RE (1999) *Educational Psychology*, 4th edn, Allyn & Bacon, Boston.
Slee, PT (2002) *Child, Adolescent and Family Development*, 2nd edn, Cambridge University Press, Cambridge.
Slee, R (1992) (ed.) *Discipline in Australian Public Education*, ACER, Melbourne.
Slee, R (2000) 'Professional partnerships for inclusive education?', *Melbourne Studies in Education*, 41(1): 1–13.
Slee, R Weiner, W & Tomlinson, S (1998) (eds) *School Effectiveness for Whom?*, Falmer Press, London.
Smith, D & Laws, K (1992) 'The communicating role'. In C Turney, N Hatton, K Laws, K Sinclair & D Smith (eds), *The Classroom Manager*, Allen & Unwin, Sydney.
Smith, D & Lovat, TJ (2003) *Curriculum: Action on Reflection*, 4th edn, Social Science Press, Sydney.
Smith, F Hardman, F & Higgins, S (2006) 'The impact of interactive whiteboards on teacher-pupil interaction in the National Literacy and Numeracy Strategies', *British Educational Research Journal*, 32(3):443–57.
Smith, J (2001) 'Gender and schooling'. In CJ Marsh (ed.), *Teaching Studies of Society and Environment*, Pearson, Sydney.
Smith, MK (2008) 'Howard Gardner, Multiple Intelligences and Education', <www.infed.org/thinkers/gardner.htm> extracted 2 October 2008.
Smith, R & Lambert, M (2008) 'Assuming the best', *Educational Leadership*, 66(1):16–21.
Smith, RK (2007) 'Unveiling a role for the EU: The "headscarf controversy" in European schools', *Education and the Law*, 19(2):111–30.

Smith, S (2008) 'A Three Legged Chair Model of Queensland's Approach to Implementary OBE', <www.teachers.ash.org.au/bce/obe.htm> extracted 22 October, 2008.

Soon, TH & Leng, SL (2006) 'Using Interactive CD-ROM to improve understanding of vocabulary in Chinese language', *Celebrating Learning through Action Research*, CLEAR Symposium, North Zone Schools, Ministry of Education, Singapore.

Spady, W (1993) 'Outcome-based education', *Workshop Report No. 5*, ACSA, Canberra.

Spady, WG (1994) 'Choosing outcomes of significance', *Educational Leadership*, 51(6):18–23.

Sparks, D & Hirsh, S (1997) *A New Vision of Staff Development*, ASCD, Alexandria.

Spaull, A (1997) 'Deprofessionalisation of state school teaching: A Victorian industrial relations saga', *Australian Journal of Education*, 41(3):289–303.

Sroufe, LA (1988) 'The role of infant caregiver attachment in development'. In R Belsky & T Nezworski (eds), *Clinical Implications of Attachments*:18–40, Lawrence Erlbaum, Hillsdale, New Jersey.

Stake, R (1987) 'An evolutionary view of programming staff development'. In M Wideen & I Andrews (eds), *Staff Development for School Improvement*, Falmer, London.

Starr, K (1991) 'What is social justice?' *Curriculum Perspectives*, 11(3):20–4.

Stecher, BM & Klein, SP (1997) 'The cost of science performance assessments in large-scale testing programs', *Educational Evaluation and Policy Analysis*, 19(1):1–14.

Stein, N (1999) *Classrooms and Courtrooms: Facing Sexual Harassment in K–12 Schools*, Teachers College Press, New York.

Stemberg RJ (2007) 'Who are the bright children? The cultural context of being and acting intelligent', *Educational Researcher*, 36(3):148–55.

Stevenson, C (1998) *Teaching Ten to Fourteen Year Olds*, 2nd edn, Longman, New York.

Stevenson, J Ling, L Berman, E & Cooper, M (1997) *Values in Education*, ACER, Melbourne.

Stewart, D (2005) 'The place of law in the leadership and management of schools', *Education and the Law*, 17(4):127–36.

Stigler, JW & Hiebert, J (1999) *The Teaching Gap*, The Free Press, New York.

Stiler, GM (2007) 'MP3 Players: Applications and implications for the use of popular technology in secondary schools', *Education*, 128(1):20–86.

Strike, K & Soltis, J (2004) *The Ethics of Teaching*, 4th edn, Teachers College Press, New York.

Stromlo High School (2001) *Stromlo High School*, Stromlo High School, ACT.

Strutt, E (2006) 'The issues with outcomes-based education', *West Australian* 26 February 2006.

Suan, M (2006) 'Ability-grouped buddy system in an English class', *Celebrating Learning through Action Research*, Ministry of Education, Singapore.

Suckling, A & Temple, C (2001) *Bullying: A Whole-School Approach*, ACER, Melbourne.

Sukhnandan, L Lee, B & Kelleher, S (2000) 'An investigation into gender differences and achievement: Phase 2 school and classroom strategies', National Foundation for Educational Research, Slough.

Summers, J & Davis, H (2006) 'Introduction: The interpersonal contexts of teaching, learning and motivation', *The Elementary School Journal* 106(3):189–91.

Sun, KT Lin, YC & Yu, NJ (2007) 'A study on learning effect among different learning styles in a web-based lab of science for elementary school students', *Computers and Education*, 50(4):1411–22.

Supovitz, JA & Brennan, RT (1997) 'Mirror, mirror on the wall, which is the fairest test of all? An examination of the equitability of portfolio assessment relative to standardised tests', *Harvard Educational Review*, 67(3):472–506.

Susinos, T Calvo, A & Rojas, S (2009) Becoming a woman: The construction of female subjectivities and its relationship with school, *Gender and Education*, 21(1):97–110.

Susskind, JE (2008) 'Limits of Power Point's Power: Enhancing students' self-efficacy and attitudes but not their behaviour', *Computers and Education*, 50(4):1228–39.

Sutton, D (2009) Correspondence with the Manager, Vocational Education, Victorian Curriculum and Assessment Authority, Melbourne, July 3, 2009.

Sutton, R (1992) *Assessment: A Framework for Teachers*, Routledge, London.

Swan, WW (1998) Local school system implementation of state policy actions for educational reform, Paper presented at the Annual Conference of the Americal Educational Research Association, San Diego.

Sweeting, H & West, P (2001) 'Being different: Correlates of the experience of teasing and bullying at age 11', *Research Papers in Education*, 16(3):225–46.

Sweetnam, G (2005) 'Interactive whiteboard trial', *P & C Journal, NSW*, 56(3):21.

Sydney Morning Herald (2005) 'Peers set to follow Yasamin's dress example', *SMH*, May 18, p. 4, Justin Norrie – reporter.

Sykes, PJ Measor, L & Woods, P (1985) *Teacher Careers: Crises and Continuities*, Falmer, London.

Sylva, K Siraj-Blatchford, I & Taggart, B (2003) *Assessing Quality in the Early Years*, Trentham, Stoke-on-Trent.

Szorenyi-Reischl, N (1981) *Values Education in Core Curriculum*, La Trobe University, Centre for the Study of Innovation and Education, Melbourne.

T

Tan, M & Pakiam, R (2006) 'The impact of video on writing skills in the foundation years', *Celebrating Learning through Action Research*, Ministry of Education, Singapore.

Tannock, R & Martinussen, R (2001) 'Reconceptualising, ADHD', *Educational Leadership*, 59(3):20–5.

Tapscott, D (1999) 'Educating the net generation', *Educational Leadership*, 56(5):6–11.

Tapscott, D (2007) 'Educating the Net generation'. In Ornstein, A, Pajak, EF & Ornstein, SB (eds), *Contemporary Issues in Curriculum*, 4th edn, Pearson/Allyn & Bacon, Boston.

Taras, M (2005) 'Assessment – summative and formative – some theoretical reflections', *British Journal of Educational Studies*, 53(4):466–78.

Taylor AL (2006) 'The Influence of Teacher Attitudes and Individual Differences on Pupil Achievement with Programmed Science Materials', *Journal of Research in Science Teaching*, 4(1):38–39.

Taylor, MD Pountney, DC Baskett, M (2006) 'Using animation to support the teaching of computer game development techniques', *Computers and Education*, 50(4):1258–68.

Teacher Standards, Quality and Professionalism Reference Group (2002) *Terms of Reference*, Reference Group, Melbourne.

Teaching Australia (2008) *Feasibility Study: Establishing a National Centre for Pedagogy*, Australian Institute for Teaching and School Leadership, Canberra.

Teese, R & Polesel, J (2003) *Undemocratic Schooling: Equity and Equality in Mass Secondary Education in Australia*, University of Melbourne, Melbourne.

Terwilliger, J (1997) 'Semantics, psychometrics, and assessment reform: A close look at "authentic" assessments', *Educational Researcher*, 26(8):24–6.

Tessmer, M & Richey, RC (1997) 'The role of context in learning and instructional design', *Educational Technology, Research and Development*, 45(2):85–116.

The Age (2005) 'Whereto the national curriculum', 29 October 2005.

The Standard (2009) Massive freebies dished out in fight for survival: School crunch, *The Standard*, 10 July, p. 1.

Thelen, H (1960) *Education and the Human Quest*, Harper & Row, New York.

Theroux, P (2001) *Enhance Learning with Technology: Differentiated Construction*, <www.cssd.ab.ca/tech/oth/learn/differentiating.htm> extracted 21 October 2008.

Theroux, P (2004) *Engaged Learning*, <www.enhancelearning.ca>.

Thompson, G (2008) 'Beneath the Apathy', *Educational Leadership*, 65(6):50–54.

Thompson, R (1989) 'Competency-based training: An industry learning experience', *Asia Pacific HRM*, 27(3):86–90.

Thornburg, D (2002) *The New Basics: Education & the Future of Work in the Telematic Age*, ASCD, Alexandria, Virginia.

Tillett, A (2009) 'Pre-school PC guide draws teachers' fire', *West Australian*, 15 April 2009, p. 13.

TIMSS (2008) *Trends in International Mathematics and Science Study*, US Department of Education, Institute of Education Sciences.

Titman, W (1997) 'Special places, special people: The hidden curriculum of school grounds', *Set 1*, 1–4, Winchester, United Kingdom.

Tobias, S & Duchastel, P (1974) 'Behavioural objectives, sequence and anxiety in CAI', *Instructional Science*, 3(2):232–42.

Tobin, K (1987) 'The role of wait time in higher cognitive learning', *Review of Educational Research*, 56(2):69–95.

Tomlinson, CA (1999) *The Differentiated Classroom*, ASCD, Alexandria, Virginia.

Tomlinson, CA (2008a) The Goals of Differentiation, *Educational Leadership*, 66(3):26–31.

Tomlinson, CA (2008b) Learning to love assessment, *Educational Leadership*, 65(4):8–13.

Tomlinson, CA & Germundson, A (2007) 'Teaching as jazz', *Educational Leadership*, 64(8):27–31.

Tomlinson, CA & Kalbfleisch, ML (1998) 'Teach me, teach my brain', *Educational Leadership*, 56(3):53–5.

Tomlinson, P & Quinton, M (1986) *Values Across the Curriculum*, Falmer, London.

Toombs, WE & Tierney, WG (1993) 'Curriculum definitions and reference points', *Journal of Curriculum and Supervision*, 8(3):175–95.

Torrance, H & Pryor, J (1995) Making sense of 'formative assessment': Investigating the integration of assessment with teaching and learning, Paper presented at the Annual Conference of the American Educational Research Association, San Francisco, California.

Towers, J (1992) 'Outcomes-based education. Another educational bandwagon?', *Educational Forum*, 56(3):291–305.

Townsend, T (1999) 'Public and private schools – new priorities and practices?', *Curriculum Perspectives*, 19(1):58–64.

Townsend, T, Clarke, P & Ainscow, M (1999) *Third Millennium Schools: A World of Difference in Effectiveness and Improvement*, Swets & Zeitlinger, London.

Trachtenberg, D (1974) 'Student tasks in text material: What cognitive skills do they tap?', *Peabody Journal of Education*, 52(2):54–7.

Travers, J (1997) 'School computing: Lessons from the past', *EQ Australia*, 4:31–3.

Travers, PD & Reborc, RW (1990) *Foundations of Education: Becoming a Teacher*, Prentice Hall, Englewood Cliffs, New Jersey.

Trepanier-Street, ML McNair, S & Donegan, MM (2001) 'The views of teachers on assessment: A comparison of lower and upper elementary teachers', *Journal of Research in Childhood Education*, 15(2):234–41.

Tronc, K (2002) 'Children 2002: They've never had it so good', *The Practising Administrator*, 2.

Tuijnman, A & Bostrum, A (2002) 'Changing of notions of lifelong education and lifelong learning', *International Review of Education*, 48(1/2):93–110.

Tullock, M (1995) 'Gender differences in bullying experiences and attitudes to social relationships in high school students', *Australian Journal of Education*, 39(3):279–93.

Turney, C Hatton, N Laws, K Sinclair, K & Smith, D (1992) *The Classroom Manager*, Allen & Unwin, Sydney.

Twigg, CA (2003) Improving Learning and Reducing Costs: New Models of Online Learning, *Education Review*, September:28–38.

Tyack, D & Cuban, L (1995) *Tinkering towards Utopia: A Century of Public School Reform*, Harvard University Press, Cambridge, MA.

Tym, A (2010) 'Is a curriculum a map or a set of survival skills? Navigation and survival in the politics of pedagogy', *Curriculum Perspectives*, 30(1), (in press).

Tzuriel, D (1992) 'The development of ego identity at adolescence among Israeli Jews and Arabs', *Journal of Youth and Adolescence*, 21:551–71.

U

Urban, H (2004) *Positive Words, Powerful Results: Simple Ways to Honour, Affirm and Celebrate Life*, Fireside, New York.

US Department of Education (2001) *Elementary and Secondary Education: No Child Left Behind* Act, US Department of Education, Washington DC.

US Department of Education (2002) *Elementary and Secondary Education: No Child Left Behind Act*, US Department of Education, Washington.

V

Values Education for Australian Schooling (2005) Research Study, VICCSO, Melbourne.

Van den Berg, R (2002) 'Teacher's meanings regarding educational practice', *Review of Educational Research*, 72(4):577–626.

Van Velzen, WG Miles, MB Ekholm, M Hameyer, U & Robin, D (1985) *Making School Improvement Work*, OECD, Leuven.

Vansteenhiste, M Lens, W & Deci, EL (2006) 'Intrinsic versus extrinsic goal contents in self-determination theory: Another look at the quality of academic motivation', *Educational Psychologist*, 41(1):19–31.

Varjas, K Henrich, CC & Meyers, J (2009) 'Urban middle school students' perceptions of bullying, cyber bullying and school safety', *Journal of School Violence*, 8(2):159–76.

Varnham, S (2001) 'Conduct unbecoming: the dilemma of a school's responsibility in respect of teacher misconduct towards pupils', *Education and the Law*, 13(2):109–23.

Verloop, N Van Driel, J & Meijer, P (2001) 'Teacher knowledge and the knowledge base of teaching', *International Journal of Educational Research*, 35(1):441–61.

Vick, M (1994) 'Parents, schools and democracy', *Education Australia*, 28:11–13.

Victorian Council of School Organisations (2005) 'The vision for school councils', *School Bell*, 58(1):1–6.

Victorian Curriculum and Assessment Authority (2005) *Essential Learning Standards*, Victorian Curriculum and Assessment Authority, Melbourne.

Victorian Institute of Teaching – Teacher Education (2009) <www.vit.vic.edu.au/content.asp?Document_ID=22> extracted 28 July 2009.

Video Education (2006) *Classroom Videos*, Bendigo Video Education, Australasia.

Vighnarajah, H Wong, S & Bakar, K (2008) 'Qualitative findings of students' perception on practise of self-regulated strategies in online community', *Computers and Education*, 53(1):94–103.

Villa, RA & Thousand, J (1992) 'How one district integrated special and general education', *Educational Leadership*, 50(2):39–41.

Vining, L (2000) 'Marketing today's schools', *The Practising Administrator*, 22(2):9.

Vinson, T (2004) *Community adversity and resilience: the distribution of social disadvantage in Victoria and New South Wales and the mediating role of social cohesion*, The Ignatius Centre for Social Policy and Research, Jesuit Social Services, Melbourne.

Volante, L (2006) 'Toward appropriate preparation for standardised achievement testing', *Journal of Educational Thought*, 40(2):129–44.

Volman, M (1997) 'Gender-related effects of computer and information literacy education', *Journal of Curriculum Studies*, 29(3):315–28.

von Glaserfield, T (1995) *Radical Constructivism: A Way of Knowing and Learning*, Falmer, London.

Vygotsky, LS (1978) *Mind in Society: The Development of Higher Psychological Processes*, Harvard University Press, Cambridge.

W

Wadsworth, D & Remaley, MH (2007) 'What families want', *Educational Leadership*, 64(6):23–7.

Wake, P & Sangster, C (2008) *Education and the Law*, 20(2):165–69.

Waks, LJ (2006) 'Globalisation, State transformation and educational re-structuring. Why postmodern diversity will prevail over standardisation', *Studies in Philosophy of Education*, 25(2):403–24.

Walberg, H (1985) 'Examining the theory, practice, and outcomes of mastery learning'. In DU Levine (ed.), *Improving Student Achievement Through Mastery Learning Programs*, Jossey-Bass, San Francisco, California.

Walker, DF & Soltis, J (2004) *Thinking about Curriculum: Curriculum and Aims*, Teachers College Press, New York.

Walker, J (1994) *Competency-based Teacher Education – Implications for Quality in Higher Education*, II R Conference, Canberra.

Walker-Dalhouse, D (2005) 'Discipline: Responding to socioeconomic and racial differences', *Childhood Education*, 81(6):24–9.

Wall, J & Ahmed, V (2007) 'Use of a simulation game in delivering blended lifelong learning in the construction industry – opportunities and challenges', *Computers and Education*, 50(4):1383–93.

Wallace, J Sheffield, R Rennie, L & Venville, G (2007) 'Looking back, looking forward: Re-searching the conditions for curriculum integration in the middle years of schooling', *Australian Educational Researcher*, 34(2):29–49.

Walsh, K & Farrell, A (2008) 'Identifying and evaluating teachers' knowledge in relation to child abuse and neglect: A qualitative study with Australian early childhood teachers', *Teaching and Teacher Education*, 24(1):585–600.

Wang, H C Chang, C Y & Li, T Y (2008) 'Assessing creative problem-solving with automated text grading', *Computers and Education*, 51(4):1450–66.

Warwick, P (2007) 'Echoes of Plowden? Opportunities and pressures evident in teachers' experience of autonomy and accountability in one school community', *Forum*, 49(1):33–8.

Wassermann, S (2001) 'Curriculum enrichment with computer software', *Phi Delta Kappan*, 82(8):592–7.

Watanabe, M (2006) '"Some people think this school is tracked and some people don't". Using inquiry groups to unpack teachers' perspectives on detracking', *Theory into Practice*, 45(1):24–31.

Watkins, C (2005) *Classrooms as Learning Communities*, Routledge, London.

Watson, I & Considine, G (2003) *Learning Experience of Students from Low-income Families*, University of Sydney, Sydney.

Watson, N Fullan, M & Kilcher, A (2000) The role of the district: Professional learning and district reform, Paper presented at the Annual Conference of the American Educational Research Association, New Orleans.

Watt, J (1989) 'Devolution of power: The ideological meaning', *Journal of Educational Administration*, 27(1):19–28.

Wayne, AJ Yoon, KS Zhu, P Cronen, S & Garet, MS (2008) Experimenting with teacher professional development: Motives and methods, *Educational Researcher*, 37(8):469–79.

Webb, R Vulliamy, G Hamalainen, S Sarja, A Kimonen, E & Nevalainen, R (2004) 'A comparative analysis of primary teacher professionalism in England and Finland', *Comparative Education*, 40(1):83–108.

Webster, RS (2009) Does the Australian National Framework for Values Education stifle an education for world peace, Paper presented at the Annual National Values Education Conference, Canberra.

Wee, E & Woo, HM (2006) 'Impact of virtual geometrical instruments on the learning of simultaneous equations using the graphical method', *Celebrating Learning through Action Research*, Ministry of Education, Singapore.

Weekend Australian (2009) 'School reporting', 28 March 2009.

Weiner, B (1986) *An Attribution Theory of Motivation and Learning*, Springer-Verlag, New York.

Weinstein, CS & Weinstein, ND (1979) 'Noise and reading performance in an open space school', *Journal of Educational Research*, 72(4):210–13.

Weiss, EM & Weiss, S (2001) 'Doing reflective supervision with student teachers in a professional development school culture', *Reflective Practice*, 2(2):125–53.

Weissbourd, R (2003) 'Moral teachers, moral students', *Educational Leadership*, 60(6):6–11.

Wescombe-Down, D (2009) Teacher quality: Benefit or blight, Unpublished paper, SA Govt.

West Australian (2008) 'Constable wants OBE review and levels axed', 23 October.

West Australian Curriculum Council (1998) *Core Shared Values*, Curriculum Council, Perth.

Westergard, E (2007) 'Do teachers recognise complaints from parents, and if not, why not?', *Evaluation and Research in Education*, 20(3):159–79.

White, J (2006) 'Arias of learning: Creativity and performativity in Australian teacher education', *Cambridge Journal of Education*, 36(3):435–53.

Whitehead, AN (1929) *The Aims of Education*, MacMillan, New York.

Whitehead, K (2001) 'Do men still manage while women teach? Using four reports on middle schooling to portray continuities and changes in teachers' work in the 1990's', *Australian Journal of Education*, 45(3):309–22.

Whitton, D, Sinclair, C, Barker, K, Nanlohy, P & Nosworthy, M (2004) *Learning for Teaching: Teaching for Learning*, Thomson, Melbourne.

Whitty, G (1994) Deprofessionalising teaching? Recent developments in teacher education in England, Occasional paper No. 22, Australian College of Education, Canberra.

Whitty, G (2006) 'Teacher professional in a new era', General Teaching Council for Northern Ireland Annual Lecture, Queen University, Belfast.

Wiggins, G & McTighe, J (2002) *Understanding by Design*, 2nd edn, ASCD, Alexandria, Virginia.

Wiggins, G & McTighe, J (2005) *Understanding by Design*, 2nd edn, ASCD, Alexandria, Virginia.

Wiggins, G & McTighe, J (2008) 'Put understanding first', *Educational Leadership*, 65(8):36–41.

Wiggins, G (1997) 'Practising what we preach in designing authentic assessments', *Educational Leadership*, 54(4):18–25.

Wiggins, G (1998) *Educative Assessment*, Jossey-Bass, San Francisco.

Wikipedia (2006) World Wide Web, <en.wikipedia.org/wiki/World_Wide_Web>.

Wiliam, D (2006) 'Does assessment hinder learning?' ETS Europe, 11 July, <www.uk.etseurope.org/home-corpo-uk/news-home/?print=1&news=13...> extracted 3 August 2006.

Wiliam, D (2008) 'Changing classroom practice', *Education Leadership*, 65(4):36–42.

Williams, M (2000) 'Connecting teachers to the Dot.Com world', *EQ*, Winter (2):9–11.

Williams, R (2001) Automated essay grading: An evaluation of four conceptual models, Unpublished paper, Curtin University, Perth.

Williamson, K (1995) 'Independent learning and the use of resources: VCE Australian Studies', *Australian Journal of Education*, 39(1):77–94.

Willingham, WW & Cole, NS (1997) *Gender and Fair*

Assessment, Lawrence Erlbaum Associates, Mahwah, New Jersey.

Willis, S & Kissane, B (1995) *Outcomes-based Education: A Review of the Literature*, Education Department of Western Australia, Perth.

Willis, S & Kissane, B (1997) *Achieving Outcome-Based Education*, ACSA, Canberra.

Wilson, B (2002) Curriculum – is less more?, Paper presented at the Curriculum Corporation Conference, Canberra.

Wilson, J (1990) *A New Introduction to Moral Education*, Cassell, London.

Wilson, S & Sproats, E (2009) 'Re-engaging young people in learning: What schools can learn from a community-based program for "at risk" students', *Curriculum Perspectives*, 29(1):29–40.

Wilson, T Williams, N & Sugarman, B (1967) *Introduction to Moral Education*, Penguin, Baltimore.

Winnicott, DW (1964) 'Review of memories, dreams and reflections', *International Journal of Psychoanalysis*, 50(1):711–16.

Winter, E (2000) 'School bereavement', *Educational Leadership*, 57(6):80–5.

Wise, AE (2001) 'Creating a high-quality teaching force', *Educational Leadership*, 58(4):18–21.

Wise, B (2008) High schools at the tipping point, *Educational Leadership*, 65(8):8–13.

Withers, G & McCurry, D (1990) 'Student participation in assessment in a cooperative climate'. In B Low & G Withers (eds), *Developments in School and Public Assessment*, ACER, Melbourne.

Witkin, HA Moore, CA Goodenough, DR & Cox, PW (1977) 'Field-dependent and field-independent cognitive styles and their educational implications', *Review of Educational Research*, 47:1–64.

Wofmann, L & West, M (2004) 'Class size effects in school systems around the world. Evidence from between-grade variation in TIMSS', *European Economic Review*, 50(3):695–736.

Wolf, SJ & Fraser, BJ (2008) 'Learning environment, attitudes and achievement among middle-school science students using inquiry-based laboratory activities', *Research in Science Education*, 38:321–41.

Wolfe, CR (2000) *Learning and Teaching on the World Wide Web*, Academic Press, San Francisco.

Wolk, S (2008) 'Joy in school', *Educational Leadership*, 66(1):8–15.

Woods, A (2007) 'Searching for equitable outcomes for all students', *Curriculum Perspectives*, 29(1).

Woods, P (1988) 'A strategic view of parent participation', *Journal of Education Policy*, 3(4):323–34.

Woods, P (1990a) *Teacher Skills and Strategies*, Falmer, London.

Woods, P (1990b) *The Happiest Days?*, Falmer, London.

Woods, P & Jeffrey, B (2002) 'The reconstruction of primary teachers' identities', *British Journal of Sociology of Education*, 23(1):89–107.

Woods, PA (2000) Redefining professionality and leadership: Reflexive responses to competitive and regulatory pressures, Paper presented at the Annual Conference of the American Educational Research Association, New Orleans.

Woolfolk, A (2008) *Educational Psychology*, 11th edn, Allyn & Bacon, Boston.

Wormeli, R (2007) *Differentiation*, Stenhouse, Portland.

Worthen, BR White, KR Fan, X & Sudwecks, R (1999) *Measurement and Assessment in Schools*, 2nd edn, Longman, New York.

Wright, RJ (2008) *Educational Assessment*, Sage, Thousand Oaks, CA.

Wyatt-Smith, C (2008) Literacy testing and quality, *Curriculum Perspectives*, 28(3):59–64.

Wyatt-Smith, C & Campbell, R (2002) 'What counts as quality literacy assessment in middle schooling? Teacher accounts of classroom-based assessment and large-scale testing', *Curriculum Perspectives*, 22(3):1–12.

Wylie, C (1995) School-site-management – Some lessons from New Zealand, Paper presented at Annual Conference of the American Educational Research Association, San Francisco, California.

Wynne, EA (1986) 'The great tradition in education: Transmitting moral values', *Educational Leadership*, 43(4):37–41.

Y

Yamada, M (2008) 'The role of social presence in learner-centred communicative language learning using synchronous computer-mediated communication: Experimental study', *Computers and Education*, 52(4):820–33.

Yamaguchi, R O'Malley, PM & Johnston, LD (2004) 'Relationship between school drug searches and student substance use in US schools', *Educational Evaluation and Policy Analysis*, 26(4):329–41.

Yaman, M Nerdel, C & Bayrhuber, H (2008) 'The effects of instructional support and learner interests when learning using computer simulations', *Computer and Education*, 51(4):1784–94.

Yang, YT Newby, T & Bill, R (2007) 'Facilitating interactions through structured web-based bulletin boards: A quasi-experimental study on promoting learners' critical thinking skills', *Computers and Education*, 50(4):1572–85.

Yates, L (1998) Feminism's fandango with the state revisited, Paper presented at the Annual Conference of the American Educational Research Association, San Diego.

Yates, L McLeod, J & Arrow, M (2007) *Self, School and Future*, UTS, Sydney.

Yeh, SS (2001) 'Tests worth teaching to: Constructing state-mandated tests that emphasize critical thinking', *Educational Researcher*, 30(9):12–17.

Yeh, SS (2007) 'Class size reduction or rapid formative assessment? A comparison of cost-effectiveness', *Educational Research Review*.

Yeh, SW & Lo, JJ (2008) 'Using online annotations to support error correction and corrective feedback', *Computers and Education*, 52(4):882–92.

Yeo, S Thiagayson, K Cheah, R & Khiang, TK (2006) 'Does peer tutoring for Sec I E during Maths lessons improve pupils' academic results?' *Celebrating Learning through Action Research*, Ministry of Education, Singapore.

Yeung, AS & McInerney, DM (2005) 'Students' school motivation and aspiration over high school years', *Educational Psychology*, 25(5):537–54.

Yon, S Ling, R & Aik, S (2006) 'The use of online questions to motivate lower secondary students learning science', *Computers and Education*, 51(1):345–63.

Yonezawa, S & Jones, M (2006) 'Students' perspectives on tracking and detracking', *Theory into Practice*, 45(1):15–23.

Yong, LF Gene, LY & Abaullah, NB (2006) 'A study on how an ICT-driven learning platform (LM5) impacts on experimental learning for Primary 5 pupils in Nan Chiau Primary School', *Celebrating Learning through Action Research*, Ministry of Education, Singapore.

Yong, LF Salleh, H Ong, A Simon, J Hui, Q & Woon, Y (2006) 'A case study of social constructionist model of teaching in a technology-enabled environment for Primary 4 pupils at Nan Chiau Primary School', *Celebrating Learning through Action Research*, Ministry of Education, Singapore.

Yost, D (1997) 'The moral dimensions of teaching and preservice teachers: Can moral dispositions be influenced?', *Journal of Teacher Education*, 48(4):281–92.

Younger, MB & Warrington, M (2006) 'Would Harry and Hermione have done better in single sex classes? A review of single-sex teaching in co-educational secondary schools in the United Kingdom', *American Educational Research Journal*, 43(4):579–620.

Z

Zady, MF Portes, PR & Del Castillo, K (1998) When low SES parents cannot assist their children, Paper presented at the Annual Conference of the American Educational Research Association, San Diego.

Zandvliet, D & Fraser, B (1998) The physical and psychosocial environments associated with classrooms using new information technologies, Paper presented at the Annual Conference of the American Educational Research Association, San Diego.

Zbar, V (1998) *Discovering Democracy: Final Report, Implementing Discovering Democracy in Schools Forum*, ACSA, Canberra.

Zembylas, M (2007) 'The power and politics of emotions in teaching', *International Journal of Research and Method in Education*, 3(4):62–75.

Zubrick, SR Silburn, SR, Lawrence, DM Mitrou, FG & Dalby, RB (2008) The Western Australian Aboriginal Child Health Survey: Are there policy implications? In Robinson, G Eickelkamp, U Goddnow, J & Katz, I (eds), *Contexts of Child Development*, Charles Darwin University, Darwin.

Zyngier, D (2003) 'A bridge not far enough', *EQ Australia*, Winter (2):9–10.

Zyngier, D (2009) 'Teachers under the pump – and over a barrel – and up the creek: Reframing the current debates about "quality: of education', *Curriculum Perspectives*, 29(1).

INDEX

AAMT 24, 25, 405–6
AATE 24, 25, 406
ability groupings 83
Aboriginal Australians *see* Indigenous Australians
academic freedom 377
academic learning time 134
ACARA 10, 14, 15, 25–6, 29, 30, 33
accommodation (Piaget) 39
accountability 151–2, 200, 336, 400
achievement
   and formative assessment strategies 315
   and gender 264–6
   and individual differences 253–4
   international rankings 363
   motivation 60–2
acoustics, of classroom 79–81
action verbs
   for activities 162, 261
   for instructional objectives 114
Adelaide Declaration (1999) 148
ADHD (attention deficit hyperactivity disorder) 229–30
advertising, to children 373–4
aesthetic needs 60
affective objectives 161
ageing, of teachers 352–4
aims, importance of 147–8
alcohol and road use (topic) 107–8, 112
alternative assessment 323
alternative schools 307
analytic questions 188
artefacts, as resource 250
Assertive Discipline Model (Canter & Canter) 222, 232, 233–4
assessment 310
   alternative 323
   assessment tasks 328–9, 330
   audiences of 312
   authentic 323–4, 329, 332, 336
   basic principles 311
   criterion-referenced measures 317
   diagnostic 315, 316
   direct observation 321–2
   formal 37, 315
   formative 313–14, 315, 316, 363
   ICT developments in 312–13

   inclusive/exclusive 320
   informal 315, 321
   internal/external 318–19
   for learning 311, 313–14, 319
   norm-referenced measures 317
   performance-based 317, 327, 336
   portfolios 237, 319, 329–33
   postmodern 320
   product *v* process 317–18, 327, 331
   reasons for 311–12
   semantic differentials 322–3
   standards 318
   strategies for a unit of work 116
   student self-assessment 318, 331
   summative 315, 316, 319
   systems in various countries 310–11
   technicist (traditional) 320
   techniques 320–1
   use of ICT tools 363–4
   value-added 315
assimilation (Piaget) 39
Assistant Teacher Program 103
associations, as resource 250
ASTA 24, 25, 406, 407
at-risk children
   and child care 33
   at secondary level 34
Attitudes and Values Questionnaire (Forster & Anderson) 290
attribution theory of motivation 62–3
audioconferencing 213
Australia Reconstructed 393
Australian Association of Mathematics Teaching (AAMT) 24, 25, 405–6
Australian Association for the Teaching of English (AATE) 24, 25, 406
Australian Bureau of Statistics 239
Australian Capital Territory
   Curriculum Framework 157
   parents push for democratic participation 295
   school councils 300–1
Australian Certificate of Education 319
Australian Council of Deans of Education (ACDE) 395
Australian Council for Educational Research (ACER) 319, 334, 335

Australian Council of State School Organisations 295
Australian Curriculum, Assessment and Reporting Authority (ACARA) 10, 14, 15, 25–6, 29, 30, 33, 148, 156, 288, 356, 363
Australian Education Council (AEC) 14
Australian education system 129
   standards ('essential learnings') 156
Australian Education Union 28
Australian Institute for Teaching and School Leadership 407–8
Australian Institute of Training and Development 399
Australian National Framework for Values Education 277
Australian Science Teachers Association (ASTA) 24, 25, 406, 407
Australian Teaching Council 341
authentic assessment 323–4, 329, 332, 336
autonomous motivation 59
autonomy
   at school level 166
   of students 210
   of teacher 175

Bachelor of Education, competency-based 404
background noise level (BNL) 80
beginning teachers
   assertiveness 233
   concern about classroom management 220–2
   establishing routines 225
   optimism and realism 6
   questioning skills 189–91
   and the school culture 360
behaviour, of students
   disruptive 221, 222, 228
   environmental influences 223
   factors affecting 221–2
   on-task/off-task 221, 222–3
behavioural objectives 158–60
belonging 60, 79, 82
benchmarking 156, 315, 399
biases 228, 239, 240, 269

bicycle safety (primary topic) 105–7, 111
   sample lesson plan 121
Bishop, Julie 18
blogs 201, 211, 229, 237, 247
Bloom, Benjamin 160–1, 162, 188, 260
   cognitive domain taxonomy for questions 188–9
board games 215, 216
Boards of Trustees (NZ) 307
body language 183, 184, 213, 226–7
Boston, Ken 16
boys, underachievement 83–4, 354
brain structure, and gender 264–5
Bruner, Jerome, cognitive growth theory 44–5, 48
bulletin boards 77, 201, 211, 213, 214
bullying 228–9, 382

cable television 247
California Software Clearinghouse 242
camera phones 381
carbon emissions, website 240
career structure 346, 349–52
caring 276
categorisation 44–5
Catholic education system 30, 345, 346
CD-ROMs 136, 214, 239, 245
   creating 245
character education 276, 369, 372
charter schools 374
chat rooms 201, 211, 213, 229
cheating 337
checklists
   achievement motivation 61
   comprehensiveness of school policy 304
   evaluation of print materials (Piper) 242, 243
   of learning outcomes 336
   lesson evaluation 126
   for student teachers 125
   students' coping behaviours 38
   use of classroom space 78
child abuse 270
child neglect 270, 383
child sex abuse 382–3
Churchill, Winston 78
citizenship 16, 275, 287, 288–90
City Learning Centre, Melbourne 34
civics education 16, 288–90
Civics Expert Group 16
class relations 355
class size, and student achievement 82
classroom behaviour
   questioning rituals 192
   teacher support 63–4
   and use of colour 79

classroom communication systems (CCSs) 186
Classroom Environment Scale 83
classroom environments 71–2
   ability groupings 83
   class size 82
   effects of physical setting 78–9, 223
   natural light 79
   noise 79–81
   psychosocial environment 83
   seating 81–2
   temperature 81, 223
   use of colour 79, 223
classroom management 220–2
   achieving balance 232
   bullying 228–9
   consistency 232
   corrective discipline 231–2
   establishing routines 224–6
   good communication 226–7
   human relations skills 224
   issues of gender/race 227–8
   models of 232–3
   on-task/off-task 221, 222–3
   positive climate 223–4, 230, 232
   preventive discipline 230
   supportive discipline 230–1
   use of signals 227, 231
   working with parents 230
'The Classroom of the Future' 71, 133, 245
classroom settings 72
   checklist for use of space 78
   communication via 183–4
   display boards 77
   for floating teachers 77
   floor space 73–4
   large furniture/equipment 74–6
   pets 77
   plants 77
   room arrangement 72–3
   students' desks 74
   teacher's desk 74
classrooms 129
   differentiated 136, 254–6
   heterogeneous 137
   open 135–6
   self-contained 135
   streamed/non-streamed 137
climate, of classroom 61, 67, 208
   creating a positive climate 223–4, 232
COAG 27–8, 278
codes of education 369
cognitive development theories 5
   Bruner 44–5, 48
   Piaget 39–42, 44, 48
   Vygotsky 45–8
cognitive equilibrium (Piaget) 40
cognitive objectives 161

collaborative learning 211
colour, use in classroom 79
commercial activity, in US schools 373
Common and Agreed National Goals for Schooling (1989) 147, 148
Commonwealth Schools Commission 295
communication 182–5, 193
   effective 186
   explaining 187–8
   interactive 185
   links within the school 183
   models of 185–6
   non-verbal 183–5, 226–7
   proactive 185
   verbal 183
   see also listening; questioning
community resources 249–50
community schools 85
competencies, generic 402
competency-based teaching (CBT) 396–8
   advantages 398–400
   'competent professional' defined 397
   disadvantages 400–2
   impartial benchmarks 399
   minimum standards 397
   national competency standards 402–4
   performance element 397
competition 61
computer adaptive testing (CAT) 336, 364
computer graphics 200, 205
computer-assisted instruction (CAI) 200–1, 258–9
computer-based resources 200–2, 242
computer-managed instruction (CMI) 200
computers
   laptops 244, 381
   PDAs (personal digital assistants) 245
   personal 136
   placement of 75, 77, 79, 225
   routines for use 225
   tablet PCs 244–5, 381
   ubiquity of 93, 225, 244
concepts 114
concrete objects, for play 42
concrete operational stage (Piaget) 41, 44
   teaching strategies 41
confidence 228
confiscations 380–1
   students' rights 385–7
conservation 43, 45
constructivism 44, 45, 151, 204, 211–12, 317

content standards 155–6
contracts 256–8
   examples 257
   strategies 257
controlled motivation 59
controversial issues 377
Convention on the Rights of the Child (UN) 380, 384
Convict Fleet to Dragon Boat (CD-ROM) 245
cooperative learning 61, 63, 141, 204
   assigning roles 143
   ICT applications 213
   Jigsaw method 142–3
   origins 141–2
   problems encountered 144
   research evidence 144
   student-teams learning approach 142
copyright law 377–8
core curriculum 11, 12, 14
corporal punishment 379, 380, 385
corporate advertising 373–4
corporate sponsorship 372, 374–5
Council of Australian Governments (COAG) 27–8, 278
creationism 371
creativity 210
crisis resolution 49
critical literacy 186
critical thinking skills 241
cultural resources 249
culturally different students 269–70
   teaching strategies 269
   and values 281
culture
   and classroom behaviour 228
   and difference 266, 269–70
   meanings of 347
   and moral stance 53
   and social stimuli 46
   and stages of development 39
culture of a school 175, 340
   in 21st century 362
   aesthetic aspects 357
   anthropological aspects 357
   behavioural aspects 359
   evolving 358
   expressed in metaphor 358, 360
   framework for analysing 359
   and leadership 360
   and new teachers 360
   stories 358
   uniform 358
   visual manifestations 358
CURASS 14, 15, 16, 24, 152
curriculum
   and authentic assessment 323
   constructivist 212
   and instruction 93
   meanings 90–4
   programs 104
   world-class 26, 29
   see also national curriculum
Curriculum and Assessment Committee (CURASS) 14, 15, 16, 24, 152
Curriculum Corporation 16, 286, 287, 289
Curriculum Development Centre (CDC) 11, 14, 295
curriculum documents, examples of 94–5
   early-grade English topic 95
   primary personal development, health and physical education 96–8
   primary studies of society and environment 95–6
   senior Economics 98
curriculum improvement strategic plan 172, 173
curriculum materials, and individual differences 263–4
Curriculum Standards and Accountability Framework (SA) 16
cyber predator teams (police) 229
cyber-bullying 229, 382
cyberphobia 200

databases 201
Dawkins, John 14
decision making
   ethical 369
   parent involvement 295
   school-based groups 177
Decisive Leadership Model (Rogers) 222, 234
defamation 378
Democracy and Education (Dewey) 141
demonstrations 204, 210
DESCA (Harmin) 64–6
Desirable Attributes of Beginning Teachers 400
detentions 379, 385
development 38–9, 48
   eight stages (Erikson) 50
   see also cognitive development theories; moral development theory; psychosocial development theory
Dewey, John 6, 141, 211, 323
diagnostic assessment 315, 316
difference
   recognition of 27
   see also diversity; individual differences
differentiated classrooms 136, 254–6
digital portfolios 331
dilemma stories 54, 282
dioramas 241
direct instruction 204, 209–10, 364
direct observation 321–2
directed questioning 204, 207–9
disabled students 266, 267–8
disadvantaged students
   in Australia 30
   equity in education 10, 27
   poor home conditions 5, 60
   at secondary level 34
   and teacher quality 32
discipline 220, 224, 379
   corrective 231–2
   good 233
   preventive 230
   routines 231
   students' rights 380
   supportive 230–1
   tip sheets 232
discomfort factor 199
'Discovering Democracy' 12, 16–17, 289, 300, 356
   project kit 240
discovery learning 43, 45, 46, 213–15
discussion 204, 212–13
   furniture layout 212
discussion forums, online see bulletin boards
disengagement, of students 31–2, 34
dislikes, of young children 5
disruptive behaviour 221, 222, 228
diversity
   in lessons 230
   pre-service teachers' reflection on 275
   in students 252–3
documents, as resource 250
domains, in teaching 397, 408
Don't Smile Until Christmas (Ryan) 350
dress codes 381–2
drop-in centres, for parents 304–5
drug testing 380–1
drug use 380–1, 387
Duke of Edinburgh Award 379
duty of care 379
DVDs 247

early childhood education, equity of access 32–3
early school leaving 31–2, 34
Early Years Learning Framework (EYLF) 33, 130
economic rationalism 133, 343
Economics 98, 278
Educate America Act 1994 154
education 393
   and private industry in Australia 374
Education Act 1988 (UK) 26

Education Act 1992 (UK) 278
Education Act 2004, 10
Education and the Human Quest (Thelen) 141
Education Network Australia 242
Education Revolution 10, 18, 28, 287, 356, 363
Educational Management Organisations 374
effective schools movement (US) 165–6
Eltis, Ken 16
email 201, 211, 246
Emotional Bank Account 227
emotional disturbance 267
empathy 372
empirical questions 188
employment discrimination 377
empowerment 175, 355
enactive representation (Bruner) 45
encouragement, strategies 65–6
engaged learning 134–5
English 20
   draft curriculum 25, 288
   framing paper 23
   performance in Reading strand 335
   proposed content 22
   reporting software 334
   standards for teaching 156, 406
English Literature 278
EQ Australia 284
Equal Opportunity Acts 377
equality of opportunity 27
equity 7, 10, 26–7, 34
   in classroom 67, 363
   for Indigenous students 27, 28–9, 363
Erikson, Erik, psychosocial development theory 48–51
Essential Learning Standards (Vic) 16, 325
Essential Learnings (Tas) 16, 151, 325
ethical behaviour, of teachers 273–4, 276
ethical relationships
   school–industry 372–5
   teacher–education system 371
   teacher–principal 371–2
   teacher–students 372
ethics 276
   of care 276
   of justice 276
   of teaching 368–70
ethnic groups 269–70, 320
ethnocentrism 228
ethos 178
evaluation strategies 116
exceptional students 266–9
   computer assistance 268

diagnostic assessments 267
   mainstreaming 268
exclusion from school 379, 380, 387–9
expert speakers 249
explaining 187–8
external assessors 318
extrinsic motivation 58–9
eye contact 185

facial expressions 185
federation, centenary 16
feedback
   checklist for student teachers 122, 125
   for students 66, 151, 227
figure–ground discrimination 80
films 247
Fitzgerald Report (Poverty & Education in Australia) 295
floating teachers 77
floor space 73–4
formal assessment 37, 315
formal operational stage (Piaget) 42, 44
   teaching strategies 42
formative assessment 313–14, 315, 316, 363
fragility, of students 5
freedom
   academic 377
   of speech 377
friendship groups 139
fundraising 300

galleries 249
Gardens for Life 85
gay rights 371
gender
   and brain structure 264–5
   and classroom relationships 227–8
   and individual differences 264–6
generalisations 114
Generation X 353–4
generic competencies 402
Geography 278
giftedness 266–7
Gillard, Julia 19, 20, 26, 27
global rankings 29
globes 241
goals
   importance of 147–8
   meaningful 67
governance activities 300–1
government publications 239
government schools
   low-SES 30
   v private schools 84
grading 311–12, 336
graphics programs 200, 205
green schools 71

group dynamics 141
group work 138–40
grouping strategies 134

hard policy 17, 18, 25, 26, 362
Harmin, Merrill, DESCA techniques 64–6
Harvard Project 278
hearing problems 80–1, 267, 268
History 20, 278
   draft curriculum 25
   framing paper 23
   proposed content 22
   standards 156
   teaching Australian 18, 26
History Summit 13, 18, 356
History Teachers Association of Australia (HTAA) 24, 25
Hobart Declaration 284, 288
Home Economics 278
home instruction, informal 300
home schooling 84
home–school notebooks 299
Howard, John 18
HTAA 24, 25
human development 38–9, 48
human relations skills 224

iconic knowledge (Bruner) 45
ICQ (software) 213
ICT Assessment Framework 313
ICT strategic plan 169–71, 173
identity, search for 48–9
idleness 221
imagery 45
independent schools 345
   high-SES 30
   popularity 346
   see also Catholic education system; private schools
independent study 204, 217, 254
Indigenous Australians
   disadvantage in school 228, 270, 363
   equity in education 10, 27, 28–9, 228
   foetal growth 39
   interest in education 302
   level of achievement 61–2
   preschool attendance 33
   teacher's attitude to 275
   whiteness as norm 270
individual differences
   and achievement 253–4
   and curriculum materials 263–4
   and exceptional students 266–9
   and gender 264–6
individualised learning 136
individualism, in Australian society 277, 299

individuals, in school environment 252–3
informal assessment 315, 321
informal teaching 135
information literacy 236, 237
injury claims, work experience 379
inner speech 46
innovative teaching 57
inquiry 204, 213–15
    disadvantages 214
    model program 233
    processes 214–15
instant messaging 211, 213
instruction
    computer-based 258–9
    direct 204, 209–10, 364
    personalised 252
    phases of 202–3
    whole-class 137–8
instructional modes 197, 203
    constructivism 204, 211–12
    cooperative learning 204
    demonstrations 204, 210
    direct instruction 204, 209–10
    directed questioning 204, 207–9
    discussion 204, 212–13
    drills 204, 206–7
    independent study 204, 217
    inquiry 204, 213–15
    lectures 204–6
    online teaching 210–11
    problem solving 204, 213–15
    role-playing 204, 215–16
    simulation games 204, 215–16
    small-group activity 204
    wheel of choice 197
instructional objectives 113, 114, 160
integrated studies 20
integration, in schools 141
intellectual disability 266, 267, 268
    teaching strategies 268
intellectual needs 60
intelligence, multifaceted 252
intelligences, multiple 260–1, 267, 331
intelligent design 371
interaction morality 282
interactional method, of planning lessons 120–6
interactive whiteboards 77
interest groups 139
International Association for the Evaluation of Educational Achievement (IEA) 29
International School Improvement Project 166
internationalisation 362
Internet 217
    interactive learning 93, 136, 237
    major teaching role 246
    and pornography 383
    posing questions 192
internship 103–4
intrinsic motivation 57–8

James, Mary 314
Japan (middle school topic), sample lesson plan 122
jargon, by teachers 302
Jigsaw method of cooperative learning 142–3
job satisfaction 347–9
journal writing 136
joyful learning 6
junk materials 241
justice 27, 276

Karmel Report 295, 393
Keating, Paul 16
Keeves Report (1982) 295
kindergartens 129–30
Know Your Rights at School 383
knowledge construction 71
Kohlberg, Lawrence 281–3
    moral development theory 51–4

language development, Vygotsky 46–7
language laboratories 77
laptop computers 244, 381
Lawstuff 383, 389
league tables 30
learning
    collaborative 211
    different ways of 252
    discovery 43, 45, 46
    goal-directed 147
    how to learn 254
    how to teach 7
    individualised 136
    joyful 6
    and non-verbal communication 183–4
    open 43
    pace of 43
    self-directed 256
    see also cooperative learning
learning activities 113
    examples of 116
    in lesson plans 119–20
learning centres 258
learning environments 71, 85
    see also classroom environments; classroom settings
learning stations 75–7
learning styles 198
    and curriculum materials 264
    matching students' with teaching style 196–9
lectures 204–6
Leisure Grid 108, 109
lesson evaluation checklist 126

lesson plans 104, 118–20
    amount of detail 119
    beginnings of lessons 119
    a detailed approach 120
    examples of 121, 122
    interactionist approach 120–6
    learning activities 119–20
    post-lesson analysis 126
    reasons for 119
    sample planners 123–4
lesson study 126–7, 259
letter-grade reporting 336, 356
libraries 249
life skills 85
listening 192–3
    interactive/reactive 192
    paraphrasing 192–3
    reflective 192
    types of 192
listservers 201
literacies, multiple 186
literacy 33, 34, 91, 131, 200, 319, 356, 363
    see also NAPLAN
litigation 376, 377, 378
Lortie, Dan 361–2
lost property 381

maps 241
marketing, of schools 374–5, 379
masculinity 228
Maslow's hierarchy of needs 59–60, 66
Master of Teaching program 404
master timetables 134
mastery learning 259–60, 401
Mathematics 20
    criterion-referenced tasks 317
    draft curriculum 25, 288
    education aims 148
    framing paper 23
    maintaining interest in 92
    proposed content 22
    standards for teaching 156, 405–6
    teacher shortage 365
    use of strands 156
Mayer Report 400
MCEETYA 17, 29, 395
McGaw, Barry 19
meaning making 5
media 279, 296
media centres 77
media literacy 186
Melbourne Declaration (2008) 148, 149, 150, 288
mentoring 221, 360
middle schools 132–3
    organisation of 133
Ministerial Council on Education, Employment, Training and Youth Affairs (MCEETYA) 17, 29, 395

misbehaviour 220–2, 230
    techniques to manage 231
mistakes, allowed 61
mobile phones 229, 381, 387
models 79, 241
moral development theory (Kohlberg) 51–4
    and values education 281–3
moral dilemma stories 54, 282
moral education 273, 275–6, 277
    pluralist morality 277
    ways of promoting 372
moral reasoning (Kohlberg) 51, 281
motivation 57
    achievement 60–2
    attribution theory 62–3
    autonomous 59
    causes of low level of 68
    controlled 59
    extrinsic 58–9
    influencing factors 66–8
    intrinsic 57–8
    main principles 68
    social 63–6
MP3 players 245, 247
multicultural books 239
multiculturalism 275
multimedia 192, 200, 207, 210, 214
    advantages 244, 331
multiple choice tests 276
multiple handicaps 267
multiple intelligences (Gardner) 260–1, 267, 331
museums 249
My Class Inventory 83
My School website 30

NAPLAN 30, 34, 363
National Action Plan for the Education of Girls 265
National Assessment Program, Literacy and Numeracy (NAPLAN) 30, 34, 363
National Board for Professional Teaching Standards 408
National Centre for Pedagogy 196
National Centre for Vocational Education Research 399
National Children's and Youth Law Centre (NCYLC) 383
    information sheets 383, 389
        discipline/punishment 384–5
        exclusion from school 387–9
        searches/confiscations 385–7
    Lawstuff online 383
National Civics and Citizenship Assessments 289–90
National Collaborative Curriculum Development project 12, 14–16

national curriculum 7, 10–11, 13, 17, 34, 147–8, 152, 364
    core curriculum 11, 12, 14
    core subject content 22
    curriculum development timelines 21
    development program 19
    Discovering Democracy project 12, 16–17, 240, 289, 300, 356
    draft curriculum (2010) 25
    and equity 29
    framing papers 23
    hard policy 363
    History Summit 13, 18, 356
    implementing 26
    National Collaborative Curriculum Development project 12, 14–16
    proposed shape of 20
    Statements of Learning 13, 17–18
    Statements/Profiles 14–15, 19, 24, 147
    vision 26
National Curriculum Board (NCB) 10, 18–25, 278
    goals and aims 148, 287–8
    joint communiqué to 24–5
    stakeholders 24
National Curriculum Development Paper 20–2
National Framework for Values Education (2005) 286
National Goals of Schooling 148
'National Goals for Schooling in the Twenty-first Century' 33
National Institute for Quality Teaching and School Leadership (NIQTSL) 341, 399
National Network of School Learning Communities (US) 297
National Office of Overseas Skills Recognition (NOOSR) 399
National Project on the Quality of Teaching and Learning (NPQTL) 395, 402–4
National Safety Council 250
National Values Education Project 285–7
    chronology 286
    nine values 287
needs, human 38, 59
    Maslow's hierarchy 59–60, 66
    social needs 63
negligence 378
Nelson, Brendan 285, 371
neo-Kohlbergian theorists 53–4
neo-Piagetian theorists 44
Net Generation 93
New Basics Project (Qld) 16
New South Wales
    new religion syllabus 278

school councils 301
Scott Report (1989) 295
standards 157, 263
values education publications 285
newspaper clippings 79
newspapers 250
NIQTSL 341, 399
No Child Left Behind Act 2001 (US) 26, 84, 91, 156, 199–200, 311, 319
noise 79–81
    and stress 81
non-verbal communication 183–5, 226–7
    see also body language
Northern Territory
    decentralised education 295
    standards 157
    teacher education board 405
numeracy 33, 91, 131, 200, 319, 356, 363
    see also NAPLAN

obedience orientation 51
objectives
    advantages of 158
    behavioural 158–60
    classifiying 160–2
        affective domain 161
        cognitive domain 161
        psychomotor domain 161
    expressive 157
    importance of 148, 150–1
    instructional 113, 114, 160
    and planning 148
    of program 107
    for teaching 150
observation, of students 38
OECD 29, 166, 352, 354, 363
off-task behaviour 221, 222–3
O'Neill, Sharyn 327
online courses 201
online teaching 210–11
online textbooks 238–9
open classrooms 135–6
open education 135
    critique of 136
open learning 43, 246
Oral History Association of Australia 250
oral presentations 204–6
Organisation for Economic Cooperation and Development (OECD) 29, 166, 352, 354, 363
orthopaedic impairment 267
outcomes 325
    advantages of 157–8
    expressive 157
    importance of 151–4
    problems with 158

outcomes statements 151, 155, 157, 325
   example 152
   planning to teach 153
outcomes-based assessment 324–5, 327, 328–9
outcomes-based education (OBE) 151, 261–3, 404
   in Australia 151–4, 262–3
   criticism of 151
   and records 333
overhead projectors 81, 247–8
   making transparencies 248

paedophilia 382–3
pamphlets 79
paraphrasing 192–3
parent involvement in schools 293–4
   Aboriginal parents 302
   activities for volunteers 306
   decision making 295
   drop-in centres 304–5
   fundraising 300
   history of 294–6
   issues for teachers to consider 306
   language difficulties 305
   need for training 303–6
   parents' rights 303–4
   participation 294, 296–9
      claims against 298
      claims in favour 297
      continuum 299–301
   practices and outcomes 301–2
   role of principal 305, 306
   school policy checklist 304
   seminars 300
   special events 300
   teacher–parent communication 305
   trust model 297
   ways of working 230, 293
Parkerville, WA 168
Participation and Equity program (PEP) 295, 393
pastoral care 68–9, 270
PDAs (personal digital assistants) 245
pedagogical questions 188
pedagogical reasoning model (Shulman) 195–6
pedagogy 195–6
peer tutoring 213
performance assessment 317, 327, 336
   assessment tasks 328–9, 330
   portfolios 329–31
performance standards 155
performance-based pay 30
performance-based teacher education 401
personalised instruction 252
   see also independent study
personality development 48–9, 51

photographs 79
physical disability 266, 268
   teaching strategies 269
Piaget, Jean 211
   and Bruner's iconic stage 45
   stages of cognitive development 39–42, 44, 51
      criticism of 43–4
      implications for teaching 42–3
      use in classroom 48
pin-up boards 77
PISA 10, 29, 319, 363
plagiarism 337
planning to teach 101–3
   creative planning 105
   'informed prescription' 102
   'informed professionalism' 102
   principles 101–2
   teacher evaluation 126
   see also program development
play activities 5
podcasting 247
policy
   hard 17, 18, 25, 26, 362
   soft 17
pornography 383
portfolios 237, 319, 329–33
posters 241
poststructuralism 355
poverty, and student achievement 31
PowerPoint 205, 206, 241, 245, 248
practice drills 204, 206–7
practicum 103, 104
preoperational stage (Piaget) 40–1
   teaching strategies 41
preschools 129–30
primary education, equity in 33
primary reinforcers 58
primary schools 130–1
   organisation of 131
   sites of private space 132
Principals Australia 166
print materials 237–41
   analysis schemes 242
   evaluation checklist (Piper) 242, 243
   selecting 242
prints 241
privacy, of students 280, 380–1, 389
private schools 84, 374
   discipline 379
   see also Catholic education system; independent schools
private speech 46
privatisation 372
privilege 34
proactive communication 185
probeware 201
probing questions 191, 208
problem solving 204, 210, 213–15

problem-based learning 211, 216–17
   see also constructivism
problem-solving skills, in group work 143
processes, and assessment 317–18
professional development 342–3, 408
   lesson study 126–7
professional learning programs 406
professionalisation 342, 343
professions
   characteristics of 342
   competency development 399
   growth of 343–4
   meanings of 340–1
program development
   alternative routes 106
   fine tuning 108–10
   headings to include 104–5
   objectives 107
   primary school example 105–7, 111
   secondary school example 107–8, 112
Program for International Student Assessment (PISA) 10, 29, 319, 363
programs 104
project kits 240
project-based learning 216–17
   individual projects 136
   student-initated 330
   use of resources 237
Promethean 248
property, lost 381
Protestant work ethic 275, 277
psychic rewards 6, 361
psychomotor objectives 161
psychosocial development theory (Erikson) 48–51
psychosocial questions 188
punishment 379
   routines 231, 232
   students' rights 380, 384–5

quality teachers 32, 393, 402, 408
   and disadvantaged students 32
Queensland
   New Basics 325
   OBE 262–3
   standards 157, 263
   teacher education board 405
Queensland Environmental Protection Agency 240
questioning 188–92
   analytic questions 188
   Bloom's cognitive domain taxonomy 188–9
   by students 191–2
   directed 204, 207–9
   empirical questions 188
   examples of question beginnings 209

pedagogical questions 188
planning 189–90
probing 191, 208
psychosocial questions 188
redirecting 191
rephrasing 191
responding to answers 191
sequence for teacher 190
valuative questions 188
wait-time 190, 204

race
   and classroom management 227–8
   reflecting on 275
racial integration (US) 141
racism 275
radio 247
reading groups 138–9
record-keeping 333–4
Red Cross 250
redistribution, of resources 27
reference books 239
reflective practice 126, 153, 221, 232
registrations, national 399
reinforcement 58
Religious Studies 278
reporting 334–6
resilience 60
resources 236–7
   CD-ROMs 136, 214, 239, 245
   checklist for teachers 238
   films 247
   for individualised learning 136
   Internet 246
   local community 249–50
   maps/globes 241
   models 241
   multimedia 192, 200, 207, 210, 214, 244
   overhead projectors 81, 247–8
   PowerPoint 205, 206, 241, 245, 248
   project kits 240
   radio 247
   reference books 239
   Smart Boards 77, 201, 241, 248
   television 247
   textbooks 237–9
   trade books 239–40
   for unit of work 117
   websites 240–1
rights
   enforcing 383
   of students 368, 380–3, 389
   of teachers 368, 376–7
Rogers, Carl 279
role-playing 108, 204, 215–16
routines 224–6, 232
   examples 225
Rudd government 10, 11, 18–19, 33, 287, 363

Safe and Friendly Environment (SAFE) school policy 229
scaffolded instruction 47
schemata (Piaget) 39, 40
School Based Review (UK) 166
school boards 301
school closures 133
school councils 295, 296, 300–1, 302, 306–8
school development planning 165–7
   agreement about aims 176
   curriculum changes 176
   difficulties 176–8
   effective schools movement (US) 165–6
   ethos 178
   leadership/management 177
   'market economy' 167
   and school culture 175
   self-management 177
   stakeholder partnerships 176
   support for change 177–8
   synergy 175
   teaching/learning styles 176–7
   team building 176
   trust among stakeholders 175
school development plans (SDPs) 165, 167–8
   examples 168, 169
school excursions 379
school improvement 166
school organisation 133–4
school performance, reporting 131
school structures 129
   kindergarten/preschools 129–30
   middle schools 132–3
   primary schools 130–1
   secondary schools 131–2
schooling
   in 1960s 361–2
   complex 93
   historical accounts 294–6
   importance in children's lives 5
   role of state in 355
   stability of 360–1
schools
   alternative 307
   autonomy 166
   climate 381
   green 71
   private 84, 374, 379
   self-managed 166–7
   single-sex 83–4
   sustainable 72
Schools Assistance Act 2008 17, 363
Schools Assistance Bill 10, 25
Schools Commission 393
Schools of the Third Millenium 166
Schoolteacher (Lortie) 361

Science 20
   draft curriculum 25, 288
   framing paper 23
   proposed content 22
   standards for teaching 156, 406–7
   teacher shortage 365
   vocabulary expectations 183
Scott Report (1989) 295
searches 380–1
   students' rights 385–7
secondary reinforcers 58
secondary school students
   nature of 5
   opinion of school 5
secondary schools 131–2
   equity in 33–4
   organisation of 131
self-actualisation 60, 67
self-assessment 318
self-contained classrooms 135
self-efficacy 6
self-esteem 59–60, 228, 318
self-evaluation, after teaching 117
self-expression 34
self-managing schools 177
self-realisation 34
semantic differentials 322–3
sensorimotor stage (Piaget) 40
service learning 85
sex stereotyping 265
   strategies to reduce 266
sexual assault 383
sexual harassment 382
The Shape of the Australian Curriculum 288
signals 227, 231
simulation games 204, 215–16, 241
single-sex classes, in coeducational schools 83–4
single-sex schools 83–4
Skilbeck, Malcolm 11, 14, 295
small-group learning 138–40
   friendship groups 139
   positioning of teacher 139, 140
   see also cooperative learning
Smart Boards 77, 201, 241, 248
social background
   and achievement 29–30
   index of 29
social inclusion 27
social interdependence theory 142
social justice education 27
social motivation 63–6
social needs 63
sociograms 139, 140
soft policy 17
sound amplification systems 81
South Australia
   bullying study 229
   Keeves Report (1982) 295

school councils 300
standards 157
teacher education board 405
values pathways 284
Spady, William 151
special needs *see* exceptional students
specialist rooms 77
speech impairment 267
sponsorship 372, 374–5
    possible arrangements 375
    what schools can offer 375
staff deployment 134
staff and resources strategic plan 173, 174
standards 151, 263, 325, 392
    competency-based 397–8
    essential learnings 156, 263
    impact of 199–200
    importance of 154–7, 336
    specialist 407–8
    statements of 155
    structures for 157, 405
    for teaching 402–5
    uses of 408
standards-based education 263
Statements of Learning 13, 17–18
Statements of Learning for Civics and Citizenship (2006) 289
Statements/Profiles 14–15, 19, 24, 147, 152
    outcome statements 325
    and record-keeping 334
    and values education 284–5
stereotyping
    by culture 269
    by gender 265
Storefront School, Ottawa 85
strategic planning frameworks (SPFs) 165, 168, 169
    curriculum improvement plan 172, 173
    essential components 170
    example 169
    futures perspective 168
    ICT strategic plan 169–71, 173
    sample summaries 171, 172
    and school culture 175
    staff and resources plan 173, 174
    strategic intents 168–70
    target setting 173
streaming 137, 398
strip searches 380
Stromlo High School, ACT 167
student achievement
    and class size 82
    and poverty 31
student disengagement 31–2, 34
student satisfaction surveys 83
students
    need to feel significant 198

privacy of 280, 380–1, 389
rights 368, 380–3, 389
values of 275–6
student-teams learning approach 142
Studies of Society and Environment 278, 280
    shared values 284
subsidiarity 175
summative assessment 315, 316, 319
suspension *see* exclusion from school
sustainable schools 72
Swan View Senior High School, WA 270
Sydney Olympic Park 249
syllabus, defined 91–2
syllabus statements 155
symbol systems 45
symbolic stage (Bruner) 45
synergy 175

tablet PCs 244–5, 381
TAFE 398, 399
Tasmania
    core set of values 285
    Essential Learnings 16, 154, 157, 285, 325
    teacher education board 405
Taylor, Tony 18
teacher education 392
    desired graduate attributes 396
    national enquiries into 394
    national registrations 399
    need for higher standards 393
    no absolute standards 402
    'occupational competence' defined 393
    performance-based 401
    pre-service 404
Teacher Education in Australia 394–5
teacher-fronted instruction 206
teachers
    ageing of 352–4
    attributes of 'good' teachers 3–6
    as change agents 408
    and class relations 355
    complex role of 392
    conditions for 364
    drop-out rate 222, 360
    duty of care 379
    empowerment 355
    ethical relationships
        with education system 371
        with principal 371–2
        with students 372
    floating teachers 77
    isolation 370
    lasting impact on students 265, 371
    loss of freedom 273
    morale 341, 356
    necessary attributes

        personal 6
        professional 6
    peer support 221
    police clearance of 383
    rights 368
    self-appraisal 409
    and social relationships 355
    social service 341
    status 344, 399
    supporting students 63–4
    use of jargon 302
    and values education 273–5, 279, 370–1
    warmth/enthusiasm 67
teacher–student relationship 63, 393
teaching
    and communicating 6
    complexity of 6–7
    deprofessionalised 343
    disempowered 355
    ethical 368–70
    factors influencing 7
    feminisation of 354–5
    gender-based patterns 265
    informal 135
    innovative 57
    learning how to 7
    legal issues 376, 377
    lifecycle phases 350–2
    as moral craft 370–1
    movement out of 222, 341
    as profession 3, 340–2, 344
    status 349, 351, 352
Teaching Australia 195, 196, 399, 406, 407–8
teaching, in Australia 344
    career structure 346, 349–52
    female-intensive 346
    full-time/part-time 345
    geographical location 346–7
    hours of work 345
    male principals 346
    male/female by age 353
    male/female proportions 345
    need for incentives 351–2
    need for male teachers in primary schools 354
    proportion in state/non-state schools 345
    reforms 362
    specialisation 346
    status as profession 349–50, 352, 399
    teacher satisfaction 347
        primary 348
        secondary 349
    teachers' earnings 344–5
teaching practice 103
teaching styles 199
    matching with learning styles 196–9

Technology, teacher shortage 365
technology use 200–2, 203
   limited take-up in schools 202
   see also computers
technophobia 200
television 247
temperature stress 81
terrorism 270, 275, 278
testing 319, 320, 363
   and commercialism 374
   computerised 336–7
   national standards 18, 33
   teaching to 33, 355
textbooks 237–9
   Internet-linked content 239
Thelen, Herbert 141
thinking
   and private speech 46
   and problem solving 43
time
   academic learning time 134
   effective use of 134
   time-on-task 134
TIMSS 10, 29, 319, 363
trade books 239–40
transitional periods (between lessons) 72
Trends in International Mathematics and Science Study (TIMSS) 10, 29, 319, 363
tutoring services 84
two-by-ten strategy 5
Tyler, Ralph 141

Understanding by Design (Wiggins & McTighe) 117–18
unit planning 110, 113–17
   content 114
   evaluation 115–17
   instructional objectives 113, 114
   learning activities 113
   resources 117
   self-evaluation 117
   Understanding by Design approach 117–18
units 104

valuative questions 188
value-added assessment 315

values 273
   assessment of 290
   and students 275–6
   and teachers 273–5, 279, 370–1
   traditional 277
values analysis approach 283–4
values clarification approach (Rogers) 279–80
   sample exercise 281
values education 273, 276, 277
   and ACARA 287–8
   analysis of curriculum designs 278–84
   moral development approach 281–3
   separate subject in curriculum 278
   set of processes across curriculm 278–9
   values analysis approach 283–4
   values clarification approach 279–80
   and Statements/Profiles 284–5
   useful websites 286
Values of NSW Public Schools 285
The Values We Teach 285
variety, in lessons 230
versatility, in lessons 230
Victoria
   approach to values education 284
   change to decentralised system 295
   deprofessionalisation of teaching 343
   Essential Learning Standards 16, 157, 263, 325, 326
   focus on essential learning 285
   outcome levels reduced 325
   parents' rights 303
   partnership with McDonald's 374
   role of principal 177
   school councils 295, 300–1
   Schools of the Future 167, 177
   Schools of the Third Millenium 166
   teacher education board 405
videoconferencing 213, 244, 246
videotapes 247
   road safety 108
violence
   and gender roles 228

   at home 270, 382
   at school 378–9
   terrorist attacks 270
virtual science laboratory 210
visual handicap 267, 268
vocal fatigue 80
Vygotsky, Lev 211
   social constructivist theory of development 45–7
   implications for teaching 47–8
   zone of proximal development 47, 48

wait-time 190, 204
websites, as resource 240–1
Western Australia
   access program for Indigenous students 270
   core shared values 285
   cross-curricular outcomes 325
   Cyber Friendly Student Summit 229
   degree of parent involvement 1909 294
   lack of support 178
   lost property procedures 381
   opposition to OBE 154, 263, 325, 327
   Outcomes and Standards 157
   rates of child sex abuse 383
   school-based decision-making groups 177
   teacher education board 405
Wheel of Instructional Choice 197
Whereas the People 288
whiteboards, interactive 77, 201, 241, 248
whiteness, as norm 270
whole-class instruction 137–8
Wilson, Bruce 153
women, in teaching 354–5, 361, 400
word processors 200–1
work centres 75–7
work ethic 275, 277
work experience, injury claims 379
work gratification 6
Work Studies 398
world-class curriculum 26, 29

zone of proximal development 47, 48